SharePoint® 2010
ALL-IN-ONE
FOR
DUMMIES®

SharePoint® 2010
ALL-IN-ONE
FOR
DUMMIES®

by Emer McKenna, Kevin Laahs, and
Veli-Matti Vanamo

WILEY

Wiley Publishing, Inc.

SharePoint 2010® All-in-One For Dummies®

Published by
Wiley Publishing, Inc.
111 River Street
Hoboken, NJ 07030-5774

www.wiley.com

Library of Congress Control Number: 2010935587

ISBN: 978-0-470-58716-4

Manufactured in the United States of America

10 9 8 7 6 5 4 3 2 1

About the Authors

Emer McKenna is the founder of N2C, Inc. a Sacramento based corporation, through which she provides independent consulting services to her clients. Emer focuses on Microsoft technologies including Microsoft Exchange, SharePoint Products and Technologies, SharePoint Workspace 2010 and Office Communications Server. Prior to branching out on her own Emer worked as a Technology Consultant for Hewlett Packard; Emer spent 15 wonderful years with HP working initially as a Digital employee, then a Compaq employee and finally as an employee of HP. Emer has had the good fortune of working with SharePoint from its initial beta release (code named Tahoe) and is the co-author of three previous SharePoint books coinciding with each major version release. Emer looks forward to continuing her exploration of Microsoft technologies and sharing her knowledge through published media. When Emer is not working she joins her husband in the wonderful, glittery, sparkly world of parenting their two little girls, Caoimhe (7) and Niamh (4). You can catch Emer on her blog `http://nut2craic.com` or through e-mail at `emer.mckenna@n2cinc.com`.

Kevin Laahs lives in Scotland and has been in the IT industry for more than 30 years. He is a Technology Strategist with HP Enterprise Services and works as astrategic advisor to many of HP's worldwide customers with his main technical focus being Messaging and Collaboration technologies. He helps clients plan, design and implement infrastructures that help them meet their business goals. Kevin is a frequent speaker at industry events and writes regularly for industry publications. Outside of his working life Kevin enjoys golf and music – neither of which he is as good at as he would like to be. Kevin can be reached at `kevin.laahs@hp.com`

Veli-Matti Vanamo is a Technical Consultant in the HP Software & Services Information Management practice. His main focus is designing, developing and deploying enterprise knowledge management systems based on Microsoft SharePoint. Veli-Matti has worked with over 20 major global customers including The Walt Disney Company, Procter & Gamble, Bank of America, World Health Organization, Sygenta, General Motors and Bank of Montreal. Veli-Matti was the Lead Technical Architect responsible for the internal HP Services Global Knowledge Management Systems and deployment of Microsoft Office SharePoint Server architecture. Veli-Matti is a member of number of Technical Review Boards, including Microsoft Developer Advisory Council for SharePoint 2010 and Microsoft Office SharePoint Server 2007. Veli-Matti is a frequent speaker at industry conferences such as Microsoft TechEd, Microsoft TechNet and MSD2D Web Casts and a co-author of three books on Microsoft SharePoint.

Dedication

This book is dedicated to our ever-patient families: Michael, Caoimhe, and Niamh; Wendy, Jenny, and Euan; Audrey, Christian, and Cora. Thanks for supporting us through yet another writing adventure.

Authors' Acknowledgments

We did it! And I say that with pride and incredulity. The pride bit is obvious. This book is the product of a lot of hard work, perseverance, dedication and determination. The incredulity comes from the fact that I actually got to write another book with Kevin — this is the fourth book I have had the pleasure of co-authoring with him and after our last book I believed him when he said that he was done writing techie books. I wasn't ready to hang up my writing boots and was resigned to the fact that I would proceed with my next book sans Kevin and Veli. Imagine my surprise when Kevin actually agreed to Veli's proposition of coauthoring another SharePoint 2010 book! Thank you for saying yes Kevin, it was an honor to write with you again, and thanks to Veli for giving you the bait. We had initially planned on going the self-publishing route, but that changed when Wiley came knocking on the door with an offer to write *SharePoint 2010 All-In-One Desk Reference for Dummies*. We jumped at the chance.

Thank you to my literary agent Carol Jelen from Waterside Productions for introducing me to Katie Feltman from Wiley Publishing. Thank you to Katie for the opportunity to write for such a wonderful series and a reputable publisher. It has been an incredibly satisfying, rewarding and educational experience. The Wiley staff are brilliant! Thank so much to Katie and Pat O'Brien for their incredible patience and support throughout this whole process. Thanks to Pat, Barry, Lisa, Laura, and Matthew for your very thorough and enlightening edits — you really brought our text to life.

Special thanks to the wonderful folks at Temple Coffee (29th and S) in Sacramento. Lori, Leslie, Bethany, Ben, Spencer and Lauren, thank you all so much for being such gracious hosts and for putting up with me for hours on end while I tapped away on my laptop. The coffee creations that you all make are true works of art, without which this book would never have been completed.

Thanks to you, the reader, for purchasing our book. We hope you find this book useful in your SharePoint journey as that's what makes all the hard work put into writing this book worthwhile. If you have any feedback or questions regarding the content, feel free to contact us and we'll try our best to help you out.

Thank you to my ever loving and supportive family. To my Mum, Dad, sisters and their hubbys, thank you for your constant encouragement. Love you all. To Caoimhe and Niamh, my sweet, sweet girls. Thank you for being so patient with me and excited for me as I completed each chapter. Your smiles and

voices light up my whole world. I love you with all my heart. And finally —
and most importantly — to my husband Michael, thank you for being, and
continuing to be, my rock. I love you.

Emer McKenna

I recall saying to myself, "Have you lost your mind?" when agreeing to
embark on yet another book. In fact I recall saying those exact words to Veli
when he first mooted the idea. And my co-authors and those closest to me
will doubtless say that I have indeed lost my mind when I tell you that,
overall, I did actually enjoy the experience. They would be correct in stating
that all the evidence during the writing process was to the contrary but, now
that our fourth book is complete, I can reflect that I enjoyed writing in a
different style to our previous books. Writing a For Dummies book is a great
way of cutting through the hype and simply explaining how to get stuff done.
To achieve this you need to learn the subject matter in great detail and then
think about it in practical terms. This is what I enjoyed from the experience
since, in the end, technology is all about making people's lives simpler. So I'd
like to acknowledge Wiley for being patient with us as we mastered the style
and for all their help in getting the book to print. Thanks to Emer for handling
all the logistics this time through and Veli – don't you ever come to me again
with such a ridiculous idea as writing another book since my wife, Wendy,
and children, Jenny and Euan, have been put through enough.

Kevin Laahs

Thanks to Emer and Kevin for once again agreeing to co-author our third
book together, once I saw SharePoint 2010 at the Microsoft Airlift in June
2009 I just knew we had to do this. I'm sorry my timelines were ever shifting,
Emer & Kevin – you will always be my favorite Goose & Maverick.

Thank you Audrey, my ever wonderful wife and our two little ones, Christian
and Cora, for putting up with me through the process and giving me the time
to put into this project. I love you guys. Thanks to my family around the
world for encouraging and pushing ever forwards, especially my mother.

Thanks to our colleagues at HP and Microsoft for being a sounding board
and an anchor throughout the process; especially Brian Carter, Eric Tipton,
Paul Turner, Doron Bar-Caspi and Kimmo Forss. Thanks to the rest of the HP
Academy crew for not making feel bad about missing few parties to finish
off the last few chapters; Wendy, Lex, Mark, Matthew and Amish. And lastly,
thanks to the best customer I could ask for; Department of Social Protection–
Helen, Dave, Pat and the rest of the crew.

Veli-Matti Vanamo

Publisher's Acknowledgments

We're proud of this book; please send us your comments at http://dummies.custhelp.com. For other comments, please contact our Customer Care Department within the U.S. at 877-762-2974, outside the U.S. at 317-572-3993, or fax 317-572-4002.

Some of the people who helped bring this book to market include the following:

Acquisitions, Editorial

Project Editor: Pat O'Brien

Acquisitions Editor: Katie Feltman

Senior Copy Editor: Barry Childs-Helton

Copy Editor: Laura Miller

Technical Editor: Matthew McDermott

Editorial Manager: Kevin Kirschner

Editorial Assistant: Amanda Graham

Sr. Editorial Assistant: Cherie Case

Cartoons: Rich Tennant (www.the5thwave.com)

Composition Services

Project Coordinator: Sheree Montgomery

Layout and Graphics: Ashley Chamberlain

Proofreaders: John Greenough, Lisa Stiers

Indexer: Broccoli Information Management

Publishing and Editorial for Technology Dummies

    Richard Swadley, Vice President and Executive Group Publisher

    Andy Cummings, Vice President and Publisher

    Mary Bednarek, Executive Acquisitions Director

    Mary C. Corder, Editorial Director

Publishing for Consumer Dummies

    Diane Graves Steele, Vice President and Publisher

Composition Services

    Debbie Stailey, Director of Composition Services

Contents at a Glance

Table of Contents

Introduction

Microsoft SharePoint Server 2010 is chock full of goodies for you to explore and leverage within your organization. When you start looking at all the functionality that SharePoint 2010 provides, you may — understandably — find yourself feeling a tad overwhelmed and frustrated. Probing at just one little area of the product reveals layer after layer of new features, making you feel like you just opened Pandora's box.

Much of the new functionality emerges as services that can be consumed by your users, and SharePoint 2010 has lots of new services available right out of the box. For example, PerformancePoint Server used to be a standalone server offering from Microsoft, but with SharePoint 2010 it has been rolled up into the product and is now provided as one of the many service applications. Understanding what each service has to offer and knowing when and how to utilize it in your organization is the key to a successful SharePoint 2010 deployment.

With *SharePoint 2010 All-In-One For Dummies,* we demystify the product and show you how to get the most out of your SharePoint deployment.

Who Should Read This Book

This book is intended for SharePoint administrators who are responsible for deploying and managing SharePoint, and also for the technically savvy business users that want to get the most out of their organization's SharePoint 2010 deployment.

Others who may benefit from this book include:

✦ **Developers:** When it comes to building solutions for SharePoint 2010, writing code is typically a last resort. By understanding and knowing how to maximize the services that ship with SharePoint, developers can save themselves a lot of time and effort, and impress their managers by quickly producing solutions with very little underlying cost.

Developers will find Books I and IV most useful to their needs.

✦ **Power Users:** Since its inception SharePoint has always been a great technology for empowering the end user, and SharePoint 2010 is no exception. Technically savvy end users, also known as Power Users, will be eager to take advantage of all the goodies that SharePoint 2010 has in store for them, and knowing what those goodies are is half the battle.

Power users will find Books I and IV of most immediate benefit to them.

Icons Used in This Book

To help you get the most out of this book, we've placed icons here and there. Here's what the icons mean:

Next to the Tip icon, you can find shortcuts and tricks of the trade that help you to understand SharePoint and have more fun using it. Also, there are references to other chapters that can expand your knowledge.

The Warning icon doesn't appear often in this book, but when it does it's to warn you of potential problems or common pitfalls.

When we want you to pay special attention to a specific detail that bears remembering, we mark it with a Remember icon. Committing these little details to memory along the way will make your SharePoint journey more enjoyable.

When we are forced to describe high-tech stuff, a Technical Stuff icon appears in the margin. You don't have to read what's beside the Technical Stuff icons if you don't want to, although these technical descriptions often help you understand how a specific feature works.

Ready, Set, Go . . . but Go Where?

So you've read the introduction and you're ready and raring to go . . . but where do you start? Well, the answer is easy. Start anywhere you'd like. If you're new to SharePoint 2010, a good place to start is Book I, Chapter 1. If you're a Power User with access to a SharePoint 2010 environment and you're ready to get your hands dirty, then any of the chapters in Book IV will work for you. If you're interested in a specific topic — for example, Access Services — take a peek at the index at the back of the book for all the chapters related to Access Services and start with the first one.

Read on!

Book I

Introduction to SharePoint

The 5th Wave   By Rich Tennant

Contents at a Glance

Chapter 1: Getting to Know SharePoint

*I*f you're new to Microsoft SharePoint, you should know it's an integrated suite of software programs designed to help organizations make the best possible use of their intellectual assets. SharePoint combines Web browsing with client-server networking to manage in-house information in some powerful ways:

✦ Discovering and sharing the important business information that lurks unused within many organizations

✦ Managing Web content by regulating access to documents and data

✦ Boosting collaboration through social networking

✦ Providing tools for *business intelligence* — turning raw data into usable business information

✦ Serving as a flexible environment for developing custom software to meet differing business needs

This chapter gets up close and personal with SharePoint, lays out how it has evolved since it first popped up in the marketplace, and gives you a glimpse of how it fits into a Microsoft strategy called Unified Communication (which some folks consider a whole new way of doing business). We figure a quick overview of where SharePoint has been will shed light on SharePoint features and functions as they are now. For example, SharePoint 2010 is highly integrated with Microsoft Office and can be deployed in a mind-boggling variety of ways — but it got to that point version by version, getting smarter with each release. A look at how this happened can give you a leg up on planning the evolution of your organization as it uses SharePoint.

Catching up with SharePoint Evolution

Every new release of any software product brings change for the people who use it — "Here it comes, ready or not." New features (and learning curves) for the end user, better and easier ways for developers to put SharePoint capabilities to work, or more options that IT professionals can tweak to support the needs of the business. If a new product release didn't bring any benefit to anyone, why spend time, resources, or money on implementing it? So goes the industry reasoning, anyway.

How much a software product changes between releases (and which features and functions ultimately make their way to the users) often will depend on the software's basic technical design — its *architecture*. That design typically has a limited lifespan. No, it isn't all planned obsolescence; rapidly changing business requirements demand new capabilities and ways of working. If a software product's architecture stays the same, sooner or later it can't accommodate that demand, and its market share shrivels.

As an example, consider what's happening to information systems in the current economic climate — in particular, *cloud computing*, which has nothing to do with the weather: Many organizations are looking to save money by moving away from maintaining their own IT infrastructures. Instead of installing more big server computers and mazes of network cable, they put their utility computing "in the cloud": The services that their end users require — including software programs they use every day — are managed and maintained by a third party and used via a secure connection to the Internet. That's a shift in platform — away from isolated, standalone computers, even away from "hard-wired" company networks. It's no wonder that software products have to change to meet business needs in new operating environments. SharePoint, in fact, can handle both the old and the new — zipping happily through network cables or going out to users via the Internet cloud. Many features, such as claims based authentication (discussed in Book II, Chapter 2), allow SharePoint to co-habitate in the different environments that you find both inside and outside of the Enterprise.

As you might expect, a software product's architecture also changes in response to how well it does in the marketplace — and not just if it fails. Many products actually get revamped because of their success — as when demand emerges for a larger-scale version of the product — and that's exactly what happened to SharePoint when support for large farms was initially introduced in SharePoint 2003.

If a software product changes its architecture between releases, that usually happens in one of two ways:

✦ **A total redesign.** Redesign tends to happen early in a product's life — often requiring a massive amount of re-engineering that has to meet a tight development deadline. Sometimes the features that end users, developers, or IT professionals looked forward to end up unfinished or dropped completely. (The much-anticipated Shared Services capability of SharePoint 2003, for example, had to wait until 2007 before it got anywhere close to delivering on its original promise.)

✦ **An evolution of the current architecture.** As a software product matures and finds its rightful place in the computing ecosystem, its architecture proves effective for a while and then changes gradually, one release at a time. This process usually results in the greatest benefits across the board.

Over the years, SharePoint has undergone both kinds of architectural changes (Table 1-1 sums them up). The current version — SharePoint 2010 — is not a redesign, but an evolution. At the core, it's much the same as its immediate ancestor with the long name Microsoft Office SharePoint Server 2007, or MOSS. In fact, SharePoint 2010 (let's hear it for simpler product names!) builds on the parts of MOSS that were tried and tested in the real world, and found to work well — in particular, these:

✦ The Site Framework: The same MOSS mechanism that supports team sites is still in the mix. (Get a look at how it works in Book I, Chapter 2.)

✦ Business Connectivity Services: The Business Data Catalog from MOSS has been enhanced to allow both reading and writing of external data — another winner. (See Book III, Chapters 2, 3, and 4.)

✦ Social Networking Features: Microsoft had connecting people together in mind when it came up with this part of SharePoint — and they called it right.

That said, SharePoint 2010 does contain some significant architectural changes — these, for example:

✦ Indexing is far more flexible. This means you can index more content and, more importantly, help users find relevant information.

✦ Service applications are available via SharePoint for the first time. The architecture allows for flexibility in deployments and sharing of resources across multiple SharePoint farms.

✦ Office Web Apps. These allow users to view and edit Office content (Word, Excel, PowerPoint) through the browser allowing fast access to such content from essentially any environment.

In effect, you can think of SharePoint 2010 as "the second release of the third generation of SharePoint" (if you like to trace lineage). This evolution has added features for end users, options for developers, and flexible deployment for the IT crew. (And the crowd goes wild!)

Whatever you call this episode of the SharePoint journey — evolution or redesign — the resulting product is, in Microsoft-speak, "The Business Collaboration Platform for the Enterprise and the Web." Clearly the product is aimed at "the cloud" but also at home on a good old-fashioned corporate intranet. And keep that "collaboration" part in mind; you'll be seeing a lot of it in this book.

Table 1-1:		The Redesign and Evolution of SharePoint	
SharePoint Version	*Release Date*	*Type of Architectural Change*	*Result*
SPS 2001 (Tahoe)	2001	N/A	A portal that could be used for knowledge management. Design favored consumers of information more than creators. Commercialized the digital dashboard that delivered content in Web pages via Web Parts.
SPS 2003	2003	Redesign	Combined SharePoint Team Services (STS) and SharePoint Portal Server (SPS) to give companies total control of their information from start to finish.
Microsoft Office SharePoint Server 2007 (MOSS)	2007	Redesign	Significant architectural changes included item-level permissions and flexible deployment options — which laid the groundwork for SharePoint 2010.
SharePoint 2010	2010	Evolution	Many new collaboration features were added to the 2007 version, including easy-to-use tools for the end user and multiple ways to deploy SharePoint — both on-site and "in the cloud".

Why SharePoint Evolution Matters to Your Company

This section takes a whirlwind look at the evolution of SharePoint, how it got to be what it is today, and how you can make best use of it.

How SPS 2001 adapted to match business needs

SharePoint Portal Server (SPS) 2001, code-named Tahoe while it was undergoing design and development, started life as an application intended for *knowledge management* — essentially coordinating business administration, IT, and the processes of doing business so that everybody in the company could have access to what they needed to know, could apply it to best advantage, and could get more efficient about sharing what they learned.

SPS 2001 commercialized the Digital Dashboard — a Web-based feature that delivered content to Web pages via Web Parts (chunks of ready-to-use computer code). This concept is still in use today; it's part of the .NET Framework, a set of programming routines used for developing custom software and extending the capabilities of Microsoft products such as SharePoint.

While SPS 2001 was being designed, an old standby product — Microsoft Exchange — was starting to have an identity crisis: Exchange 2000 had outgrown its origins as an e-mail-and-messaging program (it was an ancestor to Outlook); now it was marketed as a "Messaging and Collaboration" server product — the whole collaboration side was new. Microsoft added a slew of features to make Exchange "Web-enabled," and stuck on a plethora of APIs (Application Programming Interfaces) so developers could build complete, Web-based, *collaborative* applications based on Exchange.

Well, if a horde of people were going to collaborate online, they needed some convenient online place to keep what they were working on. Thus the Web Storage System was born.

SPS 2001 (the SharePoint ancestor) needed a database to store all the knowledge everybody expected it to manage — but still had to serve as a "portal" to the Web. So it made sense at the time to build SPS 2001 on top of the Web Storage System — but that ambitious system never caught on, probably for two main reasons:

✦ Exchange worked just fine as a messaging server — and had a big, loyal, relatively happy throng of users — so the product went back to doing what it did well, and only that: messaging.

✦ Microsoft wanted to make SQL Server the data-storage engine of choice where applicable. (Of course, there was also some loose talk back then about getting Exchange to use SQL — but that still hasn't happened, and for good reason: The input/output patterns for e-mail are more sporadic and unpredictable than those used in other applications. By using its Extensible Storage Engine (ESE), Exchange can handle those I/O patterns better than SQL (or, for that matter, SQL Server), and that's unlikely to change any time soon.

So it was back to the e-mail only focus with Exchange, and the Web Server System died on the vine (for the time being).

How SharePoint changed along with related products

With Exchange returned to its focus on messaging, Microsoft promoted SharePoint as the platform for collaborative applications — but the product's "identity crisis" continued: How would it get collaboration to work, and what else was it good for?

Of course, the SharePoint engineering team *could* have embraced the Web Storage System and started evolving WSS as the main storage product, but other factors contributed to the need for a change in SharePoint architecture.

Tucked away in a whole other product — Microsoft Front Page Server — was a little-known program that had essentially been dwarfed by the marketing given to SharePoint Services. This unassuming product — SharePoint Team Services (STS) — could do many of the same things SPS 2001 could do (for example, document publishing), but it was focused on smaller teams formed to execute specific tasks.

Slowly STS gained traction — both inside and outside Microsoft — because it could aid in the collaborative creation of business information and Web content, which SPS couldn't do. At the time, each product had its own bailiwick:

✦ SPS could connect people and information across departments and entire organizations.

✦ STS enabled small teams — practically any number of them — to create content and collaborate on team-specific information.

Surely there was potential here for a single product that would cover all the bases and give a company large-scale, detailed control of its information.

And so Windows SharePoint Services (WSS) and SharePoint Portal Server 2003 (SPS 2003) were born — which required a core architectural change in order to strengthen the "abilities" of SharePoint — scalability, availability, reliability, and manageability. Neither STS nor SPS 2001 had addressed all these features completely — but the first generation of SharePoint had piqued market interest, so version 2.0 was highly anticipated and was expected to meet the needs of the enterprise.

Three tiers, no waiting!

These days a common practice is to group multiple servers that perform similar roles into tiers. This arrangement is especially good for redundancy in the system; if you lose one server, the other servers in the same tier (which perform the same role) can take on the load.

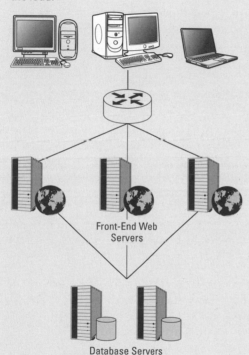

Front-End Web
Servers

Database Servers

Typically you see the following in a three-tier server architecture:

✔ The first tier also known as the *presentation tier* is normally a bank of dedicated servers that interact directly with end users, and can handle user requests interchangeably. SharePoint calls these Web Front End (WFE) servers; they receive all requests from users and applications and *render* (create and display) every Web page that makes its way to the users' screens.

✔ The third tier (we'll get to the second tier in a minute!) is also known as the *database tier*. It's where data is kept and served to the network users. Multiple applications make use of the database tier; the database itself provides data to any and all of them. Typically, large servers that run SharePoint use SQL Server as the database and achieve redundancy by using various techniques — up to and including the duplication of entire servers (*mirroring*).

✔ For many applications these two tiers — the presentation tier and the database tier — are actually sufficient; the applications run on the Web server that provides Web pages to the users. In fact, WSS runs as a two-tier application (as shown in Figure 1-1). If your company is huge (or nearly huge), however, large-scale applications require multiple servers to perform roles that they do best in tiers.

✔ Some types of processing are resource-intensive (indexing, for example, uses a lot of processor cycles and is disk intensive).

✔ Spreading the output of processing across a tier is more efficient than having each server do its own processing.

So the middle tier is usually called the *application tier* — where specific applications are provided as network services and commands to those applications are executed.

In the case of SharePoint, the best example is the Index service. No point making all those servers index the same content — so the Index service itself runs as an application in the middle tier, sending its results to all the servers that use the search service.

SPS 2001 used the Web Storage System to store data — but STS split that task, mainly using SQL to store metadata and NTFS to store content (such as documents). This design limited the scalability of WSS — and its availability to users. In effect, it was a hybrid storage system that used Web Server, the installed file system, SQL, and the Windows Registry (configuration information) to store data. To make some sense of this complexity, all Web content had to be tied to the same server — specifically, the one responsible for rendering Web pages. These days, fortunately, SharePoint 2010 handles this problem by a three tier architecture with all data being stored in SQL. This allows SharePoint 2010 to meet the needs of the smallest to the very largest of organizations.

One way to meet the expectations for SharePoint version 2.0 was to design it to run on multiple physical servers and divide up the processing among them. Doing so brought some advantages:

✦ Multiple servers allowed redundancy; if one of them failed, others could take over, which improved the reliability of the system.

✦ Organizations could scale up SharePoint as required, whether *vertically* (by adding larger servers) or *horizontally* (by adding more servers).

✦ Multiple servers could be grouped according to the roles they performed — into *tiers*.

At this point, three-tier architectures were starting to crop up nearly everywhere. So they became the starting point for the next generation of SharePoint. (For a look at how this arrangement works, see the accompanying sidebar, "Three tiers, no waiting!")

To take advantage of a tiered server structure, the second generation of SharePoint used three role-based tiers (see Figure 1-1); this model persists today in SharePoint 2010. Early on, however, that meant a big architectural change — because SPS 2003 now had to depend on WSS.

SharePoint finds a renewed purpose

The success of SharePoint Team Services told Microsoft that small teams needed better ways to collaborate than the Windows operating system could give them. Windows provided file-sharing — and sure, that meant teams could share documents — but they couldn't share much else. What they needed to share these days was richer information about documents and items that were required for stronger collaboration such as calendars, tasks, and project lists.

The grand Microsoft plan was to enhance the basic Windows operating system and augment it with collaboration services that any application could use — even non-Microsoft applications (what a concept!). The idea was to allow collaboration among a wide range of applications.

And so Windows SharePoint Services (WSS) was built on the .NET Framework harnessing ASP.NET as well as SQL Server.

"Windows" was part of the name because WSS was intended as part of the operating system (initially a free download, later an optional installable service). Figure 1-2 shows how WSS fit into the whole SharePoint picture.

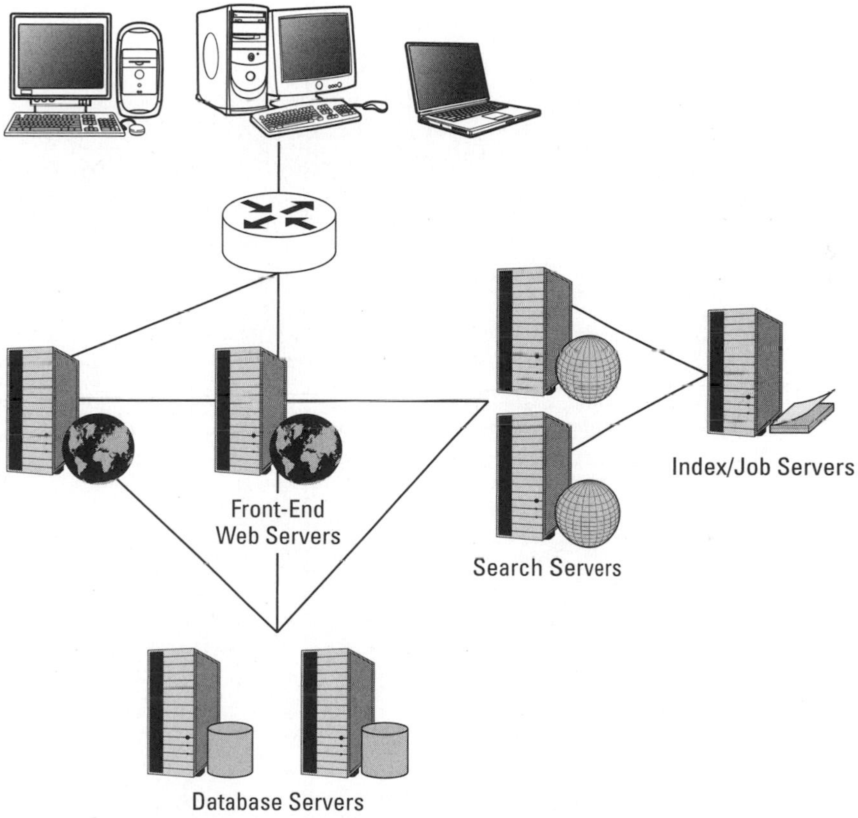

Figure 1-1:
SPS as a
three-tier
application.

Index/Job Servers

Front-End
Web Servers

Search Servers

Database Servers

Of course, this approach made WSS both part of the operating system *and* an application that used the operating system. It was really a sample of how collaborative applications could be built. Your team could use WSS to create team Web sites that took advantage of the various frameworks built into WSS:

✦ **The Web Part Page framework** could be used to build feature-rich user interfaces for various Web browsers.

✦ **The site framework** could be used to create collections of Web sites that had features based on consistent templates.

✦ **The document library and list frameworks** could be used to store data and provide flexible views of this data.

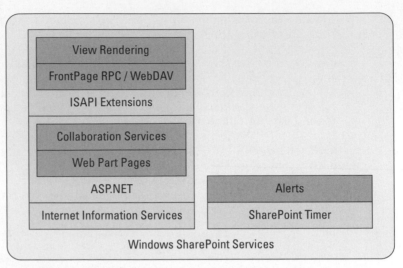

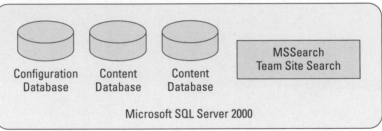

Figure 1-2:
WSS
software
architecture
is in the
upper
part of the
picture.

Teams could customize and extend the capabilities of these Web sites so multiple individuals could work on the same documents and different types of list items (contacts, tasks, calendar entries, announcements, and such). Web services and improved management of information encouraged the expansion of collaboration. The following are examples of this in action:

✦ Outlook 2003 could set up a team site as a shared workspace to accommodate online meetings linked to meeting requests.

✦ Outlook 2003 could synchronize lists; you could view, for example, a shared calendar in a team site side-by-side with your own personal calendar.

✦ Word 2003 could harness document workspaces that allowed users to see relevant related files from within Word.

✦ Both Access and Excel could synchronize SharePoint lists.

✦ The new InfoPath feature could store its forms and publish fields from those forms in a form library made available for collaborative use.

✦ Users could navigate to document libraries directly from Windows Explorer.

✦ Eventually (after Microsoft purchased Groove in 2005 and brought its features into the Office Suite) users could synchronize document libraries and lists for offline use.

So there you have it — Windows SharePoint Services formed the platform upon which SharePoint Services 2003 was built. This meant

✦ If WSS was not already present when you installed SPS 2003 the installation process would install it for you.

✦ Installing SPS 2003 on top of WSS would augment the features that your WSS team sites already made available.

✦ SPS 2003 delivered the newest version of MSSearch; it could index multiple content sources and deliver aggregated search results.

✦ With SPS 2003 in place, the scope of a search done from a team site could now include all team sites — or all sites within the organization.

SharePoint Services focused on connecting people and information. The Site Directory provided with SPS 2003 improved on WSS by giving each team site automatic awareness of the other team sites. Instead of piling up information in isolated, little-used islands and letting duplicate documents run rampant, the Site Directory kept information sources organized, tidily indexed, and searchable — automatically — from the get-go. Result: information assets were a lot easier to find, access, and use. Figure 1-3 shows the software architecture of SPS 2003, which made all this magic possible.

SharePoint gets new powers

By 2003, the third generation of SharePoint was well underway; the changes in its architecture had paid off with market success. The three-tier server architecture was flexible, but Microsoft had limited the number of physical implementations to three — for small, medium, and large server farms. But larger enterprises wanted larger-scale deployments so they could save costs by running (and supporting) fewer software products. The success of SharePoint led to a cry for more functionality — especially in the area of Web *content management* (managing the information that is ultimately published on Web pages). If enterprises could use SPS 2003 for internal Web sites, why couldn't they use it out there on the World Wide Web as well?

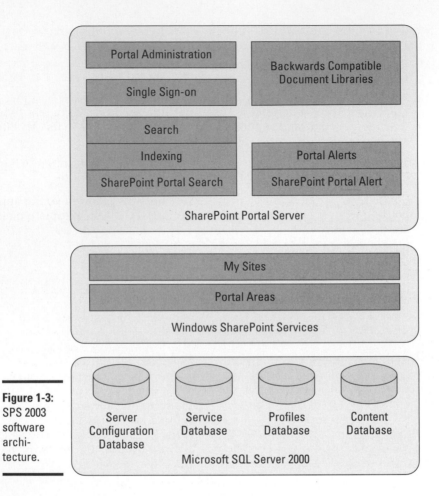

Figure 1-3:
SPS 2003
software
archi-
tecture.

Having purchased Ncompass Labs, Microsoft could address Web content management with Ncompass Content Management Server (CMS). But there was confusion in the market over whether to use SharePoint or CMS. Both software products were fine for creating content and publishing it for use with a Web browser. Much of the same functionality needed for putting external content on the Web could put internal content on internal Web sites. Microsoft figured that out and integrated CMS 2002 into SharePoint 2003. This addition, probably more than anything else, sparked the next generation of SharePoint.

As Microsoft developed the 2007 version of SharePoint — in particular, Microsoft Office SharePoint Services (MOSS) — the focus was on meeting enterprise-scale needs by getting content management to work seamlessly with collaboration. Windows SharePoint Services delivered the central platform services (in particular, storage and security). Building on this strong foundation, Microsoft targeted six "solution areas" (as shown in Figure 1-4):

✦ Collaboration: To bring collaboration up to date, WSS included more "modern" ways of collaborating through wikis and blogs.

✦ Portal: MOSS offered portal features that allowed relevant content to be targeted at people and supported the first social features in its "My Site" implementation.

✦ Search: MOSS provided search capabilities that were well suited to large Enterprises that had information held in multiple repositories.

✦ Content management: MOSS provided features that allowed you to apply policy to your information assets and workflows to help automate their life cycle.

✦ Business forms: MOSS embarked into the electronic forms arena allowing forms to be more accessible through the browser.

✦ Business intelligence: MOSS provided tools that would make it easier to analyze business data resulting in better business decisions

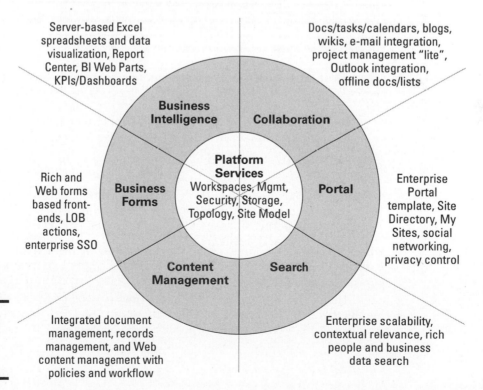

Figure 1-4: MOSS solution areas.

Server-based Excel spreadsheets and data visualization, Report Center, BI Web Parts, KPIs/Dashboards

Docs/tasks/calendars, blogs, wikis, e-mail integration, project management "lite", Outlook integration, offline docs/lists

Business Intelligence   **Collaboration**

Platform Services
Workspaces, Mgmt, Security, Storage, Topology, Site Model

Rich and Web forms based front-ends, LOB actions, enterprise SSO

Business Forms   **Portal**

Enterprise Portal template, Site Directory, My Sites, social networking, privacy control

Content Management   **Search**

Integrated document management, records management, and Web content management with policies and workflow

Enterprise scalability, contextual relevance, rich people and business data search

MOSS also changed how Web pages would be constructed: Master Pages, Page Layouts, and Content Pages worked together to ensure a consistent user interface across all sites.

Authentication was as desperately needed as the six solution areas — and because MOSS used ASP.NET 2.0 as its underlying platform, improvements were also possible in that area. After all, if your company is building Web sites that have to grapple with the wilds of the Internet, then it needs an industrial-strength authentication mechanism. Standard Windows authentication just won't cut it. So MOSS added *pluggable authentication* — authenticating users by plugging the credentials they supply into the appropriate resource — whether a simple list of names or a database that supports more elaborate verification. Authenticated users could then have authorized access to internal content.

MOSS also provided capabilities that could "light up" individual sites by giving them custom features that could be independently developed, installed on the server, and then switched on and off within each site. The simplest example was what you could do with lists: All standard lists in a team site (Announcements, Contacts, and so on) were contained in a feature called "Team Collaboration Lists" — and switching off this feature in a team site would disable access to all its standard lists. In effect, the company could now have more control over who could see what lists — and team sites could be custom-tailored to match access privileges.

To support the business intelligence and business forms, MOSS gave the server more roles to play in managing applications — chiefly these:

✦ **Excel Services** allowed Excel spreadsheets to be published to the server and provided browser access to the data they contained.

✦ **InfoPath Services** allowed InfoPath forms to be rendered on the server; end users could interact with the form data through the browser.

✦ **Business Data Catalog** allowed descriptions of external data and methods for accessing it. After data was described in the catalog, users with the correct permissions could get at it through Web Parts, as columns in a list, or as search results.

In effect, Excel and InfoPath services were server versions of the familiar Microsoft client products with the same names. A major functional difference: The server versions could process the same data and present their results through Web browsers. Figure 1-5 shows that WSS provides platform services MOSS provides service applications. SharePoint 2010 extends the concept of service applications significantly.

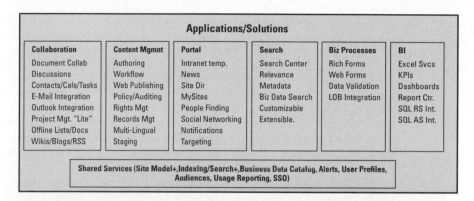

Figure 1-5:
MOSS
software
archi-
tecture.

MOSS was a great success for Microsoft. Flexible, scalable, and extensible, this version of SharePoint made possible a massive leap in functionality that we see in SharePoint 2010 to all solution areas.

Fitting SharePoint into Unified Communications

Unified Communications is (in addition to an impressive-sounding name for a Microsoft marketing strategy) largely a new way of working. It involves a new approach to the six solution areas Microsoft initially sought to address:

✦ Collaboration

✦ Portal

✦ Search

✦ Content management

✦ Business forms

✦ Business intelligence

Knowing all the parts that make up SharePoint 2010

At first glance, you may think Figure 1-6 and Figure 1-5 tell a similar story — but looks can be deceiving. SharePoint 2010 tackles every solution area with new features and possibilities.

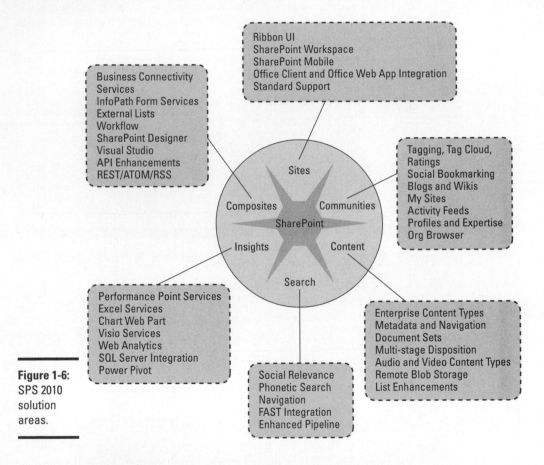

Figure 1-6: SPS 2010 solution areas.

Ribbon UI
SharePoint Workspace
SharePoint Mobile
Office Client and Office Web App Integration
Standard Support

Business Connectivity
Services
InfoPath Form Services
External Lists
Workflow
SharePoint Designer
Visual Studio
API Enhancements
REST/ATOM/RSS

Tagging, Tag Cloud,
Ratings
Social Bookmarking
Blogs and Wikis
My Sites
Activity Feeds
Profiles and Expertise
Org Browser

Sites

Composites   Communities

SharePoint

Insights   Content

Search

Performance Point Services
Excel Services
Chart Web Part
Visio Services
Web Analytics
SQL Server Integration
Power Pivot

Enterprise Content Types
Metadata and Navigation
Document Sets
Multi-stage Disposition
Audio and Video Content Types
Remote Blob Storage
List Enhancements

Social Relevance
Phonetic Search
Navigation
FAST Integration
Enhanced Pipeline

You probably won't be surprised to find some architectural changes in SharePoint 2010 when compared to MOSS. That's how software evolves (you knew that, of course). Fortunately, the core building blocks and concepts of SharePoint are essentially the same.

The newly named SharePoint Foundation — and the solutions you can build on it — works much the same as WSS, which it replaces. Along the same lines, SharePoint Server 2010 replaces Microsoft Office SharePoint Services (MOSS), and is a bit less of a mouthful to say. Fresh names also grace some of the most important SharePoint features, to go along with their expanded capabilities:

✦ **Workflow Foundation** supports the definition, execution, and management of workflows.

✦ **Presentation Foundation** supports the development of modern user interfaces, so developers can use a common technology to create custom programs for both Windows-based and browser-based client applications.

✦ **Communication Foundation** supports the building of service-oriented applications that communicate across the Web and across the enterprise.

✦ **SharePoint Foundation** supports the collaboration that helps people and information stay connected — even across organizational and geographic boundaries.

SharePoint Foundation is a very versatile application that shows itself a worthy descendant of WSS: If you install only SharePoint Foundation, you can put its considerable set of features to work right away — and add a slew of bells and whistles — on a company-wide scale — when you install SharePoint Server 2010 later.

Unlike its MOSS predecessors, SharePoint 2010 is a 64-bit application — which makes sense when you consider the scale factor; the bigger the scale, the more data has to be processed in the same (or less) time. No wonder Windows Server 2008 SP2 and Windows Server 2008 R2 are the required server platforms. And there's a welcome bonus for developers: They can install SharePoint 2010 on Windows 7 or Vista SP1 machines while developing custom capabilities for their organizations.

Putting the parts of SharePoint together for business collaboration

SharePoint has been called many things in the course of its history — which can be confusing. So here's a quick translation of the terms we use when referring to the various offerings in the SharePoint family:

Generically (and logically enough) we use "SharePoint" as the umbrella name for all things SharePoint. If version numbers can help differentiate specific families, you'll see them. For individual SharePoint products, we either use their full names or use an abbreviation from this list:

✦ SP 2010 = SharePoint 2010

✦ SPS 2010 = SharePoint Server 2010

✦ SPF 2010 = SharePoint Foundation 2010

✦ SPD 2010 = SharePoint Designer 2010

✦ SPW 2010 = SharePoint Workspace 2010

The more you read about — and eventually use — SharePoint, the clearer it shows up as part of an organizational ecosystem of collaboration and communication. You can run SharePoint services from Microsoft Office 2010 applications, use their results in Exchange Server 2010, and even use them to enhance the search capability in Windows 7. SharePoint power can be everywhere your organization needs it to be. This book shows how to make that happen.

Chapter 2: Introducing Microsoft SharePoint Foundation 2010

In This Chapter

✔ Getting familiar with SharePoint Foundation

✔ Using the site framework to start building your SharePoint site

✔ Discovering SharePoint development possibilities

Two SharePoint server products are available — SharePoint Foundation 2010 (SPF) and SharePoint Server 2010 (SPS). In this chapter, we introduce you to SharePoint Foundation — a pre-requisite for SharePoint Server that provides (and will help you get familiar with) some SharePoint Server features. We cover SharePoint Foundation's reason for being, its core architecture, and how to get started building a SharePoint site. We also touch on the components of SharePoint that make it an ideal platform for developing custom software to fit your business. This chapter takes a fairly broad, quick view of SharePoint Foundation; covering its every detail might take until we get to SharePoint 2014 (or whatever major release comes next) — and then we'd have to start over. So on with the SharePoint 2010 show . . .

Spotlighting SharePoint Foundation

It's been a long and winding road to get to the two current SharePoint products. As Book I Chapter 1 shows, SharePoint took a while to evolve into its niche and find what it did best. Now that the product has managed that feat, it's time for a name change — "so long, farewell, *auf wiedersehn,* goodbye" to Windows SharePoint Services (WSS) and "welcome to my world, won't you come on in" to SharePoint Foundation.

Why the name change? Well, start with the switch from "Services" to "Foundation". In earlier years, including SharePoint capabilities as part of the operating system services was the daring new thing. These days the emphasis is more on what you *do* with those services — the ways you can fit collaboration and content management to your business — in short, what you can build on the basis of SharePoint.

After all, a typical dictionary definition of *foundation* will only get us so far:

✦ The basis or groundwork of anything

✦ A cosmetic, as a cream or liquid, used as a base for facial makeup

✦ The natural or prepared ground or base on which some structure rests

Sure, you can make pretty-looking Web sites with SharePoint Foundation, but that's not the metaphor Microsoft had in mind. Those other two definitions suggest *building* — whether that's a structure (a platform for growth, if you will) or the activity of putting something together. Both are closer to what SharePoint Foundation is all about.

Although "Services" conveys the idea of a helpful product, a service is more something that you make use of rather than build upon. So the name change to "Foundation" suggests more of a development mindset — building solutions (that is, scripts, applications, even Web services specific to your business). Although SharePoint Foundation comes with its own set of useful features, its primary purpose in life is to support custom programs built by end-users, power users, developers, and partners. Call it a SharePoint customizing kit (minus the flame paint job).

Of course, Microsoft also dropped "Windows" from the product names, but so far as we can tell, nothing broke. In case you were worrying about a brand new price tag to go with the new name, don't: SharePoint Foundation is just as free as Windows SharePoint Services was (free when you purchase Windows that is!) and it's available as a Web download. So think of SharePoint Foundation as the free framework that supports your own custom software projects and other Microsoft products — in particular, SharePoint Server 2010.

Putting SPS on top of SPF

Figure 2-1 shows what you get when you install SharePoint Foundation by itself. Here's a bird's-eye view of the major feature enhancements you get when you install SharePoint Server after installing SharePoint Foundation.

✦ Sites: Many more Web Parts and tools to help you build even more powerful web sites.

✦ Communities: Social networking with features such as activity feeds.

✦ Content: Enterprise Content Management, metadata navigation and document sets to name a few.

✦ Search: Enterprise search capabilities including searching for people and expertise.

✦ Insights: Powerful analysis and charting tools.

✦ Composites: Features for the application developer that make it easy to build your own solutions.

Mind you, these are only the main enhancements; SharePoint Foundation provides a lot of the underlying plumbing that makes all the bells and whistles possible.

Much of this plumbing — delivered with SharePoint Foundation — is much the same as it used to be, though it works a bit differently and adds some new possibilities. An example is Business Connectivity Services, a new, free, built-in service application that takes over from the old Business Data Catalog. Under the hood, there's more good news: Business Connectivity Services is one of several built-in programs that conform to the new Service Applications framework, which means you can integrate new applications with much more flexibility. SharePoint Server 2010 includes other Service Applications (such as InfoPath and Visio Services) that are designed to take advantage of SharePoint features. Upcoming subsections give you a closer look at how some of those features help you make the most of SharePoint.

✦ You can control SharePoint sites via the familiar Ribbon interface.

✦ SharePoint Workspace makes collaboration and offline working easier.

✦ SharePoint Mobile makes the sites available to PDAs, cell phones, and other small form factor devices.

✦ Integration of Office client and Web Applications means you can use already-familiar Microsoft products to work with your SharePoint content.

✦ Communities can be established with SharePoint, which lets your business gain from everyone's experience and expertise.

✦ Dividing the site into communities.

✦ SharePoint provides tools for creating, regulating, revising, and distributing Web content that you can search more easily.

✦ By turning raw business data into Web-ready content, SharePoint helps collaborating employees arrive at useful Insights more quickly.

✦ Using SharePoint Composites, you can bring together various software capabilities and create custom applications that fit your business.

Figure 2-1 shows how SharePoint Foundation underlies the process of creating a custom solution to typical organizational problems, such as how to best exploit your information assets.

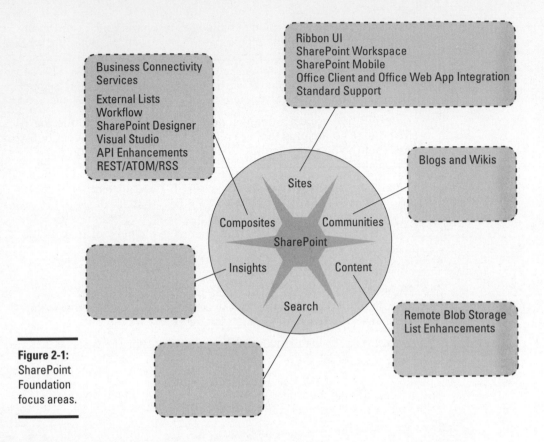

Business Connectivity Services

External Lists
Workflow
SharePoint Designer
Visual Studio
API Enhancements
REST/ATOM/RSS

Ribbon UI
SharePoint Workspace
SharePoint Mobile
Office Client and Office Web App Integration
Standard Support

Blogs and Wikis

Sites
Composites   Communities
SharePoint
Insights   Content
Search

Remote Blob Storage
List Enhancements

Figure 2-1:
SharePoint
Foundation
focus areas.

SharePoint Foundation Basics

In this section we look at what makes SharePoint Foundation work as a platform on which you can build collaborative applications to suit your organization.

Untying some commands on the Ribbon

By adding the Ribbon, Microsoft made the SharePoint user interface instantly more familiar to Office users. The Ribbon first replaced the menu-and-toolbar interface in most Office 2007 client applications; these days you can find it in all Office 2010 applications — and on almost all SharePoint Web pages, accessible via the browser. Result: The controls for a SharePoint site are more consistent with those you know from everyday Office applications such as Word and Excel. The Ribbon can also show you the exact tools you need for doing specific tasks on the SharePoint site. Handy, isn't it? (Now, there's an understatement!)

The Ribbon organizes your options with two kinds of tabs:

✦ Common actions for the tasks you do are grouped together and placed on tabs that appear as you navigate around your SharePoint site. Behind the scenes, the Ribbon finds the tools you'll probably need for wherever you end up — and puts them on the tabs for your convenience.

✦ *Contextual tabs* appear when you perform specific actions, offering a handful of commands that are related to what you're doing. Contextual tabs limit the on-screen clutter so it's easier to see what you're working on.

Figure 2-2 shows the tabs, groups, and tasks you'd see on a typical SharePoint Web page. In this example, you get five groups of commands you might use for a range of Web-page tasks:

✦ **Edit:** This is the group you use for tweaking, massaging, or otherwise fiddling with documents.

Although this is the first group in the picture, the Edit button's menu has dropped down in front of the group name. (Just goes to show that on-screen real estate is precious. But you knew that.)

✦ **Manage:** This group is for managing access to the Web page.

✦ **Share & Track:** Use this group to share content in the library with others.

✦ **Page Actions:** This group holds tools that allow you to reference the page from other locations such as marking it as your browser's home.

✦ **Page Library:** This group is where you find tools to control access to the library that the Web page resides in.

Tabs   Groups   Tasks

Figure 2-2:
The Ribbon shows tabs, groups of commands, and tasks on a Share-Point site.

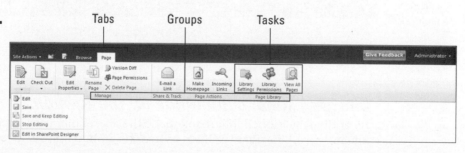

For some commands, you can see more options by clicking the down arrow next to the command. In Figure 2-2, clicking the arrow next to the Edit task put a list of editing options on-screen.

Figure 2-3 shows what a SharePoint Web page's Ribbon looks like when you click the Edit option under the Edit button. More tabs, groups of commands, and tasks appear on the Ribbon — and now you can modify the contents of the page at a detailed level (choosing fonts, formatting, and such).

Figure 2-3:
Clicking the Edit option under the Edit group brings up the Editing Tools tab.

Okay, suppose you want to shrink a picture on the page you're editing so the text fits better. You select a picture and voilá — a contextual tab appears, as shown in Figure 2-4. A new Design tab — specific to images — crops up, offering the tools you need for the job (in this case, the Horizontal Size and Vertical Size commands). Beats slogging through complex menus on a hunt for the right command.

Figure 2-4:
Clicking an on-screen object (in this case, a picture) brings up the appropriate tools on a contextual tab.

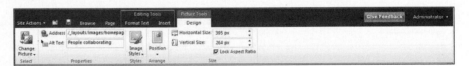

If you're one of those IT wizards who has permission to (ahem) "manage server resources," you can add custom commands and tabs to the Ribbon and download SharePoint developer documentation from the Microsoft Web site in order to find out how to do this.

If you can't find something, look closely at the Ribbon. Maybe a contextual tab has appeared with the option you're looking for! If not, try clicking the part of the Web page you want to modify. (If it's a picture of the company founder, resist the temptation to add a mustache.)

Setting up SharePoint sites

SharePoint is a Web-based application — designed to use Web sites to store and access content. The parts of SharePoint Foundation that support your Web sites make up the *"site framework."* Five major components make up the site framework:

✦ **SharePoint Farm:** This group of SharePoint servers is also known as the Web Farm (a figure of speech, similar to calling a bunch of cubicles a "cube farm" — no pitchfork required). Whether your farm has one or many servers, you can configure each one to do a specific server task — and share services throughout the farm (or with other farms).

✦ **Internet Information Services (IIS):** This service handles all requests for SharePoint content; it runs on your front-end Web server. The requests arrive in the form of a URL (Uniform Resource Locator) — such as `http://www.nut2craic.com/sites/music/default.aspx`. IIS directs each one to an appropriate "IIS Web site" (a single server can hold many of these).

✦ **Web Applications:** A Web Application is a special IIS Web site set up to serve as a host location for your SharePoint sites. Whether you create a Web Application directly or specify an existing IIS Web site as a new Web Application, you have to make sure that it exists on all Web servers in your farm that have direct contact with users. That's because the Web Application is where IIS looks to determine whether to hand off incoming URL requests to SharePoint.

The server portion of the incoming URL — in our example URL given earlier — that would be `www.nut2craic.com` — dictates which Web Application takes responsibility. This part of the URL is often referred to as the *namespace*. Each Web Application can support multiple namespaces, using a variety of techniques such as

- IIS host headers that specify names for the IIS web site.

- SharePoint's Alternate Access Mappings (AAM), which allow you to reference a single web application using multiple different namespaces.

Additionally, each Web Application can support one or more managed paths (SharePoint owned resources under which site collections are created). Managed paths also form part of the URL and in the first example given earlier, the managed path is `/sites/`.

✦ **Site Collections.** These are groups of administratively related SharePoint sites created inside Web Applications. The sites in each collection can contain subsites — sometimes a gaggle of them — and yes, it can get confusing, especially when they share resources and features. For the moment, remember that specifying certain settings for the top-level site in a collection (such as permissions) also specifies those same settings for every site and subsite in the collection by default.

✦ **Databases.** SharePoint puts most of its configuration information about the servers in your farm in one place: a single configuration database. The content that lives in each site collection (such as Web pages, documents, and lists) winds up in a different place: a separate content database (and you can have many content databases in your farm).

Although the content databases are hosted on one or more SQL servers, SharePoint doesn't manage those servers so it's debatable whether they're part of the overall SharePoint farm. You don't install any SharePoint code specifically on your SQL servers — it's all tucked away in the databases that SharePoint creates on those servers.

Remote Blob Storage

Here's a new feature that's not nearly as messy as it sounds: SharePoint Foundation 2010 can store some content outside all those SQL servers by using a technique called Remote Blob Storage (RBS). No, you're not packing away some oozing monster from a '50s horror movie. This feature stores binary "blobs" of data (such as the contents of the Word documents in a document library) in the file system or a dedicated storage space. This capability offers you a couple of immediate benefits:

- **You can make your SQL content databases smaller and more manageable.** Just keep in mind that all that content still has to be managed, and that will be the chore of the external repository.

- **You can integrate third-party applications that access content in some other way than through an SQL database.** That's especially handy if, say, you're using an archiving product that stores its content in the file system.

Remote Blob Storage may also be the only way to go if you plan on upgrading existing databases that are larger than 4 GB into a basic installation of SharePoint Foundation. The reason behind this is that SQL Server Express 2008 (the version of SQL used for a basic, single-server installation of SharePoint Foundation) can't support content databases larger than 4 GB. If, for example, you have a database that used Windows SharePoint Services 3.0 (which based its internal database format on SQL and could handle more than 4 GB of data), you have two practical choices: Shrink those databases before you migrate them to SharePoint Foundation or move them to Remote Blob Storage.

Designing your site framework

Now, when you put together all the components just described, what you get is a scalable, flexible framework that provides a home on your network for SharePoint Web sites and their contents.

✦ Each Web Application can have one or more content databases associated with it.

✦ Each site collection — and its contents — are contained in various tables in a single content database.

✦ The details of all your site collections are held in various tables in the configuration database.

✦ Every Web server that receives user requests for content knows which content database — and which corresponding site collection — to access when it responds to a request.

By default, a newly created site collection is stored, in the database that currently has the greatest number of available places to put it. That's why, when you configure a content database, you indicate the maximum number of site collections you want it to contain; SharePoint keeps a note of how many site collections are currently in each database. Of course, if you absolutely have to shoehorn some new site collections into a particular content database, here are some ways you can do so:

✦ Dramatically increase the maximum number of available places in the database you want to expand so it *always* has the most free "slots" for site collections.

✦ Set the maximum number of site collections permitted on all *other* content databases to zero.

✦ Use a command-line program (such as `stsadm` or PowerShell), rather than the browser, to create the site collection in the first place. That way you can specify the exact content database in which to create the site collection.

Because a content database contains an entire site collection, you can move that database around — from one SQL server to another, from one Web Application to another, even from one SharePoint Farm to another — without losing those site collections.

You may be tempted to put all your content "eggs" in one content database "basket" — but let's not tempt fate here. A major reason for having multiple content databases is to ensure that no individual database gets too big for its britches. A very large database can slow down performance in SQL, and can be a major headache if you have to *restore* that monster after a disaster. After all, SharePoint 2010 gives you a much handier way — Remote Blob Storage — to store content outside the content database if want to, say, back up vital data or just avoid database bloat.

A SharePoint server knows which farm it belongs to via the Windows Registry. That's because the installation process asks you whether you want to create a new farm or put your SharePoint server in an existing farm; either way, you have to indicate which SQL server houses the configuration database. This information then resides in the Registry on each SharePoint server; it's used whenever you start SharePoint. The Registry key is

```
HKEY_LOCAL_MACHINE\SOFTWARE\Microsoft\Shared Tools\Web Server
       Extensions\14.0\Secure\ConfigDB
```

As you're planning the ways your organization will use SharePoint, you'll have to decide how many server farms, Web Applications, and content databases your business needs. Before you can do that, however, you have to get a handle on your business requirements — in other words, what your business is trying to achieve with SharePoint. They influence your site design — especially in how you separate content, how many namespaces you need, and how fine-grained your management processes have to be.

Creating a site collection

After you've installed SharePoint Foundation, you can create any number of Web Applications to host any number of site collections. But first things first: To get up and running with a demo installation of SharePoint Foundation, you need only prepare a single server with the necessary prerequisites and then do a Basic installation. This process installs all the required server roles — in particular, the Web server and application server roles — on the single server. A Basic installation also installs SQL Server 2008 Express to house the configuration and content databases.

This server installation is only usable as a demo or as a playground (with SharePoint features taking the place of jungle gyms and slides). A Basic single-server installation can't be extended to make a SharePoint farm. For that matter, a farm needs a separate, full-featured (non-"express") edition of SQL Server. If you want to extend this single-server installation later on, you'll have to do an Advanced installation of SharePoint Foundation.

Here's an example in which SharePoint Foundation has been installed on a single server called `ms4`. To create a site collection called `http://www.nut2craic.com/sites/music`, follow these steps:

1. **Start SharePoint Central Administration (SCA) from the Start menu of your SharePoint server or by typing the URL to SCA into your browser.**

SharePoint Foundation created the SharePoint Central Administration (SCA) Web Application during installation. The IIS Web site associated with the SCA Web Application has a random, and unique, port number; Figure 2-5 shows the example's port number as `33805` and the Web address of SCA as `http://ms4:33805`.

2. **In the SCA window, choose Application Management➪Manage Web Applications.**

An SCA Web page appears, as shown in Figure 2-6.

Readers with previous SharePoint experience may notice that the SCA options are far easier to find than they used to be. The warning at the top of the page is a testament to the (far better) manageability of SharePoint 2010; it comes to you courtesy of a Health Analyzer that monitors and reports on critical resources — you can even customize the analyzer by adding your own rules. (See? Sometimes progress really *does* happen.)

Figure 2-5:
The
SharePoint
Central
Admini-
stration
Web site,
shown as a
window in
IIS.

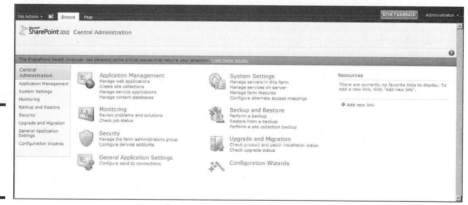

Figure 2-6:
Creating
a Web
Application
in SCA.

3. **Create a new Web Application by clicking the New button on the Ribbon.**

   The dialog box shown in Figure 2-7 appears. Although you'd have a lot of administrative decisions to make when creating a Web Application for real, it's okay to accept almost all the defaults for this example — *except* the following four:

   a. *Specify the namespace of the Web Application by typing in* `www.nut2craic.com` *as the host header (as shown in Figure 2-4).*

   b. *Although SharePoint allocated you a random port number it is now not required for uniqueness (since the host header is unique) so you can remove the port number from the Public URL section leaving you with just* `http://www.nut2craic.com` *here.*

c. *Each Web Application requires an Application Pool under which it will run and, by default, SharePoint will create a new pool for this purpose. Each Application Pool requires an account under which it will run. Best practice is to create a Managed Account for this purpose but for this exercise you can simply use the built-in Network Service account. Therefore in the Application Pool section select the predefined option.*

d. *From the Search server drop-down list, choose the server on which you've installed the demo version of SharePoint Foundation (for this example, that's* ms4*).*

The Database Name and Authentication section of the Create Web Application window is where you name the content database that will be created to host the content of all the site collections you eventually associate with the new Web Application.

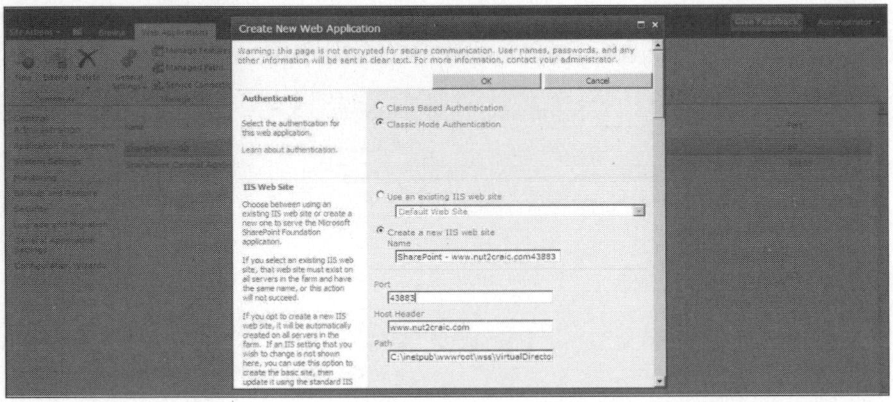

Figure 2-7:
Configuring
a Web
Application
in the Create
New Web
Application
dialog box.

The Create a New Web Application dialog box appears.

4. **Choose the option that links you to the Create Site Collections page.**

This step gets you started with (you guessed it) creating a site collection. You can also access this link from SCA itself. Either way, you get the dialog box shown in Figure 2-8.

From here you choose the Title and Description for your site collection, its managed path (/sites/), and the final portion of its URL (/music). Further down this dialog box you can choose the site template to use for this site collection, the primary site collection owner, and, optionally, a secondary site collection owner. If you've set up quota templates you can also choose that from this dialog box. Site templates are extensible components that are used to initially configure a site collection in terms of its look and feel and some of its initial content.

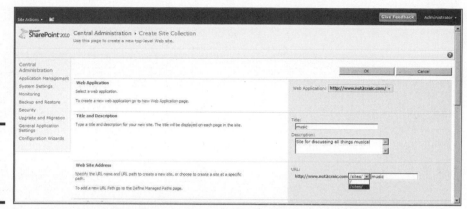

Figure 2-8:
Creating
a site
collection.

In actual practice, various SharePoint administrative dialog boxes require you to choose the correct Web Application. More often than not, SharePoint won't pre-select a current Web Application for you — and clicking the down arrow does *not* give you a list of current Web Applications (as you might naturally expect). Instead, you get a link to another dialog box — and from there, you choose the Web Application you want. (Very frustrating indeed!) But at least . . .

Your new site collection is created.

5. **Make sure that the link to** www.nut2craic.com **works.**

You should be able to access the site collection by entering http://www.nut2craic.com/sites/music into your browser's navigation box — at least that's what you'd do as a final step if this were a real installation. The idea is to ensure that the host header resolves to a suitable IP address for your server (in this case, ms4).

In a for-real installation, you'd handle this chore by adding www.nut2craic.com to the Domain Name System; for demo purposes you may be able to get away with adding it to the hosts file on the device you are running your browser on.

When you've typed in the site collection's name, you should see your brand new site collection as shown in Figure 2-9. Your top-level site comprises multiple Web pages, lists, and libraries all of which are customizable and extendable. When created you can start to populate it with content, create subsites, and tailor the whole environment for the task at hand.

SharePoint offers many ways to contribute (and tweak) the content kept in SharePoint sites, including these:

✦ Saving directly from Office client applications *and* Web Applications.

✦ E-mailing content to lists and libraries.

✦ Synchronizing content with SharePoint Workspace and Outlook.

✦ Uploading directly through browsers.

✦ Using Web Services and the Object Model to build new ways to use SharePoint.

Securing access to content

SharePoint gives you control over access to resources at many levels, including these:

✦ The SharePoint farm

✦ The site collection

✦ Individual sites

✦ Lists and libraries

✦ Items within each list or library

While you're specifying who can do what to these securable objects, keep the following concepts in mind:

✦ **Security principals:** These folks are the "who" in "who can do what" — whether an individual or a group. SharePoint supports different types of users and groups:

• Local Windows users and groups

• Active Directory Users and Security Groups

- • SharePoint Groups

- • Members and roles from any pluggable authentication methods on your network (such as using a SQL table to hold users and groups). If a resource has been secured for a group security principal, SharePoint verifies whether the requesting user is a member of that group before allowing access.

✦ **Authentication:** This is the process of identifying and verifying who the requesting user is — and whether that user has sufficient rights to perform the desired task on the requested resource. A user gets these rights in one of two ways:

- • Explicitly, through the user's security principal

- • Implicitly, through membership in a group security principal

SharePoint supports many methods of authentication — including standard Windows, claims-based, and forms-based — and you can apply any of these at the Web Application level. Whatever the authentication method, SharePoint can identify the requesting user as a security principal — so long as the user is authenticated successfully (if not, well, let's not go there).

✦ **Authorization:** This is, in effect, the official okay for the user to *do* the "what" in "who can do what." It's a process of granting specific rights to security principals to perform specific tasks. SharePoint can be as finicky as necessary about assigning rights; they show up in the user interface as assigned Permission Levels.

✦ **Permission Levels:** SharePoint checks to see whether the requesting security principal has the required authorization to perform a specific task. A default SharePoint Foundation 2010 installation provides 33 permissions that users can be granted. Here's how they work:

Some permissions are pre-requisites for others. For example, a user must have View Items permission as a pre-requisite for Manage Lists.

Server-farm administrators can control which permissions can be used within a Web Application. For ease of management, any number of permissions can be grouped together as Permission Levels.

Each security principal is associated with one or more Permission Levels; SharePoint aggregates the permissions in each level to determine the final set of permissions granted to each requesting user.

Ready-to-use Permission levels include Full Control, Design, Read, and Contribute — and you can create your own to suit your needs. Normally you assign Permissions levels to whole sites; a site can either inherit its permissions from a parent site or have them explicitly set at the level of subsites, lists, libraries, or individual items.

You can (for example) define a custom role called Publishers (using SharePoint Groups) as a group security principal, and grant its members permission to add items to a list but not to delete items. To do so for the list at `http://www.nut2craic.com/sites/music/lists/announcements`, follow these steps:

1. **Open SharePoint Central Administration to check your Web Application's available SharePoint permissions.**

   For a refresher on Central Administration, see Book II, Chapter 6.

2. **Choose Manage Web Applications to select your Web Application and then choose User Permissions on the Ribbon.**

3. **Access the site collection** `http://www.nut2craic.com/sites/music` **as a site administrator.**

4. **Choose Site Actions⇨Site Permissions.**

   SharePoint shows you a list of the default SharePoint groups and Permission levels currently in effect. None of the default Permission levels is suitable for this example's needs, so you have to create a new one. You can do so from scratch or, better still, use an existing one as a starting point. In this instance, the Contributelevel is closest to the requirement, so . . .

5. **Select Permission Levels from the Ribbon and then select Contribute to view that level's permissions; scroll down to the Copy Permission Level button and click it.**

   SharePoint now shows you the same page with the same permissions automatically selected.

6. **Name the new level** Add No Delete, **remove the Delete Items permission, and save your changes.**

   So far, so good. But none of the default SharePoint Groups are suitable for the example's purpose; any member of those groups would have permissions that were either too big or too small for the task at hand. But don't let that stop you; the next step shows how to create a new group.

7. **Return to the Site Permissions page, choose Create Group, and then specify a new group called** Publishers.

   A SharePoint group defines a *role* — anyone who is a member of the group has the role, and is allowed to execute the required task.

8. **Navigate to the Announcements list.**

   If you cannot see a quick link to the Announcements list, click the Lists option in the Quick Launch bar at the left side of the page, which shows you all lists defined in the site.

   The Announcements list is where you would typically create announcements that are relevant to your web site. You can grant access at multiple levels; in this example, you're doing so at the list level — which means the list is the only part of this site collection that use the custom permission level.

9. **To manage the permissions on the list, use the Ribbon: On the List tab, click List Permissions.**

   By default, the permissions on a list are inherited from its parent — in this case, the site collection — but for this example, you want to break the inheritance. So. . .

10. **Click Stop Inheriting Permissions.**

    A warning dialog appears reminding you that changes to the parent site will not apply to the list. After accepting the warning you are returned tot he site permissions page

11. **Assign the new Permission level.**

    A two-step operation completes this task:

    a. *Grant the permission level to your group security principal.* Choose Grant Permissions, specify Publishers in the box at the top of the dialog box, and select the Add No Delete check box at the bottom of the dialog box.

    b. *Add users to your new group.* You can do so either from the Grant Permissions dialog box or by clicking the Publishers group name (which takes you to a page where you can manage the membership). Either way, any user you add to the Publishers group can add items to the Announcements list but can't delete any items (so if they add an item in error then they'll need to find someone that has delete access to remove the item). Additionally, a user who is only a member of the Publishers group on this particular site collection can't access any other part of the site.

Lists, libraries, views, and content types

SharePoint 2010 offers a range of ways to organize the content you want to use. The following subsections give you a closer look at each of them.

Lists and libraries

Lists provide the most common (and most-used) storage mechanism for content in a site collection. You use lists for whatever purpose you like; you can use the many pre-defined lists directly or as a starting point for your own custom lists. Examples of built-in lists are Announcements, Events, and Contacts. The lists you create are only limited by your imagination (or . . . by your business needs! Exactly!). Some key concepts about lists follow:

✦ *Lists* are defined in terms of columns — in particular, by the *metadata* (data describing or defining other data) they contain. (Properties is another commonly used term for this.)

✦ Each column has a field type. Examples of field types are

   • String

- Number

- Lookup (for information that exists in another list)

- Person or Group

- Custom field type that you've developed

✦ You can optionally apply validation rules to a list to ensure consistency in usage. For example you may want to check that the sum of various columns does not exceed a particular threshold.

✦ The definition of a *list* and the contents of the list are ultimately stored in a content database.

✦ A *library* is just a special form of list where one of the columns is used to store the binary content of the item. This means that a Word document that has been stored in a document library is physically stored in the underlying content database.

✦ *Versioning* within lists and libraries is supported (this is the ability to store separate copies of items each time they are modified) and can be used for various purposes — for example in a document library it can be used to compare two versions of a document or in a wiki page it can be used to show which edits were recently made to the page.

Creating a list involves giving the list a name and then defining the columns that will comprise the list. These columns can be newly defined or chosen from existing site columns; site columns created by site administrators and in SharePoint Foundation ensure consistency across sites in a site collection. (Note that the boundary of usage here is the site collection: Site columns can only be chosen from the existing site and its parent sites — a restriction that can be overcome by installing SharePoint Server 2010 and leveraging the Managed Metadata Service.)

Views

When your list is created its contents are primarily accessed via customizable views. Views define which columns are displayed and how the items within the list are grouped, sorted, and filtered. These flexible views can be created through the browser by end users and the "All items" view is automatically created for you when you create a list.

Views are used in many places to display the data in your lists and libraries. For example:

✦ Accessing the list directly through your Web browser.

✦ On a List View Web Part to show list content alongside other pertinent content.

✦ In Office client applications such as Outlook, Excel, and Access.

✦ Accessing a library from Windows Explorer via the Explorer view.

Columns based on custom field types don't appear in Datasheet view — and they're not included when you export a list to a Microsoft Excel worksheet.

SharePoint also has support for mobile views — views that are designed to be displayed on mobile devices and are therefore much simpler in display terms. Mobile support was in previous versions of SharePoint but is vastly improved in 2010 — for example, you can see a mobile view of a team site by merely adding /m to the URL for the home page — which seamlessly redirects you to a page offering a list of the lists available in the team site you're visiting. You don't even need a mobile device; just enter the required URL into your Web browser and there you are.

Content types

Content types provide a way to group a set of site columns together and these structures can then be used for various purposes — for example, allowing a single list to hold items of different types. As you enable a list to contain a content type, the columns associated with the list are extended (along with those site columns) from the content type. These site columns can then be treated in the same way as other columns — and you can include them in the views associated with the list.

SharePoint itself uses content types for many features — such as controlling workflows and page layouts. As with site columns, each site within a collection can have its own content types and can use any content types defined in any of its parent sites. This again limits the scope of usage — a restriction which can also be overcome if you leverage the Enterprise Content Type and Syndication capabilities of the Managed Metadata Service.

Scaling your lists to fit the job

SharePoint 2010 is dramatically better at scaling lists than MOSS was. If you need a seriously big list — say, if you're an astronomer who wants to list stars in the galaxy — you can now have lists and libraries with millions of items. Two changes in SharePoint make this marvel possible:

✦ Improving the way data is indexed and queried in SQL.

✦ Modifying the behavior on front-end Web servers such that they are not compromised by queries that would generate a large amount of processing.

The second change is accomplished by setting limits on certain resources — for example the number of items that can be returned in a query or the number of unique permissions that can be applied within a list. Administrators can set these limits on a per-Web-Application level.

By default the maximum number of items that can be returned by an end user query is 5,000 items (it's 20,000 for administrators and auditors). If a user was to execute a view on a list that would return more than this number the server will not return any items for the requested view and a warning message is displayed at the top of the list. The server, in this case, is defending itself against inappropriate use.

Users who have permissions to modify the list settings will also see a warning as shown in Figure 2-10 where we have set the maximum number of items to 2,000 (which incidentally is the lowest threshold you can set in the user interface!) — as soon as there are more than 2,000 items in the list and a view is executed that returns more than this number the warning is displayed.

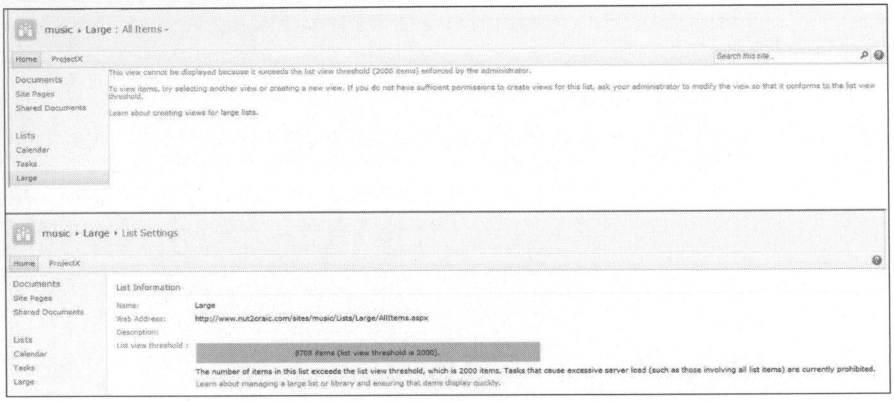

Figure 2-10:
The List
Threshold.

List view thresholds can be set separately for end-users and administrators and you can also allow custom code to override the thresholds. There is also the ability to specify time periods when the thresholds do not apply which may be useful if you have a legitimate need to run large queries on a less frequent basis.

Limiting the number of items that can be returned in a query is not only necessary but also kind. If your organization simply must have millions of items in a list, it's unreasonable to process that whole million items in one fell swoop. You could seriously overload your server (if you don't scare it to death first). And unless your users live for thousands of years, you wouldn't expect a user to step through a million items in one operation.

To keep your queries effective, you have to prevent them from tying up the server in an effort to defend itself against . . . well . . . large queries. Design your views carefully to ensure that they don't exceed the threshold. You can do so in various ways:

✦ In SharePoint Foundation you can use the filtering capability on views. For example, if you have a large list that contains the details of songs, you could create 26 views to split the content alphabetically by song title.

✦ In SharePoint Server there are more powerful ways to navigate large lists via the Managed Metadata Service. This allows you to implement faceted navigation — the ability to navigate through lists using dynamic meta-data values. For example, if you had a Genre column for your music information, you could navigate the list by the values of that column to find Country, Rock, Classical, and so on. (With SharePoint Foundation, you could only do this trick if you created separate filtered views for each Genre you expected to find in your list.)

Another feature essential for taming large lists is the capability to specify up to 20 indices for your list. By specifying the columns that are heavily used in views and filters, you can execute queries faster. In the music example, creating an index for the Genre column would improve performance when you wanted to filter a large list to show only the Country or Rock items.

SharePoint as a Development Platform

The Composites piece of the SharePoint pie is primarily focused on develop-ers. The features that contribute to this solution area encompass the whole development landscape and address developer productivity, rich plat-form services, and flexible deployment options. All these additions to the SharePoint landscape attest to its viability as a development platform that can support industrial-strength solutions on an enterprise-wide scale.

Dissecting SharePoint Web solutions

There are many elements that can be involved in a SharePoint solution — especially these:

✦ One or more Web Parts

✦ Site templates

✦ Feature definitions

✦ Assemblies

✦ Code access security policies.

To deploy of these components, you use a Web Solution Package (WSP) — a cabinet file that contains, among other things, a *Web manifest* (a definition of what's in the package and how it should be installed).

Features are a major component of any SharePoint installation and are installed via a WSP. A feature is a package of components that implements a specific piece of functionality such as:

✦ Custom lists

✦ Custom actions

✦ Default Web pages

✦ Web Parts

✦ Workflows

When features are installed in the server farm, you can turn them on and off at multiple levels, according to their scope — the scope determines where you can activate a feature in the farm. Activating a feature lights up the site with the various components contained in the feature. SharePoint itself uses features to control such functionality as managing Web content; third-party software generally extends SharePoint capabilities by building and deploying features (and other supporting components).

The best way to get a handle on what's in a .wsp is to save a team site as a template. Doing so creates a .wsp file automatically (and behind the scenes) in the Solution Gallery for the site collection. You can take the following steps to see this process in action:

1. **Access your team site as a site administrator and choose Site Actions/ SiteSettings.**

2. **From the Site Actions section, choose Save site as a template.**

   The Save Site As Template Web page appears.

3. **Give your template a filename and a name.**

   You can also choose to include the physical contents of the site in the template.

   After processing is complete, SharePoint puts a .wsp file in the Solution Gallery for the site collection; this gallery is essentially a library of solutions you've created.

4. **Open the Solutions Gallery by choosing Site Actions/Site Settings⇨Galleries⇨Solutions.**

5. **With the Solutions Gallery on-screen, click the Library tab on the Ribbon and then choose Open with Explorer.**

   Doing so takes you to a Windows Explorer view of the library, from which you can take a copy of the .wsp file.

6. **Place your .wsp file in a temporary location and rename it with a .cab extension.**

7. **Use Windows Explorer to open the .cab file.**

   You should see all the individual files it contains:

   a. Manifest.xml defines the overall contents of the solution.

   b. Individual feature.xml files define all the lists, Web Parts, and such that your solution contains.

   c. Schema.xml defines the fields and views for each of the lists contained in the solution.

The main reason for introducing you to `.wsp` files and features at this stage is to show how other developer tools can help you produce these files and deploy them across your SharePoint farms.

Developing with a browser, SharePoint Designer, and Visual Studio

SharePoint empowers people to customize their team sites in a variety of ways — end users can make simple modifications to Web pages through the browser, power users can power their way through the features of SharePoint Designer 2010, and professional developers can use Visual Studio 2010 to build complete solutions. Indeed it is now even possible to install SharePoint on a Windows 7 or Windows Vista Service Pack 1 platform for development purposes (far easier for developers to get going) and to build and deploy *sandboxed* solutions (that is, those that can only run a contained environment).

If you're concerned about "under the desk" installation, then you can prohibit installation of SharePoint on a computer by tweaking a particular Registry key in any way that's applicable to your environment (for example, using the built-in Windows Group Policy administration tool). Figure 2-11 shows the details of the `DisableInstall` Registry key.

Sandboxed solutions are a new concept for SharePoint. No, it doesn't involve pails and shovels. Rather, developers can create and upload custom code that can run safely on the server without the risk of some rogue code (or a typo in exactly the wrong place) bringing down the whole server farm. This helps SharePoint's reputation as a viable platform for building solutions; developers want to do their thing without (so to speak) betting the farm. Server-farm administrators can monitor and validate these sandboxed solutions — for example by measuring CPU execution time and memory consumption — ensuring that they do not compromise the overall health of the SharePoint environment.

Figure 2-11:
The Registry key that disables the installation of SharePoint.

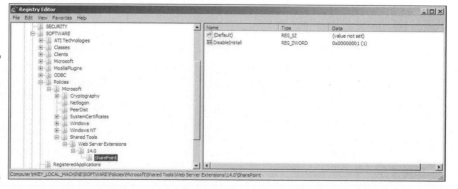

Developer capabilities are far easier to get to in SharePoint 2010 — and they work together much better — than in previous versions. For example, in previous releases you could use SharePoint Designer to significantly change the way a view rendered list data. When you did so, it was then not possible to further customize that view through the browser due to incompatibilities between Designer and SharePoint (essentially Designer used XSLT and SharePoint used CAML — Collaborative Application Markup Language — to render the view).

SharePoint 2010 does away with that incompatibility; modifying a list and/or view is as easy as clicking the "Edit List in SharePoint Designer" option from the Ribbon. From inside Designer, you can add new columns to your list, customize views, and leverage features such as conditional formatting — all of which remain compatible with browser-based manipulation of the list since SharePoint views now use XSLT rather than CAML.

And SharePoint Designer is still free of charge — so there is no excuse for not going ahead and trying out the enhancements it can bring to your SharePoint sites. (Go on — you know you want to be a power user!)

Visual Studio 2010 contains many tools for the professional developer that allow not only development, but also the deployment and debugging of complete solutions. For example, many of the designers inside Visual Studio facilitate the creation of Web Parts and Workflows, define features, support the building of sandboxed solutions, and can deploy those solutions as .wsp files.

Here's an end-to-end rundown on the development story:

1. End users can design the basic components of a team site for a specific business purpose and then save that site as a template.

2. The .wsp file generated can be imported by a power user into SharePoint Designer to have extra functionality added to it.

3. The professional developer can then import the modified .wsp file from Designer to complete and deploy the total solution.

Turning on the Developer Dashboard

SharePoint offers tools to boost the productivity of software developers — in particular, Designer and Visual Studio. But SharePoint also helps developers see a bigger picture — the effect their code has on the server — so they can fine-tune the code for better performance. The Developer Dashboard is the tool to use for debugging code and monitoring the performance of Web pages.

You can control the Developer Dashboard at the farm level, using the stsadm utility to control one of its three states: on, off, and ondemand. (Whether the developers themselves have those three states is debatable.)

Although PowerShell is the SharePoint 2010 administrative tool, the older command-line tool, `stsadm`, is still used for controlling certain features. In this case, you use it to set the value of a property called `developer-dashboard`. Log on to one of the front-end Web servers in your farm and execute the following from a command prompt (using `ondemand` as the example):

```
Stsadm -o setproperty -pn developer-dashboard -pv
    ondemand
```

`Stsadm.exe` is well hidden, deep down in a folder tree on your SharePoint servers at

```
%COMMONPROGRAMFILES%\microsoft shared\Web server extensions\14\bin
```

Make life easier for yourself by placing a shortcut on your desktop that calls `stsadm.exe` directly from this location. Simply navigate to the folder location, right-click `stsadm.exe`, and choose Create Shortcut. Then, on your desktop, modify the properties of the shortcut by prepending it with `cmd`. Executing this shortcut brings up a command window with the path already set to the location of `stsadm.exe`. (Another way to get this small chore done is to adjust the Path environment variable on the server to include the same folder location.)

If the status of the dashboard is `on` or `ondemand`, any user with Add and Customize Pages permission can see the Developer Dashboard at the bottom of each Web page visited. `ondemand` allows the user to view the dashboard on request; it isn't displayed automatically for all Web pages. A small icon appears next to the user's name in the top-right corner of each Web page; this icon toggles the dashboard for the current Web page when the dashboard status is `ondemand`. Figure 2-12 shows many details for all the components that make up the Web page — in particular, these:

✦ Times to render components on the page

✦ Page-checkout level

✦ Database query information

✦ Web Part processing times

✦ Any critical events or alerts

The dashboard is a handy tool for finding out why a page might be taking a long time to load — and Microsoft engineers actually used it to optimize all the built-in pages from real-world usage of SharePoint during its development. Take a hint from the pros at Redmond and use the dashboard to optimize your own team sites and custom solutions.

Connecting to data in various ways

Application developers have to be able to access SharePoint data program-matically or they can't build business solutions. Thus SharePoint supports common client-based and server-based techniques for accessing SharePoint data — but it also allows interaction with data stored outside your SharePoint farms.

Connecting to external data

Business Connectivity Services (BCS) are included in SharePoint Foundation and are designed to enable you to easily interact with data held in external systems from within SharePoint. After all, not all your business data will be held inside SharePoint lists and libraries — and so BCS offers an elegant way to augment your SharePoint data with data from external systems. Result: better business collaboration.

BCS is the evolution of the Business Data Catalog that was introduced in MOSS 2007 and is present in both SharePoint Foundation 2010 and SharePoint Server 2010. Richer functionality is available in SPS 2010 but the fact that you can access external data at all in SharePoint Foundation further attests to the viability of SharePoint Foundation as a development platform. BCS includes several components such as the Business Data Connectivity (BDC) Service and a pluggable connector framework that essentially permits access to data from any back-end data source within SharePoint.

Three connectors are included with SharePoint Foundation:

1. ADO.NET Connector for connecting to databases.

2. WCF Connector for connecting to Web services and WCF end points.

3. .NET Framework Assembly Connector for connecting (as you might expect) to .NET Framework connectivity assemblies.

Developers can build their own connectors that can be plugged into the framework to gain access to other data sources as required.

The external data you access — such as application-specific data held in databases (like human resource data, customer relationship management information, and product lists) — can be used for multiple purposes:

✦ You can display external data as a list within SharePoint allowing users to interact with the data in the same way they would with a SharePoint-based list. Although the data remains in the external repository, it can be writeable through the SharePoint user interface, assuming the necessary permissions are in place.

✦ You can augment SharePoint-based lists through the External Column data type. As long as the External Column is defined in the BDC, it can be added to an existing SharePoint list and display external data as appropriate. For example you may have a Customer Relationship Management application that maintains details of all your suppliers. You could then add a `Supplier` lookup column to a SharePoint list to ensure that you have consistent data usage across all your information sources.

✦ You can index the external data and have it appear in search results.

SharePoint 2010 implements BCS as a service application in its own right. That's a departure from MOSS 2007, which used Shared Service Provider (SSP) to handle all service applications. Book II provides more information on the SharePoint Service applications, including Business Connectivity Services.

Programmatic data access possibilities

SharePoint offers many ways for end users to input data — but developers must be able to access this data through the programs they create; solutions that meet varying business requirements depend on it. In previous SharePoint versions, you could use Web Services and the Server Object Model; in SharePoint 2010, these capabilities are augmented on the client side with REST APIs and a Client Object Model; in addition, SharePoint supports LINQ on the server (as described in upcoming subsections).

Client Object Model

The Client Object Model (Client OM) provides a subset of the Server Object Model APIs. The Client OM gives you access to many SharePoint objects such as lists, libraries, content types, and fields. You can call the Client OM from many places — whether from JavaScript or a .NET or Silverlight application. Using the Client OM in conjunction with JavaScript and AJAX allows you to build feature-rich Web pages that can do partial refreshes of SharePoint data displayed on the page. For example, building a tree view that lets you navigate through SharePoint data without having to refresh the whole page with each click is simple for developers to achieve via the Client Object Model.

RESTful Web Service

List data can be accessed via a REST-style (Representational State Transfer) Web Service. ListData.svc is a server-side Windows Communication Foundation service that follows the REST protocol and allows you to manipulate SharePoint list data via a URL (Uniform Resource Locator). The list data is returned as an XML-based ATOM feed — similar to RSS (Really Simple Syndication) but having advantages such as supporting binary object types. Note, however, that this service relies on ADO.Net Data Services being installed on your front-end Web servers.

The name Atom applies to a pair of related standards. The Atom Syndication Format is an XML language used for Web feeds, while the Atom Publishing Protocol (AtomPub or APP) is a simple HTTP-based protocol for creating and updating Web resources.

The REST syntax (full details of which can be found in the SharePoint SDK in the Microsoft Web site) is pretty straightforward and includes the following elements:

✦ The entity you want to work with — a SharePoint list.

✦ The identifier of the resource — item(s) in the list.

✦ The properties of the resource you want to manipulate — columns in the list.

✦ Optional query strings, which you can append to the URL in order to filter and sort the items returned, or to return data from related lists.

Therefore the syntax for calling the SharePoint REST service is

```
/_vti_bin/ListData.svc/{Entity}[({identifier})]/[{Property}]?[querystring]
```

Here are some examples of using REST to find specific items in a list called Albums in a site called Music:

✦ This syntax returns all the items in the list:

```
http://www.nut2craic.com/sites/music/_vti_bin/listdata.svc/albums
```

✦ This syntax returns the Genre column for the second item in the list:

```
http://www.nut2craic.com/sites/music/_vti_bin/listdata.svc/albums[1]/
    Genre
```

✦ This syntax returns all items whose `Genre` equals `"Country"`

```
http://www.nut2craic.com/sites/music/_vti_bin/listdata.svc/
     albums?$filter=Genre eq 'Country'
```

LINQ

LINQ (Language Integrated Query) provides an easy way for developers to query data sources using a standard syntax. LINQ itself relies on providers to query underlying data sources — and there are providers for SQL, XML, Google, Wikipedia, and Twitter. SharePoint 2010 introduces LINQ as a SharePoint tool.

LINQ can be used in server-side code (such as Web Parts, Event receivers, sandboxed code, and so on) to access list data. Behind-the-scenes LINQ queries are translated into CAML queries — which are then executed against the list data. A LINQ query can join multiple SharePoint lists together in much the same ways as you can join database tables together, which allows you to perform all sorts of sophisticated queries.

Chapter 3: Getting Started with a Basic Site

In This Chapter

✔ Creating and configuring a team site

✔ Linking lists

✔ Populating your site with content

*T*his chapter focuses on the workings of SharePoint sites and how to use content to best advantage. The SharePoint features and functions in these two areas enable end users to create team sites, *populate* them (that is, put useful content in them), and *consume* (make use of) that content in multiple ways.

Setting up SharePoint Sites

Almost all your interaction with SharePoint will be with a SharePoint Web site of some sort. So this section shows you how to create a site that suits your business purpose, how to find your way around it, and how to tailor it to your requirements.

Creating your site with templates

The first step toward collaboration is the creation of a site collection and (in particular) its top-level site. A *SharePoint site* is a specialized Web site you use to gather, organize, and present the information you put into SharePoint; a *site collection* is a related group of these sites. You can create a site collection in various ways; how you do so depends on the specifics of your SharePoint deployment. Ultimately you end up with a site collection that has an associated URL — such as

```
http://www.nut2craic.com/sites/music
```

The makeup of the URL is influenced by factors such as these, all discussed in Book I, Chapter 2 (and using the URL just given as an example):

✦ The SharePoint server farm where the site collection is located.

✦ The Web Application that hosts the site collection.

✦ The managed paths that are available within the Web Application.

When you create a site, it's associated automatically with the template that was used to *instantiate* (create an instance of) the site. Every template included in SharePoint corresponds to an intended usage of a site. Result: a suitable look and feel for that intended purpose (the Blog template, for example, has a look and feel that fits the tasks of writing, reviewing, and commenting on blog posts).

Many templates come with SharePoint, and you can add custom templates to fit your organization's activities. The default templates in your system depend on which version of SharePoint you've installed:

✦ All SharePoint 2010 versions install the templates listed in Table 3-1.

✦ SharePoint Server 2010 adds the templates in Table 3-2 and Table 3-3:

- Templates in Table 3-2 require only SharePoint Server 2010.

- If you also use the Access Database Service, you can apply templates from Table 3-3.

Microsoft designed SharePoint to work seamlessly with Access and all of Office 2010: Users can tap into SharePoint capabilities using special controls installed in their Office applications.

Table 3-1	Standard Templates in all SharePoint 2010 Installations
Template	*Description*
Team Site	A basic site containing a document library and lists for managing announcements, calendar items, tasks, and discussions.
Blank Site	No initial content — it's up to you to populate the site.
Document Workspace	A site set up for collaboration on documents — and the activities collaboration generates. This site provides a task list for assigning to-do items, and a link list for resources related to the document.
Blog	Designed for a typical blog Authors create posts and readers (visitors) can create comments.
Group Work Site	Promotes groupware activities such as creating a group calendar and finding out the whereabouts of group members.
Visio Process Repository	Stores Visio process diagrams in a document library and uses lists for review discussions.

Template	Description
Basic Meeting	A site to plan, organize, and capture the results of a meeting. It provides lists for managing the agenda, meeting attendees, and documents.
Blank Meeting Workspace	A blank meeting site with certain lists available (should you need them), such as Attendees, Objectives, and Status List.
Decision Meeting Workspace	A site for meetings that track status and make decisions.
Social Meeting Workspace	For planning social events. Contains a library for hosting pictures of the event.
MultiPage Meeting Workspace	Very similar to the basic meeting but with some blank pages for you to customize.

Table 3-2   Additional Templates with SharePoint Server 2010

Template	Description
Document Center	A site for managing a large quantity of documents.
Records Center	A site that stores data related to Information Management and Compliance. Can be used to file records automatically according to a specified filing plan.
Enterprise Search Center	A site from which Enterprise searches are executed and in which results are displayed. You can use its tabs to match the scope of your search to what you're searching for.
Personalization Site	A site you can use to display targeted content in personalized views.
Basic Search Center	A simple search site.
FAST Search Center	A site for using the FAST search capability (see Book III, Chapter 6).
Publishing Portal	A starter site that you can turn into an Internet-connected Web site offering common branding, news, press releases, and so on.
Enterprise Wiki	A site for publishing knowledge that you capture and want to share throughout your organization. It provides easy content editing in a single location, including the co-authoring of content, discussions, and project management.

Table 3-3	Templates that Require the Access Database Service
Template	*Description*
Assets Web Database	Creates a database of your organization's assets.
Charitable Contributions Web Database	Creates a database of charitable contributions.
Contacts Web Database	Creates a database of contacts.
Issues Web Database	Create a database of business-related issues.
Projects Web Database	Creates a database of projects.

Typically, you create a site as either a user or administrator, depending on the capabilities you need:

✦ An end user can create sites in one of two ways:

• Creating a self-service site if an administrator has enabled that feature.

• Creating a subsite from within an existing site.

✦ SharePoint administrators have several ways to create sites:

• Via Central Administration.

• Via the New-SPSite PowerShell cmdlet.

• Via the STSADM operations createsite or createsiteinnewdb.

When you've created a site, you select one of the templates listed in Tables 3-1, 3-2, or 3-3 as a starting point for your site.

You don't have to select a template at the moment you create a site, but you will have to choose a template when the site is first accessed.

Figures 3-1 and 3-2 show a typical experience with a standard Team Site and the Group Work Site. Only two real differences between these sites:

✦ The features that are enabled: The Group Work Site adds the Group Work Lists feature.

✦ The contents of the home page: The Team Site uses a Wiki home page; the Group Work Site uses a Web Part page.

Figure 3-1:
A typical
Team Site.

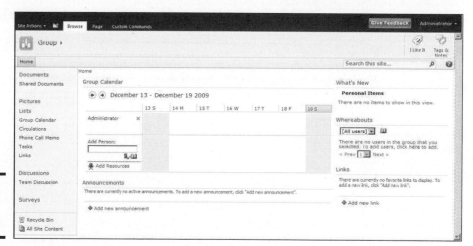

Figure 3-2:
The Group
Work Site.

TIP

The SharePoint user interface itself is lit up when you have Silverlight installed (for more about Silverlight, see the "Interesting Web Parts" section). Figure 3-3 and Figure 3-4 show two different flavors of the template selection user interface that shows up onscreen when you're creating a site. When you have Silverlight installed — as shown in Figure 3-4 — you get a user interface with far richer features (have it pick up the tab for lunch).

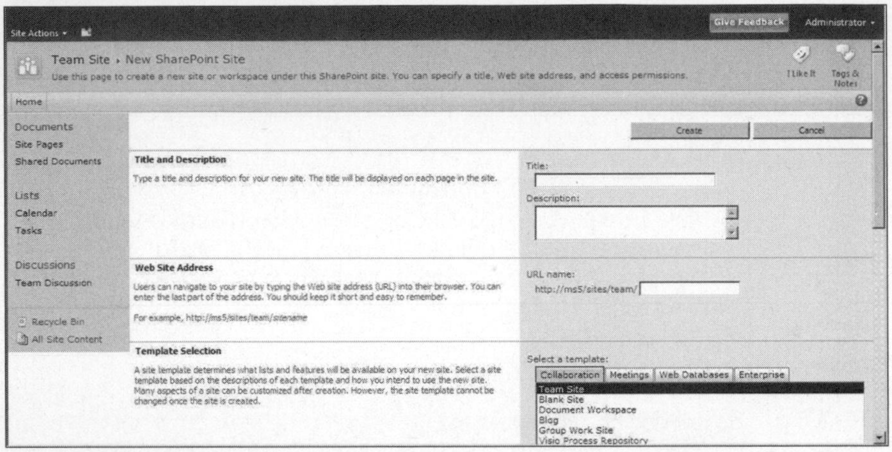

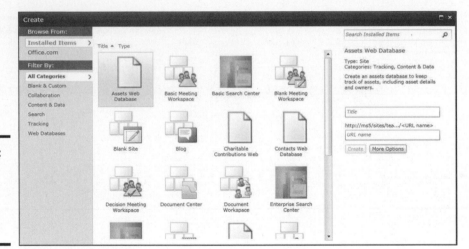

Figure 3-3:
Template
Selection.

Figure 3-4:
Template
Selection
with
Silverlight
installed.

Navigation

Navigational aids in SharePoint 2010 help you find your way through the contents of site collections. As with previous versions, *breadcrumb* trails (a series of hyperlinks that help you return to a specific Web page that you have traversed to get to the current page) are present, as are customizable vertical and horizontal quick-launch bars — but with some enhancements, so you don't have to poke around a Web page to find the options you want. More of those appear where you'd look for them intuitively (except for the Site Actions menu, which moved from the right side of each Web page to the left).

Two examples help explain the overall navigational improvements:

✦ The breadcrumb trail includes more stops along its path, list and document library views, and access to drop-down lists directly from the breadcrumb trail. You can follow a breadcrumb trail (sorry, no wicked witches included) and still have access the views of a list, as shown in Figure 3-5.

✦ You get a new Up button item beside the Site Actions option on the left side of the page. Clicking this button shows you where the current page fits into the overall hierarchy of the site; if you like, you can jump quickly to another pertinent location. In Figure 3-6, for example, we arrived at this page by selecting the Modify This View, an option shown in Figure 3-5.

Figure 3-5:
Views
from the
breadcrumb
trail.

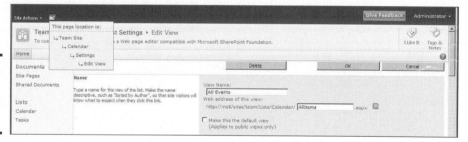

Figure 3-6:
The Up
navigational
aid.

Setting themes for your sites

Although you could set themes for your sites in previous versions, this feature is far more flexible in SharePoint 2010. Site administrators can choose from 20 built-in themes (they're in the Theme Gallery associated with each site collection) and modify such elements as these for each chosen theme:

✦ Choose a font for headings.

✦ Choose the colors to use for hyperlinks.

✦ Specify which subsites in a site collection use the theme.

This is a welcome addition; in days of yore, every site's theme had to be chosen manually.

✦ Upload new themes into the gallery to augment existing themes.

In another departure from previous versions, you no longer have to know the arcane arts of using Cascading Style Sheets (CSS) or modifying XML files on the server to make the new theme available to the site.

✦ You can build your own themes from within PowerPoint 2010 — which gives you greater consistency when you want to present a wider gamut of content — in just three steps:

1. **Select any of the built-in PowerPoint themes.**

2. **Change the font, color, or effects associated with the theme and save it as a custom theme file (with a** .thmx **extension).**

   Figure 3-7 shows an example.

3. **Upload the new** .thmx **file into the Theme Gallery and apply it to individual sites.**

Figure 3-7: Saving a theme from within PowerPoint to SharePoint.

Multiple-browser support

SharePoint 2010 supports multiple browsers — to varying degrees. The level of support depends on the browser version and the platform on which it runs. Not all browsers can support Silverlight or ActiveX controls (which enable SharePoint to deliver the widest range of capabilities).

SharePoint 2010 offers two levels of browser support, based on platform and browser:

✦ **Level 1 browsers** (see Table 3-4) give you access to all SharePoint features.

   SharePoint is a Microsoft product. Only Microsoft Windows operating systems with recent versions of Internet Explorer or Firefox have Level 1 support.

Although Firefox is considered a Level 1 browser, some features that rely on ActiveX controls won't work (for example, the Datasheet view or Multiple Upload of Documents).

✦ Level 2 browsers (see Table 3-5) are more restricted in their capabilities and may not let you use some SharePoint features you need.

✦ Unsupported browsers may work, but Microsoft hasn't put a lot of time and energy into verifying that those combinations really *do* work.

Unsupported browsers include Safari (Apple) and Chrome (Google).

Table 3-4:	Level 1 Browsers
Operating System	*Browser*
Windows XP, Windows Vista, Windows Server 2003, Windows Server 2008	Internet Explorer 7, Internet Explorer 8 (32-bit), Mozilla Firefox 3.5.
Windows 7, Windows Server 2008 R2	Internet Explorer 8 (32-bit), Mozilla Firefox 3.5

Table 3-5:	Level 2 Browsers
Operating System	*Browser*
Apple Mac OS X Snow Leopard	Apple Safari 4. *x*, Mozilla Firefox 3.5
Windows XP, Windows Vista, Windows Server 2003, Windows Server 2008	Internet Explorer 7, Internet Explorer 8 (64-bit)
Windows 7, Windows Server 2008 R2	Internet Explorer 8 (64-bit)
UNIX/Linux 8.1	Mozilla Firefox 3.5

Don't be afraid to try something out. You might be pleasantly surprised when it works!

Generating and Consuming Content

Without content, what's a SharePoint site for? Essentially nothing — after all, the purpose of a site is to host content — which means *generating* it (making it available to the organization) and *consuming* it (that is, putting it to work). In this section, we look at how you can build Web pages for your site — and how you can manage all that tasty content in your lists and libraries.

Creating pages for your site

Although you can use various applications to get at the content residing in a SharePoint site, the primary client application for the job is a Web browser. If you're authorized to edit existing pages and create new Web pages (through which you can present aggregated content to site visitors), well, you can. You can also edit the site's pages — through the browser or through SharePoint Designer 2010. Typically Designer is more of a heavy-duty tool for power users — or for adding features to your Web page that are not available directly through the browser (for example, adding a Data View Web Part).

If your organization uses software from various makers, note: SharePoint Designer 2010 can only be used to modify SharePoint 2010 sites.

There are two ways to modify pages through a Web browser: Web Part pages and Wiki pages. They're both customizable Web pages on which you can gather information from multiple locations and present it in a useful and meaningful way.

Web Part pages

Web Part pages are familiar to SharePoint veterans as a way of modifying pages within sites. Fortunately, they work fine in SharePoint 2010. Each Web Part serves a specific purpose and handles specific kinds of content.

Think of the *Web Part* as a container that had to be placed on the page before content could surface through it. For example, to place an image on your page, you would first insert an Image Web Part and then set the properties of that Web Part to point to your image.

Wiki pages

SharePoint 2010 introduces the powerful new Wiki page for ease of content creation. Wiki pages are for liberated editing — you (and your team, for that matter) can evolve the contents of the page to suit the current situation without having to jump through the usual institutional hoops.

Think of this page as a container in which you can edit content directly, using capabilities like these:

✦ Insert an image directly onto a page without having to insert a Web Part to host it.

✦ Edit and format text in a WYSIWYG fashion, as you would in a word processor.

✦ Directly edit the HTML that ultimately determines how your page looks in visitors' browsers.

Editing content directly on the page opens a whole range of powerful editing features such as these:

✦ Inserting tables into which you can edit your own content.

✦ Inserting and resizing pictures.

✦ Previewing styles in real time before you apply formatting:

   • Selecting a style changes the text on the page dynamically, so you can see the effect of a style before you apply it.

   • This is the same functionality you get with other Office applications such as Microsoft Word — an advantage in itself. The consistency of the user interface reduces learning times significantly, while letting a much wider — and non-technical — range of users author Web pages.

✦ Choosing a text layout dynamically, at any time, to organize your page and its content into headers, columns, and footers. If you change the number of columns (for example, collapse from two to one) then the contents within those columns are merged.

✦ *Versioning* compares changes and reverts to previous versions if required.

✦ Inserting Web Parts into a Wiki page.

✦ Inserting lists and libraries directly.

   Inserting a list or library dynamically inserts a List View Web Part to host the list contents. (This was a two-stage operation in previous versions of SharePoint.)

If you look at the HTML source of a newly created two-column page, you can see the Wiki containers (essentially `<div>` elements of a specific class inside a `<table>` that controls the layout). This next HTML snippet is from a two-column page with `"Steve"` in the first column and `"Earle"` in the second. Of course, this HTML becomes a bit more complex as you insert Web Parts — but (fortunately) this need not concern the casual user!

```
<div id="ctl00_PlaceHolderMain_WikiField">
 <div class="ms-wikicontent ms-rtestate-field" style="padding-right: 10px">
   <div class="ExternalClass3F6AFD518A17458F84F64A34CB0A91FB">
     <table id="layoutsTable" style="width:100%">
       <tbody>
         <tr style="vertical-align:top">
           <td style="width:49.95%">
             <div class="ms-rte-layoutszone-outer" style="width:100%">
               <div class="ms-rte-layoutszone-inner" style="min-
height:420px;word-wrap:break-word">Steve</div>
             </div>
           </td>
           <td style="width:49.95%">
             <div class="ms-rte-layoutszone-outer" style="width:100%">
               <div class="ms-rte-layoutszone-inner" style="min-
height:420px;word-wrap:break-word">Earle</div>
```

```
            </div>
          </td>
        </tr>
      </tbody>
    </table>
    <span id="layoutsData" style="display:none">false,false,2</span>
  </div>
 </div>
</div>
```

Not all site templates have this feature activated by default. That's why editing the home page of a team site is different from editing the home page of a group site — the team site offers a far more flexible editing experience. That's because the team site's template has the Wiki home page feature activated; in the group site, the Wiki page is disabled. You can change this situation and activate the Wiki home page through Site Settings.

Interesting Web Parts

There are many enticing Web Parts that can light up your sites. The three following Web Parts will appeal to the broadest range of users because of the powerful features they facilitate.

To see all the Web Parts that are available to you, just edit the home page of your team site and, on the Insert tab, choose Web Part. From here you can browse

✦ The available Web Parts that are relevant for the site

✦ The features that are currently activated

Silverlight

The Silverlight Web Part allows you to run Silverlight applications within your Web pages just as SharePoint itself does in parts of its user interface.

Silverlight is a cross-browser, cross-platform, and cross-device browser plug-in that lets you run sophisticated applications inside the browser. With Silverlight v3.0, you can build applications that run outside the confines of the browser thus allowing them to be placed on the desktop, start menu, and so on.

Using the Silverlight Web Part is straightforward:

1. **Establish the Silverlight `.xap` file on your front-end Web server.**

For this example, the `.xap` file resides in the sample's source files. You need to extract the `.xap` file and load it somewhere on your front-end Web server.

For example, you could store this file — along with some other `.xap` files that come with SharePoint — at this easily remembered (yeah, right) folder path:

```
<System Drive:>\Program Files\Common Files\Microsoft
    Shared\Web Server Extensions\14\TEMPLATE\LAYOUTS\
    ClientBin
```

And when that's done, you can configure the location of the `.xap` file in the Silverlight Web Part so it looks like this:

```
/_layouts/clientbin/fallingsnowexample.xap
```

Try it yourself and enjoy the snow (yes, snow!):

2. **Place the Silverlight Web Part on a page.**

3. **Configure the location of the file in the Web Part to point to the `.xap` file (the extension associated with Silverlight Application Packages).**

   We like a falling-snow Silverlight example on the Internet (`falling snowexample.xap` — use your favorite search engine to find it). When you find this file, you can use it to see how easily you can place a Silverlight application on your Web page by using the Silverlight Web Part.

The `.xap` file is essentially a compiled application in its own right; it contains an `AppManifest.xaml` file and the necessary `.dll` files to run the application. All you need do is to place an application package somewhere that's reachable from your front-end Web server.

Multimedia

Everyone wants to display *usable* videos in their team sites. By "usable" we mean "quick to access and easy to play." The Media Web Part does this handy trick for both video and audio. You can enable it by using the SharePoint Server Publishing Infrastructure site collection that comes with SharePoint Server 2010. (Note that this feature isn't available if you have only a SharePoint Foundation installation.)

You can insert the Media Web Part onto your page in either of two ways — the same object ends up on your Web page either way:

✦ Click the Insert Video and Audio task from the Ribbon.

   or

✦ Insert the Media Web Part.

You can choose a media file to process and upload it from your computer during configuration — or you can point to a media file in an existing accessible location, as shown in Figure 3-8. (Just make sure you click the actual media player's image so the contextual tab appears!)

If you right-click the Media control on your page, Silverlight pops up. (At least it does if you've installed Silverlight — if you haven't, then you're given a link so you can. Considerate, isn't it?) The Media Web Part is actually just a Silverlight Web Part in disguise, preconfigured with the Silverlight media player. If you followed the snow example given earlier, then you probably noticed the `mediaplayer.xap` file in the ClientBin folder. Okay, some other files live there, too, and you may want to look into them as you investigate the rest of SharePoint. The clue to their usage is in their names (for example, `picturemosaic.xap` and `hierarchychart.xap`).

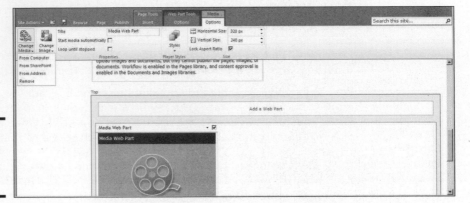

Figure 3-8: Configuring the Media Web Part.

Charting

The Chart Web Part is the last one we're taking a peek at in this section. Like the Media Web Part, it's only available with SharePoint Server 2010.

Desire springs eternal, whether it's the urge to show multimedia on your sites or the yearning to please management with nice-looking charts — and the new Chart Web Part allows you to satisfy those longings. In the past, of course, you had a few ways to achieve this kindly goal (Office Web Components and Excel Web Access are two that spring to mind) — but the new Chart Web Part is a far more powerful way to meet end users' needs. You can use it, for example, to display data from a SharePoint list in a chart. Figure 3-9 shows this feature in action, displaying the source list as well as a graphical representation of how many albums (or is that CDs these days?) were recorded by each artist.

As you configure your Chart Web Part, two wizards guide you through the process of connecting to the source data and customizing the look and feel of your chart. The source data can come from any of these places:

✦ A connected Web Part

✦ A SharePoint list within the current site collection

✦ Excel Web Services

✦ Business Data Catalog

You have available a plethora of ways for displaying and analyzing your chart — with support for multiple series, 2-D and 3-D charts, standard deviation, moving averages, and so on. All in all, what you have here is a very powerful tool that anyone can use to increase the effectiveness of intellectual assets. (The world had better look out.)

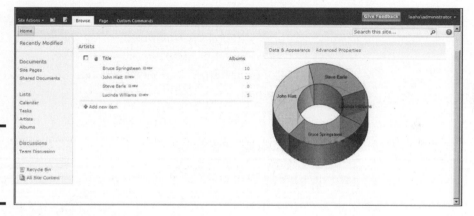

Figure 3-9: Chart Web Part in action.

Manage your libraries and lists

Lists and libraries are where you would normally store specific content related to your site.

We say "*normally* store" because you do have some choices here. You can link to information in other sources through a variety of techniques — such as the Data View Web Part — or by using service applications such as the Business Connectivity Service, Access Database Services, or Excel Web Services. But lists and libraries are the native way for SharePoint to store data, and they're flexible enough to serve a variety of purposes.

You build your lists and libraries by defining the number of columns that suit your purpose and by creating views for the list. Then users have various ways to interact directly with the list — whether through a browser or as an element embedded in a Web page alongside other pertinent information.

SharePoint offers many enhancements for managing your lists and libraries and their contents:

✦ **The Ribbon:** From here, you'll find many useful options such as creating new columns, views, workflows, and so on.

Always check the Ribbon!

✦ **Validation formulas:** You can apply these to individual columns as well as the overall item in a list or library — and you can provide custom error messages for users when validation fails. These formulas help ensure that the content gathered in the list is valid and consistent for your purposes. The validation formula can use any number of columns in an item — so, for example, you may want to check to make sure that the sum of several columns does not exceed a maximum value.

✦ **Inline editing:** You can set this option view by view for the list. It allows you to modify the columns of a list item directly from the view — no need to launch the edit form associated with the list. This feature is similar to functionality offered by the Datasheet View (but that's an ActiveX control, so it may not be available to all browsers).

✦ **Bulk management of items:** You can do this bit of magic by (first) enabling the Tabular View option for the current view. What you get is an individual check box for each item in the view. Using these check boxes, you can bulk-select items and then perform a single operation on all of them — if you want them gone (for example), you can delete them. Unlike uploading multiple documents (which requires an ActiveX control installed by Office — and that only works if you're running a Level 1 browser), multiple operations such as these work for any browser.

As you get used to SharePoint 2010, you can catch a glimpse of the effort that Microsoft has put into giving users the tools to do powerful things without having to resort to relatively mysterious "power user" tools such as SharePoint Designer or InfoPath. For instance, in previous versions of SharePoint, you could only modify the Web forms associated with a list (new, display, update) if you used SharePoint Designer. But now you can make simple modifications to these forms (say, add further instructions) — exactly the sort or capability that was a common request from the "normal" user. In SharePoint 2010, end users can modify these forms through the browser.

The Form Web Parts task in the Customize List group on the List tab gives you editing access to the forms. You can view, display, and update them, modify them to include other Web Parts, or even use them to display other lists alongside the item you're viewing. By default, these forms are launched in a dialog box rather than in a full page, which makes navigation easier.

Building a relationship between two lists

There is a simple way to build a parent-child view for related lists. To illustrate this feature, consider the very simple information in Figure 3-10. It's a typical parent/child relationship between some music albums (parent) and the tracks on those albums (child). The data is held in lists that reside on the `http://www.nut2craic.com/sites/music` site.

The following steps show you how to re-create this example:

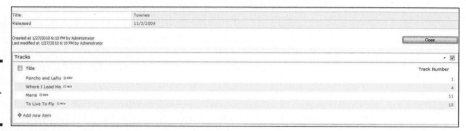

Figure 3-10:
List relation-
ships.

1. **Create the Album list.**

   a. *Navigate to the home page of your site and from the Site Actions menu click More Options.*

   If the menu and/or option doesn't appear, that means you don't have the necessary permissions to create lists on the site. You need the Manage Lists permission to be able to create lists; it's part of the Full Control permission level.

   The resulting dialog box allows you to create various structures.

   b. *You can now filter by List and choose Custom List as the type to create. On the right side, give your list a name (in the example, it's **Albums**).*

   You now have a very simple list with one column called Title.

   c. *By choosing the Create Column option from the Ribbon, you can create another column (of the Date and Time type) called **Released**.* This is sufficient for the purposes of this example, but feel free to add other columns if you like.

   d. *Create some items for the list and put them in there.*

2. **Create the Tracks list.**

   a. *Repeat the preceding steps to create a basic Tracks list.*

   b. *Add a column of the Number type to hold the track numbers.*

   c. *Create a column called **Album** of the Lookup type.*

   Doing so facilitates building the relationship between the two lists.

   d. *In the Additional Column Settings section of the dialog box, you can now choose Albums from the drop-down list labeled* Get information from.

   By default, the Title column from this list appears in the new column — but note that you can also choose to display more columns from the source list at this point. (You can, for example, show the Released column as well.) Also note that these columns are included automatically in the All Items view.

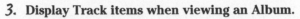

e. *Scroll further down the dialog box and you see a Relationship section that allows you to specify whether you want to maintain the integrity of the relationship.*

If, for example, you want to ensure that an Album item cannot be deleted if a Track item still refers to that album (essentially you're restricting deletion), you can. Or you can have all the Track items related to the Album deleted when the Album item itself is deleted.

This action is optional. For present purposes, we have what we need for the next step — that is, the Lookup column — but if you enforce the relationship, SharePoint indexes the column for you.

f. *Create some items in the Tracks list and note that the data for the Album column comes from the Albums list.*

3. **Display Track items when viewing an Album.**

This step customizes the default display form. You need only perform it once.

a. *Navigate to your Album list and open an item.*

A pop-up dialog box appears, showing the base columns associated with the item.

b. *Close the pop-up dialog box and go back to your Album list. In the Ribbon, click the List tab under List Tools, and then click the Form Web Parts task.*

SharePoint 2010 allows you to modify the default forms used to view and edit items through the browser — a very welcome addition. (Previous versions referred you to SharePoint Designer to make even simple changes.)

c. *Choose the Default Display Form option.*

A Web page appears where you can add other Web Parts and customize existing ones. More handy features show up on-screen at this point:

The Page Tools contextual tab appears in the Ribbon when you click the Albums Web Part.

A special user interface appears when you click the Insert task.

A Related List task gives you single-click access to any other lists that use the Albums list as a lookup field (as shown in Figure 3-11). You simply click on the Tracks list to put its related contents onscreen when you view an item in the Albums list.

d. *Including the Tracks list creates a new List Web Part that you can customize as you see fit — go for it if you like.*

For example, you could change the title and modify the view used
to display the items. Figure 3-10 shows the result when we modified
the title, applied a view sorted by Track Number, and used a Shaded
style in the display. (Fancy, isn't it?)

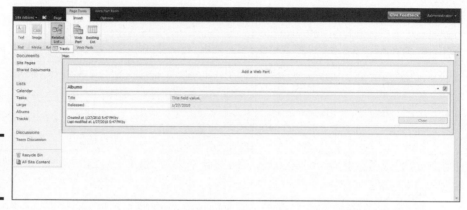

Figure 3-11:
Inserting a
related list.

If you have previous Web Part Page experience may have noticed that the
net result of the process just described is actually a Web Part Page with two
connected Web Parts on it. Fortunately, building such a page is simple and
intuitive in SharePoint 2010 (score one for improved ease of use!).

Chapter 4: Introducing SharePoint Server 2010

In This Chapter

✔ Comparing SharePoint Server to SharePoint Foundation

✔ Getting familiar with SharePoint Server features

✔ Using Web Content Management to best advantage

✔ Building an Enterprise Wiki

If your organization is looking to install SharePoint, the first order of business is to figure out which SharePoint implementation — Foundation or Server — will best fit your business needs. Earlier chapters in Book I offer a good working sense of what Foundation has to offer; this chapter does the same for SharePoint Server.

Choosing Between SharePoint Foundation and Server

A math wizard would call SharePoint Server a "superset" of SharePoint Foundation — because Server includes Foundation but has more capabilities. No surprise that budget-conscious IT honchos often ask, "Do we really *need* Server or will Foundation suffice?" Well, that depends on what you want to do with SharePoint. SharePoint Foundation provides not only the platform on which Server is built, but also some powerful features of its own — and it integrates well with Office client applications. Also, it's true that implementing Server is going to cost you more money to use; unlike Foundation, Server requires a license and a fee. So it's very tempting just to try out Foundation and see whether it can meet your needs.

Whoa, there — first things first. Trying out Foundation (or, for that matter, any new technology) before you have a solid understanding of your business requirements is usually a recipe for disaster. But one way to get a handle on whether you need SharePoint Server is to take that first step toward better business decisions: Identify and consider the information assets that are crucial to your business, imagine how your organization can exploit them to the full, and then consider how SharePoint can best help you do that.

Information assets are electronic documents and business data (some of it residing in those documents), plus your people and the tacit knowledge they possess. If you daydream over lunch about ease of discovery, simpler sharing, and better insight into all this intellectual wealth, then you should consider SharePoint Server from the outset.

First, consider relative ease of access to stored data. SharePoint Foundation holds information in team sites; SharePoint Server, on the other hand, allows the information to be discovered — and used — by any part of your enterprise that has appropriate access privileges. Although it would be unfair to call Foundation "closed" and Server "open," that's a matter of degree — of the two implementations, Server offers easier access to information, and on a wider scale.

That said, a Foundation-only implementation may fit the bill for your organization. But if your goal is to make the most of your intellectual property — while generating more of it and getting at it quickly — note that Server introduces many features such as Enterprise Search, Category-based browsing, and tagging. If you're after a "Business Collaboration Platform for the Enterprise," SharePoint Server can get you there.

 SharePoint Server requires SharePoint Foundation — so if you've installed it you also have the full power of SharePoint Foundation at hand. Installing Server installs Foundation automatically if you haven't already done so.

Looking at Core SharePoint Server Features

SharePoint Server lays on the functionality with a trowel when it builds on SharePoint Foundation. To give you a feel for all those extra features and tools, the following:

✦ **Features:** Server adds more than 180 features to Foundation.

✦ **Site Templates:** Server adds more than 37 site templates.

✦ **PowerShell cmdlets:** Server adds more than 240 cmdlets.

✦ **Team site features:** A Foundation-based team site has three features, of which one is activated by default. A Server-based team site has 20 features, of which eight are activated by default.

✦ **Service Applications:** Server adds more than 10 Service Applications to enable features such as Enterprise Search, Social Networking, and Web Analytics.

Throughout this book, we explore many of the features and network services that SharePoint Server provides. In this chapter, we home in on the features that offer you the most help in managing your information. These features are essentially SharePoint's contribution to Communities, Content, and Insights.

Managing information means finding, monitoring, modifying, controlling, and delivering information at every stage of its full lifecycle — from creation to editing, publishing, discovery, and eventual disposition.

You can see how SharePoint Server 2010 improves all stages of the information lifecycle by looking at two of its major features: Enterprise Wikis and Managing Enterprise Content. The next several sections of this chapter show how the Web Content Management platform allows you to build full-featured wikis that the entire enterprise can use — and makes the whole task easier through

✦ Simple and accessible editing of content

✦ Ease of publishing

✦ Consistency in identifying and governing information assets

✦ Discovering relevant content

✦ Maintaining quality information

✦ Leveraging the expertise of your people

Managing Web content

The features of SharePoint Server 2010 encompass a *publishing infrastructure* that gives you control of your Web-based content management. You get to choose the features you want as you're building a wide range of Web sites to suit differing needs.

Many factors can influence the ultimate design and purpose of such information sources, including these:

✦ **People:** Who is allowed to create and edit content and who is allowed to consume such content.

✦ **Content structure:** The degree to which the content should be structured. This can range from highly structured to totally unstructured.

✦ **Adherence to corporate values:** Should content adhere to any mandatory or optional corporate guidelines in terms of usage? For instance, should certain metadata (such as a timestamp) be applied to the content? If the content appears in a corporate blog, what are the restrictions?

✦ **Approval process:** Must content be approved before it can be *consumed* (put to use) — and, if so, by whom? Does it require a lightweight to heavyweight workflow-approval process?

✦ **Branding and layout:** Must the site adhere to what is known as *pixel-perfect branding* (essentially following strict internal guidelines when displaying certain intellectual property as your logo and trademarks) or can the authors choose their own lightweight branding and page layouts?

✦ **Community involvement:** Do you want to allow the community to provide feedback on the content — which can help improve the information continually?

✦ **Governance:** Does the site need to conform to corporate policies in terms of information retention, discovery, and disposition (that is, how much of what to show to whom)?

Introducing the Enterprise Wiki

You build an Enterprise Wiki site by starting with a template that uses multiple features — not only of the SharePoint Server, but also of the base platform. Multiple authors can edit the content easily, consumers can offer feedback, and you can notify all who need to know when the content is updated.

The core components of the Enterprise Wiki are

✦ **Page templates:** You can have multiple page types, each offering a different layout and structure.

This feature uses the underlying Master Page, Page Layout, and Content Type structure that is at the heart of all Web pages that are delivered via the SharePoint platform.

✦ **Web Edit:** This is the core Web-editing feature that comes with SharePoint Foundation. You can use it to edit pages directly (and easily) from a range of browsers.

The rich text editor allows Wiki linking with an auto-complete capability — which makes it simple for a document's authors to reference already-existing Wiki pages or to insert placeholders for future content.

✦ **Categories:** SharePoint offers a service that manages metadata, so authors can categorize Wiki pages for easy discovery and navigation by visitors to the site.

✦ **Ratings:** Allowing consumers to rate Wiki pages provides one important measure of the quality of the information being published. The Web Analytics feature of SharePoint uses these ratings, which gives you a head start in your own analysis and statistical reports on the data.

✦ **Social Tags and Notes:** This feature makes use of information kept in the social store to allow end users to comment on Wiki pages — and to classify the information for their own purposes. These classifications can enhance collaboration in two convenient ways:

• Making relevant content easily accessible to other end users.

• Keeping end users informed of other information that is similarly classified by others.

✦ **Scalable:** Uses the output-caching feature provided in the SharePoint publishing infrastructure to ensure that Enterprise Wiki pages can support large numbers of consumers.

Building an Enterprise Wiki

Okay, suppose you have a business that caters to music lovers. Figure 4-1 shows the home page of an Enterprise Wiki site that's designed to allow authors to create pages of information relevant to musical instruments, record albums (okay, CDs if you aren't into vinyl), and artist details — it's called Musicedia. We've pointed out some of its features in the figure; we cover those in the next section.

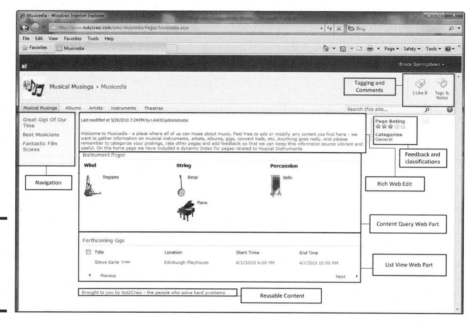

Figure 4-1:
An Enterprise Wiki home page.

Gathering required content and metadata through Page Layouts

As people create content in your Wiki sites, you'll want to ensure that each item of information has relevant metadata gathered for it. The idea is to provide adequate descriptions of the content so it can be easily discovered farther down the line. In the example shown in Figure 4-1, the Content Query Web Part that shows the Instrument Pages displays a grouped view of pages in the site that were authored with a particular page layout — one that forces each author to supply the required metadata (such as Instrument Type).

Three major components contribute to the construction of such a *Web content management* page in SharePoint:

✦ **Master Pages:** These are regular ASP.NET master pages that provide a foundation on which you build content. The master page defines the chrome of each page and the common controls — such as navigation buttons, logos, and search boxes — that will appear on all the pages in your site.

✦ **Content Types:** These provide the schema for the Web pages you want to publish. SharePoint uses Content Types to define schema for many other programming objects — in particular, container objects such as lists and libraries. The Content Type specifies the metadata required to describe both the Web page and its purpose — and organizes the metadata in columns. Each column can hold data of a different type. SharePoint provides many types of columns, including HTML content, images, and Managed Metadata columns.

Think of the Managed Metadata service in SharePoint Server as a kind of super-meticulous choice field that ensures consistency of term usage throughout your sites.

✦ **Page Layouts:** These are the settings you use to provide the template for rendering the actual content. They define what content can be authored in the page, where it should appear, and where that content comes from — whether from static text, Web Parts, or fields whose values come from the content type associated with the page layout. The default page in an Enterprise Wiki site, for example, is based on the Enterprise Wiki Page layout — which you define by using the Enterprise Wiki Content Type.

Each content type can have many page layouts, but every page layout must be associated with a content type.

In the example Wiki site shown in Figure 4-1, the page layout is created to host information about musical instruments. It builds on the Enterprise Wiki page layout, adding some mandatory metadata that forces the author to choose a value that categorizes the type of the instrument (guitar, drum, vuvuzela, or what?). This piece of metadata is handy for showing the content to users in multiple ways — as when (for example) you use the Content Query Web Part to build a dynamic table of contents for the Wiki site.

Figure 4-4 shows an Instrument Web page being created to describe the guitar. Here the Managed Metadata service offers the author a list of instrument types from a pre-defined term set as part of the creation process.

The following steps give you a bird's-eye view of how to build an Instrument Web page; the major objects you create will be a content type, a term set, and a page layout:

1. **Create a site using the Enterprise Wiki template (on the Publishing tab of the site-creation page); add yourself as the site owner.**

This template has all the required publishing features activated.

2. **Create a content type to describe a Musical Instruments page.**

a. *From the Site Actions menu, choose Site Settings✦Galleries✦Site Content Types; when a Web page appears, click the Create button.*

b. *Name your content type* **Instrument Page**.

As you're using this content type primarily for a page layout, select Page Layout Content Types from the parent content type's drop-down list.

c. *Choose Enterprise Wiki Page as the parent content type.*

You want your layout to inherit all the standard columns associated with a Wiki page.

d. *Choose Page Layouts Content Types as the group in which your new content type will be placed and then click OK.*

You now have a new content type, to which you want to add a mandatory column that contains the type of instrument.

e. *At the bottom of the page, click the link labeled Add from new site column.*

f. *Name your column* **Instrument Type** *and choose Managed Metadata as its type.*

g. *Scroll down the page to the Term Set Settings section and choose the Customize your term set radio button.*

A term set called Instrument Type appears in the dialog box.

Pre-defined term sets can be created using the Metadata Management Service — but in this example, you're dynamically creating your term set for a specific purpose.

h. *Hover your mouse pointer over the Instrument Type option.*

A down arrow appears; clicking it allows you to start adding terms to the set.

i. *Add three terms —* **String**, **Wind**, *and* **Percussion** *— and click OK.*

You've completed the creation of the new column (as shown in Figure 4-2).

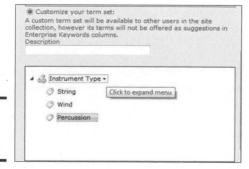

Figure 4-2:
Editing a
term set.

3. **Create a page layout that uses the Instrument Page content type:**

    a. *Navigate to Site Settings and choose Galleries⇨Master Pages and Page Layouts.*

    b. *Click the Documents tab in the Ribbon, pull down the New Document task, and select Page Layout.*

    A new page layout appears.

    c. *Choose Page Layout Content Type for the Content Type Group.*

    d. *Choose Instrument Page for the Content Type Name.*

    e. *Type **Instrument** for the URL and **Instrument Details** for the Title, and then click OK.*

    You've completed the creation of your page layout.

4. Customize the page layout:

This is a process of indicating what content you want on your page. The page layout is essentially derived from the Enterprise Wiki page layout — so the simplest course of action is to copy that layout's content to use as your starting point (you can modify it later). Doing so also gives you a consistent page layout for all pages on your site.

A simple way to kick-start your customizing is to access your page layouts via Windows Explorer — and then use good old Notepad to copy and paste the relevant content:

    a. *Click the Library tab in the Ribbon, followed by the Open with Explorer task in the Connect And Export group.*

    A Windows Explorer window appears.

    b. *Open the file* `EnterpriseWiki.aspx` *with Notepad; copy its entire contents into the Windows Clipboard.*

    c. *Open* `Instrument.aspx` *and replace its entire contents with the contents of the Clipboard.*

    d. *Save and close* `Instrument.aspx`.

5. Add the Instrument Type **field to your page layout.**

You now need to add an actual field to the page layout that will be used to gather the Instrument Type that the page is referring to.

Adding a new field is no big deal. The page layout is just an `.ASPX` page that you can edit with many different tools — but the easiest approach is to use SharePoint Designer. (After all, if you've installed Designer, it's available directly from the SharePoint user interface.)

    a. *Install SharePoint Designer 2010 on the device that runs your browser.*

    Designer is available as a free download from the Microsoft Web site.

b. *From your browser, navigate to the Master page and Page Layouts page as you did in Step 3.*

c. *Hover your mouse pointer over the* Instrument.aspx *item and click the Edit in Microsoft SharePoint Designer option from the drop-down list.*

Designer is launched.

d. *Choose to open the page in advanced mode.*

e. *In Designer, click the Insert tab on the Ribbon.*

A list of options appears.

f. *Choose the Show Toolbox option from the drop-down list on the SharePoint task in the Control group.*

At the bottom of the toolbox, you'll see all fields available for insertion into the page layout. From here you can drag the field to a suitable place.

g. *Drag the Instrument Type field to where you want it in the page layout.*

Doing so inserts the field, as shown in Figure 4-3: The field has been inserted directly underneath the Name field in the Edit Mode Panel.

h. *Save the page in Designer and close Designer.*

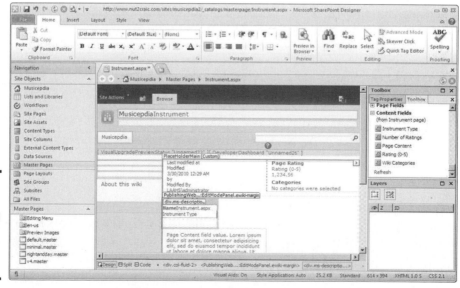

Figure 4-3:
Adding a
content field
to a layout
through
Designer.

6. **Check in — and approve — the customized page layout.**

The SharePoint publishing infrastructure not only requires items to be approved before they can be seen by all users, but it also supports implicit check-out when you edit certain items. Therefore check your page layout and have the person in charge of the SharePoint site approve it. (Given that *you're* the site owner in this example, you can both check *and* approve your page layout. Convenient, isn't it?) Here's the sequence:

    a. Return to your page layouts and note the approval status for your Instrument page layout is currently Draft.

    b. Hover your mouse pointer over your page layout and choose the Check In option from the drop-down list.

    Be sure to check in a major version — that is, the version of the page you want the users to see. After this operation, the approval status changes to Pending.

    c. From the drop-down list, choose Approve and Reject⇨Approve.

    Doing so approves your page layout.

7. Enable your Instrument Page to be a valid page layout for the Pages document library:

    a. From the Site Actions menu, click the option labeled View all site content; *then navigate to the Pages library.*

    b. Click the Library tab on the Ribbon followed by the Library Settings task on the Settings group.

    c. In the Content Types section, click the link labeled Add from existing site content types.

    d. Navigate to the Page Layout Content Types, add the Instrument page, and then click OK.

8. Indicate that pages in your site can use your new page layout:

    a. From the Site Actions menu, choose Site Settings⇨Look and Feel⇨Page layouts and site templates.

    A Web page appears.

    b. In the Page layouts section of the Web page, add the Instrument page.

9. Create and edit an Instrument page in your Wiki:

    a. Navigate to the Pages library and click the Documents tab in the Ribbon.

    b. From the New Document task click the down arrow and then click the newly added Instrument Page option.

    A dialog box appears.

    c. In the dialog box, name your page — for example, **Guitar***.*

The Instrument page layout is chosen automatically.

d. *Click to choose your new item in the Pages library.*

SharePoint displays a page that contains the same controls as the default Wiki page (for example, Rating and Categories).

e. *Click [Edit this page].*

Now not only can you add formatted text to your page, but you can specify the Instrument content type (to match the kind of form you're creating), as shown in Figure 4-4.

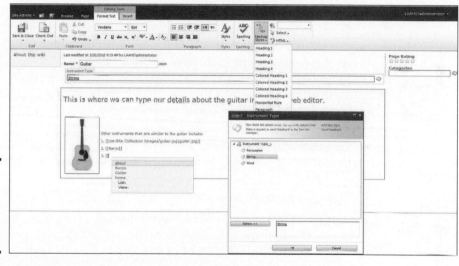

Figure 4-4:
Creating
content with
the new
page layout.

Creating rich content on your pages

The Web Edit feature is new to SharePoint 2010. Both Foundation and Server support rich Web editing but the publishing infrastructure includes some extra features — such as inserting reusable content. When you edit page content, you're populating a column defined in the schema of that page. Foundation provides a type of column that allows rich text editing and the publishing infrastructure augments this with another column type that allows "Full HTML content with formatting and constraints for publishing". As you build your Web pages you can decide which column type suits your needs.

Many Web-editing features are available on the Ribbon after SharePoint is installed. For example, you can edit Web content in the SharePoint publishing environment (as when you edit an Enterprise Wiki page): You can launch the text editor by using the Edit task on the Page tab of the Ribbon or by using the Edit shortcut that appears next to the Site Actions button. Other powerful SharePoint capabilities are also available on the Ribbon:

✦ **Automatic recognition of linked content:** Figure 4-4 shows this feature in action alongside the picture of the guitar. You enter a link to other pages by enclosing a reference to the linked content within two opening and closing square brackets. As you type the opening square brackets, the editor recognizes them as the start of a reference — and shows you matching content from your site as you type more characters.

This user interface allows you to navigate to not only other existing pages in your site but also to items and views held in lists and libraries within your site. As the page is rendered, any link to content that does not exist is highlighted on the page with a dashed line so you can click that link and create that content.

✦ **Insert and resize images:** From the Insert tab on the Ribbon, you can insert an image from your computer, insert a URL leading to an image, or browse your site for images that may have previously been uploaded.

When an image is on your page, you can resize it by dragging its edges or format it further by using the context-sensitive Picture Tools tab that appears when you select your image. In addition, you can position your image in line with text, resize it to exact proportions, and style it with borders.

✦ **Format using Styles:** You can choose any of several built-in styles from the Ribbon if you need to format content in a hurry. Both the Styles and Markup Styles tasks can be used for this purpose.

Refer to Figure 4-4 to see the Markup Styles options.

✦ **Edit the HTML source:** If none of the built-in styles suits your immediate needs, you can edit the HTML that the editor has produced for you and fine-tune it to do what you have in mind.

✦ **Insert reusable content:** Many Web sites — particularly those used for Web sites that face the Internet — demand adherence to corporate branding and company guidelines. Often standard content must appear on all Web pages — logos, disclaimers, and the like. The SharePoint publishing infrastructure can identify and store reusable content for your Web site. Reusable content is contained in a special list set up during the site-creation process. By navigating to All Site Content, you can add items to your Reusable Content list — and you can insert this content onto each page that requires it; just choose the Reusable Content task on the Ribbon's Insert tab.

When you define your Reusable Content during installation, you indicate whether to enable automatic updates — in which case, a link appears on the page as a way to reference the content when you insert it on your page. This approach ensures that your page will update automatically if the reusable content changes. Refer to Figure 4-1 for a sample of reusable content inserted at the bottom of the Web page.

Inserting Web Parts onto your page

You can enhance your Web pages by inserting Web Parts that gather their content from many different places on your organization's network — such as the lists and libraries in your site, or even external content from the wild Web wilderness out there. There are many different Web Parts that come with both Foundation and Server and you can use the following three tasks from the Web Parts group on the Insert tab of the Ribbon to insert an appropriate Web Part:

✦ **Web Part:** This option allows you to browse all the Web Parts that are available to your site. A publishing-enabled site can have many interesting Web Parts — for example, Excel Web Access for analyzing content, Tag Clouds for social computing, and Audio and Video Web Parts to handle multimedia.

✦ **Existing List:** Every list and library on your site has a corresponding List View Web Part dynamically created for it. The purpose of this dynamic Web Part is to insert views of the underlying list into other pages. When you've placed the List View Web Part on your page, you can configure it to use an existing view of your list — or use it to create a new view for displaying the content. You can insert the List View Web Part from the Web Part option mentioned earlier.

✦ **New List:** This option allows you to create a new list dynamically and have its List View Web Part inserted after you've created the list.

Figure 4-1 shows an example: a Calendar list inserted as a List View Web Part, with the view customized to show only forthcoming events.

If you hover your mouse pointer over a List View Web Part and select the check box that appears on the right side, the Ribbon presents you with relevant options for managing the content of the list.

Using the Content Query Web Part

Take another look at Figure 4-1 to see the dynamic table of contents for Musical Instrument pages created inside the sample Enterprise Wiki. You can get a table like that by using the Content Query Web Part, which is only available with SharePoint Server 2010. (It's part of a collection of Web Parts designed to aggregate content from within your site collection and display the content suitably.) You can configure the Content Query Web Part to display only the content that has a particular content type and filter; you can also group and sort such content on the basis of column values.

To get the table shown in Figure 4-1, follow these steps as you edit a page:

1. **Insert the Content Query Web Part onto your page (you will find it in the Content Rollup Category).**

2. **Enable the Web Part Tool Pane.**

You configure Web Parts using a tool pane that you can open in several ways:

- On the inserted Web Part, click the link labeled (you guessed it) *Open the tool pane.*

  or

- On the right side of the inserted Web Part, click the Edit Web Part option that appears when you click the down arrow.

  or

- Select the Web Part using the check box.

  or

- Find the context-sensitive tab on the Ribbon called Web Part Tools, from which you can choose the Web Part Properties task.

3. **With the tool you've chosen, expand the Query category to define the criteria you want the items display to meet.**

You can choose items according to their locations within the site collection, the types of lists they occupy, and their content types. You can filter to retrieve only those items that match a particular criterion — for example, an Instrument Type property that equals Percussion. (Figure 4-5 shows the query for the Instrument pages.) Here's the sequence:

a. *Choose List Type⇨Pages Library.*

b. *Choose Page Layout Content Types from the Content Type Group.*

c. *Choose the Instrument page from your chosen Content Type.*

4. **Configure the Presentation Settings.**

The Presentation category allows you to control the display of the items. You can group and sort the items, apply display styles, and indicate which columns you want to display. Refer to Figure 4-5 to see the details required to display the items.

Inserting Navigational Aids

Navigational aids help users find relevant information. SharePoint offers many such aids, such as the breadcrumbs and Browse icon discussed in Book I, Chapter 2.

On a standard SharePoint team site, you can modify the horizontal top link bar and the vertical Quick Launch bar, but a publishing-enabled site replaces these controls with a single Navigation page. Using that page, you can control both Global Navigation (horizontal) and Current Navigation (vertical) for any and all sites in the site collection.

You can build Dynamic navigation elements from the pages residing in a Page Library — and from any subsites in a site collection — by choosing Site Settings⇨Look and Feel⇨Navigation. If you want to control specific items in both the Global and Current navigation controls, you can. Figure 4-6 shows the example Enterprise Wiki configured to show Pages in the Global Navigation — and the resulting effect on the navigation bar.

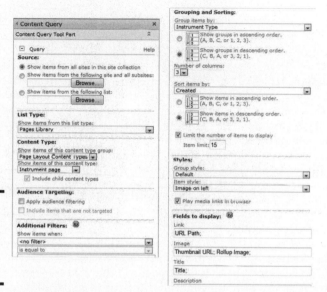

Figure 4-5:
Configuring the Content Query Web Part.

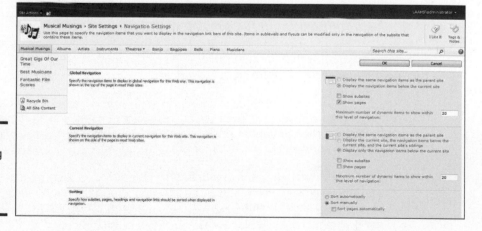

Figure 4-6:
Configuring dynamic global navigation.

Navigating by using Categories and a taxonomy

The Enterprise Wiki Content Type includes a column called Wiki Categories of the type Managed Metadata. The Wiki Categories column is included on the Enterprise Wiki page template, which ensures that the Categories control appears consistently on every page in the Wiki.

The Wiki's multiple authors categorize each page using terms that are defined in the term store; each of these is associated with the Wiki Categories column. The *term store* is part of the Managed Metadata service; it's where the owners of the Enterprise Wiki can specify, manipulate, or fine-tune the terms used to identify the Wiki Categories.

In this instance, think of the term store as providing a structured hierarchy of agreed-upon terms (a *taxonomy*), such that information is labeled consistently throughout the entire Enterprise Wiki. In fact, other sites in your SharePoint farm may use the same terms from the Enterprise Wiki term store — which increases the scope of the consistency you've established for your terms. This arrangement makes information retrieval more effective, ensuring that relevant information is returned — and helps you avoid the confusion of using the same term to define different information types.

As the owner of an Enterprise Wiki site, you control the term set used for the Wiki Categories column in each of your Web pages by editing the column definition. Editors can then apply any terms they need from the set to any page in the Wiki, using the term-set user interface (refer to Figure 4-2 for a look at it). If viewers want to find all pages in the Wiki that have been categorized with the same term, they merely click the term; related content then appears on-screen serendipitously.

Navigating using a folksonomy and tags

Here's another way to get around your SharePoint site: Using tags to build a *folksonomy* that gathers the expressed opinions of people who consume a specified piece of information.

Social tagging is a capability unique to social networking: Users can categorize any information as they see fit, resulting in a *social tag*. Clicking a social tag brings the relevant content to you, rather than making you invoke a search to find it.

In addition to tagging information, SharePoint Server also builds *tag clouds* that emphasize the terms used most heavily in the folksonomy; a user can click one of those terms to call up the most relevant content. After all, if many users tag the same content with the same terms, it's very likely that the content is actually related to that term! (And if it wasn't related before, it is now — because they tagged it!) You can get this capability easily by placing the Tag Cloud Web Part on your Web pages; better yet, you can set the Web part to go get content that matches either the tags used by an individual user or by all users.

When you're browsing the content of a site and you want to tag an item of content, you use the Tags and Notes option on the Ribbon. As you type in your tags, SharePoint consults the term store (and previously entered tags, which at this point have been filed under "Keywords"), and then offers you some suggestions for your new tag. This feature helps ensure consistent usage of social tags. Additionally, you can use an I Like It button to tag your favorite content with a single click.

Social tags are held in the *social store,* a special storage area that's part of the social networking capability in SharePoint Server 2010.

Getting feedback about your content through Ratings

To help improve the quality of your information sources — and to assist users in understanding the value that others place on information — SharePoint Server 2010 introduces a rating mechanism. This is, again, part of the overall social networking capability, and can be used to rate any item in a SharePoint site.

SharePoint offers some components that control the rating process and keep it consistent:

✦ **A site column called Rating (0-5)** appears as a set of five stars; it allows consumers to rate any item that contains this column by clicking the appropriate number of stars. Each user's rating is stored in the social store, and this column represents the current average rating. Hovering the mouse pointer over the Rating control shows you the number of stars in your rating. As long as you have at least View access to an item, you can rate it.

✦ **A site column called Number of Ratings** stores the number of people who have rated the item in question.

✦ **A scheduled timer job called User Profile Service Application — Social Data Maintenance Job** runs on the front-end Web servers (by default, every hour on the half hour). It aggregates all the ratings that users have input since the last run, and calculates the average rating for each item.

✦ **A scheduled timer job called User Profile Service Application — Social Rating Synchronization Job** runs on the front-end Web servers (by default, every hour on the hour). It writes the aggregated data from the social store back to the content databases in which the rated items reside.

The rating columns are included in the Enterprise Wiki Content Type; the Rating (0-5) column is included in the Enterprise Wiki page layout. Therefore, from the moment you set up any Wiki page, it can be rated by anyone visiting your Wiki site.

You can also enable rating (just as easily) on any list or library within your site:

1. **Navigate to your list and click the List tab on the Ribbon.**

2. **Click the List Settings task in the Settings group.**

   A Web page appears.

3. **Click the Rating settings link under the General Settings section.**

4. **Select the Yes dialog box and then click OK.**

These steps add the two site columns to all the content types defined for your list or library. They also insert the Rating (0-5) column into the default view. You can add the column to other views to suit your purposes — and you may also want to consider adding the Number of Ratings column to your view to show your viewers how many people's opinions are expressed in the average rating value. Figure 4-7 shows the effect of applying these actions to a Discussion list — and adding a Number of Ratings column manually while you're at it.

If you apply ratings to a document library that hosts Office 2010 content, then the two rating columns also show as properties inside all client applications integrated with SharePoint.

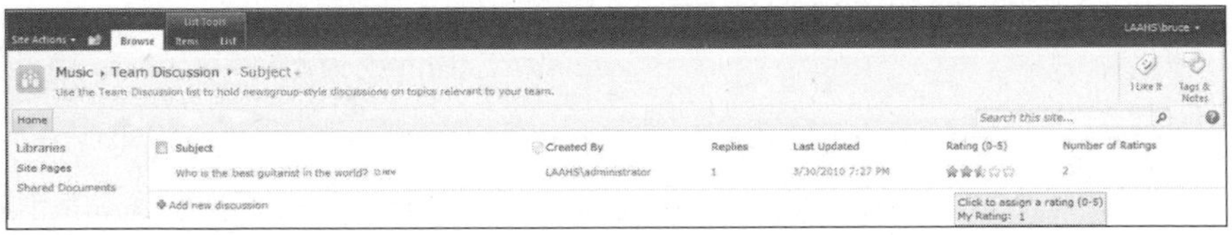

Figure 4-7: Ratings in action.

Getting feedback about your content through Notes

The SharePoint social feedback capability also gives you Notes — a convenient way to comment on information sources such as list items, documents, Web pages, and even links to external sources. Notes are public comments; they're viewable by everyone. You enter them by using the Tags & Notes task on the Ribbon. The resulting user interface, shown in Figure 4-8, shows you all comments — yours and everyone else's — on the item you're reviewing.

You can also enter Notes through Office 2010 client applications.

Notes are also handy for other purposes, such as writing comments on other user's My Sites — much like the Wall in Facebook.

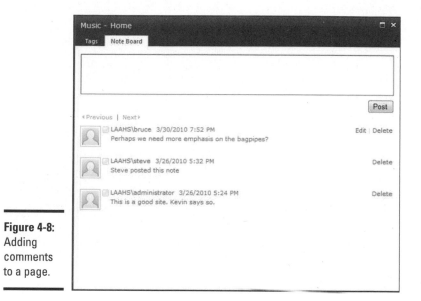

Figure 4-8:
Adding
comments
to a page.

Chapter 5: Enterprise Content Management

In This Chapter

✔ **Getting started with Enterprise Content Management**

✔ **Dealing with large document libraries**

✔ **Controlling the lifecycle of your information assets**

*1*n the language of Enterprise Content Management (ECM), *content* is information that you work with in your organization's day-to-day activities. That information is usually in the form of Office documents — and almost always at the heart of any business process where Office applications rule. In SharePoint, those documents get used heavily for collaborative purposes.

Chapter 4 discusses *Web* Content Management — where "content" refers primarily to the Web pages you construct from many information sources (and ultimately publish for consumption by their users). Those sources include, but aren't limited to, Office documents.

ECM is all about managing the *lifecycle* of your content — its whole journey through your business processes, from the moment someone dreams it up until it's put to use. SharePoint Server 2010 and Office 2010 deliver many features that make it easy for end users to participate in the ECM process. Lifecycle *management* refers to activities such as these:

✦ Creating content

✦ Storing content

✦ *Discovering* content (that is, finding it as needed, in a timely way)

✦ Sharing content

✦ Working with large quantities of content

✦ Ensuring that your content adheres to your corporate policies and complies with regulatory requirements

This chapter looks at the major ECM features of SharePoint Server 2010 — and offers pointers on how your organization can wield them to make efficient use of its content. These features work together to deliver an overall ECM capability — and they take advantage of many other SharePoint services and features (such as the Managed Metadata service, Enterprise Search, and content rating).

Generating and Finding Content

SharePoint Server 2010 allows you to store millions of items in lists and libraries — which is all well and good, so long as users can easily contribute to, and navigate, these giant files to find relevant information quickly. From the perspective of Enterprise Content Management, some interesting new features make this vital task possible — in particular, the Document Center, document IDs, Document Sets, and using metadata for navigation. The upcoming subsections take a closer look at these features.

The Document Center

The Document Center is designed to act as a repository for large quantities of documents. It provides a site template you can use to build a Document Center site that brings together various SharePoint ECM features. You can use such a site for many purposes — for instance, as a central knowledge base.

Figure 5-1 shows a typical Document Center. Note in particular the following major components, all geared to helping you contribute and find information:

✦ **Document Upload button:** This Web Part is a content editor that calls the standard `upload.aspx` page.

✦ **Find Document by ID:** This Web Part locates items by unique Document ID.

✦ **Newest Documents:** This Content Query Web Part shows the most recent documents posted to the Documents library (sorted by date created).

The example shows the Title field added — but you can configure the Newest Documents Web Part to suit your needs. For example, you can configure it to show content from the whole site collection instead of just the Documents library in the current site.

✦ **Highest Rated Documents:** This Content Query Web Part sorts content by the values contained in the Rating column.

In the example, this Web Part has been configured to center the Title of the content and display the value of a custom column called Profile Type.

✦ **Modified By Me:** This is a Content Query Web Part that shows only the documents in which the Modified By property equals the current user.

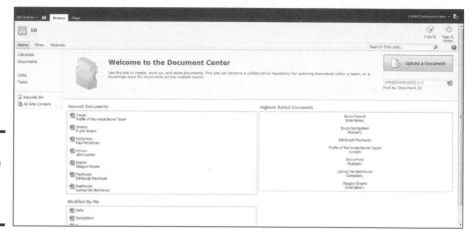

Figure 5-1:
An example
of a
Document
Center site.

Assigning unique Document IDs

Documents tend to be living creatures; commonly they move around a lot
during their lifetime — especially in a large corpus. This mobility poses
issues for any user or application looking for the document in its original
location. Previous versions of SharePoint had no built-in way to identify a
document uniquely wherever it resided.

✦ The most common working practice today is to identify content by its
URL — but that approach encompasses the name of the site in which
the document resides, as well as the actual name of the document. The
problem is that the site name, and even the document name, can change
as documents are renamed or moved to different sites.

✦ Another technique, though less used, is to use the ID metadata column
to identify the item of content. Every item you put in a SharePoint list or
library picks up a unique ID column automatically — but the scope of
this ID is limited to the list or library where the item resides. If you move
the item to another library, its ID will change.

As large-scale document libraries and lists have become more common, individual items of content get harder to find. What's needed is a single reference
that won't change — so SharePoint Server 2010 introduces a feature called the
Document ID service. This feature, installed and activated by default in the
Document Center site template, has the following characteristics:

✦ **Its scope is the site collection.** Each unique ID generated and maintained is consistent for all sites in the collection.

✦ **It adds a column called Document ID** to all content types defined in the
site collection.

✦ **Document ID is exposable in any view** of any list or library in the collection.

✦ **Event receiver registered** that generates the unique Document ID as content is created.

✦ **Feature receiver registered** that fixes up the unique Document ID if the service is disabled or enabled.

✦ **The administrators of a site collection can specify the first four to twelve characters of the Document ID** to help ensure that an item in another site collection will never get the same ID as an item in this one.

This configuration option emphasizes that the scope of any Document ID in SharePoint is the individual site collection!

Although the Document ID feature is also installed with site templates other than the Document Center template, it's inactive in those other templates. To apply a Document ID to an existing site collection, follow these steps while logged on as that site collection's administrator:

1. **Access your site collection and choose Site Actions⇨Site Settings.**

The Site Settings page appears.

2. **From the Site Collection Administration section, choose the link labeled** *Site collection features.*

Another Web page appears.

3. **Activate the Document ID service feature and return to the Site Settings page.**

In the Site Collection Administration section, the page now shows a new link called Document ID Settings.

4. **Click Document ID Settings.**

The resulting page is where you can choose the initial characters of the unique ID.

SharePoint chose a random value for you, which you can change if you want.

If you change this value later on, be sure to follow up with this action: Check the box in Document ID Settings that resets all existing Document IDs for this document to match the new value you specified.

5. **Click the OK button.**

All content types in your site collection show a Document ID column added. If you visit any list or library (including libraries such as Pages that hold your Web pages in a publishing site) and modify any view, you can add the Document ID to the view. Any content you create now — in any list or library — gets a unique Document ID automatically.

Note that none of the existing content shows the Document ID column as populated — not at this point, anyway. First, every item of existing content must have a unique ID. To assign all those IDs, you have to a schedule *Document ID assignment job* to run — for every one of the Web applications that run on your front-end servers; the next step shows how.

In the example's configuration, this job runs daily between 10:00 p.m. and 10:30 p.m.

6. **Test-run the Document ID assignment job via Central Administration.**

   Here's the procedure:

   a. *Access SharePoint Central Administration; in the Monitoring section, choose the option labeled* Check job status.

   b. *From the resulting Web page, choose Job Definitions on the Quick Links pane (at the left) to see all jobs.*

   c. *Scroll down until you see the Document ID assignment job for the Web Application in which your site collection resides; then click its link.*

   d. *In the resulting dialog box, click the Run Now button.*

   The job runs and assigns a Document ID to every item of existing content.

If you reconfigure your Document ID settings later, you'll have to run the job called *Document ID enable/disable* and do these steps again to assign the new settings.

The Document ID is a piece of metadata associated with a specific document in a library, as such it's also *propagated* (added identically) to the metadata of documents produced in Office 2010 client applications. In fact, the Document ID is *persisted* (kept) as a custom property in the underlying Office document — which means you can check the Document ID for any copies of an Office document you have extracted from SharePoint. You can see this in Figure 5-2: The actual value is shown in the Backstage view of the Word document; SharePoint also stores a hashed value in a custom Office property called _dlc_DocIDItemGuid.

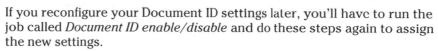

Figure 5-2: A unique Document ID, shown in Backstage view and as a property.

If you upload an Office document that already contains a Document ID, the uploaded document only retains the same Document ID if you're overwriting the original file. If the upload results in the creation of a *new* document in the site collection, then SharePoint generates a new Document ID for the uploaded document.

Figure 5-1 shows a Find Document by ID option on the home page of the Document Center. This option activates a Web Part in which you enter the ID of the document you're looking for. If a document with that specific ID exists somewhere in the site collection, the Web Part locates and opens it for you.

The Find Document by ID option only works if the SharePoint Search Query service is running on your front-end Web servers. If that service is unavailable for any reason, SharePoint gives you an error message.

You can add the Find Document by ID Web Part to other pages in your site collections; it's an especially handy addition to document library views.

Utilizing Document Sets

Document Sets — a new feature of SharePoint 2010 site collections — are groups of items related to the same subject matter. After all, a document usually isn't isolated; it requires other content — such as spreadsheets and presentations — to complete the full picture.

Document Sets contain one or more child content types. You can group any content together — say, text, images, and sales figures for a new product — and treat the group as a single entity for various operations (such as generating reports, presentations, or promotional materials). Document Sets have some very handy major features:

+ For each item in the set, the metadata columns apply to all documents in the set.

+ You can add content of any type derived from the Document content type to the set.

+ When you create a document of a type not already included in the set, you can *provision* (that is, supply) the set with documents of that type.

+ The Home Page for every Document Set is a customizable Web Part page.

Figure 5-3 shows a home page produced by a Document Set that holds the full details of a particular artist's life and works. To create a Document Set that produces a similar kind of home page, follow these steps:

1. **Define a new Document Set for your site.**

Here's the procedure:

a. *Choose Site Actions➪Site Settings➪Galleries➪Site content types.*

b. *Click the Create option at the top of the page.*

c. *Give your Document Set a name by typing it into the Name text box.*

d. *Click/right-click?*

The Parent Content Type drop-down list appears.

e. *Choose Document Set Content Types, and then choose Document Set as the Parent Content Type.*

f. *Choose Document Set Content Types as the Group for your new Document Set, and then click the OK button.*

You're now at the Details page for your new content type. You can choose to add any existing site columns or create new columns that you want to apply to your new Document Set content type. The columns you choose can be propagated to all content in your new Document Set.

2. **On the Details page, choosing Settings➪Document Set to define the content types your Document Set will contain.**

From this page, you can add the content types you want in your Document Set. In the Document Set shown in Figure 5-3, we added three content types: Artist Profile, Album Details, and Gig Guide.

3. **Define initial templates to use for each document.**

The Default Content section offers you the option of specifying templates to use for each content type. These templates will be used to format the individual documents in the Document Set.

4. **Define common properties for all content in the set.**

The columns you associate with the Document Set Content Type can be propagated to every individual item in the set: Just use the Shared Columns section to specify which properties to propagate. A Timer Job called the *Document Set fields synchronization job* does the actual propagating.

5. **Define how the Document Set's welcome page will look.**

Each Document Set has a Web Part page that appears when you click an item created from that Document Set.

You can modify this Web Part page in various ways, including these:

- To include other content — perhaps a Media Web Part that displays a video of how to use the items in the set.

- To define the columns that appear by default, depending on how you set the Welcome Page Columns and Welcome Page sections.

6. **Enable the Document Set.**

After you define the content type for your new Document Set, you can enable it within any library in your site by using the link labeled *Add from existing content types.* You can find this link on the library's settings page (available from the Ribbon while viewing your library); using it puts a new option on the New button's drop-down list that allows you to create a Document Set.

If you're on the home page of a Document Set and you click the New button, you can only create content already defined in the Document Set's specified content type (defined in Step 2).

Document Sets also inherit settings from the library in which they're stored. For example, if you've enabled version control (also known as *versioning*) in the document library, you can maintain versions of each Document Set it contains. That way you can capture all documents in the set at a particular point in time. You can use this SharePoint functionality only when you're viewing a Document Set.

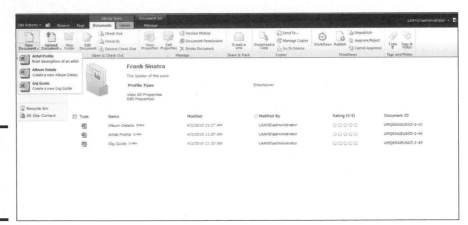

Figure 5-3:
Working with Document Sets.

Navigating by metadata

End users need to get something back when they enter metadata. After all, if they don't understand the value of entering this "data about data," then they won't enter it — and half a chunk of metadata is actually worse than none at all. This is where SharePoint services like the Managed Metadata service come into play by making it easy for users to enter relevant — and consistent — metadata. Once this vital data resource is available, it's also easier for users to find the information they're looking for — which is especially useful in large document libraries — and get a practical reward for their efforts.

SharePoint Server 2010 improves navigation for the end user by introducing *metadata navigation* for lists and libraries — users can move from one document to another by filtering content by using the values set in certain columns:

✦ A column used for this purpose — called the *navigable column* — must contain a known set of possible values — for example, data appropriate for the Choice, Content Type, and Managed Metadata column types.

✦ The valid values for the navigable column appear in a Navigation control on the left side of the page.

Figure 5-4 shows metadata navigation enabled, using the Profile Type column. Here the user filters the view of the library to show only those artists whose Profile Type is that of Entertainer. You can also choose to filter the content further by specifying individual properties for each item.

Metadata navigation is a feature you activate site by site. It's activated by default in a Document Center — but it can also be activated on other SharePoint Server 2010–based sites. You configure metadata navigation at the level of an individual list or library by using the settings page of the list or library in question.

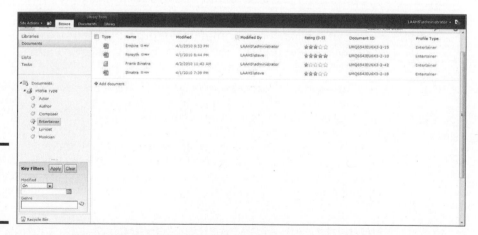

Figure 5-4:
Metadata
navigation
in action.

Doing the Right Thing by the Regs

Today many organizations must meet certain regulations that specify limits or requirements for the management of information sources. These can be legally mandated requirements or policies that your organization dictates to meet certain business needs. For example, many organizations have Standards of Business Conduct (SBCs) that lay out certain behaviors expected of employees — and not just whether you can wear a Hawaiian shirt on Friday. In particular, some SBCs mandate how you manage information that the organization owns — its *information assets* — of which business records are a good example. An SBC that covers business records usually details how, where, and for how long you should keep business records that may subsequently be required for some legal or forensic investigation. "Look before you leap" has a business equivalent: "Check (the SBC) before you shred."

Compliance means, in effect, meeting such requirements and following their attendant rules. SharePoint Server 2010 introduces some flexible compliance features that help your organization — and its users — adhere to policies (both internal and external) in a way that suits your business needs:

✦ **Information Management Policies:** You can define the rules and processes that information should adhere to — and alert users to any special care they should take when they're dealing with certain types of information. ("Do I shred, copy, or eat this memo? Better check.")

✦ **Content Organizer:** This very powerful feature files content automatically on the basis of metadata. You can use it for multiple business purposes, but the main idea is to ensure that content finds its way to the appropriate locations.

✦ **Records Management:** You can define any item as a business record and have it retained and/or disposed of in a controlled fashion.

✦ **Holds and eDiscovery:** This feature helps you handle documents in a way that's usually required if your organization is under litigation and must (a) find relevant information quickly *and* (b) ensure that it can't be changed.

✦ **Automation of processes:** You can create SharePoint workflows that use any — or all — of the features in this list so your users don't have to remember a tangle of manual processes.

You can check the current compliance status of an item by viewing it from the Compliance Details menu option that appears in the drop-down list when you hover your mouse pointer over an item in a Document Set. Figure 5-10 is an example of what you see when you choose the Compliance Details option.

Information Management Policies

You can define policies at the level of content types, and (if necessary) override them with policies defined at the level of individual lists or libraries. SharePoint comes with some ready-made policies that apply to content types. Whether you modify these policies or build your own, you can specify the following attributes:

✦ **Policy Statement:** This is text that appears in pertinent places — say, in the Information panel in Office applications — to remind users of what they should and should not do with content of this type.

✦ **Retention Stages:** You can define one or more *retention stages* that spell out how long you have to keep particular content — and what to do with it as it meets various expiry dates (such as permanently delete it, start a workflow to deal with it, or declare it as a record).

✦ **Auditing:** This feature controls whether audit logs are kept for a particular content type — and if so, for which type(s) of events. It's a way to keep track of who's doing what with your content. In a high-security environment, you can even see who's been reading the content. ("So — checking the UFO files again, are we?")

✦ **Barcodes:** You can specify that a barcode be automatically generated and inserted as a column whenever someone creates content of a particular type.

Office client applications can write this barcode into the underlying Office document.

✦ **Labels:** You can specify a label to apply automatically to documents as they're saved and/or printed. You can build the label's text from any columns defined in the content type.

You apply policies to content types from the Information Management Policy settings on the content type's Details page (Site Actions⇨Site Settings⇨Site collection policies). You can either

✦ Create an individual policy for a content type

or

✦ Apply a policy that you previously defined at the level of the site collection by choosing Site Actions⇨Site Settings⇨Site collection policies.

Each content type can only have one policy applied to it.

You can also override a policy set for a content type by defining library-level retention policies on individual lists or libraries. To do so, you use the option labeled *Information management policy settings* on the Library Settings page. This enforces the library retention policy against all content in the library, regardless of its content type. This option also allows you to generate a *file plan report* for your library — an Excel workbook that shows you detailed information about the library (such as the content types it supports and the retention policies currently applied).

Content Organizer

The Content Organizer is a site feature you can use to create metadata-based rules that move the content submitted to the site into the libraries and folders you choose.

This feature helps users follow the approved filing practices defined for the site.

The Content Organizer defines a single drop-off point to which users can upload content. From this drop-off point, the content is filed automatically to an appropriate location — which can be any folder in any library in any site the administrator chooses.

The Content Organizer offers a generic capability that is harnessed by multiple SharePoint features such as a Records Center.

Other applications (especially those in Microsoft Office) that can store information automatically in SharePoint can also make use of the Content Organizer. Behind the scenes, the Organizer is a Web service (`official file.asmx`) — used in places like the R2 File Classification Infrastructure of Windows Server 2008 — to move files automatically into SharePoint. In theory, the Content Organizer could move other repositories (such as Exchange Public Folders or Notes databases) into SharePoint. (We wouldn't suggest doing that, however, until somebody else has proved that it works.)

The Content Organizer is inactive on most sites by default. That's because it's a little allergic to willy-nilly trial and error. The Organizer works best only *after* you've put some serious thought into your overall filing plan. When you get to the point of configuring the Content Organizer, you'll need answers to the following questions, based on your business requirements:

✦ What libraries will host the content?

✦ How will you determine which content goes to which library?

✦ Will you require subfolders within the libraries?

✦ How will you determine which subfolder your content is filed in?

✦ Will you require content to be filed in libraries in multiple sites?

✦ Will you support e-mailing content for filing?

As content arrives at your site, the Organizer looks at its metadata (or prompts the user for the required metadata if it isn't already present in the content). Then, according to the rules you've defined, the Organizer moves the content to the desired destination automatically.

Three major components facilitate this automatic filing of content; you enable them when you activate the Content Organizer feature: the Drop Off Library, the Organizer's rules, and its settings. Here's a quick look at each of them.

The Content Organizer relies on other ECM features such as Document ID — which the Organizer uses to locate content regardless of the actual library it's stored in.

Drop Off Library

The Drop Off Library is a document library that you set up and provision automatically when you activate the Content Organizer. This document library is essentially a hub for incoming content that should be filed automatically — the single drop-off point referred to in the previous section. The Content Organizer inspects all content uploaded to this library, and then files the content according to rules that you have defined.

Users can choose to upload any content type for which a rule is defined in the Organizer; they see those types indicated in the user interface. Content that has the required properties makes the grade; the Organizer files it automatically.

Content Organizer Rules

When the Content Organizer is activated, it offers the Content Organizer Rules option, which you can access by choosing Site Actions➪Site Settings➪ Site Administration. This is where you define the rules that determine how incoming content is filed. You can define multiple rules and assign a priority to each one. Should incoming content match more than one rule, the rule with the highest priority takes precedence.

The conditions associated with a rule are constructed using the properties (columns) associated with a particular content type. Therefore the scope of a rule is at the level of content type — with two caveats:

✦ You can associate multiple content types with the same rule.

✦ You can require unknown content types to match a specific rule.

This arrangement caters to situations in which the same underlying content goes by different names in various parts of your organization — say, "Movie" in some departments and "Film" in others.

You can have as many conditions as you need in a rule. Keep in mind, however, that your content must match *all* conditions in order to match the rule in question. To help make this happen, use a list of pre-defined operators such as greater-than (>) or equals (=) to define your conditions.

The final part of a rule is the destination library — the place where matching content will be filed. But first things first here:

✦ You must have the destination library already set up, configured to allow the same content types as the rule, and ready *before* you start sending content to it.

✦ You can choose to provision folders automatically in the destination library for each unique occurrence of a property in the incoming content.

For example, more than one artist may have been born in a given year, so you can have a rule create a folder for every unique Year Of Birth property on incoming content tagged as an Artist Profile.

✦ The Content Organizer Settings determine whether the destination library can be in a different site collection. Those settings are the next topic.

Content Organizer Settings

This option is available when you choose Site Actions⇨Site Settings⇨ Site Administration⇨Content Organizer Settings. You use it (logically enough) to specify global settings for the Content Organizer. The main settings to consider are these:

✦ **Redirect users to Drop Off Library.** This is used to help avoid the content organizer being bypassed thus ending up with content being filed in the wrong place.

  If this option is enabled then any attempt to upload directly to a library that is defined as a destination in a rule will result in the user being redirected to the Drop Off Library instead.

✦ **Send to another site:** This option allows you to control whether the destination library in a rule can be in a different site collection.

✦ **Folder Partitioning:** If you anticipate a lot of incoming content, use this option to have the Organizer partition the destination libraries automatically, ordering their folders by item count.

✦ **Duplicate submissions:** You use this option to control what happens when different items of content with the same filename arrive in a destination library. You can

  • Use versioning

    or

  • Treat each file separately, in which case each filename gets a unique ID appended.

Setting up the Content Organizer

The following steps show you how to enable automatic filing of incoming content to a Document Center site that supports a specific content type. In this example, Artist Profile is the content type; the content is filed in one of two destination libraries, depending on the value of the property called Gender. The Gender property can take one of two values: Male or Female. Here's how to get automatic filing underway:

1. **Create two document libraries with different names (in this case, `Male` and `Female` and configure the libraries to permit the Artist Profile content type.**

2. **Activate the Content Organizer site feature by choosing Site Actions⇨ Site Settings⇨Site Actions⇨Manage site features.**

3. **Configure the Content Organizer Rule settings as follows:**

   a. *Create two rules called `Gender-Male` and `Gender-Female`.*

   b. *Specify the Artist Profile content type.*

   c. *Specify the `Gender` property in Artist Profile by using the equal sign (=) as the operator*

   d. *Specify the Male and Female libraries (created in Step 1) as the destination libraries for their corresponding rules.*

   Figure 5-5 shows the `Gender-Female` rule at work.

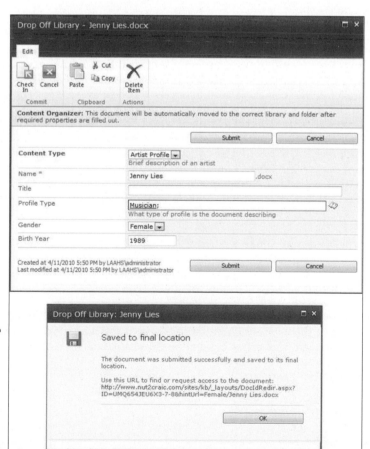

Figure 5-5:
The Content Organizer in action, nagging the user for properties.

Now, when any content is uploaded directly through the browser to any of three document libraries (Drop Off, Male, or Female), the end user sees the user interface in Figure 5-5. (If you've created a rule that refers to more than one content type, the user interface allows you to choose the content type you want to associate with the content you're uploading.) When upload is complete, the content is filed to the correct location. Then the user is shown a URL that refers to the uploaded content by its unique Document ID (as shown in Figure 5-5).

A similar user interface appears if you upload content interactively through other SharePoint 2010 aware applications such as the Office 2010 clients. If you don't complete all the required metadata, a timer job called Content Organizer (which runs daily) sends you a nagging e-mail to tell you the content couldn't be filed. The e-mail also provides you with a link to the content as it languishes in the Drop Off Library; you can easily access the offending content and provide the required properties. (Figure 5-6 shows a sample e-mail error message.) This latter functionality, the Content Organizer timer job, also requires that outgoing e-mail be configured through Central Administration.

Sending content via e-mail

SharePoint Foundation can receive e-mailed content and organize it into lists and libraries. This capability monitors a drop folder where you can tell your e-mail system to place all e-mail messages destined for SharePoint. You use System Settings in Central Administration to configure incoming e-mail for the server farm; when that's done, end users can assign e-mail addresses to individual lists and libraries. Here's what that does for them: As incoming e-mail is processed, the content in each message is sorted and routed according to the type of list or library to which it's destined. For example, if the destination is a document library, then any attachments to the e-mail are detached and inserted in the library as individual items of content; for a discussion list, the body of the e-mail itself is posted as an item.

Integrating your e-mail system with the Content Organizer gets both to work together. Then users can e-mail content directly to your repository and have that content filed automatically in the appropriate location(s). The users need not know a thing about the filing structure.

Activating the feature adds a configuration option to the Submission Points section of the Content Organizer Settings page. There you can set the e-mail address and other generic e-mail options such as

✦ Who is allowed to use e-mail to submit content

✦ Whether to save the original e-mail (in addition to processing its attached content)

SharePoint applies these settings to a hidden list called Submitted E-mail Records. The Content Organizer monitors this list and processes the listed items accordingly. Should any of the received items have missing properties, an e-mail goes out to the nag the sender, just as when uploaded content slouches into the Drop Off Library with incomplete metadata.

Figure 5-6: E-mail message indicating incomplete metadata for Content Organizer.

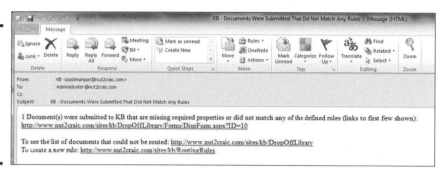

Managing records with SharePoint

Managing your business records boils down to marking an item of content *as* a business record — usually the intent that the content be discoverable and tamper-proof should it be required for later investigative purposes. (And that's about as delicately as we can put it. Such matters look cruder in the news.) SharePoint Server 2010 supports two methods for marking content as records: In Place Records Management and a Records Center site template.

In Place Records Management

Using the In Place Records Management feature, you can mark an item as a record in three ways:

✦ With a single click

✦ As an automated retention policy

✦ As an automated workflow

This process is known as *declaring* a record — in this case, the item remains in its current location. That's different from moving or copying the item to a central repository of records (which is the kind of site you create when you use the Records Center site template).

Your business requirements dictate whether you use in-place management, a Records Center, or a combination of both. SharePoint gives you the choice.

SharePoint provides In Place Records Management as a feature available for site collections. When activated, this feature adds some capabilities:

✦ **Records Declaration Settings at the site-collection level:** Choose Site Actions➪Site Settings➪Site Collection Administration to declare records for all sites in the collection. You get the following configuration settings:

- **Restrictions that are placed on an item that is marked as a record:** You can control what access rights are placed on a record. You may choose to leave the item as is, let it continue being edited but forbid deletion, or set the item to a read-only status, which blocks any edits or deletions.

- **Availability:** Use this setting to control which lists and libraries are allowed to have manual in-place records management. This effectively controls whether end users can mark an item manually as a record or whether such marking is restricted to automated retention policies and/or workflows.

- **Declaration:** Use this setting to control who is allowed to declare and undeclare records manually. You can allow this access to all contributors and administrators, to administrators only, or to policy actions only.

✦ **Records Declaration Settings at the list or library level:** On the Ribbon, choose Library Settings➪Permissions and Management if you need to override the Availability setting on specific lists or libraries. You can also indicate whether all new items added to the list or library are automatically considered records.

✦ **Information Management Retention Policies are augmented:** This setting beefs up your automatic retention policies so you can specify different retention stages for records and non-records. If a retention-stage action marks a non-record as a record (that is, declares a new record), then the stages or actions defined for records subsequently apply to the item that has become a record.

✦ **Declare Record:** This command appears on the Documents tab of the Ribbon when you select an item in a list/library that is enabled for manual declaration of records.

Using this command incorrectly brings down hassles on your head:

- If you choose Declare Record (the action that turns a non-record into a record) and you haven't yet activated In Place Records Management, that's a big SharePoint faux pas. You get an error message that nags you to (you guessed it) activate In Place Records Management.

- You can only use the Declare Record task on programming objects that are not containers — that is, on individual items of information. This means, for example, that you cannot declare a folder, a Document Set, or a discussion item as a record, because these are all container objects. (Note that you *can* declare the individual items inside a Document Set as records.)

✦ **Declared As Record:** This is a property made available on all items in a list or library, provided at least one item is already declared as a record. Declared As Record is a date/time property that indicates when the item was marked as a record. When you've added this property to an item, subsequently you can use it in various ways: in views, as a filter in meta-data navigation, or as part of a search query to find all items that are declared as a records.

Of course, if you're like us, you may not *want* to have records scattered around all over your site collections, but that can happen if you implement In Place Records Management — unless you do some centralizing first. That's what the Records Center (detailed in the next section) is for.

Records Center

If you want a central location for all business records so they're not only easier to find and manage, but also (possibly) integrated with some other third-party applications that discover documents . . . well, now you have one.

In SharePoint 2010, the Records Center gives you the capability to declare an item as a record in any site collection — *and* have that record placed in a central repository called (with relentless logic) the Records Center. The original item can be copied, moved altogether (deleted from its original location), or moved and replaced with a link to its new location. The Records Center uses various SharePoint features — some basic, others specific to ECM — to create a repository that acts as a long-term archive — governed by a structured filing plan yet still easily accessible to end users. Here's a list of the most important Records Center components:

✦ **Document ID Service:** This feature ensures that every item in the repository can be easily retrieved, regardless of where it resides in the filing plan. When the action that sends an item to the Records Center is configured to move the item itself, and leave a link in its place, that link utilizes the item's unique Document ID.

✦ **Content Organizer:** This SharePoint feature helps you build a filing plan that stores incoming content automatically in the correct location for your business needs. Activating the Records Center configures the Organizer automatically to create subfolders and notify rule managers whenever incoming content doesn't match a rule.

✦ **Metadata Navigation:** This feature is a natural for the Records Center; it ensures that content can be easily navigated and found.

✦ **In Place Records Management:** Activating the Records Center configures this feature automatically to declare all new items as records.

✦ **Dashboard management page:** This feature is handy for defining your file plan in terms of Content Organizer rules. It also helps you monitor the Records Center repository (available from the Site Actions menu).

✦ **Incoming E-Mail support:** This feature enables end users to e-mail records to the repository.

✦ **Send To location support:** This feature allows items from any site collection to be copied to the repository by using the Send To command on the Ribbon.

To create and configure a Records Center follow these general steps:

1. Ensure that incoming e-mail has been configured for your server farm (via Central Administration) if you want to support the e-mailing of records.

2. Using Central Administration, create a site collection and choose the Records Center template from the Enterprise tab.

3. Configure Send To Location support from the *Configure send to connections* link in the General Application Settings in Central Administration.

   You configure these locations at the level of individual Web Applications; you can enter any number of connections to each Web Application's Content Organizer. To add a Send To location for your Records Center, you would enter the URL for your Records Center's Content Organizer. This is actually a Web Service called `official file.asmx`; you can obtain the full URL value from the Submission Points section of the Content Organizer settings for your Records Center. The net result will be something similar to what you see in Figure 5-7. Figure 5-8 shows the result when you use the Send To feature to send an item to the Records Center.

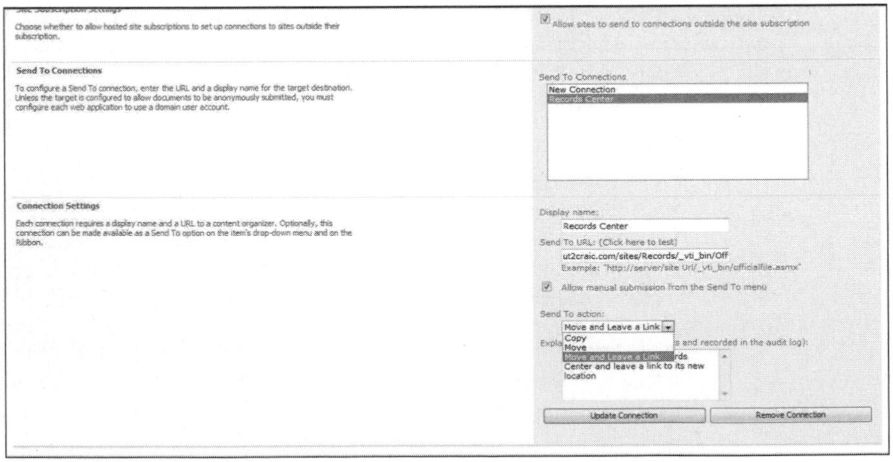

Figure 5-7:
Configuring
Send To
locations
for your
Records
Center.

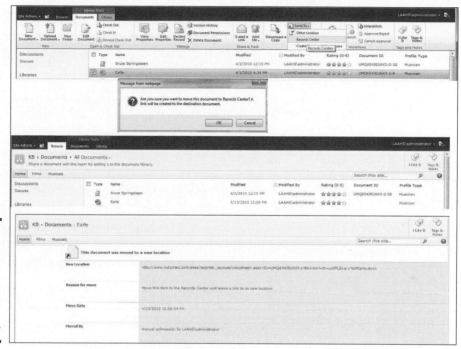

Figure 5-8:
Sending an
item to the
Records
Center —
before and
after results.

Holds and e-Discovery

Holds and e-Discovery facilitate compliance. You use these features to gather pertinent content together for situations such as litigation. You may have to take care of some serious chores such as these:

✦ Provide a compliance officer with proof of certain information assets — that they exist, your organization has them, and they're accessible.

✦ Ensure that, during the investigation period, the disposition of such assets is suspended. (Translated from the legalese, this means you have to make sure nobody tinkers with, shreds, loses, or otherwise messes with the documents.)

SharePoint provides many features to help you achieve compliance — and implements Holds and e-Discovery as a site feature. When you activate this feature, you can create and populate *holds* with items that match a particular search query. Then you can either copy matching items to a hold in another location (using the Content Organizers in those locations) or configure the hold to reference the matching items in place.

Items can be of any type and can come from anywhere within the site collection — this means you can identify not only documents but also blogs, discussion forums, and other such items that match the search query.

When items of content are safely tucked into a hold, they become (in effect) read-only; nobody can modify content while it's in a hold. This also means that information-management policies won't apply to items in holds; the idea is to avoid any dispositions that might occur as part of a retention stage of the policy being executed.

During the creation of a hold, you specify who is allowed to manage the hold; only those users will be allowed to view the hold, add more items to the hold, release the hold, and view a *hold report* (containing details of when the hold was created and the items it contains):

✦ The hold report is an Excel spreadsheet that the authorized users can view conveniently by using Office Web Apps (Figure 5-9 shows a sample).

✦ A timer job called Search and Process actually creates the hold; the job runs daily.

✦ Another timer job called Hold Processing and Reporting creates hold reports.

✦ When a hold is created, whoever maintains the hold is notified and the items in the hold are marked as read-only.

To create and populate a hold, follow these steps:

1. **Activate the Hold and e-Discovery site feature by choosing Site Actions⇨Site Settings⇨ Hold and e-Discovery.**

Doing so adds a new section to Site Settings called Hold and eDiscovery.

2. **From the Hold and eDiscovery section click the link labeled** *Discover and hold content*.

3. **At the bottom of the page, click the link labeled** *Add a new hold*.

4. **Give your new hold a name, description, and one or more users who can manage the hold. Click the Save button.**

5. **Specify search criteria to use to find the items you want to place in the hold, and then choose the hold you just created.**

This example creates a *local hold*. If you want to copy the items to a *remote hold*, you can control the list of possible destinations via the Send To connections defined for the Web Application you're using (as described previously).

6. **Click the link labeled** *Add items to hold*.

Your hold is now created and working. After the timer jobs run, it will be populated with the details of matching items — and those items will be locked. You will also be able to navigate to the hold report by clicking either the Holds or the Hold Reports option when you choose Site Actions⇨ Site Settings.

You can see a sample hold report in Figure 5-9 — and how a hold affects an item that is in the hold (via its Compliance Details) in Figure 5-10. The hold report shows that two search queries have been executed to find items for the hold — and that the actual list of items is available from the Items On Hold worksheet.

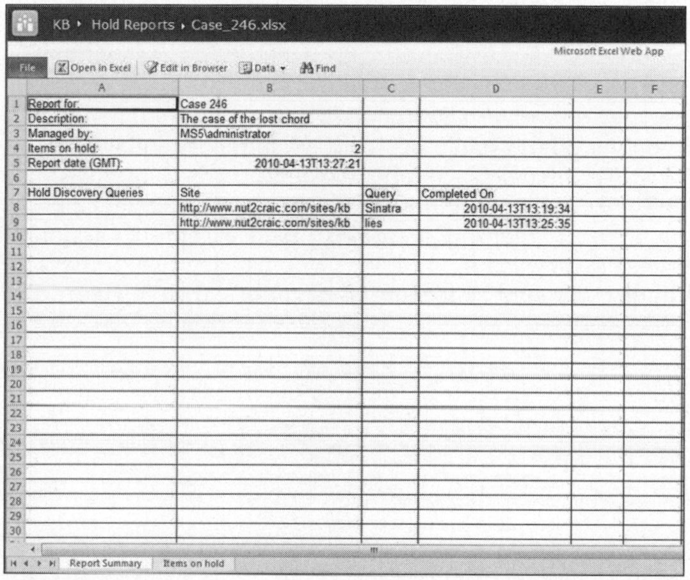

Figure 5-9:
A Hold
Report.

Figure 5-10:
Compliance
details.

If you don't want to wait for the timer jobs to run, you can access them via Central Administration and run them dynamically.

Automating with workflows

Of course, the handiest way to ensure that users do the right thing is to do it for them automatically. So SharePoint allows you to integrate compliance features into workflows. You can, for example, build user actions such as the disposition and declaration of records into your overall business process.

You can use SharePoint Designer 2010 to build such workflows and publish them to your SharePoint sites — for example, you may want to send any item that has a particular status to the Records Center Repository automatically. Workflows can harness timesaving compliance features such as moving items to alternate locations (using a Content Organizer) and leaving a link behind for each item moved. You can see this process in the workflow design we created in SharePoint Designer (shown in Figure 5-11).

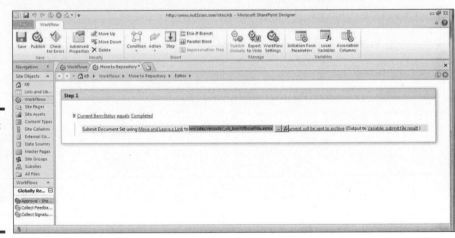

Figure 5-11:
A workflow that makes use of SharePoint compliance features.

Chapter 6: Office 2010 and Office Web Applications

In This Chapter

✓ Integrating SharePoint and Office 2010 client applications

✓ Using Office Web Applications (what's different and what isn't)

This chapter covers the integration points between the major Office 2010 client applications and SharePoint. It also discusses Office Web Applications — which you can use to view and edit Office documents through your browser — a capability that complements the client applications and gives you a much broader reach toward your information assets.

Office 2010 Integration

The integration between SharePoint and Office applications is the best we've seen so far; Office 2010 and SharePoint 2010 get along like old pals. Earlier releases never followed the "big bang" approach to spraying users with new features every time out — it's more like each SharePoint feature slowly crept into a place where end users just might stumble upon it one day. But Office 2010 puts a lot more SharePoint 2010 power into the hands of the end user — offering much wider, and deeper, integration points:

✦ **Wider** in the sense that more Microsoft Office products have integration points (a brand new product called SharePoint Workspace helps make this happen — more about Workspace later in this chapter).

✦ **Deeper** in the sense that (unlike earlier SharePoint versions that used lists and libraries as their main integration points), SharePoint 2010 lets you use *service applications* to reach into the bowels of your Enterprise data and *surface* the content (that is, display it conveniently) in Office 2010 client applications. It's efficient, fast, and less gory than it sounds.

An example: You can use Business Connectivity Services to ensure consistency for metadata properties across many end-user applications. If you have an enterprise-level database that holds (say) product names or customer account numbers, you can put those items in lookup lists for display within the Information panel in client applications such as Word 2010 — ensuring that everyone uses the same values for metadata.

It's clear that Microsoft put more thought into the big picture than in previous SharePoint releases. For example, you can now enable or disable some client integration at the list and library levels — controlling such details as whether an offline client application can access the content in a particular library. In previous versions, this was an all-or-nothing operation that you had to do with a Web Application.

In this chapter, we take a look at some generic integration points that most Office 2010 client applications have in common (and zoom in on some specifics as appropriate). Then we offer a quick tour of SharePoint Workspace — the newest SharePoint aware application.

Going Backstage

Office 2010 client applications (including SharePoint itself) have a feature called the Microsoft Office Backstage View. You get to it via the File tab on the Office 2010 Ribbon; Backstage View is the place to go when you want to do something with (or to) the formatting or other properties of the content you have onscreen. Here's a short list of functions to give you a sense of what you can do in the Backstage View of a Word document:

✦ Save and print

✦ Save to SharePoint

✦ Publish as a blog post

✦ Manage versions

✦ Manage properties and other related data

Backstage is context-sensitive, so developers can extend it to suit your business needs. The exact details of what you see when you go Backstage depend on what you're currently doing and the environment in which you're working. Figure 6-1 shows an example.

Some things you see here only show up because the source document being edited resides in a SharePoint 2010 document library. In such a case, you'd see these SharePoint options:

✦ **The Note Board:** This social networking feature of SharePoint 2010 allows you to add comments to list, libraries, items, and so on as you view them through your browser.

The Note Board feature is available in any Office 2010 client application that can open items stored in SharePoint 2010.

✦ **Managed Keywords:** Accessible from the Info option, this allows you to select terms from the Managed Metadata Service and apply them to your document.

✦ **Versions and Check Out:** You can compare versions of an item in a version-enabled document library — and check those versions out or in.

✦ **Properties/Show Document Panel:** You can view and manage the columns (metadata) from the underlying SharePoint library — including Rating information (if this feature is enabled in your document library).

✦ **People Currently Editing:** You can see and communicate with others who may be editing the document at the same time as your are.

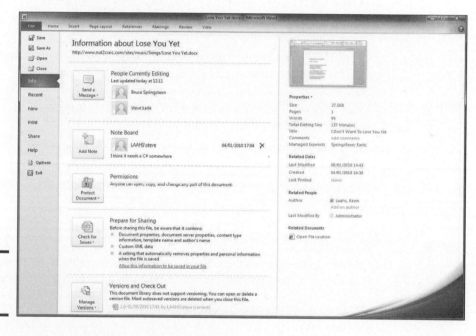

Figure 6-1:
Backstage
View.

Locating SharePoint Sites

As the popularity of SharePoint increases inside an organization, users find themselves becoming members of multiple sites — usually far too many to remain intimately aware of what they are all used for let alone the libraries and lists they contain. That said there are usually some core sites that users work with more frequently than others and there is now a simple way for you to identify these sites and subsequently navigate to them from within Office applications.

This capability exists in MOSS (the ancestor of SharePoint 2010) but it's hidden pretty well from end users. (No wonder it isn't used much.)

In SharePoint 2010 you have a much more robust and manageable feature that puts the sites that you care for most at your fingertips.

The ability to have Office applications display shortcuts that are maintained in SharePoint is accomplished via the User Profile Service. If this is enabled then the following steps will ensure that a particular library is displayed in the Open, Save As, and Share dialog boxes that appear in Office 2010 applications.

1. Using your browser, access the document library that you want to appear in Office 2010 applications.

2. From the Library tab in the Ribbon select the Connect To Office task.

   This indicates that you want a shortcut to the library to appear in your Office applications.

3. The library is added to a SharePoint list called QuickLinks that is stored within your MySite.

4. You can manually maintain this list from your MySite and administrators can also automatically populate the list by targeting links to audiences via the User Profile Service application.

5. Items in your QuickLinks list now appear in Open, Save As, and Share dialog boxes.

There are several components that come into play here to make all this work, as depicted in Figure 6-2:

1. Office needs to know how to read the QuickLinks list that is held in the users' MySite. This is achieved via a registry entry on the computer where Office is running. The registry entry is created the first time a user clicks the Connect To Office task. On a Windows 7 platform this registry entry is located at HKEY_CURRENT_USER\Software\AppDataLow\Microsoft\Office\14.0\Common\Portal and contains the URL to the user's MySite.

2. In the same registry hive there is another value called LinkPublishingTimeStamp and this controls when any Office application should ask SharePoint for a list of links.

   By default this occurs once a day but you can force it to occur by removing the LinkPublishingTimeStamp value and restarting an Office application (useful for troubleshooting!).

3. After Office has read the list of links it publishes them into another registry hive located at HKEY_CURRENT_USER\Software\Microsoft\Office\14.0\Common\Server Links\Published\My Site.

4. There are different types of links published and each Office application knows which links are relevant to it.

   - Synchronization links tell Outlook which lists and libraries to synchronize for offline access.

   - File access links appear in the File Open/Save As dialog boxes for most Office applications such as Word and Excel.

As an example of what this ultimately means to the end user take a look at Figure 6-3. This is the dialog box that is presented to the user when they go Backstage and click the Share/Save to SharePoint option. No longer do they need to fumble around trying to remember URLs to SharePoint sites — the ones they care about are right there in the user interface and easily accessible.

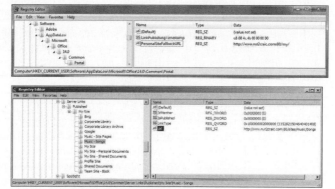

Figure 6-2:
Connect
To Office
Registry
entries.

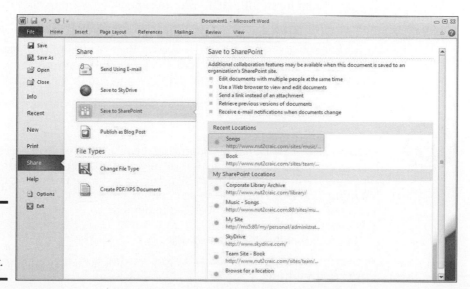

Figure 6-3:
Sharing
directly to
SharePoint.

Multi-user editing

Some Office 2010 client applications, such as Word and OneNote, support multi-user editing when used in conjunction with SharePoint 2010. This means that two or more users have the ability to perform simultaneous editing of content. You can see an indication of this in the Backstage view shown in Figure 6-1 where both Steve and Bruce are editing a document with Word 2010 at the same time. Further indication of multiple editors is given in the status bar at the bottom of the Office application and in the body of the content.

Office Documents Cache and MS-FSSHTTP

Multi-user editing is made possible by the support for incremental file updates and progressive synchronization in the core SharePoint Foundation platform. This uses the MS-FSSHTTP protocol (File synchronization via SOAP over HTTP) as the client to server communication method and a file provider runs on your front-end Web servers to process the delta changes. This protocol allows a client to call a service request that allows for the uploading or downloading of file changes, along with related metadata changes to and from a server.

The Office Documents Cache (ODC) is a general purpose local store for Office documents and, by default, is used as the Save location for all client applications with the exception of OneNote (it has its own cache as it did in Office 2007). The ODC is used to store offline copies of server-side documents and to facilitate synchronization of such documents.

MSOSync.exe is the process that maintains the ODC and you can use the Settings option in the Upload Center (as shown in in Figure 6-5) to clear the cache should you want to.

Many Office 2010 client applications and Office Web Applications are MS-FSSHTTP aware and can therefore use this file synchronization architecture, but the manifestation of end user features are targeted at specific use cases for each client application.

OneNote 2007

OneNote 2007 is designed for capturing ideas quickly without necessarily worrying about details such as formatting, and correctness of content. The co-editing features mirror this design and do not inflict anything on the user that would interfere with this ease of editing approach. Therefore the following co-editing features have been implemented:

✦ Changes synchronized automatically

✦ Synchronization frequency changes according to the number of authors currently editing

✦ All authors allowed to freely modify all content.

Word 2010

Word 2010 is generally used to create finished documents that are subsequently published. As you author content in Word you're usually concentrating on the subject at hand and don't want to be interrupted. With this use case in mind the implementation of co-editing in Word 2010 is necessarily different to that of OneNote 2010:

✦ **Each paragraph is locked** as a user edits it — remaining locked until that user saves the document back to the document library. The user can concentrate on the current part of the document he or she is working on — which reduces worry about conflicting edits.

✦ **Other users are notified** of (a) who has the paragraph locked and also (b) when that user saves the document (see Figure 6-4).

✦ **Each time a user saves a document**, any changes the user made to the document are pushed to the server; any pending changes made by others are pulled down and merged into the local copy.

✦ **A visual indication** is given when any changes have occurred on the server allowing each user who is currently editing to push their own changes and pull the new ones down.

Excel 2010

The main use case for Excel 2010 is that of a single author who designs and builds the workbook with all its formula and business logic and of multiple users analyzing the completed workbook concurrently. Therefore multiple users need to be able to interact with and analyze the workbook as well as be able to contribute data to the completed workbook at the same time — for example multiple departments contributing a row of data representing their own results.

This use case results in the Excel Web Application running in the browser being used as the tool for multiple users to interact with the workbook and the full blown client still being single user editing focused. Through the Excel Web Application multiple users can contribute data, which is reflected in real time across all user sessions. Therefore, for example, if one sheet of the workbook contains a list of products that are used as a lookup in another sheet, one user could add a new product and another user could then immediately select that new product.

PowerPoint 2010

PowerPoint 2010 in SharePoint usually is a publishable piece of content that is presented to multiple users, so the co-editing features are similar to those in Word.

PowerPoint 2010 works well with large SharePoint libraries such as an Asset library containing images, because it can use the same metadata navigation paradigm that you get in SharePoint itself. For example when you want to insert an image into your slide you can navigate to a SharePoint Asset library and then choose to filter its content based on some metadata contained within that library. This can also be done when inserting Video and other content types. This provides you with a very simple way to navigate a large corpus of information to find relevant content.

A very exciting new feature aids the presentation aspect of the finished slide deck. You can now present your slide deck over the Web using SharePoint as the server for this capability. This is known as PowerPoint Broadcast. The only requirement for viewing the broadcast slide show is a Web browser and Office Web Applications installed on your SharePoint Server.

So synchronized viewing across multiple users is no longer achieved by distributing your presentations via e-mail and instructing users to "please now move to slide 10". Instead you can now use the Broadcast Slide Show task from within PowerPoint, which publishes the presentation and issues a URL that users can access to view the live slide show. By default this URL points to your local SharePoint server but you can also broadcast via a public service if you need to reach viewers outside of your own organization. The presenter uses the PowerPoint 2010 client application whereas the viewers use PowerPoint Web Application, which is a great example of the ultimate power of Office 2010, Office Web Applications, and SharePoint 2010 working together.

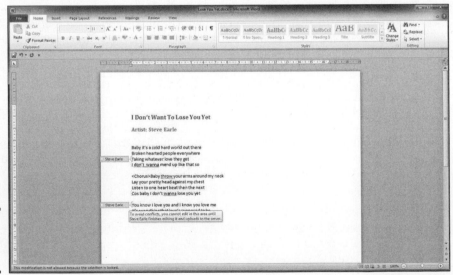

Figure 6-4:
Co-editing in
Word 2010.

These co-editing features require Office 2010 client applications or Office Web Applications, and the source of the content being edited must reside in a SharePoint 2010 library.

Offline Working via the Office Documents Cache

Offline working is possible with Office documents stored in SharePoint, and change synchronization is performed the next time the online repository is available. The Office 2010 client applications utilize the Office Documents Cache by default for storing a copy of the master server-side document both for faster viewing and for synchronization purposes. This is a general purpose store that is used by many Office 2010 applications. If there are any issues with synchronization you can access the cache to view issues and to retry the uploading of pending changes using the Upload Center, which is installed as part of the Microsoft Office 2010 Tools.

You can see this in Figure 6-5 where Word 2010 could not save local changes to the server — in the Upload Center, you can view all cached documents, retry uploads, and clear cached content.

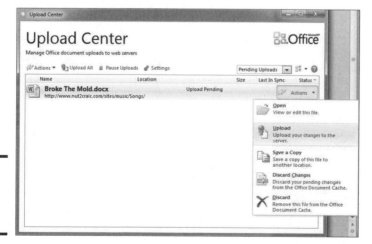

Figure 6-5:
Office
Document
Cache.

Of course, if your organization has an entrenched way of saving documents, you can set the Save location to accommodate the way you work. Figure 6-6 shows a choice not to use the Office Documents Cache as the default Save location — in this case, reverting to a legacy mode (saving in a local Drafts folder).

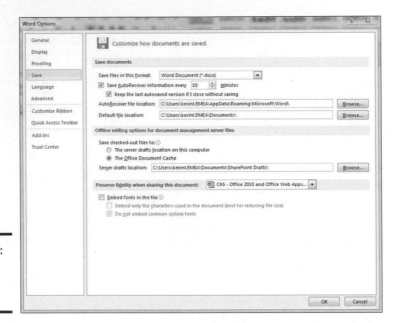

Figure 6-6:
Setting
the Save
location.

The exception to this use of the Office Documents Cache is the OneNote application. OneNote 2007 and OneNote 2010 already have the capability to do joint editing regardless of where the shared master copy resides. OneNote has its own client cache, so the master copy can hang around on any shared resource it likes (such as a simple file share or a Web site), so as long as it's accessible to all users who want to edit the content.

Working with lists and libraries

Many Office applications can work with data stored in SharePoint lists and libraries in some way. Libraries can do duty as the repository for content generated by end-user productivity applications — *and* host the source of InfoPath forms. This arrangement gives you many ways to interact with list content. The next few subsections examine some examples of client applications that can manipulate content held in lists and libraries.

Excel 2010

Excel can be used to analyze list and library data by selecting Export to Excel on the Ribbon.

The important word here is *Export*, because you're essentially using a disconnected copy of the list in its current form; there's no automatic synchronization of changed content. You can, however, create a new list by importing a spreadsheet (using the Import Spreadsheet option from the Create Item page).

Access 2010

Access is an effective tool for working directly with the contents of a list. You can ensure that any changes made in Access are replicated back in the source list on the SharePoint server. Choosing Link To Access on the Ribbon does the trick.

Project 2010

You can publish a project plan created in Project 2010 to a Projects Task List on a SharePoint site. When the plan is published, any changes made to either source item get re-synchronized from within Project.

Any conflicts that arise from editing the same data in both places must be resolved manually.

From within Project, you click File/Save & Send/Sync with Tasks List. Doing so connects your project plan with a SharePoint list. After the initial synchronization, you can use the Info option in the Backstage View to specify the fields to use (including custom fields) from the lists that are synchronized.

Outlook 2010

Outlook allows two-way synchronization between list types it has in common with SharePoint 2010. Result: You can work offline with the data in SharePoint repositories, and synchronize the changes when you connect to the server again. This capability allows you to view data in SharePoint lists side by side with data held in your Outlook mailbox or public folders — for example, a group calendar and a personal calendar — and you can drag and drop items between the lists.

You can also connect libraries to Outlook so you can view this content inside Outlook, using its viewer. If you've used this feature before, you know you can also use the application originally associated with the content to do an offline edit — and still have that application synchronize changes back to the server. (Pretty slick, isn't it?)

Although you can use Outlook as a conduit to certain SharePoint data, keep in mind that it was never designed to be a complete offline client application for SharePoint (even though Outlook used to be called "the Smart SharePoint Client"). The good news is that there is a *new* client — specifically designed for offline work with list and library content — called SharePoint Workspace. It's next up.

SharePoint Workspace

This newest member of the Office family has its roots in Groove — the product that came with the company (called Groove Networks) that Microsoft bought back in 2005. (Or was it Ray Ozzie they actually bought and got Groove as a freebie? A mystery for the ages.) Groove was promising, but had some limitations (as recalled in the accompanying sidebar).

But all that is now in the past — because SharePoint Workspace provides you with a very robust environment that gives you fast, anywhere-and-any-time access to collaborative content held in your SharePoint sites.

Groove and SharePoint Workspaces

Within SharePoint Workspace, you can create different kinds of workspaces to host content — because SharePoint supports both its own workspaces and those created the old way in Groove. You can control what type of workspace a user can create by setting a group policy.

Groove workspaces function in a peer-to-peer fashion — they're completely separate from any SharePoint workspaces you might create. SharePoint workspaces are brand new; although they work much the same way as Groove (offline, providing automatic synchronization, and so on) they're built differently: SharePoint workspaces use client-to-server synchronization via the MS-FSSHTTP protocol. Bottom line: A SharePoint workspace will only work with a SharePoint 2010 back-end server.

For the rest of this discussion, we focus on the SharePoint workspaces you can manage with the SharePoint Workspace application. ("Groovy!" No, no. SharePointy.)

Workspace benefits everyone

SharePoint Workspace offers benefits to everyone — not only the mobile user — because you can get access to your SharePoint content even if your server is unavailable.

Think of SharePoint Workspace as much like Outlook running in cached mode: The system synchronizes content as (and when) it can, contacting the server behind the scenes as (and when) required.

SharePoint Workspace also harnesses other products and services in the whole Microsoft ecosystem — such as InfoPath to display items and Business Connectivity Services to access content that's external to SharePoint.

Remembering Groove

Groove is/was a peer-to-peer application that let teams collaborate securely across network boundaries — while maintaining fully synchronized content online *or* offline. Its real power lies in helping small teams of people share the same online working space, no matter where they might be on the corporate network or the public Internet.

Groove operates securely across corporate firewalls and proxies (even on ad hoc infrared networks). It connects team members seamlessly, without any user intervention. Users work within a "workspace"; the content is stored locally. Any changes to the workspace are replicated, automatically and seamlessly, to the local workspace on other users' devices.

Microsoft Office Groove 2007 was brought to market as part of the Office 2007 family. Although you *can* connect Office Groove 2007 to SharePoint, you do run into some practical restrictions that limit its use:

✔ The integration point itself is essentially a tunnel from a single user's local workspace to the back-end SharePoint site.

✔ Content can only flow in both directions via that particular user's workspace.

✔ What you have here is a single point of failure; if it fails, you're in trouble. That means the content can never really be trusted to be completely up to date.

SharePoint Workspace doesn't offer a full offline replica of your team sites — it doesn't have to. Instead, it offers offline access to collaborative content within the sites that are of interest to you. So it works with the following data sources from SharePoint team sites and your MySite:

✦ Document libraries

✦ Most standard types of lists that Microsoft supports

✦ Custom lists

✦ Lists containing external data

Getting Started with SharePoint Workspace

Getting started with SharePoint Workspace is easy: After you've installed it on your local device, you see a Sync to SharePoint Workspace task light up in the Ribbon when you visit an appropriate page. (That's because a SharePoint Workspace extension is installed in your browser automatically, the first time you visit such a page after installation.)

You can see how this looks in Figure 6-7, which also shows the corresponding result in SharePoint Workspace after you synchronize. This arrangement gives you fine-grained control over what content is synchronized into the workspace from the site. But why stop there? You can also synchronize all the content in a site if you use the SharePoint Workspace Launchbar to create the workspace.

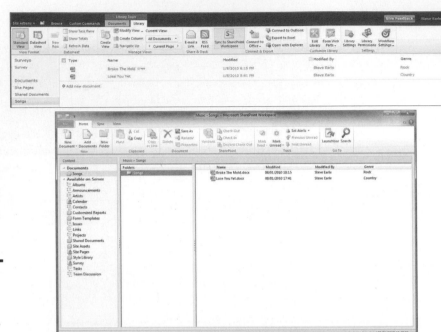

Figure 6-7:
Sync to
SharePoint
Workspace.

You can also see (in Figure 6-7) that SharePoint Workspace shows the content from each team site you currently have offline — as well as other content available to you on the server. SharePoint Workspace knows you have this stuff available. That's because the first thing it downloads is the schema associated with the SharePoint site. So, at any point in time, you can choose to download additional content from your site and have whatever stuff you need at your fingertips.

SharePoint Workspace presents you with a very Office-like representation of the site that's easy to navigate (partly because it utilizes common components such as the Ribbon). In addition to list content, Workspace also downloads list views, while still honoring the difference between public and private views. You can view the version history, but only the latest version is actually synchronized — and list items are displayed in a preview pane that uses InfoPath forms to render the items.

All server-side policies are obeyed; you can only synchronize content to which you have at least "read" access. If your permissions to certain content are revoked, then you're out of luck if you try to synchronize that content (though you'll still have any existing content you already have in SharePoint Workspace).

Searching your workspaces locally

Content stored locally in SharePoint Workspace is indexed and searchable. The application that does the job is Windows Desktop Search (as is the case with your mailbox data cached in Outlook).

The installation of SharePoint Workspace installs a protocol handler that knows how to crack open the local content store. After Workspace pulls that caper, the items it finds in the content store show up in the index. This is a great feature that really extends the SharePoint search experience into the desktop. If you're fond of pulling in information from everywhere, you can execute queries against list and library content residing in multiple site collections.

How synchronization works

Synchronization is automatic — and only changes are sent over the wire. This avoids clogging the network with large files that have undergone only small changes. The frequency of synchronization adapts to the current working environment as follows:

✦ For workspaces that are physically open in the user interface, the sync happens every 10 minutes.

✦ For workspaces closed in the user interface, the sync happens every 20 minutes.

✦ *On-demand synchronization* occurs as you change local content and view list content — which is much the same way Outlook deals with offline lists.

SharePoint Server will also tell you how healthy it is, which also plays a part in how frequently SharePoint Workspace does the synchronization. Essentially the server indicates how well it can deal with synchronization requests by a issuing a health number between zero and ten. Depending on this number, SharePoint Workspace takes appropriate action — which may mean backing off for a while until the server is less swamped with synchronization requests. As you can see in Figure 6-8, this could mean backing off for up to three hours.

Synchronization status is shown in the user interface; errors can be quickly identified and acted upon. Note that SharePoint Workspace puts a limit on the maximum number of items in any single list that it will synchronize. That number is 30,000; if the list on the server exceeds that number, you receive an error message during a synchronization attempt.

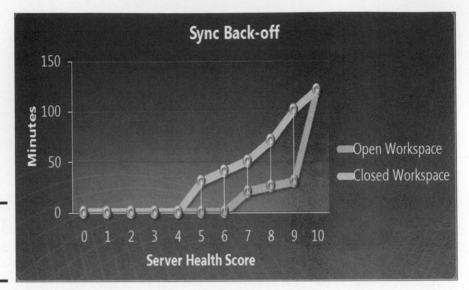

Figure 6-8:
Server
Health and
Backoff.

To ensure that content is synchronized wherever you happen to be, SharePoint Workspace attempts to contact the SharePoint server using all the URLs defined in the Alternate Access Mappings (AAM) settings. You can see this attempted contact in the SharePoint Workspace Backstage View: All defined AAM URLs are listed and, assuming your AAM settings are correct, synchronization occurs whether you're inside or outside your network. As long as there is a published URL that can access your SharePoint server from wherever you happen to be, then SharePoint Workspace will synchronize.

Where content is stored

Behind the scenes, SharePoint Workspace uses three different stores for content:

✦ The Office Document Cache (ODC) facilitates synchronization of all documents held in a workspace.

✦ List items are held inside SharePoint Workspace's own relational database.

✦ Information about external content is accessible via Business Connectivity Services.

In all cases, only the updates to content are synchronized (you cannot update the schema, for example). That means you can't create new lists or libraries from SharePoint Workspace; if you could, it would require an update to the schema residing in the back-end team site.

Working with content and populating your workspaces

There are multiple ways to populate your SharePoint workspaces. You can fill them up with

+ Items created by using built-in InfoPath forms.

+ Documents dragged and dropped from Windows Explorer.

+ Content from any Office 2010 client authoring application that has a Save To Workspace option.

+ Content saved directly to the server — which, in turn, synchronizes with the workspace.

Even though the end result of all this populating is a document in the workspace that *appears* to synchronize with the server, the actual document that synchronizes is physically held in the ODC.

As you edit documents held in the SharePoint workspace, the client applications are not actually aware that you launched the edit from SharePoint Workspace. The client application thinks the document came from the server-side document library — so each client application just deals with the document as if you had selected your browser's Edit in *<application>* option. All client applications use the ODC to store local versions — for fast access and to ensure that these local copies get synchronized when network connectivity permits.

Because the underlying application thinks it's editing a copy of a server-side document from the cache, we get all the goodness of the SharePoint integrations (such as co-editing), even if we launch the content from SharePoint Workspace. Therefore, each time you edit a document from your SharePoint workspace, you're actually editing the content through the ODC. (The ODC performs any pending uploads required via the Upload Center.) If the upload is successful, SharePoint Workspace synchronizes the newly updated content on the server with what's on your workspace.

You can see this process in action in Figure 6-9: Initially there's no valid network path to the SharePoint server — and no pending uploads. Then a user typing away furiously in Word 2010 creates a new document and saves it directly to the Songs library in the workspace called Music. The title of the document is `Hill Billy Highway`: Even though the document is saved directly to the workspace, it's actually being uploaded to the server, using the correct URL for the document library in the team site.

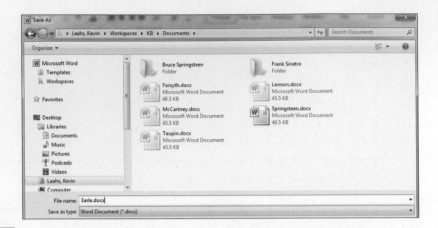

Figure 6-9:
Saving
directly to
workspace
though it
doesn't look
that way.

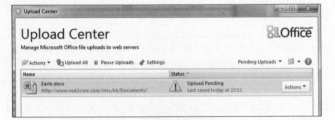

Of course, here the current working mode is offline — so it isn't possible to actually upload the content at this time. So the content remains in the Upload Center while it waits around for upload — but SharePoint Workspace still displays the document as if it were already uploaded (albeit the status bar shows you when the last attempt was made to upload the document, and whether it succeeded). When the network connection is available again, the Upload Center can successfully upload the document — which makes all the other instances of SharePoint Workspace synchronize with the newly created content.

The user interface can tell you whether the current application thinks it's editing a document that has a master copy in a SharePoint site. Figure 6-10 shows two copies of the same document open for editing. One copy is stored in SharePoint and the other not. Take a quick squint at them.

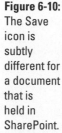

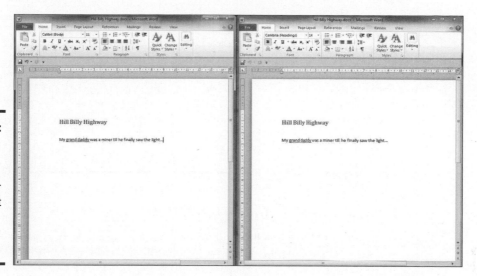

Figure 6-10:
The Save
icon is
subtly
different for
a document
that is
held in
SharePoint.

The Save icon on the Quick Launch bar under the Ribbon is subtly different in each screenshot. In this case, if you hover your mouse pointer over the Save icon in the picture at the right, you see a tip: `Save this document and refresh it with updates made by other authors.` (Aha!) If you aren't editing a master copy in a SharePoint site, you don't see that tip; what you see is the Save icon is it appears in the picture on the left.

Office Web Applications

Office Web Applications (often called Office Web Apps) are an optional add-on to both SharePoint Foundation 2010 and SharePoint Server 2010. Both offer the capability to view and edit Office content stored in SharePoint; both use a browser instead of an actual client application.

When you're using the Office Web Apps, you don't even need any Office 2010 client applications installed on the device that's running your browser. At the time of writing, the license to use Office Web Apps is included in your Office 2010 license.

In this section, we review how the Office Web Apps work, how to configure them, and the features they bring to end users (aside from the minor verbal confusion mentioned in the accompanying sidebar).

What's in a name?

The reason we're using the name Office Web Apps instead of the OWA acronym is, well, obsolescence: For years, "OWA" has been associated with Outlook Web *Access* — the Web client that comes with Microsoft Exchange. Exchange 2010 asserts that OWA is now known as Outlook Web *App* (to align with the main four Web App names). But to old-school Windows users, the OWA acronym will always be synonymous with Exchange.

Introducing the Office Web Apps

SharePoint 2010 has four Office Web Apps — Word Web App, Excel Web App, OneNote Web App, and PowerPoint Web App — all of which offer a high-fidelity viewing experience and a natural editing experience ("Gee, it feels just like a real application!") when you're tweaking Office content through your browser.

Okay, "natural editing experience" means the tools you use to edit content are almost exactly the same as the tools you'd use in the corresponding client application. It doesn't mean you get to take your laptop outside. (Tea break's over. Back to work.)

Viewing content is as simple as following a URL link; a resulting Web page displays the content. Then you can start editing the content in one of two ways: in your browser (assuming you have permissions to modify the content) or in the associated client application (assuming you have that application installed on the same device that's running your browser).

There are many benefits to implementing Office Web Apps. Try these on for size:

✦ **Access to your information — from anywhere:** As long as you have access to a browser and you have physical network connectivity to your SharePoint server, then you can view content stored in SharePoint. You don't have to have any particular version of Office installed on the device you're using to run your browser. Although Internet Explorer, Firefox, and Safari are the *officially* supported browsers, you can use almost any browser that supports basic HTML to view content. This includes browsers that you might run on your Smart Phone (mobile access to content, anyone?).

✦ **Sharing content is simplified:** You no longer need to worry over whether consumers of your content have the necessary tools to view it. Previous SharePoint versions had difficulty with backward compatibility when users viewed content in client applications, but (fortunately) that concern is resolved in the current version: All you need is a browser to view the content. So now you can use the full features of a client application and share the document confidently — without worrying that your creation will suffer when someone tries to view it but doesn't have the same application.

✦ **Parity with client applications is built in:** You can use either the browser or the client application to edit your content, while maintaining full fidelity. Therefore, even though the Web Apps' editing features aren't as extensive as those available in the client apps, you won't break anything if you edit your content in the browser. Digital watermarks provide a good example: Although you can't edit these in the browser, you *can* edit a document that contains watermarks; they're retained when the document is saved and synchronized.

✦ **Co-authoring is possible:** Some Web Apps support this kind of collaboration; Excel Web App and OneNote are the prime examples.

✦ **Encourages users to store content on the server, not locally.** Office Web Apps make working with server-based content easier than before — and this can help encourage people to store content in SharePoint instead of on their local drives. That's an advantage in the age of regulatory compliance and e-discovery. Of course, you get all the collaborative benefits of SharePoint as well — because your content is merely an item in a library and adheres to all the workflows, security, and versioning features this enables (to name a few).

✦ **Reduces need for sharing via attachments.** Many folks create content locally and then use e-mail to send it around to others for comments. Being able to just send a URL link instead is an improvement — especially when clicking the link provides a full-fidelity view of the content. One happy result is an easing of mailbox-bloat. Less mail to wade through makes for a more efficient way of working.

Office Web Apps use essentially the same code as the Office client applications. The main difference is that the code runs on the server — which keeps content on the server almost identical with the content you're editing. This near-parity of content is especially evident in

✦ **Lists, tables, images, and other inserts:** You can insert text-based and graphic-based content with the same ease.

✦ **Formatting and proofing tools:** Layouts, grammar checking, autocorrect, and spell checking offer the same experience.

✦ **Formulas:** Use of formulas in the Web App is consistent with the formula support in Excel.

✦ **Smart Art:** When you brighten up your PowerPoint presentations with these graphics, the new look shows up on the version of the presentation that others can see on the server.

This arrangement makes viewing content a high-fidelity (nearly pixel-perfect) experience; actual images of the rendered content appear in the browser instead of an HTML representation. (Figure 6-11 and 6-12 compare a PowerPoint 2010 presentation being edited in the browser with the same on-screen image in the client application — and neither one looks like a bad clone.) If you want to use tags and apply notes when you're viewing content through Office Web Apps, no problem: You use the same buttons that appear on the Ribbon when you're viewing standard Web pages from your SharePoint sites.

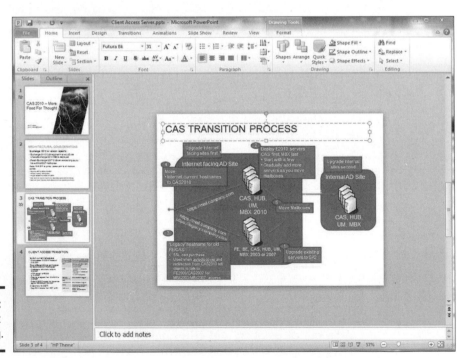

Figure 6-11:
PowerPoint
2010 editing.

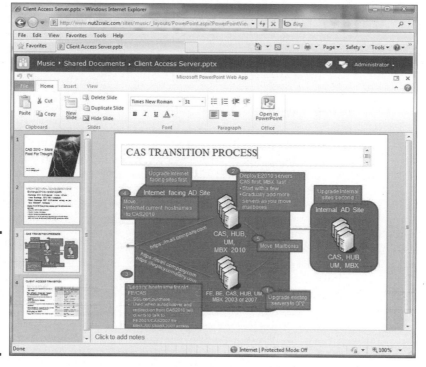

Figure 6-12:
PowerPoint
Web App
editing —
looks just
like the real
thing!

The Office Web Apps support the most common formats. (You could even say they really love those formats, but let's not get personal.) Here's a quick list:

✦ Open XML formats are supported natively.

✦ .DOCX, .PPTX, .XLSX, .DOCM, .XLSB, .XLSM, .PPSX — bring 'em on.

✦ Legacy formats are converted automatically for viewing.

✦ DOC, .PPT, .DOTM, .PPTM, .POTX, .PPAM, .PPSM, .PPS — no problem.

✦ Any recalcitrant legacy formats can be converted to Open XML for editing.

Almost all documents are compatible with Office Web Apps — but there are some exceptions. The holdouts include these:

✦ Information Rights Management: IRM-protected documents cannot be viewed or edited.

✦ Spreadsheets that depend on DDE (Dynamic Data Exchange) cannot be viewed.

✦ VBA (Visual Basic for Applications) commands aren't executed when you're viewing content. (Oh, well, at least VBA isn't destroyed when you're editing content through Office Web Apps. That would be a real bummer.)

✦ Documents that are set to track changes can be viewed but not edited.

Word Web App

Word Web App supports both the viewing and editing of content. When you're editing content, the layout of the content may be different to that of the client application — for example, tables may be shown on separate lines instead of being shown right-justified. This is due to the way that the HTML and Javascript are generated while displaying the page for editing. Nevertheless, editing such objects doesn't destroy their positioning in the underlying document — so you can edit confidently, knowing the content will look fine when viewed.

All the normal editing tools are available to you, including grammar checking, spell checking, and automatic list creation. You can even insert tables and images. The Ribbon also provides common options such as cut and paste.

Editing works in all supported browsers — but some options may not work for certain scenarios in certain browsers. For example, clicking the Copy button on the Ribbon works in Internet Explorer but not in Firefox. That's because Firefox doesn't support using a mouse to copy content to the Clipboard.

When Office Web Apps are enabled, you'll notice one particular change at the document-library level if the device that's running your browser doesn't have Office installed: The New Document option launches a Word Web App editing page. (After all, it doesn't have Word available.)

OneNote Web App

OneNote Web App works almost exactly the same as the client version — so multiple people can view and edit the content and still have automatic saving and synchronization.

Versioning is also built in; you can easily undo edits or revert to previous incarnations of the notebook.

PowerPoint Web App

PowerPoint Web App offers viewing and editing, as well as a Slide Show mode that supports animation. You can broadcast a slide show and other users can follow along merely by connecting their browsers to the published

URL for the broadcast. The result is exactly the same as you'd get via the client application — because the PowerPoint rendering engine is running *on the server*.

Just putting the rendering engine on the server makes it simple to present a deck of slides to multiple users without using a third-party application. SharePoint itself handles the broadcast; if the consumers can reach your SharePoint server(s), they can behold the presentation in all its glory.

To broadcast a presentation, follow these steps:

1. **Open your presentation in the PowerPoint 2010 client application.**

2. **From Backstage View, click Save & Send/Broadcast Slide Show.**

The Broadcast Slide Show dialog box appears, as shown in Figure 6-13.

3. **Select an existing Broadcast Service or add a new one (as we're doing in Figure 6-13).**

The Broadcast Service is a site collection on a SharePoint farm; it's controlled via the PowerPoint service application. A single broadcast site is created for you when you install Office Web Apps — but you can create more using the `New-SPPowerPointApplication` PowerShell cmdlet and following up by using `Set-SPPowerPointApplicationService` for configuration. You can also control the list of broadcast services that the end user sees in PowerPoint by specifying those services in a Group Policy.

4. **Click Start Broadcast.**

Several processes happen:

a. Your presentation is uploaded to the Broadcast site.

b. The PowerPoint service application generates all the images required to represent your presentation in Slide Show mode.

c. A URL link is created to the Power Point Web App viewer, and returned to you for distribution to the people who want to view the presentation. You can distribute this link by whatever means you like.

5. **Click Start Broadcast and run your presentation.**

Just relax and run it the way you usually would. During the broadcast, any user who connects to the URL will see the same slide in the browser as you see while you're broadcasting from your client application.

Figure 6-13:
Broad-
casting a
presen-
tation using
PowerPoint
Web App.

Excel Web App

Excel Web Apps build on Excel Services, which are a component of SharePoint Server 2010. If you install Office Web Apps on SharePoint Foundation 2010, Excel Services are installed automatically for you.

Excel Web Apps support multi-user viewing *and* editing. As you enter data into your spreadsheet, the Excel calculation engine that's running in the service application gets busy: It auto-saves your changes, re-calculates the result, and displays the updated sheets to everyone who's currently viewing the same spreadsheet.

Multi-user editing is only available through the Web App — and if any user opens the spreadsheet in Excel 2010, the Web App cannot edit it. This is a feature, not a bug: Limiting editing this way allows one user to edit the master spreadsheet while others use the Web App for analysis and what-if scenarios. (Efficient collaboration, anyone?)

You can enter formulas into cells and they will autocomplete just as they would with the full-featured client application. You can also easily insert tables, analyze their contents, and put them through activities such as filtering, sorting, and conditional formatting. Any objects that are only editable if you're using the full-blown client (for example, Charts) are still viewable during your editing session; they'll update to reflect any changes made by any current author. You get a glimpse of all this hubbub in Figure 6-14.

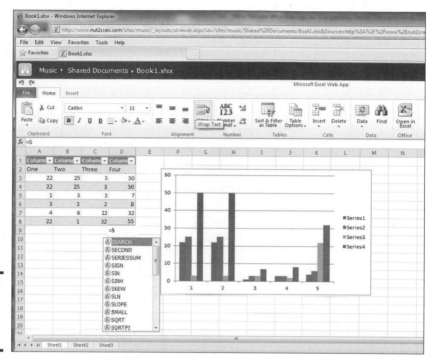

Figure 6-14:
Editing via
Excel Web
App.

A brief look at Web App architecture

Office Web Apps are built to use many of the standard services offered by
SharePoint Foundation:

✦ The service application framework is used to support the viewing of
  Word, Excel, and PowerPoint content, as well as the editing of Excel and
  PowerPoint content. Service applications are involved for heavier processing activities — such as calculating formulas for Excel or generating
  images that represent content created in Word and PowerPoint.

✦ ASP.NET handlers and Web pages on the front-end Web servers support
  the viewing of all content — as well as the execution of less process-
  intensive operations such as Word and OneNote editing.

✦ Many features are installed to configure the end-user experience. For
  example, Office Web Apps enables options in the drop-down list that
  appears when you hover your pointer over items in a library.

✦ MS-FSSHTTP is used to support editing and co-authoring.

✦ The site framework is used to cache content for viewing, as well as for
  broadcasting PowerPoint presentations.

✦ Many PowerShell cmdlets are installed for administration purposes.

Viewing

The goal of the Web App viewing architecture is to represent content in a Web page by using native browser objects (such as images, HTML, and Javascript).

Generating the content

Think of the Web App as converting Office content into browser components and then presenting them through a Web page. Result: The end user can use a browser to navigate the content — no need to switch applications. That's because the user sees onscreen images that represent the major content in Word and PowerPoint documents; the service applications convert the content into these images as, and when, required. Essentially each page or slide in your document is represented as a separate image.

Also, to avoid unnecessary processing, the converted content is stored in an Office Web Apps Cache. That's where the Web App goes to retrieve any converted content not deemed to be stale. This cache is actually just a site collection (one per Web Application) that's created automatically — and a library within that site collection that stores all the images and surrounding objects in a compressed format. You can see where the Office Web Apps cache is (and control the timeout for items in the cache) by using the `Get-SPOfficeWebAppsCache` and `Set-SPOfficeWebAppsCache` PowerShell cmdlets.

The conversion process generates two types of images:

✦ PNG (Portable Neutral Graphics). These are used if the browser you're using to view a document doesn't have SilverLight installed. In this instance, you also get a warning message in the viewing page that tells you you're missing out — because SilverLight offers a better viewing experience!

✦ XAML. These are SilverLight representations of the individual pages and slides within the Word and PowerPoint documents. SilverLight is not mandatory, but if you've installed it, you get some nice benefits:

- Faster loading due to compression of XAML content.
- Improved text fidelity and zoom.
- Improved accuracy of hit highlighting when using Find.
- Smoother animations in PowerPoint.

Presenting and navigating the content

By default, the Web page used to display the content appears in the chrome of the SharePoint site in which the content is stored. Standard breadcrumb navigation is available so you can get back quickly to the library in which the content is stored. You can see this in Figure 6-12.

Navigating large documents from within the viewing Web page is an efficient process: Only the images that represent content approximating the page you're currently viewing are pulled down in the background. As an added benefit, navigating from the first page to the last doesn't take long because you have no need to download the full document; all you need pulled from the server is the image that represents the last page.

The viewing page also allows you to use Find to access content — essentially just as you would from within a client application. Each page you're viewing is actually an image, so some supporting XML data is also downloaded. That's needed so the Web App can find the words on the current page and know exactly where to put them relative to the image. The extra bit of XML also enhances hit highlighting — and that's one of the ways SilverLight offers a better view than you'd get with PNG images.

Editing content

When you edit content through the browser, it's usually saved automatically for you — and any images required to view the content (logos and disclaimers, anyone?) are re-generated.

The Word Web App requires you to click a Save button to commit your changes to the underlying documents.

The OneNote and Word Web Apps render content for editing via .ASPX pages installed on your front-end Web servers. These pages (OneNote.ASPX and WordEditor.ASPX) translate the .ONE and .DOCX files into lightweight HTML and Javascript — and that's what the user edits. A ballet of asynchronous processing goes on behind the scenes to make the editing experience seem easy and natural. For example, inserting pictures can take some time if you're uploading a large image from your device — but all that toil goes on in the background while you continue to edit to your heart's content.

For Word and PowerPoint, the service applications re-generate the required views while you're editing — and then auto-save the content to the underlying document library. (Busy, aren't they?)

In all cases, the editing experience feels much the same as it does when you're using the underlying application, especially with user-interface elements such as the Ribbon (see Figure 6-14) lending familiarity.

Configuring the end user experience

When Office Web Apps are installed, an ordinary click in a document library undergoes a change in its default behavior: The click launches the corresponding Web App viewer (provided your content type supports it). Of course, if you're having an old-school moment, you can revert to the previous behavior (launching the underlying client application) in one of two ways:

✦ You can activate the `OpenInClient` feature at the site-collection level, either manually for each site collection or by harnessing PowerShell to do this as it slogs through all your site collections.

The following PowerShell script could be used for this purpose:

```
$WebAppsFeatureId = $(Get-SPFeature -limit all | where {$_.displayname
        -eq "OpenInClient"}).Id
Get-SPSite -limit ALL |foreach{
        Enable-SPFeature $WebAppsFeatureId -url $_.URL }
```

✦ You can override the default behavior at the document-library level by editing the settings for each library you're editing.

You might want to do this for special-purpose document libraries whose content won't render correctly in Office Web Apps (for example, IRM-enabled document libraries). Behind the scenes, using this approach sets the `DefaultItemOpen` property of the document library to `false`.

You can also tweak the drop-down list that appears when you hover your mouse pointer over an item in a document library. Just use the Edit In Browser and View In Browser options that you find in the `OfficeWebApps` feature. If you've already installed Office Web Apps, this feature is already activated by default for all new site collections created after the installation.

You can, of course, use PowerShell to activate the `OfficeWebApps` automatically for existing site collections. If you prefer, you can activate the feature manually though the browser. Either way, you get access to the feature in the user interface. Figure 6-15 shows what you see before and after activating the feature.

Figure 6-15:
Drop-
down list
additions.

Book II

Architecture and Planning

Contents at a Glance

Chapter 1: The Framework

In This Chapter

✓ Examining the roles of the servers in a SharePoint farm

✓ Reviewing the fundamental components of a SharePoint farm

✓ Introducing the new service application architecture

*S*harePoint 2010 builds on the success of its predecessor by introducing a suite of new service offerings and architectural improvements. For example, SharePoint 2010 provides Visio Services so you can store your Visio diagrams in SharePoint and view those diagrams directly in your browser — without having to install Visio client software on your computer. (Let's hear it for progress!)

SharePoint 2007 introduced Excel Services so users could collaborate on Excel data directly through the SharePoint browser interface. SharePoint 2010 beefs up Excel Services with improvements in performance and functionality. For example, in SharePoint 2007, if you made a change to the data that affected only two out of five Web Parts on your Web page, the entire page was refreshed — and you had to wait for all the Web Parts to reload before you could see the updates. (Yawn.) Excel Services in SharePoint 2010 takes advantage of AJAX (asynchronous JavaScript and XML) technology so you can refresh specific elements of the page, instead of having to refresh the entire page.

At the heart of the new SharePoint service offerings is a new service-application architecture that replaces the Shared Services Provider (SSP) model used in SharePoint 2007. Its an open architecture, embedded in the underlying SharePoint Foundation platform — so now you can develop expanded services in-house or get them through third-party vendors.

Although the services architecture has received a major overhaul, the fundamentals and basic terminology of the product remain the same. A SharePoint *farm* is still composed of Web servers, application servers, and database servers, with nary a pitchfork in sight (unless it's an item in a database). And logical elements such as Web applications, site collections, and Web sites are still very much alive. So we begin this chapter by examining the overall framework of SharePoint Server 2010, explaining how the components work together, and taking a closer look at the new service application model. Then we discuss the underlying architecture that's common to all services in SharePoint 2010.

Understanding the Server Roles

You can give your server three basic roles in a typical SharePoint deployment:

✦ Web server

✦ Application server

✦ Database server

Depending on the size of your implementation, a single server may assume more than one role. For example, if you have a very small SharePoint installation that doesn't require load balancing or redundancy capabilities, you could have all three roles on one server. Roles aren't directly assigned to a particular server computer; instead, a server assumes a specific role *in your configuration*, depending on the components it has installed, the services it runs, and its location within your server farm.

Two additional roles you can give to your servers are specific to the Search Service: a crawl server and a query server.

The *crawl server* is a new term for the role that SharePoint 2007 called the Index server. SharePoint 2010 can now host multiple crawls and multiple query components on a single server.

Where the servers physically reside in your infrastructure — and how many you need — will depend on the network topology you're implementing. For example, if you have a medium-size farm topology, you probably have three tiers — one for each of the basic server roles. Each tier probably has multiple servers that provide load balancing, fault tolerance, and optimal performance. When demand increases down on the ol' server farm, you can add servers to each of the tiers as needed. Result: a scalable architecture. (You can read more about planning your SharePoint 2010 topology in Book II, Chapter 4.)

Don't put all your roles on a single server for a production deployment. (Think of what happens to too many eggs in one basket.) Instead, use a single server only for testing or development.

Web server

The Web server (also known as a *front-end Web server*) hosts all the Web pages, Web Parts, and Web services that go into action when the farm receives a request for processing.

When you access a SharePoint site, it's the Web server's job to receive that request — and ultimately to present you with the requested Web page. If the

Web page contains information such as an Excel Web Access Web Part, that information requires further processing by an application server. The Web server directs the request to the appropriate application server, receives the results, and presents the information to you on the page.

Application server

The application server hosts the services running in the farm, such as Visio Services, Excel Services, and Business Data Connectivity Services.

The first server you install in a SharePoint 2010 farm is, by default, an application server — and it hosts the Central Administration application. Servers added to your farm assume the role of application server when they host service applications. You can click the *Manage services on server* link in Central Administration to configure which servers run which services.

Figure 1-1 shows the page that appears after you click the *Manage services on server* link.

 You can also manage service applications by using PowerShell. (You can find the steps involved in managing the SharePoint services in Book III, Chapter 8, and you can read more about managing SharePoint 2010 by using PowerShell in Book III, Chapter 7.)

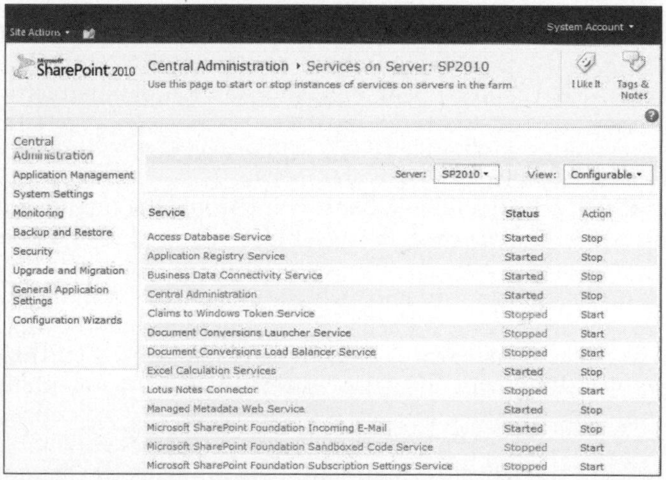

Book II
Chapter 1

The Framework

Figure 1-1:
Managing services on a server.

Service	Status	Action
Access Database Service	Started	Stop
Application Registry Service	Started	Stop
Business Data Connectivity Service	Started	Stop
Central Administration	Started	Stop
Claims to Windows Token Service	Stopped	Start
Document Conversions Launcher Service	Stopped	Start
Document Conversions Load Balancer Service	Stopped	Start
Excel Calculation Services	Started	Stop
Lotus Notes Connector	Stopped	Start
Managed Metadata Web Service	Started	Stop
Microsoft SharePoint Foundation Incoming E-Mail	Started	Stop
Microsoft SharePoint Foundation Sandboxed Code Service	Stopped	Start
Microsoft SharePoint Foundation Subscription Settings Service	Stopped	Start

Central Administration ▸ Services on Server: SP2010
Use this page to start or stop instances of services on servers in the farm

Server: SP2010 ▾   View: Configurable ▾

Central Administration
Application Management
System Settings
Monitoring
Backup and Restore
Security
Upgrade and Migration
General Application Settings
Configuration Wizards

Database server

The database server stores most of the data associated with a SharePoint 2010 implementation, including

✦ Configuration information

✦ Administration information

✦ Data associated with the service applications

✦ User content

SharePoint 2010 has a lot more databases than any previous version. The main contributor to this increase is the new service application architecture (well, okay, *framework*). Gone is the old SSP model; now each individual service that needs to store data has its own dedicated database.

With SharePoint Server 2007, the services used by a Web Application were housed in a Shared Services Provider (SSP) — which typically had one database to store the data for all the services that used the SSP. If you wanted to back up the changes you made to one of the services, you had to back up the entire SSP.

When you begin use specific service applications, such as Search, on a larger scale, you may have to dedicate an entire server to some of the service's databases. For example, the crawl component of the Search Service application handles a lot of inputs and outputs, so it's CPU-intensive. If you have a sizeable SharePoint implementation, you want to host the crawl databases on a separate, dedicated database server.

By default, SharePoint stores all its user content data in SQL databases that include files *and* metadata. For example, a document in a SharePoint document library has a physical file and metadata (such as the name of the document, the size of the document, and when it was uploaded to the site).

Storing Binary Large Objects (BLOBs)

When you upload a document, SharePoint stores the metadata as relational data — and stores the actual file as a BLOB (Binary Large Object). A *BLOB* is what the database uses to store unstructured data (such as a file) as a single entity (presumably some techie wag named it after a movie monster). In SharePoint terms, a BLOB is a container in the database that holds the file you upload. SharePoint stores both the metadata and the BLOB in the content database. When you view the content of your document library, you can see the document name, the date the document was created, and the author of the document. SharePoint doesn't need to query (ask) the BLOB for that information; it retrieves the information by querying the metadata. When you want to open the document or upload a new version of the document, SharePoint accesses the BLOB.

BLOB data usually takes up a large percentage of the SQL storage in a typical SharePoint implementation — especially if the organization is utilizing the collaboration features available in SharePoint.

External BLOB Storage (EBS)

First introduced with SharePoint 2007, External BLOB Storage (EBS) at least had one thing in common with the old monster movie: It tried to move the BLOB (or, in this case, BLOB data) elsewhere for storage. EBS offered Application Programming Interfaces that third-party vendors could use to provide the functionality that would handle the job.

Remote BLOB Storage (RBS)

With SharePoint 2010, EBS has matured into Remote BLOB Storage (RBS). Microsoft provides RBS as a downloadable component available in the SQL Server 2008 R2 Feature Pack. After you have RBS running, you can separate the BLOB data from your content databases and store it in a different storage mechanism (popular storage vendors, such as EMC, AvePoint, and CommVault, are implementing RBS provider support for SharePoint 2010).

**Book II
Chapter 1**

The Framework

Okay, why move the BLOB? Well, putting all that data in a different storage mechanism has the potential to improve the performance of your farm by reducing the load on your database servers. It may also reduce cost, especially if the storage mechanism you choose is cheaper than SQL storage.

Search server roles

SharePoint 2010 includes a Search Service application that, when configured, endows your SharePoint farm with enterprise search capabilities. The Search Service application is a self-contained unit of search — although a SharePoint farm can host multiple Search Service applications. This arrangement is helpful when you want to provide dedicated Search Services to specific Web applications. For example, if your HR department requires its Search Service to be completely isolated from the rest of your organization's search capability, then you can create a dedicated Search Service application and map it to the Web application that hosts the HR Web site.

The Search Service application has three main areas:

✦ **Administration:** Stores the Search application's general settings (such as the Managed Properties you define), in the Search Administration database.

✦ **Query:** This capability is implemented through one or more query components and one or more property databases.

 • The property databases store the metadata (such as the properties of documents) associated with the items in the index.

 • The query component stores the search index.

 SharePoint 2010 allows you to partition your index across multiple query components, increasing scalability and boosting the performance of your search.

✦ **Crawl:** Implemented through one or more crawl components and one or more crawl databases. Crawl components produce the index partitions and propagate them to the query servers. The crawl component keeps track of all the query components in the farm — and propagates the right data to the right component. The crawl database manages crawl operations and stores the crawl history.

While your farm grows, you can increase the scale of your Search Service by distributing the components to multiple dedicated search servers. The role a server assumes depends on the components or services that it runs — and a single server can host multiple roles.

Query server

The query server is responsible for querying the index, finding matching content, and then sending the content back to the Web servers for presentation to the user.

The first step of increasing the scale of your search is to segregate the query component to improve response time (and to make sure the server has the memory it needs). After you segregate your query components, you can then partition them to match your chosen scale — which means you can distribute your query components across multiple query servers.

Crawl server

The crawl servers run one or more crawl components. A crawl component is associated with only one crawl database; however, a crawl database can be associated with more than one crawl component. The crawl database stores a list of all the URLs that the associated crawl components should crawl — that database is the driving force behind the crawl components, and it directs each component to the content it should crawl.

The crawl function of search isn't as memory-intensive as the query component — but it does get busy with a lot of inputs and outputs, and it's CPU-intensive. You can improve the performance, availability, and accuracy of your search by taking two steps:

✦ Adding crawl components and crawl databases to your implementation.

✦ Distributing these components across multiple servers.

You can find out how to configure the Search Service application in Book III, Chapter 6. (Preferably before you use it. But you knew that.)

Understanding the Farm Components

Many components work together behind the scenes to keep your farm up, running, and serving content. A SharePoint farm contains of one or more

Web Applications that use the same set of SharePoint services. That's possible because those services are built to be shared across multiple Web Applications. Each Web Application is associated with

✦ One or more Web sites in Internet Information Services (IIS).

✦ An application pool.

✦ One or more content databases.

Each Web Application can contain multiple site collections — which in turn can contain multiple sites. The following sections provide more detail on each of these components. Figure 1-2 shows a high-level overview of the major players in a SharePoint 2010 farm.

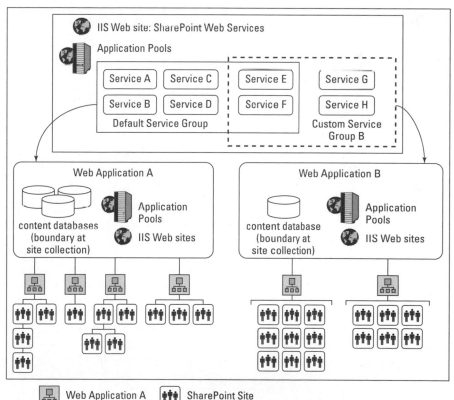

Figure 1-2: Many components work together in a SharePoint farm.

Internet Information Services (IIS) components

Suppose you install SharePoint 2010 on a Windows 2008 server configured with the Windows 2008 *application server role* — it hosts and manages applications that communicate with systems on the network, such as Web applications and services. Windows 2008 servers configured with this role support Web servers through Internet Information Services (IIS). IIS hosts internal and external Web sites, as well as the Web services that communicate over Hypertext Transfer Protocol (HTTP). SharePoint uses IIS to host its Web sites and Web services.

Application pool

An IIS Web site runs under an *application pool* — a group of one or more URLs that

✦ Run under the same identity.

✦ Are served by the same worker process(es).

✦ Provide a protective barrier for the applications they contain.

This arrangement means that applications running in one application pool aren't affected by applications running in another.

SQL databases

SQL Server plays an integral role in a SharePoint implementation by storing much of the configuration and administration information, as well as end-user content. SharePoint SQL databases fall into the following categories:

✦ **Configuration:** The configuration database stores the information that specifies your SharePoint farm's configuration — such as when timer jobs are scheduled, and version information for the servers in the farm.

✦ **Services:** Many service applications, such as Managed Metadata Service, have one or more dedicated databases that store information related to the specific service each one offers.

✦ **Search:** Search databases also belong to the services category, but they're worth special mention because they play a vital role in the scalability and performance of your SharePoint implementation. The Search Service application has at least two configuration databases:

• *An administration database:* This database stores the general settings of the Search Service application, such as the Managed Properties that you define.

• *One or more property and crawl databases:* This database manages crawl operations and stores the crawl history, and the property database stores the metadata of crawled content.

✦ **Content database:** When you create a Web Application by using the Central Administration browser interface, you specify a database that the Web Application should use to store its content.

The content database stores the data for all the sites and site collections within the associated Web Application — including user content, files, list data, and security information.

Central Administration is an example of a regular SharePoint site collection; it stores its data in its own content database.

As your SharePoint implementation matures and its usage increases, your content databases grow. They can become so large that you have to add more content databases to your Web Application. For example, if you have Service Level Agreements that state your databases can't be any larger than 100GB, then you must add content databases to a Web Application when it nears the 100GB limit. You can do so by using one of two methods:

- The Manage Content Databases page on the Central Administration Web site.

- The PowerShell commands `New-SPContentDatabase` and `Mount-SPContentDatabase`.

A Web Application can span multiple content databases — but a site collection resides on a single content database and can't span multiple content databases.

Web Application

In SharePoint, a *Web Application* is an application server's Web site that runs under an application pool, such that

✦ The Web Application is mapped to one or more content databases.

✦ The content databases store the content for all SharePoint site collections hosted by the Web Application.

✦ A SharePoint farm has multiple Web Applications.

✦ Each Web Application is associated with one or more service applications.

Web Applications are at the heart of any SharePoint deployment because they provide access to all the SharePoint sites in the farm — including administrative sites such as Central Administration.

A SharePoint Web Application includes several underlying components:

✦ One or more IIS Web sites

✦ One or more IIS application pools

✦ One or more SQL content databases

Creating a Web Application

When you install SharePoint 2010 for the first time, the installation creates a number of Web Applications by default, including the Central Administration Web site.

You can create additional Web Applications in your farm by using either of these methods:

✦ The Web Applications management page in Central Administration.

   You can access this page by clicking the Manage Web Applications link from the Applications Management section in Central Administration.

✦ The PowerShell command `New-SPWebApplication`

Extending a Web Application

You can extend a Web Application across multiple IIS Web sites, presenting the same content to users through different URLs and authentication settings.

Extending a Web Application is particularly useful in an extranet scenario when different users access the same content by using different domains. When you extend a Web Application, the content database remains the same, but the IIS application pool and IIS Web site may be different. You can create additional Web applications in your farm by using either of these methods:

✦ In Central Administration, choose Application Management⇨Manage Web applications.

✦ In PowerShell, use the `New-SPWebApplicationExtension` command.

Site collection

A *site collection* in SharePoint is a collection of SharePoint sites that have the same owner and share administration settings. Individual SharePoint sites occupy one of these two basic categories:

✦ The first site created in a site collection is its *root site* or *top-level site*.

✦ Additional Web sites created in a site collection are *subsites* (or simply *SharePoint sites*).

SharePoint provides built-in navigational components, which allow you to easily move between the sites in a site collection. When you navigate to the administration settings of a subsite, you're presented with a subset of administrative options available for that specific site — along with a link to the top-level site's settings page. Figure 1-3 shows the settings page for a SharePoint team site.

Figure 1-3:
SharePoint sites share administrative settings with the top-level site.

Creating a site collection

A Web Application can contain multiple site collections, and each site collection resides in a single content database.

Site collections can't span multiple content databases.

You can create a site collection in one of two ways:

✦ In Central Administration, choose Application Management➪Create site collections. Then use the Create Site Collection page.

✦ In PowerShell, use the `New-SPSite` command.

Each site collection in a Web Application has its own administration and navigational structure — but has no built-in way to navigate between site collections. Therefore each collection can provide an additional level of security.

When you create a site collection, you create a new top-level Web site. Any subsites you create within that site collection have the navigational and administration settings of the top-level site.

Deleting a site collection

When you delete a site collection from a Web Application, you say a permanent goodbye to the top-level site and all its subsites. All the content contained in the site collection is permanently deleted, including

✦ Subsites and their contents

✦ Document libraries and the documents they contain

- ✦ Lists and list data, including
  - Surveys
  - Discussions
  - Announcements
  - Events
  - Custom lists
- ✦ Site configuration and settings
- ✦ Roles and security information

You can delete a site collection in one of two ways:

- ✦ In Central Administration, choose Application Management⇨Delete a site collection. Then use the Delete Site Collection page.
- ✦ In PowerShell, use the `Remove-SPSite` command.

Before deleting a site collection, make absolutely sure that you have a backup copy of the site collection and all its contents.

Moving a site collection with PowerShell

If your site collection grows too large for the content database where it resides, you can move the site collection from one content database to another. You can move a site collection to a different content database by using either

- ✦ The PowerShell command `Move-SPSite`
- ✦ The `Stsadm` command-line tool

`Stsadm` is *deprecated,* which means Microsoft plans to eliminate it or stop supporting it. The `Stsadm` command-line tool is in the SharePoint 2010 administrator's toolkit, but Microsoft recommends using the PowerShell commands when possible.

Unfortunately, SharePoint 2010 doesn't offer a built-in graphical user interface for moving site collections. If you're allergic to the command line, however, you're not out of luck: Third-party vendors (such as AvePoint and Quest) offer tools that provide a graphical interface.

SharePoint site

Keep a few key points in mind while you're busily creating SharePoint sites:

Book II
Chapter 1

The Framework

✦ **A SharePoint site has many names.** Microsoft's SharePoint documentation uses many different words to refer to a Web site that resides in a SharePoint site collection, including

- Team site

- Web site

- Site

- Subsite

- Web

- Subweb

✦ **All Web sites in SharePoint are SharePoint sites.** You can think of every Web site in a SharePoint implementation as a SharePoint site, including

- The Central Administration Web site

- The top-level site in a site collection

- A subsite in a site collection

✦ **There are many different types of SharePoint sites.** When you create a SharePoint site, you select a site template that best represents the type of site you want to create. The site template determines the lists and features that are available on your site. For example, if you want to create a site where members of your IT department can blog about their technical experience, then you'd probably choose the Blog site template when creating your site. (You can find the list of the site templates that come with SharePoint in the "SharePoint site template" section, later in this chapter.)

✦ **The first site in a site collection is special.** The first site created in a site collection is the *root Web site* that sits at the top level of the site collection.

✦ **SharePoint developers need to be specific in their terminology.** When writing code for SharePoint, developers need to know when they're using a SharePoint *site* and when they're using a SharePoint site *collection*. When developers talk shop about SharePoint sites, they use nicknames for their programming objects: *Web* means the SPWeb object (a SharePoint site) and *site* means the SPSite object (a site collection).

Here's a quick summary to help you tell a site from a site collection:

- A *SharePoint site* is simply a Web site that's powered by SharePoint.

- A *site collection* contains SharePoint sites. Each site it contains has the same administration and navigational components as the top-level site.

- The *top-level site* is the first SharePoint site created in the site collection. It pops into existence automatically when the site collection is created. All subsequent sites created in the site collection are *subsites*.

Creating a SharePoint site

After you create your top-level site, you can create additional SharePoint sites by using one of two methods:

✦ Choosing Site Actions⇨New Site on your SharePoint site.

✦ Using the PowerShell `New-SPWeb` command.

Figure 1-4 shows the Site Actions menu with the New Site option highlighted.

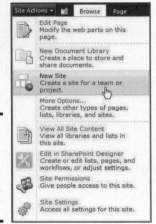

Figure 1-4:
Creating new sites by using the Site Actions menu.

Deleting a SharePoint site

If you want to remove a SharePoint site from your site collection, you can delete it by using either of these methods:

✦ Choosing Site Settings⇨Delete site.

✦ Using the PowerShell `Remove-SPSite` command.

Deleting the top-level Web site of a site collection removes the entire site collection. Check first to be sure you want to pitch the whole thing.

Scoping a SharePoint feature

A *feature* in SharePoint — say, a list, a set of Web Parts, or a complex work-flow — is a package of components that has a specific job to do in your SharePoint deployment.

SharePoint provides its built-in functionality as a set of features that you can activate and deactivate, as necessary. For example, all the default SharePoint lists (including Calendars, Tasks, Contacts, and Discussion lists) are features.

Installing a feature adds an entry to the configuration database of the SharePoint farm. *Scoping* a feature — specifying the scope of its operation — determines where in the farm it can be activated. For example, if a feature is scoped to the Web-site level, you can activate it from the Site Settings page of your site. You can scope a feature to the following levels:

✦ **Farm:** Available for activation from the Manage Farm Features page in Central Administration.

✦ **Web application:** Available for activation from the Manage Web Application Features dialog box in Central Administration.

✦ **Site collection:** Available for activation from the Site Collection Settings page at the root (top) level of the site collection.

✦ **Web site:** Available for activation from the Site Settings page of each individual site within a site collection.

Creating a SharePoint site definition

A *site definition* is a set of files that establishes the composition of a site in SharePoint from which other sites are created. The site-definition files for SharePoint reside in the folder at the end of this path:

```
\Program Files\Common Files\Microsoft Shared\Web server extensions\14\TEMPLATE\
    SiteTemplates
```

In the `SiteTemplates` folder, each subfolder represents a single site definition.

A site definition does its job by describing the components (such as navigational structure and activated features) that make up a site. The site-definition files and folders reside on each front-end Web server in your SharePoint deployment.

Before you can use any additional (custom) site definitions you create, you have to install them on all your front-end Web servers.

With that caveat in mind, here's where you can get creative. SharePoint comes with a plethora of site definitions that you can use as the basis for any custom site definitions you want to create. You'll rarely need to create a site definition from scratch. To create a custom site definition, follow these steps:

1. **Navigate to the site-definition folder on the front-end Web server.**

   You can find this folder at

   ```
   \Program Files\Common Files\Microsoft Shared\Web server extensions\14\
       TEMPLATE\SiteTemplates
   ```

2. **Make a copy of the folder (including the contents) for an existing site definition that comes close to the functionality that you want your site definition to provide.**

3. **Rename the newly copied folder to reflect your custom site definition.**

4. **Customize the site-definition files and feature associations for your new site as necessary.**

   For example, you can change the navigational structure or identify a specific set of features you want activated automatically during site creation.

5. **Register your custom site definition and any associated configurations as custom site templates.**

   The following section explains what a site template is — and how to create one for a custom site.

Don't directly modify any of the standard site definitions that come with SharePoint; that's asking for a headache. Microsoft won't support such modifications officially (and probably doesn't like them much anyway).

SharePoint site template

When creating SharePoint sites — including the top-level site in a site collection — you're presented with a list of templates on which to base your site. They show up onscreen grouped by display category, and they're called *site templates.*

When SharePoint creates a site, it looks for a site definition on your SharePoint front-end Web server in the following directory:

```
\Program Files\Common Files\Microsoft Shared\Web server
extensions\14\TEMPLATE\<localID>\XML
```

You have several XML files in this directory that have the WEBTEMP prefix. They are the site-template registration files. Their job is to inform SharePoint of the available site-definition configurations when you're creating a SharePoint site. SharePoint pulls information from these files to determine what to put on the list of site templates it shows you when you're creating a site or a site collection.

The following sections describe the site templates that are available with SharePoint 2010 — the heading of each section corresponds to a display category in SharePoint.

Collaboration site templates

The Collaboration site templates create sites that enable multiple users to work together (that is, collaborate) on a SharePoint file. The SharePoint collaboration site templates include

✦ **Team Site:** A site where teams can organize, author, and share information (quickly, of course). This site provides a document library and lists for managing announcements, calendar items, tasks, and discussions.

✦ **Blank Site:** A site you can customize according to your requirements.

✦ **Document Workspace:** A site for colleagues to work together on a document. It provides a document library for storing the primary document and supporting files, a task list for assigning to-do items, and a link list providing access to resources related to the document.

✦ **Blog:** A site where a person or team can post ideas, observations, and expertise; site visitors can then comment on the posts.

✦ **Group Work Site:** A site using groupware to enable teams to create, organize, and share information quickly and easily. It includes Group Calendar, Circulation, Phone Call Memo, Document Library, and other basic lists.

✦ **Visio Process Repository:** A site where teams can quickly view, share, and store Visio process diagrams. It provides a document library for storing controlled versions of documents — for example, process diagrams and lists for managing announcements, tasks, and review discussions.

Meeting site templates

The Meeting site templates create sites that help put together group meetings. They offer such tools as agenda lists and preconfigured task lists. The SharePoint Meeting site templates include

✦ **Basic Meeting Workspace:** A site where you can plan, organize, and capture the results of a meeting. It provides lists for managing the agenda, meeting attendees, and documents.

✦ **Blank Meeting Workspace:** A meeting site you can customize to meet your requirements.

✦ **Decision Meeting Workspace:** A site for documenting your meetings. It provides lists for creating tasks, storing documents, and recording decisions.

✦ **Social Meeting Workspace:** A site for planning social occasions. It provides a list for tracking attendees, providing directions, and storing pictures of the event.

✦ **Multipage Meeting Workspace:** A site you can use to plan, organize, and capture the results of a meeting. It provides lists for managing the agenda and meeting attendees, in addition to two blank pages you can customize according to your needs.

Enterprise site templates

The Enterprise site templates create sites that facilitate activities that help the organization run well and make use of its information. For example, you can create an area for the central management of enterprise content. The SharePoint Enterprise site templates include

✦ **Document Center:** A site that stores and manages the organization's documents in a central location.

✦ **Records Center:** A site specifically tailored to managing records. Record managers can configure the routing table to direct incoming files to specific locations. The site provides capabilities that specify whether records can be deleted or modified after they're added to the records repository.

✦ **Business Intelligence Center:** A site that supports collaboration with other site members, the management of information, and the development of business intelligence through tools such as scorecards and interactive dashboards.

✦ **Enterprise Search Center:** A site focused on enhancing the search capabilities of your whole enterprise. You can customize its standard SharePoint pages to meet your specific search needs.

✦ **My Site Host:** A site that hosts personal sites (My Sites) and the public People Profile page.

You may use this template only once per User Profile service application. (You can find out how to configure the User Profile Service application in Book III, Chapter 7.)

✦ **Basic Search Center:** A site tailored to delivering an improved search experience. The site includes pages for search results and advanced searches.

✦ **FAST Search Center:** A site that specializes in the FAST search feature. If you have FAST Search Server for 2010 configured in your SharePoint environment, the FAST Search Center provides a better visual experience during the search. For example, it displays document previews and thumbnails in your search results.

Publishing site templates

The Publishing site templates create sites that target a large audience. The publishing site templates include

✦ **Publishing Portal:** This site gives you a starting point for creating a public, Internet-facing portal or a large intranet portal. It includes a starting page, a sample press-release subsite, a Search Center, and a login page. Typically, sites built on this template have more readers than contributors; Web pages are published through the approval workflow method.

✦ **Enterprise Wiki:** A site for publishing knowledge that you capture and want to share throughout your organization. It provides a single location for coauthoring content, discussions, and project management.

Custom site templates

You can add your own custom templates to the standard SharePoint collection of site templates — largely because each site template has a specific configuration spelled out in a site-definition file. Suppose you have a custom site definition that contains a configuration you really like. You want this configuration to appear as a choice in the SharePoint user interface when you're creating a site or a site collection. Can do. But first you have to register your site template. Follow these steps to register a custom site template:

1. **Navigate to the XML directory.**

   You can find this directory at

   ```
   \Program Files\Common Files\Microsoft Shared\Web server extensions\14\
       TEMPLATE\<localID>\XML
   ```

2. **Make a copy of the file** `webtempvispr.xml`, **which holds the registration for the Visio Process Repository site template.**

   If you're using SharePoint Foundation, make a copy of `WEBTEMP.XML` instead.

3. **Rename the newly copied file to reflect your site template.**

   Doing so ensures that you keep the `WEBTEMP` prefix. For example, you can name the file `WEBTEMPMusic.XML`. The capitalization of the filename doesn't matter.

4. **Customize the content of the file to reflect your own registration.**

   Make sure the XML elements in the `WEBTEMP` file are as follows:

   • The `Name` attribute of the `Template` element should match the folder of your custom site definition.

   • The `ID` attribute of the `Template` element should use unique values greater than 10,000 to avoid conflict with existing Microsoft templates.

A few Microsoft template registrations do fall into this range, such as the `offile` template that holds Records Center registrations. Try to avoid them too. As a best practice, you should verify that the value isn't already used for a Microsoft template before you specify it.

- The `ID` attribute of the `Configuration` element maps to a specific configuration in your custom site definition.

- The `Title` attribute defines the name of the site template as it should appear in the list of available site templates in the SharePoint user interface.

- The `DisplayCategory` attribute determines under which tab the site template appears in the list of available site templates. You can add your own custom category by simply assigning your custom name to the `DisplayCategory` attribute.

Don't directly modify any of the standard SharePoint site-template registrations; Microsoft doesn't support such modifications.

Shared Services Provider (SSP) limitations

SharePoint 2007 introduced the Shared Services Provider (SSP) model so you could configure services such as Search Services, Excel Services, and the Business Data Catalog as a single SSP.

Although the SSP architecture made SharePoint services easier to share widely, it did have its limitations, including these:

✦ **Services aren't easily reusable.** With SharePoint 2007, when you created a Web Application, you associated that SSP with a Web Application. If you needed a new dedicated search for another Web Application, you could create a new SSP, configure the search, and map it to your Web Application. The search functionality in the first SSP was isolated from the second SSP — providing an easy and secure way of dedicating services.

The problem with this method is that it doesn't promote reusability; when you created a new SSP, you got a new instance of all the services in that SSP and had to configure every service you wanted to use. For example, if you created two SSPs (SSP1 and SSP2) and wanted the SSP2 search configuration to be different from that of SSP1, then you simply applied your new configuration settings to the SSP2 search. But if you wanted the remaining services (such as Excel Services and the Business Data Catalog), to have the same configuration as the corresponding SSP1 services, you couldn't simply reuse the services from SSP1. Instead, you had to configure every service in SSP2 to have the same settings as it had in SSP1. (Pass the aspirin, will you?)

✦ **Limited scalability.** When you created an SSP, all the data relating to the services within that SSP were stored in the same SSP database.

✦ **Not extensible.** After all that work within the limits of the SSP model, you couldn't extend it; Microsoft didn't provide the hooks into the SSP architecture that would have allowed developers to build their own service offerings. (There was gnashing of teeth behind IT doors.)

If you're still running SharePoint 2007, watch out for these limitations.

Service application architecture

SharePoint 2010 introduces a fresh approach to services architecture. Gone are many limitations of its predecessor. Developers cheer its more robust, scalable, and flexible platform.

Here's a quick list of architectural improvements to the 2010 release — specifically in the area of services:

✦ Web Applications are no longer confined to a single SSP. For that matter, the services are no longer bound to a single SSP. Instead, services are free to roam throughout your SharePoint farm and, in some cases, even across farms — helping out where they're needed.

✦ Services in SharePoint 2010 exist independent of one another in the farm; you can pick and choose which services you want your Web Applications to use.

✦ A Web Application can use a combination of dedicated and shared service applications. For example, you can have two Web Applications that use the same service applications — such as Excel Services and Business Connectivity Services — and you can configure the same two Web Applications to use a unique Search Service application.

✦ The new service-application architecture provides the flexibility for you to increase the scale of your services when demand grows within your organization. If need be, you can load-balance multiple instances of the same service across multiple application servers within the farm. (Pretty fancy.)

✦ You can share many standard SharePoint services — such as the Search Service and the Managed Metadata Service — across multiple farms. (Figure 1-5 shows an example.)

✦ One important way that SharePoint 2010 improves on SharePoint 2007 is by offering an open service-application architecture. In SharePoint 2010, this open architecture is part of the underlying SharePoint Foundation platform. Result: You can expand on your service offerings through in-house development or third-party vendors.

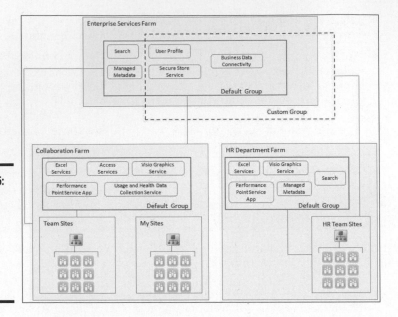

Figure 1-5:
Services
can be
easily
shared
across
multiple
farms.

SharePoint service

In SharePoint, a *service* is a set of program files that you deploy to the application servers within your farm to provide data or processing resources to SharePoint. The program files can exist in a variety of forms, such as

✦ A set of Web services, assemblies (.DLL files), executables, and databases that work in unison to answer a specific need.

✦ A set of assemblies that you build and install in your SharePoint environment to communicate with your line-of-business (LOB) applications.

Both SharePoint Foundation and SharePoint 2010 are equipped with services out of the box. The SharePoint product offerings that you own determine the number of services available. For example, SharePoint Foundation contains a small subset of the service offerings that SharePoint 2010 provides, such as the Business Data Connectivity service. Table 1-1 lists the service offerings that come with SharePoint, version by version. Note in particular that

✦ Most enterprise service offerings from Microsoft are standard with SharePoint 2010.

✦ The underlying service-application architecture enables you to create custom services in both SharePoint Foundation *and* SharePoint 2010.

Table 1-1   SharePoint Services Available Out of the Box

Service	Description	SharePoint Foundation	SharePoint 2010 Standard	SharePoint 2010 Enterprise
Access Services	Allows viewing, editing, and interacting with Access Services databases in a browser.			X
Application Registry Service	A backwards-compatible Business Data Connectivity (BDC) API.			X
Business Data Connectivity Service	Provides the SharePoint farm with the ability to upload BDC models that describe the interfaces of your line of business applications. After the BDC models are uploaded, you can access data from these systems by using SharePoint.	X	X	X
Excel Services Application	Allows viewing of and interactivity with Excel files in a browser.			X
Lotus Notes Connector	A search connector that crawls the data in a Lotus Notes server.			X

(continued)

Book II Chapter 1

The Framework

Table 1-1 *(continued)*

Service	Description	SharePoint Foundation	SharePoint 2010 Standard	SharePoint 2010 Enterprise
Managed Metadata Service	Provides access to managed taxonomy hierarchies, key-words, and social tagging infrastruc-ture, as well as Content Type pub-lishing across site collections.		X	X
Performance Point Service Application	Supports the moni-toring and analytic capabilities of PerformancePoint Services, such as the storage and publication of dash-boards and related content.			X
Search Service Application	Indexes content and serves search queries.		X	X
Secure Store Service	Provides capabil-ity to securely store data (such as user names and passwords) and associate it with a specific identity or group of identities.		X	X
State Service	Provides temporary storage of user session data for SharePoint Server components, such as InfoPath.		X	X

Service	Description	SharePoint Foundation	SharePoint 2010 Standard	SharePoint 2010 Enterprise
Usage and Health Data Collection	Collects farm-wide usage and health data, and allows you to view usage and health reports.	X	X	X
User Profile Service Application	Adds support for personal sites, user profile pages, and other social-computing features. Some of the features offered by this service require other services, such as Search Services and Managed Metadata Services, to be configured.		X	X
Visio Graphics Service	Enables viewing and refreshing of Visio Web drawings.			X
Web Analytics Service Application	Processes and analyzes usage data to provide insight into Web usage patterns. The Web Analytics Service Application requires the Usage and Health Data Collection Service and the State Service to be configured in the farm.			X
Word Automation Services	Provides server-side conversion of documents into formats that are supported by the Microsoft Word client application.			X

You may need to create a set of services that are shared across multiple farms. For example, Figure 1-5 shows a services farm dedicated to managing and maintaining cross-farm services — such as the Search and Managed Metadata services for an entire organization.

Not all services can be shared across multiple farms — but the following services can be:

✦ Business Data Connectivity Service

✦ Managed Metadata Service

✦ Search Service application

✦ Secure Store Service

✦ User Profile Service application

✦ Web Analytics Service application

Additional services

The hardworking SharePoint services included in the core service application architecture. That means they're available in both SharePoint Foundation *and* SharePoint 2010. Here's a list of these additional service offerings:

✦ **Application Discovery and Load Balancer Service:** Also known as "the topology service," this one is at the heart of the service-application architecture. Its features allow you to browse and connect to service applications.

   The Application Discovery and Load Balancer Service is installed — and started — automatically on every SharePoint server in the farm.

✦ **Claims to Windows Token Service:** This SharePoint version of a security token service (STS) supports claims-based security, handling authentication requests by issuing security tokens based on user account information.

   The Claims to Windows Token Service is installed automatically and started automatically on each SharePoint server in the farm.

✦ **SharePoint Foundation Subscription Settings Service:** A service that supports site subscriptions. Sites that are members of a site subscription can share settings and configuration information.

A site collection can be a member of only one site subscription; after you set that subscription, it can't be changed.

Site subscriptions are typically used in hosting scenarios, where data and services are partitioned to accommodate multiple tenants.

A subscription ID maps the features, services, and sites to the tenants and assists in partitioning the service data accordingly. The Subscription Settings Service keeps track of partitioned services and the associated subscription IDs.

Services program files

Microsoft uses two WebServices directories to host the program files associated with the standard SharePoint services:

♦ `\Program Files\Common Files\Microsoft Shared\Web Server Extensions\14\WebServices`

This directory stores the files for the Business Data Connectivity Service, the Claims to Windows Token Service, and the Application Discovery and Load Balancer Service.

♦ `\Program Files\Microsoft Office Servers\14.0\ WebServices`

This directory stores files for more service offerings including, but not limited to, the Lotus Notes Connector Service, the Search Service, the User Profile Service, the Access Database Service, Excel Calculation Services, and the Visio Graphics Service.

Figure 1-6 shows the WebServices directory located in the Web Server Extensions tree, with the Topology folder expanded to reveal its contents. Figure 1-7 shows the corresponding Windows Communication Foundation (WCF) service hosted in IIS.

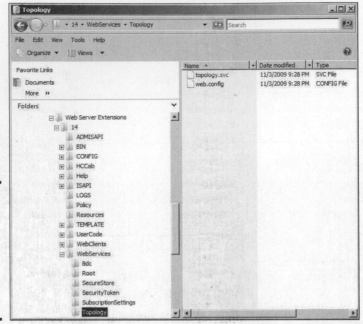

Figure 1-6:
The folders in the Web-Services directory correspond to a service application.

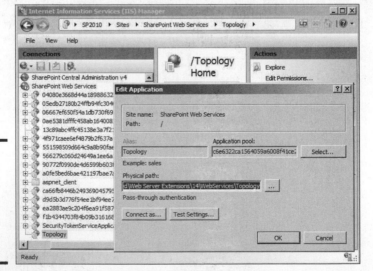

Figure 1-7:
The Topology WCF Service running in IIS.

Service application

A *service application* is a configured logical representation of a service in SharePoint. For example, SharePoint comes equipped with a Managed Metadata Service, but you can't use this service until you assign it some resources (such as the application pool where it will run and the databases it will use).

SharePoint 2010 provides a Farm Configuration Wizard that walks you through the process of configuring service applications for each of the services that come with SharePoint 2010. This wizard helps you select the services you want to run in your farm — *and* create your first site — so you can get your SharePoint environment up and running as quickly as possible. After you select the services, the wizard configures each service application with the default settings, sets up the necessary Web Application associations, and starts the services on the servers in your farm. Figure 1-8 shows some of the available services you can choose on the SharePoint 2010 farm-configuration page.

Figure 1-8:
The initial
Farm
Config-
uration
Wizard
configures
a set of
service
offerings.

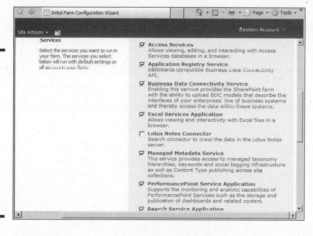

For more customized environments, you can use Central Administration to apply your own settings to existing service applications, create new service applications, and associate the services with specific Web Applications.

How a service instance works

You can deploy a service on multiple servers within your SharePoint farm that does a neat trick: It installs the physical bits required to run the service. When you start a service on a specific application server, SharePoint starts a physical instance for each service application associated with that service.

A *service application* is a logical representation of a service, and a *service instance* is a physical representation (or instance) of a service. For example, if you create multiple search service applications, each application has its own configuration settings. Starting the Search Service on a server launches an instance of the service for each defined Search Service application.

Each instance is managed by a software load balancer provided by the Application Discovery and Load Balancer Service. The load balancer uses a simple round-robin load-balancing algorithm to keep track of all the running instances of a service. When a request comes in from a front-end Web server for a particular service, the load balancer selects the next server in the round-robin schedule that contains an instance of the service application. Then the load balancer links the chosen instance to the front-end Web server; the link provides communication.

Communicating by service application proxy

When you create a service application in SharePoint, a service-application connection (a *service application proxy*) is created automatically. The service application proxy is the mechanism that allows a Web Application to communicate with a service application.

Here's what happens:

1. When a front-end Web server receives a request from a client for a specific service application, that front-end Web server passes the request to the service application proxy.

2. The service application proxy informs the farm that it needs to communicate with a specific service application.

3. SharePoint's built-in load balancer determines the next service instance available to service requests and hands the Uniform Resource Identifier (URI) of that specific service instance to the service application proxy for direct communication.

Service application proxy group

When you create a Web application, you specify the service applications that the Web Application will use by selecting an application proxy group. There are two types of application proxy groups:

✦ **Default:** A farm-wide group that contains a list of the service applications available by default to all the Web Applications within that farm.

Each farm has only one default group.

✦ **Custom:** You can use the custom group to associate a different set of service application proxies with your Web Application; you can create one custom application proxy group per Web Application in your farm.

Figure 1-9 shows the Service Application Connections section of the Create New Web Application page in Central Administration.

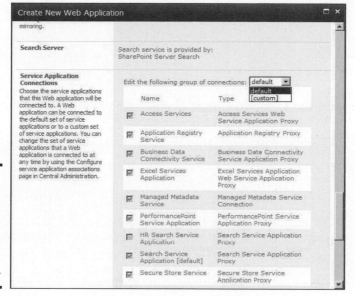

Book II
Chapter 1

The Framework

Figure 1-9:
Connect
your Web
Application
to a specific
application
proxy group.

Service application associations

When you map a Web Application to an application proxy group, you create associations between the Web application and the service application proxies that belong to the proxy group. These associations are *service application associations* or *service application connections.* They define which service applications a Web Application will use. You can customize the application proxy groups by using the Service Application Associations page in Central Administration. (If you're itching to configure service application associations, flip to the "Connecting to a local Service Application" section of Book II, Chapter 8.)

Figure 1-10 shows the service application proxy groups and the corresponding service application proxies for three Web Applications in a sample SharePoint farm. Here's what the major players are up to:

✦ The Web Application running on port 80 is using the service applications listed in the default application proxy group.

✦ The Web Application running on port 8090 is using the four service applications listed in its custom application proxy group.

✦ The Web Application running on port 8095 is using a custom application proxy group that has a different combination of service applications from the (whole different set of) Web Applications running on port 8090 and port 80.

The whole thing looks busier than a convention of ambidextrous puppeteers.

If you want to change the number of busy Web Apps, here's how: Click the Application Proxy Group link on Service Application Associations page to add and remove application proxies from the group.

Figure 1-10: Control the Web Application-to-proxy-group associations.

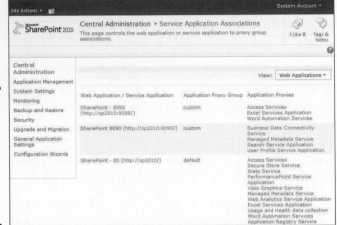

Remote connections

Some service applications that come with SharePoint, such as the Business Data Connectivity Service and the Search Service, can be shared across multiple farms. (It's like sending a really competent hired hand around from farm to farm. Only faster.)

But whoa, there. Before you can make a service application available to other farms, you have to publish the service — and then the other farms have to respond. Here's an overview of what goes on:

1. You publish a service by clicking the Publish command on the Service Applications management page in Central Administration.

   When you publish a service application, it's available for use by other farms.

2. For another farm to use the service application, that farm has to connect to the service by using the service's published URL (or a URL to the farm's Discovery Service).

3. You set up a connection to a published service by clicking the Connect command on the Service Applications management page in Central Administration.

You can find the detailed steps involved with publishing a service and connecting to a published service in Book II, Chapter 8.

Chapter 2: Assessing Authentication Options

In This Chapter

✔ **Understanding claims-aware applications**

✔ **Configuring authentication modes**

✔ **Implementing multiple authentication methods**

*U*sing a corporate network is all about authorization (but you knew that). In Book I, Chapter 2 we discuss how to authorize access to the content in your SharePoint sites. To enforce that authorization, SharePoint has to be able to identify which user is trying to get at the content. Similarly, user identity is crucial in providing services (such as User Profiles); the user's online identity controls what he or she can do with personal home pages and social features.

Authentication is part of the overall process of establishing a user's identity. When you're dealing with computer networks, it's never enough just to say, "I *am* somebody." Ultimately, the requesting user presents some form of *token* (call it a digital voucher) to SharePoint that proves identity. SharePoint then uses this token to associate the user with an internal programming object (called `SPUser`) that authorizes access to content (saying, in effect, "Okay, you are somebody. Now you can look at this pie chart.").

In previous versions of SharePoint, the user's identifying token could be one of these:

✦ A standard Windows security token, representing an Active Directory user object or security group.

✦ A token generated by an ASP.NET membership and role provider — these allow you to essentially write your own authentication and authorization methods to suit your needs.

Although SharePoint 2010 still supports these classic (please don't say "old-fashioned") Windows-based identities, the support now extends to *claims-based identity* — an identity model supported by the .NET Framework that allows claims about a user to be used for authentication purposes.

Support for claims-based identity brings some advantages:

✦ SharePoint can participate in authentication systems that *aren't* based on Windows (what a concept).

✦ Identities become easier to delegate to back-end applications (for example, delegating an update task to a Human Resources application).

✦ The environment for in-house software developers becomes simpler and more consistent.

In this chapter, we look at SharePoint as a *claims-aware* application (one that can handle claims-based identities) — and the options you have for authenticating users and providing claims about their identities — which you can also re-use in your back-end applications.

Understanding Claims-Based Identity

In the claims world (on the other side of the looking glass), a user's *identity* consists of any number of attributes that describe the user — such as e-mail address, full name, groups the person belongs to, country he or she lives in, and even more personal attributes such as passport or driver's-license numbers. Authorities that you explicitly trust issue claims about these attributes and their values.

Here software acts like people: Claims-aware applications have an explicit trust relationship with an issuer (usually another application configured by some honcho in the organization). A claims-aware application only believes a claim about a user if the application trusts the entity that issued the claim. If that trust is in place, then the application doesn't care how the claim-issuing entity authenticates the user — or where the entity gathers the attributes and their values — which means the application doesn't need to include authentication logic in its code.

This abstraction of authentication allows the application to work in almost any authentication infrastructure, doing no more than processing claims presented to it to establish users' identities. The trusted authorities that perform authentication are called *identity providers* or *authentication providers*.

The notion of explicit trust here is important. Without it, claims-based identity systems wouldn't be possible. Your application has to pick the authorities whose claims it will trust. For example, consider the attribute of age. Your application might trust a person to provide his or her age in response to a routine request for information (if, for example, the application is setting up a retirement party). But if the information were needed to calculate an age-related payment (say, of an auto-insurance premium), then you'd want the answer to come from a more authoritative source — say, an agency such as a governmental records office that could back up the claim with an official birth certificate.

As a claims-aware application, SharePoint 2010 doesn't give a hoot about how the user is authenticated. All it cares about is receiving a *SAML* (Security Access Markup Language) token that provides values for attributes it can use to figure out the user's identity. (More about SAML in a minute.) This obsession on the part of SharePoint actually offers some flexibility while it saves some work:

✦ You can deploy SharePoint in environments that may require more Internet-friendly authentication techniques than a purely Windows-based system can provide.

✦ You can make changes to the available authentication methods no need to re-code, recompile, or reconfigure SharePoint — or any integrated solutions.

Book II
Chapter 2

Security Assertion Markup Language (SAML) is an XML-based standard for exchanging authentication and authorization data between security domains; that is, between an identity provider (a producer of assertions) and a service provider (a consumer of assertions). SAML is a product of the OASIS Security Services Technical Committee.

In a *really* general way, claims-based identity is like the process you go through when you board an airliner:

1. As you approach the departure gate, you hand over your boarding card to the agents.

2. The agents check (discreetly, of course) to make sure the boarding card isn't a forgery by verifying (via a barcode or magnetic strip) that the airline issued it.

3. Because the agents trust the airline, they trust the details on the boarding card (such as your seat number, name, and flight number).

4. The agents authorize you to board the airplane.

Okay, we left out the part about surrendering any pointy objects, but you get the idea. (Every metaphor has limits.) You have various ways to get your boarding card — by online check-in or by walking up to a ticket desk. In either case, you must provide some credentials to prove your identity before you can have a boarding card issued to you — a booking reference if you're online, or an actual passport or driver's license if you're at the ticket desk.

In essence, the boarding card is a set of claims about you that have been issued and verified by an authority that the agents at the gate trust. The agents don't care how you got the boarding card — or (by implication) how you proved your identity to the issuing authority. This is a real-world analogy that suggests how claims-based identity systems deliver a major benefit: They separate the whole authentication process (including maintenance such as managing passwords) from the application.

In software terms, the "set of claims" is called a *security token*. Each token is signed by the issuer. A claims-based application considers users to be authenticated if they present a valid, signed security token from a trusted issuer. No matter what authentication protocol was used, the application gets a security token in a simple and consistent format (SAML) that it can use to determine authorization and permission levels for that user. Ultimately, the application can authorize access to its resources by using any of the claims the user presents (provided, of course, that the authority has validated them).

SharePoint 2010 supports two methods of identifying users:

✦ **Classic mode:** Windows identities identify users and the system supports only one authentication provider: Windows itself.

✦ **Claims-based mode:** Claims identify users and the system supports three authentication providers:

 • Windows

 • Forms-based authentication (FBA)

 • Trusted identity providers

You specify your preferred authentication method at the Web Application level. Naturally, the first order of business here is to enable and configure the method you want SharePoint to use. The next sections of the chapter take a closer look at your various options.

Classic Mode Authentication

Although SharePoint has dealt with Windows identities since its first release, the process of authenticating an identity has always been distinct from the SharePoint code itself. In fact, Microsoft Internet Information Services is the application that performs the actual authentication — and then passes the user's SID (security ID) to SharePoint. SharePoint, in turn, uses the SID to establish an `SPUser` object whose purpose is to authorize access to content.

Windows identity support is still available in SharePoint 2010. The idea is to provide enough backward compatibility to cater to legacy systems (which may have some solution that expects Windows identities to be presented to it, and gets surly if they're not forthcoming). Also, some organizations haven't migrated to claims-based authentication but still want to use SharePoint.

You *can* still use Windows as the identity provider in a claims-based scenario. Just keep in mind that claims-based authentication has some advantages over Windows classic authentication — for example, having multiple authentication providers in the same zone. (For more about that handy feature, see the "Configuring Claims-Based Authentication" section later in this chapter.)

You determine an identity mechanism for SharePoint to use at the Web Application level: During the creation of a Web Application, the first option you choose is whether you want Claims-based or Classic-mode authentication.

You can't change the identity mechanism for a Web Application after you create it! If you subsequently change your mind you will have to delete your Web Application and recreate it (which, of course, will mean that any sites created in the Web Application will also have to be recreated which is not something that anyone would enjoy).

Classic mode supports only Windows as its authentication provider — which means it also supports the following standard IIS Windows authentication modes:

✦ **Anonymous:** Allows access to content in SharePoint sites without the user having to provide authentication credentials. Enabling Anonymous access reveals a new task on the Ribbon that permits site administrators to indicate the parts of their site to which they want to allow anonymous access. The options (shown in Figure 2-1) are as follows:

- Entire Web Site

- Lists and Libraries

- Nothing

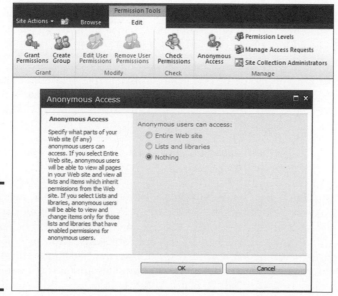

Figure 2-1:
Setting
Anonymous
Access
at the site
level.

The default is to allow no access: Even though Anonymous access is enabled at the Web Application, individual site administrators still control how their own content is accessed. If a user chooses either of the other options, a Sign-In button appears onscreen so the user can access the content after being authenticated.

✦ **Basic:** Requires Windows account credentials, which a Web browser can present when making a request during an HTTP transaction. The credentials are attached in an Authentication HTTP header and are sent over the network in plaintext.

✦ **Digest:** This option works the same as basic authentication, except the user's credentials are encrypted as an MD5 message digest instead of being sent over the network in plaintext. Although Digest authentication is stronger than Basic without the Secure Sockets Layer (SSL provides a layer of encryption thus securing the inherently insecure plaintext that is used in the conversation), Digest mode does have some disadvantages; for example, it has to store passwords in a reversible encryption format on the server.

✦ **Client Certificates:** This mode supports the exchange of public-key certificates using Secure Sockets Layer (SSL) encryption over HTTP. Client certificates are issued by a Certificate Authority (CA), and they must conform to the Public Key Infrastructure (PKI).

✦ **NTLM:** Microsoft NT LAN Manager authentication is required for networks that receive authentication requests from client computers that don't support Kerberos authentication (Kerberos is a standard authentication protocol that is stronger than NTLM since it supports features such as mutual authentication in which both the client and server have to verify each other's identity). NTLM is based on encrypting user names and passwords before sending the encrypted credentials over the network.

✦ **Negotiate (Kerberos or NTLM):** Enables clients to select between Kerberos authentication and NTLM authentication. Negotiate mode tries to use Kerberos authentication unless either of these conditions applies:

  • Kerberos authentication isn't supported in the deployed environment.

  • The calling application doesn't provide sufficient information to implement Kerberos authentication.

Creating a Web Application that uses Classic Mode Authentication is very straightforward. By accepting all the SharePoint default values presented during a New operation from the Manage Web Applications page in Central Administration, you end up with an NTLM authentication provider for the default zone (see "Implementing Multiple Authentication Methods through Zones," later in this chapter, for more about zones and authentication methods).

The New Web Application page only allows you to select either NTLM or Kerberos as the authentication options for Classic mode. If your system requires support for other authentication modes, then you have to use IIS to configure them manually.

Claims-Based Authentication

You could have many reasons to use something other than Windows identities for authentication in your SharePoint system. For example:

✦ You may want to offer controlled access to content elsewhere on the Internet, to people who don't have accounts in your Active Directory domain.

✦ Your organization may have been through a merger but doesn't yet have a trust relationship between the formerly separate server forests — which rules out Windows authentication for the time being.

✦ You have to integrate your system with a back-end security application that doesn't run on Windows, so somehow you have to delegate the processing of a user's identity from SharePoint to the back-end application.

Book II
Chapter 2

Assessing
Authentication
Options

These are just three examples of where a claims-based identity system can be beneficial.

SharePoint 2010 uses the Microsoft Windows Identity Foundation (WIF) to implement claims-based identity. WIF is a set of .NET Framework classes that enable the creation of claims-aware applications. Applications created with WIF can process authentication requests created to comply with the WS-Federation authentication protocol.

WS-Federation builds on two other standard protocols: WS-Trust and WS-Security. WS-Federation supports the token-based authentication architecture that enables a Web application to require a security token for authenticated access to resources. During its development, WIF was known as the Geneva framework.

With claims-based identity, SharePoint isn't hard-coded to use only a specific set of identity providers. (Such was the case with SharePoint 2007, which offered only Windows Active Directory and ASP.NET as authentication providers.) Instead, you can use any identity provider you like — as long as it's been designed and implemented in accordance with the WS-* Security Standards. This means you can use identity providers such as Windows LiveID, OpenID providers (such as Google and Yahoo), and Active Directory Federation Services.

But SharePoint goes further than even this degree of openness; it can also accept Windows and Forms-based Authentication requests (FBA – another name for ASP.NET membership and role providers as described at the beginning of this chapter) and convert them into a claim. Such a claim can then be used inside SharePoint, for communicating with service applications and for delegation to other back-end applications that support claims. In addition, SharePoint provides a "Claims to Windows Token" service that can convert a claim back into a Kerberos ticket for integration with non-claims-based applications.

Understanding SharePoint's Security Token Service

SharePoint has its own Security Token Service (STS) for taking care of two essential claims-based chores:

✦ Dispatching unauthenticated requests for SharePoint resources to an identity provider (IP).

✦ Converting security tokens received from the IPs into claims (that is, into SAML tokens).

The STS is a Web Service that comes into play for any Web Application that has been enabled for claims-based authentication. Figure 2-2 shows what happens when a user attempts to access a SharePoint resource using either a Web browser or an Office 2010 application.

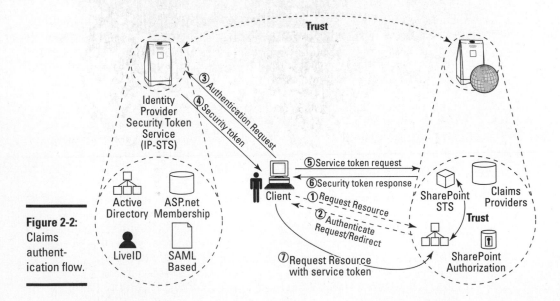

Figure 2-2: Claims authentication flow.

Here's the process, step by step:

1. An unauthenticated HTTP request comes to the URL of the SharePoint resource.

2. SharePoint responds, indicating that the request isn't authorized — and provides the calling application with a URL it can go visit to get authenticated.

The URL that SharePoint offers depends on which authentication providers have been enabled in SharePoint. The calling application could, for example, end up redirected to a Windows LiveID logon page. If more than one authentication provider is available, the URL will be to a sign-in page where the user can select the type of identity provider you want to perform the authentication.

3. The IP authenticates the user against the relevant resource — be it Active Directory (for Windows), a membership and role provider (for Forms-based Authentication), or a SAML-based system (such as ADFS or LiveID).

4. The identity provider returns the security token specific to its authentication method.

5. The IP-specific security token is presented to the SharePoint Security Token Service (STS).

    The STS verifies that it trusts the issuer of the security token, gestures hypnotically (not really), and turns the security token into a SAML token suitable for use in SharePoint (or regenerates the incoming SAML token if the identity provider was already SAML-based).

    Note that the attributes of the SAML token depend on which IP was used. At this stage, you could require that the SAML token be augmented with your own claims provider before it's passed back to the calling user. This is a useful way to ensure that claims for other applications (such as a back-end Customer Relationship Manager application) are already included in the user's list of claims.

6. The SAML token is returned to the user.

7. The HTTP request goes to the original URL with the SAML token attached. SharePoint then uses the SAML token to determine whether the user is authorized to access the requested resource.

SharePoint's STS is a Web service called `SecurityTokenServiceApplication` — refreshingly obvious, isn't it? — which is installed on your front-end Web servers in the IIS Web site called SharePoint Web Services.

Configuring Claims-Based Authentication

You configure claims-based authentication when you create a Web Application. (Sorry, but you can't change the authentication mode after creation. It's one of those decisions you have to make beforehand.)

Claims-based authentication is slightly more complex to configure than Classic mode. That's because you must also think about the identity providers you will use. Follow these steps to specify basic settings for claims-based features in the new Web Application process:

1. **From the Manage Web Applications page in Central Administration, select the New task on the Ribbon.**

   The New Web Application page appears.

2. **Choose the Claims-based Authentication radio button at the top of the page.**

3. **In the Claims Authentication Types, select the identity providers you want to support — whether Windows, FBA, or a Trusted IP.**

   In Figure 2-3, we've selected Windows and the LDAP ASP.NET membership and role provider that comes with SharePoint. The "Implementing Forms-based Authentication" section in this chapter shows you how to complete the configuration of FBA providers.

   If you specify more than one IP, then you can override the default sign-in page via the Sign In Page URL section if necessary.

To see claims authentication in action, refer to Figures 2-3, 2-4, and 2-5. These show what happens when a user attempts to sign in to a SharePoint site set up for claims authentication with a Windows and FBA (LDAP) provider. The home page on the SharePoint site has a custom Web Part on it (developed by Steve Peshka) that displays the resulting claims that the requesting user has.

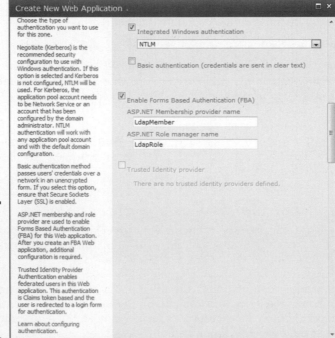

Figure 2-3: Configuring authentication providers for a claims-based Web Application.

The differences between the claims displayed in Figure 2-6 and 2-7 came about because different identity providers were used to authenticate the user. Even though the same actual data source was used for authentication (the same user object in the Active Directory) Windows authentication returned more attributes than did the LDAP authentication.

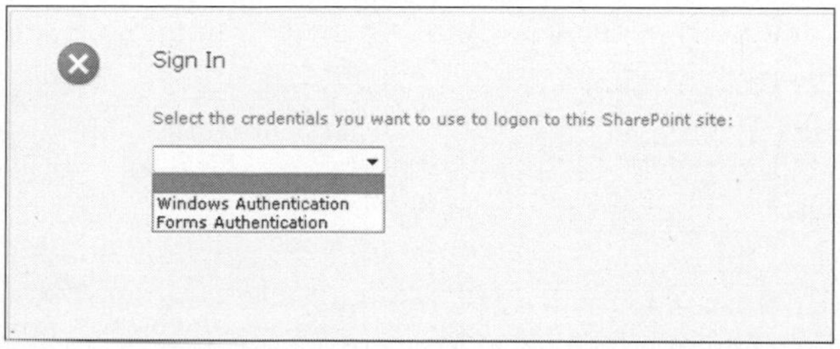

Figure 2-4: Sign in page when multiple authentication providers are enabled.

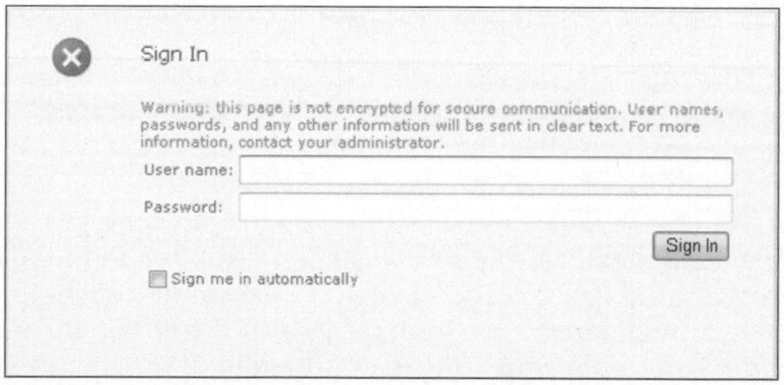

Figure 2-5: FBA Sign in page.

Figure 2-6: Claims associated with FBA authentication.

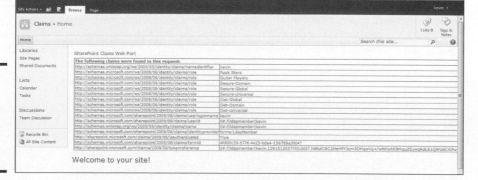

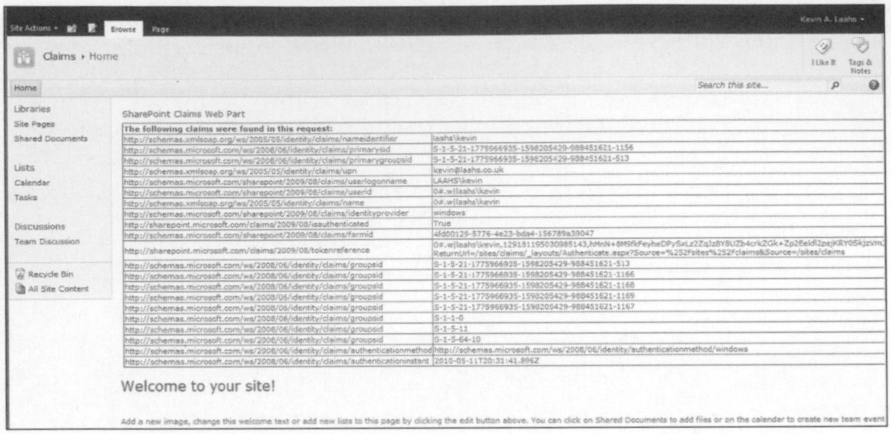

Figure 2-7:
Claims associated with Windows authentication.

Implementing forms-based authentication

SharePoint 2007 introduced support for FBA.

The SharePoint approach to FBA support was to make use of ASP.NET plug-ins to enable authentication against non-Windows systems. This feature can verify who someone is by consulting a simple list of user names and passwords (held in a file or database) or by consulting an Enterprise Directory System of your choice. This arrangement requires a *membership provider* (and optionally a *role provider*) — an application that checks the repository that holds user credentials and then validates whether a particular user exists (in a validated condition, anyway) by hunting for the username and password that the requesting user supplied. If the membership provider finds what it's looking for, the authentication is successful. If not, gnashing of teeth ensues (users tend to get upset when told they don't exist).

In SharePoint 2010, you still have the option of using FBA — but the net result is a claim rather than an ASP.NET generic identity. That's why FBA is integrated into SharePoint claims-based authentication instead of muddling along as a separate feature. SharePoint still includes an LDAP membership and role provider, and ASP.NET includes a built-in SQL membership.

Of course, this process isn't exactly automatic. In addition to providing the names of the membership provider(s) and role provider(s) while you're configuring the Web Application (refer to Figure 2-3), you must also define these providers in the `Web.config` files for every Web Application in which you expect to use FBA, including the SharePoint Security Token Service and Central Administration.

You must define the providers in the `Web.config` files if you want to add FBA-based security principals to (say) user policies for the whole server farm. (In fact, the Security Token Service is the part of SharePoint that actually calls the membership provider during the authentication process.)

The following XML snippet shows the basic details you need to add to those aforementioned `Web.config` files to complete the configuration of FBA. Insert this code into the `<system.Web>` nodes that will already be present in the `Web.config` files — but before you do so, note that you'll have to change the `"server"` and `"userContainer"` attributes so they point to your own domain controller and to the organizational unit against which you want to authenticate incoming claims. So, without further ado, there's the snippet:

```
<membership>
     <providers>
       <add name="LdapMember"
           type="Microsoft.Office.Server.Security.LdapMembershipProvider,
  Microsoft.Office.Server, Version=14.0.0.0, Culture=neutral, PublicKeyToken=7
  1e9bce111e9429c"
           server="dc1.nut2craic.com"
           port="389"
           useSSL="false"
           userDNAttribute="distinguishedName"
           userNameAttribute="sAMAccountName"
           userContainer="CN=Users,DC=nut2craic,DC=com"
           userObjectClass="person"
           userFilter="(ObjectClass=person)"
           scope="Subtree"
           otherRequiredUserAttributes="sn,givenname,cn" />
     </providers>
  </membership>
<roleManager>
    <providers>
        <add name="LdapRole"
            type="Microsoft.Office.Server.Security.LdapRoleProvider, Microsoft.
  Office.Server, Version=14.0.0.0, Culture=neutral, PublicKeyToken=71e9bce111e
  9429c"
            server="dc1.nut2craic.com"
            port="389"
            useSSL="false"
            groupContainer="CN=Users,DC=nut2craic,DC=com"
            groupNameAttribute="cn"
            groupNameAlternateSearchAttribute="samAccountName"
            groupMemberAttribute="member"
            userNameAttribute="sAMAccountName"
            dnAttribute="distinguishedName"
            groupFilter="(ObjectClass=group)"
            userFilter="(ObjectClass=person)"
            scope="Subtree" />
    </providers>
  </roleManager>
```

Implementing Multiple Authentication Methods through Zones

Zones provide access to a Web Application through multiple URLs, each of which represents a different logical path to the same physical application. Each Web Application can have up to five Zones defined — and each Zone can have its own authentication providers defined. (If you suspect that some complexity is afoot, you're right.) In practice, each Zone is represented by an IIS Web Site; whenever you create a Web Application, what you're actually defining is the default Zone for the Web Application.

In SharePoint 2007, if you had the need to allow your content to be accessed through different authentication schemes, you had to implement multiple zones because each zone could only support one authentication provider (Windows or FBA). Not only did this result make heavier use of server resources (because you needed multiple IIS Web sites), it also meant that end users had two URLs to deal with.

Because you can host multiple authentication providers in a claims-enabled Web Application, you can now implement a single URL that different authentication schemes can use. Wait a minute — that sounds *less* complex. Sure enough, this approach removes complexity for end users and makes more efficient use of available server resources. Of course, if you also want to define different URLs to access the same content, you can: Just implement multiple Zones.

You configure a new Zone using the Extend Web Application option from the Manage Web Applications page. During this process, you can define the authentication providers to be used within that Zone. You can create up to five Zones, and each one has a pre-defined name given to it:

✦ Default

✦ Intranet

✦ Internet

✦ Extranet

✦ Custom

The name is simply used for descriptive purposes; it doesn't affect the configuration of the Zone. (Sorry, no "Twilight" Zone is available yet.)

If you want the content in your Web Application to be available in the SharePoint Search Index, the SharePoint search engine must be able to use NTLM authentication. Therefore, make sure that at least one Zone for your Web Application has NTLM enabled.

Chapter 3: Considering the Logical Architecture

In This Chapter

✔ Planning SharePoint 2010 logical architecture

✔ Understanding SharePoint 2010 topology components

✔ Working within software limits and best practices

*L*ogical architecture is a widely used term in the IT industry, though the meaning is often adapted by technology vendors to their specific product's technology-planning process. Although the definition varies slightly, *logical architecture* commonly defines how technological components of a solution are organized and integrated in a specific deployment.

Logical architecture typically defines

✦ **Software components,** which encapsulate the cohesive piece of software that executes a function on one or more hardware components via a set of services on one or more interfaces

✦ **Data components,** which define the basic data stored and manipulated by the application, and the user interfaces and Web sites used to display information to the users

✦ **Logical relationships,** which define the relationships between the software and data components, and their connection mechanisms and protocols

 Your logical architecture is like a map to your information systems deployment — it shows the geographical features (software components), population areas (data components), and the roads between them (logical relationships).

Logical architecture takes into account the business requirements of the solution without going into detail about the actual physical implementation, so it provides common ground and understanding between the business owners and the IT resources.

Logical architecture design allows you to navigate from your initial requirements gathering phase to your design and planning phase, and then carry on to the actual physical deployment.

The goal of the logical architecture is to

✦ Summarize the overall architecture

✦ Drive the physical architecture design

Logical Architecture Design for SharePoint 2010

You can choose from an almost endless variety of ways to deploy and implement SharePoint 2010 in your organization. Before you start to consider the physical server architecture and deployment plans, you need to understand

✦ What you plan to use SharePoint for

✦ How you'll implement SharePoint to meet the business requirements and the needs of the users

An easy way to approach logical architecture design is to consider it as your high-level blueprint for the overall deployment of SharePoint 2010. It should include SharePoint functionality and deployment options, which may not be part of the initial phase of the project (such as extranet connectivity or My Sites functionality) because the option to include these scenarios in the future may influence the physical architecture design. By including possible future additions early in the logical-architecture-design phase, you can avoid having to go through possibly disruptive infrastructure changes in the future.

Think of designing a logical architecture like designing a new house for your family — you probably want to consider adding extra rooms for possible future additions to the family before you build the house so that you can avoid having to deal with adding that new extension later.

We cover the major logical-architecture components in greater detail in Book II, Chapter 4, but the SharePoint 2010-specific logical-architecture components include

✦ **Server farms:** Technically, a server farm isn't a logical-architecture component, but it's included in SharePoint-specific logical-architecture components because it's the top-level container for other design elements, such as service applications. A server farm also provides physical data isolation, which can be used to meet any regulatory or policy restrictions on the type of data stored on the SharePoint environment, such as documents that contain Social Security numbers or employment records.

The most common reason for using multiple server farms is driven by network infrastructure WAN performance, which may require you to deploy servers close to the major end user hubs in order to achieve expected end user performance targets. We cover geographically distributed deployment scenarios in detail in Book II, Chapter 4.

Server farms can also be used to dedicate operational responsibility to different business IT departments, although you can now delegate administration to some extent by utilizing SharePoint 2010's multi-tenancy features.

✦ **Service applications:** SharePoint 2010 introduces a powerful model for sharing service applications, such as Search and Managed Metadata Service, moving away from the previous monolithic, single-farm-specific models of the past. The new service applications can be shared across Web Applications within the farm, and even across multiple farms within an organization, thus providing interesting new scenarios for logical architecture designs in SharePoint 2010.

All the out-of-the-box service applications can be individually configured, and third parties who develop add-ons for SharePoint 2010 can use the framework to provide flexible service offerings on the SharePoint Foundation. Each Web Application can connect the service applications that you deem appropriate for your business requirements, and you can even deploy multiple instances of the same service within a farm.

For example, you can create an enterprise-wide Managed Metadata Service, which all Web Applications hosted on the server farm must consume, while still allowing the Manufacturing Department to connect and maintain their own business-specific Managed Metadata Service, as well. You can also configure your enterprise-wide Managed Metadata Service to be shared outside of your main server farm — in case the HR department, for example, requires a separate server farm of its own for data protection.

✦ **Application pools:** Used by Internet Information Services (IIS) to provide process isolation and identity services for Web sites hosted on Microsoft Windows Server. Each application pool runs in its own worker process, using a configurable service account to prevent two processes from interacting with each other and to provide isolation in case a worker process should crash.

You can use application pools to isolate both individual and groups of SharePoint Web Applications and service applications so that they can't interact with other processes on the physical Web server. Each of the application pools can be configured with an individual service account to limit the effect of a service account getting locked out in the Microsoft Active Directory.

Although the number of application pools is typically limited only by the amount of memory on the physical server, Microsoft recommends following a general guideline of no more than eight application pools per server. Most modern deployments could handle more, but each of the application pools and service accounts used adds to the operational complexity of the SharePoint environment, so carefully consider and plan your application pools.

As a general guideline for planning application pools and service accounts, plan to separate each of the main SharePoint Web Applications into its own application pool with a unique service account. Also, consider isolating service applications that connect to sensitive external data via Business Connectivity Services, such as an HR employment database.

✦ **Web Applications:** A Web Application is essentially an IIS Web site that SharePoint 2010 has extended to include the SharePoint-specific virtual directories, configuration settings, and an ISAPI filter. The ISAPI filter directs the processing of incoming requests to the SharePoint application pages.

You can extend an existing Web site by using the SharePoint Central Administration Web Application Management page or by creating a new Web site from the Central Administration provisioning pages — which automatically creates and configures the necessary IIS settings on each of the physical front-end Web servers.

Although a Web Application is typically associated with a single IIS Web site, you can extend up to four additional IIS Web sites and map each to an existing Web Application. These extended IIS Web sites are referred to as *zones* in the SharePoint logical-architecture components.

✦ **Zones:** In terms of logical architecture design, zones are used to provide logical separation between distinct access points to a SharePoint Web Application. SharePoint 2010 defines five zones that can be used to extend IIS Web sites to provide connectivity to an existing Web Application over different network access points:

- Default

- Intranet

- Internet

- Extranet

- Custom

Each zone can be configured with its unique authentication provider and Web Application policy, thus giving you flexibility in your deployment. For example, you can give partners read-only access to your SharePoint Web Application by using Forms Authentication via SSL encryption on the extranet, while still allowing internal content publishers to have read/write access on the internal network.

✦ **Alternate access mappings (AAM):** Support zones and can be used to map multiple URL addresses to a given zone. You typically use AAM for *vanity URLs* (friendly addresses, such as `http://portal.nut2craic.com` rather than `http://server245.nut2craic.com`). You may also use alternate access mappings to provide SSL termination on a physical network device in extranet scenarios by providing a mapping for both HTTPS and HTTP protocols.

✦ **Policy for Web Applications:** Policies are included as topology elements because they provide isolation and access options that override all other site and content security settings for a given SharePoint Web Application. Policy can be assigned to specific users or Windows Active Directory user groups in a given Web Application or zone.

You can use policies to enforce security settings, such as restricting read/write access for anonymous users, even if the site-collection owners have enabled it for their site. For example, you can restrict contractors from being given read access to a Web Application that hosts confidential information or restrict all write access for Partners on an extranet portal.

Policies can also give access to IT and Operations staff for all sites and content within a SharePoint Web Application for support purposes without having to ask the site-collection administrator or farm administrator to assign permissions to the help desk when its staff is troubleshooting issues for end users.

✦ **Content databases:** Although content databases fall under server-architecture planning and storage sizing, they're typically also included in a logical architecture plan because, from a topology configuration perspective, each site collection is located within a content database connected to a SharePoint Web Application. Each Web Application may have multiple content databases attached to it in order to distribute site collections on multiple SQL databases. So, the number of content databases is largely driven by the number and size of planned site collections because Microsoft's best practices recommend storing no more than 200GB within a single content database.

The site collection itself can't span multiple content databases, but by distributing multiple site collections across available content databases, you can achieve some balance on the amount of content stored, thus allowing you to plan for larger topologies. We talk about the sizing aspect of content database planning in Book II, Chapter 4.

✦ **Site collections:** A site collection represents a top-level site, which can in turn contain multiple subsites. Site collections are separated in topology design from regular sites because each site within a site collection inherits security settings from the top-level site itself, thus creating a logical security boundary. A site collection may be assigned to a specific content database and can be backed up and restored directly from the SharePoint Central Administration and Management Shell by a farm administrator.

All subsites within a site collection share the same site collection administrators and may inherit site security settings from its parent. Other site collection artifacts include SharePoint features and template files, such as master pages and page layouts.

Site collection design is particularly important for team and group collaboration deployments because quota templates can be assigned only at a site-collection level. Therefore, if you want to plan your storage growth and reinforce good working practices, each team and group-collaboration site must be created as a site collection.

On the other hand, enterprise-portal and Web content-management deployments often use a single site collection that has multiple subsites in order to use the built-in SharePoint navigational features, such as the navigation bar and breadcrumbs. For these types of single-site repositories, such as a Records Center and Enterprise Documents Center, Microsoft has extended its best-practices limit for a content database up to 1TB from the previous 100GB limit.

✦ **Sites:** Everything in SharePoint resides within the context of a site, so a site is the lowest-level design element within a topology. Lists, libraries, and the actual items and documents they store are all hosted within a site. Although a site resides under a site collection, and therefore inherits the site collection specific settings and artifacts, each site can still be configured with unique permissions and features.

✦ **My Sites:** Typically defined as a unique lowest-level design element within a topology (even though there are technically sites underneath) because each user account usually has only one My Site.

These personalized sites are the core element in SharePoint 2010's extensive social functionality, and they integrate directly with search and user-profile functions within a farm. Users can also edit their profiles and manage their tags, comments, and links from their My Sites, in addition to being able to store both shared and personal content on the site.

Although SharePoint logical design includes numerous design elements, the topology is typically fairly straightforward, as illustrated in Figure 3-1. The sample topology is very typical for a small to medium-size organization of up to 20,000 users, which has a single SharePoint farm deployment that hosts three Web Applications for enterprise-portal, My Sites, and team-collaboration purposes.

All the service applications provided in the sample topology run under a single application pool and belong to the default group that's hosting all the services to the Web Applications. Access is provided through a default zone for intranet users that uses NTLM or Kerberos authentication because many organizations have deployed a wider VPN-based access mechanism for off-site employees to connect to the internal network.

The enterprise portal hosts the divisional content within sites by using a single site collection in order to present common look and feel, and navigation. Team sites are provided as site collections in order to both enforce quotas and provide the site owners with a degree of autonomy to organize their content in sites and workspaces. The My Site Web Application provides knowledge workers with both a personalized workspace and social features.

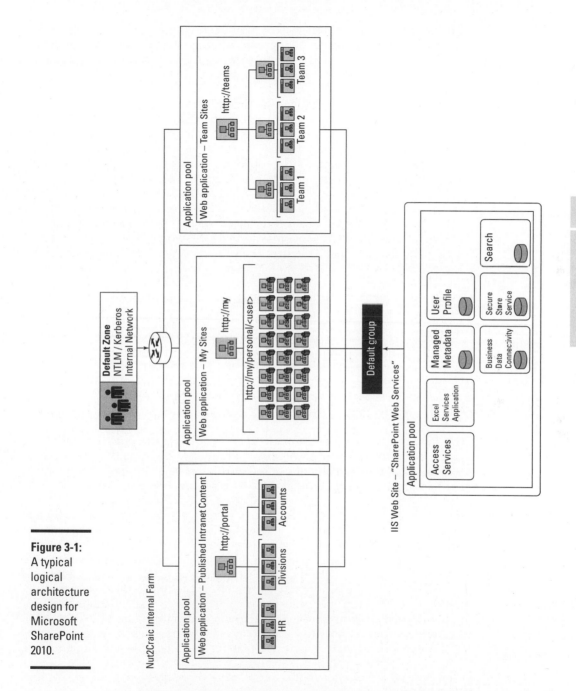

Figure 3-1:
A typical
logical
architecture
design for
Microsoft
SharePoint
2010.

Although the sample topology in Figure 3-1 covers the needs of a typical organization, SharePoint 2010 is increasingly moving up the corporate-application
food chain and increasing in importance and value. So, you need to carefully

consider possible future expansions and needs within your organization when you design your deployment. For example, in Figure 3-1, it isn't clear where you would host line-of-business (LOB) applications that have been developed by using the powerful new SharePoint InfoPath functionality.

Even if you aren't planning to use all the provided functionality in the product set initially, it does make sense to plan ahead and have a clear strategy for functionality if the business requirements arise to warrant it. For example, even if you aren't planning to move your corporate portal to a SharePoint-based solution during the initial phase of your deployment, it still makes sense to design your topology to include possible future additions.

Similarly, even if LOB applications that use Business Data Connectivity (BDC) Services and sandboxed code aren't on your organization's radar just yet, the business sponsors may ask whether you can develop a new or updated solution by using the new SharePoint 2010 application framework. Consider whether these LOB applications should

✦ Reside under the Portal Web Application as separate site collections (thus sharing the IIS application pool with the main portal site).

✦ Use a new Web Application that has a different BDC Service application running under its own Web Application pool in order to provide process isolation in case a custom component misbehaves.

Planning for Application Limits and Best Practices

Although most of the limits and best practices apply directly to the hardware sizing, which we cover in Book II, Chapter 4, you should be aware of the limits and recommendations related to the logical-architecture components in order to design around them or note down exceptions.

Because some of the recommendations are guidelines, rather than absolute hard limits, you can choose to accept the risk and exceed the proposed threshold. For example, Microsoft's best practice for content databases is 200GB when multiple site collections are used and 1TB for a single large site collection within a content database (for example, for Documents Center functionality). These best practices stem from the time it takes to back up and restore a content database, so you can choose to exceed it because no technical limitations prevent you from storing more than 1TB within a content database. However, if you do exceed the best-practice storage limit, note the increased restore time and plan for the exception accordingly.

Microsoft gives guidance in three categories for SharePoint 2010 best practices and application limits:

✦ **Boundaries:** Actual hardcoded limits that Microsoft has imposed on the product or depending service that you can't overwrite or exceed. These limits are "by design" in the released product, though Microsoft has increased certain boundaries in subsequent Service Pack (SP) release for previous versions of SharePoint.

The most-used example of a boundary is the document size limit, which in SharePoint 2010 has been set to 2GB. In SharePoint 2003, the initial boundary was increased by the SP1 release. However, the current boundary is set to mirror Microsoft SQL Server limits, so this time the boundary is unlikely to change.

✦ **Thresholds:** Configurable options that are initially set to Microsoft's best-practice limits. The farm administrator can overwrite these limits. For example, the out-of-the-box document-upload size defaults to 50MB, although the boundary is actually 2GB.

To increase the limit, a farm administrator must configure the document-size limit in the Web Application general settings, keeping in mind organization-specific bandwidth issues and user behavior.

✦ **Supported limits:** Microsoft best practices against which the product team has tested the SharePoint 2010 application. Exceeding them on currently available hardware and software architecture may decrease performance of certain aspects of the application and could therefore affect the overall performance profile of the environment.

If you plan to exceed any of the supported limits, conduct thorough performance testing on your environment to ensure that exceeding the limits doesn't cause bottlenecks in operation of the SharePoint farm.

A good example of supported limits is the number of users in a SharePoint group, which Microsoft defines as 5,000 users per SharePoint group. Although you can technically exceed this limit without the system generating error messages, Microsoft's testing has shown decreased performance past the supported limit.

Microsoft determines the limits by first defining baseline performance characteristics in a lab environment, using an automated performance testing application to generate simulated user load on the SharePoint farm. This baseline is then used as a reference point to evaluate individual-feature impact on the system by systematically throttling up the feature usage until noticeable performance degradation is recorded.

For example, to come up with the earlier example limit of 5,000 users in a given SharePoint group, the system test engineers may have started off with the system under stress, running at baseline-performance levels, and then programmatically added users to the SharePoint group through the administrative user interface until the response time of the administrative page started to slow down or the baseline system performance started to degrade.

Although the slowdown in response time under stress probably started to be noticeable somewhere around 2,000 users, the software vendors define acceptable response times based on how real-world users are likely to behave. For example, an end user might consider an extra 5-second wait for a page to load acceptable, but if that wait time increases to longer than 20 seconds, the end user might think there's something wrong and navigate away from the page before the operation actually completes.

No performance test in lab conditions is ever 100-percent representative of the real world, especially because every deployment is always slightly different in the hardware used, as well as the deployment topology and software configuration selected. Therefore, Microsoft (just like most software vendors) uses a generalized usage case that features a typical software and hardware configuration in order to provide general guidance for customers.

If you have a business requirement that means you have to exceed any of the limits marked as Supported, you can do so as long as you're prepared to run your own performance tests to ensure acceptable system performance and stability on your specific hardware and software topology.

Microsoft maintains an up-to-date list of software boundaries and limits on the TechNet Web site. Service packs and cumulative updates may address or increase specific feature limits or provide guidance on the subject. If you plan to go anywhere near the stated limits, check the latest published guidance about the feature to see whether Microsoft has released updates and corrections.

Web Application and site limits

Table 3-1 lists the important best practices and software limits related to SharePoint Web Applications, site collections, and sites.

Although most of the listed limits are far beyond the reach of normal deployments, even the smaller deployments of SharePoint 2010 are likely to reach the content-database size limit because of today's increasingly graphical content in Microsoft Office files. Therefore, plan on including multiple content databases from the start for all Web Applications that host multiple site collections. The exact number of content databases depends on the expected size and number of site collections within your organization. We cover the topic in greater detail in Book II, Chapter 4.

For larger deployments, you should note down the application pool-related best practice because you can easily create a new application pool for each

Web Application and separate service applications to run under their own application pool, which provides process isolation for custom code and sensitive data.

From a content-author perspective, the most notable limit in Table 3-1 may be the best practice to include no more than 25 Web Parts on a given page. Although 25 Web Parts may seem like a lot, it's easy to include numerous Web Parts on a corporate portal Web page unless you consciously group dynamic information.

Table 3-1	Web Application and Site-Related Software Limits and Best Practices		
Topology Object	*Limit Value*	*Limit Type*	*Notes*
Content database	300 per Web Application	Supported	To use Microsoft's best-practice recommendation of 200GB per content database, larger deployments must distribute site collections over multiple content databases.
			A supported limit of 300 content databases per Web Application therefore provides you with 60TB of potential storage space for a Web Application if you want to remain within the support boundaries.
			Microsoft states that administrative operations performed via Central Administration on site collections will degrade if you exceed the supported limit; however, as an alternative administrative option, you can use PowerShell to manage the Web Application.

(continued)

Table 3-1 *(continued)*

Topology Object	Limit Value	Limit Type	Notes
Content database size	200GB per content database	Supported	Microsoft best practice recommends keeping content database sizes below 200GB when multiple site collections, such as team collaboration sites, are hosted on the Web Application.
			The supported database size is increased up to 1TB for single site-collection applications, such as the Enterprise Document Center and Records Center, that often store large amounts of documents.
			This limit is mainly in place for system-backup and restore reasons, and exceeding the stated limit affects only the length of time it takes to back up and restore a given content database. So, many organizations run multi-terabyte content databases that have advanced hardware-based disaster recovery plans in place to reduce the impact of database backup and restore functions.
Site-collection size	100GB per site collection	Supported	Microsoft recommends that site collections remain smaller than 100GB, unless it's the only site collection within the Web Application, such as a Records Center or Documents Center; in this case, a 1TB supported limit applies.
			Exceeding the stated limit can impact backup and restore functions performed from the Central Administration, so if you plan to exceed the supported limit, you need to use alternative disaster recovery methods.

Topology Object	Limit Value	Limit Type	Notes
Zone	5 per Web Application	Boundary	Zone names have been hardcoded to Default, Intranet, Extranet, Internet, and Custom, and they can't be extended or renamed.
Application pool	10 per server	Supported	The Microsoft recommendation for application pools per server is largely driven by the typical amount of RAM installed on front-end Web servers. Each application pool consumes 30-50MB of memory before any SharePoint-specific components are even loaded into memory. A typical application pool uses at least 800MB when it has SharePoint applications loaded and cached under system stress, and its memory use can reach up to 10GB if the resources are available on the system. We cover memory usage and server sizing in more detail in Book II, Chapter 4.
Site	250,000 per site collection	Supported	Microsoft has significantly increased the recommended limits for sites in SharePoint 2010 when compared to previous versions of the product, and SharePoint now supports up to 250,000 sites within a single site collection, as long as those sites are held in nested structures that have no more than 2,000 sites per level. The number of nested site structures is limited only by some browsers' URL addressable space of 256 characters. Typically, this character limit translates to about ten levels deep, unless efforts are taken to reduce the URL address for each site.

Book II
Chapter 3

Considering the Logical Architecture

(continued)

Table 3-1 *(continued)*

Topology Object	Limit Value	Limit Type	Notes
Subsite	2,000 per site view	Threshold	By default, the site view displays only up to 2,000 sites within a site because exceeding the threshold impacts the performance of the All Site Content page and the Tree View Control. So, sites should be nested within logical structures, with each nested site hosting less than 2,000 sites.
User profiles	2 million	Supported	Because each user profile in SharePoint 2010 comes with social features, such as tagging, notes, and comments, Microsoft has set an acceptable performance limit on user profiles to support full usage of the social capabilities of SharePoint 2010.
			The social database supports up to 500 million social items, along with the 2 million profiles limit (which is largely driven by backup and restore time). You can reduce the time impact of exceeding the stated limit by using alternative database disaster recovery options.
			If you plan to synchronize user profiles from Active Directory, Microsoft supports up to 2 million synchronized identities without significant performance degradation. If you're using custom profile import components, performance test them to ensure they can support the expected number of profiles and frequency of synchronization.

Topology Object	Limit Value	Limit Type	Notes
Web Parts	25 per page	Threshold	The number of Web Parts on a given page is largely driven by the type and complexity of the Web Parts used. Custom Web Parts should be adequately performance tested on a case-by-case basis as part of your overall change management process so that you can ensure they don't affect overall system performance.
Business Connectivity Services (BCS) connections	500 per Web server	Boundary	BCS is, by default, configured to limit the number of active external system connections to 200, with the option to increase the limit up to 500 open/active connections on a given server. You can configure different BCS applications to run on dedicated servers in the SharePoint farm.

List and item limits

Microsoft invested considerable effort in improving the underlying SQL queries and data libraries in SharePoint 2010 in order to improve list- and item-related limits to meet the needs of the enterprise electronic content management (ECM) and records management deployments.

The most impressive improvement in SharePoint 2010 list- and item-related limits (which you can find in Table 3-2) may be the number of list items, now broadly defined simply at "tens of millions of items per list" by Microsoft. This new limit is a more-than-tenfold improvement over the previous version of the SharePoint platform, thanks to the improved SQL queries and database-related indexing tuning included in SharePoint 2010. The old limit was largely imposed by the list-view functions, which have now been separated from the underlying data-storage functions by throttling the queries and limiting the number of items that list views are allowed to return to the end users.

From an end-user perspective, the new items in the limits list worth noting are the Items in a List View entry and Items in a List View for Auditors and Administrators entry. These new thresholds have been set fairly low, by default, when you take into account the number of items the underlying list is actually able to store. But from an end-user's perspective, it's fairly difficult to find the right information in a flat list that displays over 1,000 items. Users are very likely to search or use the new filtering functionality provided by the SharePoint 2010 lists framework to pare down the data within a list. Of course, there may be exceptions to this rule, so the new list-view limits support fairly comprehensive options to exceed the thresholds on specific lists or at configurable daily time windows. For example, you can allow users to have unrestricted list views between 6pm and 6am daily. In addition, auditors and administrators are, by default, allowed to return 20,000 items, which can also be increased by the system administrator.

Document libraries now support a respectable 50 million items per library, which allows even large enterprises to consider a single records or documents center in SharePoint 2010. In the past, Microsoft recommended that you split content on departmental sites to work around some of the limitations, but with the new metadata and taxonomy features that help users navigate to the relevant data, there are no technical or user-interface restrictions to force the separation of data. However, the old file-size limit of 2GB still applies because of underlying SQL Server limitations.

Table 3-2		**List- and Item-Related Software Limits and Best Practices**	
Topology Object	*Limit Value*	*Limit Type*	*Notes*
Items	Tens of millions per list	Supported	SharePoint 2010 significantly increases the limit of list items stored within a list because of new list-view filtering options that have significantly optimized the underlying SQL queries used to return items from the content database.
			Microsoft's recommendation is intentionally vague because the number of columns, the security options, and even the type of columns used on the list all affect the specific performance characteristics. Most out-of-the-box list types perform well up to 50 million list items, but custom lists that include lookup columns that extend beyond 10 million items should be performance tested to ensure system stability and performance.

Topology Object	Limit Value	Limit Type	Notes
Documents	50 million	Supported	Because documents are simply list items underneath the hood, the performance benefits from significantly improved list views are automatically inherited by document libraries.
			However, if you plan to use a number of custom columns and lookup columns as part of your document library metadata definition, with the expected number of documents exceeding 10 million items, you should test to ensure system stability and performance.
Items in a list view	5,000	Threshold	To provide large list support, the SQL queries that construct list views for end users have been tuned to limit the returned items to 5,000 items by default. Given SharePoint 2010's new ad-hoc filtering and metadata-based list-item navigation functionality, the threshold is unlikely to matter to most end users.
			However, if you plan to store more than 5,000 items that all need to be returned to end users in a single flat list, you need to request that the farm administrator set up an exception for your site collection or increase the default limit.
			Administrators can also define that unrestricted views be allowed during daily time windows — for example, for batch processing or reporting purposes.

(continued)

**Book II
Chapter 3**

**Considering the
Logical Architecture**

Table 3-2 *(continued)*

Topology Object	Limit Value	Limit Type	Notes
Items in a list view for auditors and administrators	20,000	Threshold	Administrators and auditors are, by default, allowed to view up to 20,000 list items in a flat view. You can increase this limit for a given list if you have a business requirement that needs to return more than 20,000 list items in a flat view without applying filtering or paging.
File size	2GB	Boundary	By default, the maximum file size limit for Web Applications is 50MB. However, farm administrators can increase the limit in the Web Application general settings to up to 2GB. If you plan to allow large files to be uploaded to your SharePoint environment, you may need to increase IIS timeout settings to meet your expected WAN and LAN performance levels.
Business Connectivity Services (BCS) items	2,000 per database connector	Threshold	By default, BCS database connectors have been configured to return no more than 2,000 items from the external database. However, each application can increase the limit to up to 1 million records via execution context.

Security limits

Although it's hard to find deployments in which the security limits have become an issue, it's still worth taking note of the major limits listed in Table 3-3. Most limits stated in Table 3-3 apply only in scenarios in which users are assigned directly to a SharePoint site or group in order to grant them permissions to access the container.

In most deployments, in which Windows Active Directory is used to authenticate users, you should consider using Active Directory security groups, rather than SharePoint groups, because Active Directory was designed and built to manage user and group permissions. If your organization has invested in an automated Active Directory management product, such as Microsoft Forefront Identity Lifecycle Manager (ILM), your IT department may already have existing Active Directory groups that your SharePoint environment can leverage to grant permissions — for example, for a specific business unit, such as HR or Accounts. The true benefit of using Active Directory security groups is in the automation of the group membership management through products such as ILM.

On the flipside, if your organization doesn't maintain automatically generated Active Directory security groups, SharePoint 2010 group functionality provides an easy Web-based user interface and self-management functionality perfect for small to medium-size organizations. If you plan to use SharePoint groups, take note of the number of groups to which a user can belong, which is driven largely by the size of the access control list (ACL) and the number of SharePoint groups within a single site collection.

Table 3-3		Security-Related Software Limits and Best Practices	
Topology Object	*Limit Value*	*Limit Type*	*Notes*
Users per site collection	2 million	Supported	Although you can add millions of users individually to a given site collection, it quickly becomes unmanageable to do so without using Windows Active Directory security groups.
			Alternatively, consider using PowerShell-based scripts to manage access for a large number of users within a site collection because the Web-based user interface was designed with only thousands of users in mind.
SharePoint groups to which users can belong	5,000	Supported	Because SharePoint 2010 uses access control lists (ACLs) to grant permissions for objects, the number of groups a user belongs to increases the user token size and can affect caching and security-check performance.

(continued)

Table 3-3 (continued)

Topology Object	Limit Value	Limit Type	Notes
Active Directory users and groups in a SharePoint group	5,000	Supported	SharePoint groups allow both Active Directory user objects and group objects to be added to the group membership. Because SharePoint needs to validate permissions when a user is requesting access to a secured object, such as a site or document library, Microsoft has defined the acceptable performance to peak at 5,000 users or groups per SharePoint group.
			If you plan on exceeding the stated limit, performance test both access to secured objects and group membership management to ensure acceptable performance and system stability.
SharePoint groups	10,000 per site collection	Supported	The limit for the number of SharePoint groups per site collection is driven by the user interface and browser performance, rather than any database- or access control list (ACL)-related performance impact.
			If you need to create more than 10,000 SharePoint groups for a given site collection, you can do so by using PowerShell-based management scripts.

SharePoint Search topology limits

SharePoint 2010 Search provides vast improvements in both scale and accuracy of results, as well as possibly — and most importantly — user interface enhancements to perform queries and filter search results.

Although the underlying query engine in SharePoint has always supported complex queries by using the typical AND/OR operations common to popular search engines such as Bing and Google, in the past SharePoint was always somewhat betrayed by the lack of out-of-the-box user interface to perform these queries.

The SharePoint 2010 user interface that allows end users to perform queries leaps forward with vast improvements compared to previous SharePoint releases. These improvements are matched on the backend to scale both the query and the indexing engines to meet the needs of enterprise and internet-deployment scale. Of course, with the new scale and features provided by the Search Service application come design decisions about how best to apply this new technology in your organization. We cover the SharePoint 2010 Search Service application features in more detail in Book III, Chapter 6.

Table 3-4 lists some of the major limitations and best practices related to the SharePoint 2010 Search Service application.

There are now two main engines included in the SharePoint 2010 Enterprise framework:

✦ SharePoint Search Service application

This chapter focuses on the SharePoint 2010 search engine that most deployments likely adopt at the start of their deployment cycle.

✦ FAST for SharePoint service application

We cover FAST in more detail in Book III, Chapter 6.

With up to 100 million indexed items per service application, SharePoint 2010 Search should meet the scale of large enterprises because a single farm supports up to 20 service applications. In SharePoint 2010, if you deploy search query components to multiple servers within the farm, each of the query servers holds only part of the actual search index, which is referred to as an *index partition*. Each index partition can handle up to 10 million items within the acceptable sub-millisecond query-return throughput.

We go into detail on search-topology design and administration in Book III, Chapter 6.

Book II
Chapter 3

Considering the
Logical Architecture

Table 3-4 **SharePoint Search-Related Software Limits and Best Practices**

Topology Object	Limit Value	Limit Type	Notes
SharePoint Search applications	20	Supported	Although Microsoft recommends only up to 20 Search Service applications to be hosted per farm, the search supports cross-farm service application connectivity, which allows dedicated resource farms to provide extra capacity, if required. SharePoint 2010 allows Search Service applications to be assigned to specific servers within the farm and use multiple database servers in order to scale to large hosting service-provider requirements. However, typical enterprise deployments are unlikely to reach anywhere near the stated limit because of vastly improved indexed-items limits per Search Service application.
Index partition	20 per Search application	Threshold	SharePoint 2010 Search allows the search index to be partitioned to up to 128 components. Each partition is hosted on a SharePoint query server, therefore reducing the disk and memory footprint in a multiple query server deployment scenario because each of the query servers hosts only part of the full search index at any given time.

Topology Object	Limit Value	Limit Type	Notes
Indexed items	100 million per application; 10 million per index partition	Supported	SharePoint 2010 supports index partitions that contain part of the search corpus, with each partition containing up to 10 million items.
			Search partitions allow the total index corpus to reach an impressive 100 million items per Search Service application.
			Because a server farm supports up to 20 Search Service applications, the theoretical limit of indexed items on a SharePoint farm increases up to 2 trillion items.
Content sources	50 per Search application	Threshold	The boundary for content sources is 500, but the limit is set to 50 by default in order to keep within the concurrent crawls threshold.
			If you plan to increase the limit for content sources, carefully plan the crawl schedule for each content source so that you keep within the crawl-related limits.
Concurrent crawls	20 per Search application	Threshold	Although the limit for crawls in progress at any given time can be increased, Microsoft testing has shown that performance degradation occurs beyond 20 concurrent crawls.
			If you have multiple content sources that require a high frequency of crawls, you need to carefully observe how long those crawls take to complete and set schedules accordingly to avoid a negative impact on overall system performance.

(continued)

Table 3-4 *(continued)*

Topology Object	Limit Value	Limit Type	Notes
Start addresses	100 per content source	Threshold	The absolute boundary for start addresses is 500, but plan to keep well below the limit by bundling up Web sites to a simple HTML page that contains a link to each of the desired crawl locations. This method of bundling crawl locations eases administration and allows you to delegate administration of the crawl locations to the actual content owners without the need to grant them access to the SharePoint Search administration interface.
Scopes	200 per site	Threshold	Although you can configure up to 200 search scopes, the end users are unlikely to use the exceedingly complex drop-down list for selecting a scope.
Display groups	25 per site	Threshold	Display groups allow you to group search scopes together — for example, by business function or technology. The threshold is set at 25 by default. Try to avoid exceedingly complex search-scope groupings because end users probably don't use groups unless those groups are easy to use.
Keywords	200 per site collection	Supported	The boundary for keywords is set to 5,000, but Microsoft has observed performance degradation on the administrative Web-user interface when managing over 200 keywords.

Topology Object	Limit Value	Limit Type	Notes
Alerts	1 million per Search application	Supported	Although Microsoft has tested up to 1 million alerts based on search results, alerts currently don't have a boundary or an observed performance impact if you exceed the stated limit. If you plan to exceed the stated alert limit significantly, first conduct case-specific performance tests to ensure acceptable system performance and stability.

Chapter 4: Designing the Logical Architecture

In This Chapter

✔ **Planning SharePoint 2010 site and services topology**

✔ **Using multiple SharePoint server farms**

✔ **Choosing service applications and Web Applications**

✔ **Designing site collections**

*A*lthough you might be tempted to fast-forward the planning stages to the actual SharePoint deployment, with a plan to start small and grow with the requirements, you have some good reasons to dare to think big from the beginning — especially when deploying SharePoint 2010.

The best reason of all can be summarized in a single word — change. Change is inevitable in business, but most system administrators who have dealt with storing data can undoubtedly tell you that change is always painful and, more importantly, usually costly. Not necessarily in actual currency, but most definitely in effort and time.

SharePoint has matured in how it manages organizational change without significant disruption to end users or reclassification of data, but you still need to carefully consider the site topology to avoid having to move data across site collections or Web Applications. These moves can lead to issues with features such as hyperlinks, bookmarks, and embedded document links, as well as certain metadata fields such as Create At and Created By. For example, Unique Document IDs allow users to open documents by clicking a hyperlink that contains the ID number. That ID number stays the same, even if the underlying file is moved to a new folder on another site — as long as that new folder resides within the same site collection. The Site Content and Navigation feature even allows you to move complete sites and lists freely within a site collection, although the URL of the moved object is updated during the move.

You can find third-party products and solutions that move content between site collections, and even server farms, while retaining the Created At and Created By information. These solutions can even fix embedded links within Office documents. But the best solution of all is to plan ahead in order to minimize the need for change. Even if you're planning to start with team collaboration for a small number of users for specific business groups or purposes, by thinking about the possible future extensions, you can design and prepare your environment to grow with your requirements.

In this chapter, we focus on planning the site topology and service-applications architecture, keeping in mind software and best-practices limits (which we cover in Book II, Chapter 3).

The key message of this chapter is simple: Dare to think big.

Getting Started with SharePoint Site and Services Topology Planning

Although a more complex SharePoint 2010 deployment can include many topology components (as we discuss in Book II, Chapter 3), SharePoint topology planning boils down to four main sections:

✦ **Server farms:** The top-level containers for all other design elements and functionality. Each physical SharePoint server infrastructure can have only one server farm, although multiple SQL Servers can share back-end SQL Servers.

✦ **Service applications:** The new, flexible model for sharing services, such as Search and Managed Metadata, across multiple Web Applications hosted on the server farm, and even across server farms.

✦ **Web Applications:** The top-level containers for the actual content held within SharePoint and the connection to service applications. These containers are usually accessed through a single URL (for example, `http://intranet`), but they can be extended across multiple IIS Web Applications or IIS bindings to provide URLs with access to the same content.

✦ **Site collections:** Site containers, which can contain multiple levels of nested sites, each with any number of actual lists and document libraries holding content. Site collections are an important design element for both end users and system administrators because SharePoint system settings such as quotas are applied at this level.

Every SharePoint 2010 installation, complex or simple, has at least one server farm on a single server or a load-balanced high-availability infrastructure. On the server farm, in order to provide services for users (for example, SharePoint Search functionality), you need to provision at least one service application that's consumed by at least one Web Application, which must have at least one site collection in order to store data in lists or libraries. This simple view of the basics of topology components appears in Figure 4-1.

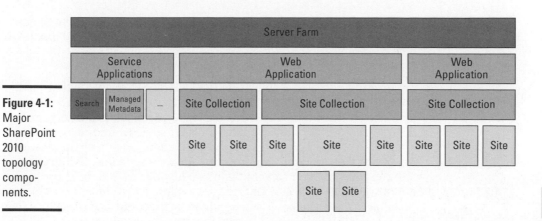

Figure 4-1:
Major
SharePoint
2010
topology
compo-
nents.

The topology concept starts to get a little more complex when you move beyond the single Web Application and single site collection model, following that "dare to think big" motto. Even if you plan to provide team-collaboration functionality for a specific user group, you may want to prepare for the requests you'll probably receive for similar spaces from other business groups or new projects.

"What if?" and "What about?" are good questions to constantly keep at the back of your mind when you go through your own or your customer's business and end-user requirements.

You need to gather requirements upfront if you want to successfully implement SharePoint without getting bogged down with the myriad of software and system features the platform provides. You can often best preface the software feature design decisions with a simple demonstration of the capabilities and features of the platform so that you can get the stakeholders thinking about the possibilities with just the standard functionality and potential future states. For example, by simply importing the enterprise directory with a few key members' organizational information (including expertise and pictures) into user profiles, demonstrating the new contact card that comes with the People Search functionality, you can probably prompt the stakeholders to consider providing My Sites for all users within the organization.

Although you can provide My Sites on the same Web Application as team collaboration spaces, consider separating these fundamentally different SharePoint uses to their own individual Web Applications for both visual and technical reasons:

✦ **Visual:** Users access each Web Application by using a URL, which you can give a meaningful DNS alias, often referred to as a *vanity URL,* so that users can remember it and associate it with the provided service. For example, `http://teams` for Team Sites and `http://my` for My Sites describe what content and functionality you'll likely find on a Web page.

Consider raising awareness and making the end users feel like they're part of the process by holding a competition to come up with the best vanity URL for each provided service, such as the enterprise portal, team collaboration site, or My Site functionality.

✦ **Technical:** Each Web Application is a separate IIS Web site that resides within an application pool that provides process and resource usage isolation on the physical server. So, most system administrators probably want to ensure that the enterprise portal has dedicated resources and an IIS worker process that won't be affected by other web applications hosted on the farm (for example, the self-service team-collaboration site). In addition, you can configure each application pool to run under an individual service account, thus providing isolation and resilience to possible account-lockout issues, which might occur occasionally in even the most carefully planned Active Directory environments.

Each application pool uses at least 300MB of system memory, so Microsoft recommends limiting the number of application pools to no more than eight per server. When you plan Web Applications and associated application pools, plan to share application pools between multiple Web Applications in large topologies.

Figure 4-2 shows a straightforward logical architecture for SharePoint 2010, which is a safe bet for both small and large implementations. In this typical topology, the intranet portal, My Sites, and self-service team-collaboration services are host by separate Web Applications, with each Web Application consuming the same set of default service applications, which are all hosted on a single server farm.

Daring to think big doesn't mean you have to over-engineer the solution.

Preparing SharePoint Server Farms

Why would you ever need more than a single farm? That question is probably the foremost thought on most architects minds when planning SharePoint topologies because of the IT industry's drive for consolidation and more efficient use of hardware. We cover the performance characteristics of SharePoint 2010 in Book II, Chapter 5, but from a performance point of view, SharePoint 2010 can't really justify multiple farms for anything aside from meeting high-availability requirements that use cross-site failover features which we will deep dive into later in Book II, Chapter 5.

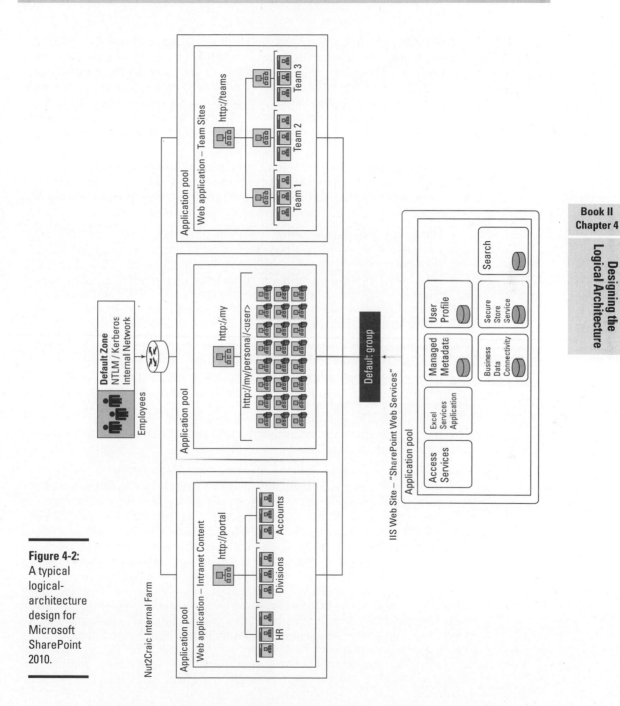

Figure 4-2:
A typical
logical-
architecture
design for
Microsoft
SharePoint
2010.

Therefore, non-performance-related requirements largely drive the need for multiple SharePoint farms:

✦ **Quality assurance, test, and development environments:** Consider deploying multiple farms, if for no other reason than because industry best practice governance policies dictate separate development and quality-assurance environments. In managed environments, before any customizations or line-of-business applications can be deployed to production, they must be thoroughly tested and verified by the business users to meet the required functionality and features.

In addition to managing and testing custom developments, you need to prepare for service-pack and hotfix deployments by testing the process on a test environment that's as close to your production environment as possible so that you can identify and address any possible issues or complications ahead of deploying updates to production.

✦ **Divisional IT departments:** Multiple SharePoint environments traditionally require neither a technical nor particularly logical design driver — for political or operational reasons, the environment needs to be maintained by separate operating divisions within an organization. In an organization where the operating business unit directly provides the funding for an internal IT department, you may not be able to find the resources and commitment to centralize SharePoint to a single farm.

✦ **Geographically dispersed organizations:** Many organizations deploy multiple SharePoint environments to address their global needs because they operate in multiple locations around the continent or the world. Although the world has become smaller (at least, in IT terms) with the proliferation of high-speed Internet links that can create inexpensive virtual private networks for internal data traffic, places around the world have bandwidth (and especially latency) at a cost far exceeding that of a locally deployed and managed application infrastructure.

✦ **Industry- or country-specific requirements for isolation:** In certain industry sectors and countries, the governing body regulations dictate a level of physical isolation for types of information that can be stored and managed on SharePoint deployments. Although SharePoint 2010's features related to process isolation and multi-tenancy reduce the need to deploy multiple farms, if the regulation dictates stringent data or process isolation for information stored on your SharePoint environment, then you can address this by deploying multiple server farms.

SharePoint 2010's new features for improving centralization — including the new service application model, process isolation, multi-tenancy, sandboxed code services, and reduced network bandwidth usage — significantly reduces the arguments for multiple-server farms, but carefully consider your server farm requirements because splitting a single farm later to multiple instances involves time consuming migration effort.

Planning for change management

Change management refers to the systematic way of dealing with changes to controlled IT infrastructure so that you can ensure standard methods and processes are followed, hopefully reducing the number and impact of issues that arise after you implement the changes. For example, SharePoint offers a number of ways to deploy a Web Part to a server, including manually installing the .NET binary to the Global Assembly Cache and adding the relevant lines to the `web.config` file, or packaging the Web Part as a *SharePoint Feature file* (a compressed CAB file with an XML manifest file that SharePoint understands). By standardizing a deployment method, you can limit the number of issues that occur when you install hotfixes, updates, and new versions to custom Web Parts on your infrastructure.

You must address the impact of your server farm topology on your change-management policies and how you approach your farm topology planning. After all, without a quality-assurance farm, you can't easily implement a change-management policy that includes a staged deployment process for system updates and changes, such as service packs and hotfixes (illustrated in Figure 4-3).

**Book II
Chapter 4**

Designing the
Logical Architecture

Figure 4-3:
A typical change-management process for enterprise applications.

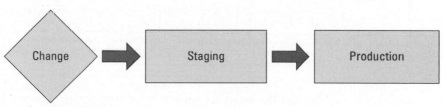

Although you can accommodate the staged deployment process for system patches, application patches, and updates by using two server farms, if you plan to customize your SharePoint environment now or develop custom applications in the future, consider expanding on the change-management process to include a full development lifecycle plan.

Figure 4-4 shows an example of a development lifecycle plan in which the Administrator must follow these steps for all customer applications and Web Parts:

1. **Gather requirements.**

Before you can design and develop the customization, you have to undertake a requirements-gathering process to discover and document the exact business requirements. You may find this documentation worth its weight in gold years later, when you have to upgrade the application to support a new version of the platform (especially if the original business sponsor has moved on). Without documented requirements, you may also find it difficult to perform functional testing to ensure the developed customization actually meets all the original goals. This stage doesn't need a separate SharePoint farm in the topology design.

2. **Design and develop the application.**

Large customizations and applications should include a design document, especially if the application connects to external data sources. Without a design document, operational staff can't easily troubleshoot issues without involving the original developer in the process. Ongoing support can become extremely painful and time-consuming, especially if the original application developer was a third-party provider or has moved on from your organization because you have to decompile the application code, line by line, to first understand what the application should be doing so that you can figure out what's at fault. Complete this stage on either developer workstations or on a dedicated development farm in the topology design.

3. **Perform functional testing.**

All customizations should go through a functional test period to make sure they fulfill the business requirements and goals stated at the onset of the process. This stage typically involves actual end users accessing the application so that you can ensure the functionality is user friendly and meets the needs of the actual end users. Although this stage is traditionally done on a dedicated User Acceptance Test (UAT) farm, you can also do it on the Quality Assurance farm, as long as you don't run systems tests for performance or reliability at the same time.

4. **Perform system testing.**

All custom code and applications should go through systems testing to ensure that they don't have any reliability or performance issues when you place the applications under simulated load. Run this stage on a Quality Assurance farm in the topology design, which mirrors production as closely as possible, so that you can ensure the tests reflect how the application is likely to behave when you put it into production.

5. **Deploy application to production.**

The last stage of the cycle involves deploying the application to the production environment. Perform this deployment during scheduled maintenance windows that the business owners have agreed to use in order to avoid disrupting production system operation.

Figure 4-4:
The typical lifecycle of customizations and custom applications.

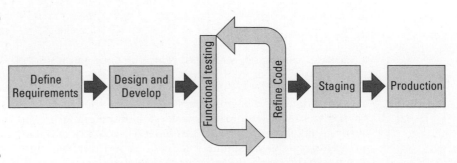

Although you might argue against the need for rigorous change management for your line-of-business applications — thanks to new SharePoint 2010 sandboxed-code functionality and the ability to create no-code line-of-business applications by using power-user tools such as SharePoint Designer and InfoPath 2010 — you can still also make a case for deploying a separate development farm on which you can develop and test these applications. And a separate farm for development gives you the ability to verify the impact that your service pack upgrades may have on your custom applications, even those applications that have been created without using custom .NET code. If nothing else, it forces developers to think about their applications holistically and discourages changes on your production environment after users are actively using your line-of-business application.

No-code customizations and line-of-business applications are a gray area of SharePoint change management, and you may need to handle them on a case-by-case basis, instead of trying to force them to your SharePoint environments change-management policies and procedures which have traditionally been geared towards more extensive custom developments. But if you plan to create custom SharePoint artifacts (such as master pages, Cascading Style Sheets, and custom code that you created by using Visual Studio 2010), you may want to add a development farm to your farm topology. Technically, you can double your staging environment as a development environment, but this setup quickly becomes tricky to manage — especially if multiple developers or groups are working on artifacts at the same time — because you need to avoid developers accidentally affecting concurrent testing or development activities.

Another important consideration for both no-code line-of-business applications and custom Visual Studio applications revolves around security and access to the eventual underlying data that the application processes. Although both SharePoint Designer power users and Visual Studio developers require site-collection administration privileges when they actively develop the application or artifact, what happens after the application or artifact has gone to production? What if the line-of-business application in question is an HR yearly performance management application? These questions quickly become important in the context of a developed application that stores sensitive data. One of the typical reasons for implementing a lifecycle-management process for no-code line-of-business applications involves developing these applications in a separate environment, where the power users or developers can retain administrative access to the applications without jeopardizing potentially confidential or sensitive data stored on the production environment.

You need dedicated server farms for change management and development purposes, but you also need to resist the urge to over-architect the server farm topology. You don't want to create significant administrative overhead and delay to operational management of the SharePoint farms. Remember, a managed process should ensure that you develop artifacts and customizations in an environment as close to the actual production environment as possible so that you can catch potential issues or conflicts with other custom developments or applications. On the operational side you must deploy updates, patches, and new versions of all applications and customizations on all of the server farms. Therefore, the more server farms you add, the longer it takes to deploy changes to production and the more effort (and cost) you need to spend on the operations side.

Often, multiple development groups request separate server farms because they're worried about other developers or groups potentially affecting their timelines and progress by working on the server farm at the same time. Consider these requests carefully and try to move to a process where developers have locally installed SharePoint instances on their development Windows 7 workstations and deploy releases to the shared development farm only when they're ready for first-pass review.

 Multiple server farms require dedicated server instances on which they can run, but they don't have to add to your physical server architecture requirements thanks to SharePoint 2010's full support for virtualization technologies, such as HyperV and VMWare. We cover virtualization options in Book II, Chapter 5.

Getting familiar with process isolation

A SharePoint server farm offers physical server-level process isolation to meet the more extreme needs typically associated with custom development and regulatory compliance. The server farm itself also has multiple levels of isolation options. And SharePoint 2010 adds to the more familiar application-pool and content-database-level isolation by introducing sandboxed solutions for custom code deployment and service-partitioning functionality with multi-tenancy.

Multi-tenancy refers to the ability to partition shared service applications in order to allow *tenants* (also called *subscribers*) to administer the service applications assigned to them. You may be familiar with multi-tenancy from shared hosting environments, such as SharePointOnline.com; you can use the same functionality for internal enterprise deployments and divisional IT environments. For example, by partitioning the Managed Metadata Service, you can allow divisional portals or team sites to manage their own metadata without having to create multiple instances of the service application.

You have process isolation and partitioning options when you plan server farms because you no longer need to deploy a different server farm in order to limit what information different groups of users have access to or are allowed to administer. For example, you can allow separate business division IT departments to administer only their own service applications, such as Search and Business Data Connectivity Services, without even being able to view information outside of their division. Previously, certain services required farm administrator privileges, which data owners sometimes weren't prepared to share between IT departments.

You can choose from several logical topology options when you design Shared Services infrastructures in SharePoint 2010.

Application pools

IIS application pools are used throughout the SharePoint application to provide process isolation for both service applications and Web Applications. An *application pool* is simply an IIS worker process that refers to the Windows service executable under which all the code and page processing runs on the physical server. The IIS worker process runs on every SharePoint 2010 server's task manager process list as the w3wp.exe executable. After you install a SharePoint 2010 Standard single server and run the Farm Configuration Wizard, five w3wp.exe processes (or application pools) typically start for Central Administration: a Topology Service, Security Token Service, shared process for all other SharePoint service applications, and the SharePoint – 80 default Web Application that the wizard creates.

Each of the Web Applications can, and should, run as a dedicated service account to keep them protected and isolated from accidental account lockout scenarios. You don't get any performance benefit by sharing service accounts across application pools, although from an account management perspective, try to keep the number of managed service accounts to a minimum so that you can cut down the effort required to comply with account security policies, such as organization password-change policies.

Service applications

Service applications support process isolation through application pools and data partitioning through multi-tenancy. A service applications can be shared within a farm or even across multiple farms if that service application supports multi-tenancy.

The Farm Configuration Wizard places all service applications in a single application pool. You can configure isolation to meet your requirements after you run the wizard, or you can choose to provision service applications manually during the installation — which we recommend if you've gone through the effort of planning your service applications before deploying the SharePoint environment, so you can use all of the right service accounts and application pools right off the bat.

Web Applications

Because you access Web Applications through IIS Web sites, Web Applications support process isolation by using the IIS application pools. You can extend Web Applications across multiple IIS Web sites, each of which can have its own application pool if you wanted to go into this level of process isolation. For example, you can provide connectivity to multiple networks, such as the extranet and the intranet in different IIS worker processes.

Any given server farm can host multiple Web Applications (for example, for different business divisions). And because the new service-application and multi-tenancy features can also have their own associated services, their own IT divisions can manage and configure their service application settings, thus reducing the need for divisional server farms.

We cover Web Applications and associated application pools in the "Planning Web Applications" section, later in this chapter.

Sandboxed solutions

Sandboxed solutions in SharePoint 2010 add another layer of isolation and management functionality that focuses on custom applications and Web Parts that built on top of the SharePoint framework. Sandboxed solutions execute code in a dedicated worker process under the SPUserCodeWorkerProcess. exe service in order to protect the main Web Application pool from being affected and to limit what the code can access on the server. Any site-collection owner can deploy sandboxed solutions when they're enabled. As a result, security becomes of paramount importance when SharePoint deals with sandboxed solutions because you don't want custom applications from being able to access secure information on web application or make modifications to the system files. For example, if the code can modify or access system files or configuration information on the physical SharePoint servers, it could upload malicious software on the server in order to gain administrative access.

The Sandboxed Solutions Service automatically monitors and controls the resource usage (such as memory and CPU) allowed each custom application. The system administrator can configure thresholds to suit the characteristics of the overall farm, and the administrator can even assign the sandboxed solutions server affinity so that you can offload those solutions to a dedicated server within the SharePoint farm.

In SharePoint 2007, process-heavy custom applications might have warranted a separate server farm. By using sandboxed solutions in SharePoint 2010, you can consolidate even custom applications to your main SharePoint farm, knowing that they can't adversely affect the overall server-farm performance or run in the same application pool context as your main portal Web Application and thus potentially gaining full access to information stored on the portal.

Preparing for geographically distributed deployments

Geo-distributed deployments, in this age of data-center consolidation and cloud-based services, is becoming a fleeting memory of the days when the best practice was to deploy SharePoint collaboration servers at each of the major user base hubs for multinational organizations. Even in the previously challenging Asia Pacific region, you can now provide centralized IT services relatively easily, and the network conditions are set to become only improve in the future. Multinational organizations also used to deploy server farms in certain key countries, such as Japan and China, because of language considerations, but SharePoint 2010's ability to localize service applications on a centralized server farm has removed the need for this site-collection-specific consideration.

Deploying multiple server farms across multiple locations really is rarely technical, but largely driven by country-specific regulations and divisional/country-based IT organizations. However, a few cases still exist in which groups of end users access the corporate network by using narrow-band or high-latency connections over satellite links in remote or moving locations (such as oil rigs or moving ships). If you intend to use the platform for large publishing-driven and multimedia-intensive operations, you could benefit from replicated copies of the content near large user bases thus enabling faster access to the information.

SharePoint 2010 addresses these more exceptional circumstances by providing new geo-friendly key functionality for dispersed deployments:

✦ **Cross-farm service applications:** Several key service applications support and have been designed to work across server farms and over network distances. For example, Microsoft specifically developed and designed the Managed Metadata Service so that Web Applications that are running on geographically dispersed locations can easily consume that service.

✦ **Read-only farms:** SharePoint 2010 supports asynchronous SQL log shipping, which can be configured to replicate content across datacenters, and even across continents. Because you can replicate these databases only one direction, the database in the remote location is in read-only mode. SharePoint 2010's new Ribbon interface, as well as the drop-down lists, detect the content database state and allow users to perform only actions that don't require users to write data back to the content database. A read-only farm allows users only to browse, search, and download documents and line-of-business application content. To update or checkout a document, the user has to visit the central farm.

In addition to server-farm-specific geo-friendly features, Office 2010 Professional ships with the SharePoint Workspace application, which can take SharePoint sites offline and synchronize them back when network connectivity is restored. By using a mixture of client-based synchronization and replicated read-only farms, you can meet the needs of smaller satellite offices while providing full read-only functionality to larger sites by using SQL log shipping and read-only farms, as illustrated in Figure 4-5.

**Book II
Chapter 4**

Designing the
Logical Architecture

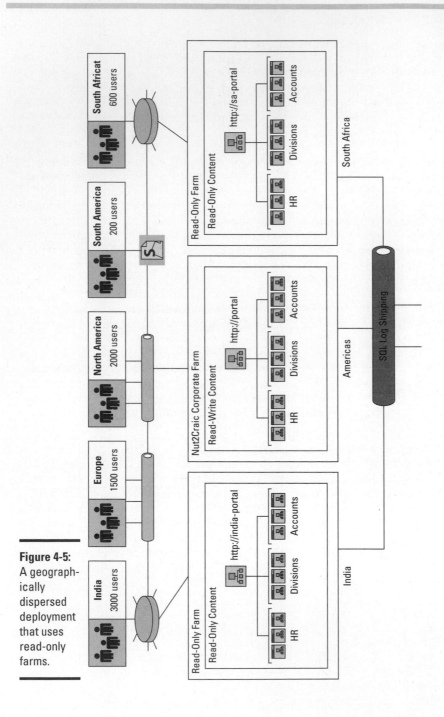

Figure 4-5:
A geographically dispersed deployment that uses read-only farms.

Operational considerations

Someone has to manage all the server farms in your environments. And, more importantly, someone has to ensure that they're all patched for operating system and application updates. You can automate part of the operating-system and SharePoint patching by using Windows Server Update Services (WSUS), but SharePoint updates are performed in two stages: one for bit upgrade and the other for database upgrade. WSUS can automatically download and install the bit upgrade, but the server administrator must perform the database upgrade manually. You can automate application patches, but remember that deploying custom solution updates requires either a manual change-management process or a custom automated process based on PowerShell scripts.

So, each server farm in your deployment architecture adds administrative overhead and maintenance. Unlike Exchange 2010, SharePoint 2010 doesn't have a centralized management console from which you can manage multiple SharePoint environments. Administrators have to remember and access each farm's Central Administration site specifically to manage that farm, although you can run PowerShell scripts to manage farms remotely from the same command-line console.

Consider carefully each additional server farm deployment; the farm administrators will thank you for it.

Planning Service Applications

In previous versions of SharePoint, planning services mainly revolved around the Search Service because to provision multiple search indexes for different divisions, you needed to create multiple Shared Service Providers (SSPs). However, SharePoint 2010's new service-application model doesn't have the previous versions' barriers and design drivers, essentially giving you a clean slate to design your service-application topology to meet the needs of the business, instead of bending the business requirements around the technology options.

Such open architectures can become challenging to design without over-architecting a solution. And too much architecture becomes difficult for the IT operations responsible for the ongoing support of the environment to manage. For example, you might want to create a Search Service application for each team that asks for a customized list of sources from which they want to get search results. But managing 20 dynamic team or business-group search applications can become difficult, mainly because of the sheer overhead involved in ensuring each search application's indexes and Best Bets are relevant and up to date. So, design a basic services topology that meets your needs now and that you can easily expand on later (when more business divisions come on board) without necessarily needing a new set of service applications. To design an extensible services architecture, you need to dare to think big and consider the business as a whole, even if you're currently deploying SharePoint for only a specific business unit or function.

Service-application topology design essentially boils down to four main topics:

+ Deciding what service applications you want to utilize
+ Planning service-application groups
+ Preparing for process isolation and data partitioning
+ Providing distributed services for multiple farms

Although you need to design your service-architecture framework up front to prevent uncontrollable proliferation of service applications, you don't have to build and deploy all your planned architecture right away. The key is to have a plan so that you can deal with requests and changes when they arise; but thanks to the new service-architecture flexibility, you can start small and grow your provided services however the requirements dictate. Plan for the future, but build for now.

Deciding on provided services

First and foremost, you need to figure out which of the numerous service applications that come with SharePoint you plan to deploy now or in the future. Because we cover all the major service-application functionality in other chapters in this book, we now focus on the planning-specific points of interest.

You don't have to deploy most of the services immediately thanks to the flexible pick-and-mix architecture for services in SharePoint 2010. In fact, because Web Applications connect to your provisioned services through service groups, you may not need to configure your Web Applications to use the newly provisioned service application at all.

You can decide whether to provision all your service applications during SharePoint installation or manually configure them afterwards when the need arises, although most system administrators would advise avoiding wizards and opt for the manual configuration approach in order to control application pool and service account settings.

What service applications you have at your disposal depend on the type of license for your version of SharePoint 2010 and additional expansions, such as Office Web Applications. And so, unless you have an enterprise agreement that covers all Office and SharePoint product licenses in your organization, you need to find out and decide on your SharePoint license type. Although discussing SharePoint licensing would take a chapter of its own, from the planning perspective, you have different service applications available depending on which SharePoint license and application package you have. Talk to your local Microsoft licensing representative when you price and purchase SharePoint licenses because Microsoft has a certain level of flexibility built-in; for example, with the Office Web Applications and the extranet/Internet facing deployments.

Figure 4-6 lists the service applications that come with SharePoint 2010, including the additional Office Web Service applications that you can install and use if you have Office 2010 client-access licenses in your organization. Excel appears in both the Enterprise Edition and Office Web Applications columns on Figure 4-6; you can deploy Excel support on SharePoint Foundation and SharePoint Standard, even if you don't have the Enterprise license, and you can use Excel Web Parts and calculation services on SharePoint Enterprise without having to install or license the wider Office Web Applications built to open and edit Office documents in your browser.

Figure 4-6: SharePoint 2010 and Office Web Applications service applications.

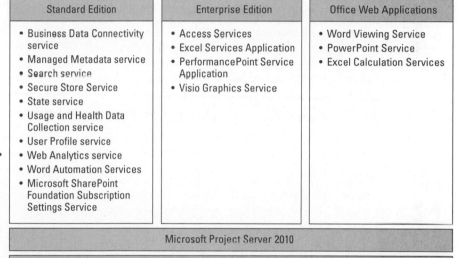

Standard Edition	Enterprise Edition	Office Web Applications
• Business Data Connectivity service • Managed Metadata service • Search service • Secure Store Service • State service • Usage and Health Data Collection service • User Profile service • Web Analytics service • Word Automation Services • Microsoft SharePoint Foundation Subscription Settings Service	• Access Services • Excel Services Application • PerformancePoint Service Application • Visio Graphics Service	• Word Viewing Service • PowerPoint Service • Excel Calculation Services

Microsoft Project Server 2010

FAST Search Server 2010 for SharePoint

FAST Search Server 2010 for SharePoint also may install a number of service applications, depending on the role of the server you're installing. In production FAST Search Server 2010 for SharePoint deployments, Microsoft recommends using separate servers for FAST, with the Content and Query Service applications running on the SharePoint farm itself.

In previous releases of SharePoint, Microsoft Project Server was a separate product, which partly built on top of Windows SharePoint Services. Projects Server 2010 moves fully into the SharePoint family by becoming a service application, just like PerformancePoint and FAST Search Server 2010 for SharePoint. To install Project Server 2010, you need a SharePoint Enterprise license. So, consult your local Microsoft licensing specialist about licensing options — especially if you were previously licensed for Project Server 2007 under the Software Assurance and don't plan to purchase SharePoint Enterprise licenses.

Service applications and groups

Service-application groups connect Web Applications and individual service applications, and you can freely modify these groups at any given time without interrupting the Web Applications or service applications on the server farm. For example, if you create and configure Business Connectivity Services after initial go-live and assign it to the Default service group, all the Web Applications connected to the Default group automatically gain access to the functionality.

All the service applications automatically belong to the Default group, unless you specify otherwise when you create a new service application. You might not want a service application to belong to the default group if you need to make that service application dedicated. It is possible to freely change the Default group service applications later by using the Central Administration Service Application Associations Management — so you don't have to get the settings right from the get-go.

There are two types of service application groups: Default and Custom. Custom groups can pick services freely, as illustrated in Figure 4-7. Each Custom group is specific to a Web Application, and service applications can belong to any number of Custom groups within a server farm. Therefore, you can most effectively use service-application groups when you're creating Web Applications, though you can change a particular Web Application's groups later by using Central Administration Web Application Management.

Only the Web Applications connected to the Default group automatically inherit new service applications connected to that group. You have to manually connect all the Custom groups to the newly provisioned service application, as required.

Partitioning and isolating services

Although all service applications are physically deployed within a single Web Application in IIS, SharePoint still offers process isolation by using application pools, as illustrated in Figure 4-7. Essentially, each service application becomes a virtual directory within the service application IIS Web site, which can be configured to run under individual application pools or share them with other service applications. When service applications share the same application pool, they utilize fewer memory resources. However, if the application pool crashes for any reason or the Active Directory account that the application pool runs as gets locked out, then all service applications configured to share the pool become unavailable.

In addition to operational considerations, you may want to establish process isolation for security reasons — especially for key security that relates service applications, such as the Secure Store Service, which provides single sign-on (SSO) Services to external data stores. Because potentially malicious custom code can run in the IIS worker process context, the malicious application could run code by using the worker process identity or read information held in memory. Protect against potential confidential data leaks by isolating the Web Applications and service applications that hold potentially confidential information to separate application pools.

IIS Web site–"SharePoint Web Services"

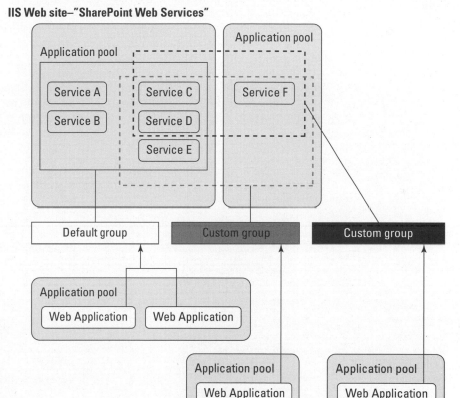

**Book II
Chapter 4**

Designing the
Logical Architecture

Figure 4-7:
SharePoint 2010 has a flexible pick-and-mix services architecture.

On the flip-side of security-related process isolation is the need to control and administer the functionality and data provided by certain service applications, such as Managed Metadata and Search. You typically have to isolate information for functional reasons, rather than purely for security, so service applications' partitioning features can provide a functional alternative to creating separate service applications to meet the isolation needs of some teams or business divisions.

SharePoint 2010 refers to partitioning as *multi-tenancy*. Although developers designed multi-tenancy to enable the online/cloud hosting model, you can also use it in internal enterprise deployments to provide partitioning and reporting capabilities for organizations. This setup provides centralized IT services for divisional business units that have their own IT staff as an alternative to creating multiple service applications or deploying multiple server farms.

For example, by partitioning the Search Service, rather than creating multiple instances of the Search Service, you can reduce the overhead associated with data and management isolation. Because each service-application instance provisions associated databases and scheduled tasks, running multiple instances of the same service application comes with administrative overhead, as well as some performance overhead. So, if you plan to provide customized service offerings to your business divisions, or even to specific projects, partitioning gives you the flexibility to provide the services without having to deal with the associated administrative and resource requirements of full-blown service applications.

The left side of Figure 4-8 illustrates the standard service applications that support partitioning, and the service applications that don't store any data (which you can therefore share without the need for partitioning) appear on the right.

Figure 4-8:
Service applications that support either partitioning or stateless sharing.

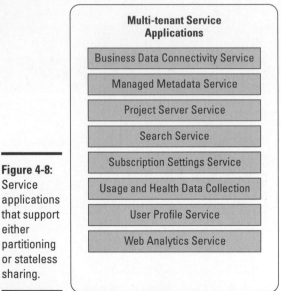

Multi-tenant Service Applications

Business Data Connectivity Service

Managed Metadata Service

Project Server Service

Search Service

Subscription Settings Service

Usage and Health Data Collection

User Profile Service

Web Analytics Service

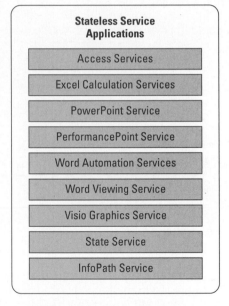

Stateless Service Applications

Access Services

Excel Calculation Services

PowerPoint Service

PerformancePoint Service

Word Automation Services

Word Viewing Service

Visio Graphics Service

State Service

InfoPath Service

With the exception of FAST Search Server 2010 for SharePoint, every standard SharePoint 2010 service application either supports multi-tenancy or is a stateless processing engine that doesn't need to store data and therefore doesn't require partitioning. SharePoint 2010 was designed for use in *hosted deployments,* where hundreds (if not thousands) of customers share the same server farm and have access to almost all the functionality that SharePoint 2010 offers.

Unless you're a hosting provider, however, you have significantly fewer situations in which multi-tenancy is applicable because you're in an enterprise where SharePoint enables mostly collaboration and knowledge sharing. The one logical exception involves an enterprise's Managed Metadata Service, which adds value for both the cross-enterprise scenario and for cross-divisions or large projects. We will cover the Managed Metadata Service and its value in Book III, Chapter 5.

If you're planning to create multiple Web Applications on the same server farm for entity-specific uses (such as divisional portals, larger projects, or teams), consider deploying a partitioned Managed Metadata Service that can support each of the hosted Web Applications, in addition to the enterprise-wide Managed Metadata Service. Figure 4-9 shows a partitioned Managed Metadata Service scenario.

Providing distributed services

If you plan to deploy multiple server farms or are deploying a new farm in an organization that has a separate central SharePoint 2010 service, you need to consider where services, such as User Profiles, are hosted because the service application framework now supports cross-farm connections. In fact, a number of key service applications that come with SharePoint 2010 support cross-farm connections, so they can provide centralized services and share features, such as managed metadata, between farms. Because the service application framework supports third-party custom applications, more cross-farm service applications may be developed in the future. However, not all service applications need to provide cross-farm access, potentially over regions or even continents.

The standard SharePoint 2010 service applications that you can share across farms are

+ User Profile Service
+ Managed Metadata Service
+ Business Data Connectivity Service
+ Search Service
+ Secure Store Service
+ Web Analytics Service

The User Profiles Service and Managed Metadata Service are the two most common cross-farm service applications, with the Search Service trailing closely behind. For example, large multinational organizations need to provide a centralized User Profile store because they likely need multiple farms, perhaps hosted in multiple continents. By connecting to a central User Profile store, the divisional or regional farms don't need to provision their own and duplicate information. For example, they don't have to crawl the Active Directory individually or synchronize user profile properties. Also, having one single central My Site that's connected to each of the regional or divisional content farms can streamline social features such as tagging and comments without the need to synchronize social content.

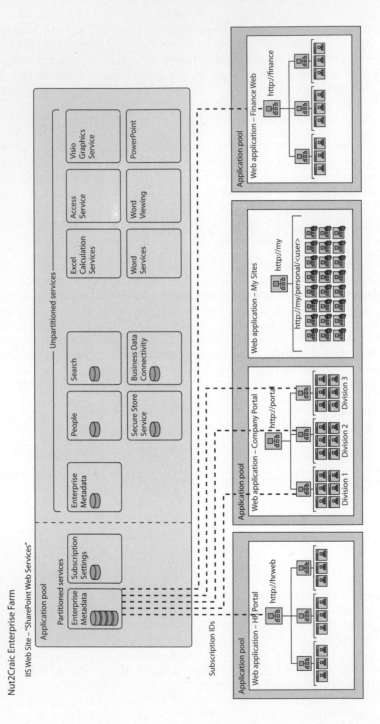

Figure 4-9:
This enterprise scenario features partitioned Managed Metadata Services.

While a single User Profile Service across the enterprise makes sense due to the benefits to united social collaboration functionality across the enterprise, the Managed Metadata Service typically needs both enterprise and local instances in order to meet both the enterprise and the divisional metadata requirements. For example, a product-engineering division wants to classify their documents by using enterprise keywords, but they also want division-specific managed metadata for product-specific information, which the enterprise as a whole doesn't need to use when classifying their documents.

Figure 4-10 illustrates the extreme scale that the services architecture can go to in SharePoint 2010 when a large enterprise uses distributed service applications.

**Book II
Chapter 4**

In the example in Figure 4-10, the central IT provides a dedicated Enterprise Services farm (Farm A) for all business units, as well as the centralized collaboration farm, which the other farms can connect to for centralized user profiles, and enterprise managed metadata and search functionality. In addition, the central IT provides Farm B and Farm C with access to key enterprise applications by using Business Data Connectivity Services and a Secure Store Service that's configured to provide single sign-on capabilities between Active Directory accounts and the external databases.

**Designing the
Logical Architecture**

The product engineering division deployed their own SharePoint farm (Farm B) because they operate under divisional business IT support and fund their own physical server infrastructure. However, they want to use User Profile, Managed Metadata, and Enterprise Search Services from the Central IT farm (Farm A). Because they want to classify documents with both the enterprise and divisional metadata, they also provisioned a local Managed Metadata Service, along with Excel Services and Office Web Application support.

Because the product engineering division (Farm B) connects to the enterprise services farm's (Farm A) User Profile service, Farm B can provision new My Sites on the Enterprise Collaboration farm (Farm C), in addition to the centrally provided ad-hoc team collaboration capability (Farm C). Users' tags, notes, and links are accessible on both Farm B and Farm C because the User Profile service on Farm A stores this information.

Although the sample in Figure 4-10 applies to a large enterprise, it does provide a good picture of the scale to which you can take service applications. The number of farms that connect to the Central Enterprise Services farm (Farm A) is limited only by the number of farms that a large enterprise can manage and support.

So no matter how big you dare to think, service applications can likely keep up!

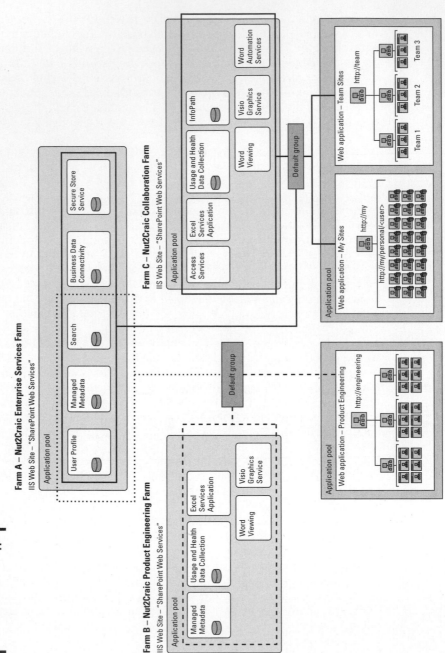

Figure 4-10:
An
enterprise
cross-farm
service-
application
scenario.

Planning Web Applications

Web Applications aren't simply containers for site collections. You need to carefully plan Web Applications (for both topology and technical reasons) before you figure out how to store the actual data in the underlying site topology. SharePoint 2010 uses the Web Application layer as an important middle tier in the topology. For example, Web Applications provide both authentication services and the crucial connections to service applications.

You could create a single Web Application that has access to all SharePoint 2010's functionality, including My Sites, team sites, divisional portals, and an enterprise search center. But, because of scale, performance, and visual benefits, most organizations create at least three Web Applications when they deploy SharePoint. Here are the typical three Web Applications:

✦ Portal Web Application (`http://portal`)

✦ Team Collaboration Web Application (`http://team`)

✦ My Site Web Application (`http://my`)

In addition to these typical Web Applications, organizations may decide to deploy business-unit-specific Web Applications, as well as Web Applications that facilitate security isolation (for example, for secure collaboration). Planning Web Applications typically revolves around

✦ **Descriptive service brand URLs (also called *vanity URLs*):** You access each Web Application by using a unique domain name, so you can create meaningful service-oriented or company-specific vanity URLs that the end users hopefully recognize and remember without having to refer to Web browser bookmarks or sticky notes spread across their monitors.

For example, `http://teams` and `http://portal` describe the content and functionality that the user can find on a Web page — and those addresses are considerably more user-friendly than the physical server name (such as `http://cskspfe01`).

Vanity URLs don't have to be descriptively named — you can make them otherwise memorable or branded. For example, one of our customers named their enterprise portal Solas, which is Irish for Light, symbolizing a new start after a move from a green-screen legacy environment. Because the organization chose the entry from a large number of employee suggestions (they ran a staff competition for naming suggestions) a bit of a buzz had already been generated before the SharePoint environment ever went live. Solas has become recognized within the organization as the go-to place for all corporate information.

✦ **Process- and data-isolation requirements:** Because each Web Application runs in an application pool and connects to content databases assigned to the Web Application, you may want to establish both process and data isolation so that you can divide sensitive or business-specific content between Web Applications.

✦ **Authentication requirements:** You can configure each Web Application with different authentication providers or enable them for anonymous access (for example, if you want to use it mainly for Web-content publishing). SharePoint 2010 supports both classic mode authentication against Active Directory or new claims-based authentication that can use a number of authentication providers. Claims-based authentication also provides a framework that you can use to create custom providers.

You can choose between classic and claims-based authentication when you first create the Web Applications — but you can't change the authentication method after you provision it. Therefore, consider the authentication requirements beforehand so that you don't have to recreate Web Applications in order to enable authentication against other identity stores.

✦ **Operational manageability requirements:** Because you access each Web Application by using a unique URL, you can use that URL to separate Service Level Agreements and support plans for the different types of service.

At the Web Application level, you control a number of general settings, such as Recycle Bin and Maximum Allowed File Size, which allows you to customize each service's specific settings separately. For example, you can limit the My Site's maximum file upload size to the default 50MB so that you can prevent users from uploading .PST files, while increasing the file upload size to 1GB files on the divisional portal.

Addressing authentication

SharePoint 2010 introduces a new claims-based authentication mechanism that builds on the Microsoft Windows Identity Foundation (WIF) .NET framework, while maintaining the previous Windows authentication model that uses classic mode authentication. SharePoint uses classic mode authentication when upgrading from Microsoft Office SharePoint Server 2007 to SharePoint 2010, and SharePoint also uses it as the default authentication mode when you create a new Web Application. Because you can select the authentication mode only when you create a new Web Application, as shown in Figure 4-11, you need to determine what authentication scenarios will apply to your Web Applications before you provision them.

If you know a Web Application will require only Windows authentication, then you don't need to select the Claims Based Authentication radio button when creating the Web Application. However, if you think the Web Application may, in the future, require multiple forms of authentication, even if you need to enable only Windows authentication right now, turn on Claims Based Authentication to avoid having to rebuild the Web Application when you need the additional forms of authentication.

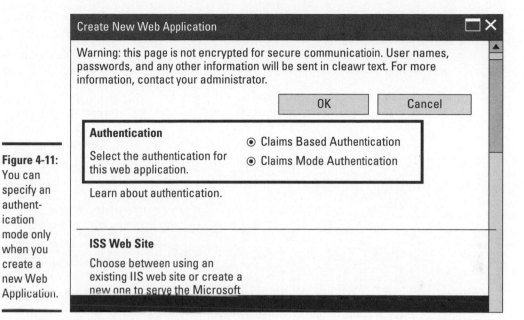

Figure 4-11:
You can
specify an
authent-
ication
mode only
when you
create a
new Web
Application.

Claims-based authentication supports the same Windows-based authentication schemes as Classic mode; however, it adds a number of other authentication providers, as well as allowing you to use custom or third-party
solutions, as shown in Figure 4-12. Therefore, you can select the Claims
Based Authentication radio button when you create a Web Application but
initially use only Windows-based authentication modes until you need to
allow external users to access the Web Application.

SharePoint 2010 allows you to use multiple authentication methods by using
zones. You can create up to five zones per Web Application by extending
an existing Web Application and selecting one of the predefined zones.
A zone is actually a new IIS Web site, which means that each zone has a
unique domain name. You can configure a zone to function over different IP
addresses and ports in IIS Manager Web site bindings.

In Figure 4-13, the SharePoint architecture extends a single Web Application
over multiple zones, with different authentication mechanisms configured for
each type of user group accessing the Engineering Portal Web Application.

In the example in Figure 4-13, the three zones are configured with different
authentication mechanisms to address the types of users accessing the
Engineering Web Application. The internal users access the Web Application
by using internal Active Directory authentication from the internal network.
The contractors use Forms Based Authentication (FBA) that has usernames
and passwords held in an existing SQL database. Because Forms Based
Authentication submits usernames and passwords over the network,
the sample architecture uses SSL encryption for the communication.

Finally, partners have their own Active Directory that has Active Directory Federation Services 2.0 enabled for Claims Based Authentication to the Engineering Web Application. All the different user groups can access the same user interface and data stored on the Web Application.

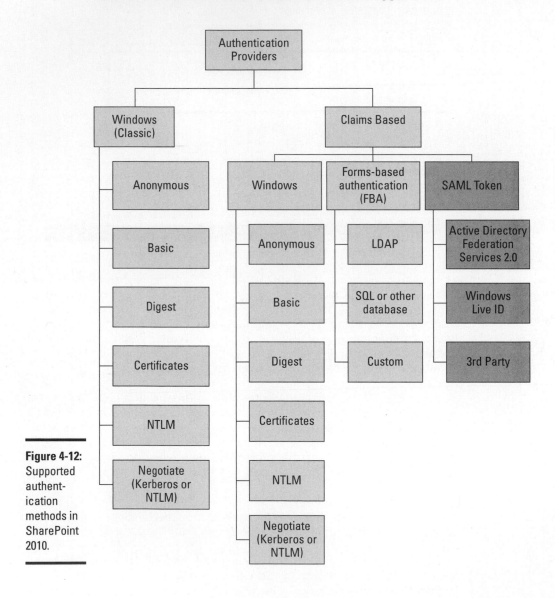

Figure 4-12: Supported authentication methods in SharePoint 2010.

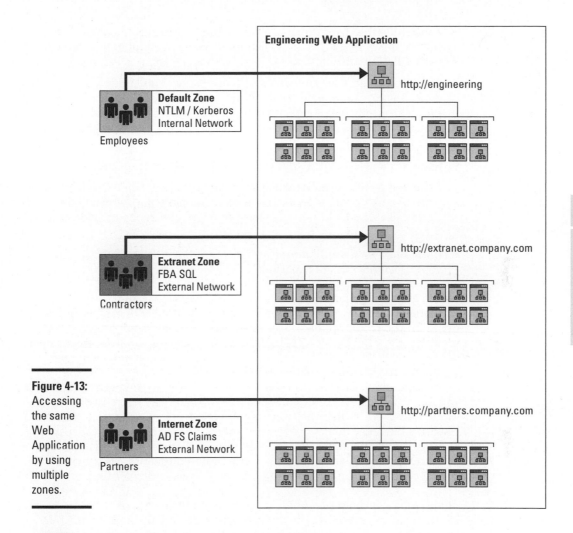

Figure 4-13:
Accessing
the same
Web
Application
by using
multiple
zones.

You can use claims-based authentication for the new zones only if you
originally created the Web Application with the Claims Based Authentication
radio button selected.

Planning zones and policies

You can use zones' authentication-specific features to manage these important
access-related settings:

✦ **Authentication provider:** As we mention in the section "Addressing Authentication," earlier in this chapter, you can configure each zone with different authentication.

✦ **Anonymous access:** Control whether to allow anonymous access per zone. So, for example, you can allow anonymous access for content publishing only when a user accesses it through the internal network, while requiring users to authenticate when accessing this feature from external networks.

✦ **Secure Sockets Layer (SSL):** Enforce SSL on all external zones.

✦ **Different public URL:** Because a zone is technically an IIS Web site, each zone must be configured with a unique domain name, which allows you to create an easily identifiable alias that you can use to provide external access.

✦ **Policy for Web Application:** Assign each zone different policies to govern user access permissions.

Policies are essentially permission levels that you can assign to specific user accounts or groups, and apply across all the site collections, sites, and lists hosted on the Web Application. Importantly, you can use policies to both block and allow permissions globally within a Web Application when a user accesses the Web Application through the zone to which you've applied the policy. The granularity of custom permission policy levels (which we covered in Book I, Chapter 2) goes all the way down to the permission levels available within SharePoint. For example, you can deny users the ability to view versions only when they access the Web Application from an external network. (We don't think you'd ever want to do such a thing because why would you limit the ability to read previous versions of documents if the user can read the document itself; we just wanted to illustrate the depth of custom permission levels.)

Policies can allow all SharePoint support staff full control of all the sites and lists within a given Web Application, or perhaps only through a zone that enforces SSL encryption. And because policies can both grant and deny access, you could assign contractors the Deny All access policy to a Web Application that hosts confidential information, regardless of how the site or list administrators configure access to a part of that Web Application.

Policies can help you enforce your information security best practices in extranet scenarios because policies allow you to control which user groups are allowed or denied access to the Web Application, regardless of what permissions they have when they're working on the internal network, as illustrated in Figure 4-14.

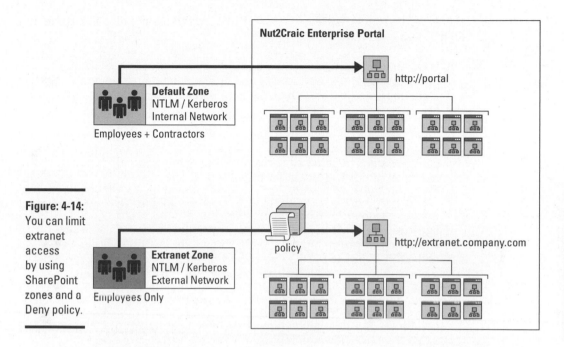

Figure: 4-14:
You can limit
extranet
access
by using
SharePoint
zones and a
Deny policy.

In the example in Figure 4-14, the contracted staff have internal Active Directory accounts and can access the corporate portal when they're within the company network, working on desktop PCs provided and controlled by the IT department. However, because IT has no control over contractors' personal PC equipment when they are working from home, they block contractors' access from the Internet by using a Deny policy on the extranet zone for the Enterprise Portal Web Application.

Because you can use only five zones, you need to plan the use of policies and zones carefully so that you don't have to redesign your zone topology in the future.

Policies overrule all site, list and item permissions. Users or groups that receive access with a policy exception gain access to all sites, lists, and items when they access the Web Application by using the defined zone URL.

Planning SharePoint Site Topology

Even though site collections and sites are at the bottom of the logical-architecture design, you need to plan them carefully because the actual data is always associated with a site within a site collection. One of the more difficult aspects of site-topology planning involves the terminology: the difference between a site collection, site, subsite and a top-level site.

Here are the concepts related to site topology (which are also illustrated in Figure 4-15):

✦ **Site:** All the data (except service applications) stored in SharePoint reside in a site; it's the lowest-level design element within a topology. Lists and libraries, as well as the actual items and documents in both, are all hosted within the site.

✦ **Site collection:** A site (often referred to as a *top-level site*) that can contain multiple sites. (Those multiple sites in a site collection are often called *subsites* because they reside within a hierarchy directly under the top-level site or nested under other subsites.)

A site collection is separated in topology design from regular sites because each site within a site collection inherits security and artifact settings from the top-level site (the site collection) itself, so a site collection creates a logical security boundary. All sites within a site collection share the same site collection administrators and can inherit site security settings from their parent site collection. (You can also configure unique permissions for each site, instead.)

You especially need to plan site-collection design for team and group collaboration deployments because you can assign quota templates (which control how much data you are allowed to store on a site) only at a site-collection level. Therefore, if you want to plan your storage growth and reinforce good working practices — create each team and group collaboration site as a site collection.

On the other hand, you may want to use a single site collection that has multiple subsites for Enterprise Portal and Web Content Management deployments so that you can build in SharePoint navigational features, such as the navigation bar and breadcrumbs.

✦ **Content database:** Although content databases relate to server-architecture planning and storage sizing, they're typically also associated with a logical-architecture plan, because site collections are located within one of the provisioned content databases per SharePoint Web Application and they cannot be moved from one content database to another without performing a manual backup/restore operation for the Site Collection.

When you design a site topology, remember the Microsoft best-practice recommendation of 100GB per site collection, unless the content database doesn't contain any other site collections, in which case, increase the limit up to 1TB in size.

The number of content databases is largely driven by the number and size of planned site collections because Microsoft best practices recommend that you store no more than 200GB within a single content database. Content databases allow you to place site collections in multiple databases within a Web Application, which allows you to plan topologies far exceeding 200GB.

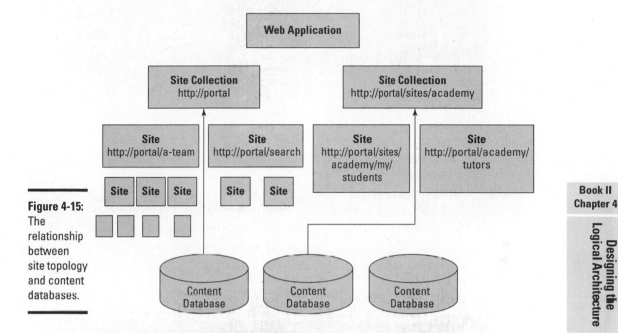

Figure 4-15:
The relationship between site topology and content databases.

Organizing sites and site collections

When you have to decide what to make an individual site collection and what to include in a site collection usually comes down to the functionality and synergy between information that you want to create.

Site collections share functionality between all the sites in the hierarchy, including

✦ **Site-collection galleries:** Take advantage of a number of galleries and libraries, such as a the unified Master Page and Images Gallery, across all the sites within a site collection in order to provide branded look and feel, and a common user interface, to the end users.

✦ **Site-collection administration:** Site-collection administrators are granted full control over every site, list, and library in the site collection, so they can assist and fix issues resulting from accidental subsite administrator actions. A number of SharePoint capabilities (such as Features, Recycle Bin, Policies, Search Settings, and Variations) are administered at the site-collection level. You can access a number of reports, including the Web Analytics Reports and the Audit Log Reports, for all sites in the site collection contained in the top-level site administration interface.

✦ **Content authoring benefits:** Content and page authors can take advantage of shared site columns, content types, Web Parts, workflows, and other authoring resources in order to provide a consistent authoring environment, regardless of where in the site hierarchy the author adds or edits the content.

✦ **Site collection navigation:** The site navigation control that comes with SharePoint 2010 provides dynamic navigation across the site collection without requiring that you maintain static links or create custom controls.

You don't want to create every site under a single site collection for a number of reasons:

✦ **Quota enforcement:** You can enforce and monitor quota only at a site-collection level.

✦ **Access control:** Because site collection administrators have access to all the content stored on the site hierarchy, you need to place confidential information in a site collection that only the authorized administrators can access.

✦ **Database sizing:** From a purely storage-sizing perspective, the only way to limit individual content database growth is to spread content between multiple site collections. Every site collection is stored within a content database, and you can't divide the content of a single site collection over multiple content databases. However, you can create multiple content databases and put different site collections on each database — or even assign a particularly large site collection to a content database of its own, with every other content database going to separate databases. You can even put content databases on multiple physical SQL servers to provide massive scale-out capability on the back-end SQL infrastructure.

Because we give a lot of technical reasons to create unique site collections, you may not think that the end users can benefit if you create their team sites as site collections, rather than subsites. However, most end users probably don't know or care whether the document library to which they upload content is hosted on a site collection, rather than a subsite. So, don't hesitate to create site collections for specific business units or projects if you have concerns about content database sizes or want to enforce specific quotas for those sites.

From a functional point of view, the decision between a site collection and a hierarchical site structure comes down to three basic types of sites typically hosted on a SharePoint Web Application:

✦ **Team site:** The fundamental definition of a *team site* is a site to which only a certain set of users have access so that they can collaborate or share information relating to a specific project, division, or task. The type of information created and stored on a team site is typically dynamic, so team members continue to work on it until it is ready for publishing. A team site doesn't typically have a large number of subsites, but team sites created for large projects or business units may have a hierarchical structure of subsites — for example, for sub-team, project-task, or meeting purposes.

The owning party typically manages and administers team sites, which can contain confidential information over which the team needs to maintain tight control.

We recommended creating team sites as separate site collections in order to provide overarching administration and quota management features for team sites.

✦ **Publishing site:** You can find a wide variety of site templates for content publishing, ranging from Publishing Portals and Enterprise Wikis to Document and Record Centers. But the fundamental definition of a *publishing site* is a site where a large number of users have access to view the information that site contains. An enterprise or divisional portal is a prime example of a publishing site, where information is targeted to a wide audience, with a small subset of content authors who can edit and publish information after it has been approved by the content area owner.

A wiki is the complete opposite of the typical publishing portal, since everyone is allowed to edit and add on to a wiki site, but either all company employees or a large portion of them (such as a specific business unit) still access the information.

Publishing sites benefit from a unified look and feel, as well as from a common navigation structure, and they're typically managed centrally by either an IT group or a specific information management group, whereas subsites typically have specific content managers.

We recommend creating Publishing sites within a single site collection in order to provide out of the box navigation for the end users and content restructuring capability for the portal owners.

✦ **My Site:** Personal spaces, with a public section of the site where everyone can access person-specific profile information, as well as publicly shared documents. You can link the My Site–specific template to the User Profile Service application, from which you can store and display user profile data. If you enable self-site creation for the Web Application that hosts the My Sites top-level site collection, users can create personal site where they can store data and create SharePoint lists.

The personal areas of My Sites that the My Site template creates are always site collections.

Because you can choose from dozens of standard site templates, which you can use to create sites that have their own unique features, look and feel, and usage characteristics, you need to plan the types of sites that you want to offer to users within a Web Application. The type of sites you plan to create within the Web Application determine the number of site collections that you need to create to hold them. Therefore, from a planning perspective, you need to figure out

✦ The type of sites you plan to provide within the Web Application

✦ The number of site collections these sites will spread across

For example, if you're planning to create an Enterprise Publishing Portal that includes a number of divisional subsites, as well as a central document center and a records management center, then you probably want to use a single site collection so that you can take advantage of the site-collection navigation controls and the ability to move and link to content within the same site collection. And because you know the site collection is likely to require a lot of storage space, you can limit the first content database to one site collection so that you can keep that content database within the Microsoft best-practices recommendation of no more than 1TB of data. You'd therefore create subsequent site collections on new content databases, which you can expand on, as required.

On the other hand, if you plan to use the Web Application for which you're planning a site topology primarily for team collaboration, each individual team site likely requires unique permissions and site artifacts. From an operational point of view, you probably want to enforce quotas to limit the storage growth and to enforce good working practices that involve cleaning old or no-longer-relevant content. So, if you want to remain within Microsoft best-practices recommendations, you need to configure the content-database site-collection limits according to your quota limits. For example, if you want to establish a moderate 200MB site-collection quota limit, you set a limit between 1,000 and 2,000 site collections so that you can remain within the 200GB content-database recommendation. Because every single site collection probably won't reach the quota limit, you need to guess a little when making the estimation, especially because exceptions for exceeding the default quota limit can occur in changing business environments. Still, at this stage, rough estimates are perfectly acceptable. (We go into the sizing subject in more detail in Book 2, Chapter 5.)

Multilingual considerations

SharePoint 2010 supports different languages through site language packs and content variations, which you're probably familiar with if you've deployed multilingual support for Microsoft Office SharePoint Server 2007. And although SharePoint 2010 includes new features and support for multiple languages in Managed Metadata and Search, the important site-topology-related design decisions focus on the two concepts of language packs and variations.

Language packs provide localized SharePoint sites for internal collaboration and content portals, where users or country-specific business units can use the central collaboration farm to create sites or site collections in their native languages. The created site, apart from SharePoint-specific error messages, provides all the SharePoint functionality localized to a specific language, even down to the system-generated home page, featuring the selected language. Of course, the content that users subsequently enter is unique because the system doesn't provide automated translation for content such as Microsoft Office files. And after you provision a site or site collection by using a language template, you can't change that template.

However, SharePoint 2010 allows you to enable Multi-Lingual User Interface (MUI) to provide alternate languages for specific sites, regardless of the language template that you used when you originally created the site. The MUI changes the user interface, or *Chrome* (elements such as the Ribbon and navigation), so that it displays the user-selected language. The new Managed Metadata Services application supports the MUI and displays the language-specific metadata, as long as you provided that metadata when you created the taxonomy and metadata information. Of course, the content that users enter in rich-text pages and the actual files stored on the site aren't translated to the selected language, but at least the user can read the interface in his or her native language.

If you want to provide completely localized content, including the rich-text content on Web pages and the files stored on your site, then you can use variations feature for SharePoint that provide support for both how the users navigate the translated information and how SharePoint automates the content-creation tasks. SharePoint doesn't have a magic bullet for translating content, so the variations simply automate the translation of the content by providing workflows to assign the translation tasks to language-specific editors. SharePoint enables variations at the site-collection level because organizations typically use these variations on publishing sites. After you select the source language (which is referred to as a *source label*) in site administration, you can't change it.

Variations create a complete mirror of the site structure behind the scenes, with associated workflows for new content and timer jobs to ensure that SharePoint keeps content synchronized. Because there is no automatic translation functionality in SharePoint, don't enable variations support for a site that already has a lot of existing content since there would be a lot of empty pages in the new variations language site. You need to plan for the future when you use variations. Get to know the ins and outs of the variations functionality before you embark on this labor-intensive multilingual-content path for your publishing sites.

Chapter 5: Planning for Performance and Scalability

In This Chapter

✔ **Planning SharePoint 2010 physical architecture**

✔ **Sizing SharePoint 2010**

✔ **Planning for high availability**

*E*arlier SharePoint implementations emphasized the physical architecture of the computer system and how best to manage its performance and capacity. Although that concern stays constant, more recent SharePoint versions shifted the emphasis (slowly but surely) from physical to logical. These days you design your logical topology first — guided by a short list of goals that benefit the whole enterprise — and then figure out the physical infrastructure needed to support your SharePoint implementation.

Naturally, physical and logical have to work together — and here's where they start: SharePoint 2010 uses a 64-bit code base exclusively (that's "x64 architecture" if you want to sound hip). x64 offers better memory management — which for SharePoint and SQL databases means more in-memory caching to speed up processing.

The time was right for SharePoint 2010 to move to 64-bit. Since the old days of SharePoint 2007, more hardware is available in 64-bit designs. CPU processing power has grown exponentially, improved multicore chips proliferate, and SharePoint 2010 (a multithreaded software architecture) can take full advantage of it all. SharePoint 2010 offers x64-friendly features to improve the delivery of some ambitious goals that the physical infrastructure must also meet:

✦ High system availability.

✦ Reliability that meets the increased demand for information.

✦ Business continuity and disaster recovery with minimal interruption.

✦ Enterprise-wide information-handling capabilities (including line-of-business applications).

✦ Content management that enhances collaboration and controls versions.

This chapter gives you a closer look at some design aspects that a highly available SharePoint infrastructure just can't do without. Stay with us through the maze of terms, and you can

✦ Give your operations team better control over managing your system's capacity and performance.

✦ Give your organization the full benefit of SharePoint's 64-bit powers.

Core Terms and Concepts for SharePoint Planning

Many of the most adept IT gurus agree that a plan for the physical architecture of your SharePoint system must rest on the four pillars of planning wisdom shown in Figure 5-1.

Figure 5-1:
Behold the pillars of terminology for perform-ance and capacity planning.

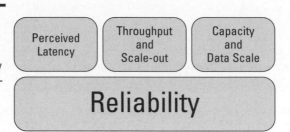

The following subsections offer a closer look at each pillar (don't worry — nothing will fall on your head).

Latency

Latency is, in essence, how long you have to wait before you get a response to an action. In the context of SharePoint, latency encompasses both the end-user action and the SharePoint system response — for example, how long a view takes to render on a user's browser to after a user visiting a team site clicks the document library link. This is where the user's perceptions come to play: Long before the document library view appears in the browser, the SharePoint server has already completed the request. Of course, to a computer, a "long" time can range from a fraction of a second to a few seconds. If the user "needs the information yesterday," the *perceived* latency can seem almost endless. By and large, end users don't know why the page was slow to render — they just know it was slow — so latency is often as much a reflection of the user experience as it is a performance issue.

Throughput

Throughput is the typical number of operations an application can process in a second. In a SharePoint context, it's a measure of how many requests the server is processing every second. Requests in SharePoint cover every action the server takes in response to a user action. Loading the home page of a team site, for example, actually performs numerous requests to fetch the data and compile the page before sending the response (which looks like a one-piece page) to the user. You can increase throughput by finding and eliminating bottlenecks in system performance that slow down operations.

If you're looking for SharePoint service applications to separate from the same physical server as your front-end Web server, a great place to start is the search-indexing and crawl component — it's the most CPU-intensive component of the search framework. (For more about the crawl component, see Book 3, Chapter 6.)

Book II
Chapter 5

Planning for
Performance and
Scalability

Capacity and data scale

The concepts of *capacity* and *data scale* are related: You're likeliest to hear about data scale if your organization needs a bigger one — which usually means increasing capacity. SharePoint treats those concepts this way:

✦ **Capacity** includes measures of how fast the available resources on the system can process data and how much room they have to store that data.

✦ **Data scale** refers not only to how big a body of data the system can search, but also to how much actual data the system can manage.

You can increase data scale by *scaling up* and/or *scaling out.* These expressions may sound similar, but one is more drastic than the other:

✦ **Scaling up** (the somewhat-less-drastic approach) means increasing the throughput rate of a physical server by adding resources — think CPUs and processing power — so it can operate on a grander scale.

✦ **Scaling out** means adding more physical servers to help your main server with the swarms of incoming processing requests. Doing so increases total throughput by putting more server computers on the job.

Quite aside from whether you can actually lift the components that you have to put in place (hint: new servers are heavy), scaling *up* a SharePoint system differs from scaling *out* in these respects:

✦ When you scale up, you're beefing up one server. When you scale out, you add whole new servers, and you do so *dynamically* without system downtime or interruption to the system operations.

✦ When you scale up, you're trying to get one server to do multiple jobs better. When you scale out, you dedicate additional servers to different purposes: Some become front-end Web servers; others are devoted to individual service applications. (Scaling out moves the features that consume a lot of system resources to dedicated servers.)

✦ Scaling up is limited by how much it can increase one machine's total application throughput (you can only cram so many CPUs into a single server). Scaling out is limited only by the network bandwidth available to process the requests and serve them to end users. (Okay, the *cost* of hardware is also a limit, but if you assume an unlimited budget . . . yeah, right. Nice daydream, isn't it? Back to work.)

SharePoint supports scaling out your data by giving you these options:

✦ You can add more content databases hosted on multiple SQL servers.

✦ Using remote-storage BLOB support, you can move scads of binary data from SQL databases to other (less expensive) storage devices.

For more about BLOBs (as data objects, not gloppy movie monsters), see Book 1, Chapter 2.

Regardless of whether you scale up or out, you still have to do some *capacity planning.* That means deciding just how to store the data your SharePoint system generates — not only the actual content stored in the environment, but also the metadata and full-text index associated with every content file stored in SharePoint. Oh, yeah, *and* (depending on the backup strategy) figuring out where and how to store your backups as well. Not to worry; we take a closer look at capacity planning later in this chapter.

Reliability

Underpinning the other pillars you always find issues of *reliability:* Your system's performance has to meet agreed-upon targets for throughput and latency — and do so consistently.

Reliability targets are typically agreed upon in a *Service Level Agreement (SLA)* between the business and the IT Operations groups. In practice, reliability targets are measurements done with such tools as Microsoft Systems Center Operations Manager (SCOM) or HP OpenView (which monitors and reports on all servers in an enterprise data center).

To maintain reliability, you have to keep the system's high availability in mind as you plan. That means outsmarting the next disaster by adopting *business continuity* measures that have no obvious single point of failure that could torpedo the whole system. For example, you can double up on all SharePoint servers and utilize SQL Server Clustering or Database Mirroring to minimize the likelihood of downtime due to server hardware issues. You can even split your SharePoint farm between multiple locations in order to avoid datacenter wide issues from affecting availability, but more on that later on in the chapter.

In addition to all these fundamental concepts of SharePoint performance and capacity, you'll run into these terms as you're drawing up your plan:

✦ **Requests per second (RPS):** Sometimes given as Operations per Second (ops/sec), this unit of measure represents how many requests the server can process in a second. A single Web page may actually require several operations to compile, depending on how many Web Parts are on the page.

✦ **Spike:** A *spike* is a short period of increased load due to a sudden increase in system usage. During a spike, typical usage (and therefore load) can increase tenfold compared to traffic during normal business hours. Fortunately, spikes are often predictable; in most organizations, they typically occur first thing in the morning or after e-mail announcements. Spikes on already-busy infrastructure may lead to a severe drop in perceived performance (at least from where the end user sits) and other spike-like jumps in both perceived latency (as discussed earlier) and gripes about the network.

✦ **Peak hours:** Most organizations have predictable periods of usage, usually attuned to the normal working hours of the end users. In organizations that span multiple time zones, of course, peak hours can be tougher to identify — but when working hours in different time zones converge (one regional office is trying to finish a working day while another is just starting up), expect a higher load on the system. That's one place you'll find your peak hours of usage.

If you avoid running system maintenance or other resource-intensive tasks during peak hours, usually you can minimize the effect on end users, steer clear of performance issues, and reduce grousing.

✦ **Off-peak hours:** In all organizations, even those that span multiple continents, periods that generally see reduced traffic are *off-peak hours*. These are prime time for long-running system-maintenance tasks or reporting operations that require considerable system resources. Performing these tasks during off-peak hours not only eases the impact on end users, but also takes less time than it would during a workday (that's because the system isn't under end-user load).

✦ **Bottleneck:** In every application, sooner or later, some component starts to limit overall throughput. If a network can only carry so much traffic before its limited bandwidth can't handle the demand, what you get is a traffic jam of information — a *bottleneck*. The usual cause of a bottleneck is not enough CPU processing power or disk I/O throughput to meet the demands of SQL Server. Those components will reach their limits long before the network becomes an issue. Of course, what's "typical" changes as times and technology change. With SharePoint 2010's improved scale-out architecture, don't assume that the CPU will lag before that madly growing network of yours starts getting too big for its britches.

Software Architecture Building Blocks

Before we dive into the performance characteristics and sizing formulas, is important to understand both the SharePoint services as well as the underlying platform dependencies which the application relies on to function. Modern software architectures are complex series of components and interlinked services, which all add up to the overarching performance of the deployed solution.

Main Platform Components

SharePoint 2010 builds on the shoulders of giants — namely Microsoft Windows, Internet Information Services (IIS), and SQL Server — products that SharePoint uses as primary architectural components. This design has four main goals:

✦ Deliver a three-tiered application infrastructure (see Book 2, Chapter 1 for more about tiers).

✦ Use *stateless* front-end Web servers to render content to end users.

✦ Execute CPU-intensive operations (such as search queries and indexing) on middle-tier application servers.

✦ Store the actual data in a relational database.

Here's a list of the most important components that affect SharePoint 2010 deployments — with a look at each one's role and impact:

✦ **Microsoft Windows Server 2008/R2 x64:** SharePoint 2010 fully supports Windows Server 2008 and R2. Both are used throughout the farm to provide the underlying platform (through Windows services) and scheduled tasks for SharePoint service applications. Although SharePoint supports multiple authentication providers and user directories, the underlying SharePoint farm requires a domain infrastructure; all communications between service applications must be authenticated against the domain. If you're running multiple servers and you don't have a Windows domain already deployed in your organization (or if you're deploying a completely isolated server farm connected to an extranet — or to the Internet) you still have to join the servers to a domain.

✦ **Microsoft Internet Information Services (IIS):** IIS provides the communications framework for SharePoint Web Applications and Web services. You can use both IIS 6.0 (Windows Server 2008) and IIS 7 (Windows

Server 2008 R2), though SharePoint eases the administrative burden by provisioning all SharePoint Web sites and Virtual Directories from Central Administration.

One exception to this rule is Alternative Access Mappings (AAM), which enable you to map multiple URLs to a single Web Application — for example, vanity URLs (discussed in Book II, Chapter 4). Although you can configure AAMs from Central Administration, you must configure Bindings separately, from IIS Manager.

✦ **Microsoft SQL Server 2005/2008/2008 R2 x64:** Both SQL Server 2005 and 2008 are fussy about the patch levels they'll accept:

- SQL Server 2005 requires the SP3 Cumulative Update 3 (CU3).

- SQL Server 2008 requires the SP1 CU2 or later.

Both SQL Server versions are fully supported as long as they're deployed on x64 server infrastructure.

Okay, *technically* you could deploy those SQL Sever versions on x86 SQL infrastructure . . . but don't. No, seriously, don't even attempt it. Microsoft doesn't support that kind of deployment, and has very good reasons for that reluctance (they'd fill another book).

A bit of good news, as of this writing: No need for further patches if you're deploying Microsoft SQL Server 2008 R2; it was released after SharePoint 2010 and is already up to date.

✦ **Microsoft SQL Server Reporting Services 2008 R2 x64:** If you're planning to use the SQL Server Reporting Services integration — or, for that matter, Access Services — in your SharePoint 2010 environment, keep in mind that SQL Server 2008 Reporting Services R2 needs a higher-level patch (as mentioned earlier). This is especially important if you plan to upgrade an environment that has SQL Server 2008 Reporting Services integration components installed for Microsoft Office SharePoint Server 2007. (Just trust us on that one, okay?)

SharePoint Platform Components

Although it's wise to get familiar with the core platform components, the SharePoint application components are just as important to include in your performance and capacity planning.

To safeguard your system's performance, pay close attention to these aspects of SharePoint:

✦ **SharePoint Foundation Service:** This is the main service-providing site; it's where you find list and library functionality for collaboration and publishing services. If you're planning a highly available deployment, make sure you distribute this component on two or more servers.

✦ **Central Administration Web Site:** Sure, Central Administration requires minimal system resources to operate, but consider deploying this component on multiple servers anyway — to provide redundant access to the administration interface. (Good insurance in case a component on one server goes haywire.)

✦ **Logging Service:** The logging service collects data on usage and system health from all the servers in your farm and stores its findings in a central usage-logging database. From a performance perspective, this service puts considerable disk I/O load on the SQL Servers. If you're running a very large topology that has a lot of disk I/O load on its content database, consider moving the logging databases to a dedicated SQL Server platform.

✦ **SharePoint Search Query:** The search application has two distinct roles: Query and Indexing.

In large organizations where you expect users to do a lot of search queries, consider scaling out the Query roles to dedicated servers in your infrastructure.

✦ **SharePoint Search Indexing:** The indexing component of the SharePoint Search application is typically the first target for moving to dedicated servers. That's because it needs a lot of disk, network, and CPU resources when indexing and crawling content.

✦ **Office Web Applications (Word Viewing, PowerPoint, Excel Calculation):** If you plan to deploy Office Web Applications on your infrastructure, you've installed these services on your farm. By default, all office files open in the Office Web Applications — and that feature can put considerable load on the environment in large-scale deployments. Therefore consider moving those Web Apps to the application tier — and enabling them on multiple servers for high availability and a lower hassle-factor.

✦ **PowerPivot for SharePoint:** If you're planning to deploy Microsoft SQL Server 2008 R2 as the database engine, you can enable PowerPivot so it displays a PowerPivot-enabled Excel worksheet directly from the browser. But that convenience has a price . . .

This service can put considerable load on your environment, so be sure to estimate and allocate sufficient system resources to the service application.

✦ **Visio Service Application:** New Visio data-connected diagrams offer powerful functionality to the end users and can be used to create line-of-business applications with visualization.

In larger deployments, if you want to provide high availability and ensure that the service is deployed on multiple servers, move this service application to the servers in the middle application tier.

✦ **Access Services:** Access Services requires Microsoft SQL Server 2008 R2 Reporting Services server to be deployed in your infrastructure. If you have that arrangement, you can use R2 to import, store, and run Access database applications on the SharePoint infrastructure. If you're planning to move important legacy Access databases to the SharePoint infrastructure, be sure to enable the service application on multiple middle-tier application servers.

✦ **User Profile Service Application:** User profiles utilize three databases for synchronization, profile storage, and social data (such as comments and tagging). In large deployments, all this activity adds to the load, so you need higher disk I/O and performance requirements in your SQL Server infrastructure.

✦ **Managed Metadata Service Application:** The Managed Metadata Service has only a minimal effect on system performance. It can coexist comfortably on any server in your farm's topology.

✦ **Web Analytics Service Application:** The Web Analytics service aggregates and stores usage statistics from all the servers in your farm. Busy and large-scale . . . yep, this service can put considerable load on your SQL server in a large deployment.

✦ **Business Connectivity Service Application:** In busy environments, using Business Connectivity Services adds to both CPU and memory requirements on the server. To provide adequate system resources for the service, consider deploying it to middle-tier application servers.

✦ **InfoPath Forms Service Application:** Rendering InfoPath Forms is a relatively inexpensive operation; you can co-locate it with other service applications on your physical farm topology.

✦ **Word Automation Service Application:** Automation services can convert Microsoft Word files to other formats such as PDF — a useful but (you guessed it) resource-intensive activity.

If visions of a heavily used Automation Service haunt your planning, scale out this service application across multiple application-tier servers. The goal here is to preserve performance and high availability.

✦ **PerformancePoint Service Application:** If you plan to use PerformancePoint Services for business intelligence, consider scaling out the service to the application tier in your farm. While you're at it, be sure to allocate extra memory on the server for the service application.

✦ **Timer Service:** Almost every scheduled task in SharePoint 2010 runs in the Timer Service. Although existing farm servers can handle the standard timer jobs, some organizations need to develop custom timers as service applications. If that's your plan, carefully consider the impact and isolation requirements for this service application.

✦ **Sandboxed Solutions:** The service enables you to isolate custom code components so they run in a restricted environment where you can control execution with defined thresholds and automated quotas. You can scale out the sandboxed solutions so they run on multiple servers — a useful approach if you plan to add resource-intensive custom applications to the sandboxed code when it executes in the real environment.

Performance and Capacity Management

In traditional client-server applications, such as Microsoft Exchange, emphasis for server sizing is on the number of users and type of clients they are using. Typically, the types of actions users can perform are limited; thus the performance impact of each user can be precisely estimated. Often the resource cost of maintaining every client connection throughout the session is the limiting factor. You see that cost expressed as memory usage per connection. A high-availability Exchange deployment has well-defined numbers of users that a specific hardware configuration can support.

Because users' primary access to SharePoint is through a Web browser, they make fewer constant connections to the SharePoint server. New features take advantage of those off-again-on-again connections — in particular, new protocols and new ways to integrate with SharePoint 2010 from client applications (such as SharePoint Workspace and the new Outlook 2010 Social Connector). The client applications constantly poll the server for updates while they're running, regardless of whether the user is actually interested in the information at the time. Of course, while that's going on, the applications generate a consistent load on the SharePoint servers — even though that load is less than what Web-browser access imposes. Of course, as with Outlook 2010 and Exchange 2010, Office 2010 client applications defer to the SharePoint 2010 server health information returned during the data polls — they'll back off if the server is under stress.

The Web browser's intermittent (asynchronous) connection with SharePoint — in conjunction with the wide array of functionality that comes with SharePoint 2010 — can make capacity planning a challenge (headache) to say the least. That's because the performance impact of each request varies, depending on the type of action performed. Each type of action has a different resource cost; to devise an accurate, overall picture of resource requirements, you'd have to predict just how the environment will be used — which is almost a black art in itself.

When you're planning performance and capacity management, pay special attention to understanding the types of actions your users are likeliest to perform — and the ways they'll utilize the service applications.

Essentially, performance and capacity management for SharePoint 2010 goes through four distinct phases (illustrated in Figure 5-2).

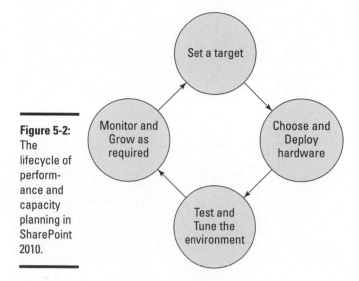

Figure 5-2:
The
lifecycle of
perform-
ance and
capacity
planning in
SharePoint
2010.

Although managing performance and capacity is similar to riding herd on other enterprise applications, it's good to familiarize yourself with some SharePoint-specific concepts. The evaluation cycle of capacity and performance management is constant; these pointers should help:

✦ **Set performance and capacity target for your environment.** Even though it's now easy to add to your system's physical architecture as your demand grows, you have to start somewhere — and the starting place may as well be based on educated guesses (it beats a blind shot in the dark). Try to estimate the expected load on your environment prior to going live. When you do go live, monitor the usage so your system can grow with the demand. This is especially important if you don't have a deep pool of resources to draw from but still have to meet increased demand *tout de suite* — because the lead time for getting hold of new hardware (and subsequently deploying it to a data center) is often a matter of weeks rather than hours.

✦ **Choose hardware to support the number of users on your logical architecture.** When you have a performance and capacity target, you can estimate the size of the physical hardware required to meet those targets — keeping in mind the logical architecture design that has to withstand the user load. This exercise boils down to ballpark numbers — in particular, required CPU cycles, disk I/O operations per second (IOPS), and memory requirements — your hardware must meet for the initial deployment.

✦ **Test and tune your environment to meet the initial targets.** When the hardware is deployed, SharePoint installed, and the service applications configured to the (doubtless brilliant) design of the logical architecture, try running load tests on the environment *before* you unleash the end users to start using it in production mode.

SharePoint 2010 has several levels of caching — which you can configure and optimize to fit your deployment, with an eye toward increasing performance. It's one way to meet the initial performance targets for your SharePoint environment. For more information of optimizing the caching settings for your deployment, we recommend reading the most up-to-date guidance on Microsoft TechNet.

✦ **Monitor and grow your environment to meet demand.** SharePoint differs from other enterprise applications (such as Exchange) in how you extend it to meet increased demand. Unlike Exchange — in which you may need to move mailboxes manually to other servers to free up resources — SharePoint offers a sort of dynamic scale-out: You can scale out SharePoint to multiple servers without the end users even noticing that the underlying farm has changed. Even if you start with a single-server SharePoint environment, you can add more servers to the farm while the users are still accessing the first deployed server. When the new server roles and services are configured, the application simply takes advantage of the increased processing power — and load-balances incoming requests to the new servers ("Here you go, guys — you deal with 'em!").

Although SharePoint manages its own service applications, be sure you configure your chosen front-end Web server's load balancing to include those new front-end Web servers you've put in the available server pool.

Overview of Performance Requirements

If SharePoint 2010 is your first deployment of SharePoint, trying to estimate its initial usage in your organization — accurately, anyway — can be, um, an *exciting challenge*. (In other words, brace yourself.)

Actually it's not that bad. Your estimates can be educated guesswork based on your understanding of two factors:

✦ The users (in particular, their work patterns).

✦ The content and applications you're going to make available to the users.

Fortunately, you may have some surprising resources you can draw upon when you make your estimates:

✦ **Other Web sites and collaboration applications:** Your estimates improve quite a bit if your users have had experience with Web or collaboration environments before, and you happen to have access to them (say, static Web sites or third-party collaboration systems such as eRoom). For example, by analyzing the usage logs of an existing HR static Web site that you're planning to migrate to SharePoint 2010, you can estimate more accurately the number of requests during a day, as well as the hourly usage patterns and peaks.

✦ **Existing usage figures:** If you have access to your existing SharePoint deployment's usage statistics — even if those belong to particular business units or workgroups — you can mine them for SharePoint-specific usage patterns. For example, you can find how many search queries users executed and how many operations they performed during a typical browsing session.

Even in a best-case scenario, estimating SharePoint usage is largely educated guesswork. That's because the functionality and the available features change significantly from version to version. For example, the new Outlook 2010 Social Connector adds a new constant-access client that generates load on your SharePoint environment while users are simply working on their e-mail clients.

Estimating requirements boils down to getting a handle on some basic factors that add load to your environment — which gives you a glimpse of the trends that go with that load:

✦ **Expected active users per day:** End users are the folks who access SharePoint day in and day out over asynchronous HTTP protocol, a pure estimate of users per day can give you a generic access profile that helps you to determine the network and server hardware requirements for your deployment. Although the total number of users in your environment doesn't matter from a performance perspective, the number of estimated *active* users during a day does — because these users will perform a certain average number of operations.

✦ **Peak hours and spike trends:** Unless your user base is distributed all over the planet, or works in 24-hour shifts (let's not even go there), it's a pretty sure bet that you have a quantifiable peak period of access to the SharePoint infrastructure. With those peaks come *spike trends* — short periods of significantly increased user load on the environment. A good example is the typical 9:00 a.m. start of the workday: Generally users are more likely to be accessing the system at the same time, which adds up to a temporary spike of usage. Although (nowadays, anyway) these spikes are often evened out by flexible working hours and multiple time zones, you'd be wise to consider them a fact of working life: Try to identify any previous or estimated trends of usage that put an unusually high load on the environment.

✦ **Features and functionality available:** Perhaps the most difficult estimate of all is the "how" part of this simple question: "Exactly *how* are users going to use the infrastructure?" If you don't have an existing MOSS 2007 infrastructure to analyze usage patterns for specific service applications (and lack clairvoyance), this estimate is tough to do. Sometimes the best you can do is list the features and functionality you plan to make available, put the list on a questionnaire, send it to a number of end-users, and poll them on how much they expect to use what you're offering. You know — *ask*.

✦ **Client applications used to access the environment:** With the added client-side protocols and Office 2010's integration features, client access in SharePoint 2010 has significantly changed from that of past versions (where Web browsers were the primary client application used to access SharePoint). Client applications laden with features can generate a significant load on the infrastructure.

If you're planning to deploy Office 2010 (or, for that matter, just Outlook 2010), keep in mind that you have a couple of load-generating culprits to ride herd on:

- The Outlook 2010 Social Connector constantly retrieves activity feeds from SharePoint.

- The Office 2010 Upload Center saves and synchronizes files in the background (as discussed in Book I, Chapter 6).

In addition, you can use SharePoint Workspace (part of Office 2010 Professional) to take complete sites offline.

Estimating Requests per Second

After you've gathered enough information to get a good handle on your expected usage profile, you can use it to estimate and calculate the performance requirements that can help guide your selection of physical hardware.

Unless you're upgrading from an existing MOSS2007 infrastructure, you may have a tough time estimating the RPS requirements for your new SharePoint 2010 infrastructure. To come up with a rough estimate for expected load generated on the SharePoint environment (with little or no input from existing collaboration or Web-publishing sites in your organization), you can use the old operations-per-second (ops/sec) formula from MOSS 2007. Then you could convert the resulting ops/sec figure to the newfangled Microsoft RPS measurement with a masterful math trick: Multiply it by 4. Here's why: RPS is actually a measurement of throughput in .NET requests per second; testing has shown that each user request takes about a quarter of a second, which gives you an average of four .NET requests per second.

The old formula used to estimate user operations per second was:

number of users	X	percent of active users per day	X	number of actions per active user	X	spike factor
360,000			X	number of peak hours per day		

Here's where the 360,000 figure comes from: 100 (for percent conversion) times 60 (number of minutes in an hour) times 60 (number of seconds in a minute). The idea was to distill the number of operations per second for estimated active users. A *spike factor* was thrown in to provide some leeway so the system could meet occasional spikes without affecting the end users' perceived performance levels (you don't want too much apparent latency creeping in).

As mentioned before, the result represents the number of average user operations per second, which you can multiply by 4 to get the RPS figure.

For example, if we take a medium-scale enterprise of 5,000 users who are very active in team collaboration *and* on the enterprise portal — say, in a single time zone, operating from 9:00 a.m. to 5:00 p.m., with the browser homepage set to the corporate portal homepage (hey, sometimes normal is beautiful) — the following formula could provide a very rough estimate for RPS requirements:

$$\frac{5000 \quad X \quad 80 \quad X \quad 30 \quad X \quad 4}{360,000 \quad X \quad 8} = 16.66 \times 4 = 67 \text{ RPS}$$

Estimating SQL Server Requirements

Because all SharePoint content and service-application data is stored and accessed from the SQL infrastructure, you have to keep the SQL part of your system from becoming a performance bottleneck. That means coming up with a good working estimate of disk capacity and performance. Although the ins and outs of Microsoft SQL Server sizing could almost fill a whole other book, certain SharePoint 2010-specific metrics and characteristics can help you size and plan your SQL platform requirements.

As you plan your SharePoint implementation, keep in mind these three major aspects of sizing SQL:

+ **Disk I/O operation requirements (IOPS):** These days you have a multitude of available storage architectures to choose from. Regardless of which one you choose, you have to take into account the required IOPS rate. That's especially true if you're planning to utilize a shared storage architecture such as Storage Area Network (SAN) or Network Attached Storage (NAS).

Directly Attached Storage (DAS) is still often utilized for SQL Servers because it has dedicated I/O bandwidth and can deliver high IOPS rates reliably. But increasingly this approach is giving way to shared storage solutions that can be extremely cost-effective. Even so, the first question most shared-storage administrators will ask you is the required IOPS throughput requirement — even before they ask how much storage you need. No mystery here: Although storage space is easy to increase, disk I/O throughput is often limited — and much harder to increase in shared storage, especially if other I/O-intensive applications such as Exchange are vying for resources on the same platform.

At the time of this writing, Microsoft is still working on effective IOPS-estimation formulas based on real-world data and ongoing performance testing. Visit the Microsoft TechNet topic on the SQL Server planning section for SharePoint 2010 for up-to-date information on disk subsystem IOPS planning.

✦ **Disk storage requirements:** In an era of plentiful low-cost storage, often you can meet your disk storage requirements simply by carving the space you need out of the shared storage infrastructure. But hold on there. Estimating your disk storage needs before you start slicing and dicing is still important — and it's just as vital to monitor those disks carefully as they start to fill up.

If your SQL Server environment runs out of storage for your log files or your databases, SharePoint will become unavailable to all end users of the environment. Unhappy users become the next headache pretty quickly.

By default, SharePoint 2010 stores the file objects *and* their associated metadata in the same content database. Here's a formula to help you ensure that your storage calculation takes both the file and its metadata into account:

```
File storage requirements + metadata storage requirements = required
    storage space
```

To estimate the approximate size of SharePoint content databases, we recommend utilizing the following formula for deriving the file and metadata storage requirements:

```
File storage requirements = (Number of documents × number of versions) *
    average size of documents
```

```
File metadata storage requirements = 10 KB × (Number of list items +
    (number of versions × number of documents))
```

The reason metadata storage is isolated into a separate formula goes back to SharePoint 2010's support for remote BLOB storage of file content. If you only size the content database, you end up storing only the file metadata. (For more about BLOBs, see Book 2, Chapter 1.)

✦ **System performance requirements:** Industry performance testing has shown that you need to have roughly five SharePoint processors for every SQL Server processor you deploy. This effectively means a single SQL Server CPU won't become a bottleneck until you've maxed out five SharePoint front-end Web server cores. That's a load of processing, no argument there. Although this scenario may seem unlikely in most deployments, imagine you have a very large infrastructure that utilizes multiple SharePoint front-end Web servers in a scaled-out farm. Got the picture? Okay, divide the total CPU cores available on the SharePoint front-end tier by five. There's your estimate of how many SQL server CPU cores you'll need.

Proactive Planning

Arguably the most important part of the ongoing juggling act that balances capacity and performance is all that (equally ongoing) monitoring and adjustment you have to do in response to how your end users actually utilize the platform. Keep in mind that you can scale out SharePoint 2010 without any impact on system availability or user-perceived performance. That means you can add to your physical server infrastructure to keep pace with usage — as long as you carefully monitor usage and plan upgrades proactively, keeping an eye on your organization's needed lead time for new hardware.

Naturally, in virtualized environments, you can meet the increased requirements quickly by carving more capacity from the virtualization pool. With Microsoft SQL Server 2008 R2, you can even increase CPU capacity and memory allocation dynamically — without having to bring down the environment (which can be a real drag).

Although virtualization and utility-based computing represent an increasing trend in the industry, as of this writing Microsoft hasn't settled on a final virtualization and utility-based computing model for SharePoint 2010. But keep an eye on both Microsoft and on hardware providers as the technology matures. Monitor these particular performance counters to help identify trends:

✦ **Processor — % Processor Time:** Don't exceed an 80-percent level of constant CPU utilization on any server in your SharePoint farm. Industry testing has shown that throughput starts decreasing beyond this level of system load.

✦ **Disk — Average Disk Queue Length:** If the disk queue is gradually getting longer, your infrastructure may be suffering from reduced disk I/O throughput. If so, then increasing disk IOPS throughput (say, by adding disks or upgrading to faster disks in your storage architecture) may solve the problem.

✦ **Disk — % Free Space:** When your disks start filling up and the amount of free space dips to about 30 percent, either increase the disk capacity or clean up old data from your SharePoint environment.

✦ **Memory — utilization in terms of pages/sec:** You should increase your system memory if the pages/sec counter reaches 10.

✦ **Memory — available megabytes of space:** Available memory is still useful to monitor, even though most modern server applications simply grab all available memory for caching purposes.

Add this counter to your front-end Web servers and SharePoint application servers to identify possible memory leaks. Leave it out for your SQL Servers.

✦ **Paging File — % Used and % Used Peak:** The server paging file (also known as the *swap file*), holds virtual memory on disk. Page faults occur when a process has to stop and wait while the required virtual resources are retrieved from disk into memory — a process that's significantly slower than accessing those resources directly from memory.

If the paging file is in constant use, add more system memory to avoid paging to disk.

✦ **ASP.NET — Requests Queued:** The ASP.NET framework queues requests automatically for the SharePoint application servers to process.

If this queue exceeds 700 requests queued consistently, consider adding more SharePoint front-end Web servers or application servers to distribute the load and respond to user requests in a timely manner.

✦ **ASP.NET — Requests Wait Time:** This important ASP.NET counters indicates the amount of time the server has to wait for requests to be processed.

If the number showing on this counter is consistently high, consider adding more SharePoint front-end Web servers or application servers to scale out the environment.

✦ **ASP.NET — Requests Rejected:** If the number on this counter is consistently above 0, then your system is either under a significant load or you have some other important issues to troubleshoot.

Designing Server Topologies

After you've estimated your capacity and performance requirements, the last step in the process is to select the hardware topology and the physical server architecture that can meet the needs of your planned deployment. Planning the physical arrangement of your servers means working out a three-tier architecture for SharePoint 2010:

+ **SharePoint front-end Web servers** respond to end-user requests and render SharePoint Web Part pages.

+ **SharePoint Application Servers** process service-application loads, such as search query and indexing.

+ **SQL Database Server back-end servers** store and retrieve all content and configuration data.

Even though you can (technically) install all three of these roles on a single physical server, as a rule you shouldn't. (Hint: If you carry all your eggs in one basket, Murphy's Law will put an unseen banana peel on the floor.) For production environments, separate the SharePoint and SQL Database components and put them on different servers. When the times comes to scale out the environment, you'll be able to do it effortlessly (as illustrated in Figure 5-3) — or at least with vastly reduced hassle.

**Book II
Chapter 5**

**Planning for
Performance and
Scalability**

Figure 5-3:
Single-
server
SharePoint
2010
topology.

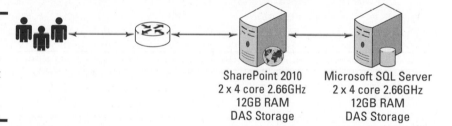

SharePoint 2010
2 x 4 core 2.66GHz
12GB RAM
DAS Storage

Microsoft SQL Server
2 x 4 core 2.66GHz
12GB RAM
DAS Storage

In Figure 5-3, all SharePoint 2010 application roles are consolidated to the single server; a separate SQL back-end database server stores all the data. This topology allows you to scale up easily to 200 RPS (at least that's the result of industry performance testing that used high-end server platforms with 8 cores and directly attached storage). Now, modern servers can easily be scaled up to run at least 16 CPU cores — so you probably have enough capacity to scale *up* rather than *out* — that is, increase total throughput without having to add more servers to the topology. Bottom line: Most small to medium-size organizations looking to increase performance haven't much reason to scale out — which simplifies the planning of hardware architecture pretty quickly. If that's your situation, you can move on and consider high availability as the main factor in your physical server topology.

Designing for high availability

As requirements go, *high availability* (in essence, being available 24/7 with minimum downtime — like that exec with the corner office and the thousand-yard stare) is essential to the physical architecture of a SharePoint system. SharePoint 2010 is no exception; throughput for single-server architectures on modern server platforms can easily surpass 200 RPS. Small deployments (10–50 users) that host critical data and line-of-business applications present even more of a demand for a highly available architecture.

In the context of SharePoint, high availability boils down to two essential components:

✦ **SharePoint Farm:** Multiple servers can be the basis of a SharePoint server farm, where all components are distributed on two or more servers. The resulting infrastructure offers no single point of failure.

✦ **High-availability SQL Server:** This server must support both SQL Clustering and SQL Mirroring. Result: high availability with automatic failover to a secondary server that will resume operations in case the primary server has gone down..

SharePoint 2010 High-availability topologies

In SharePoint 2010, you can scale out all the service-application roles to meet your requirements for high availability *and* performance. You're free to design and deploy your architecture to meet your specific needs. Keep in mind two common scenarios that can serve as starting points for your plan; they're illustrated in the next two figures.

In Figure 5-4 — a basic high-availability physical topology — the SharePoint 2010 application servers run all the configured service applications as well as the front-end Web server. The SQL Servers may utilize either SQL Mirroring or Clustering so the back-end database server has no single point of failure. This scenario offers a simple topology, no single point of failure, and excellent performance — and you can scale it out easily to provide more capacity or resilience.

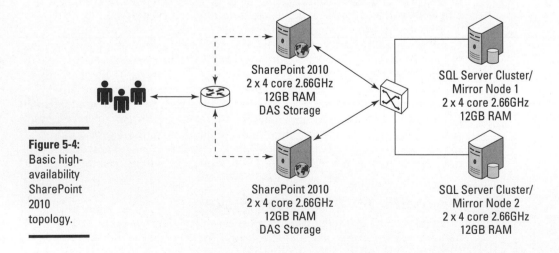

Figure 5-4: Basic high-availability SharePoint 2010 topology.

SharePoint 2010
2 x 4 core 2.66GHz
12GB RAM
DAS Storage

SharePoint 2010
2 x 4 core 2.66GHz
12GB RAM
DAS Storage

SQL Server Cluster/
Mirror Node 1
2 x 4 core 2.66GHz
12GB RAM

SQL Server Cluster/
Mirror Node 2
2 x 4 core 2.66GHz
12GB RAM

Figure 5-5 shows a medium-high-availability SharePoint 2010 farm topology. Here the front-end Web server and service-application components have been scaled out to provide added capacity and resilience for service applications such as search and user profiles. Though this comprehensive three-tier server topology is more complex, it offers (this will sound familiar) no single point of failure, excellent performance, and the option of being scaled out easily to provide more capacity or resilience. Yep, there's a pattern here — doing what works — and this topology is the most common high-availability deployment we've encountered in the field.

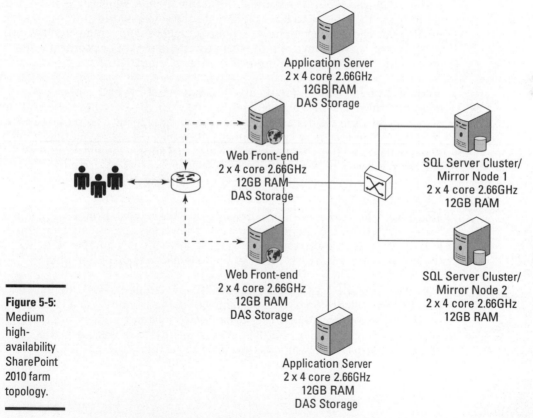

Figure 5-5:
Medium high-availability SharePoint 2010 farm topology.

Microsoft SQL Server high-availability options

If you want automatic failover with standard SharePoint 2010 support for Microsoft SQL Server, you have two options: SQL Server Cluster and SQL Server Mirroring. Here's a closer look . . .

SQL Server Cluster

Clustering technology has been around for a long time and matured considerably along with Microsoft Windows. Microsoft SQL Server 2005, 2008, and 2008 R2 all support clustering technology; it's the most common enterprise choice for highly available SQL configurations. No wonder. It's a mature technology with management techniques that are well established and familiar.

The only downside to SQL Clustering is its reliance on hardware-based shared storage. Clustering works on the principle that you have to put the underlying disks wherever you put the application — which in turn requires all nodes in the cluster to be connected to the same shared storage array. If this is your chosen design, be sure your SQL servers are connected to DAS, SAN, or NAS shared storage that meets the standards of performance and disk latency that Microsoft supports for SharePoint 2010.

If you want to provide failover capabilities for multiple data centers, you must carefully plan the required hardware topology — getting Microsoft support specialists in on the act with your networking team. The requirements your system has to meet are stringent — but (like eating vegetables) it's for your own good: That way your system remains supportable in stretched SQL cluster scenarios.

SQL Server Mirroring

SharePoint 2010 now fully supports software-based synchronous SQL mirroring, which (unlike clustering) has no hardware requirements to set up and operate. This approach is still in its relative infancy compared to SQL Clustering. Server mirroring isn't exactly simple to manage and operate.

SQL Mirroring still has network bandwidth and latency requirements. That's because every write operation is committed synchronously to all mirror participants. Your system must have a network latency of no more than 1ms and (recommended) 1 GB of network bandwidth available between the mirror participants — which can be hard to achieve if you want to provide failover for all your data centers.

Chapter 6: Touring Central Administration

In This Chapter

✔ Touring the Central Administration Web site

✔ Monitoring your SharePoint system's health

✔ Recovering from disaster and managing software patches

SharePoint 2010 significantly improved and organized the Central Administration site, gave its design a sizable facelift, and included new functionality to give you better insight into the health of your SharePoint deployment. In earlier SharePoint versions, Central Administration used to serve as more of a launching pad to feature-specific administration pages (such as Search). SharePoint 2010 fully integrates the administration panel into all standard SharePoint features and service applications. Result: streamlined administration in a single user interface. It's not only slick, it works better.

In this chapter, we walk through the Central Administration Web site and highlight some of the new enhancements intended to smooth operations and simplify the management of your SharePoint 2010 farm.

Accessing Central Administration

In SharePoint 2010, Central Administration actually bucks tradition. Earlier Microsoft enterprise products have always included Management Consoles to handle administrative chores in such products such as Microsoft Exchange and SQL Server. SharePoint was one of the first Microsoft products to depart from that approach: It introduced a Web-based user interface in SharePoint Team Services 1.0 and followed up by integrating Web-based management into SharePoint Portal Server 2003.

Of course, this relatively newfangled Web-based approach has both benefits and drawbacks. On the plus side, consider these advantages of a Web-based management interface:

✦ **No need to install extra software to run the management console.** The arrangement is almost too simple: The administrative interface is just a Web site. A Web browser is the only software requirement. No extra bells, whistles, or buggy whips required. (What a concept.)

The latest versions of browsers such as FireFox and Internet Explorer are your best bet because they provide modern JavaScript and HTML support — which makes the user experience more like using familiar client software.

✦ **Remote access to the management console.** As long as you've configured the Central Administration Web site to respond on an IIS port that isn't blocked by a firewall, all workstations in the network have access to Central Administration. (Simpler. Faster. Nice.) You can even publish the Central Administration site for extranet users or remote managers; they can connect by using your preferred extranet access method (such as reverse proxy).

On the downside, a Web-based management interface does have some limitations:

✦ **By default, security is questionable.** That's likely to stay a default condition for as long as the Internet remains something of a wild frontier. Any Web site accessed through a standard Web browser is as vulnerable as other Web Applications unless you beef up security.

If you're dealing with sensitive data — and sooner or later, most organizations have to — consider protecting the communication channel with SSL encryption, which secures the connection by encrypting the traffic between the end user workstation and the web server.

• Encryption is especially important if you plan to utilize authentication providers other than NTLM, which is the widest used Microsoft Windows protocol for authentication against the Active Directory.

• You should encrypt communication if you plan to conduct all network administration remotely.

• You can configure or reset your service-account usernames and passwords on the Central Administration Web site.

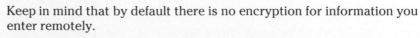

Keep in mind that by default there is no encryption for information you enter remotely.

You can conduct the management tasks related to the service accounts on the server console locally, while performing all other management tasks remotely from your workstation Web browser since the other data is of little interest to potential malicious users eavesdropping on your communication.

✦ **The user experience is still not quite as good as the one offered by a purpose-built user interface.** Web development and browser support are light-years ahead of where they used to be in terms of the usability they provide — but Central Administration is still a Web site designed for publishing content, not for controlling applications with fluid ease. You won't see a quickly expanding management-tree structure responding, almost in real time, to your mouse clicks. Instead, your click starts a more complex process: The server has to render every management page — and your Web browser has to render that page again — before you can see whether you clicked the wrong link by mistake. Getting back to where you once belonged requires another page load, even if you just click the Back button on your browser.

Configuring access and granting permissions

You set up the Central Administration Web site during the farm-configuration process, as shown in Figure 6-1. The first time you run your farm configuration on a server, the `psconfig.exe` utility program prompts you for a database name and an HTTP port for your Central Administration Web site. Moral of the story: Figure out in advance what you want that name and that port to be. Here are some characteristics of Central Administration to keep in mind (along with some practical pointers):

✦ Although the port is dynamically assigned by default, you can overwrite it with your own preference during setup.

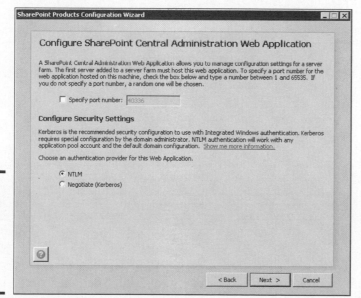

Figure 6-1:
Configuring the port for the Central Administration Web site.

✦ Unless you're deploying only a single server instance, one of your first tasks during deployment should be to create a second instance of Central Administration on another server in your SharePoint farm for high availability.

You never know where and when you might need quick access to Central Administration, so select a HTTP port that's easily memorable, such as 8088 or 911. You can change the port later, through the Central Administration Web site, using `stsadm` and PowerShell.

✦ If you're running multiple Central Administration Web Applications on your server farm, a good practice is to standardize on a single port instead of using the default dynamically assigned port.

✦ By default, only the installation user account and the Central Administration service account are allowed to log on and administer the SharePoint deployment.

SharePoint, like other enterprise applications, doesn't allow either Windows local administrators or domain administrators access to the management site. Therefore you should create a SharePoint or Active Directory group for all operations team members who require access to Central Administration. You can assign them Farm Administrator privileges on the Central Administration home page by choosing Security⇨ Manage the farm administrators group.

Administering SharePoint 2010

After you've created and configured you Central Administration site, you can access it on any of the SharePoint 2010 servers via one of two methods:

✦ Choose Start⇨Program Files⇨SharePoint⇨Central Administration.

or

✦ Enter the server name and port in any Web-browser client connected to the same network.

You're prompted for authentication and cheerfully greeted with a Central Administration Web page (shown in Figure 6-2).

Figure 6-2: SharePoint 2010 Central Administration Web site.

SharePoint 2010 groups similar administrative tasks under seven headings:

✦ **Application Management:** This group brings together the management tools for your Web Applications, site collections, service applications, and databases.

✦ **Monitoring:** This section brings together the new Health Reports, Timer Jobs, and Reporting functionality.

✦ **Security:** Here's where you find user-management options for farm administration, service accounts, distribution groups, and information-management policies.

✦ **General Application Settings:** This group contains farm-level options for External Connections, InfoPath service, SharePoint Designer, Reporting Services integration, and content deployment.

✦ **System Settings:** This section provides links to Server and Service management pages and allows e-mail and mobile phone related service options to be configured.

✦ **Backup and Restore:** This section provides links to farm-backup management pages, as well as the user interface for exporting sites and lists.

✦ **Upgrade and Migration:** This section provides insight into managing software patches in SharePoint 2010, and offers (among other features) the option of doing separate upgrades for your binaries and your content database.

**Book II
Chapter 6**

**Touring Central
Administration**

Managing SharePoint Applications

The Application Management section shown in Figure 6-3 contains four subsections to further divide the tasks associated with application management in SharePoint 2010:

✦ **Web Applications:** Use this subsection to create, extend, and delete Web Applications in addition to managing Web Application-specific Policies and settings such as self-site creation and blocked file types.

✦ **Site Collections:** Use this subsection to create, delete, and manage site collection-specific settings such as quota templates and site administrators.

✦ **Service Applications:** Use this subsection to create, delete, and manage service application instances such as search and user profiles on your farm. Some of the service applications have their individual administrative sections you can access through here.

✦ **Databases:** Use this subsection to add and manage content databases for your Web Applications and modify data-connection settings.

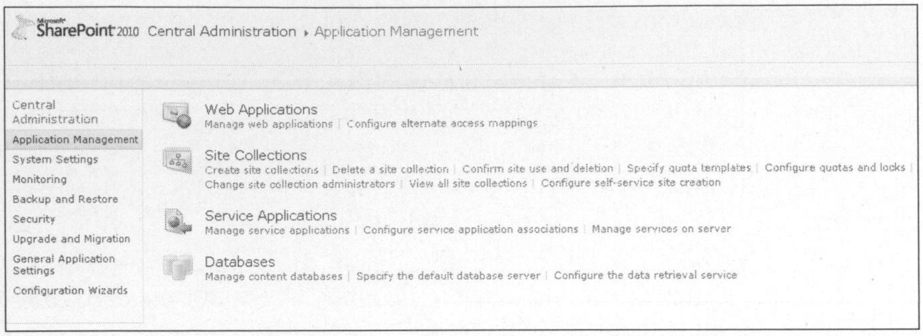

Figure 6-3:
Manage
Web
Applications
from here.

We cover the management of Web Applications and site collections in Book I, Chapter 3; see Book II, Chapter 7 for more about managing service applications.

Monitoring SharePoint 2010

The Monitoring section (shown in Figure 6-4) covers new services which are part of SharePoint 2010's new analytics capability geared for site administrators. This section provides you access to the following subsections:

✦ **Health Analyzer:** Use this subsection for access to the new health reports and associated rule definitions — which you can customize to suit your environment and needs.

✦ **Timer Jobs:** Use this subsection to review scheduled jobs that are about to start, check the status of currently running jobs, and look at the details of recently completed jobs.

✦ **Reporting:** Use this subsection to review and report on policies (administrative, diagnostic, and information management), on the health of your SharePoint system, and on Web-site usage.

Figure 6-4:
Monitoring
SharePoint.

Health Analyzer

SharePoint 2010 Health Analyzer (shown in Figure 6-5) provides you with the proactive monitoring capabilities built into SharePoint so you can easily identify and review problems — and decide how best to tackle them.

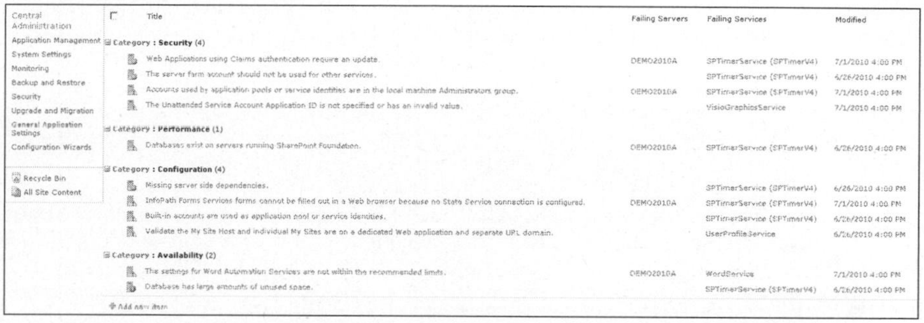

Figure 6-5: SharePoint 2010 Health Analyzer.

The Health Analyzer sorts problems into four categories: Security, Performance, Configuration, and Availability. In each category, you can find some vital troubleshooting information:

✦ Critical, Warning, or Information warning symbols indicate how serious each currently detected problem is. *Critical* means your system is already in trouble; *Warning* means trouble is on the way, though often you can still intervene; *Information* means you'd be wise to pay attention to a particular issue before it starts growing fangs.

✦ The Analyzer identifies both the server and service instance where the detected problem is occurring.

✦ You can click each identified problem to bring up more information — specifically about how to solve the problem, as shown in Figure 6-6.

The problem illustrated in Figure 6-6 shows an Information-level issue that two databases (content and Web Analytics) have space available to reclaim if you use a DBCC `ShrinkDatabase` command in SQL Server Management. No big problem yet, but you don't want to let those databases fill up with unused space. At this point, you have some options:

✦ You can edit the problem if you want to include further information on the identified issue.

✦ If you've enabled the SMS Transport Web service in the Central Administration System Settings page, you can choose to be alerted (via e-mail or SMS text message) if the issue ever occurs again.

✦ If the system can resolve the issue for you, you can give the go-ahead to fix the problem with the recommended solution.

Review problems and solutions – Database has large amounts of unused spa... □ ×

View

Edit Item · Version History · Manage Permissions · Delete Item · Alert Me · Reanalyze Now · Repair Automatically

Manage · Actions · Health

Title	Database has large amounts of unused space.
Severity	3 - Information
Category	Availability
Explanation	Following databases have large amounts of space allocated on the disk but not in use. This may be due to recent deletion of data form the database, or because the database has been pre-grown to a larger size. This database will take up a larger amount of space on the file system unless it is shrunk down to a smaller size. WSS_Content_e58f8446cde041318a305696f040d32a on demo2010a, WebAnalyticsServiceApplication_ReportingDB_e0ab6211-8b16-4b9f-9e19-a0cd4c6aefc1 on demo2010a
Remedy	The database can be shrunk in size using the DBCC ShrinkDatabase command or the Shrink Database wizard in SQL Server Management Studio. For more information about this rule, see "http://go.microsoft.com/fwlink/?LinkID=167144".
Failing Servers	
Failing Services	SPTimerService (SPTimerV4)
Rule Settings	View

Version: 3.0
Created at 4/16/2010 12:11 PM by System Account
Last modified at 6/26/2010 4:00 PM by System Account

[Close]

Figure 6-6:
SharePoint 2010 Health Report Issue Resolution.

Timer Jobs

SharePoint 2010 uses *timer jobs* (small, automatic, timed events that work somewhat like printer jobs) for all task scheduling and execution. Timer jobs can handle a range of tasks from content publishing to feeding User Profile service activity. Timer Job Status allows you to see an overview of scheduled tasks, currently running jobs, and the history of recently completed jobs (as shown in Figure 6-7). In addition, the Timer Job Status page provides links to further details of the job history — and a list of all timer-job definitions — so you know what's going on (because, after all, somebody has to).

Figure 6-7:
Timer Job Status monitoring page.

Timer jobs are a crucial part of a healthy SharePoint 2010 environment, and they're the first place to check to make sure everything is operating normally.

If you find a miserable trail of frequently failing timer jobs in the Job History page, investigate by clicking the failed job definition. What you get is some good starting points for troubleshooting:

✦ Error messages associated with the task.

✦ The server it was run on.

✦ The Web Application it was created for.

Book II
Chapter 6

Touring Central
Administration

Reporting

SharePoint 2010 comes with improved Web analytics. This feature uses information from the usage-logging database to produce reports and spot usage trends in your SharePoint farm. These administrative reports give you insight into

✦ How Search is being utilized in your SharePoint environment.

✦ How well the service application is handling the user load.

For example, the Health Reports shown in Figure 6-8 give you a glimpse of the worst offenders in your farm in terms of page performance. To head off further trouble, you can follow up to find out what may be causing those slow average page-load times. If a page takes a consistently long time to render in response to a high number of SQL database queries, the Web Parts added to the page may be causing excessive load that slows page loading. You can further troubleshoot slow pages by enabling the Developer Dashboard (in on-demand mode) to discover which stored procedures or Web Parts take longest to render and disable them or contact the developers for assistance and updates.

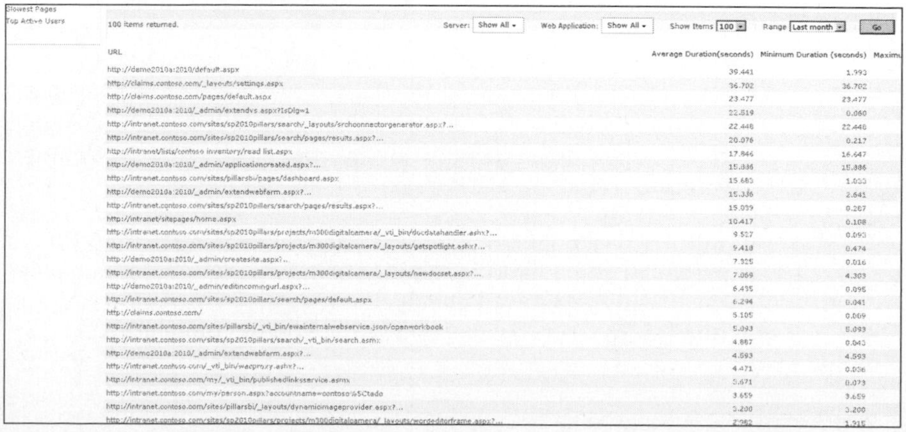

Figure 6-8:
Slowest
Pages
administrative
report.

The Reporting subsection also contains the familiar Web-usage reporting feature, which offers you at-a-glance lists of usage summaries — one for each Web Application hosted on your farm — and a *drill-down* capability if you want to take a look at further details such as usage patterns, frequently visited pages, or downloaded documents.

Reviewing Security

The Security section, shown in Figure 6-9, allows you to manage the service account, user policy, and information policy related settings in a single handy page with the following subsections:

✦ **Users:** Use this subsection to manage the farm administrators group, perform administrative tasks on distribution groups, and provide links to Web Application user policy settings page.

✦ **General Security:** Use this subsection to focus on tasks related to the security of service accounts and Web Applications. Examples include configuring managed and service accounts, password-change settings, and antivirus settings.

✦ **Information policy:** Use this subsection to configure Digital Rights Management (DRM) system integration with Microsoft Windows Digital Rights Management Services. Here you can also configure Information Management Policies at the farm level.

Figure 6-9: Security Management for SharePoint 2010.

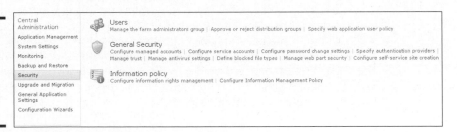

Managing service-account settings

SharePoint 2010 makes service accounts considerably easier to manage by providing a unified Credential Management feature. You activate it from the Central Administration site by choosing Security➪Configure service accounts.

On the Credential Management page (shown in Figure 6-10), you can configure the account used for application pools or services by selecting one of the already-registered managed accounts or by registering a new account for the Web App or service application you're configuring.

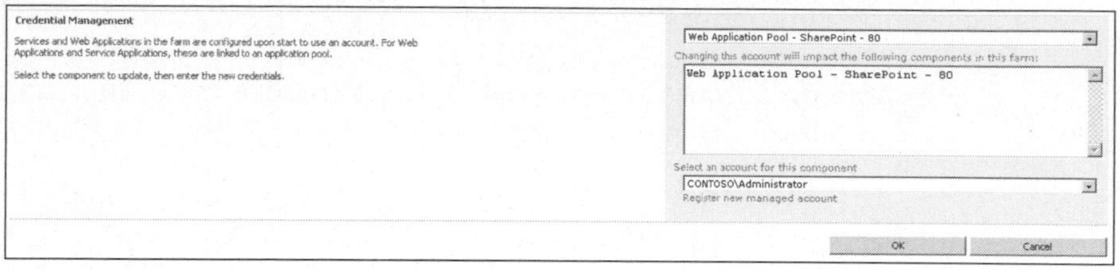

Figure 6-10:
The
SharePoint
2010
Credential
Manage-
ment page.

Book II
Chapter 6

Touring Central
Administration

To simplify the management of service-account passwords, SharePoint 2010 introduces managed service accounts that feature automated password reset and a strong password generator. Most organizations include a password-reset policy for all Active Directory accounts, including the application service accounts. Figure 6-11 shows the page for managing password changes; here you can change the service-account password immediately or schedule a recurring password-reset policy that e-mails the administrator whenever a managed service account's password is reset.

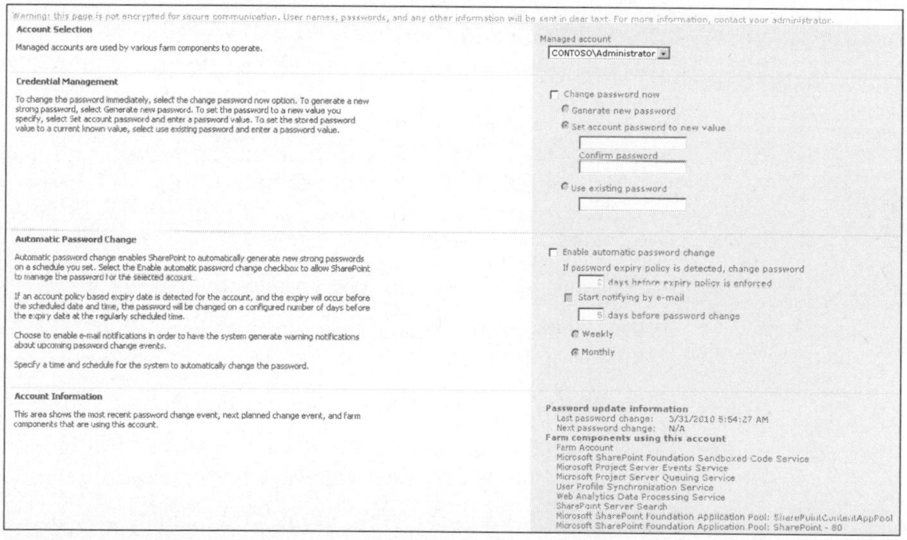

Figure 6-11:
Automated
password
manage-
ment in
SharePoint
2010.

The password-management page shown in Figure 6-11 also reports the last password update and next scheduled change — along with every farm component currently using that service account. SharePoint notifies the user if the page is accessed over unencrypted HTTP protocol (as opposed to SSL-encrypted HTTPS protocol). That's necessary because any user names and passwords entered here may be sent over connections that malicious users can intercept.

Choosing Your General Application Settings

The General Application settings page (shown in Figure 6-12) is where you configure farm-wide settings that don't quite fit under the other categories. The subsections of this page include

✦ **External Service Connections:** In this subsection, you can manage the Send To connections that deliver content to central repositories such as an enterprise document center. The Document Library drop-down menu (which appears when you hover on top of a file in the library) is where you find the actions you can take on this page. One of your options is to manage automated document conversions from office files to other formats (such as PDF).

✦ **InfoPath Form Services:** Use this subsection to configure farm-wide service applications and upload such resources as global form templates and connection files. (We cover InfoPath Form Services — including administrative tasks — in more detail in Book III, Chapter 4.)

✦ **Site Directory:** In this subsection, you configure a central Site Directory that prompts all applications to create an entry in its list whenever new site collections are created.

✦ **SharePoint Designer:** In this subsection, you can completely disable (or only partly allow) the use of SharePoint Designer. Although intended as a business productivity tool, Designer used to inspire some (shall we say) unusual business applications that tended to get users into trouble. (More about that brouhaha in the next subsection of this chapter.) As you might imagine, SharePoint administrators have been looking for SharePoint to offer a feature they could use to rein in Designer at the farm level — and now they have it.

✦ **Search:** In this subsection, you can configure

Farm-wide Search providers (such as FAST Search Server 2010 for SharePoint).

Find links to all the search service application administration pages.

✦ **Reporting Services:** In this subsection, you can configure the integration settings for SharePoint 2010 and SQL Reporting Services 2008 R2.

✦ **Content Deployment:** Here's where you manage and configure Web-content deployment schedules and settings.

Configuring SharePoint Designer (carefully!)

Although SharePoint Designer is an immensely powerful tool in the right hands, it has been the bane of SharePoint Administrators from the very start (when it was still called FrontPage Designer). SharePoint Designer allows power users to design and deploy feature-rich line-of-business applications in almost no time — complete with workflow and Business Data Connectivity links to external data — as well as edit master pages and site layouts to customize the look and feel to their own preferences.

Figure 6-12:
General
Application
settings
page in
SharePoint
2010.

Of course, from a system-management perspective, all this spawning of applications amounted to a migraine in the making. Customized applications tended to crop up willy-nilly, with little or no concern for wider SharePoint operations. Result: It was like trying to run a taxi fleet full of hot rods. Heavily modified sites ran into trouble when SharePoint Service Packs were installed — because IT had no way to test the impact of the upgrade properly (or, for that matter, to notify the site owners to prepare for the upgrade). In addition, users routinely shot themselves in the foot by modifying the Master Page or site template (a *major* no-no) until their sites wouldn't render anymore. Of course, they still sought support from IT, and were (at best) puzzled when IT couldn't revive those modified sites. No surprise that most large organizations chose to block the use of SharePoint Designer completely — or decided they would no longer support any sites touched with Designer, not even if the users paid for the extra aspirin.

With SharePoint 2010 came a set of fine-tuned controls. System administrators can now decide what they'll allow SharePoint Designer to do at the level of individual Web Applications, as shown in Figure 6-13.

Figure 6-13:
Managing
SharePoint
Designer
settings
for Web
Applica-
tions.

Web Application	
Select a web application.	Web Application: **http://finweb.contoso.com/** ⏷
Allow SharePoint Designer to be used in this Web Application	
Specify whether to allow users to edit sites in this Web Application using SharePoint Designer.	☑ Enable SharePoint Designer
Allow Site Collection Administrators to Detach Pages from the Site Template	
Specify whether to allow site administrators to detach pages from the original site definition using SharePoint Designer.	☑ Enable Detaching Pages from the Site Definition
Allow Site Collection Administrators to Customize Master Pages and Layout Pages	
Specify whether to allow site administrators to customize Master Pages and Layout Pages using SharePoint Designer.	☑ Enable Customizing Master Pages and Layout Pages
Allow Site Collection Administrators to see the URL Structure of their Web Site	
Specify whether to allow site administrators to manage the URL structure of their Web site using SharePoint Designer.	☑ Enable Managing of the Web Site URL Structure
	OK · · · · · Cancel

Access to SharePoint Designer can be enabled or disabled by using the following settings:

✦ Enable SharePoint Designer

✦ Enable Detaching Pages from the Site Definition

✦ Enable Customizing Master Pages and Layout Pages

(Hint: It's this kind of editing that often gets users and their hot-rodded sites into trouble.)

✦ Enable Managing of the Web Site URL Structure

If you plan to allow the use of SharePoint Designer for a particular Web Application in your environment, consider disabling the editing of Master Pages.

Investigating System Settings

The System Settings section (illustrated in Figure 6-14) contains farm-wide options for managing servers and services, configuring the SharePoint messaging options, and managing the farm features and sandboxed code.

Wait a minute — why a sandbox on a farm? Relax. It's another one of those metaphors that jazz up IT-speak. *Sandboxing* code means running the custom code in a dedicated process utilizing an unprivileged system account so it is unable to perform harmful actions to the system and should it crash — will not affect the core SharePoint system processes.

Figure 6-14: System settings for SharePoint 2010 farms.

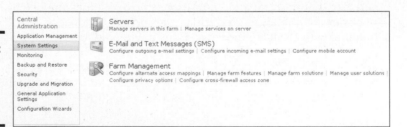

The settings you can manage from the System Settings subsection (try to say *that* three times fast) include these:

✦ **Servers:** Use this subsection to control services on individual servers in the farm and view the farm topology.

✦ **E-mail and Text Messages (SMS):** You configure farm-wide e-mail (both inbound and outbound) in this subsection. You can also enable SMS messaging, but only if you've subscribed to a third-party text-message service (it's not a built-in SharePoint feature).

✦ **Farm Management:** This subsection contains links to all the configuration containers that hold your farm-level settings. In addition, here's where you manage any customized features, solutions, and sandboxed code (user solutions) deployed on your SharePoint system.

Disaster Recovery with Backup and Restore

Most organizations that deployed SharePoint in the past chose to use either the backup-and-restore features of SQL Server or third-party products from vendors such as AvePoint, Quest, and HP. That was largely because MOSS 2007 could only back up or restore the content database from the Central Administration site.

Sure, you could back up and restore individual site collections by using the command-line `stsadm` application, but typically you had to do so case by case, one site collection at a time. Some administrators still tried to automate backup by creating a `stsadm` batch job — even though the tool was unreliable at best (it didn't provide good, detailed error information if an operation failed). Would an attempted backup or restore operation end in downtime and despair? Nobody knew for sure.

SharePoint 2010 offers a new Backup and Restore feature (shown in Figure 6-15) that beefs up Central Administration with some serious recovery functionality, including better support for troubleshooting.

**Book II
Chapter 6**

**Touring Central
Administration**

Figure 6-15:
The
SharePoint
2010 Backup
and Restore
page.

Here are some of the new backup-and-restore powers you can wield:

✦ **Restore from unattached content database:** This option may save your hash someday. It's wise to remember that SharePoint site collections don't go to the Recycle Bin when they're deleted; they simply disappear. Even so, a common problem used to be (and probably will continue to be) accidental deletion of site collections. No matter how many times SharePoint warns end users that they're about to delete a database and all its content, somebody will nuke one by mistake.

To restore a single site collection in MOSS 2007, you had to restore the content database to a whole other environment — and then attach the content database to a Web Application — before you could use `stsadm` to do a backup operation on the deleted site collection. This was extremely time-consuming — which was why most large enterprises that had to be able to recover site collections chose third-party solutions for disaster recovery.

Although SharePoint 2010 makes restoring accidently deleted site collections a little easier, you still need to locate the correct SQL backup file and restore that under a new name (or on a different SQL server) before you can use this feature.

✦ **Export sites and lists:** Export and Import functions previously only available through `stsadm` now move to the Central Administration Web site with the expected scheduling and status in tow. However, from a functional perspective there are still issues you may counter with exported application content, such as workflows which won't work properly after import. If you're purely interested in moving content from sites or lists however, the functionality is a welcomed addition to the out of the box backup and restore suite.

✦ **Backup and restore history:** SharePoint 2010 monitors and logs all backup and restore jobs automatically; the logs contain history information and such operational details as any error messages associated with the job run.

Managing Upgrades

Sooner or later, the time of upgrading your SharePoint system to a new service pack or hotfix arrives. Back in the day, it was an occasion of some dread — because every SharePoint patch used to update the database schema and upgrade the binaries at the same time. *Patch management* — installing, configuring, and tweaking software patches and updates — had to be carefully planned, tested, and executed over weekends to minimize its impact on end users. Very large content databases could take hours to complete, requiring long maintenance windows that typically came around only during weekends.

SharePoint 2010 has a unified management site for Upgrade and Migration (shown in Figure 6-16). You can use it not only to upgrade from SharePoint Standard to Enterprise, but also to manage product and patch installations.

Figure 6-16: SharePoint 2010 Upgrade and Patch Management site.

SharePoint 2010 offers patch management suitable for the entire enterprise, largely because you can install updates in two parts:

✦ Binary upgrade

✦ Database schema update

For this approach to work in a multi-server environment, the upgraded binaries must be *backward-compatible* with the existing database — able to keep working both before and after the database schema update. SharePoint 2010 patch management fulfills this condition — which means you can do a *rolling upgrade* if your servers have to be constantly available: You upgrade the binaries in your front-end Web and application servers one machine at a time, and bring each one back up in a backward-compatible mode until you've upgraded the whole server (including the database schema) to run the latest patch.

**Book II
Chapter 6**

**Touring Central
Administration**

After binaries are upgraded, the system administrators can schedule a suitable time for giving the SharePoint databases a rolling upgrade (one database at a time) to minimize overall system downtime. The Upgrade and Patch Management section of Central Administration includes a handy reporting subsection (shown in Figure 6-17) that can show you current status for both the binary and database upgrades.

Figure 6-17:
SharePoint 2010 Database Upgrade Status report.

Central Administration	SQL Instance	Database	Type	Status
Application Management	demo2010a	Claims_WSS_Content	Content Database	No action required
System Settings	demo2010a	SharePoint_AdminContent_374dd25d-d4f2-4dba-aa80-95a75ee9e788	Content Database	No action required
Monitoring	demo2010a	WSS_Content_03e4c46c479a4e069b60145b1a985769	Content Database	No action required
Backup and Restore	demo2010a	WSS_Content_6b8e9ad10bde4099f3b0fbfbb6ef95	Content Database	No action required
Security	demo2010a	WSS_Content_o4ed960e12a4e94969b0dff161c5928b	Content Database	No action required
Upgrade and Migration	demo2010a	WSS_Content_ece4c0fa5c06fa5ade84dfb295d43	Content Database	No action required
General Application Settings	demo2010a	WSS_Content_cbfdf6ff98a4928b4dbb7e9d0c506	Content Database	No action required
Configuration Wizards	demo2010a	WSS_Content_98fb6e6dde041318a30569d040d92a	Content Database	Database is up to date, but some sites are not completely upgraded.
	demo2010a	Application_Registry_Service_DB_49efe2032d174372a1fb07ca0d0d69d1a	ApplicationRegistryServiceDatabase	No action required
	demo2010a	Bdc_Service_DB_v95fedfb9b6cb43fbb1e44eu6f029107d	BdcServiceDatabase	No action required
	demo2010a	FASTContent_CrawlStoreDB_7266d5b76ae3463b89f3429420ec7	SearchGathererDatabase	No action required
	demo2010a	FASTContent_DB_86dee0120c95479189de90b9286ca4e6	SearchAdminDatabase	No action required
	demo2010a	FASTContent_PropertyStoreDB_463d1c96d4e445b5ab9bf19bef8ae1ce	SearchPropertyStoreDatabase	No action required
	demo2010a	FASTQuery_CrawlStoreDB_737fe9e174eaa49e4f4d4d4bff0366fb1b	SearchGathererDatabase	No action required
	demo2010a	FASTQuery_DB_ed8c2e60d0504111fb7897a47e0157b6e	SearchAdminDatabase	No action required
	demo2010a	FASTQuery_PropertyStoreDB_10ece821d79246dab04a35bcb8d4d4	SearchPropertyStoreDatabase	No action required
	demo2010a	Managed Metadate Service_8cbadae18a7647b6ac190419f6cd27f9	MetadataWebServiceDatabase	No action required
	demo2010a	PerformancePoint Service Application_4a91194ec395e8978890752132924349	BIMonitoringServiceDatabase	No action required
	demo2010a	Search_Service_Application_CrawlStoreDB_sd12268adcc47cabf45970eb7ea51b6	SearchGathererDatabase	No action required
	demo2010a	Search_Service_Application_DB_dd12ba14e7bb4ffaafcc3ee26e73c949	SearchAdminDatabase	No action required
	demo2010a	Search_Service_Application_PropertyStoreDB_b566dce49c514f8899ae51e503889389	SearchPropertyStoreDatabase	No action required
	demo2010a	Secure_Store_Service_DB_f6f93cafd0e54693babfd1e12ef26191	SecureStoreServiceDatabase	No action required
	demo2010a	SharePoint_Config	Configuration Database	No action required
	demo2010a	StateService_023458a051374afa89eb028bfef9d07f	StateDatabase	No action required
	demo2010a	User Profile Service Application_ProfileDB_987e27f4752344ee939de2328d85a9ad	ProfileDatabase	No action required
	demo2010a	User Profile Service Application_SocialDB_ed99aadd9603429561319f1fb7b3f3a	SocialDatabase	No action required
	demo2010a	User Profile Service Application_SyncDB_b693fa07f51b44289940d82d4069bddb	SynchronizationDatabase	No action required
	demo2010a	WebAnalyticsServiceApplication_ReportingDB_e0ab6211-4b16-4b9f-9e19-a0cd4c6aefc1	WebAnalyticsWarehouseDatabase	No action required
	demo2010a	WebAnalyticsServiceApplication_StagingDB_26c092db-3437-427b-9d8c-744248149d59	WebAnalyticsStagerDatabase	No action required
	demo2010a	WordAutomationServices_36972c0afbd846bc9ad913feff0a08575	QueueDatabase	No action required
	demo2010a	WSS_Logging	SPUsageDatabase	No action required

The executable file that actually performs database upgrades (psconfig. exe), checks the status of all servers in the farm before allowing a database upgrade to proceed. The idea is to prevent unpatched servers from trying — and failing — to connect to an upgraded database. That's because the backward compatibility of this feature is one-way: New binaries can connect to old database schemas, but old binaries can't connect to upgraded databases.

If you're restoring an old content database to patched servers, that works — provided the content database is up-to-date enough for SharePoint 2010 to support. In practical terms, that means your database can't lag behind the current patch by more than two or three patch releases. If your database meets that condition, no problem: After the restore operation is complete, SharePoint 2010 upgrades the restored database to the current patch schema.

The Upgrade and Patch Management section of Central Administration also includes a subsection (shown in Figure 6-18) that reports on upgrade status. If an upgrade fails, a descriptive error message is written to the upgrade-status log with the database, object, and server information, along with recommended remedies and detailed information on where to find the log file. That's a vastly improved starting point for troubleshooting.

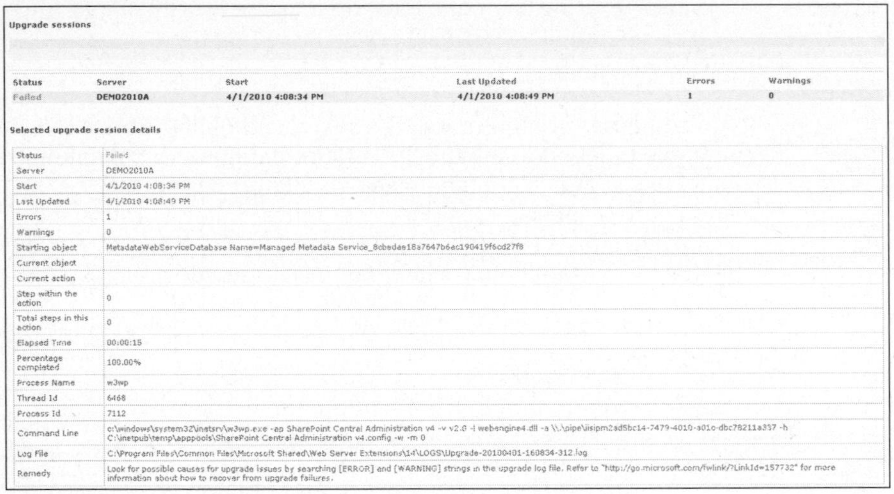

Figure 6-18: Failed patch-installation session.

Upgrade sessions

Status	Server	Start	Last Updated	Errors	Warnings
Failed	DEMO2010A	4/1/2010 4:08:34 PM	4/1/2010 4:08:49 PM	1	0

Selected upgrade session details

Status	Failed
Server	DEMO2010A
Start	4/1/2010 4:08:34 PM
Last Updated	4/1/2010 4:08:49 PM
Errors	1
Warnings	0
Starting object	MetadataWebServiceDatabase Name=Managed Metadata Service_8cbadae18a7647b6ec190419f6cd27f8
Current object	
Current action	
Step within the action	0
Total steps in this action	0
Elapsed Time	00:00:15
Percentage completed	100.00%
Process Name	w3wp
Thread Id	6468
Process Id	7112
Command Line	c:\windows\system32\inetsrv\w3wp.exe -ap SharePoint Central Administration v4 -v v2.0 -l webengine4.dll -a \\.\pipe\iisipm2ad5bc14-7479-4019-a01c-dbc78211a357 -h C:\inetpub\temp\apppools\SharePoint Central Administration v4.config -w -m 0
Log File	C:\Program Files\Common Files\Microsoft Shared\Web Server Extensions\14\LOGS\Upgrade-20100401-160834-312.log
Remedy	Look for possible causes for upgrade issues by searching [ERROR] and [WARNING] strings in the upgrade log file. Refer to "http://go.microsoft.com/fwlink/?LinkId=157732" for more information about how to recover from upgrade failures.

Chapter 7: Automating with PowerShell

In This Chapter

↳ **Getting to know PowerShell**

↳ **Using the SharePoint cmdlets**

↳ **Automating administrative tasks with PowerShell**

A fter previous SharePoint versions largely ignored PowerShell — a command-line interface that can handle the automation of management tasks — SharePoint 2010 finally jumps on the PowerShell bandwagon, which adds another tool to the administrator's toolbox. If the assimilation of PowerShell into SharePoint follows the same pattern as other Microsoft products have (such as Exchange and SQL Server), don't be surprised if PowerShell becomes the only command-line tool that administrators require in the future. If you're administrating a SharePoint system, a wise move you can make now is to get familiar with PowerShell — and get comfortable using it.

In this chapter, you get a closer look at PowerShell, get some pointers on how to start using it (in basic or fancy ways) to automate those laborious and tedious tasks that you doubtless have to perform today.

Introducing PowerShell

Before the advent of PowerShell, one of the weakest areas of the Windows operating system — any version — was its *command-line interface* (CLI) which hadn't changed much since the DOS command language of the 1980s. Even while the Windows graphical interface grew fancier throughout the '90s, a command typed at the C: prompt was still the most emphatic way to tell the system what to do. Windows provided access to the C: prompt in — what else? — a window.

Such a simple CLI for a desktop operating system might just be acceptable to some folks, but most definitely not for a server-based operating system — as any mainframe administrators worth their salt will tell you!

Given the number of servers, applications, and services that system administrators must deal with on a daily basis — while still urged toward IT consolidation and resource optimization — one lonely C: prompt in a little window just won't do the job. Administrators need a first-class CLI that can be used from a central console to control and automate the management of all IT assets. PowerShell, first released in late 2006 and now in its second release, is Microsoft's primary CLI for all versions of Windows. It offers great flexibility in managing many aspects of the operating system itself — and many of the applications that run within. Built on the Microsoft .NET Framework, PowerShell provides both an interactive shell and a rich scripting language you can use to automate many management tasks.

Furthermore, PowerShell is extensible — third parties can add commands tailored to manage specific applications or services. Indeed, many Microsoft applications now include their own PowerShell commands — providing a handy, built-in way to administer the application. The first major application to do this was Exchange 2007 which included a couple of high-powered administrative tools:

✦ **Exchange Management Shell (EMS):** Here's where the administrator gets to tell the machine exactly what to do. A *shell* (command interface) is where you run interactive, Exchange-specific (and built-in) commands and execute scripts.

✦ **Exchange Management Console (EMC):** This graphical user interface (GUI) triggers PowerShell commands from within Exchange. When you execute a command through the EMC, it gets busy behind the scenes, calling an Exchange PowerShell command to do the task at hand.

These tools highlight a stellar benefit of PowerShell: Other applications — such as Exchange, SQL Server, and System Center Operations Manager, and now SharePoint — can call PowerShell commands. This means, for example, that a .NET developer can build solutions that use application-specific PowerShell commands — a very powerful combination, indeed. Doubtless many other Microsoft server applications will harness PowerShell. The current version of PowerShell, V2, is available on all the versions of Windows that support SharePoint 2010. (Today the server, tomorrow the world! Oops. Got a little carried away there.)

Getting Started With PowerShell

In this section, you get a closer look at the basic operation of PowerShell, and take in some essential concepts that you'll need to be comfortable with in order to use the power of PowerShell to its fullest. The version of PowerShell we are working with is Version 2.

Learning the Language

In PowerShell, a command is called a *cmdlet* (pronounced *commandlet*) — not because it's little and cute, but because it represents the smallest unit of functionality. Cmdlets are executable programs that perform a specific function; generally they're very simple and (well, yes) small.

The designers of PowerShell wisely established a consistent naming convention for cmdlets that follows a verb-noun sequence. For example, the cmdlet Get-Process lists the current processes running on a system where the cmdlet Set-Date sets the system date and time. Many verbs come in pairs — such as Get and Set, Stop and Start, and Add and Remove.

Most cmdlets take one or more parameters that determine not only the object(s) to use but also the action(s) to take on the objects in question. Although there are exceptions, the normal way to provide parameters is to specify the parameter name, followed by its value. For example, this instruction sets the startup type of the DHCP service to Disabled on the computer MS2:

```
Set-Service –Name DHCP –ComputerName MS2 –StartupType
    Disabled
```

There's a quick way to find valid values for parameters. Just enter garbage for the parameter in question and the error message will (more often than not) indicate what values are expected! You can see this shameless pampering in action in Figure 7-1.

Book II
Chapter 7

Automating with PowerShell

Figure 7-1:
An error message can remind you how to perform the task.

Talking with PowerShell

PowerShell cmdlets can be invoked in three ways:

+ Interactively

+ Through the execution of a script written in the PowerShell scripting language.

+ Through the execution of a .NET application that calls the PowerShell Application Programming Interface (API)

The first step toward bossing PowerShell around is, therefore, to start an interactive session with it through a command-line shell.

Access to PowerShell depends on your version of Windows:

+ It's installed natively on Windows 7

+ It's available as a feature in Windows Server 2008 R2.

+ It can be downloaded from the Web and installed on other Windows versions.

Starting the shell is simple:

1. **Click the Start button.**

2. **In the Start menu search box, enter PowerShell.**

Items on your computer that match the word *PowerShell* appear.

3. **Select Windows PowerShell.**

The shell looks much like a legacy command window from the late twentieth century, complete with a prompt that awaits your input. Many keystrokes and mouse clicks do exactly as you'd expect — for example, the arrow keys recall previous commands — but at least one nonconformist command does something different: Right-clicking your mouse does cut-and-paste operations while you're working in a shell — a most useful click to have.

Asking for Help

To get a really good handle on what cmdlets can do, you need to be able to access the help system. Might as well do so with a cmdlet: Execute `Get-Help`. The text that appears onscreen explains how to use the help system to find out more details about cmdlets.

Cmdlets are case-insensitive — `Get-Help` is just as valid as `get-help`. That said, most documentation uses what's called "camel notation" — the first letter of each distinct word within the cmdlet is uppercased, giving the name a humped appearance (hence "camel" — hey, it makes more sense than "aardvark notation"). Here's a suitably humpy example:

```
Test-ComputerSecureChannel
```

Every cmdlet has its own help (or *should* have if its creator has followed all the documented guidelines for kindly and useful programming) which is constructed according to a schema that contains Name, Synopsis, Syntax, Description, and so on. You can display parts of a cmdlet's help by using parameters — for example, you may want to review just the examples of a particular cmdlet or just the detailed description. As an example refer to Figure 7-2 where we've asked for examples of using the Get-Process cmdlet using the -Examples parameter. The SharePoint cmdlets have fairly comprehensive help examples — so they're always a good place to start when you're figuring out how to use a particular cmdlet.

TIP

When you see the - - More - - prompt onscreen, you can use the Return/Enter key to step through the output one line at a time, the Spacebar to step through a page at a time, and Ctrl+C to interrupt the output.

```
Administrator: Windows PowerShell

PS C:\> help get-process -examples

NAME
    Get-Process

SYNOPSIS
    Gets the processes that are running on the local computer or a remote computer.

    ---------------------- EXAMPLE 1 ----------------------

    C:\PS>Get-Process

    Description

    This command gets a list of all of the running processes running on the local computer. For a definition of each co
    lumn, see the "Additional Notes" section of the Help topic for Get-Help.


    ---------------------- EXAMPLE 2 ----------------------

    C:\PS>Get-Process winword, explorer | format-list *

    Description

    This command gets all available data about the Winword and Explorer processes on the computer. It uses the Name par
    ameter to specify the processes, but it omits the optional parameter name. The pipeline operator (|) passes the dat
    a to the Format-List cmdlet, which displays all available properties (*) of the Winword and Explorer process object
    s.

    You can also identify the processes by their process IDs. For example, "get-process -id 664, 2060".


    ---------------------- EXAMPLE 3 ----------------------

    C:\PS>get-process | where-object ($_.WorkingSet -gt 20000000)

    Description

    This command gets all processes that have a working set greater than 20 MB. It uses the Get-Process cmdlet to get a
    ll running processes. The pipeline operator (|) passes the process objects to the Where-Object cmdlet, which select
    s only the object with a value greater than 20,000,000 bytes for the WorkingSet property.

    WorkingSet is one of many properties of process objects. To see all of the properties, type "Get-Process | Get-Memb
```

Figure 7-2:
Using the help system.

You may have noticed that the command used in Figure 7-2 is help and not get-help. That's because PowerShell supports the use of aliases. Many of the built-in commands have aliases and you can assign your own. Aliases allow you to make the shell more familiar and appropriate for your needs. How do you find out what aliases are currently available? Use the get-alias cmdlet, of course (and set-alias to create new ones). See how habit-forming all this cmdlet stuff is?

Wildcards can also be used with many commands — these, for example:

✦ get-help about_* lists all available help files

✦ get-help s* lists all commands starting with s

One of the most helpful commands you'll encounter is get-command. You can use it to discover all the cmdlets currently available to you — and then you can use get-help to find out what they're for and how to use them. Here are a couple of examples that use get-command:

✦ get-command -noun service lists all cmdlets that operate on the service object.

✦ get-command -verb s* lists all cmdlets whose verb start with s.

While you're putting cmdlets together, the Tab key is your best friend. You can use it to complete a command or to toggle through the possible parameters of a cmdlet.

✦ For example, in a PowerShell command window, type **get-c** followed by the Tab key. Each time you press Tab, you're taken to the next cmdlet that begins with get-c.

✦ The same trick works with wildcards: so get-*log* followed by Tab will toggle through all cmdlets that have log as part of the noun.

✦ Try pressing Tab after you specify the hyphen (–) parameter — you'll loop through all the possible parameters.

Yes, folks, the Tab can save the skin on your fingertips, so don't forget it!

Understanding the Pipeline, Objects, and Variables

Here are some basics that will give you a good working sense of what PowerShell can do:

✦ The *pipeline* is a programming technique used to string multiple cmdlets together — you feed objects output from one command into another command as input. The pipe character (|) shows up in our previous example, being used as each object returned from Get-Process is fed into the Format-List cmdlet which then shows us all the properties of each object.

✦ PowerShell is built on the .NET Framework and almost everything you work with is a .NET object. Although the output of a cmdlet may appear to be just a piece of text, it's not — it's an object in its own right. You can manipulate it further by using other cmdlets or standard .NET methods. For example, you can format a `string` object by using the `String.Format` method from the .NET Framework. (Check out the MSDN Web site for details on the .NET Framework.)

An object has two foundational members:

- A *property* represents the state of a given object
- A *method* is an executable action you can perform on this object.

✦ To find out what methods and properties an object supports, you can use the `get-member` cmdlet. By piping any object into this cmdlet you'll get a display of all the wonderful things you can do with the object. Try it with `get-process | get-member` and check out the results. You can use `get-member` to explore the properties and methods of any object returned by a command. Once you know the structure of the object, it enables you to manipulate the information more easily. For example, to learn more about the `string` object or the `integer` object, you can simply execute the following:

```
"1" | get-member      #returns all string methods and properties
1 | get-member        #returns all integer methods and properties
```

✦ In PowerShell, you create an object by assigning a value to a variable and casting it to a predefined type. You can also use the cmdlet `new-object` to create .NET or .COM objects which further extends the power of PowerShell. A common practice is to select some of the properties of the returned object and use them for further processing. A simple way to see all the properties of a returned object is to "pipe" the object into the cmdlet called `Format-List` (which has an alias of `fl`). You can also select specific properties of an object by using the `Select-Object` cmdlet (whose alias is `Select`). You can see this little wonder in action by executing the following commands:

```
Get-Process
Get-Process | fl
Get-Process | select Name
```

✦ You use *variables* to declare constants or store a reference to an object (or objects) for use later on. Variables are identified through the use of the $ character. PowerShell supports multiple types of variables including objects, strings and integers and you can also declare arrays or hash tables for use in your scripts. *Hash tables* are arrays that can use any kind of key as the index. As an example of setting up a variable, consider the following commands:

```
$c = get-process #Creates an array of objects in
    variable $c
$c[2].Name    #Gets the name of the third object in the
    array
```

If there's one variable you'll get to know intimately, it's this one: It consists of a dollar sign and an underscore ($_). It refers to the current object in the pipeline. Use it when you want to perform an enumeration or filtering of all the objects returned by a particular cmdlet.

Understanding PowerShell Usage with SharePoint

PowerShell is designed to be extended; many applications — such as Exchange Server and SQL Server — already deliver their own cmdlets that are useful for management and automation tasks. SharePoint 2010 now joins that club; this section outlines how SharePoint makes use of PowerShell — and gets you started using the SharePoint cmdlets. With this knowledge, you have the power to simplify and automate operational tasks before they turn you into an end-of-day zombie.

Positioning STSADM and PowerShell

STSADM is the legacy command-line utility for SharePoint but it still ships with SharePoint 2010 for two reasons:

✦ Some procedures still have to be done with STSADM commands (for example, enabling the developer dashboard).

✦ You have to use STSADM to manage legacy SharePoint servers in your environment; it's all they know how to use.

That said, it's highly likely that STSADM will be phased out with subsequent SharePoint releases — and PowerShell will be the sole command-line utility for management. Not only is PowerShell far more flexible than STSADM, it offers superior batch-processing performance. Of course, you could write scripts that leverage poor old STSADM nearly to death with multiple operations — but each of those would have to physically invoke the STSADM executable file. With PowerShell and an up-to-date SharePoint server, you can put the lever away: PowerShell can process a large number of objects after being invoked once.

STSADM could be extended to run commands you create (it had a total of 182 commands in MOSS 2007) — but this extensibility is also true of PowerShell: You have many ways to extend the standard set of SharePoint cmdlets — and to write your own cmdlets that take advantage of the server-side API. All told, even though STSADM is still alive and kicking, all SharePoint administrators should discreetly prepare to become PowerShell experts.

Accessing the SharePoint cmdlets

When SharePoint is installed on a server, so is a swarm of SharePoint PowerShell cmdlets — but you wouldn't see a list of them if you were simply to execute `get-command` in a standard shell. That's because the PowerShell cmdlets come with nifty accessories. To augment the built-in commands, you add what are called *snap-ins* (even though you hear no snap when you install them) — prepared functions that act like interchangeable attachments for a tool. A command called `Add-PSSnapin` is used for this very purpose — that is, adding a snap-in — and a complementary command called `Get-PSSnapin` shows which snap-ins are loaded for the current shell.

Relax. You don't have to sit around and snap every one of them in. The SharePoint installation conveniently adds a shortcut to the "SharePoint 2010 Management Shell" — which, when executed, launches a shell and adds the SharePoint snap-in.

The actual command behind the shortcut is

```
C:\Windows\System32\WindowsPowerShell\v1.0\PowerShell.exe  -NoExit  " & ' C:\
    Program Files\Common Files\Microsoft Shared\Web Server Extensions\14\CONFIG\
    POWERSHELL\Registration\\sharepoint.ps1 ' "
```

(Whew. At least you don't have to read it aloud.) Looking at this long string, you can derive that the `sharepoint.ps1` script is executed after a shell is loaded. Inside the `sharepoint.ps1` script, you'll find a cmdlet with a long name (`Add-PsSnapin Microsoft.SharePoint.PowerShell`) is executed.

You can see all this in action in Figures 7-3 where we've invoked a shell, counted the available cmdlets, added the SharePoint snap-in and then recounted the available cmdlets. Figure 7-4 then shows some of the SharePoint-specific cmdlets that are available. So (as you can see), a basic SharePoint Server 2010 installation adds a whopping 531 cmdlets (SharePoint Foundation only adds 244). You can use any, most, or all of them to manage your environment (though probably not at the same time). In fact, the number of cmdlets increases as you layer on other features such as Office Web Applications, FAST search, or PerformancePoint. They start to pop up all over the place.

If you want to list only the SharePoint cmdlets (as in Figure 7-4), then one way to do so is to use the `Module` parameter on the `get-command` cmdlet, as follows:

```
get-command –Module Microsoft.SharePoint.PowerShell | ft name
```

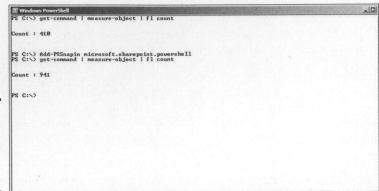

```
PS C:\> get-command | measure-object | fl count

Count : 410

PS C:\> Add-PSSnapin microsoft.sharepoint.powershell
PS C:\> get-command | measure-object | fl count

Count : 941

PS C:\>
```

Figure 7-3:
Adding and
counting the
SharePoint
cmdlets.

```
Get-SPWebAnalyticsServiceApplication
Get-SPWebAnalyticsServiceApplicationProxy
Get-SPWebApplication
Get-SPWebApplicationHttpThrottlingMonitor
Get-SPWebPartPack
Get-SPWebTemplate
Get-SPWorkflowConfig
Grant-SPBusinessDataCatalogMetadataObject
Grant-SPObjectSecurity
Import-SPBusinessDataCatalogDotNetAssembly
Import-SPBusinessDataCatalogModel
Import-SPEnterpriseSearchTopology
Import-SPInfoPathAdministrationFiles
Import-SPMetadataWebServicePartitionData
Import-SPSiteSubscriptionBusinessDataCatalogConfig
Import-SPSiteSubscriptionSettings
Import-SPWeb
Initialize-SPResourceSecurity
Initialize-SPStateServiceDatabase
Install-SPApplicationContent
Install-SPDataConnectionFile
Install-SPFeature
Install-SPHelpCollection
Install-SPInfoPathFormTemplate
Install-SPService
Install-SPSolution
Install-SPUserSolution
Install-SPWebPartPack
Install-SPWebTemplate
Merge-SPLogFile
Mount-SPContentDatabase
Mount-SPStateServiceDatabase
Move-SPBlobStorageLocation
Move-SPProfileManagedMetadataProperty
```

Figure 7-4:
SharePoint
cmdlets
being listed.

If you just want a listing of all the cmdlets that act on a particular noun —
say, anything to do with a site — then you execute the following:

```
get-command -noun *site*
```

Before you can use the SharePoint cmdlets, your user account has to meet
some minimum required privilege levels. Depending on the cmdlets you
want to run, you have to be a member of the SharePoint_Shell_Access
SQL role on the farm-configuration database and/or individual content databases. In addition, you have to be a member of the WSS_ADMIN_WPG local
group on the server where you want to run the cmdlets — and some cmdlets
(such as Get-SPFarm) require that you also be designated as a farm administrator before you can use them.

There is a cmdlet called Add-SPShellAdmin that can be used to achieve
these pre-requisites and it will ensure that the user is added to the WSS_
ADMIN_WPG local group on all front-end Web servers. Before a user can

execute cmdlets that access details in a content database, he or she must be a member of the `SharePoint_Shell_Access` role on said content database. Thus the `Add-SPShellAdmin` cmdlet supports the `-Database` parameter so you can specify content databases(s) to which you want to allow the user access via cmdlets. We can see this in action in Figures 7-5, 7-6, and 7-7 — which show the "before" and "after" situation when you're enabling two users for shell access — one explicitly to a content database (`bruce`) and the other to the configuration database (`steve`). Although both users can see some details about all the content databases in the farm, only the user who has been explicitly granted access to a content database can execute the `Test-SPContentDatabase` cmdlet successfully on that database.

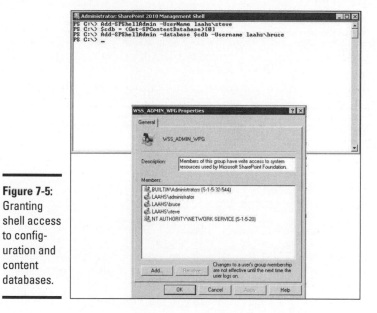

Figure 7-5:
Granting shell access to configuration and content databases.

PowerShell V2 supports remote execution which essentially means you don't have to physically log in to one of your SharePoint servers to execute cmdlets — you can run a local PowerShell on your workstation and execute commands remotely on your SharePoint server(s). Remote PowerShell makes use of Windows Remote Management — a feature of the OS that requires configuration on both the client workstation and the SharePoint server(s). As there are many different ways to set this up (and many ways to call cmdlets remotely), we won't go into exhaustive detail here. But we do urge you to read the many articles that are available on the Internet regarding remote PowerShell. It's just too slick to ignore. From a farm-administration perspective, in fact, remote PowerShell is essential if you want to execute cmdlets on all your SharePoint servers without having to log in to each one.

In general, the cmdlet you use most with remote PowerShell is `Invoke-Command`, in which one of the parameters you specify is the computer on which to run the command. You can also create a session on a remote computer using `New-PSSession` and pass that to the `Invoke-Command` cmdlet which allows you to load the SharePoint snap-in and maintain state. Following that you can either pass SharePoint cmdlets directly through the `Invoke-Command` cmdlet or, better still, import the remote session to your local session. Doing so means you can freely enter SharePoint cmdlets into your local session that execute as part of the remote session.

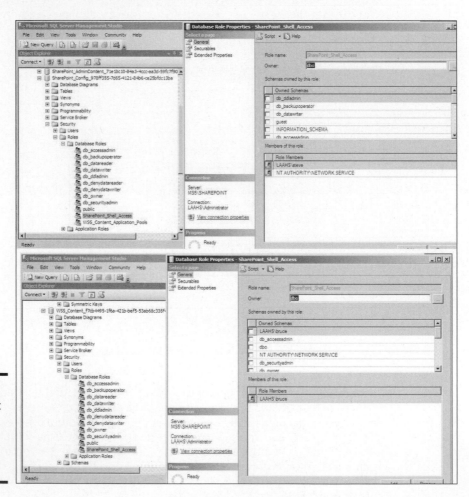

Figure 7-6: SharePoint shell-access roles on databases.

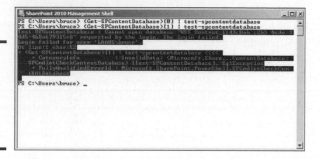

Figure 7-7:
Attempting
to access
content
inside
databases.

So, for example, if we assume you have PowerShell configured for remote usage, then you could use the following commands on a client computer to execute SharePoint cmdlets on a remote computer called RS:

```
$c = Get-Credential #Ask the user for some credentials
$r = New-PSSession RS -Authentication CredSSP -Credential $c
Invoke-Command -Session $r -ScriptBlock {Add-PSSnapin
    Microsoft.SharePoint.PowerShell}
Import-PSSession $r
```

Using SharePoint PowerShell cmdlets

Five hundred and thirty-one cmdlets is a lot — clearly, far too many to describe in this section. So here's a list of our top ten cmdlets to whet your appetite (listed alphabetically so none of them gets jealous). After this list of all-star examples, we get into using the Get-SPSite cmdlet — and take a closer look at some important points to keep in mind when executing SharePoint cmdlets.

✦ `Enable-SPFeature`: Use this cmdlet to enable installed features on sites within your farm. You can use the cmdlet to enable features at various levels — farm, site collection, or Web — and it's a fast way to light up all your sites with a newly installed feature.

✦ `Get-SPContentDatabase`: This cmdlet is a simple way to get the names of all the content databases in your farm and the number of site collections contained inside each one. Can also be used to connect to unattached databases (those that aren't part of your farm) for backup-and-recovery purposes.

✦ `Get-SPFarm`: Lists the name of your configuration database when used by itself. When used with a pipe and the fl parameter (`Get-SPFarm | fl`), this cmdlet displays lots of details about your SharePoint Farm — including the names of the servers in the farm. (You didn't really name one "Old MacDonald," did you?)

✦ `Get-SPSite`: Lists site collections. The cmdlet takes many parameters, including wildcards and regular expressions, to give you fine-grained control over which site collections you're interested in.

✦ `Get-SPLogEvents`: Use this to view and extract details from the SharePoint Unified Logging Service (ULS) trace-log files. As these logs tend to be very big, be sure to use parameters to limit the scope of the search to just the log entries you're looking for (for example, use `-StartDate` and `-EndDate`), or filter the result set using any of the columns returned (such as `Category`).

✦ `Get-SPTimerJob`: Lists all timer jobs running on your farm. You can use the corresponding cmdlet (`Start-SPTimerJob`) to kick-start a timer job if you need to run one outside its current schedule.

✦ `Merge-LogFiles`: Gathers all the ULS trace-log files from multiple servers into a single location so you can process them as a single entity with the `Get-SPLogEvents` cmdlet.

✦ `Move-SPSite`: Use this to physically move the contents of a site collection from one content database to another. This is very useful command especially if your content databases are growing out of control. You can use `Get-SPSite` to find large site collections and use the output in conjunction with this cmdlet.

✦ `New-SPUser`: Use this to add users to SharePoint sites with appropriate permissions. This cmdlet makes it easy to automate the mass addition of a group of users to a group of sites.

✦ `Set-SPDesignerSettings`: Use this to control which features of SharePoint Designer are permitted on a Web Application.

Here's a quick list of some common considerations to keep in mind while you're tinkering with SharePoint cmdlets:

✦ **It's all about objects.** Almost all cmdlets act on an object of some kind, be it a content database, a site collection, user account, or Web site (to name a few). Thus you have to use one or more parameters to define which object is the target. If you look at the help file for a cmdlet, you'll discover the different ways in which it can be called. For example, the syntax for `Get-SPSite` reveals four different ways in which you can call it — therefore you can choose the most appropriate one for the task at hand. For instance, you can specify a content database as the target object for this cmdlet — in which case, all site collections within the specified content database will be listed. Some cmdlets are global in execution, so you can run them on any server in the farm (for example, `New-SPSite`); others are local and only affect the server on which they're run (for example, `Start-SPServiceInstance`).

✦ **PipeBind gives you more options.** Specific to SharePoint cmdlets is an object type called a `PipeBind` — which you have to supply as the value of some parameters — for example, the `-Identity` parameter if you use it with the `Get-SPSite` cmdlet. For every noun supported, there is a corresponding `PipeBind` object. This object type accepts multiple formats — thanks to the handy fact that you can uniquely reference a SharePoint object in multiple ways. For example, you can use the URL *or* the GUID (globally unique identifier) for a site collection. The `PipeBind` object type ensures that you have the flexibility to use whatever unique identifier is appropriate for the current operation.

✦ **Little cmdlets can do big things.** Many innocuous cmdlets can operate against a very large number of objects — for example the `Get-SPSite` cmdlet with no parameters will enumerate all the site collections in the farm which could result in some performance issues. That's why most cmdlets have an built-in limit on the number of objects they'll return; it's up to you to explicitly override the limit by using the `-Limit` parameter, which takes a non-negative number or the word `ALL` as its value. (For `Get-SPSite`, the built-in limit is 200.)

✦ **Be sure you know what a cmdlet is going to do.** As you execute cmdlets (especially those that perform write operations) you may want to be sure that you know what the outcome of the operation will be. (It's one of the many ways SharePoint administration is different from bungee-jumping.) PowerShell supports a parameter called `-whatif` that allows you to see what an operation would do if you were to execute it without the `-whatif`. As an example of its use, consider the following command:

```
Get-SPSite -Limit 20 | Remove-SPSite -whatif
```

You can't know for sure what the twenty returned sites would be, so piping them willy-nilly into a destructive cmdlet could be disastrous. But hold on: In this case, –whatif means the command won't actually be executed. (Whew. That was a close one.) Of course, this is a very simple example of a command. But as you gain experience with the criteria you use to select objects in your command line, you'll want to have the –whatif safety net in place to make sure all your filters and selection criteria do exactly what you anticipate before you execute that potentially career-limiting command ("You did *what* to *what?!*").

✦ You have various possible ways to work with only a subset of the objects returned by a particular cmdlet:

- Some cmdlets allow you to specify parameters that limit the scope of its execution (to, say, the farm, Web Application, or content database) or the actual number of returned objects. For example Get-SPSite supports both the –WebApplication and the –Limit parameters.

- Client-side filtering using properties of the objects is possible via the where-object cmdlet (aliased as ?) in the pipeline and you can see an example of this in action in Figure 7-8. This allows you to look at every object that is returned but only process those that match the specified criteria. While this is useful be aware that this is all done as client-side processing which means that all objects are actually returned initially and the filtering is done on the client. This approach could end up wasting a chunk of server processing.

- Some cmdlets support server-side filtering — usually through a –Filter parameter (though not always). The –Filter parameter is used to perform the filtering of objects during execution of the cmdlet on the server — before the result set is sent to the client. This approach works better for all concerned — and the Get-SPSite cmdlet (as well as others such as Get-SPWeb) support it. A very good example of this approach is to execute a command that returns all sites in your farm that were created with the Blogs template, as shown in Figure 7-8.

- The Get-SPSite, Get-SPWeb and Get-SPSiteAdministration cmdlets also supports wildcards: You can use an asterisk (*) at the end of the URL (via the –Identity parameter value) and at the end of a regular expression (via the –RegEx parameter). Both of these options result in server-side filtering, so their use is encouraged.

Check out Figure 7-8 for these techniques in action and refer to help Get-SPSite –full for all the gory details.

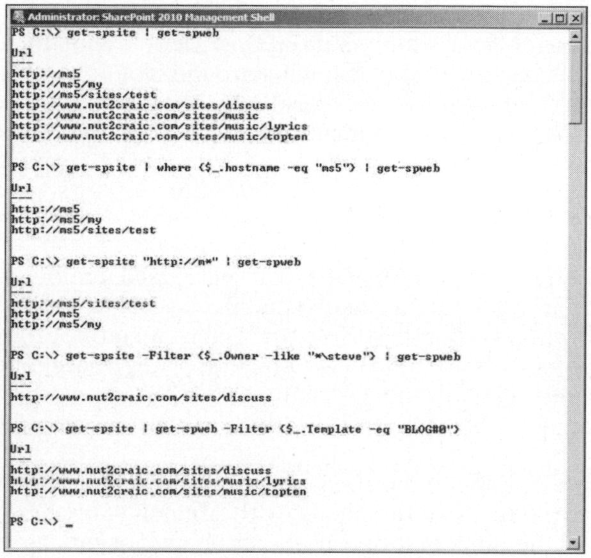

Figure 7-8:
Client-side
and server-
side filtering
in action.

Automating Tasks with PowerShell

So far, we've only looked at executing interactive commands in the shell, but PowerShell provides a more muscular approach to automation: Its scripting language offers a host of statements for controlling the execution of commands — and you can tuck them all into a simple text file called a *script*. In this section, you get started building scripts that will ease your administrative load.

Understanding SharePoint and Variables

If you've used the API in previous versions of SharePoint to develop solutions, you'll be familiar with the need to dispose of certain objects you create — specifically, `web` and `site` administration objects — to avoid exhausting the server's memory. Keep those same considerations in mind when you store these objects in variables for use within the shell or within scripts. Note that this particular issue doesn't occur when you use these objects interactively in the shell in a single line command since they'll automatically disposed of properly once that single command is complete. Therefore the following command line in the shell is perfectly okay and won't cause any disposal issues:

```
Get-SPSite | Get-SPWeb
```

However if we were to execute the following two commands where we first assign some sites to a variable, we'd run the risk of leaving the structures associated with the $s variable just lying around, not being disposed of correctly — which (just as in the real world) can cause issues farther down the line. Here's what those two commands look like:

```
$s = Get-SPSite
$s | Get-SPWeb
```

This won't be an issue if you're just executing a small number of commands that only affect a small number of objects. But it will become an important consideration when you write scripts that run frequently and touch many objects — or spend lots of time in the shell assigning SharePoint objects to variables. Therefore take heed, O Administrator, of a new practice that can keep all this mucking about under control . . . :

Whether you're working in the shell or writing a script, be sure you let the system know when you're finished with a bunch of objects — so it can then dispose of the objects properly and clean up. Essentially you do so by indicating when you're going to start assigning variables and when you're finished with those variables — using the Start-SPAssignment and Stop-SPAssignment cmdlets. These create structures called *assignment collectors*.

There are two ways to use these cmdlets.

✦ Use –Global as the single parameter on both these cmdlets indicating that you want to use the global assignment collector.

   This is the simplest option.

   When PowerShell encounters the Start-SPAssigment cmdlet, it starts tracking any subsequent assignments — until it encounters the Stop-SPAssignment cmdlet. Then it disposes of all objects assigned in the meantime. Any variables that contained objects will no longer contain those objects.

The disadvantage of running a cmdlet globally to track SPA assignments is that every object will be kept — regardless of whether it's assigned to a variable. Therefore operations that generate hordes of objects will cause you problems — in particular, your shell will eventually run out of memory. At least SharePoint warns you of this possibility, as you can see in Figure 7-9.

✦ Create individual assignment collectors and explicitly use this collector when generating objects you want to store for later manipulation.

Figure 7-9 shows an assignment-collector variable called $o that (in turn) is what you use to create a variable $s that contains a list of sites.

Book II
Chapter 7

Automating
with PowerShell

Figure 7-9:
Using assignment collectors.

Choosing looping and selection options

There will be many times when you want to loop through multiple objects and perform certain operations on either all or some of them. The major cmdlets that you'll therefore need to use to achieve these aims are where-object, select-object, sort-object, and foreach-object — which all work on a collection of objects (also referred to as an *array*) passed to them through the pipeline.

The system variable called $_ (introduced earlier in this chapter) refers to the object currently being processed within an array of objects.

Many cmdlets have aliases predefined for your use. To find out what aliases exist for a cmdlet use the get-alias -Definition <cmdlet> command.

where-object

The where-object cmdlet (aliased as just where or ?) does client-side filtering on a collection of objects using certain properties of the objects as filter criteria. So, for example, you could filter all sites on the basis of host-name.

select-object

The `select-object` cmdlet (aliased as `select`) is used to either select properties from an object, or to select unique objects from an array or to select a set number of objects from either the beginning or end of an array. You can also generate calculated properties and use them to further process returned properties — say, to display those properties in a useful format. For example, perhaps you want to translate a property value stored in bytes into gigabytes, or convert a date from American format (date-month-year) to European format (month-date-year).

Sometimes you have to use calculated properties. A common example is when a property value is actually a collection of values — such as the `Usage` property of a site-collection object (which contains details of site usage — including bandwidth, storage, and number of visits to the site).

Calculated properties are defined using a hash table that contains the Name you want to give to the calculated property and the Expression you want to apply to generate the calculated property. To see this in action execute the following two commands — you'll note that the first one doesn't return any useful information from the `Usage` property — but the second one allows you to define a new calculated property based on the `Usage` property called Storage.

```
Get-SPSite | select URL, Usage
Get-SPSite | select URL, @{Name="Size";Expression={$_.Usage.
    Storage}}
```

sort-object

The `sort-object` cmdlet (aliased as `sort`) is used to sort an array of objects by property values. This can be very useful when used in conjunction with selecting a set number of objects — for example you could return the top five team sites based on the size of the content held with the sites.

foreach-object

The `foreach-object` cmdlet (aliased as `foreach` or `%`) is used to loop through a set of input objects and perform further processing on each object through a script block. The input can come from cmdlets that generate arrays (such as `Get-SPSite`) or can be controlled with a manually entered array such as `1..10` (which would pass the values 1 through 10 to the execution pipeline).

The `foreach-object` cmdlet also supports executing commands before the input objects in the set are processed — and after the processing is complete. The `-Begin`, `-Process` and `-End Parameters` are what do this bit of magic — which facilitates operations such as timing how long it takes to process a set of objects or place headers and footers in the output stream.

TIP

Note that (confusingly) you can also call `foreach` as a PowerShell statement rather than as a cmdlet. Of course, if you go that route, the results of the operation at hand will be the same — but the performance and memory usage may differ. The `foreach` statement doesn't use the pipeline; therefore all objects are loaded into memory first and *then* passed to the execution script block. Not nearly as quick as the `foreach` cmdlet, which does support the pipeline (so only one object at a time is required in memory). As an example of usage, consider the following two commands that generate exactly the same output — a list displaying the name of every file in the current directory.

```
foreach ($file in Get-ChildItem) {$file.Name}
Get-ChildItem | foreach {$_.Name}
```

Figure 7-10 shows examples of recursion and selection techniques in operation.

Figure 7-10:
Recursion and selection techniques.

Understanding Operators

You use operators to manipulate values in arithmetic, assignment, and comparison operations. For example, you use comparison operators to define criteria for filters (or for passing to the `where-object` cmdlet) and assignment operators to place values into variables. Operators are available in a vast range of types — for use on objects, arrays, hash tables, strings, and numbers (for openers!). If you want to use SharePoint and PowerShell to the full, become adept at using operators. Table 7-2 lists some of the more common comparison operators — but that's just a good start. For a deeper look into the world of operators, turn to a shell and type **help about_ operators**.

Table 7-2	Comparison Operators	
Comparison Operator		*Definition*
Non-case-sensitive	*Case-sensitive*	
-lt	-clt	Less than
-le	-cle	Less than or equal to
-gt	-cgt	Greater than
-ge	-cge	Greater than or equal to
-eq	-ceq	Equal to
-ne	-cne	Not Equal to
-contains	-ccontains	determine elements in a group
-notcontains	-cnotcontains	determine excluded elements in a group
-like	-clike	Like - uses wildcards for pattern matching
-notlike	-cnotlike	Not Like - uses wildcards for pattern matching
-match	-cmatch	Match - uses regular expressions for pattern matching
-notmatch	-cnotmatch	Not Match - uses regular expressions for pattern matching
-band		Bitwise AND
-bor		Bitwise OR
-is		Is of Type
-isnot		Is not of Type

Making use of .NET and COM objects

If you want to get fancy, you can include .NET and COM objects in your PowerShell scripts. But if you're like us, you wouldn't use these types of objects just to show off. Instead, you'll find they give you access to a wide array of functionality that can hot-rod your scripts and enhance your management operations.

The .NET Framework on which PowerShell is built brings a couple of hefty advantages:

✦ **Pre-coded solutions to common requirements** and management of the execution of programs written specifically for the Framework (commonly known as *managed code*).

✦ **The .NET library:** A collection of classes, interfaces and value types that are included in the .NET Framework. This library provides access to system functionality and describes the system classes available within PowerShell.

.NET objects

The `new-object` cmdlet provides a way to create objects of a specific class from the .NET library. You can use the `-type` qualifier to specify the .NET library class for the new object. As a simple example here is how you would create a time object and find out what you can do with it in terms of properties and methods.

```
$time = new-object -type System.DateTime
$time | get-member
```

The `get-member` cmdlet reveals the many methods that date and time objects supports. One such method is AddDays which allows you to add any number of days to a date variable. That might come in handy if you want to inform users of a particular future date when their site collections might be unavailable due to maintenance.

As an example that you may well use in your day to day operations consider that you might want to write a PowerShell script that could execute some management chores on a SharePoint Web server and then send an e-mail to all users of that Web site to let them know what you had done. Alas, SharePoint has no cmdlet for sending e-mail — but luckily the .NET Framework has a class called `System.NET.Mail`. All you need is to know the name of an SMTP server and the following code would do the trick:

```
$SmtpClient = new-object -type system.net.mail.smtpClient
$SmtpClient.host = "MySMTPServer"
$web = Get-SPWeb "http://somewebsite/"
$From = "Me@mymail.com"
Get-SPUser -web $web | foreach {$To += $_.Email + ";"}
$Title = "Your site"
$Body = "Hi, I've done something to your site"
$SmtpClient.Send($From, $To, $Title, $Body)
```

The .NET library is literally huge and is outside the scope of this book. Documentation to help you understand the contents of the library is available on the Web via the Microsoft Developer Network (MSDN).

COM objects

Besides telling .NET objects what to do, PowerShell also supports .COM objects. .COM objects enable administrators to invoke and communicate with applications running on your local machine and this allows you to, for example, launch Internet Explorer at the end of a script to view some results. (Or you might invoke your favorite media player to play you a nice tune as a reward for all that management work you've dispatched with a couple of PowerShell commands!) To instantiate a .COM object, add the `-com` parameter to the `new-object` cmdlet.

Using data providers to access data stores

The Windows operating system contains various types of data stores that you can access by using different tools — these, for example:

+ Use `regedit` to access the Registry store.

+ Use an MMC snap-in to manage the Certificates store.

  For more about snap-ins, flip back to the "Accessing the SharePoint cmdlets" section of this chapter.

+ Use the `Set` command to access Environment variables and hold them in a store.

PowerShell supports the concepts of *data providers*, which present data from different stores to the standard cmdlets in a consistent manner. Many such providers are available in SharePoint; to discover which ones are in your toolbox, use the `Get-PSProvider` cmdlet. The `Get-PSDrive` cmdlet shows you the drives that you can navigate to using standard commands such as `CD` and `DIR`. It's a natural way to get at data in other stores.

Navigating the Registry is (believe it or not) fairly simple. Here's an example: You can discover the configuration database that a SharePoint server belongs to. Just execute the following steps from a shell:

1. **Type** `CD HKLM:` **and press Enter.**

   Your prompt changes to `HKLM:>` before your very eyes.

2. **Type** `CD \SOFTWARE\M`, **press Tab, and then press Enter.**

   Your prompt changes to

   `HKLM:\Software\Microsoft>`

3. **Type** `CD '.\shared tools'` **and press Enter.**

   Your prompt changes to

   `HKLM:\Software\Microsoft\Shared Tools>`.

4. **Type** `CD web`, **press Tab, and then press Enter.**

   Your prompt changes to

   ```
   HKLM:\Software\Microsoft\Shared Tools\Web Server Extensions>
   ```

5. **Type** `CD 14.0\Secure` **and press Enter..**

   Your prompt changes to

   ```
   HKLM:\Software\Microsoft\Shared Tools\Web Server Extensions\14.0\Secure>
   ```

   Yes, the prompts are getting longer as you add more of the path. But what the prompt may lack in brevity it makes up for in precision.

6. **Type** `Get-item configdb | get-itemproperty | fl dsn` **and press Enter.**

   The `dsn` value from the Registry key is displayed. This contains the name of the configuration database and the SQL server that houses it.

   Figure 7-11 shows examples of data providers in action.

Figure 7-11:
Data providers in use.

Building and running PowerShell scripts

In essence, a script is nothing too fancy. It's simply a list of statements and commands stored in a text file with a `.ps1` extension. You build scripts when you want to automate tasks thus avoiding having to type in all the individual commands interactively into the shell each time.

You can build your script using any appropriate method you like — be it a script editor such as Notepad, a purpose-built application such as the free PowerShell ISE (Integrated Scripting Environment) from Microsoft, or third-party GUI tools such as PowerGUI.

Passing parameters to your scripts

Many times your scripts will perform a series of operations on particular objects and so you'll want to pass parameters to your script to indicate the object(s) that the script should use as input.

There are two common ways of passing parameters to scripts:

✦ Provide parameters on the command line when you invoke your script. The parameters are loaded into an array called $ARGS, which you use inside your script to gather the supplied parameters. $ARGS[0] contains the first parameter, $ARGS[1] the second, and so on.

Although this is the quickest way to support parameters in your script, the person executing the script has to know the exact order in which to supply parameters — and you cannot have any optional parameters.

✦ Use named parameters via the param keyword that you place at the top of your script. The variable names you place here will be used as named parameters to your script. For example assume we have a script called FindUser.ps1 where the first line contains the following:

```
param (
    [string]$user,
    [string]$site
)
```

Unlike using the $ARGS array, this method allows us to pass the parameters in any order and to omit parameters — as in this example:

```
FindUser -Site "http://site/" -User Laahs
```

Utilizing functions

Functions can be used to help you organize blocks of code within your scripts and to make your scripts more readable. They also allow you to call script blocks multiple times within a script thus cutting down on the physical size of the script and avoiding the need for you to repeat repeat yourself.

Because PowerShell parses scripts sequentially, you have to define your functions before you can call them in the body of the script. You *declare* a function (predictably enough) by typing the Function keyword, followed by the function name and any parameters, followed by the script block.

For Example:

```
function MultiplyByNine {
$temp = $args[0] * 9
Write-Output $temp
}
```

Parameters can be parsed inside your functions by using the same techniques as described in the previous section.

An example of a simple script that uses functions is shown in Figure 7-12.

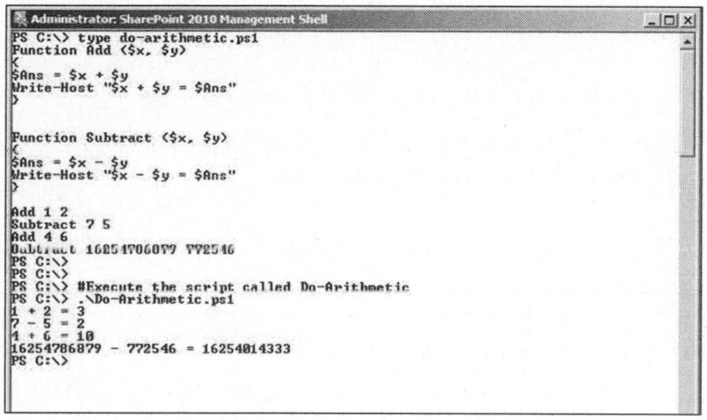

**Book II
Chapter 7**

**Automating
with PowerShell**

Figure 7-12:
PowerShell
functions.

Running your scripts

When you've written your scripts you'll want to execute them to see what they can do. Before you launch that first script, take a spin through this handy list of pointers:

✦ By default, scripts are actually not allowed to run (that's a safety feature in case you're tricked into running something that you're not aware of). Therefore you have to set the execution policy on the machine you're using to run your scripts so it allows certain types of scripts to run — for example, in a production environment, you might want only signed scripts to be executable. In a development environment you should be safe enough to execute the following command which will allow you to run your own scripts but won't run any downloaded from the Internet unless they're signed by a trusted publisher. You only need to execute this cmdlet once for each machine you want to run PowerShell scripts on.

```
Set-ExecutionPolicy RemoteSigned
```

✦ You can't just double-click your .ps1 file and expect it to run. You might *expect* it to run, of course, but it won't; instead, double-clicking your .ps1 file opens your script for editing. That's just as well: Scripts have to be told in which shell they're going to run. To execute a script by double-clicking it, first you need to create a shortcut that launches PowerShell and then passes your script to it. You can use this same technique to run PowerShell scripts as scheduled tasks. Note, however, that the following example shouldn't be used that way; the –noexit means the shell window remains open (you won't want that parameter for a scheduled task!):

```
powershell.exe -noexit & 'c:\my scripts\test.ps1'
```

✦ Invoking a script manually from within a shell is possible. The shell needs to know the full path of the script and you can do this using one of the following three techniques:

a. Make sure you type the full path to the script.

b. Use ".\" in front of the script name to indicate it resides in the current directory (as shown in Figure 7-12).

c. Ensure the directory that holds your script is also in your Windows Path environment variable

✦ Understanding "dot-sourcing". When you execute a script, the variables and functions inside the script are local. Thus, when the script terminates, those variables and functions are no longer available to the shell in which you ran the script. But if you run the script by "dot-sourcing" it (which means you execute it by typing a dot and a space in front of it before you press Enter, like this: . yourscriptgoeshere), then you're essentially loading all the functions and variables for use throughout the shell session. Therefore if you have a lot of functions that you regularly use you can place them in a script and have that script "dot-sourced" every time you invoke a shell.

✦ You can have certain functions and scripts executed every time you invoke a shell through your PowerShell profile. Your profile is merely another script that is executed at shell invocation time. And it's located through the system $profile variable so if you merely type **$profile** into a shell, you can locate where your startup script should be. Neither the folder nor the file exists by default so you have to go physically create it and, of course, the easiest way to do this is to use PowerShell as follows:

```
New-Item -path $profile -type file -force
Notepad $profile
```

Thus you can create all your favorite functions in a single script and "dot source" it through your profile meaning that all your functions will be available to all your shells all of the time. Also by ensuring that the location you keep your scripts in is included in your windows path environment variable (and you can set this up in your profile script) you can execute all your scripts by just entering their names — regardless of the current directory your shell may be pointing to.

For examples of these techniques, look at Figure 7-13 — where we've defined a function called `Get-Storage` that will return the storage used by the site collection(s) that we pass as a parameter. Enjoy!

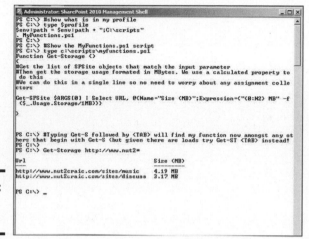

**Book II
Chapter 7**

**Automating
with PowerShell**

Figure 7-13:
Scripts in
action.

Remember the Tab key — your old buddy from earlier in the chapter? Well, he even works for your own script names and loaded functions — go ahead and try it!

Chapter 8: Using Service Applications

In This Chapter

✔ Adding and removing service applications

✔ Configuring service applications

✔ Administering service applications

✔ Connecting to remote service applications

SharePoint 2010 ships with an impressive collection of services right out of the box — Access Services, Excel Services, and Business Connectivity Services, to name a few. All the services share the same underlying service architecture and administrative architecture.

The great thing about this similarity, from an administrator perspective, is that the methods you use to manage, configure, and provision one type of service are common across all services. For example, the context-sensitive Ribbon menu in Central Administration allows you to easily manage all your service applications from a single page. The content on the pages varies depending on the service, but the basic method of accessing the administrative pages is the same. For example, when you click the Manage command for Access Services, a different list of settings appears than if you click the Manage command for Excel Services, but the method of getting to the management page for both services is the same.

In this chapter, we introduce you to the service-application management pages and show you how to create, configure, manage, and use the services in your farm.

Using the Service Application Management Pages

When you first install SharePoint Foundation and SharePoint 2010, you have the option to use the Farm Configuration Wizard to help you get your service applications and initial Web Application up and running. For more advanced and complex installations, you can forego the wizard and manually configure your farm. Regardless of which option you choose, you need to understand how to create, configure, manage, and use the service applications in your farm.

Central Administration provides numerous pages for managing the entire service application lifecycle. The Application Management page in Central Administration provides a central point for managing service applications by consolidating the service application–related links under a single Service Applications section. Figure 8-1 shows the links to the service application management pages.

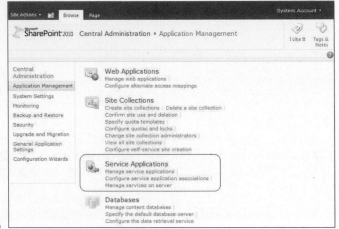

Figure 8-1:
You can manage service applications from a central point.

Three links are available under the Service Applications section:

✦ **Manage Service Applications:** Allows you to create or manage service applications

✦ **Configure Service Application Associations:** Allows you to specify the service applications used by each Web Application

✦ **Manage Services on Server:** Allows you to select the services that will run on each server in the farm

Creating a Service Application

The Farm Configuration Wizard creates and configures service applications for each of the out-of-the-box services so that they're available for your Web Applications to use. This wizard is great for initial setup and configuration of your farm, but you may eventually need to create additional service applications. For example, you may want to create a separate Search Service for your HR department.

REMEMBER

You need to be a member of the Farm Administrators groups to be able to create a new service application from Central Administration.

Follow these steps to create a new service application by using Central Administration:

1. **Navigate to the Central Administration home page.**

2. **In the Application Management section, click Manage Service Applications.**

The Manage Service Application page appears, as shown in Figure 8-2. The actions that you can perform at a given moment appear on the Ribbon menu. The Ribbon menu is context sensitive, which means that commands on the menu turn on and off depending on what you select. For example, in Figure 8-2, a service application hasn't been selected, so the only active menu options are New and Connect.

Figure 8-2:
The Manage
Service
Application
page
provides
a context-
sensitive
menu.

3. **In the Ribbon menu, click New.**

A list of services appears, from which you can choose the type of service application to create.

4. **Select the type of service application that you want to create.**

For example, if you want to create a new Search Service application, click Search Service Application.

5. **Enter the property information required by the service application.**

   The page that loads is specific to the type of service application that you're creating. For example, if you're creating a new Search Service application, the Create New Search Service Application page appears.

   You can later change the settings that you specify on this page by clicking the Properties command in the Manage Service Applications page.

6. **Click OK to create the service application.**

   A status page appears, informing you of the progress while your changes are being processed. Depending on the type of service application you're creating, this process may take a long time. The final status should be a message indicating that the service application was created successfully.

7. **Click OK to return to the Manage Service Application page.**

   Your new service application now appears in the list of service applications on the Manage Service Application page. Part of the service-application creation process includes the creation of a service application proxy for the service application. This application proxy allows you to connect your Web Application to the new service application.

Editing Service Application Properties

When you create a service application, you specify its configuration settings, such as the description of the service application, the application pool under which it will run, and the database it will use to store its data. These settings are known as the *service application properties.*

Follow these steps to edit a service application by using Central Administration:

1. **Navigate to the Central Administration home page.**

2. **In the Application Management section, click Manage Service Applications.**

   The Manage Service Applications page appears. At this point, most commands on the context-sensitive ribbon are inactive because you haven't selected a service application.

3. **Select the service application that you want to edit.**

   When you select a service application, commands on the Ribbon menu activate. If your service application doesn't have common properties that are editable from the properties menu, the Properties command remains inactive.

4. **In the Ribbon menu, click Properties and in the page that appears edit the service application properties, as desired.**

   The page that loads is specific to the type of service application that you're editing. For example, if you're editing the properties of a Search Service application, the Edit Search Service Application page appears.

5. **Click OK to save the changes to the service application.**

   A status page appears, informing you of the progress while your changes are being processed. Depending on the type of service application you're editing, this process may take a long time.

   The final status should be a message indicating that the configuration changes to the service application were applied successfully.

Managing Service Application Settings

The Manage provides you with access to a service management pages. For example, for a Search Service application, you can click the Manage command to access the Search Administration pages, where you can configure settings such as the content sources for the crawl, the server name mappings, and the crawl rules. Depending on what service application you're managing, clicking the Manage command also can give you access to informational data relating to the service application, such as the log files and analytical reports.

Follow these steps to access the management pages of a service application by using Central Administration:

1. **Navigate to the Central Administration home page.**

2. **In the Application Management section, click Manage Service Applications.**

3. **From the Manage Service Applications page, select the service application that you want to manage.**

   When you select a service application, the Manage command on the ribbon menu activates.

4. **In the ribbon menu and in the page that appears, click Manage and configure the service application, as desired.**

   The page that loads is specific to the type of service application that you're managing. For example, if you're managing a Search Service application, the Search Administration page specific to that Search Service application appears.

5. **Click OK to save any changes to the service application.**

   If you made configuration changes when you were managing the service application, you must save the changes before they can take effect.

Service Application PowerShell cmdlets

You can use PowerShell cmdlets to manage the service applications in your SharePoint farm. The following sections list some of the cmdlets that you may find useful when you manage service applications.

If you're new to PowerShell and need a quick starter guide, read Book II, Chapter 7.

Retrieving service application information

You can use the PowerShell Get cmdlets to retrieve information that you need to perform many of the service-application administrative operations. For example, many of the service application PowerShell commands require the identity of the service application with which you want to work. You can use the `Get-SPServiceApplication` cmdlet to return a list of all the service applications defined in your SharePoint implementation. The list that's returned provides the display name of each service application, the type of service it is, and its identity in the form of a Globally Unique Identifier (GUID). You can copy, or *pipe,* the GUID information of the service application so that the GUID can feed into subsequent PowerShell commands.

Table 8-1 lists some useful cmdlets related to retrieving service application information.

Table 8-1	**PowerShell cmdlets to Retrieve Information**
cmdlet	*Description*
`Get-SPServiceApplication`	Returns the service application specified by the Identity parameter. The Identity parameter identifies an object, in this case the service application. If no parameter is specified, then the cmdlet returns all the service applications in the farm.

cmdlet	Description
`Get-SPServiceApplication Proxy`	Returns an instance of the service application proxy specified by the Identity parameter.
`Get-SPServiceApplication ProxyGroup`	Returns a list of the application proxy groups in the farm. You can display a specific application proxy group by including the Identity parameter to the command.
`Get-SPServiceInstance`	Returns the services instance specified by the Identity parameter for a specific server. If the Server parameter isn't specified, the cmdlet returns results for the entire farm.
`Get-SPTopologyService Application`	Returns the URL for the farm's Topology Service. You can use this URL for the FarmUrl parameter in the `Receive-SPS erviceApplicationConnectionI nfo` cmdlet.
`Get-SP<specific service type property>`	Retrieve specific property settings for the type of service application specified in the cmdlet. For example, if you want to retrieve the `ServiceApplicationPool` property settings for a Visio Services service application, use the `Get-SPVisioServiceApplication` cmdlet; if you want to retrieve the property settings associated with the performance of a Visio Services service application, use the `Get-SPVisioPerformance` cmdlet.

Creating service application components

You can use the PowerShell New cmdlets to perform many of the tasks associated with creating a service application. For example, when you create a service application, you typically assign it its own application pool. Note, this is a special type of application pool (a Web Service application pool); it is not the same type of application pool used for a Web Application. The cmdlet `New-SPServiceApplicationPool` creates a new Web Service application pool for the service application in Internet Information Services (IIS).

Table 8-2 lists some useful cmdlets related to creating service applications.

Table 8-2   **PowerShell cmdlets to Create Components**

cmdlet	Description
`New-SPServiceApplicationPool`	Creates a new Web Service application pool in IIS.
`New-SPServiceApplicationProxyGroup`	Creates a new service application proxy group specified by the Name parameter.
`New-SP<name of the service type>`	Creates a new service application for the type of service application specified in the cmdlet. For example, if you want to create a new Visio Services Service application, use the `New-SPVisioServiceApplication` cmdlet; if you want to create a new Business Data Connectivity (BDC) Service application, use the `New-SPBusinessDataCatalogServiceApplication` cmdlet.
`New-SP<name of the service type>Proxy`	Creates a new service application proxy for the type of service application specified in the cmdlet. For example, if you want to create a new BDC Service application proxy for a BDC Service in your farm, use the `New-SPBusinessDataCatalogServiceApplicationProxy` cmdlet. Not all services have their own dedicated cmdlet for creating a new service application proxy. For those that don't, you can use the `New-SPServiceApplicationProxyGroup` cmdlet.

Removing service application components

You can use the PowerShell Remove cmdlets to perform many of the tasks associated with removing a service application. For example, if you're removing a service application and want to remove all the associations with that service application, then in addition to removing the service application, you can also remove the application pool assigned to the service application, along with the service application proxy and its associated proxy groups.

Table 8-3 lists some useful cmdlets related to removing service applications.

Table 8-3   PowerShell cmdlets to Remove Components

cmdlet	Description
`Remove-SPServiceApplication`	Deletes the service application specified by the Identity parameter.
`Remove-SPServiceApplicationPool`	Deletes the Web service application pool specified by the Identity parameter.
`Remove-SPServiceApplicationProxy`	Deletes the service application proxy specified by the Identity parameter.
`Remove-SPServiceApplicationProxyGroup`	Deletes the service application proxy group specified by the Identity parameter.
`Remove-SPServiceApplicationProxy GroupMember`	Removes one or more proxies from the specified service application proxy group.

Managing service application components

You can use PowerShell cmdlets to perform many of the tasks associated with managing a service application. For example, you can use the `Start-SPServiceInstance` cmdlet to start the instance of a service on a specific server in your farm.

Table 8-4 lists some useful cmdlets related to managing service applications.

Table 8-4   PowerShell cmdlets to Manage Components

cmdlet	Description
`Add-SPServiceApplicationProxy GroupMember`	Adds a service application connection to the service application proxy group.
`Publish-SPServiceApplication`	Publishes the service application specified by the Identity parameter so that it's available for use by remote farms.

(continued)

Table 8-4 *(continued)*

cmdlet	*Description*
`Receive-SPServiceApplication ConnectionInfo`	Returns a list of the published service applications from the Topology Service specified in the FarmUrl. You can use the command to retrieve the URL of the remote service application to which you want to connect.
`Set-SPServiceApplication`	Set properties of a service application, such as the application pool used.
`Set-SP<specific service type property>`	Sets specific properties for the type of service application specified in the cmdlet. For example, if you want to set the `ServiceApplicationPool` property for a Visio Services service application, use the `Set-SPVisioService Application` cmdlet; if you want to set the properties associated with the performance of a Visio Services service application, use the `Set-SPVisioPerformance` cmdlet.
`Unpublish-SPServiceApplication`	Stops publishing the specified service application. The service application can't be accessed consumed by remote farms.
`Start-SPServiceInstance`	Starts the service instance for a service on the specified server or on the farm.
`Stop-SPServiceInstance`	Stops the service instance for a service on the specified server or on the farm.

Assigning Service Application Administrators

You can specify users or groups of users who have rights to administer a specific service application. The users to which you assign administrator rights receive limited access to the Central Administration site, and they can manage settings related to that specific service application.

Figure 8-3 shows the Manage Service Applications page that appears for a domain user who appears in the list of administrators for the HR Search Service application. Members of the Farm Administrators group, by default, have rights to manage all service applications.

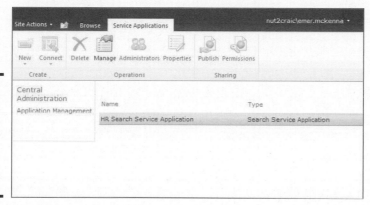

Figure 8-3:
You can
allow users
to manage
a specific
service
application.

When you add a user to the list of administrators for a particular service application, that user receives access to the Central Administration site, from which he or she can manage only that particular service application.

Follow these steps to assign administrators to a service application by using Central Administration:

1. **Navigate to the Central Administration home page.**

2. **In the Application Management section, click Manage Service Applications.**

3. **In the Manage Service Applications page, select the service application to which you want to assign administrators.**

   When you select a service application, the Administrators command on the ribbon menu activates.

4. **In the ribbon menu, click Administrators.**

The Administrators control that loads is specific to the service application that you're managing. Figure 8-4 shows the administration control for the sample HR Search Service application.

Administrators for HR Search Service Application

Specify the users who have rights to manage this service application. These users will be given access to the Central Administration site and will be able to manage settings related to this service application. Members of the Farm Administrators group always have rights to manage all service applications.

To add an account, or group, type or select it below and click 'Add'.

Add

Emer McKenna
Kevin Laahs

To remove an account, or group, select it above and click 'Remove'.   Remove

Permissions for Emer McKenna:

Full Control   ☑

OK   Cancel

Figure 8-4:
Add administrators to and remove them from your service application.

5. **Add and remove administrators, as needed.**

   To add users to the list of administrators for your service application, enter the account name or security group, and then click Add. Next, select the name and select the Full Control check box in the permissions section.

   To remove users from the list of administrators for your service application, select the account or security group from the list, and then click Remove.

6. **Click OK to save changes to the service application's Administrators list.**

   If you made changes to the list of Administrators, you must save the changes before they can take effect.

Assigning Service Application Permissions

You can specify the accounts or other security principals that have access to invoke a service application. For example, you may want to give a user or group of users read access to the term store in your Managed Metadata Service application. The set of permissions defined for the Managed Metadata Service application include the Read Access to Term Store permission.

Follow these steps to grant users permissions to a service application by using Central Administration:

1. **Navigate to the Central Administration home page.**

2. **In the Application Management section, click Manage Service Applications.**

3. **In the Manage Service Applications page, select the service application to which you want to grant permission.**

   When you select a service application, the Permissions command on the ribbon menu activates.

4. **In the ribbon menu, click Permissions.**

   The Connection Permissions control that loads is specific to the service application that you're managing. Figure 8-5 shows the permissions control for the out-of-the-box Managed Metadata Service application. The permissions available are specific to the service.

Book II
Chapter 8

Using Service
Applications

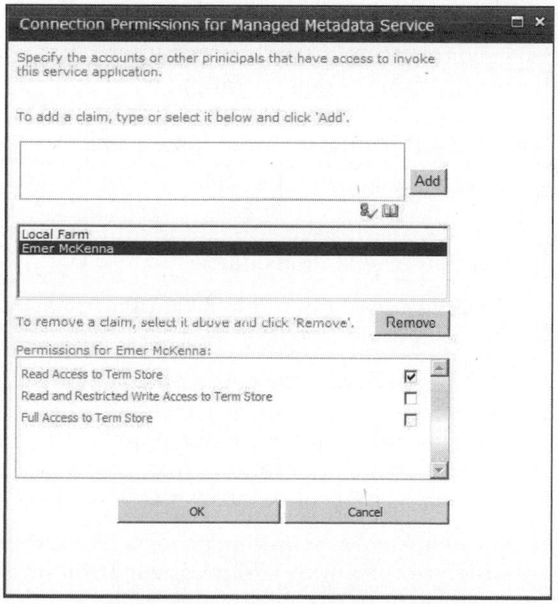

Figure 8-5:
Add and remove permissions, as needed.

5. **Add and remove permissions, as needed.**

   Use the following instructions to add and remove permissions:

   • To grant users or groups permissions to your service application, enter the account name or security group, and then click Add. Next, select the name and the permissions that you want to apply.

- To remove permissions for a user or group, select the name of the user or group, and then uncheck the permissions that you want to revoke.

- To remove a user or group entirely from the permissions list, select the user or security group from the list, and then click Remove.

6. **Click OK to save the changes you made to the service application's Permissions.**

    If you made changes to the permissions, you must save the changes before they can take effect.

Connecting to a Local Service Application

Before a Web Application can use a service application, you need to set up a service application association. When you create a Web Application, you connect the Web Application to service applications by selecting a proxy group. The service application–to–Web Application associations are very flexible, allowing you to add additional service applications to a Web Application after it has been created.

Follow these steps to connect a previously created Web Application to a service application by using Central Administration:

1. **Navigate to the Central Administration home page.**

2. **Click Application Management.**

    The Application Management page appears, giving you easy access to the Service Application Associations link.

3. **In the Service Applications section, click Configure Service Application Associations.**

    The Service Application Associations page controls the Web Application or service application–to–proxy group associations. The selected view determines the contents of the page. The Web Applications view displays a list of Web Applications, the application proxy group to which they can be mapped, and the list of application proxies for the proxy group.

4. **In the Service Application Associations page, select either the Web Application to which you want to add an association or the application proxy group mapped to that Web Application.**

    The Configure Service Application Associations page appears, allowing you to edit the associations for the application proxy group.

5. **From the Configure Service Application Associations page, select the service applications that you want to connect to the Web Application.**

    Figure 8-6 shows the Configure Service Application Associations page for the custom application proxy group for a Web Application. You can add and remove service application associations, as needed.

Configure Service Application Associations		
Edit the following group of connections: custom		
Name	**Type**	
☑ Access Services	Access Services Web Service Application Proxy	
☐ Application Registry Service	Application Registry Proxy	
☐ Business Data Connectivity Service	Business Data Connectivity Service Application Proxy	
☑ Excel Services Application	Excel Services Application Web Service Application Proxy	
☐ Managed Metadata Service	Managed Metadata Service Connection	
☐ PerformancePoint Service Application	PerformancePoint Service Application Proxy	
☐ HR Search Service Application [set as default]	Search Service Application Proxy	
☐ My Search App [set as default]	Search Service Application Proxy	
☐ Search Service Application [set as default]	Search Service Application Proxy	
☐ Secure Store Service	Secure Store Service Application Proxy	
☐ State Service	State Service Proxy	
☐ Usage and Health data collection	Usage and Health Data Collection Proxy	
☑ User Profile Service Application	User Profile Service Application Proxy	
☑ Visio Graphics Service	Visio Graphics Service Application Proxy	
☐ Web Analytics Service Application	Web Analytics Service Application Proxy	

Figure 8-6:
Add and remove service application association-tions, as needed.

**Book II
Chapter 8**

**Using Service
Applications**

6. **Click OK to save changes to the group of connections.**

If the application proxy group you're editing is the default application proxy group, any changes you make affect all Web Applications that leverage that proxy group.

Follow these steps to connect a previously created Web Application to a service application by using PowerShell:

1. **On the server that's running SharePoint 2010, ensure that the person executing the PowerShell commands is a member of the SharePoint_Shell_Access role on the configuration database and a member of the WSS_ADMIN_WPG local group.**

You can find more information about the PowerShell prerequisites in Book II, Chapter 7.

2. **From the Start menu, choose All Programs⇨Microsoft SharePoint 2010 Products⇨SharePoint 2010 Management Shell.**

3. **At the PowerShell command prompt that appears, type the following command, and then press Enter.**

```
Add-SPServiceApplicationProxyGroupMember [-Identity
    <your service application proxy group>] [-Member
    <the members to add to the service application proxy
    group>]
```

Follow these steps to remove the association between a Web Application and a service application proxy by using PowerShell:

1. **From the Start menu, choose All Programs⇨Microsoft SharePoint 2010 Products⇨SharePoint 2010 Management Shell.**

2. **At the PowerShell command prompt that appears, type the following command, and then press Enter.**

```
Remove-SPServiceApplicationProxyGroupMember [-Identity
    <your service application proxy group>] [-Member
    <the application proxy to remove from the service
    application proxy group>]
```

Handling Remote Service Connections

Several service applications can be shared across farms, including

✦ Business Data Connectivity Service

✦ Managed Metadata Service

✦ Search Service

✦ Secure Store Service

✦ User Profile Service

✦ Web Analytics Service

Before you can share service applications across farms, several steps need to be taken on both the provider farm and the consuming farm.

The provider farm is the farm that contains the service application and the consumer farm is the remote farm that uses the service application.

At a high level, here are the steps required:

✦ The farm that provides the service application and the farm that consumes the service application must exchange trust certificates.

✦ The provider farm must publish the service application.

✦ The consumer farm must connect to the service application.

These steps enable the farms to share information securely, ensuring that only authorized farms can connect to your service applications.

Exchanging trust certificates

Before a farm can consume services from another farm, both farms must exchange trust certificates. Exchanging trust certificates involves exporting and copying the certificates from one farm to the other and establishing trusts on each farm.

Follow these steps to exchange trust certificates by using PowerShell:

1. **Check that the servers meet the certificate export prerequisites.**

The servers that you use from each farm must be running Windows PowerShell 2.0, and the same server should be used for the duration of the exchange process. If your server has the User Account Control (UAC) turned on, you need to run the PowerShell commands with administrative rights.

2. **On the server that's running SharePoint 2010 in both farms, ensure that the person executing the PowerShell commands is a member of the SharePoint_Shell_Access role on the configuration database and a member of the WSS_ADMIN_WPG local group.**

You can find more information about the PowerShell prerequisites in Book II, Chapter 7.

3. **Export the root certificate from the publishing farm.**

Use the following instructions to export your root certificate:

a. From the Start menu, choose All Programs⇨Microsoft SharePoint 2010 Products⇨SharePoint 2010 Management Shell.

b. At the PowerShell command prompt that appears, type the following commands, pressing Enter after each command.

```
$rootCert = (Get-SPCertificateAuthority).
    RootCertificate
$rootCert.Export("Cert") | Set-Content <c:\PubRoot.cer>
    -Encoding byte
```

You can replace <c:\PubRoot.cer> with the path to which you want to save the exported certificate. Remember where you place the file as you'll need it again in step 6.

4. **Export the root certificate from the consuming farm.**

Use the following instructions to export your root certificate:

a. From the Start menu, choose All Programs⇨Microsoft SharePoint 2010 Products⇨SharePoint 2010 Management Shell.

b. At the PowerShell command prompt that appears, type the following commands, pressing Enter after each command.

```
$rootCert = (Get-SPCertificateAuthority).
    RootCertificate
$rootCert.Export("Cert") | Set-Content <c:\ConRoot.cer>
    -Encoding byte
```

You can replace <c:\PubRoot.cer> with the path to which you want to save the exported certificate. Remember where you place the file as you'll need it again in step 6.

Book II
Chapter 8

Using Service Applications

5. **Export the security token service (STS) certificate from the consuming farm.**

The consuming farm needs to provide two certificates to the publishing farm — the root certificate and a security token service certificate. Follow these steps:

a. *From the Start menu, choose All Programs⇨Microsoft SharePoint 2010 Products⇨SharePoint 2010 Management Shell.*

b. *At the PowerShell command prompt that appears, type the following commands, pressing Enter after each command.*

```
$stsCert = (Get-SPSecurityTokenServiceConfig).
   LocalLoginProvider.SigningCertificate
$stsCert.Export("Cert") | Set-Content <c:\ConSTS.cer> -
   Encoding byte
```

You can replace `<c:\ConSTS.cer>` with the path to which you want to save the exported certificate. Remember where you place the file as you'll need it again in step 6.

6. **Copy the certificates.**

Copy the root certificate and the STS certificate from the consuming farm to the server in the publishing farm, and copy the root certificate from the publishing farm to the server in the consuming farm. There's nothing special about the copying process; you can use the same technique that you use when copying a file from one server to another.

Remember to copy the consumer certificates to the server that was used to export the publisher root certificate, and copy the root certificate from the publishing server to the server that was used to export the consumer certificates.

7. **Establish trust on the consuming farm.**

To establish the trust relationship on the consuming farm, you need to import the root certificate from the publishing farm, and then create a trusted root authority on the consuming farm. You can use Central Administration or PowerShell to set up the trust relationship.

Follow these steps to perform these tasks by using PowerShell:

a. *At the PowerShell command prompt, type the following command and press Enter.*

```
$trustCert = Get-PfxCertificate <c:\PubRoot.cer>
```

You can replace `<c:\PubRoot.cer>` with the path of the root certificate that you copied from the publishing farm. This step imports the root certificate from that publishing farm.

b. *At the PowerShell command prompt, type the following command and press Enter.*

```
New-SPTrustedRootAuthority <PublisherFarm> -Certificate
    $trustCert
```

When you create a trusted root authority, you must give it a unique name. You can replace `<PublisherFarm>` with a unique name that represents the publishing farm.

Figure 8-7 shows the expected output from the SharePoint 2010 Management Shell.

Figure 8-7:
You receive confirmation when the trusted root authority is created.

c. Manage the trust relationships by using Central Administration.

If you don't want to use PowerShell to establish your trust relationships, follow these steps to perform the same tasks by using Central Administration:

a. In the Security page in Central Administration, click Manage Trust.

The Trust Relationships page appears and lists the trust relationships that you currently have established in your farm.

b. Click New to create a new trust relationship in your farm.

Figure 8-8 shows the Establish Trust Relationship page that appears.

c. Import the root certificate and, if you're the publishing farm, the STS certificate for the relationship.

The browse buttons allow you to select the certificate files that you copied from the farm with which you're trying to establish a trust.

Because you're creating the trust on the consuming farm, you need to import only the trust certificate for the publishing farm; you don't need to provide an STS certificate.

Establish Trust Relationship □ ×

General Setting
The name for this trust relationship.

Learn about trusts.

Name:
PublisherFarm

Root Certificate for the trust relationship
This is mandatory regardless of whether you want to provide to or consume trust from the other farm. Please add the Root Certificate for the other farm with which you want to establish a trust relationship.

Learn about certificates.

Root Authority Certificate

C:\PubRoot.cer   Browse...

Security Token Service (STS) certificate for providing Trust
This step is optional. Only add this certificate if you want to provide trust to another farm.

☐ Provide Trust Relationship
Token Issuer Description:

Token Issuer Certificate

Browse...

Figure 8-8:
You can manage trust relationships directly from the security pages.

8. **Establish trust on the publishing farm.**

Establishing the trust relationship on the publishing farm is similar to the process of establishing a trust on the consuming farm, in that you need to import the root certificate from the consuming farm and then create a trusted root authority on the publishing farm. However, an additional step is required to complete the trust relationship: You need to import the STS certificate from the consuming farm and create a trusted service token issuer on the publishing farm.

TIP

Follow these steps to perform these tasks by using PowerShell:

a. At the PowerShell command prompt, type the following command and press Enter.

```
$trustCert = Get-PfxCertificate <c:\ConRoot.cer>
```

You can replace `<c:\ConRoot.cer>` with the path of the root certificate that you copied from the consuming farm. This step imports the root certificate from the consuming farm.

b. At the PowerShell command prompt that appears, type the following command and press Enter.

```
New-SPTrustedRootAuthority <ConsumerFarm> -Certificate
    $trustCert
```

When you create a trusted root authority, you must give it a name. You can replace `<ConsumerFarm>` with a unique name that represents the consuming farm. An output similar to that shown in Figure 8-7 should appear.

c. Type the following command and press Enter.

```
$stsCert = Get-PfxCertificate <c:\ConSTS.cer>
```

You can replace `<c:\ConSTS.cer>` with the path of the STS certificate that you copied from the consuming farm to import that STS certificate.

d. *Type the following command and press Enter.*

```
New-SPTrustedServiceTokenIssuer <ConsumerFarm>
   -Certificate $stsCert
```

When you create a trusted root authority, you must give it a name. You can replace <ConsumerFarm> with a unique name that represents the consuming farm. Figure 8-9 shows the expected output from the SharePoint 2010 Management Shell.

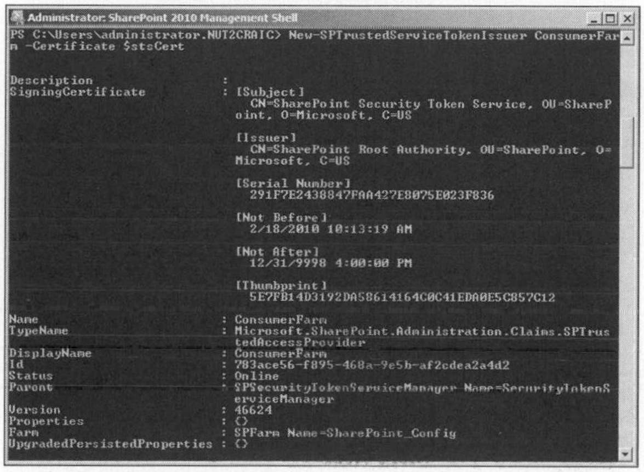

Book II
Chapter 8

Using Service Applications

Figure 8-9:
You receive confirmation on the creation of the trusted service token issuer.

If you don't want to use PowerShell to establish your trust relationships, follow these steps to perform the same tasks by using Central Administration:

a. *From the Security page in Central Administration, click Manage Trust.*

The Trust Relationships page appears and lists the trust relationships that you currently have established in your farm.

b. *Click New to create a new trust relationship in your farm.*

Figure 8-10 shows the page that appears — the Establish Trust Relationship page for the publishing farm.

When the publishing farm establishes a trust with the consuming farm, you need to provide both the root certificate and the STS certificate of the consuming farm.

c. *In the Establish Trust Relationship page, import the root certificate and, if you're the publishing farm, the STS certificate for the relationship.*

The browse buttons allow you to select the certificate files that you copied from the farm with which you're trying to establish a trust.

     d. When the publishing farm establishes a trust with the consuming farm, provide both the root certificate and the STS certificate of the consuming farm.

     Because you're creating the trust on the publishing farm, you need to import both the trust certificate for the consuming farm and the STS certificate.

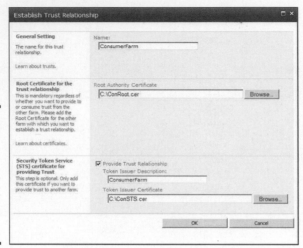

Figure 8-10: The publishing farm needs the root certificate and the STS certificate.

You're now ready to publish and connect to service applications between the publishing farm and the consuming farm.

A farm can assume the role of both a publisher and a consumer.

Publishing a service application

If you want to make a service application accessible to other farms, you need to publish the service application.

Not all service applications can be shared across farms. For example, you can't share an Excel Services application. The Publish command still activates for services that don't support cross-farm sharing, but the Publish Service Application control that appears doesn't contain the Publish to Other Farms option, nor does it provide a published URL.

Follow these steps to publish a service application by using Central Administration:

1. **Navigate to the Central Administration home page.**

2. **In the Application Management section, click Manage Service Applications.**

3. In the Manage Service Applications page that appears, select the service application that you want to publish.

When you select the service application, the Publish command on the ribbon menu activates.

4. In the ribbon menu, click Publish.

The Publish Service Application control loads, as shown in Figure 8-11. Select whether you want the connection to use HTTP or HTTPS, and select the Publish This Service Application to Other Farms option.

5. (Optional) Provide a description for the service application and a Web site URL for more information about the service.

**Book II
Chapter 8**

Using Service Applications

The descriptive information and Web site URL are visible to the administrators of remote farms, who may want to connect to your service application.

SharePoint automatically generates the published URL information, which is the URL that you pass on to the administrators of remote farms so that they can connect to your published service application.

6. Click OK to complete the publishing process.

The Manage Service Applications page reappears. The service application is published and ready to for use by your remote farms.

The *published URL* is the URL that remote farms use to connect to a published service application.

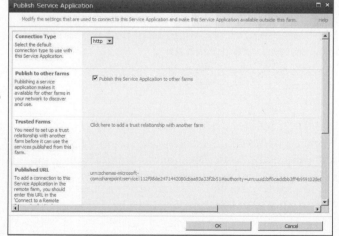

Figure 8-11: The Publish Service Application page allows you to connect the service.

You can access the published URL at any time by simply selecting the service application and clicking the Publish option again.

Follow these steps to publish a service application by using PowerShell:

1. **On the server that's running SharePoint 2010, ensure that the person executing the PowerShell commands is a member of the SharePoint_Shell_Access role on the configuration database and a member of the WSS_ADMIN_WPG local group.**

2. **In the Start menu, choose All Programs⇨Microsoft SharePoint 2010 Products⇨SharePoint 2010 Management Shell.**

   When publishing a service application, you need to know the service application's GUID. An easy way to get this information is to use the `Get-SPServiceApplication` cmdlet, either copying it for use in the next cmdlet or storing it in a variable by using the `Get-SPServiceApplication` cmdlet.

3. **At the PowerShell command prompt that appears, type the following command, and then press Enter.**

   ```
   Publish-SPServiceApplication -Identity <service
       application GUID>
   ```

4. **Type the following command, and then press Enter.**

   ```
   Get-SPTopologyServiceApplication
   ```
   This step retrieves the publishing farm's Topology Service URL so that you can give it to the administrator of the consuming farm.

Follow these steps to stop publishing a service application by using PowerShell:

1. **From the Start menu, choose All Programs⇨Microsoft SharePoint 2010 Products⇨SharePoint 2010 Management Shell.**

2. **At the PowerShell command prompt that appears, type the following command, and then press Enter.**

   ```
   Unpublish-SPServiceApplication -Identity <service
       application GUID>
   ```

Connecting to a remote service application

After a farm has established a trust with a remote farm, it can use the published service applications from that remote farm.

To consume a remote service application, you must create a connection to that service application by using its published URL.

Granting access to the publishing farm's Topology Service

For a consuming farm to make a connection to a service application on a remote farm, the consuming farm must have permissions to access the Topology Service of the publishing farm. The Application Discovery and Load Balancer Service application provides the Topology Service. To grant access to the consuming farm, you need to use the Permissions dialog box to grant the consuming farm full control of the service. Having full control gives the consuming farm permission to browse the list of published applications.

Follow these steps to grant the appropriate rights to the consuming farm:

1. **In the consuming farm, on a server that's running SharePoint 2010, ensure that the person executing the PowerShell commands is a member of the SharePoint_Shell_Access role on the configuration database and a member of the WSS_ADMIN_WPG local group.**

2. **In the Start menu, choose All Programs⇨Microsoft SharePoint 2010 Products⇨SharePoint 2010 Management Shell.**

**Book II
Chapter 8**

**Using Service
Applications**

3. **At the PowerShell command prompt that appears, type the following command, and then press Enter.**

   ```
   (Get-SPFarm).Id
   ```

   Copy the Id that appears to a file for use later. You'll need to be able to access this Id from the publishing farm.

4. **Using your browser, navigate to the Central Administration home page of the farm that contains the published service application.**

5. **In the Application Management section, click Manage Service Applications.**

6. **In the Manage Service Applications page that appears, select the Application Discovery and Load Balancer Service application.**

   When you select the service application, the Permissions command on the ribbon menu activates.

7. **In the ribbon menu, click Permissions.**

   The Connection Permissions dialog box appears.

8. **Add the farm Id of the consuming farm.**

   In the first input box, enter the Id that you copied in Step 3, and then click Add. Next, select the remote farm entry that you just added and check Full Control in the Permissions list box that appears at the bottom of the Permissions dialog box.

9. **Click OK to save the changes you've made to the service application's Permissions.**

   You must save the changes before they can take effect.

Granting access to the published service application

For a consuming farm to make a connection to a Published Service application on the remote farm, the consuming farm must have permissions to access the Published Service.

Follow these steps to grant the appropriate rights to the consuming farm:

1. **In the consuming farm, on a server that's running SharePoint 2010, ensure that the person executing the PowerShell commands is a member of the SharePoint_Shell_Access role on the configuration database and a member of the WSS_ADMIN_WPG local group.**

2. **In the Start menu, choose All Programs⇨Microsoft SharePoint 2010 Products⇨SharePoint 2010 Management Shell.**

3. **At the PowerShell command prompt, type the following command, and then press Enter.**

   ```
   (Get-SPFarm).Id
   ```

   Copy the Id that appears to a file for use later. You'll need to be able to access this Id from the publishing farm.

4. **Using your browser, navigate to the Central Administration home page of the farm that contains the published service application.**

5. **In the Application Management section, click Manage Service Applications.**

6. **From the Manage Service Applications page that appears, select the published service application to which you want to grant permission.**

   When you select the service application, the Permissions button on the ribbon menu activates.

7. **In the ribbon menu, click Permissions.**

   The Connection Permissions dialog box appears.

8. **In the first text box, enter the Id of the consuming farm, which you copied in Step 3, and then click Add.**

   The Id of the consuming farm is added to the list of identities that appears immediately below the text box.

9. **In the list of identities, select the identity you added in Step 8 and, from the permissions list box, check the permissions you want to grant.**

10. **Click OK to save the changes you've made to the service application's Permissions.**

    You must save the changes before they can take effect.

Configuring the connection

Follow these steps to connect to a remote service application from Central Administration:

1. **Using your browser, navigate to the Central Administration home page.**

2. **In the Application Management section, click Manage Service Applications.**

3. **In the ribbon menu, click Connect**

   The Connect to a Remote Service Application control appears.

4. **Enter the published URL for the remote service application in the Farm or Service Application Address text box.**

   The administrator of the remote farm that hosts the service application can provide this information to you. Figure 8-12 shows the Remote Service Application control for the consuming farm with the URL to the remote service application that was published in Figure 8-11 entered in the text box.

   You can consume services from a remote farm as long as the consuming farm supports the service offering. For example, a SharePoint Foundation farm can't consume SharePoint 2010–specific service applications, such as a Managed Metadata Service application.

Book II
Chapter 8

Using Service Applications

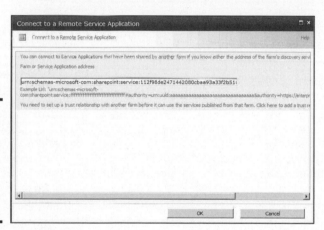

Figure 8-12:
Enter the published URL to connect to a remote service.

5. **Click OK.**

   A list of available service applications from the publishing server appears.

6. **Select the service application to which you want to connect.**

7. **(Optional) If you want to add the service application to the default application proxy group, select the Add this service application's proxy to the farm's default proxy list check box.**

   Adding the service application to the default application proxy list makes it available by default to all the Web Applications in your farm. If you don't check this setting, you must manually associate the service application with your Web Applications.

   Figure 8-13 shows the dialog box that appears, listing the available service applications.

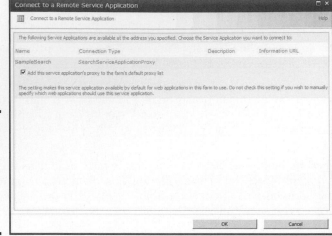

Figure 8-13:
Select the
service
application
to which
you want to
connect.

8. **Click OK.**

You're given the option to give the connection a name to identify it in the consuming farm. You can choose to keep the default name or change it to something more meaningful. The connection is now complete.

If you didn't choose to add the service application proxy to the default application proxy group, you must manually add it to your Web Applications before you can begin using the service. The Connecting to a Local Service Application section at the start of this chapter shows you how to associate a service application with an existing Web Application.

Follow these steps to connect to a remote service application by using PowerShell:

1. **On the server running SharePoint 2010, ensure that the person executing the PowerShell commands is a member of the SharePoint_ Shell_Access role on the configuration database and a member of the WSS_ADMIN_WPG local group.**

You can find more information on the PowerShell prerequisites in Book II, Chapter 7.

2. **From the Start menu, choose All Programs⇨Microsoft SharePoint 2010 Products⇨SharePoint 2010 Management Shell.**

3. **Retrieve the load balancer URL of the Topology Service of the publishing farm by using the `Get-SPTopologyServiceApplication` cmdlet on the publishing farm.**

After you have the Topology Service URL, you need to retrieve the URI of the published service application to which you want to connect.

4. **At the PowerShell command prompt, type the following command, and then press Enter.**

   ```
   Receive-SPServiceApplicationConnectionInfo -FarmUrl
       <the load balancer URL of the publishing farm's
       topology service>
   ```

   A list of the published service applications from the publishing farm appears.

5. **In the list, find the service application to which you want to connect and copy the URI.**

6. **At the PowerShell command prompt, type the following command, and then press Enter.**

   ```
   New-<SPServiceAppProxyType> -Name "<Your Service
       Application Proxy Name>" -URI "<the URI of the
       published service application>"
   ```

Book II
Chapter 8

**Using Service
Applications**

   Replace <SPServiceAppProxyType> with the cmdlet specific to the type of service application proxy to which you're connecting. For example, if you're connecting to a BDC Service proxy, use the New-SPBusine ssDataCatalogServiceApplicationProxy cmdlet. The cmdlets for each of the cross farm capable service applications are

   - New-SPBusinessDataCatalogServiceApplicationProxy
   - New-SPEnterpriseSearchServiceApplicationProxy
   - New-SPMetadataServiceApplicationProxy
   - New-SPProfileServiceApplicationProxy
   - New-SPSecureStoreServiceApplicationProxy
   - New-SPWebAnalyticsServiceApplicationProxy

7. **At the PowerShell command prompt, type the following command, and then press Enter.**

   ```
   Add-SPServiceApplicationProxyGroupMember [-Identity
       <your service application proxy group>] [-Member
       <the members to add to the service application proxy
       group>]
   ```

   This step associates the remote service application proxy with a local Web Application.

Deleting a Service Application

When a service application is no longer in use or no longer needed in your SharePoint implementation, you can delete it by using PowerShell or Central Administration. Before deleting a service application, take the time to make sure it isn't being used by Web Applications; otherwise you risk upsetting your users by removing services that they may be using.

Remove all existing connections, including remote connections, before deleting a service application. If you want to use the service again in the future, consider backing up the service application before deletion.

Follow these steps to delete a service application by using Central Administration:

1. **Navigate to the Central Administration home page.**

2. **In the Application Management section, click Manage Service Applications.**

3. **In the Manage Service Applications page, select the service application that you want to delete.**

When you select the service application, the Delete command on the ribbon menu activates.

4. **In the ribbon menu, click Delete.**

The Delete Service Application page appears. Confirm that the service application listed on the page is the service application that you want to delete.

5. **(Optional) To delete all data associated with the service application you're deleting, select the Delete data associated with the Service Applications check box.**

For example, if you're deleting a Search Service application, selecting this option deletes the databases, administration pages, and application pools associated with the service application.

If you're confident that you no longer need this data, then select the check box; however, if you think you may need to re-create the service application in the future, don't select this check box.

6. **Click OK to delete the service application.**

A status page appears, informing you of the progress while your changes are being processed. Depending on the type of service application you're deleting, this process can take a long time.

The final status should be a message that indicates the service application has been deleted. The service application no longer appears on the Manage Service Applications page. If you chose to delete the data associated with the service application, verify that the data has been removed.

Follow these steps to delete a service application by using PowerShell:

1. **On the server running SharePoint 2010, ensure that the person executing the PowerShell commands is a member of the SharePoint_ Shell_Access role on the configuration database and a member of the WSS_ADMIN_WPG local group.**

You can find more information on the PowerShell prerequisites in Book II, Chapter 7.

2. **From the Start menu, choose All Programs⇨Microsoft SharePoint 2010 Products⇨SharePoint 2010 Management Shell.**

3. **At the PowerShell command prompt, type the following commands, pressing Enter after each command.**

```
$OldSPApp = Get-SPServiceApplication -Name "<Exact
    display name of the service application you want to
    delete>"

Remove-SPServiceApplication $OldSPApp -RemoveData
```

The `-RemoveData` switch parameter deletes the service application and all associated data, such as any databases associated with the service application. If you don't want to delete the data associated with the service, run the cmdlet without the `-RemoveData` switch parameter.

A confirmation prompt, as shown in Figure 8-14, appears, asking whether you're sure you want to delete the service application and whether you really want to delete all the associated data.

4. **Type Y and press Enter to delete the service application.**

Book II
Chapter 8

Using Service
Applications

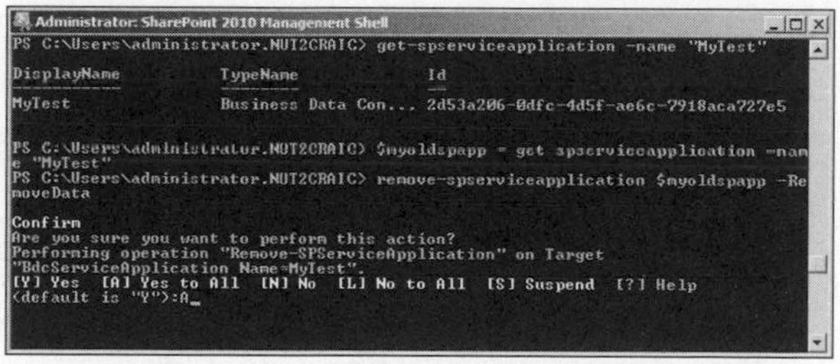

Figure 8-14: When you delete a service application in Power- Shell, you're prompted before proceed- ing with the action.

When you delete a service application, you automatically delete all associated connections. Any local or remote Web Applications consuming the service application will no longer have access to it.

Book III

Services Configuration and Management

"Configuring it has been a little tougher than we thought."

Contents at a Glance

Chapter 1: Analyzing Access Services

In This Chapter

✔ Admiring Access Services architecture

✔ Specifying Access Services settings

✔ Configuring SQL Reporting Services

A s one of the Office applications, Microsoft Access is a great tool for rapidly building database applications. One of its greatest features — much to the chagrin of the IT department — is that it's easy to use making it an accessible development tool for business users. Business users can take advantage of the many wizards that come with Access to quickly create custom database applications, complete with sophisticated query and reporting capabilities. When the database is up and running, you can post it to a network share and grant users access to the application.

The fact that Access is so easy to use and can produce results quickly makes it very popular among business units that have an urgent need, a limited budget, and don't want to go through all the red tape of getting a supported application developed through the official service request channels within their organization. From an IT perspective the unfortunate side effect of this popularity is that you have lots of unmanaged, unsupported applications dispersed throughout your organization, consuming your network resources. As business users become more and more dependent on their Access applications, the risks of using unmanaged applications that aren't within the purview of the IT department really start to pile up. For example, Access applications typically don't have fault tolerance, load balancing, or disaster recovery capabilities built into them and, at the end of the day, if an Access database becomes corrupt the IT department is expected to leap into fire-fighting mode and save the day.

Some organizations try to prevent the negative impact that Access databases can inflict on their environment by placing an organizational ban on the use of Access; however, this type of restriction is akin to throwing the baby out with the bathwater and ends up creating animosity between the IT department and their customer: the business users. And, in the unlikely event that all the business units conform to such a restriction, it doesn't remove the need for rapid application development to respond to their business requests — the IT department is often inundated with requests that they aren't equipped to meet.

Most IT organizations aren't so restrictive and recognize that a balance between governance and business needs must be found. In an effort to find this balance they often end up providing their users with guidelines and best practices on implementing Access databases within their organization, and keep their fingers crossed that their users follow those guidelines. Ideally, the best solution is one that allows the business users to continue to develop their applications in a tool such as Access, and for IT to have an easy way to backup, monitor, and spread the load of those applications across the infrastructure. Drum roll, please: Introducing Access Services!

Access Services — a new feature that comes with SharePoint Server 2010 Enterprise Edition — brings the power and agility of Access applications into the flexible, scalable, and reachable SharePoint environment. Business users can continue to be empowered by developing their applications in Microsoft Access 2010 and can extend the reach of their applications to the Web by publishing them to SharePoint Server 2010. IT administrators can ensure that the applications and their associated data remain secure and are scaled appropriately across the organization.

In this chapter we take a look at the architecture behind Access Services and examine the settings that can help keep both your Access applications and your SharePoint environment running smoothly. We also examine the underlying components required to bring the sophisticated reporting capabilities of Access to your Web-enabled Access databases. Book 4, Chapter 1 goes on to show you how easy it is to publish your Access applications to SharePoint Server 2010.

Access Services Architecture

SharePoint Server 2010 — Enterprise Edition — implements Access Services as a service application within the service application framework. The Access Services service application has many server-side components working together behind the scenes to surface your Access client applications through the browser in SharePoint. At the heart of the architecture is the Access Services Web service. The Access Services Web service, and its associated session service, acts as the interface between the backend query processing and data access layer, and the presentation layer. Figure 1-1 shows a high-level overview of the architecture and the components involved, which include:

✦ **Access Forms and Reports:** All the forms and reports that Access Services presents to users take advantage of the Data Form Web Part to render data in the browser. The Data Form Web Part is a standard Web Part that comes with SharePoint; you can add it directly to your SharePoint Web pages using SharePoint Designer. The page navigation and presentation of data in the Access Services architecture uses AJAX (Asynchronous JavaScript and XML) and JavaScript. The use of AJAX and JavaScript means that you don't have to wait for the Web page to refresh when navigating through large datasets — which ultimately translates to good performance and happy users.

✦ **Project Datasheet:** All of the datasheets that you create in your Access database application render in the browser using the Project Datasheet control that allows you to present a large amount of data in a single datasheet view.

✦ **Access Services Session:** The Access session service is based on Excel services and manages all the session and authentication information for the users inside of SharePoint. The Access Services session sends all data requests to the Access Services Web Service.

✦ **Access Services Web Service:** The Access Services Web service is the application service that sits on top of SharePoint and uses the SharePoint Service Application framework. The service application manages the Access query processor and data access layer.

✦ **Query Processor:** The query process extends the query processing capabilities of SharePoint allowing you to create more complex queries that work with your Web-enabled Access applications.

✦ **Data Access Layer:** The data access layer handles adding and retrieving data to and from SharePoint lists. Any field validation, expressions, and referential integrity defined in the Access database application is implemented using the standard features of SharePoint lists.

✦ **In-memory Cache:** When you add and retrieve data to and from SharePoint, Access stores the data in a data store in memory on the server. When users work with data in the Access application, Access Services uses the store to present that data to the users very quickly.

✦ **Access Services Event Handlers:** The Access Services architecture includes event receivers on it that trigger when certain events take place within your application. For example, if you update one of the forms in your Access database and synchronize your changes back to SharePoint, the event receivers kick off and create a new Web page to display to your users; when you update the macros in your published application, an event receiver kicks off and updates the corresponding SharePoint workflows.

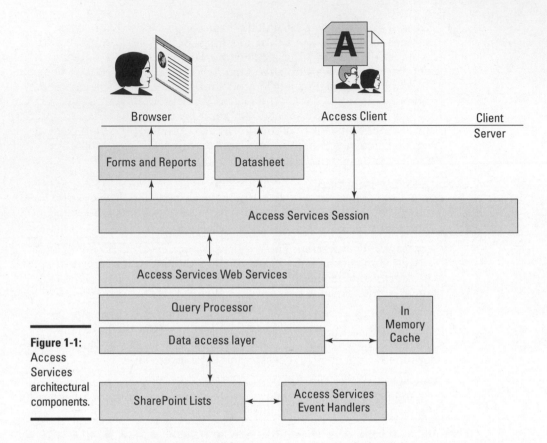

Figure 1-1:
Access
Services
architectural
components.

Managing Access Services

Although you can start leveraging Access Services right away, there are numerous configuration settings that allow you to fine-tune your implementation. For example, you can specify the maximum number of records that a table in an Access Web Application may contain — the default setting is 500,000. The Manage Access Services page in Central Administration contains the configuration setting for Access Services, and can be accessed using the following steps:

1. **Navigate to the Central Administration home page.**

2. **From the Application Management section, click Manage service applications.**

   The Service Applications page appears, listing all of the available service applications in alphabetical order.

3. **Select Access Services and from the Ribbon menu, click Manage.**

   The Manage Access Services Web page appears. Alternatively you can simply click the Access Services link, which also brings you to the Manage Access Services page.

Lists and Queries Settings

The Lists and Queries section of the Access Services management page allows you to manage the queries that are performed against your SharePoint lists, which ultimately helps you manage the performance of your Access Services application. The Lists and Queries settings include:

✦ **Maximum Columns Per Query:** This setting determines the maximum number of columns that can be referenced in a query. Some columns are automatically referenced by the query engine and consequently are included in the setting limit.

   The default value for this setting is 40; valid values for this setting are numbers ranging from 1 to 255.

✦ **Maximum Rows Per Query:** This setting determines the maximum number of rows that a list used in a query may have, or that the output of a query may contain.

   This is a very important setting when it comes to managing the overall performance of your service. You may have an Access Services application that hosts one million records, but chances are you will not need to view all one million records at one time from your browser; rather, you will filter the records to view a specific subset at a time. The Maximum Rows Per Query allows you to set a limit on the maximum number of records that can be returned in a query. If you query returns more records than specified in this setting, you will receive a message notifying you that the query is too expensive to run.

   The default value for this setting is 25,000; valid values for this setting are numbers ranging from 1 to 200,000.

✦ **Maximum Sources Per Query:** This setting determines the maximum number of lists that may be used as input to one query.

   The default value for this setting is 12; valid values for this setting are numbers ranging from 1 to 20.

✦ **Maximum Calculated Columns Per Query:** This setting determines the maximum number of inline calculated columns that can be included in a query. This setting applies to both the calculated columns in the query itself, and any sub-queries on which a query is based. The calculated columns that come with the native SharePoint lists architecture aren't included.

The default value for this setting is 10; valid values for this setting are numbers ranging from 0 to 32.

✦ **Maximum Order By Clauses Per Query:** This setting determines the maximum number of Order By clauses allowed in a query.

The default value for this setting is 4; valid values for this setting are numbers ranging from 0 to 8.

✦ **Allow Outer Joins:** This setting determines whether to allow left and right outer joins in a query. Inner joins are always allowed.

The setting is enabled by default.

✦ **Allow Non Remotable Queries:** This setting determines whether to allow queries that can't run remotely on the database tier. If you clear this setting it means that you allow remote queries to run in your environment; whereas selecting this setting means that only non remotable queries are allowed to run.

The setting is disabled by default.

✦ **Maximum Records Per Table:** This setting allows you to set a limit on the number of records that a table within Access Services may contain. This setting effectively allows you to determine how big applications that use Access Services can get, allowing IT to ensure that when an application reaches the specified limit that it's managed correctly from an organization and policy perspective. For example, if your organization embraces the adaptive and flexile nature of Access Services for small to medium sized database applications, but has a different platform or environment dedicated to large database applications, you can set the Maximum Records Per Table setting and prevent large database tables from being created in Access Services.

The default value for this setting is 500,000; valid values for this setting are –1 (indicating no limit) or any positive integer value.

Application Objects Setting

The Application Objects section of the Access Services management page allows you to set limitations on the types of objects an Access Services application can contain. Currently, this section contains only one setting: the Maximum Application Log Size setting. You can use this setting to set the maximum number of records that the Application log list associated with an Access Web database application may contain. The default value for this setting is 3,000.

Session Management Settings

The Session Management section of the Access Services management page allows you to manage the behavior of the Access database service sessions. The settings include:

✦ **Maximum Request Duration:** Use this setting to specify the maximum duration (in seconds) allowed for a request from an application.

The default value for this setting is 30 seconds; valid values for this setting are –1 (indicating no limit), and numbers ranging from 1 to 207,360 seconds (24 days).

✦ **Maximum Sessions Per User:** Use this setting to specify the maximum number of sessions allowed per user. If the maximum session limit is reached, Access Services deletes the user's oldest session when a new user session is started.

The default value for this setting is 10; valid values for this setting are –1 (indicating no limit), and numbers ranging from 1 to any positive integer.

✦ **Maximum Sessions Per Anonymous User:** Use this setting to specify the maximum number of sessions allowed per anonymous user. If the maximum session limit is reached, Access Services deletes the oldest session when a new session is started.

The default value for this setting is 25; valid values for this setting are –1 (indicating no limit), and numbers ranging from 1 to any positive integer.

✦ **Cache Timeout:** Use this setting to determine the maximum time (in seconds) that a data cache can remain available. The cache timeout is measured from the end of each data request in the cache.

The default value for this setting is 1,500 seconds (25 minutes); valid values for this setting are –1 (indicating no limit), and numbers ranging from 1 to 207,360 seconds (24 days).

✦ **Maximum Session Memory:** Use this setting to determine the maximum amount of memory (in MB) that a session can consume.

The default value for this setting is 64; valid values for this setting are 0 (indicating the setting is disabled), and positive integers ranging from 1 to 4,095.

Memory Utilization settings

On the Memory Utilization section of the Access Services management page, you can specify how much memory to allocate to the Access database service. Currently, this section contains only one setting: Maximum Private

Bytes. You can set a different value for the maximum number of private bytes (in MB) to set aside for the Access database service process to use.

The default value for this setting is –1, which means that Access Services can use 50 percent of the server's physical memory, and no more; valid values are –1 or any positive integer.

Templates settings

In the Templates section of the Access Services management page, you can find settings for configuring the management of Access database *templates* (ACCDT). These are Access database applications packaged in a reusable (template) form and published to SharePoint, where your users can then use them to create SharePoint sites. As an administrator, you can use the Maximum Template Size setting to determine the maximum size (in MB) that you will allow for any Access templates published to your SharePoint environment.

The default value for this setting is 30 MB; valid values for this setting are –1 (indicating no limit) or any positive integer.

Running Reporting Services

Access Services uses SQL Server 2008 R2 Reporting Services for (well, yes) its report-rendering capabilities. Before you can take advantage of this feature, you have to install the SQL Server 2008 R2 Reporting Services Add-in for Microsoft SharePoint Technologies 2010.

Relax — the add-in is available for download from the Microsoft Web site. If you run the prerequisite installer as part of your SharePoint installation, the Reporting Services add-in is installed for you automatically.

Reporting Services Modes

When you've downloaded and installed Reporting Services, you can configure it in one of two modes:

✦ **Local mode:** This mode is a relatively small-scale solution suitable for standalone servers or small server farms (say, a farm containing only one front-end Web server). Install the Reporting Services Add-in for SharePoint in this mode if you don't need a Report Server in the background. Using Local mode, your users can view reports, but won't have access to the more advanced server-side aspects of Reporting Services (such as subscription capabilities).

✦ **Connected mode:** This mode is the default for running Reporting Services in SharePoint Server. To use it, your environment has to run SQL Server 2008 R2 Report Server along with the Reporting Services Add-in. Configuring Reporting Services to run in Connected mode gives you the flexibility to scale your report service to match your business needs.

Reporting Services Components

After the SQL Server 2008 R2 Reporting Services Add-in for SharePoint is installed, your users can get at it and use it via the following components:

✦ **Reporting Services Management User Interface:** Central Administration presents a user interface for managing the integration of Reporting Services. Using this interface, you can specify server name, instance of Report Server, and Reporting Services settings such as timeouts and how many snapshots to keep in the report history.

You can access the Reporting Services management options from the General Application Settings page of Central Administration.

✦ **Reporting Services proxy:** This Web service provides the appropriate communication channel between SharePoint and SQL Report Server.

✦ **Report Viewer Web Part:** Activating the Reporting Services feature in a SharePoint site collection adds the Report Viewer Web Part to the site collection's Web Part Gallery. The Report Viewer Web Part is an AJAX-enabled Web Part that renders your reports in the browser.

Scaling out Reporting Services

If you're using Local mode for your reporting services, the Report Viewer Web Part communicates directly with your SharePoint content database to handle requests and render reports. Local mode is fine for standalone installations, or small Web server farms that only require one front-end Web server. For larger environments, implement Reporting Services in Connected mode. If you're using Connected mode, Reporting Services communicates with a separate Report Server database, getting the requested information from the SharePoint content database. As your environment grows and your business users start creating reports left and right, harnessing all those lovely reporting capabilities, you may have to partition your Report Server components to handle the demands of your users. If the scale gets large enough (and the report-makers get busy enough), you can use Connected mode to configure your environment to handle multiple dedicated Report Servers throughout your enterprise. Figure 1-2 shows a SharePoint server farm with Access Services and Reporting Services load-balanced across multiple application servers.

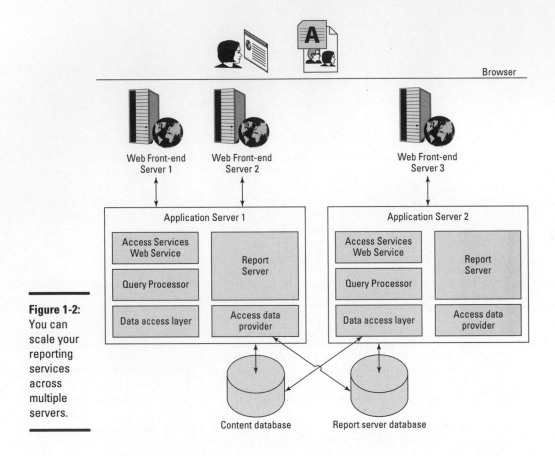

Figure 1-2:
You can
scale your
reporting
services
across
multiple
servers.

The sample farm environment shown in Figure 1-2 consists of the following components:

✦ **Web Front-End Servers:** These servers host the various Access services components such as the Web Parts, the Access Services AJAX components, and the *data-source control* that communicates with the application and figures out to which server it should transmit the requests.

✦ **Application Servers:** These servers host the back-end Access Services components that communicate with the content database and handle service requests from the front-end servers. Report Server can run on the same application server as Access services — or it may run independently on its own dedicated server. The Report Server communicates directly with the Report Server database.

✦ **Content database:** This database holds all the end-user data that SharePoint and Access Services store.

✦ **Report server database:** This database runs in SharePoint Integrated mode — and stores the metadata and objects associated with reports. Running your SQL Reporting Services in SharePoint Integrated mode allows you to manage your SQL Reporting Services reports directly from SharePoint. Having a dedicated report database takes the burden of reporting requests away from the content database, which improves the performance of your SharePoint farm.

Installing Reporting Services

Installing and configuring Reporting Services in your SharePoint environment involves the following general stages:

1. Install and configure your SQL Report Server to run in SharePoint integrated mode.

2. Install the Reporting Services Add-in on your Web front-end servers.

3. Using Central Administration, configure the Reporting Services Integration settings.

When you're configuring the Web Service URL and the Report Manager URL for your Report Server, be sure to use a different URL from the one your SharePoint server farm uses. Reporting Services provides default values for each of those URLs; double-check them so they don't conflict with the URLs you plan to use in your SharePoint implementation.

If you're installing and configuring Reporting Services in Connected mode, the path of least resistance is having your Report Server up and running *before* you install SharePoint. This one preparatory measure makes the whole installation process a lot more straightforward. Here's a prime example: While you're installing SharePoint, you can use the SharePoint Products Preparation tool to install the SQL Server 2008 R2 Reporting Server Add-in for SharePoint. Of course, if circumstances demand that you install the Add-in first, you can — and we show you how next.

Installing the Add-in before installing SharePoint

Here's how to install the SQL Server 2008 R2 Reporting Services Add-in for SharePoint before you have your SharePoint farm up and running:

1. **If your server has Internet access, run the Microsoft SharePoint Products Preparation tool.**

• The SharePoint Products Preparation tool installs all the SharePoint 2010 software prerequisites — including the SQL Server Reporting Services Add-In for SharePoint.

- If your server doesn't have Internet access, download the Reporting Services Add-in (rsSharePoint.msi) from the Microsoft Web site onto your network, transfer the file to your server, and run the Installation Wizard. You will need to run the Installation Wizard using an account that has administrator privileges.

2. **Configure the Report Server integration settings and feature activation.**

   To take care of that bit of business, jump ahead to the "Configuring Reporting Services" section of this chapter.

When you install the SQL Server 2008 Reporting Services Add-in for SharePoint Technologies before you install SharePoint, you won't have to install it every time you add a server to your SharePoint farm. The SharePoint farm configures and activates the Reporting Services Add-in automatically for each new server you add.

Installing the Add-in after installing SharePoint

The following instructions show you how to install the SQL Server 2008 R2 Reporting Services Add-in for SharePoint Technologies after you have your SharePoint farm up and running:

1. **Download the Reporting Services Add-in (**rsSharePoint.msi**) from the Microsoft Web site.**

2. **On only one SharePoint front-end Web server, run the** rsShare-Point.msi **Installation Wizard.**

   If you're installing the Add-in on an existing SharePoint farm, you can run the Installation Wizard on just one SharePoint front-end Web server. The rest of your front-end Web servers require no more than a files-only installation of the Add-in.

3. **On each of the remaining SharePoint front-end Web servers in your farm, run the files-only installation of the add-in.**

   You can use the following steps to run the files-only installation:

   a. *Using Administrator permissions, open a command prompt.*

   b. *Run the following command:*

   ```
   msiexec –i rsSharePoint.msi SKIPCA=1
   ```

   The files-only installation installs all the necessary files on the server but skips the custom action steps of the installation.

4. **Configure the Report Server integration settings and feature activation.**

   You can find this process defined in the "Configuring Reporting Services" section of this chapter, up ahead.

Configuring Reporting Services

You can use the following steps to configure Reporting Services for SharePoint integration and Access Services support:

1. **Using your browser, navigate to the Central Administration home page.**

2. **Click General Application Settings.**

The General Application Settings page appears.

3. **From the Reporting Services application section, click Reporting Services Integration.**

The Reporting Services Integration page appears.

4. **In the Report Server Web Service URL setting, enter the URL for your Report Server Web service.**

This URL should match the setting configured in your Report Server Configuration Manager.

5. **In the Authentication Mode setting, select the authentication mode you want to use.**

You should only use Windows Authentication mode if you have

- A standalone installation of the Report Server and SharePoint

  or

- A Kerberos-enabled system (see Book 2, Chapter 2 for information on SharePoint's authentication options)

Otherwise, choose Trusted Account as your authentication mode.

6. **In the Credentials setting, enter the user name and password of a user who is a member of the Administrator group on the computer that hosts the Report Server.**

7. **In the Activate the Reporting Services Feature setting, determine in which site collections you want to activate the Reporting Services feature.**

Selecting the Activate feature in specified site collections displays a list box that shows you all the available site collections in which you can activate the feature.

8. **Using Windows Explorer, navigate to the Report Server directory.**

The Report Server directory is located at

```
\Program Files\Microsoft SQL Server\MSRS10_50.MSSQLSERVER\
ReportingServices\ReportServer
```

9. **Edit the** `rsreportserver.config` **file; in the** `<Extension>` **node (located under the** `<Data>` **node), add an Access Data Server (**ADS**) extension.**

You can add the ADS extension by using the following code:

```
<Extension Name="ADS" Type="Microsoft.Office.Access.Reports.
    DataProcessing.AdsConnection, Microsoft.Office.Access.Server.
    DataServer, Version=14.0.0.0, Culture=Neutral, PublicKeyToken=71e9bc
    e111e9429c"/>
```

If you haven't added the ADS extension to the `rsreportserver.config` file, you'll hear about it: When you try to view a report in your Web-enabled Access database, you'll receive the cheerful little error message shown in Figure 1-3.

Figure 1-3:
SQL Server
Reporting
Services
Error
indicating
missing ADS
extension.

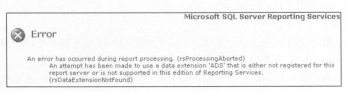

Microsoft SQL Server Reporting Services

Error

An error has occurred during report processing. (rsProcessingAborted)
   An attempt has been made to use a data extension 'ADS' that is either not registered for this
   report server or is not supported in this edition of Reporting Services.
   (rsDataExtensionNotFound)

10. **In the same directory, edit the** `rssrvpolicy` **file, and add the ReportExpressionDefaultPermissionSet.**

Add the following XML code set to the `<NamedPermissionSets>` node:

```
<PermissionSet class="NamedPermissionSet" version="1" Name="ReportExpress
    ionsDefaultPermissionSet">
<IPermission class="SecurityPermission" version="1" Flags="Execution" />
<IPermission class="Microsoft.Office.Access.Server.Security.
    AccessServicesPermission, Microsoft.Office.Access.Server.Security,
    Version=14.0.0.0, Culture=neutral, PublicKeyToken=71e9bce111e9429c"
    version="1.0" Flags="CalculationCallback" />
</PermissionSet>
```

11. **In the** `rssrvpolicy` **file, locate the UnionCodeGroup class with the name** `Report_Expressions_Default_Permissions` **and change its** `PermissionSetName`.

Change the `PermissionSetName` from `Execution` to the following:

```
<CodeGroup class="UnionCodeGroup" version="1" PermissionSetName="Report
   ExpressionsDefaultPermissionSet" Name="Report_Expressions_Default_
   Permissions" Description="This code group grants default permissions
   for code in report expressions and Code element. ">
```

12. Enable Remote Errors for Reporting Services.

Here's the drill:

a. Using SQL Management Studio, connect to the Report Server.

b. Right-click the Report Server node and click Properties.

c. Click Advanced to display the Advanced page.

d. From the Security section, set EnableRemoteErrors *to* True *and click OK.*

Remote Errors are now enabled for your report server, which means that Reporting Services will display additional information if errors occur on your remote servers.

Report Server content types

Reporting Services includes a set of predefined Report Server content types that are used to manage files associated with reports, including:

✦ **Shared data-source files (**.rsds**):** These files contain the necessary connection information to external data sources that your reports use.

Shared data-source files are particularly handy for any data sources used in common within your organization; use them to share the connection information across multiple reports.

✦ **Report models (**.smdl**):** These files are specific to the SQL Report Builder tool. They provide a business description for an underlying database used to create ad-hoc reports and data source for reports. The purpose of the report model is to create a model of the relationships between the entities in a database so that business users can create the reports they need without having to understand the inner workings of the database.

✦ **Report definition files (**.rdl**):** These files — written in an XML markup language known as Report Definition Language — contain all the information needed to generate a report in Report Server including:

• Field definitions

• Parameters and database connections

- Report style including tables, images, graphs, and other objects that your report may require.

Report definition files can be rendered in SharePoint using the Report Viewer Web Part.

In order for SharePoint to be able to recognize and handle each of these files correctly, a content type in SharePoint must be created for each file. When you activate the Reporting Services feature for a site collection through Central Administration, the appropriate Report Server content types are automatically created in the site collection.

Adding Report Server content types to a document library

Adding the Report Server content types to a document library in SharePoint allows you to launch reports and report building tools directly from SharePoint.

Follow these steps to add the Report Server content types to a SharePoint document library:

1. **Ensure the Reporting Services feature is enabled for the site that contains your document library.**

2. **Using your browser, navigate to the SharePoint document library for which you want to add the Report Server content types.**

3. **On the Library tools Ribbon, click the Library tab.**

   The Library ribbon menu appears.

4. **On the Settings Ribbon group, click Library Settings.**

   The Document Library Settings page appears.

5. **From the General Settings section, click Advanced Settings.**

   The Advanced Settings page appears.

6. **From the Content Types section, select Yes to enable the management of content types for the document library.**

7. **Click OK.**

   The Document Library Settings page appears.

8. **From the Content Types section, click Add from existing content types.**

   The Add Content Types page appears.

9. **From the Select Content Types section, in the Select site content types from drop-down list, select Reporting Services.**

   The list of available content types filters to display the content types relating to Reporting Services.

10. **In the Available Site Content Types list, select the Report Builder, Report Model, and Report Data Source content types, and click Add.**

    The content types appear in the Content Types to add list

11. **Click OK.**

    The Document Library Settings page appear, and the Reporting Services content types are listed in the Content Types section.

You must be either a site collection administrator, or have Full Control permissions before you can add content types to a library in SharePoint.

Creating reports

When you have Reporting Services up and running in your SharePoint environment you can upload and publish Report Server content types to your SharePoint libraries and then view and manage your reports directly from SharePoint.

Microsoft provides a number of tools for creating reports, including these:

✦ **Report Builder 3.0:** SQL Server 2008 R2 Report Builder 3.0 is a report authoring tool that provides an easy to use, Microsoft Office like experience for building reports that can be published to your Report Server, or SharePoint site. When you have the Report Server content types mapped to a SharePoint document library you can click the New Report Builder option from the library menu to launch the Report Builder application and create new reports that will be saved directly to the library.

✦ **Business Intelligence Development Studio (BIDS):** BIDS is a version of Visual Studio 2008 that comes with a set of Business Intelligence project templates, one of which is a Report Server Project template. The Report Server Project template enables you to create reports within Visual Studio that you can then directly deploy to your SharePoint site running Reporting Services.

    BIDS 2008 R2 comes with SQL Server 2008 R2.

✦ **Microsoft Office Access 2010:** When you create an Access Web database application and publish it to SharePoint any reports that you create in your database application are published and rendered using Reporting Services. Figure 1-4 shows an example of a report in an Access database that is published to a SharePoint site. The report is leveraging the reporting services integration capabilities of Access Services. You can find more information on how to publish your Access databases to SharePoint in Book IV, Chapter 1.

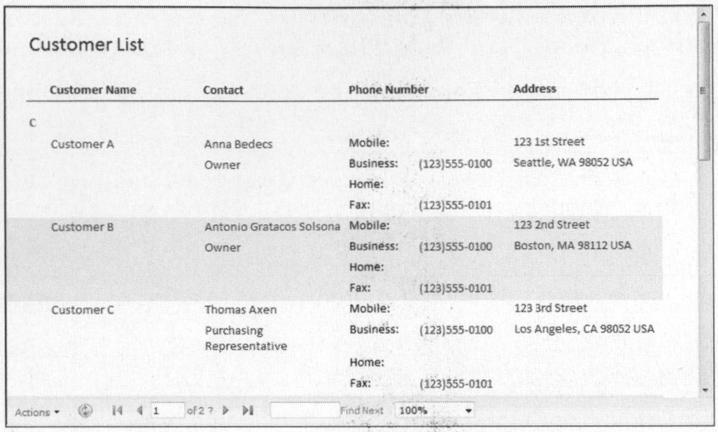

Figure 1-4:
An Access database report rendered through Reporting Services.

Chapter 2: Burrowing into Business Connectivity Services

In This Chapter

✔ Getting familiar with the Business Connectivity Services terminology

✔ Understanding the Business Connectivity Services architecture

✔ Managing Business Connectivity Services by using Central Administration

*B*usiness Connectivity Services (BCS) is the evolution of the Business Data Catalog that was introduced in Microsoft Office SharePoint Server 2007. Business Connectivity Services allows you to easily work with information stored in your back-end line-of-business applications directly from SharePoint and Microsoft Office. For example, if you have a custom solution that you developed in-house that stores its data in an Oracle database, you can connect your SharePoint 2010 environment to that system so that users can work with the Oracle data directly from SharePoint in much the same way they would a SharePoint list. You're no longer confined to the read-only view of your external data from SharePoint, now you can both view and also update your external data directly from SharePoint. The read/write capability is only the tip of the iceberg with respect to the improvements that BCS introduces.

Business Connectivity Services Overview

Business Connectivity Services (BCS) is the new and improved version of the Business Data Catalog that ships with the SharePoint 2010 products and technologies. BCS brings external data into SharePoint and Office so that your users can interact with their data in the applications that they spend most of their days using.

If you're a SharePoint administrator, BCS allows you to centrally manage and control access to data in your back-end systems. The connections that you configure are reusable throughout your enterprise, which means that all the external content types defined for a BCS application can be consumed across multiple farms.

Limitations of the SharePoint Server 2007 Business Data Catalog

Microsoft Office SharePoint Server 2007 introduced the Business Data Catalog, which provided you with a method of presenting data stored in your back-end line-of-business applications directly in SharePoint.

This very powerful feature of SharePoint 2007 did come with some limitations:

- **Read-only access to your data:** You could surface the data from external systems, but it was a read-only view. If you wanted to make changes to the external data, you had to access the external system directly or develop your own interactive Web Parts and back-end Web services to handle the updates.

- **Cumbersome to configure and manage:** To get the connection to your external system up and running, you built an application definition file. An *application definition file* is an XML file that provides information about the external system, including where the data is stored (for example, in a database or a Web service) and the format of the stored data (for example, the primary keys and data types of the data).

  Even though Microsoft provided a Business Data Catalog Definition Editor with SharePoint Server 2007 to help create and manage the application definition XML files, it still remained a cumbersome task with plenty of room for improvement.

- **Limited by the SSP:** The Business Data Catalog was accessible through the Shared Services Provider (SSP) and, consequently, inherited the limitations of the SSP architecture, such as not being able to share a Business Data Catalog across multiple SSPs.

- **Not available with WSS 3.0:** The Business Data Catalog isn't available in the Microsoft Windows Services 3.0 platform. If you wanted to have access to the Business Data Catalog functionality with SharePoint 2007 products and technologies, you needed to purchase either Microsoft Office SharePoint Server 2007 Enterprise Edition or Microsoft Office SharePoint Server 2007 for Internet Sites.

- **Data surfaced through the Business Data Catalog wasn't accessible offline:** Being able to access external content directly from SharePoint 2007 was great, but there was no out-of-the-box method for easily accessing that data offline. SharePoint 2007 provided offline synchronization capabilities to lists, such as discussion boards and calendars, but this capability didn't extend to custom lists and external data sources.

Business Connectivity Services: The new and improved Business Data Catalog

Addressing the Business Data Catalog limitations listed in the "Limitations of the SharePoint Server 2007 Business Data Catalog" sidebar, BCS includes (but isn't limited to) the following improvements:

✦ **Read and write access to your data.** You can now read and update the business data in your back-end applications directly from SharePoint. BCS allows you to connect to external data and present it to your users as a SharePoint list. The users can work with your data in the same way they work with a regular SharePoint list. They can view and edit the properties of items stored in the external database. Figure 2-1 shows data from an external database surfaced through the SharePoint browser interface as an external list. You can perform Create, Read, Update, and Delete actions on the items in the list, just like they were regular SharePoint items.

The beauty of this scenario is that when you make updates to the items in the list or add new items, these changes are immediately reflected in the external system. You can read more about how to create external lists in Book IV, Chapter 3.

Figure 2-1:
You can work with data from external systems in the same way you work with items in a regular SharePoint list.

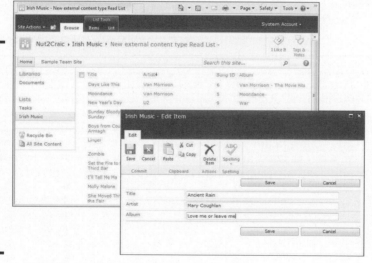

✦ **Supports the new service application architecture.** SharePoint 2010 introduces a fresh approach to the services architecture that removes many of the limitations of its predecessor, thus providing a robust, scalable, and flexible platform.

Web Applications are no longer confined to a single SSP, and the services are no longer bound to a single SSP. Instead, the services can roam throughout your SharePoint farm and, in some cases, even across farms; BCS is a prime example of a service that has cross-farm capabilities. You can find more information about the improvements that the new service application architecture offers in Book II, Chapter 1.

✦ **Available with SharePoint Foundation Server.** Connecting to external systems and being able to work with the data through SharePoint is a powerful and much-sought-after capability. Microsoft has responded to this need by making BCS a fundamental part of the base product platform. You no longer need to purchase the Enterprise version of SharePoint Server 2010 to use this capability; SharePoint Foundation comes with BCS right out of the box.

You can find more information about the service offerings that are available with each version of SharePoint 2010 in Book II, Chapter 1.

✦ **Data that's surfaced through BCS is accessible offline.** BCS allows you to work with external data in the same way you do a regular SharePoint list. The lists that present data from external systems are known as external lists and offer much of the functionality provided by a regular list, such as adding and removing items, and viewing and editing item properties. And because it is, in effect, just a SharePoint list, you can access it offline by using SharePoint Workspace 2010. Figure 2-2 shows the external list from Figure 2-1 synchronized into a SharePoint workspace.

In addition to being able to read your external list data offline, you can create, edit, and delete items directly from SharePoint Workspace 2010, and the next time you connect to the network, your changes are synchronized with the external list in SharePoint, ultimately updating the back-end external database. Of course, you may not want users to take the external data offline in every situation — for example, if the external list contains sensitive data and your company has a directive prohibiting taking this type of data offline. Fortunately, when you create an external content type, you can choose whether you want to enable offline access to the external list that's generated from the content type.

Figure 2-2:
You can take an external list offline by using SharePoint Workspace 2010.

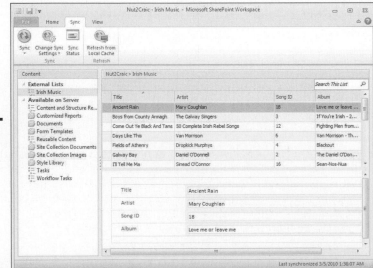

Understanding the Business Connectivity Services value proposition

Figure 2-3 shows Microsoft's value proposition for SharePoint 2010: SharePoint 2010 is a business collaboration platform that offers a rich set of integrated solution areas, including Sites, Communities, and Composites. BCS falls into the Composites solution area and is also a key player in the developers platform. Composites focus on providing end users with an easy way to create no-code collaborative solutions that allow those end users to respond to business needs efficiently and effectively. So, the IT department can focus their resources on managing and maintaining the infrastructure. The IT department can maintain control over end user-based solutions, the tools they use, and the service applications to which they have access, so IT can ensure that the solutions conform to their standards and regulations, as well as protect the infrastructure resources.

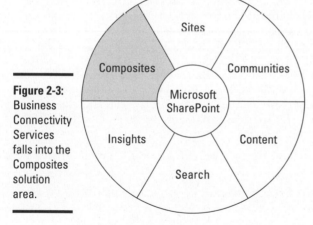

Figure 2-3: Business Connectivity Services falls into the Composites solution area.

Book III
Chapter 2

Burrowing into Business Connectivity Services

You can find more information about the SharePoint 2010 solution areas, and the capabilities that each area provides, in Book I, Chapter 1.

Interpreting the Business Connectivity Services lingo

The following list gives an overview of some commonly used terms when discussing BCS.

✦ **External system:** Refers to a back-end system that hosts data and resides outside the SharePoint application. An external system can be any number of things, such as an external database, a line-of-business application, or a Web service. You can have one or more instances of an external system defined in Business Connectivity Services. An *instance* includes connection and authentication information for the external system. Having multiple instances allows you to set different security parameters on connections to your external systems so that SharePoint can support multiple ways to connect to the same system. For example, if you have an external SQL Server database that you want to leverage in your SharePoint environment, you can configure an instance that uses the user's identity (pass-through) for its authentication mode and another instance of the same external system that uses Windows impersonation.

✦ **Business Connectivity Services (BCS):** The umbrella term that refers to everything related to Business Connectivity Services, including the external systems to which you're connecting and the components that work behind the scenes to allow your users to consume the data stored in those systems.

✦ **Business Data Connectivity (BDC):** The connectivity pieces, or the plumbing, of BCS. The BDC Service application provides a mechanism for storing and securing external content types and BDC models.

✦ **External content type:** A new term introduced with SharePoint 2010 that refers to the building blocks of BCS. But the concept isn't entirely new; if you're familiar with the SharePoint Server 2007 Business Data Catalog, think of the external content type as similar in function to the entity object. For example, if you had a line-of-business system that stored information about employees in an employee table, you'd create an Employee entity object in SharePoint 2007, and you'd create an Employee external content type in SharePoint 2010. The external content type defines the fields and methods of the external data source, in addition to defining how the external content type behaves in both SharePoint and Microsoft Office.

The XML definition of an external content type can include the following information:

- *Fields:* Data that is associated with the object being defined. For example, an Employee external content type may contain fields such as an Employee ID, First Name, Last Name, and Job Title.

- *Methods:* Operations to create, read, update, query, or delete the object.

- *Actions:* What users can do to an object, allowing you to link your business data to external URLs, such as search engines. For example, if you have an external content type named Artists that's implemented in SharePoint as an external list, you can define an action that pipes the name of the artist through to Wikipedia for more information on the artist.

  In the section "Adding actions to an external content type," later in this chapter, we show you how to define external content type actions by using Central Administration.

✦ **BDC model definition file:** An XML file that contains descriptions of one or more external content types defined for an external system, as well as the information specific to the systems environment, including authentication and connection information.

A BDC service may host multiple BDC models. For example, if you have two external applications to which you want to connect and whose data you want to access through SharePoint, you may have two BDC models in your BDC Service application — one for each external application. Alternatively, you may have information pertaining to both systems collated into a single BDC model.

If you're familiar with the SharePoint 2007 Business Data Catalog, think of the BDC model as the next generation of the application definition file.

Figure 2-4 shows a copy of the BDC model for the connection to a simple external SQL database. The BDC model in this example was generated by SharePoint Designer and contains two external content types: Irish Music – Songs and Irish Music – Artists. You can find more information about how to create a BDC model by using SharePoint Designer in Book IV, Chapter 2.

Figure 2-4:
The BDC model XML file contains elements that describe the external systems and the external content types relating to those systems.

```xml
<?xml version="1.0" encoding="utf-16" standalone="yes" ?>
- <Model xmlns:xsi="http://www.w3.org/2001/XMLSchema-instance"
  xsi:schemaLocation="http://schemas.microsoft.com/windows/2007/BusinessDataCatalog
  BDCMetadata.xsd" Name="MultipleBDCIrishMusic"
  xmlns="http://schemas.microsoft.com/windows/2007/BusinessDataCatalog">
  - <LobSystems>
    - <LobSystem Type="Database" Name="IrishMusic">
      + <Properties>
        <Proxy />
      - <LobSystemInstances>
        - <LobSystemInstance Name="IrishMusic">
          + <Properties>
          </LobSystemInstance>
        </LobSystemInstances>
      - <Entities>
        - <Entity Namespace="http://sp2010" Version="1.1.0.0"
          EstimatedInstanceCount="10000" Name="Irish Music - Songs"
          DefaultDisplayName="Irish Music - Songs">
          + <AccessControlList>
          + <Identifiers>
          + <Methods>
          </Entity>
        - <Entity Namespace="http://sp2010" Version="1.0.0.0"
          EstimatedInstanceCount="10000" Name="Irish Music - Artists"
          DefaultDisplayName="Irish Music - Artists">
          + <Properties>
          + <AccessControlList>
          + <Identifiers>
          + <Methods>
          </Entity>
        </Entities>
      </LobSystem>
    </LobSystems>
  </Model>
```

The BDC service supports two types of application definition files:

- *Application models:* Have a `.bdcm` file extension and contain the descriptions of one or more external content types.

- *Resource files:* Have a `.bdcr` extension and enable you to import or export only the localized names, properties, and permissions for one or more external content types.

The great thing about the application definition files is that they're reusable; you can import a `.bdcm` or `.bdcr` file into another SharePoint farm and instantly have access to the external data sources defined in the model — of course, assuming that the farm has the appropriate connectivity and permissions to access the external data sources.

✦ **External list:** A new type of SharePoint list that allows you to bring external data into SharePoint. When you create an external list, you can work with the external data items like they're regular items in a generic SharePoint list. You can create external lists by using the SharePoint browser user interface, using SharePoint Designer, or through code.

When you create an external list, select the external content type that you want to use as the data source for the list. Whether you're creating your external list by using the SharePoint browser's user interface or SharePoint Designer, you can easily browse the available content types defined in your BDC Service.

Figure 2-5 shows the External Content Type Picker object that appears in the browser's user interface when you create an external list; the two external content types match the external content types defined in the BDC model in Figure 2-4.

Figure 2-5:
You can browse the available external content types by using the External Content Type Picker.

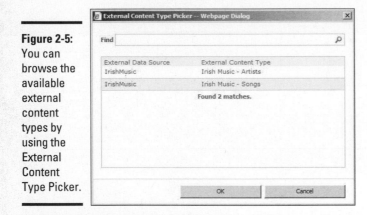

Examining the Business Connectivity Services Architecture

BCS has many components that work together behind the scenes so that you can access external data seamlessly from SharePoint and Microsoft Office.

The Business Connectivity Services architecture consists of

✦ Server-side components that help surface external data into SharePoint

✦ Client-side components that help surface external data in Microsoft Office applications, such as Word, Excel, and Outlook

SharePoint server-side components

BCS includes both server-side components and client-side components. In this section, we discuss the server-side components.

Figure 2-6 shows the main components that encompass the BCS server-side architecture. The SharePoint application servers host the BDC Service and the Secure Store Service, and each service stores its data in its own back-end SQL database that resides on the database servers.

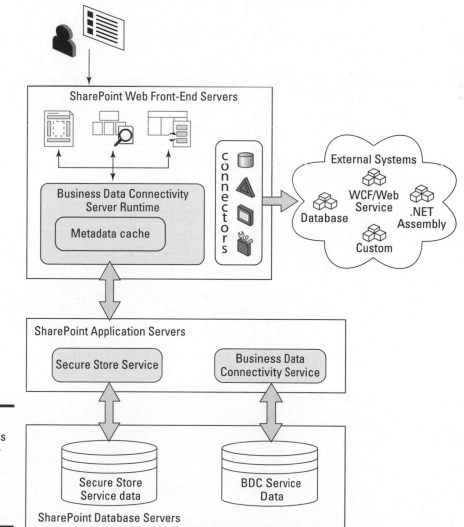

Figure 2-6: The Business Connectivity Service server-side components.

The BDC Service stores the information SharePoint needs to connect to external systems. The Secure Store Service, which ships with SharePoint Server 2010 (it's not available with SharePoint Foundation), stores the user credential information for external systems. The BDC server runtime sits on the front-end Web servers and uses the BDC data to connect to external systems.

SharePoint ships with multiple out-of-the-box connectors that the BDC Service can leverage when it connects to external data sources. For example, the database connector enables the BDC service to connect to back-end databases, such as SQL Server databases.

Users can interact with the external systems through the browser in a number of different ways:

✦ Web Parts, including BDC Web Parts and search-based Web Parts, such as the Content Query Web Part

✦ Generic searches

✦ External lists

The following sections provide more detail about each of the server-side components.

Business Data Connectivity Service

The BDC Service represents the BDC Service application and its application proxy. All versions of SharePoint, including SharePoint Foundation, ship with a BDC Service.

In a typical SharePoint installation, a BDC Service application and an associated service application proxy are created by default. The BDC Service application proxy is then mapped to the default proxy group, which in turn connects your Web Application to the BDC Service application. The BDC Service application provides you with a central place from which you can manage all your external content types and BDC models.

Before you can leverage Business Connectivity Services (BCS) in your SharePoint sites and in Microsoft Office, you must have the service up and running.

You can have multiple BDC Service applications defined in your SharePoint implementation and can associate separate Web Applications with its own BDC Service. A Web Application can use only one BDC service at a given time. In an application proxy group that has multiple BDC Service associations, a Web Application uses the BDC Service application proxy that's marked as the default application proxy.

Business Data Connectivity metadata store

The BDC Service stores its data — including information about your BDC models and the associated external content types — in the BDC metadata store, a database using SQL.

When you create a BDC Service application, you specify the name of the database that SharePoint will create and use as the BDC metadata store for that particular service application. You can view or change the database setting by accessing the Properties dialog box for the service application. Figure 2-7 shows the Properties dialog box for the default BDC Service application.

Figure 2-7:
You can edit the Business Data Connectivity Service application properties.

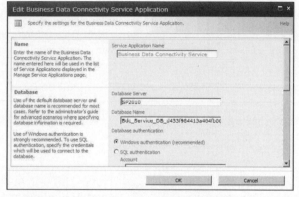

Secure Store Service application

The Secure Store Service is SharePoint Server 2010's replacement for the Single Sign-On service that's part of SharePoint Server 2007. The Secure Store Service enables you to map user credentials for an external system directly to the associated user profile in SharePoint, which provides users with a single-sign-on-type experience.

The Secure Store Service is a great complement to BCS, allowing users to connect to an external system and interact with its data directly from SharePoint without being prompted for their username and password.

Business Data Connectivity server runtime

The BDC server runtime uses the data stored in the BDC metadata store to understand how to interact with the back-end systems. For example, it determines the operations that you can perform on the data (such as Create, Read, Update, and Delete operations), and it determines who has access to the data.

Microsoft Office applications use the BDC server runtime to synchronize with the BDC metadata store and the Secure Store Service data.

Metadata cache

The BDC metadata cache provides caching of the runtime BDC service data.

Connectors

SharePoint ships with multiple connectors that the BDC Service can leverage when it connects to external data sources:

✦ **Database connector:** Similar to the database connector that shipped with SharePoint Server 2007, the 2010 version allows you to connect the BDC Service to external databases, such as a SQL Server database.

✦ **WCF/Web services connector:** New with SharePoint 2010. It allows you to connect to WCF-based services or to Web services.

✦ **.NET assembly connector:** Another new connector that ships with SharePoint 2010. You can create an assembly that collates data from a variety of sources, and then use the .NET assembly connector to connect to the assembly and access the data the assembly provides directly from SharePoint and Microsoft Office.

✦ **Custom connector:** Also new in SharePoint 2010, this connector is useful when you're connecting to a data source that has a dynamic interface, such as a database that frequently has columns added. In this instance, it doesn't make sense to use the .NET assembly connector because you'd have to recompile and redeploy your assembly files, in addition to the model, each time there's a change in the back-end.

By using the custom-connector approach, you need to update the BDC model only when changes occur on the back-end.

Client-side components

Part of the BCS architecture includes client components that allow supported Microsoft Office 2010 products to interact with external systems. The following Microsoft Office 2010 products support integration with BCS:

✦ Access 2010

✦ InfoPath 2010

✦ Outlook 2010

✦ SharePoint Workspace 2010

✦ Word 2010

Figure 2-8 shows the client-side components that make the integration between the Office applications and the BDC Service possible. The components include

✦ **BDC client runtime:** At the heart of the client-side architecture, it's basically the client-side equivalent of the BDC server runtime. The client runtime allows supported Microsoft Office applications to leverage the connections already defined in the BDC Service and connect directly to back-end systems. The client doesn't need to connect to SharePoint in order to interact with external data.

The client-side runtime and server-side runtime have a lot in common. For example, the object model is common to both, so if you know how to code to the client-side runtime object model, then you know how to code to the server-side runtime object model.

✦ **Connectors:** The BDC runtime uses the same out-of-the-box connectors that the server runtime uses:

- Database connector
- WCF/Web service connector
- Microsoft .NET assembly connector
- Custom connector

✦ **Client data cache:** The Client data cache uses a SQL Compact Edition (SQL CE) database to cache data from the external systems. The client runtime stores data in the cache when you're working offline and then commits the data back to the external systems the next time you're online.

If you use Microsoft Outlook as your e-mail client, this method of storing data in an offline cache is very similar to the cached-mode experience that you get with Outlook and Exchange.

Book III
Chapter 2

Burrowing into
Business Connectivity
Services

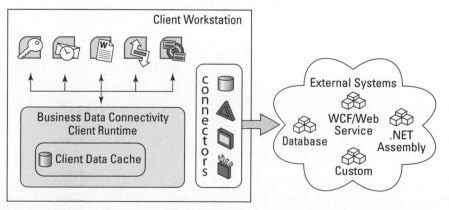

Figure 2-8:
The Business Connectivity Services client-side components.

Managing Business Connectivity Services

Central Administration provides a place from which you can manage and maintain your Business Data Connectivity (BDC) Service application and its associated data. In the following sections, we walk you through some common management tasks associated with the BDC Service.

To create service applications, you must be a farm administrator. To manage a service application, you must either be a farm administrator or an administrator of the specific service application that you're managing.

Starting the BDC Service

Before you manage and use your BDC Service, you must have an instance of the BDC Service started on at least one server in your farm.

Follow these steps to start the BDC Service from Central Administration:

1. **Navigate to the Central Administration home page.**

2. **From the Systems Settings section, click Manage Services on Server.**

   The Services on Server Web page appears, from which you can start and stop instances of the services running on the servers in your farm.

3. **In the Server drop-down list, select the server on which you want to start the service.**

4. **In the list of services, locate the Business Data Connectivity Service.**

5. **In the Action column, click the Start link to start the BDC Service.**

   A Stop link, rather than a Start link, in the Actions column means that the service is running on the selected server.

Creating a BDC Service application

You can use the Manage Service Applications page in Central Administration to access and manage the out-of-the-box BDC Service application. If you don't have a BDC Service application up and running, you need to create one before you can leverage BDC services in your SharePoint implementation.

Follow these steps to create a BDC Service application from Central Administration:

1. **Navigate to the Central Administration home page.**

2. **In the Application Management section, click Manage Service Applications.**

   The Service Applications management appears, listing all the service applications that you have configured for your server farm.

3. **In the Ribbon menu, choose New⇨Business Data Connectivity Service.**

   The Create New Business Data Connectivity Service Application Web dialog box appears, listing all the settings required for the BDC service.

4. **Complete the required fields.**

   Provide values for each of the following BDC service application settings. The settings you specify can be changed at any time.

   - *Name:* Enter the name of the new BDC Service application. The name you enter in this field is the name that will appear in the list of service applications.

   - *Database Server, Database Name, and Authentication Information:*

     Enter the name of the database server that will host the BDC Service application database, the name of the database that you want to give to the BDC metadata store, and the credentials that the BDC service will use to connect to the database. When you name the database, ensure that you select a name that's unique to your implementation.

   - *Application Pool:* Select the application pool that you want to use for the service application. You can choose an existing application pool or create a new one.

5. **Click OK.**

   Your newly created BDC Service application and an associated service application proxy should appear in the list of service applications.

Assigning BDC administrators

You can specify users or groups of users who have rights to administer your BDC Service application. The users to whom you assign administrator rights receive limited access to the Central Administration site, can manage the BDC Service application settings, and have permissions on the entire metadata store for that specific service application instance.

Members of the farm administrators' group, by default, have rights to manage all service applications.

Follow these steps to assign administrators to your BDC Service application by using Central Administration:

1. **Navigate to the Central Administration home page.**

2. **In the Application Management section, click Manage Service Applications.**

3. **In the Manage Service Applications page that appears, select the Business Data Connectivity Service application to which you want to assign administrators.**

When you select the BDC Service application, the Administrators button on the Ribbon menu activates.

4. **In the Ribbon menu, click Administrators.**

   The Administrators for Business Data Connectivity Service control loads.

5. **Add and remove administrators, as needed.**

   To add users to the list of administrators, enter the account name or security groups, and then click Add. Next, select the name and select the Full Control check box in the Permissions section.

   To remove users from the list of administrators, select the account or security group from the list, and then click Remove.

6. **Click OK to save changes to the BDC Service application's Administrators list.**

   If you made changes to the list of administrators, you must save the changes before they can take affect.

Accessing the BDC management page

After you create your BDC Service application and get an instance of that service running on at least one server in your farm, you can start managing and using your service application.

Follow these steps to access the Central Administration management page for your BDC Service application:

1. **Navigate to the Central Administration home page.**

2. **In the Application Management section, click Manage Service Applications.**

   The Service Applications management appears, listing all the service applications that you have configured for your server farm.

3. **From the list of service applications, select the BDC Service application that you want to manage.**

   When you select a service application, the Manage button becomes active on the Ribbon menu.

4. **In the Ribbon menu, click Manage.**

   A page similar to that shown in Figure 2-9 appears, listing your external content types. If you haven't created your external content types, then you see a message that indicates no external content types are currently present. The Ribbon menu displays the menu options relevant to managing a Business Data Connectivity service application.

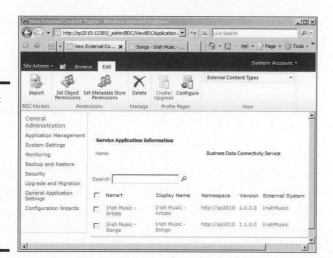

Figure 2-9:
You can centrally manage your external content types and BDC models.

Setting permissions on the BDC metadata store

Before you create external content types, assign permissions to allow administrators, and possibly other designated users, specific access rights to the BDC metadata store. For example, in order to create an external content type, a user must have Edit permissions so that he or she can edit the BDC model.

You can assign the following BDC metadata-store permissions to an account, group, or claim:

✦ **Edit:** Edit external systems, BDC models, and external content types.

✦ **Execute:** Execute operations on external content types. Operations include

- Create
- Read
- Update
- Delete
- Query

✦ **Selectable in Clients:** Create external lists of any external content type.

✦ **Set Permissions:** Set permissions on external content types, external systems, and BDC models.

Follow these steps to assign permissions on your BDC Service application's metadata store by using Central Administration:

1. **Access the Management page for your BDC Service application.**

    You can follow the instructions in the preceding section.

2. **In the Ribbon menu, click Set Metadata Store Permissions.**

    The Set Metadata Store Permissions dialog box appears.

3. **Enter the account, group, or claim to which you want to grant permissions, and then click Add.**

    The security principal appears in the list of added accounts.

4. **Ensure that the security principal you just added is selected.**

5. **Select the permissions that you want to apply to the security principal.**

    A list of the available permissions appears in the permissions box at the bottom of the dialog box.

6. **Select Propagate Permissions, if needed.**

    Select this option if you want to apply the permissions to all the BDC models, external systems, and external content types in the BDC metadata store for your BDC Service application.

7. **Click OK to save the changes.**

    Permission changes take affect when you click the OK button.

Choosing to propagate permissions overwrites existing permissions on the BDC metadata store.

Switching between views

When you access the management page for your BDC Service application, SharePoint presents you with a list of all the external content types stored in your BDC metadata store by default. The Ribbon menu includes a group named View, which shows you the currently selected view of objects in the BDC metadata store. The view is set to External Content Types by default. You can switch between three views when you manage your BDC Service application:

✦ **BDC Models:** Presents a list of all the BDC Models in the metadata store of the BDC Service application that you're managing. The Ribbon in SharePoint is context sensitive, so switching to the BDC Models view leads to changes in the Ribbon menu. For example, an additional menu option named Export appears that allows you to export the selected BDC model to an XML file that you can then import into another SharePoint system.

✦ **External Systems:** Presents a list of all the external systems defined in the metadata store of the BDC Service application that you're managing. Switching to the External Systems view allows you to manage settings specific to your defined external systems. Clicking the external system name in this list displays an additional management page where you can manage the external system instances and change settings such as the authentication mode for the instance.

✦ **External Content Types:** The default view for the BDC Service application management page. It lists all the external content types defined in the metadata store of the BDC Service application that you're managing. You can use this view to manage the external content types and perform specific tasks, such as configuring a profile page host for the external content type. The section "Configuring the profile page host" in this chapter explains how to set up a profile page host for you BDC service.

Follow these steps to switch between views in the BDC Service application:

1. **Access the management page for your BDC Service application.**

   You can follow the steps in the section "Accessing the BDC management page," earlier in this chapter, to navigate to this page.

2. **On the Edit tab, in the View group, click the arrow to the right of the view name to display the available views in a drop-down list.** Figure 2-10 shows the drop-down list that appears when you click the View arrow in the Ribbon menu.

3. **Click the view that you want to display.**

   For example, if you want to display a list of all the BDC models defined in the metadata store for the BDC Service application that you're managing, then click BDC Models.

Figure 2-10:
You can switch between views of the data in the BDC metadata store.

Setting object permissions

In addition to being able to set permissions on the entire BDC metadata store, you can set more granular permissions on individual objects within the store. For example, if you want to give some users the ability to manage an external content type but don't want them to manage other content types, then you can give the users special permissions on the external content type.

Follow these steps to assign permissions on objects in the BDC metadata store by using Central Administration:

1. **Access the management page for your BDC Service application.**

    If you don't know how to navigate to the management page, use the steps in the section "Accessing the BDC management page," earlier in this chapter.

2. **Change the view to list the object on which you want to set permissions.**

    You can select one of three out-of-the-box views when managing metadata store items:

    -   If you want to apply permissions to a BDC model, change the view to BDC Models.

    -   If you want to apply permissions to an external system, change the view to External Systems.

    -   If you want to apply permissions to an external content type, leave the view set to External Content Types.

3. **Select the object to which you want to apply the permissions.**

    You can't select more than one object when you set object permissions.

4. **In the Ribbon menu, click Set Object Permissions.**

    The Set Object Permissions dialog box appears, where you can apply permissions to specific accounts, groups, and claims.

5. **In the Add Account text box, enter the account, group, or claim to which you want to grant permissions, and then click Add.**

    The security principal appears in the list of added accounts.

6. **Ensure that the security principal you just added is selected.**

7. **Select the permissions that you want to apply to the selected security principal.**

    A list of the available permissions appears in the permissions box at the bottom of the dialog box.

8. **Select Propagate Permissions, if needed.**

   Selecting this option applies the permissions to all the components of the selected object. The Propagate Permissions setting applies to

   - *External content types:* Propagates the permissions to all the methods of the external content type
   - *External systems:* Propagates the permissions to all the external content types that belong to the external system

9. **Click OK to save the changes.**

   Permission changes take affect when you click the OK button.

Choosing to propagate permissions overwrites existing permissions on the child elements of the selected object.

Adding actions to an external content type

Actions are a very powerful feature of Business Connectivity Services (BCS) that was carried forward from SharePoint 2007. Actions allow you to define actions that a user takes on an object, such as performing searches on the selected item or piping the selected item over to another enterprise application for additional processing. You can add actions to your external content types by using Central Administration.

When you add a new action to an external content type, the action isn't available to existing external lists of that external content type. Only new external lists of the external content type to which the action is applied display the action in the shortcut menu.

Follow these steps to add an action to an external content type by using Central Administration:

1. **Access the management page for your BDC Service application.**

   The section "Accessing the BDC management page," earlier in this chapter, explains how to navigate to this page.

2. **Ensure that the View is set to External Content Types**

   The External Content Types view is the default view shown in the BDC Service management page and displays a list of all the external content types.

3. **Locate the external content type to which you want to add an action and click the arrow to the right of that content type.**

   The drop-down list for the selected external content type opens.

4. **In the drop-down list, click Add Action.**

   The Add Action page appears, where you can enter the details of the action that you want to apply on the external content type.

5. **Enter the action name in the Action Name text box.**

   The action name will appear on the shortcut menu of an item associated with the external content type in SharePoint. Figure 2-11 shows the shortcut menu for an external content type that has a custom action named Search Artist defined.

6. **Enter the URL in the Navigate To This URL text box.**

   Type the URL that you want to navigate to when you click the action from the shortcut menu. If you want your URL to vary depending on the item a user selects in your SharePoint list, you can pass parameters to the URL. To pass parameters into your URL, simply type a number in braces, such as **{0}**, in the Navigate To This URL text box. In the example shown in Figure 2-11, the action URL passes the Artist field of the currently selected item to the SharePoint search by using the site-relative URL `/_layouts/OSSSearchResults.aspx?k={0}`.

7. **Assign a property to each parameter in the URL.**

   If you use parameters in the URL in Step 6, you need to assign a property to use for each parameter. For example, if you use the parameters `{0}` and `{1}` in your URL, you need to map `{0}` to a property and `{1}` to another property.

   Follow these steps to add a parameter:

   a. *In the URL Parameters section, click Add Parameter.*

      A parameter drop down list appears displaying a list of available properties that you can select to pass as parameters in your URL.

   b. *Click the Property arrow and select the property that you want to map to the parameter from the drop-down list that appears.*

      For example, in Figure 2-11, the action we created has the Artist property mapped to parameter `{0}`.

8. **(Optional) Select an Icon that you want to appear next to the action.**

   The icon that you set appears next to the action name on the shortcut menu of an item associated with the external content type in SharePoint. If you don't want to display an icon next to the action, you can keep the default setting of No Icon.

   If you do want to provide an icon, you can either pick one of the standard icons that SharePoint provides, or you can enter the URL location of a custom icon that you want to use.

SharePoint provides the following standard icons:

- Delete

- Edit

- New

9. **(Optional) Select the Default Action setting if you want the action to be the default action for the external content type.**

Setting an action as the default action for an external content type means that when a user clicks an item of the associated external content type, he or she doesn't have to navigate the shortcut menu to select the action — instead, the action is launched automatically.

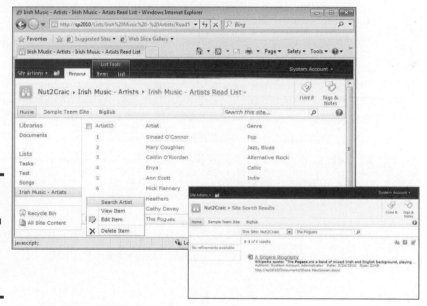

Figure 2-11: The Search Artist action invokes a search on the artist in SharePoint.

Book III Chapter 2

Burrowing into Business Connectivity Services

Configuring the profile page host

A profile page displays information for the selected item of an external content type, including any custom actions that you've defined. When you create a profile page, a View Profile action is also created and added to the shortcut menu, as shown in Figure 2-12. The View Profile action is set as the default action for the external content type, overwriting any previously defined action that you may have assigned as the default.

Before you can create a profile page for your external content types, you must configure a profile page host. The *profile page host* is a site that stores your profile pages.

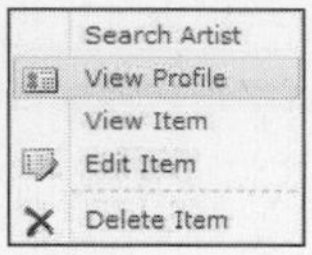

Figure 2-12:
Creating a
profile page
adds the
View Profile
action to
the shortcut
menu.

Follow these steps to configure the profile page host for your BDC Service application, using Central Administration:

1. **Create a SharePoint site that you'll use to host the profile pages.**

   Create a dedicated SharePoint site to assume the profile-page-host role.

   When creating your site, ensure that the site's permissions are set appropriately:

   • Users who plan to create profile pages need design permissions, at minimum, to allow them to add and customize pages at the host site.

   • End users need read access to the site.

2. **Access the management page for your BDC Service application.**

   If you're unsure how to navigate to the management page, you can use the steps in the section "Accessing the BDC management page," earlier in this chapter.

3. **In the Profile Pages group on the Ribbon menu, click Configure.**

   The Configure External Content Type Profile Page Host Web dialog box appears.

4. **Select Enable Profile Page Creation and, in the Host SharePoint Site URL text box, enter the URL of the site that will host your profile pages.**

5. **Click OK.**

Creating and upgrading profile pages

After you configure the profile page host for your BDC Service application, you can create and upgrade your profile pages.

Creating a profile page for an external content type creates a special Web page in the site that's specified as the profile page host. The external content type profile page displays information about an item selected from an external list in SharePoint, including the item's fields and custom actions. Figure 2-13 shows the default profile page generated by SharePoint for the Irish Music – Artists external content type.

Figure 2-13:
The profile page displays information about the selected item.

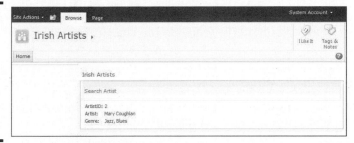

Updating a profile page simply updates the previously created page to reflect any changes made to the external content type, such as the addition of a new field. The update process follows the exact same steps as creating a profile page does.

Follow these steps to create (or update) a profile page for an external content type by using Central Administration:

1. **Create a SharePoint site to host the profile pages.**

   Microsoft recommends that you create a single, dedicated SharePoint site to assume the profile-page host role.

   When creating your site, ensure that the permissions for the site are set appropriately:

   • Users who need to create profile pages must have design permissions, at minimum, to allow them to add and customize pages at the host site.

   • End users need read access to the site.

2. **Access the management page for your BDC Service application.**

   We describe how to get to this page in the section "Accessing the BDC management page," earlier in this chapter.

3. **Ensure that the view is set to External Content Types.**

   The External Content Types view is the default view in the BDC Service management page, and it displays a list of all the external content types.

4. **Select the external content type for which you want to create a profile page.**

   You can select more than one content type during this process by selecting the check box next to each content type.

5. **In the Profile Pages group on the Ribbon menu, click Create/Upgrade.**

   Creating and upgrading profile pages from the Ribbon command is great when you're creating or upgrading for more than one external content type at a time. If you're performing the operation on only a single external content type, you can also access the Create/Upgrade option by clicking the arrow to the right of the selected external content type, and then clicking Create/Upgrade Profile Page from the shortcut menu that appears.

6. **Select or deselect the option Allow Overwriting of Existing Profile Pages, depending on your needs.**

   If you're upgrading your profile page and want to overwrite the previous version of the page, select this option.

   If you're upgrading your profile page and want to create a new version of the page while keeping a copy of the previous version, deselect this option.

   If you opt to overwrite your profile page, SharePoint permanently deletes all previous customizations of the page.

7. **Click OK.**

   The profile page is created on the profile page host site, and the default action for the external content type is set to the new profile page.

Importing a new BDC model or resource file

The BDC Service application supports the importing and exporting of BDC models into the metadata store. Exporting and importing BDC models provides portability and extensibility to your external connections because you can export a BDC model from one SharePoint environment and import it into another. This export/import scenario is particularly useful when you're developing your BDC models because it allows you to work out the kinks in your development. After you feel satisfied that the model works for you and meets your business needs, you can export it from your development or testing environment, and import it into production.

Follow these steps to import a BDC model by using Central Administration:

1. **Access the management page for your BDC Service application.**

   You can find the steps for this process in the section "Accessing the BDC management page," earlier in this chapter.

2. **In the BDC Models group on the Ribbon menu, click Import.**

   The Import BDC Model page appears.

3. **Browse to the BDC model or resource file that you want to import.**

4. **From the File Type section, select the type of definition file that you're importing.**

   When you import a BDC model, you can import one of two definition files:

   - *BDC model definition file:* An XML file that contains descriptions of one or more external content types defined for an external system and the information specific to the systems environment, including authentication and connection information.

   - *Resource definition file:* A file that contains the localized names, properties, and permissions for one or more external content types. You can use the file to add definitions to an existing external content type. For example, if you have defined an external content type that has a set of properties and you want to add one additional property to the definition, you can simply import a resource definition file that contains the XML definition of the new property.

5. **If you're importing a resource definition file, in the Advanced Settings section, select the resources that you want to import.**

   You can select one or more resource types to import, including

   - *Localized Names:* Import localized names for the external content types in a particular locale. The localized names that you import are merged with existing localized names in the BDC metadata store.

   - *Properties:* Import the properties for external content types. Imported properties are merged with the existing property descriptions in the BDC metadata store.

   - *Permissions:* Import the permissions for external content types. Imported permissions are stored with the existing information in the BDC metadata store.

6. **Click Import.**

   The newly imported BDC model appears in the list of BDC models, and its associated external content types and external systems appear in the External Content Types view and the External Systems view, respectively.

Use caution when importing permissions. Imported permissions overwrite any existing access control lists for the external content type.

When you import a BDC model, you don't need to change the view; the Import option appears on all views. If you want to export a BDC model, you need to switch the view to BDC Models.

Exporting a new BDC model or resource file

The BDC Service application supports the importing and exporting of BDC models into the BDC metadata store.

Follow these steps to import a BDC model by using Central Administration:

1. **Access the management page for your BDC Service application.**

Check out the section "Accessing the BDC management page," earlier in this chapter, to find out how to navigate to this page.

2. **Switch to the BDC Model view.**

The BDC Model view displays a list of all the defined BDC models in the metadata store for the BDC Service application that you're managing.

To switch to the BDC Model view, follow these steps:

a. *In the View group on the Ribbon menu, click the arrow to the right of the view name to display the available views in a drop-down list.*

b. *Select BDC Model.*

3. **From the list of BDC Models that appears on the page, select the BDC model that you want to export.**

You can export only one BDC model at a time.

4. **In the BDC Models group on the Ribbon menu, click Export.**

Alternatively, you can click the arrow of the selected BDC model, and then select Export from the shortcut menu that appears.

The Export BDC Model page appears.

5. **Select the type of definition file that you're exporting.**

You can choose to export

• BDC Model definition

• Resource definition

The preceding section explains the difference between these two files.

6. **If you're exporting a resource definition file, in the Advanced Settings section, select the resources that you want to export.**

You can select one or more resource types to export:

• *Localized Names:* Export the localized names for the external content types in the BDC model for a particular locale.

• *Properties:* Export the properties for the external content types in the BDC model.

- *Permissions:* Export the permissions for the external content types in the BDC model.

- *Proxies:* Export an implementation-specific proxy that the BDC service uses to connect to the external system.

7. **Click Export.**

   The File Download dialog box appears.

8. **Click Save to download the definition file.**

   If you're exporting a BDC model, the File Download dialog box prompts you to save the file with a .bdcm extension.

   If you're exporting a resource definition file, the File Download dialog box prompts you to save the file with a .bdcr extension.

Chapter 3: Exploring Excel Services

In This Chapter

✓ Looking into the Excel Services architecture

✓ Sizing Excel Services to fit the scale of your business

✓ Configuring Excel Services

Microsoft Excel is one of the most pervasive and powerful pieces of analytical software widely adopted by end users for business intelligence. Users from every walk of life — from high-powered business executives sharing financial data to the local soccer coach sharing league schedules and results — have been sharing all kinds of data using Excel for many years. Microsoft Excel is so intuitive and easy to use that end users can get hooked on its capabilities very quickly. And that can be a problem.

The upside of Excel's popularity is that it encourages people to collaborate, share and capture their intellectual knowledge, and think in terms of spreadsheets. The downside is that managing and governing the proliferation of Excel workbooks can turn into a world-class headache. Those pesky workbooks crop up in mutant versions all over the organization — often containing sensitive business data. Ensuring that any shared data is accurate, appropriate for its user, and up to date is . . . *challenging* to say the least. Some organizations try to resolve this issue by forcing their users to "give up" their spreadsheets, requiring them to use a centralized Business Intelligence platform that has little or no integration with Excel. This attempt at corralling the use of Excel often results in unhappy users, which ultimately results in bad or incomplete data.

The introduction of Excel Services with SharePoint 2007 was a welcome addition, and a step in the right direction — that is, toward providing an effective, secure method of exchanging and analyzing business data, while at the same time providing IT with an easy way to manage, monitor, and secure all that sensitive data being shared across the organization. SharePoint Server 2010 Enterprise Edition builds on those capabilities providing more functionality, security, and scalability. Excel Services integrates better than ever, offering easy hooks into other services such as PerformancePoint Services. Result: a powerful, easy-to-use platform for business intelligence.

In this chapter we take you behind the scenes to show you the workings of Excel Services — and examine the settings that can help you keep users of Excel workbooks from getting disgruntled (you might even "re-gruntle" them) and your SharePoint environment running smoothly.

Chapter 4, Book IV shows you how easy it is to publish your Excel workbooks to SharePoint Server 2010.

Admiring the Excel Services Architecture

SharePoint Server 2010 Enterprise Edition implements Excel Services as one of various service applications (for more about those, see Book II, Chapter 1). As a service application, Excel Services has many server-side components that work together behind the scenes to give users access to Excel workbooks in SharePoint — through the browser.

Understanding the Excel Services Components

At the heart of Excel Services is the number-crunching capability: Excel Calculation Services. Figure 3-1 shows a general overview of how this service's components are put together.

As with many SharePoint services, Excel Services is a *multi-tier* service application (see Book II, Chapter 1); components residing at each level work together.

Excel Services Web Front d Server Tier

Your organization's front-end Web server handles incoming requests from your users for their Excel workbooks; Excel Services provides that access. Here's how it works: The front-end Web server communicates with Excel Calculation Services, which is running on the application server. The front-end Web server translates any responses it receives from the application server into the appropriate HTML for rendering in the browser.

The front-end Web server hosts a number of components, including these:

✦ **Excel Web Access:** This component resides on your front-end Web servers and renders your Excel workbooks in your browser. Excel Web Access provides the authentic look and feel of the Excel client application. Result: Your users get a consistent (and familiar) Excel experience in an application running on the server.

✦ **Excel Web Services:** Your organization's developers are the users most likely to encounter this component: It's the application programming interface (API) to Excel Services.

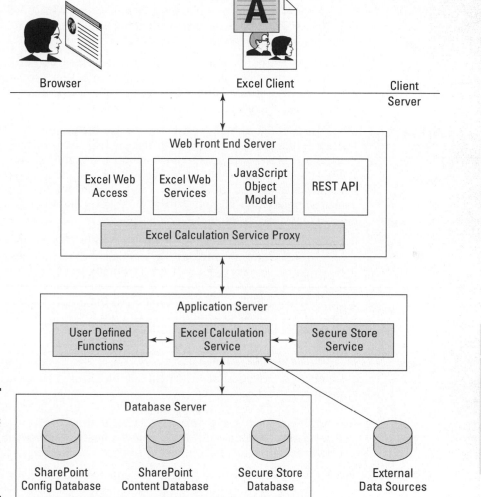

Figure 3-1: Components of the Excel Services architecture.

Book III
Chapter 3

Exploring Excel
Services

You can use Excel Web Services to automate Excel calculation activities, such as updating the workbook data.

✦ **JavaScript OM:** Excel Web Access has been part of the Excel Services architecture for a long time — but a new addition for SharePoint 2010 is the JavaScript object model. That's because the workbooks that Excel Web Access renders in the browsers are programming objects; JavaScript OM allows you to manipulate them as if they were ordinary Excel files.

You can put your JavaScript code in a Web Part (such as the Content Editor Web Part) on the same page as your Excel Web Access Web Part. If you do so, that code automatically affects and manipulates the contents of the Excel Web Access Web Part.

✦ **REST API:** Using this component of Excel Services, you can easily access parts of your workbook directly through a URL; there you can perform workbook operations (such as the retrieval and update of workbook data) by using standard HTTP operations.

REST (Representational State Transfer) is a technique for interacting with systems using the Hypertext Transfer Protocol. SharePoint 2010 comes with a set of REST services, which it implements by using ADO.NET Data Services. You can use REST to add, delete, and query items in SharePoint lists — all by using standard HTTP. If you're using REST, you can manipulate SharePoint content without having to grapple with the SharePoint object model.

✦ **Excel Calculation Services Application Proxy:** This component connects to and communicates with Excel Calculation Services (which is — say it with us — a service application running on the application server). The proxy regulates incoming requests to balance the load of calculations and send them to the right Excel Services applications. When you create an Excel Services service application in SharePoint, the application proxy is created automatically for you.

Excel Services Application Server Tier

Excel Calculation Services is at the heart of the Excel Services architecture, whichever way the data is flowing:

✦ The front-end Web server uses Excel Calculation Services to send requests for calculations — which the application server then receives and processes.

✦ Excel Calculation Services processes requests that the front-end Web server receives, and returns data that matches those requests.

For example, if a user wants to open an Excel workbook in SharePoint, the front-end Web server receives the request and submits it to Excel Calculation Services for processing. Excel Calculation Services retrieves the requested workbook content from the database and sends it back to the front-end Web server for rendering in the browser. If the workbook connects to external data, Excel Calculation Services handles the connection, update, and retrieval of data going to and coming from the data source.

Excel Calculation Services performs all the tasks that happen when you interact with an Excel workbook — in particular, these:

✦ Loading your workbooks

✦ Security and verification of authorizations

✦ Connecting to external data

✦ Refreshing your workbook data

✦ Updating and retrieving your workbook data

✦ Performing calculations and retrieving any user-defined functions that are implemented in the workbook and stored in SharePoint

✦ Managing session information, including the caching of data

Excel Services Database Server Tier

To do its magic with numbers, Excel Services makes use of several databases:

✦ **SharePoint configuration database:** This database holds Excel Services configuration information — the settings that regulate how this service application behaves.

✦ **SharePoint content database:** This database stores the Excel workbooks that Excel Services saves to SharePoint.

✦ **Secure Store Database:** Excel Services can use an unattended service account to connect to external data. It's actually called (wait for it) the Unattended Service Account (for more about how it works, see the section called "Configuring the Secure Store," later in this chapter).

The credentials that keep this account secure have to be stored somewhere — and that's the job of the Secure Store Service database. Excel Services communicates with the Secure Store Service to retrieve those credentials as needed.

Scaling Excel Services

Excel Services sits at the top of the SharePoint 2010 platform; you can use it to take advantage of all the benefits of SharePoint — especially if you want to scale your service implementation up or down to match your business needs.

When you're running Excel Services, there's nothing to stop you from having a single server function as both the front-end Web server *and* the application server — but most organizations don't. They separate those roles, and that requires multiple servers. (It's a variation on not putting all your eggs in one basket — you wouldn't want to sacrifice that one lonely server to Murphy's Law.)

The Excel workbook is the focal point of Excel Services; without a workbook, Excel Services is just a bunch of components sitting around on some servers. When you consider scaling Excel Services to fit your business, you need to have a handle on what kinds of workbooks your users are generating — and how they access those workbooks. Here are some typical examples:

✦ An organization that runs several front-end Web servers, along with two application servers (for redundancy) that run Excel Calculation Services, could have the following profile:

  • The majority of users create workbooks that contain lots of data, charts, and images.

  • Normally the users view their workbooks through the browser.

  • The workbooks don't contain many built-in calculations.

  • The workbooks don't connect to external data.

✦ An organization that runs several application servers (each one running Excel Calculation Services) and two front-end Web servers (for redundancy), could have the following profile:

  • The majority of users create workbooks that contain lots of calculations.

  • The majority of workbooks connect to external data.

  • The workbooks make use of user-defined functions.

  • Just about everybody uses custom applications to access workbook data, running lots of calculations on the server and then pulling the results back to the custom application.

✦ An organization that has two or more front-end Web servers *and* two or more application servers (each one running Excel Calculation Services) could combine both of the previous two scenarios.

 Understanding the type of workbooks your users are generating — and how they want to store and access those workbooks — is critical when you're scaling your Excel Services implementation.

Managing Excel Services

Fortunately, creating an Excel Services service application follows the standard rules and processes that developers observe when they're tinkering up service applications. That consistency comes in handy. If you use the SharePoint Farm Configuration Wizard while installing SharePoint Server Enterprise Edition, you can select an option that creates the Excel Services service application and its associated proxies automatically. (Progress can be beautiful.)

If you want to create the Excel Services application manually — or associate the service application with another Web application — jump to Book II, Chapter 7, which shows you how to work with service applications.

When you have Excel Services up and running, you can manage it as a regular service application through Central Administration.

Although you can start using the capabilities of Excel Services as soon as its application service is up and running, you may want to configure it before you use it. Numerous configuration settings allow you to fine-tune your implementation. For example, you can specify the maximum number of Excel Calculation Services sessions allowed per user — the default setting is 25.

The Manage Excel Services page acts as the home page from which you can access the management pages for Excel Services, including these:

✦ **Global Settings:** You can use the Global Settings management page to specify the configuration settings for Excel Services. The settings listed on this management page affect the entire service — which is why it's called "global" (sorry, there's no way to regulate the planet yet).

✦ **Trusted File Locations:** You can use the Trusted File Locations management page to specify locations you deem safe, from which users may use their browsers to open Excel workbooks.

✦ **Trusted Data Providers:** You can use this management page to specify the data providers that Excel Service workbooks may use to connect to external data.

✦ **Trusted Data Connection Libraries:** You can use this management page to specify SharePoint data-connection libraries that you deem safe, from which Excel can retrieve connection information when it's connecting to external data.

✦ **User-Defined Function Assemblies:** You can use this management page to register managed code assemblies that contain custom functions (such as complex formulas or calculations) that you want to use in your Excel workbooks.

You can access the Manage Excel Service page by following these steps:

1. **Navigate to the Central Administration home page.**

2. **From the Application Management section, click Manage service applications.**

The Service Applications page appears, listing all your available service applications in alphabetical order.

Book III
Chapter 3

Exploring Excel
Services

3. **Select Excel Services and from the Ribbon menu, click Manage.**

The Manage Excel Services Web page appears.

Alternatively, you can click the Excel Services link, which also brings you to the Manage Excel Services page.

Configuring the Global Settings

The Global Settings link gives you access to the Excel Services Application Settings page. From this page, you can specify configuration settings such as the load-balancing method Excel Services should use, and how Excel Calculation Services should handle external data connections.

You can access the Excel Services Application Settings page by following these steps:

1. **Using your browser, navigate to the Central Administration home page.**

2. **From the Application Management section, click Manage service applications.**

The Service Applications page appears, listing all available service applications in alphabetical order.

3. **Select Excel Services and (from the Ribbon menu) click Manage.**

The Manage Excel Services Web page appears.

Alternatively, you can click the Excel Services link, which also brings you to the Manage Excel Services page.

4. **From the Manage Excel Services Application page, click Global Settings.**

The Excel Services Application Settings page appears from which you can perform configuration settings such as specifying the load-balancing method to use and configuring the Unattended Service Account settings (about which we offer details later in this chapter).

The list of configuration settings that you can define from the Excel Services Application Settings page includes:

✦ **Security: File Access Method**

You can use the File Access Method in the Security section of the configuration page to specify the authentication method you want Excel Calculation Services to use when it's retrieving workbooks from trusted locations that aren't SharePoint-based (such as an NTFS file share).

You have two options for defining this setting:

- **Impersonation:** Setting the File Access Method to Impersonation tells Excel Calculation Services to authorize users when they try to access any workbook stored in a UNC or HTTP location that isn't a SharePoint location.

- **Process Account:** Setting the File Access Method to Process Account tells Excel Calculation Services that the user account cannot be impersonated; instead it must use the *process account* (the security context of the process that owns the current thread).

Impersonation is the default value for the setting. It's more secure.

✦ **Security: Connection Encryption:** Use this setting to determine whether to require encryption for the communication between client computers and the Excel Services components residing on the front-end Web servers. If you require encryption, then Excel Services only allows data communication between the client machine and the front-end Web servers to take place over SSL connections.

The default value for this setting is Not Required.

✦ **Security: Allow Cross Domains:** You can use this setting to determine whether workbooks from a different HTTP domain can be rendered in the browser.

The default value for this setting is unchecked, which prohibits the rendering of workbooks from a different domain.

✦ **Load Balancing:** This setting specifies the method that Excel Calculation Services processes must use for load-balancing sessions.

You can choose from among these three methods:

- **Workbook URL:** With this method, the Excel Services proxy examines the URL of the requested workbook and ensures that all requests are routed back to the same session.

  When you initially request an Excel workbook from Excel Services, Excel Calculation Services takes two actions: (a) it stores a copy of the workbook in the workbook cache for later reuse and (b) it creates a session in memory on the server. The next time the front-end Web server receives a request for the same workbook, the application proxy examines the URL and then load-balances the request to match the same Excel Calculation Services process that made the request.

- **Round Robin with Health Check:** This load-balancing method is new with Excel Services 2010. As requests are received by the front-end Web server, the application proxy routes them from one Excel Calculation Services process to the next, in an ordered round-robin sequence. The workbook being requested has no impact on the load-balancing process. The round-robin process continues; requests go from one Excel Calculation Services process to the next, until it finds an unhealthy process. In this instance, the application proxy routes the request to the next healthy Excel Calculation Service process in line.

- **Local:** This load-balancing method ensures that the Excel Calculation Services process occurs on the same front-end Web server that received the request.

Excel Calculation Services does load balancing by workbook URL as its default method.

✦ **Memory Utilization: Maximum Private Bytes:** You can use this setting to specify (in MB) the maximum number of private bytes allocated to an Excel Calculation Services process. This setting tells Excel Calculation Services exactly how much memory it can consume on the server.

This setting is especially important if these two conditions apply:

- Your organization usually has a lot of complex Excel workbooks performing many calculations.

- The servers that run Excel Calculation Services must also run other services and custom applications.

In such a case, you'll want to ensure that Excel Calculation Services doesn't become a bottleneck for other applications and services.

The default value for this setting is -1, indicating that the limit is set to 50% of the physical memory on the machine; valid values include any positive integer (theoretically, anyway).

✦ **Memory Utilization: Memory Cache Threshold:** You can use this setting to specify a percentage of the maximum number of private bytes that Excel Calculation Services can allocate to *inactive* objects (those not used in the current session). If this threshold is reached, Excel Calculation Services releases the cached objects that are no longer in use.

The default value for this setting is 90 minutes; valid values for this setting include numbers ranging from 1 to 95. A setting of 0 disables the caching of inactive objects.

✦ **Memory Utilization: Maximum Unused Object Age:** You can use this setting to specify the time (in minutes) that inactive objects remain in the memory cache.

The default value for this setting is -1, indicating that there is no limit; valid values for this setting include numbers ranging from 1 to 34560 minutes (that is, 24 days).

✦ **Workbook Cache: Workbook Cache Location:** When you use Excel Services to request a workbook from SharePoint, Excel Services creates a copy of that workbook in the workbook cache for reuse. You can use the Workbook Cache Location setting to specify a file location on the server in which Excel Services should store the workbook cache.

This setting is blank by default, which tells Excel Services to use a subdirectory in the system's temporary directory on the server as the workbook file cache.

If you open a workbook in your browser and then take a peek at the location you specified in this setting — or take a look at the system's TEMP directory if you left the setting blank — you'll see a file that represents a copy of the workbook.

✦ **Workbook Cache: Maximum Size of Workbook Cache:** You can use this setting to specify the maximum disk space (in MB) allocated to

- • Workbooks that are currently in use by Excel Calculation Services.

- • Recently used workbooks that aren't currently open. Excel Services caches unused workbooks only if you've specified a Caching of Unused Files setting.

The default value for this setting is 40960 (40 MB), and valid values include any positive integer.

✦ **Workbook Cache: Caching of Unused Files:** You can use this setting to tell Excel Services whether it should cache workbooks that it's no longer using.

Selecting this setting tells Excel Services to cache unused workbooks; clearing the setting means Excel Services won't cache any workbooks it's no longer using.

The Caching of Unused Files setting is selected by default.

✦ **External Data: Connection Lifetime:** This setting specifies (in seconds) how long a connection to an external data source should remain open. Connections that exceed the specified limit close; the next query reopens them.

The default value for this setting is 1800 seconds (30 minutes); valid values range from 0 through 2073600. A value of -1 tells Excel Services not to recycle any external connections.

✦ **External Data: Unattended Service Account: Application ID:** Excel Services uses the Unattended Service Account (which is a single account defined for the entire service application) for retrieving or refreshing data when connected to an external data source. The credentials for this account are stored in the Secure Store Service database.

To configure the Unattended Service Account for Excel Services, you must first create a target application in Secure Store Services and define the credential information for the account. When you have the target application up and running, you enter the target application identifier into the Application ID field in the External Data section of the Excel Services Application Settings page.

Two later sections of this chapter — "Configuring the Secure Store" and "Configuring the Unattended Service Account" — show you how to, um, attend to getting the Unattended Service Account up and running in Excel Services.

Your workbooks can't connect to external data unless you've already defined a trusted file location to which you'll allow external data connections. The next section shows you how to take care of that matter.

Defining your trusted file locations

The Trusted File Locations link gives you access to the Trusted File Locations settings page, from which you can define a list of locations that you consider safe — and from which it's okay to open Excel workbook files. Excel Services only loads workbooks from locations specified in the Trusted File Locations list. If you try to use Excel Services to open an Excel workbook from a location that isn't on the list, Excel Services denies the request.

Figure 3-2 shows an example of the error message you receive if you try to open a workbook from a SharePoint document library that isn't listed as a trusted file location in Excel Services. (At least it doesn't make a rude noise.)

Figure 3-2:
Locations must be defined in the Trusted File Locations list.

If your document library isn't listed as a trusted file location, you can still save the workbook to the document library — and even edit the workbook using the Microsoft Excel client application. But if you want to use any function that requires Excel Services, such as opening the workbook in the browser, you're out of luck unless your document library is listed as trusted.

When you define your trusted file locations, Excel Services supports multiple types of storage, including these:

✦ Servers running Microsoft SharePoint Foundation server, which is the default — and recommended — setting.

✦ File shares, accessible using UNC paths.

✦ Web folders, accessible using HTTP paths.

Setting trusted file locations

The Trusted File Location Settings page offers you a slew of options that you can use to control workbooks uploaded to that location. For example, you can prohibit workbooks that connect to external data from being uploaded to your location, and even set a size limit (in MB) for the workbooks that *are* uploaded to your trusted location.

Here's a summary of the settings you specify when you're creating a new trusted file location in Excel Services:

✦ **Location:** You can use this section of the Add Trusted File Location page to specify

  • The path to the location from which Excel Services may access workbooks.

  • The location type (SharePoint, UNC, HTTP).

  • Whether to include any child libraries or folders in the trust.

✦ **Session Management:** Use this section to define how Excel Calculation Services should behave when using workbooks from your trusted location. Settings in this section include these:

  • **Session Timeout:** Use this setting to specify the maximum time that an Excel Calculation Services session can remain open *and* inactive after the request ends.

  • **Short Session Timeout:** Use this setting to specify the maximum time that an Excel Web Access session stays open without any further interaction from the user (that is, how long it can remain inactive) before it's shut down. The interval is measured from the end of the original Open request.

  • **New Workbook Session Timeout:** Use this setting to specify the maximum time that an Excel Calculation Services session for a new workbook stays open without any further interaction from the user (how long it can remain inactive) before it's shut down. The interval is measured from the end of the last request.

**Book III
Chapter 3**

**Exploring Excel
Services**

- **Maximum Request Duration:** Use this setting to specify the maximum duration of a single request in a session.

- **Maximum Chart Render Duration:** Use this setting to specify the maximum time spent rendering any single chart in a workbook.

✦ **Workbook Properties:** This section defines the resources used when Excel Services opens workbooks.

Settings in this section include

- **Maximum Workbook Size:** Use this setting to specify (in MB) the maximum size of a workbook that Excel Calculation Services can open.

- **Maximum Chart or Image Size:** Use this setting to specify (in MB) the maximum size of a chart or image in a workbook that Excel Calculation Services can open.

✦ **Calculation Behavior:** This section defines the calculation modes in Excel workbooks from the trusted location you're defining.

Settings in this section include these:

- **Volatile Function Cache Lifetime:** In Excel terms, a *volatile function* is a function whose value cannot be assumed to remain the same — even if any of its parameters remain unchanged. A good example is the `Now()` function, which returns the current date and time. The current date and time are always changing, therefore this function is volatile. Use the Volatile Function Cache Lifetime setting to specify the maximum time that a computed value for a volatile function is cached for use in automatic recalculations.

- **Workbook Calculation Mode:** Use this setting to specify the calculation mode that Excel Calculation Services uses in workbooks.

The settings you specify here — excep the File setting — override the workbook settings.

✦ **External Data:** You can use the External Data section to inform Excel Services how to handle the data connections to external data sources from the workbooks in the trusted location you're defining.

Settings in this section include these:

- **Allow External Data:** Excel workbooks can connect to external data sources by using embedded connections stored within the workbook — and by using data connections defined in a data-connection library. You specify a connection type in the actual workbook. Excel Calculation Services uses the workbook settings — combined with settings on the server (such as the Allow External Data setting) — to determine how to handle connections to external data.

Use this setting to specify whether connections to external data sources are permitted within workbooks — and if so, the type of data connections that are supported.

If you choose to allow data connections from data-connection librar-ies, you must include each such library in the Trusted Data Connection Libraries list in Excel Services.

- **Warn on Refresh:** Use this setting to specify whether to display a warning to your users before the external data in the workbook they're using is refreshed. Selecting this option prevents external data from being refreshed automatically with the user's consent.

- **Display Granular External Data Errors:** Use this setting to specify whether detailed error messages appear when external data issues arise.

This setting is great for troubleshooting connectivity issues that may crop up with your workbooks in Excel Services.

- **Stop When Refresh on Open Fails:** Use this setting to specify whether you want Excel Services to stop loading the workbook if the connection to an external data source fails.

- **External Data Cache Lifetime:** Use this setting to specify how long Excel Calculation Services can use query results from external data sources.

- **Maximum Concurrent Queries Per Session:** Use this setting to spec-ify the maximum number of queries that Excel Calculation Services can run at the same time during a single session.

- **Allow External Data Using REST:** Use this setting to specify whether to allow requests from the REST API to refresh external data connections.

✦ **User-Defined Functions:** This setting specifies whether user-defined functions may be called from workbooks.

If you allow user-defined functions to be called, first you must register those user-defined functions in the User-Defined Function Assemblies list on the server.

Adding a trusted file location

You can use the following steps to identify a trusted file location in Excel Services:

1. **Using your browser, navigate to the Central Administration home page.**

2. **From the Application Management section, click Manage service applications.**

   The Service Applications page appears, listing all available service appli-cations in alphabetical order.

3. **Select Excel Services and from the Ribbon menu, click Manage.**

   The Manage Excel Services Web page appears.

   Alternatively, you can click the Excel Services link, which also brings you to the Manage Excel Services page.

4. **From the Manage Excel Services Application page, click Trusted File Locations.**

   The Trusted File Locations page appears, listing the file locations presently identified as trusted in SharePoint.

5. **From the Trusted File Locations page, click Add Trusted File Location.**

   The Add Trusted File Location page appears; here you can configure the settings associated with that file location.

6. **Configure each setting on the Add Trusted File Location page according to your needs.**

   The "Trusted File Location Settings" section of this chapter describes each of the settings you can define when you add your trusted location definition.

7. **Click OK.**

By default, the list of trusted file locations includes a definition stating that all built-in SharePoint locations are trusted. From a security perspective, you may want to review that setting and apply a more restrictive setting to your list of trusted file locations.

Defining your trusted data providers

The Trusted Data Providers link gives you access to the Trusted Data Providers settings page; there you can add or remove the data providers to be used when connecting to external data from Excel workbooks stored in SharePoint. The Excel Services service application comes preconfigured with a slew of data providers already defined.

Most deployments can get away with using only the providers shown on this well-defined list. But if your organization uses a data provider that doesn't appear on the list, you can add that provider to the list: Just use the Add Trusted Data Provider link on the Trusted Data Providers management page.

Microsoft has provided a comprehensive list of data providers defined as trusted. Adding trusted providers is fairly rare — unless you have a custom data provider that you use for your custom applications and you want to retrieve data from those applications in your workbooks.

Defining your trusted data-connection libraries

The Trusted Data Connection Libraries link gives you access to the Trusted Data Connection Libraries settings page. There you can define a list of connection libraries in SharePoint that you trust — which gives Excel Services the go-ahead to retrieve data-connection information from them.

This setting goes hand in hand with the external data settings in your trusted file locations. If those settings specify that *only* trusted data-connection libraries can process external data connections, then you also have to specify the data-connection libraries to use. You do so (logically enough) by adding those libraries to the Trusted Data Connection Libraries list in Excel Services.

You can add a trusted data-connection library by following these steps:

1. **Navigate to the Central Administration home page.**

2. **Choose Application Management⇨Manage service applications.**

The Service Applications page appears, listing all available service applications in alphabetical order.

3. **Select Excel Services and, from the Ribbon menu, click Manage.**

The Manage Excel Services Web page appears.

Alternatively, you can click the Excel Services link, which also brings you to the Manage Excel Services page.

4. **Click Trusted Data Connection Libraries.**

The Trusted Data Connection Libraries page appears. Here you can see which data-connection libraries are currently listed as trusted; you can also add new data-connection libraries.

5. **Click Add Trusted Data Connection Library.**

The Add Trusted Data Connection Library page appears.

6. **In the Address field, enter the URL to the SharePoint document library that contains the data connections you want to trust.**

7. **In the Description field, enter a description that explains the purpose of the data-connection library you're listing as trusted.**

8. **Click OK.**

When your new trusted data-connection library is added successfully to your list of trusted libraries, you can use data sources in your Excel workbooks from that location.

Registering your user-defined function assemblies

The User-Defined Function Assemblies link gives you access to the User-Defined Function Assemblies page. That's where you register *user-defined functions* — managed code assemblies that contain custom functions (such as complex formulas or calculations) that you want to use in your Excel workbooks. When you need to perform a calculation defined in a user-defined function, you simply call the function from your workbook. User-defined functions can be reused in multiple Excel workbooks.

Before you can do anything with a user-defined function in Excel Services, you must first register that function's code assembly in SharePoint.

As a built-in feature of Excel Services, Microsoft has already registered a code assembly that represents user-defined functions so you can retrieve Web-analytics report data. Here are the nuts and bolts of registering your user-defined function's code assembly:

1. **Navigate to the Central Administration home page.**

2. **Choose Application Management⇨Manage service applications.**

The Service Applications page appears, listing all available service applications in alphabetical order.

3. **Select Excel Services and, from the Ribbon menu, click Manage.**

The Manage Excel Services Web page appears.

Alternatively, you can click the Excel Services link, which also brings you to the Manage Excel Services page.

4. **Click User-Defined Function Assemblies.**

The User Defined Functions page appears. Here's where you view the list of currently registered code assemblies for user-defined functions, and register the assemblies for new user-defined functions.

5. **Click Add User-Defined Function Assembly.**

The Add User-Defined Function Assembly page appears. It's where you enter the settings for the .NET assembly that contains the user-defined functions you want to use in your workbooks.

6. **In the Assembly field, enter the strong name or the file path for your assembly.**

A strong name is a way of uniquely identifying your .NET assembly so that when it comes to deployment time you know the assembly is from a trusted, reliable source. You can find out the steps to strongly name your assembly on the MSDN Web site.

7. **In the Assembly Location, select where you want Excel Services to deploy your user-defined function's code assembly.**

   You can deploy your assembly to either of these places:

   - **Global Assembly Cache (GAC):** Select this option if you want Excel Services to deploy your user-defined assembly to the GAC.

     The *Global Assembly Cache* (GAC) is a machine-wide cache that stores assemblies and makes them accessible to multiple applications. Assemblies deployed to the GAC have all the necessary permissions required to run on the server.

     Make sure that any assemblies you deploy to the GAC are from a legitimate, reliable, and trusted source.

   - **File Path:** Select this option if you want Excel Services to deploy your user-defined assembly to a specific file location — such as a directory on the application server or on a network share.

8. **In the Enable Assembly setting, choose Assembly enabled.**

9. **In the Description setting, enter text that describes the purpose of the assembly and the user-defined function it contains.**

10. **Click OK.**

    Your assembly appears in the list of user-defined function assemblies.

    By default, user-defined functions are enabled for SharePoint. If you have changed this setting when defining your trusted file locations, before you can start using your registered user-defined function assembly, you have to make sure that the trusted location in which you'll be storing your workbooks has user-defined functions enabled. If it doesn't, then you'd better change that; read on.

You can use the following steps to enable user-defined functions in your trusted file location:

1. **Using your browser, navigate to the Central Administration home page.**

2. **Choose Application Management⇨Manage service applications.**

   The Service Applications page appears, listing all available service applications in alphabetical order.

3. **Select Excel Services and, from the Ribbon menu, click Manage.**

   The Manage Excel Services Web page appears.

   Alternatively, you can click the Excel Services link, which also brings you to the Manage Excel Services page.

4. **From the Manage Excel Services Application page, click Trusted File Locations.**

   The Trusted File Locations page appears, listing the file locations presently trusted in SharePoint.

5. **From the Trusted File Locations page, click the trusted file location that will store workbooks that make use of your user-defined functions.**

   The Edit Trusted File Location page appears.

6. **From the User-Defined Functions section, select Allow User-Defined Functions.**

7. **Click OK.**

   Your registered user-defined functions are now ready for use in workbooks stored in the trusted location you've designated.

Defining your trusted data-connection libraries

When connecting to external data in your Excel workbook, you can embed the connection information in the workbook, or use a data-connection file stored in a *data-connection library* — a place SharePoint provides where you can centrally store, secure, and manage your data-connection files. Files stored there can be reused in multiple workbooks. If the connection information in a particular data-connection file changes, all workbooks linked to that file have their connection information updated automatically.

If you want workbooks accessed by Excel Services to use the data connections kept in a data-connection library, you must ensure the following (as described earlier in this chapter):

✦ The data-connection library must be listed in the Trusted Data Connections Library list.

✦ Excel Services must be configured to allow external data connections from data-connection libraries.

Configuring the Secure Store

Unless you have Kerberos defined in your environment, your Excel Services configuration will use a shared domain account — the Unattended Service Account (a vital security feature with a goofy name) — for authenticating to data sources. Excel Services uses the Secure Store Service to store the user name and password for the Unattended Service Account. The Secure Store Service provides the storage and mapping of account names and passwords to facilitate seamless connection to external data.

Of course, before you can use the Unattended Service Account in Excel Services, you have to configure the Secure Store Service so Excel Services can use it. Other SharePoint service applications that make business intelligence work — such as PerformancePoint Services and Visio Services — also use the Secure Store Service. To configure the Secure Store Service for use with all SharePoint service applications, follow these steps:

1. **Using your browser, navigate to the Central Administration home page.**

2. **From the Application Management section, click Manage service applications.**

   The Service Applications management page appears listing all the service applications in your SharePoint implementation.

3. **From the list of service applications, select Secure Store Service Application.**

   The management page for the Secure Store Service appears. If this is your first time using the Secure Store Service, the page displays a message to tell you (in effect) "first things first" — that before you create a new Secure Store Target Application, you must first generate a new key for the Secure Store Service. (Nag, nag, nag.)

   • If you've already generated a key for your Secure Store Service, you're ahead of the game — skip to Step 5.

   • If the Secure Store Service application doesn't appear in your list of service applications, whoa there. You'll have to create the service application and its associated proxy before you can get past this point.

4. **On the Edit tab, in the Key Management group, click Generate New Key.**

   The *key* (short for *encryption key*) is a piece of code that encrypts and decrypts the credentials stored in the Secure Store database. And if you're accustomed to mere pass*words*, well, industrial-strength security calls for something longer and tougher to crack: Be prepared to concoct a *pass phrase*.

   The Generate New Key Web dialog box appears, as shown in Figure 3-3, requesting a pass phrase from which to generate a new key.

5. **In the Pass Phrase field and the Confirm Pass Phrase field, enter your pass phrase.**

   The pass phrase is case-sensitive and must contain the following different types of characters (at least three of each type):

   • Uppercase letters

   • Lowercase letters

**Book III
Chapter 3**

Exploring Excel Services

- Numerals
- At least one of the following special characters:

  "! " # $ % & ' ( ) * + , — . / : ; < = > ? @ [\ ] ^ _ ` { | } ~

The system doesn't store the pass phrase you enter, and doesn't care if that's inconvenient. You'll have to remember the pass phrase the next time you refresh the key — and you'll need to refresh the key when (for example) you add a new application server to your server farm. If you forget the pass phrase, you're locked out. So write down the pass phrase if you have to, but keep it secure.

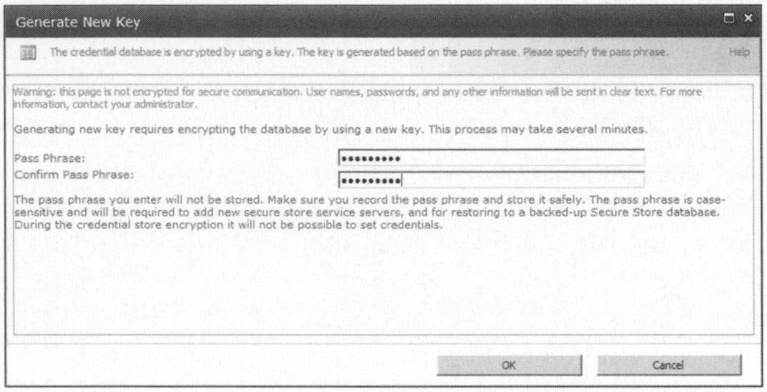

Figure 3-3:
Make sure you record the pass phrase you use to generate your key.

> Generate New Key
>
> The credential database is encrypted by using a key. The key is generated based on the pass phrase. Please specify the pass phrase.   Help
>
> Warning: this page is not encrypted for secure communication. User names, passwords, and any other information will be sent in clear text. For more information, contact your administrator.
>
> Generating new key requires encrypting the database by using a new key. This process may take several minutes.
>
> Pass Phrase: ●●●●●●●●●
> Confirm Pass Phrase: ●●●●●●●●●
>
> The pass phrase you enter will not be stored. Make sure you record the pass phrase and store it safely. The pass phrase is case-sensitive and will be required to add new secure store service servers, and for restoring to a backed-up Secure Store database. During the credential store encryption it will not be possible to set credentials.
>
>   OK   Cancel

After you enter the pass phrase, the Secure Store Service generates a new key — and at last you can begin creating target applications for use by the services in your SharePoint farm.

Configuring the Unattended Service Account

When a user accesses a workbook that contains data connections to SharePoint lists, Excel Services uses the identity of the current user to access those resources. When Excel Services renders workbooks that contain data connections to data sources external to SharePoint, those data sources have to be authenticated. Excel Services handles that chore in a variety of ways:

- ✦ **Integrated Windows Authentication:** You can use this method of authentication if you have Kerberos up and running in your environment.

- ✦ **Secure Store Service:** You can use this method to map the current user's credentials to a different credential that has access to the database. The Secure Store Service handles the mapping. This authentication method is only usable by workbooks that use an ODC file to define the connection data including the target application used for credential mapping.

✦ **Unattended Service Account:** From an administrative perspective, telling Excel Services to use the Unattended Service Account for authentication is the easiest way to configure secure access to data sources used in your Excel workbooks. The Unattended Service Account is a low-privilege account that has access to the data sources to which you want to connect.

As an administrator, you can create a target application in the Secure Store that stores the account details and maps all users to the account. Then, when connecting to an external data from a workbook, Excel Services can impersonate the Unattended Service Account to retrieve the data. (Sounds underhanded, but it actually works. Stay tuned for details.)

Creating a target application ID in Secure Store

In order to configure the Unattended Service Account for use with Excel Services, first you have to create a target application in the Secure Store Service.

Follow these steps to add a Target Application ID to the Secure Store:

1. **Using your browser, navigate to the Central Administration home page.**

2. **From the Application Management section, click Manage service applications.**

   The Service Applications management page appears listing all the service applications in your SharePoint implementation.

3. **From the list of service applications, select Secure Store Service Application.**

   The Secure Store Service management page appears. If this is your first time using the Secure Store Service, the page will display a message stating that before creating a new Secure Store Target Application, you must first generate a new key for the Secure Store Service. If you see this message, then follow the steps in the "Configuring the Secure Store" section earlier in this chapter.

   If you do not see this message then you have already generated a key for the Secure Store Service and may proceed to the next step.

4. **On the Edit tab, in the Manage Target Application group, click New.**

   The Create New Secure Store Target Application page appears.

5. **In the Target Application ID field, enter a unique identifier for your application.**

   The Target Application ID field is used to map the service application, such as Excel Services or Visio Services, to the Unattended Service Account.

The value that you enter in this field is the value that you enter in the Application ID setting on the Manage the Excel Services service page.

6. **In the Display Name field, enter a description name that will be used as the display name for the target application.**

7. **In the Contact e-mail field, enter a valid e-mail address for the person that you want to be the contact for the target application.**

8. **In the Target Application Type field, select whether the application uses a group mapping or an individual mapping.**

9. **Select a value for the Target Application Page URL field.**

   The Target Application Page URL field may be used to set the credential information for the target application by individual users.

10. **Click Next.**

    The Specify Credentials page appears, in which you can specify the fields you use when authenticating the Unattended Service Account.

11. **Add or remove the fields that you would like to use for authenticating the Unattended Service Account.**

    The default fields defined are:

    • Windows User name

    • Windows Password fields.

    You can remove a field by clicking the delete icon next to the field.

    You can add additional credential fields by clicking Add Field. When you click Add Field, a new row is added to the page with two text boxes: one representing the Field Name, and the other representing the field type.

12. **Click Next.**

    The Specify the membership settings page appears.

13. **In the Target Application Administrators field, enter the list of the users that you want to have access to manage the target application settings.**

14. **Click OK.**

    The target application is created, and you're returned to the Secure Store Service management page. You should see your newly created target application listed on the page.

Mapping the target application's credentials

With your trusty target application created, the next order of business is to use Set Credentials to configure the credential mappings. For example, if your target application is configured with a Windows user name field and a Windows password field, you'd use the Set Credential menu option to set user-name and password values. SharePoint uses credential information from the target application when it needs to use the Unattended Service Account for a service application that's been mapped to the target application.

Here are the steps that map your target application's credentials:

1. **On the Store Service management page, click the down arrow next to the name of your new target application.**

A shortcut menu appears.

2. **From the shortcut menu, click Set Credentials.**

The Set Credentials for Secure Store Target Application page appears.

3. **In the Credentials Owner field, enter the identity of the owner of the target application.**

4. **In the remaining fields, enter the valid credential settings for your Unattended Service Account.**

If you used the default user name and password-credential fields, then enter the user name and the password of the account that you want to assume the role of the Unattended Service Account.

The account that you specify must have access to the data sources to which you want Excel Services to connect.

5. **Click OK.**

Your target application and Unattended Service Account are now ready to be associated with the Excel Services service application. The next heroic task to undertake is to add the target application ID to Excel Services.

Adding the target application ID to Excel Services

To get the Unattended Service Account to do its work when you're connecting to data sources from your workbooks, you have to let Excel Services in on the act. You do so by configuring the Excel Services service application with the application ID created for the Secure Store Service target application (you know — the application you created to store the credentials for the Unattended Service Account).

Before your workbooks can connect to external data, you must enable the definition of your trusted file location to allow external data connections. You can find out how to do this in the "Defining your trusted file locations" section earlier in this chapter.

You can use the following steps to map your Excel Services service application to a target application in your Secure Store:

1. **Navigate to the Central Administration home page.**

2. **Choose Application Management➪Manage service applications.**

   The Service Applications page appears, listing all available service applications in alphabetical order.

3. **Select Excel Services and, from the Ribbon menu, click Manage.**

   The Manage the Excel Services Web page appears. Alternatively, you can simply click the Excel Services link, which also brings you to the Manage Excel Services page.

4. **Click Global Settings.**

   The Excel Services Settings page appears, from which you can specify the application ID of the Secure Store Service target application.

5. **In the Application ID field, enter the application ID of the Target Application in the Secure Store that hosts the Unattended Service Account credentials.**

6. **Click OK.**

   The Unattended Service Account is now ready for use when connecting to data sources from your workbooks.

Chapter 4: Investigating InfoPath Forms Services

In This Chapter

🖊 Understanding InfoPath Forms Services

🖊 Configuring InfoPath Forms Services

🖊 Deploying and managing form templates

Paper forms are everywhere! You'd be hard-pressed to find a process or even an activity these days that doesn't require the completion of a form of some kind. For example, in today's litigious society, if your child happens to scrape his or her knee on the playground, most establishments provide you with a detailed report — which you must sign — of the event, along with how your child was comforted.

One of the biggest advantages of paper forms is that you can collect a physical signature on the form. Conversely, when it comes to electronic forms, the collection, authorization, and verification of signatures has been a big obstacle — ensuring the validity of an electronic signature requires interoperability from both a technical, organizational, and legal perspective. Fortunately, with the advances in digital signature technology, electronic forms are becoming broadly accepted, both from a legal and usage perspective.

In the modern world, people (and organizations) are becoming more environmentally friendly and aware. Large corporations and government entities are taking stock of the environmental impacts their products and processes have, and they're making the appropriate changes. A common goal for these environmentally friendly organizations is to reduce the number of paper documents and forms that those organizations create and consume. One of the most rewarding aspects of converting paper-based forms to their electronic counterparts is the contribution to saving the environment. However, electronic forms provide many additional benefits, such as an improvement in the accuracy of the data collected on forms and the ability to include a form in an automated workflow process. SharePoint 2010 aligns perfectly with the goals of a paperless initiative by providing a scalable, searchable, and customizable repository capable of storing a variety of electronic content, including electronic forms. Out-of-the-box workflow capabilities make it easy to automate your business processes, and insight capabilities help you build reports and statistics on the collected data.

The service applications that are available out of the box with SharePoint Server 2010 provide service offerings, such as Business Data Connectivity Services, Visio Services, and Excel Services, to name a few. InfoPath Forms Services doesn't appear in Central Administration along with the aforementioned service applications. At first glance, you may think that it's been demoted in this release, no longer A-list material. However, despite all appearances to the contrary, InfoPath Forms Services is alive and kicking, and deeply ingrained in the overall SharePoint 2010 architecture and vision. In fact, you can now easily customize your regular SharePoint list forms with the InfoPath client — there's even a menu option for it in SharePoint!

In this chapter, we introduce you to InfoPath Forms Services and explain each of the configuration settings that help you manage the performance of forms within your SharePoint farm. We then show you how to deploy and manage your administrator-approved form templates

Evolving InfoPath Forms Services

Microsoft Office InfoPath 2010 is a client application that allows you to develop sophisticated XML-based forms. The InfoPath client was first introduced with the Office 2003 suite, in which InfoPath provided integration capabilities with SharePoint Portal Server 2003. For example, by using the InfoPath 2003 client, you could publish an InfoPath client directly into a SharePoint document library, allowing users who have access to the document library to access your forms.

Although the forms technology introduced with InfoPath 2003 was exciting and offered some integration with SharePoint, it was not widely embraced in the SharePoint Portal Server 2003 arena. One of the factors that impeded its adoption was the fact that to use the forms published to the SharePoint document library, you needed to have the full-blown InfoPath client installed on your desktop. This limitation alone introduced a number of obstacles for organizations, such as the cost of deploying InfoPath to every user's desktop and the training costs related to teaching users InfoPath when they really just needed to fill in a form. The good news is that the InfoPath technology has come a long way since then.

InfoPath Forms Services

In addition to the InfoPath client, Microsoft offers InfoPath Forms Services as part of its Enterprise Edition of SharePoint; InfoPath Forms Services isn't available if you have only the SharePoint Server 2010 Standard Edition license. InfoPath Forms Services — first introduced with SharePoint Server 2007 — enables you to store and manage forms and form templates from a central location within SharePoint Server 2010. The introduction of InfoPath Forms Services overcame the limitation of the InfoPath 2003 client by allowing form authors to create browser-enabled form templates that can be stored in SharePoint and used in a browser by users who have the appropriate permissions. Users don't need to have InfoPath installed on their desktops to use this functionality.

Here are the differences between InfoPath form templates and InfoPath forms:

✦ **InfoPath form template:** An .xsn file that contains the basic structure and design of the form, similar in concept to a Word template (a .dot file).

✦ **InfoPath browser-enabled form template:** Form templates that you can publish to InfoPath Forms Services (also known as browser-compatible form templates). Browser-enabled form templates allow users to fill out and view forms by using the browser rather than the InfoPath client.

Browser-enabled forms have some limitations in the types of controls that you can place on the form. For example, the Signature Line control enables the signer of a form to digitally sign a form. You can use the Signature Line control only when you design forms that will be filled out in InfoPath Filler; browser-enabled form templates don't support the Signature Line control.

✦ **InfoPath form:** An .xml file, this form is actually an instance of the form template; a single form template can have multiple form instances. If the form template is an InfoPath Filler form template, then users can fill out the form only by using InfoPath Filler. If the form template is a browser-enabled form template, then users can fill out the form by using either InfoPath Filler, or their browser via InfoPath Forms Services.

You can use the InfoPath client to create a browser-enabled form template and publish the template to a SharePoint form library. When a user accesses the form library, he or she can create new forms based on your form template. You can store your form templates centrally within your SharePoint farm or disperse them in libraries throughout your SharePoint environment.

TIP

When it comes to enterprise deployments, you may want more control over the form templates that are published to the server. InfoPath Forms Services can be configured to allow only administrators to deploy and centrally manage form templates. We discuss the configurations options available with InfoPath Forms Services in the "Configuring InfoPath Forms Services" section, later in this chapter.

Microsoft Office InfoPath client

Although InfoPath Forms Services provides the mechanism for storing, managing, and serving up forms and form templates, the actual form authoring still takes place on the InfoPath client — specifically, versions InfoPath 2007 and InfoPath 2010.

The Microsoft Office 2007 suite introduced a version of the InfoPath client, named Microsoft Office InfoPath 2007, that made developing forms straightforward. InfoPath 2007 enabled form authors to create InfoPath form templates that they could publish to SharePoint Server 2007, and end users could now view and edit those templates by using their browsers; the full-blown client was no longer a requirement for consuming InfoPath forms from SharePoint. This led to an increase in the adoption and acceptance of InfoPath as a technology for developing sophisticated, intelligent forms for SharePoint applications.

InfoPath 2010 builds on the success of InfoPath 2007, extending its integration with SharePoint Server 2010 to not only SharePoint form libraries, but also to regular SharePoint lists. If you want to quickly and easily customize the default Edit Item page for your SharePoint list, you can open the form in InfoPath 2010 with the simple click of a button, make your modifications, and save the customized edit page, ready for use, back to SharePoint. We cover this capability in more detail in Book IV, Chapter 7.

When you use InfoPath, you either

✦ Design InfoPath form templates that can be used throughout your organization.

✦ Use InfoPath to fill forms with data.

When you install the InfoPath 2010 client, your Program menu bar displays two InfoPath program options that correspond to each use case:

✦ **Microsoft InfoPath Filler 2010:** Allows users to fill out InfoPath forms by using the InfoPath client. Not all users are form designers; having the InfoPath Filler program as a separate application allows organizations to keep these two sets of users separated. You can configure your desktop deployments according to the user types. For example, if only a handful of the users in your organization will be form authors, then you can configure most of you desktops to offer only the InfoPath Filler option, which should reduce confusion among the user population about which program they should use.

The Microsoft InfoPath Filler 2010 program option is a shortcut link to the `InfoPath.exe` application file. If you browse to the Office directory and double-click the InfoPath icon, the InfoPath client opens in InfoPath Filler mode.

✦ **Microsoft InfoPath Designer 2010:** InfoPath Designer allows form authors to design InfoPath form templates that can be deployed throughout your organization. The Microsoft InfoPath Designer 2010 program option is a shortcut link to the `InfoPath.exe` application file appended with a design command line switch.

For example, entering the following command in the Run command on your Start menu launches InfoPath Designer (replace C with your system drive letter, and if you are running the 64bit version of Office remove x86 from the path):

```
"C:\Program Files (x86)\Microsoft Office\Office14\InfoPath.exe" /design
```

Configuring InfoPath Forms Services

The functionality of InfoPath Forms Services is enabled when you activate the SharePoint Server Enterprise feature set. The Enterprise features for a SharePoint installation are available if you have a SharePoint Enterprise license. After you install or upgrade SharePoint with an Enterprise license, InfoPath Forms Services is up and running, and ready for use.

Although you can start leveraging InfoPath Forms Services right away, configuration settings allow you to fine-tune your implementation. For example, you can use the configuration settings to prevent form authors from deploying browser-enabled form templates to SharePoint. In this scenario, form authors have to package their form template for approval and deployment by a SharePoint administrator.

If you're a developer or a form author, become familiar with the InfoPath Forms Services configuration settings so that you can improve the success rate of your forms. For example, if you try to deploy a form template by using InfoPath Designer and the administrator has disabled this capability in the configuration settings, you know to package the form for administrator deployment. If the timeout settings have been set too low and your form is timing out when you try to submit it to SharePoint, then you can pinpoint the problem with your administrator and come up with a solution.

When developing form templates for InfoPath Forms Services, we recommend that you have access to a development SharePoint environment that you can use to freely publish your templates and check for compatibility issues. The InfoPath Forms Services configuration settings in the development environment should mimic, within reason, the production environment.

Accessing the InfoPath Forms Services Configuration page

Follow these steps to access the InfoPath Forms Services configuration page:

1. **Navigate to the Central Administration home page.**

2. **In the Quick Launch menu, click General Application Settings.**

The General Application Settings page appears.

3. **In the InfoPath Forms Services section, click Configure InfoPath Forms Services.**

   The Configure InfoPath Forms Services page appears.

The following sections take you through each of the configuration settings available on the page and explain their purpose and effect on your SharePoint implementation.

Configuring form template settings

From an administrator perspective, InfoPath form templates fall into two categories:

✦ **User-deployed form template:** Doesn't require approval by an administrator in order to be deployed to SharePoint. For example, when a form author deploys a form template to SharePoint directly from the InfoPath client, the form template is a user-deployed form template. If a form template contains managed code, then the administrator must grant it the appropriate level of trust.

One method of gaining this trust, while maintaining the user deployment capability, is to leverage the sandboxed solutions functionality of SharePoint and publish the form template into a sandbox. InfoPath form templates that contain code that has domain trust may be published to SharePoint as a sandboxed solution.

A sandbox isolates your solution within your SharePoint farm, preventing any code that your solution contains from affecting the rest of your SharePoint environment. A sandbox environment has specific restrictions in place, such as preventing access to resources in a different site collection, so it may not be the ideal deployment solution for your form template. You can find more information about sandboxed solutions in Book II, Chapter 4.

✦ **Administrator-approved form template:** An administrator must approve and deploy a form template that requires full trust. A form that has full trust security can execute code behind the scenes without displaying an annoying security message to the user. For example, when a user saves a form, the form could automatically run code that updates a SharePoint list with data from the form. The approval and deployment process of an administrator-approved form template requires that the administrator verifies, uploads, and activates the form template. After the form template is activated, the site collection administrator can activate it.

The User Browser-Enabled Form Templates section of the InfoPath configuration page provides you with two settings that you can use to control whether users can deploy or render browser-enabled form templates:

✦ **Allow Users to Browser-Enable Form Templates.** This setting determines whether users can deploy browser-enabled form templates to InfoPath Forms Services. If this setting is unchecked, users must prepare the form templates for administrator deployment, and then provide the template to the administrator. For example, you may use this setting if your organization wants to control the form templates published to InfoPath Forms Services by requiring all form templates to be deployed to a central location by an administrator.

✦ **Render Form Templates That Are Browser-Enabled by Users.** This setting works with the preceding setting. If you've had your SharePoint 2010 implementation running for a long time and decide to take control of the browser-enabled form template deployment process to prevent users from being able to publish forms without administrator approval, selecting this check box allows you to provide users with the ability to render forms that have been created from pre-existing user-deployed form templates. If you deselect both settings, users can't deploy browser-enabled form templates, nor can they view or edit existing forms that were generated from previously deployed templates.

Although it's an unlikely scenario, you can actually configure InfoPath Forms Services so that the preceding setting is selected and this setting is cleared. Doing so means that users can deploy browser-enabled form templates to InfoPath Forms Services, but they can't view or edit those forms in a browser — which sort of defeats the purpose of deploying the form template to InfoPath Forms Services in the first place.

Configuring data-connection settings

Data connections allow you to connect components of a form template, such as a list box, to an external data source, such as a SQL database or a SharePoint list. When a user instantiates a form, the data connection retrieves data from the external data source and presents it to the user in the appropriate location on the form.

By using InfoPath 2007 and InfoPath 2010, you can define different types of connections:

✦ **Submit connections:** A connection that pushes data to an external data source from the form

✦ **Query connections:** A connection that retrieves data from the external data source for presentation in the form

Data connection timeout and response settings

How form templates deployed to InfoPath Forms Services handle data connections come with a few special concerns:

✦ The connection to the external data source is established by the server, not by the client. Therefore, the identity used for the connection is the account that runs the Web Application — which is ultimately a security risk because the account that runs the Web Application typically has elevated privileges when compared to the user who initiates the request.

✦ Data connections require additional resources, which may potentially add load to the server and the network.

✦ If the data source to which you're connecting is slow, then a user can potentially launch a denial-of-service attack by overloading the server with connection requests.

You can mitigate the preceding security concerns by assigning the appropriate data connection timeout settings. The Data Connections Timeouts and the Data Connection Response Size sections of the InfoPath Forms Services configuration page provide the following configuration settings:

✦ **Default Data Connection Timeout (Milliseconds):** Defines the default timeout for all data connections on all forms; however, if your form template requires a different timeout setting you can override this value by using the InfoPath Code Editor to add code to your form template that updates the DefaultDataConnectionTimeout property. Accessible from the Code Editor command in the Code group on the InfoPath Designer Developer tab)

✦ **Maximum Data Connection Timeout (Milliseconds):** Because the Default Data Connection Timeout setting can be overridden, administrators need a way of further defining timeouts to prevent denial-of-service attacks. This setting sets the maximum connection timeout for a form to which all data connections must adhere, regardless of the default data-connection timeout configured in the form template's code.

✦ **Data Connection Response Size:** Defines the maximum size of the responses that data connections are allowed to process. The default setting is 1500K. This setting helps prevent malicious attacks on the server; it also helps reduce the load on the server, ultimately improving performance.

Data connection authentication settings

Typically, connections to external data sources require some means of authentication, such as Windows-integrated authentication or basic authentication.

The following configuration settings help you control the authentication methods deployed in form templates:

✦ **Require SSL for HTTP Authentication to Data Sources.** If your data connection requires use of basic or digest authentication, it means that the password that you use is susceptible to being intercepted; therefore, we recommend that you use SSL to protect all such data connections. This setting is enabled by default, and to keep your connection information encrypted and secure, leave this setting enabled. Data connections that use alternative means for authentication, such as Windows-integrated authentication, aren't affected by this setting. With the setting enabled, if a data connection defines an HTTP connection but doesn't use SSL, the form will fail when the data connection is invoked.

✦ **Allow Embedded SQL Authentication.** When you design your form templates, you may be tempted to embed SQL usernames and password strings into the form. To protect against this type of behavior, administrators can control whether embedded SQL authentication is allowed by using this setting, which is deselected (meaning disabled) by default. If an administrator enables this setting and then a user views or edits a form, InfoPath Forms Services executes data connections by using the saved credentials.

We discourage embedding SQL usernames and password strings into your form template; this practice introduces a security risk because passwords are exposed during form execution.

Don't embed SQL authentication in your form templates. Instead, use a trusted connection that uses Windows-integrated authentication to identify the client to the SQL server.

✦ **Allow User Form Templates to Use Authentication Information Contained in Data Connection Files.** SharePoint provides a special type of document library, known as a *data connection library,* that allows you to store data connection file definitions. A data connection file takes the format of an XML file that has a `.udcx` or `.xml` extension and can hold authentication information, such as explicit usernames and passwords. This setting determines whether InfoPath Forms Services permits a user-deployed form template to use the authentication information associated with a specific data connection. This setting doesn't affect administrator-approved form templates.

✦ **Allow Cross-Domain Data Access for User Form Templates That Use Connection Settings in a Data Connection File:** By default, user form templates permit access to data within the realm of the domain and zone settings, as defined by Internet Explorer. Access to data external to the domain through the use of data connections requires cross-domain access rights. This setting is disabled by default, but when selected, it allows user form templates that have server-defined data connections to access data from another domain.

Configuring postback settings

Postbacks play a key role in forms development, regardless of whether you're developing ASP.NET forms or InfoPath forms. A postback is the process of submitting data to the server for processing, in other words you are *posting* data *back* to the server. This process allows a form to exchange data with the server during form processing, and requires the user to wait for the process to complete.

InfoPath Designer provides a number of tools that can help you determine and limit the use of postbacks in your form templates. For example, the InfoPath Design Checker displays warnings for controls that trigger postbacks to the server. Additionally, you can set the postback option on individual controls to manage when a postback occurs. The postback settings appear on the Browser forms tab in the properties pane for a control.

Three options allow you to specify whether the control will send data to the server when the control value changes or when a button is clicked:

✦ Never

✦ Always

✦ Only When Necessary for Correct Rendering of the Form (Recommended)

Figure 4-1 shows the postback settings options for a Text Box control.

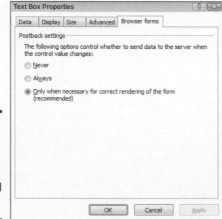

Figure 4-1:
You can control postbacks on individual controls.

InfoPath Forms Services provides a number of configuration options that can help you control the form template postbacks in the SharePoint server farm:

✦ **Number of Postbacks per Session:** Use this setting to limit the number of postbacks in a given form session; the default setting is 75. A well-designed form template should not require more than 75 roundtrips to the server; in fact, the number should be considerably lower, and well below 30. If you use the default setting, as soon as a form executes its 76th postback within a given session, the session is terminated and a server log is generated. In addition, an error is logged in the Windows event log, alerting you to investigate the possibility of a malicious attack.

✦ **Number of Actions per Postback:** When a user updates a form in InfoPath Forms Services, each action is recorded in a temporary log file, which means that the user can continue working on the form without having to wait for the form to reload with every action. During the next postback request (such as a user clicking an Update button), the log file is sent back to, and the actions replayed on, the server. The server subsequently sends updated data back to the browser. This architecture means that when postbacks are required in InfoPath Forms Services, they rarely involve a full page postback; instead, the HTML on the page is updated incrementally, thereby reducing the amount of communication required between the client and the server.

You can define the maximum number of actions that can be replayed on the server in a single postback by specifying this setting. The default setting for this option is 200, which should be more than enough for even the largest form. This setting helps prevent malicious attacks, such as denial-of-service attacks.

**Book III
Chapter 4**

Investigating InfoPath Forms Services

The use of unnecessary postbacks can considerably affect the overall performance of your SharePoint servers.

Do your best to prevent or eliminate as many postbacks as possible when designing your form templates because eliminating postbacks can improve the overall performance and user satisfaction of your forms.

Configuring session state

By default, InfoPath Forms Services uses the session state provided by the State Service to store temporary data generated when a user fills out a form. The State Service is a shared service that InfoPath Forms Services uses to temporarily store session data across related HTTP requests in the SharePoint State Service SQL database. This service allows the Web front-end servers to remain stateless between roundtrips to the server, relieving the postbacks from carrying large amounts of session-state data during form processing.

InfoPath Forms Services can be configured to use the State Service (the default setting), or the Form view (an ASP.NET view state). The State Service is typically used when you have a large number of potential users or have low-bandwidth users. The State Service maintains the session data in the SharePoint State Service SQL Server database, whereas the data associated with a Form view session is maintained on the client browser, and all the data (up to 40kb by default) is included in each postback to the server.

Most enterprise deployments leverage the default State Service to maintain session state. If you configure your SharePoint farm to use Form view and the session data exceeds 40kb, InfoPath Forms Services reverts to using the State Service instead.

Configuring the State Service

When you install SharePoint 2010, the Farm Configuration Wizard walks you through the configuration process for getting the State Service up and running in your environment. The Farm Configuration Wizard creates and configures the necessary service, service application, service application proxy, and associated database for the State Service. If you didn't configure your State Service when you installed it, you can get it up and running by either running the Farm Configuration Wizard again or using Windows PowerShell. If you have the State Service already up and running in your environment, you must use Windows PowerShell to perform any further configurations on the service.

Follow these steps to retrieve the list of cmdlets available for managing the State Service:

1. **From the Start menu, choose All Programs⇨Microsoft SharePoint 2010 Products⇨SharePoint 2010 Management Shell.**

2. **At the PowerShell command prompt that appears, type `gcm *state*`, and then press Enter.**

The State Service has a default ASP.NET session state timeout of one hour, which is basically a measurement of how long a session is inactive. When you design forms for optimal performance you limit the number of times that your form has to contact the server. SharePoint may find it difficult to detect when an optimized form is actually being used because a user can be happily updating the form, which subsequently logs actions to be replayed later during a required postback (such as when the user finally saves the form). Typing data onto an optimized form doesn't register as activity when it comes to measuring an active session because it reduces the amount of communication with the server. That's great for performance purposes but may ultimately lead to SharePoint mistaking a session for idle and timing out the session. After a session times out, the data associated with that session is lost, which means that the user must re-enter the fields that he or she has completed.

 Let your users know that they should save their forms intermittently while they enter their data, particularly if your form has a lot of freeform text that would be cumbersome to re-enter. Saving the form during a session resets the counter against which the timeout session is measured while maintaining the session; it also initiates a postback. Any activity that requires a postback ultimately resets the session timer, thus preventing timeout.

The following configuration settings help you specify the time and data limits for user sessions stored by the SharePoint State Service:

✦ **Active Sessions Should Be Terminated after (Minutes):** When a new form is created or opened for editing in Forms Services, a new session is created that contains information about the form. This setting determines the *total* length of time that the session is kept alive. The default value for this setting is 1440 (one day), which should be ample time for a user to fill in a form.

If you multiply the default timeout session of the State Service (60 minutes) by the number of postbacks allowed in a given session (75), a session could potentially be kept alive for 4500 minutes (about three days)! To prevent sessions from lasting for so long, InfoPath Forms Services offers this setting, which provides another level of management. This setting defines the timeout for a session, regardless of whether it's active or inactive, which effectively translates to the total session timeout.

You can change the default setting of one day, depending on your needs.

✦ **Maximum Size of User Session Data (Kilobytes):** This setting sets a limit on the amount of data that can be stored to maintain a user's session. As far as protecting the server is concerned, this setting is of paramount importance because if you set it too high, the server is at risk of running out of disk space or memory. For example, the File Attachment control is resource-intensive and, depending on the size of the attached file, could require a lot of session state space. If numerous sessions are active simultaneously, all requiring equally large session-state resources, the server can potentially experience an outage. Configuring this setting to the appropriate number, given your organization's requirements, can prevent such outages from occurring; the default setting of 4096 kilobytes should be adequate for most environments.

Understanding Data Connections

InfoPath form templates contain one or more connections to data sources. The *main data source* is the default data source and stores the data entered onto the form by the user. You can associate additional data sources with the form to help populate controls on the form, such as a drop-down list box. For example, you may have a list box on your form that retrieves its contents from a SharePoint list when the form is opened. Additional data sources are known as *secondary data sources*.

You configure data sources through the use of data connections, also known as *query connections*. You can store your data connections directly with the form template or in a data-connection library. A *data-connection library* is a special type of document library that comes with SharePoint Server 2010 — and are also available with SharePoint Server 2007 — and stores data-connection files.

Data-connection files

Two types of data-connection files can be stored in the data-connection library:

✦ **Office Data Connection (ODC) file:** Leveraged by other office applications, such as Excel, ODC files store information about database connections. The ODC file contains all the information needed to form a connection to the database, such as a server name, table name, and query.

✦ **Universal Data Connection (UDC) file:** Can store information about several different types of data connection, such as a Web service or a database. InfoPath form templates use UDC-type data connections. A UDC file may have a .udcx or .xml extension. The UDC file format has been around since FrontPage 2003. Office applications use two versions of the UDC file format; InfoPath uses the V2.0 format.

Data Connection Wizard

If you want to create a UDC data connection file for use with InfoPath form templates, you have a couple of options:

✦ Build the .udcx file from scratch by using an editor, such as Notepad. Details on the exact steps involved with this method is outside the scope of this book, however, you'll find plenty of guidance and examples on Microsoft's MSDN Web site.

✦ Leverage the Data Connection Wizard that comes with InfoPath Designer 2010.

The Data Connection Wizard provides tools with which you can set up a connection and store it directly into a data connection library on the SharePoint server. Figure 4-2 shows an example of a data connection file that was generated by using the Data Connection Wizard in InfoPath Designer. The data source in this particular example is a SharePoint list named Colors.

InfoPath allows you to store connection information with your form template. However, creating a UDC file instead has a number of advantages:

✦ **Share connection information.** UDC files allow you to share the same data connection information among many form templates, without requiring each template to hold its own copy of the connection data.

✦ **Maintain and update more easily than storing connection information directly in your form.** UDC files improve the maintenance and upkeep of connection information; if the data source moves, you have to update the data connection information in only one file, instead of editing each form template that uses the data connection.

```
Colors - Notepad
File  Edit  Format  View  Help
<?xml version="1.0" encoding="UTF-8"?>
<?MicrosoftWindowsSharePointServices
ContentTypeID="0x010100B4CBD48E029A4ad8B62CB0E41868F2B0"?>
<udc:DataSource MajorVersion="2" Minorversion="0"
xmlns:udc="http://schemas.microsoft.com/office/infopath/2006/udc">
        <udc:Name>Colors</udc:Name>
        <udc:Description>Format: UDC V2; Connection Type: SharePointList; Purpose: ReadOnly;
Generated by Microsoft InfoPath 2010 on 2010-04-26 at 10:15:22 by NUT2CRAIC
\Administrator.</udc:Description>
        <udc:Type MajorVersion="2" Minorversion="0" Type="SharePointList">
                <udc:SubType MajorVersion="0" Minorversion="0" Type=""/>
        </udc:Type>
        <udc:ConnectionInfo Purpose="ReadOnly" AltDataSource="">
                <udc:wsdlurl/>
                <udc:SelectCommand>
                        <udc:ListId>{6C74C1EA-0042-4E3B-85A6-1508743D7D60}</udc:ListId>
                        <udc:WebUrl>http://spdev01/</udc:WebUrl>
                        <udc:ConnectionString/>
                        <udc:ServiceUrl UseFormsServiceProxy="false"/>
                        <udc:SoapAction/>
                        <udc:Query/>
                </udc:SelectCommand>
                <udc:UpdateCommand>
                        <udc:ServiceUrl UseFormsServiceProxy="false"/>
                        <udc:SoapAction/>                          /
                        <udc:Submit/>
                        <udc:FileName>Specify a filename or formula</udc:FileName>
                        <udc:FolderName AllowOverwrite=""/>
                </udc:UpdateCommand>
                <!--udc:Authentication><udc:SSO AppId='' CredentialType=''
/></udc:Authentication-->
                </udc:ConnectionInfo>
</udc:DataSource>
```

Figure 4-2:
A data-connection file stores information about the connection.

+ **Support cross-domain connections.** Data connections stored in a UDC file support cross-domain connections, which means that you can connect to data outside of the current domain boundary. If your form template makes use of cross-domain connections, then you must use a UDC file and enable the Cross-Domain Access for User Form Templates setting in InfoPath Forms Services.

Centrally managing data connections

SharePoint provides a central repository, known as the central store, for hosting data connection files. You can upload, manage, and maintain your data connection files in the central store by using Central Administration.

When you upload a data connection file to the central store, SharePoint stores the file in its configuration database. Access to the central store — and the data connection files it contains — is handled by InfoPath Forms Services. Unless you have specific security restrictions within your organization, most data connection files are probably stored in data connection libraries. That said, data connections defined in the central store have some advantages to those stored in a site collection data connection library, including

+ Form templates can leverage cross-domain data connections defined in the central store without requiring the form to be fully trusted.

+ All site collections across the entire server farm can access data connections defined in the central store through InfoPath Forms Services.

+ Data connections defined in the central store have increased security because only users who have access to Central Administration can modify and upload data connection files to the central store.

Creating a UDC file for the central store

Before you upload a data connection file to the central store, you must first create the physical .udcx file. InfoPath Designer provides an easy mechanism for creating data connection files that you can upload to the central store. At a high-level, here's the process:

1. **Create the data connection.**

   The Data Connection Wizard steps you through the process of creating the initial connection to your data source. For example, you can connect to a SharePoint list, specifying the fields that you want to use on your form template. Book IV, Chapter 6 walks you through the process of creating the connection to your data source.

2. **Convert the data connection to a connection file.**

   This step tells your form template to look to the data connection file for connection information, instead of storing the connection information with the form template. So, if your data connection information changes, you don't have to modify your form template, you can simply update the associated data connection file.

Follow these steps to create the .udcx file, which you can then upload to the central store:

1. **Open your form template in InfoPath Designer.**

2. **At the bottom of the Fields task pane, click Manage Data Connections.**

   The Data Connections dialog appears displaying a list of the current data connections for the form template.

3. **From the data connections list, select the connection that you want to convert, and then click Convert to Connection File.**

   The Convert Data Connection dialog box appears.

4. **In the URL field, enter the URL to the data-connection library where you want to create your data-connection file.**

   The URL that you specify here *isn't* the URL to the central store. You can't upload files to the central store directly from InfoPath; you must first create the file in a SharePoint data connection library in a site to which you have access. Storing the file in the data connection library is only a temporary requirement — you no longer need to store the file after it's uploaded to the central store.

5. **In the Connection Link Type section, click Centrally Managed Connection Library (Advanced).**

   Clicking this option doesn't create the data connection file in the central store, it simply tells InfoPath and InfoPath Forms Services that the connection information for the specific data connection is in the central store.

6. **Click OK.**

   SharePoint stores the data-connection file in the data connection library that you specified in Step 4.

7. **Download the newly created `.udcx` file from the data-connection library to the SharePoint administrator.**

   The SharePoint administrator (who may be you) then uploads the file to the central store.

After the data connection file is uploaded to the central store, you can delete the data connection file that was created in your data connection library.

Uploading data-connection files to the central store

If you are the SharePoint administrator, after you have the physical `.udcx` file, you can upload it to the central store.

Follow these steps to upload a data connection file to the central store:

1. **Navigate to the Central Administration home page.**

2. **In the Quick Launch menu, select General Application Settings.**

   The General Application Settings page appears.

3. **In the InfoPath Forms Services section, click Manage Data Connection Files.**

   The Manage Data Connection Files page appears, displaying a list of the currently uploaded UDC files.

4. **In the Library menu, select Upload.**

   The Upload Data Connection File page appears.

5. **In the Select File section, browse to and select the `.udcx` file that you want to upload.**

6. **In the Category field, enter the name of the category in which you want to file your UDC file.**

7. **In the Web Accessibility section, set the Allow HTTP Access to This File setting, as needed.**

   Select this setting if you want to allow clients, such as Microsoft InfoPath, to access the UDC file over HTTP. Otherwise, leave the setting deselected to ensure that only browser forms can use the UDC file.

8. **Click Upload.**

   SharePoint examines the data connection file to ensure that it is in the correct format. If the file you upload isn't the correct format, you receive an error and the file doesn't upload to the central data connection library.

**Book III
Chapter 4**

**Investigating
InfoPath Forms
Services**

If the file is the correct format, it appears in the list of data connection files in the category specified in Step 6. Figure 4-3 shows a list of data connection files in the central store, grouped by category.

Data connection files need meet the Universal Data Connection 2.0 XML file format. You can find details about this specification on Microsoft's MSDN Web site.

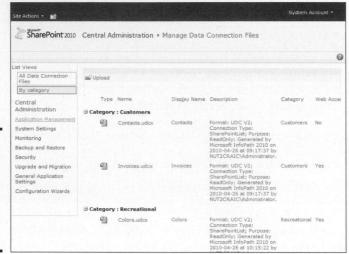

Figure 4-3:
You can view the UDC files in the central store by category.

If you create form templates that leverage data connection files in the central store, you must publish the template as an administrator-approved form template.

Managing Administrator-Approved Form Templates

As a SharePoint administrator, it's your job to thoroughly evaluate the form templates that you upload and deploy to the farm. Unless your organization requires that an administrator approve and deploy all form templates, form templates that require administrator approval generally require higher privileges and are therefore a greater security risk than user-deployed forms. For example, form templates that contain managed code and have full trust to the domain require administrator approval before being deployed because the code contained in those templates could be malicious.

After you know that the form template is worthy of deployment and won't wreak havoc on your SharePoint farm, you can upload that form template to the server and activate that template to your site collections.

Uploading form templates

You can upload browser-enabled form templates to the server by using the Upload Form Template page in Central Administration. SharePoint provides a verification option that allows you to ensure that the form template doesn't contain errors and that it'll upload correctly. For example, if a form author gives you an InfoPath Filler form template — which means it isn't browser-compatible — then the error shown in Figure 4-4 appears during the verification process. If the verification process passes, you can proceed with the template upload.

When you upload an administrator-approved form template into Central Administration, the solutions framework works behind the scenes to package the feature up so that it's easily deployable across all the servers in the farm. SharePoint creates a feature to deliver the form template and then wraps the feature in a SharePoint Foundation solution package (a .wsp file). On the Solution Management page (which you can navigate to by choosing Central Administration⇨System Settings⇨Manage Farm Solutions), your form-template solution package appears in the list of the solutions deployed across your farm with a status of Deployed.

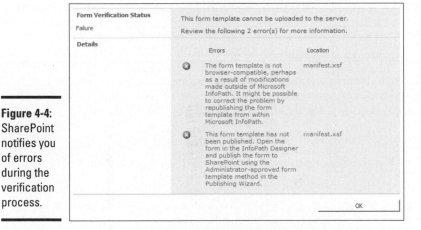

Figure 4-4: SharePoint notifies you of errors during the verification process.

**Book III
Chapter 4**

**Investigating
InfoPath Forms
Services**

As part of the solution-deployment process, SharePoint pushes all the associated feature files to the Features directory on all the front-end Web servers in the farm. The feature files include a file that represents the administrator-approved form template uploaded to the server. Figure 4-5 shows the feature files for an administrator-approved form template. When you upgrade a form template, SharePoint maintains the previous versions in subfolders within the feature directory. In the example in Figure 4-5, the folder contains several subfolders; each subfolder hosts a different version of the form template.

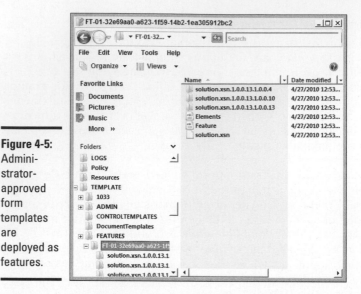

Figure 4-5:
Admini-
strator-
approved
form
templates
are
deployed as
features.

The Features directory is in located in the `C:\Program Files\Common Files\Microsoft Shared\Web Server Extensions\14\TEMPLATE\ FEATURES` directory (replace C with your server's system drive letter). The feature folder that represents your form template has a name prefix of "FT-01-" followed by the feature GUID.

Follow these steps to upload a new form template by using Central Administration (if you're upgrading an existing form template, jump to the "Upgrading Form Templates" section, later in this chapter):

1. **Navigate to the Central Administration home page.**

2. **In the Quick Launch menu, select General Application Settings.**

   The General Application Settings page appears.

3. **In the InfoPath Forms Services section, click Upload Form Template.**

   The Upload Form Template page appears.

4. **Browse to and select the administrator-approved form template that you want to deploy.**

5. **Click Verify.**

   SharePoint verifies the form template and provides status about whether the form template is ready to upload to the server.

6. **In the status-notification page, click OK.**

   If you received any errors or warnings during the verification process, correct them before proceeding to Step 7.

7. **Browse to and select the administrator-approved form template that you want to deploy.**

    When the verification process completes (even if your form template is error free), the File Name field is blank again, so you have to browse to and select the file again.

8. **Click Upload.**

    InfoPath Forms Services provides the status of the upload process. If the process goes smoothly, you receive a status that notifies you when the form template has been successfully uploaded; otherwise, you receive a status that notifies you of any errors that occurred during the upload process.

9. **From the status-notification page, click OK.**

    SharePoint redirects you to the Manage Form Templates page, which lists all the uploaded form templates.

    In the Manage Form Templates page, you can manage your form template from its initial activation through to its removal. The rest of this chapter shows you how to manage your administrator-approved form templates.

Follow these steps to upload a new form template by using PowerShell:

1. **From the Start menu, choose All Programs⇨Microsoft SharePoint 2010 Products⇨SharePoint 2010 Management Shell.**

2. **At the PowerShell command prompt that appears, type the following command, and then press Enter.**

    ```
    Install-SPInfoPathFormTemplate -Path <path to your form template file
        location>
    ```

After you successfully upload your template, you can activate the form template to the site collections of your choosing.

Categorizing form templates

When you upload administrator-approved form templates to InfoPath Forms Services, you have the option of editing the properties of the uploaded file and populating the category field associated with the form template. Populating the category field for your form templates allows you to view the list of uploaded templates with the By Category view.

Follow these steps to categorize an administrator-approved form template by using Central Administration:

1. **Navigate to the Central Administration home page.**

2. **In the Quick Launch menu, select General Application Settings.**

    The General Application Settings page appears.

3. **In the InfoPath Forms Services section, click Manage Form Templates.**

   The Manage Form Templates page appears, listing all the uploaded form templates.

4. **On the Manage Form Templates page, click the name of the form template that you want to categorize, and then click View Properties.**

   The Form Template Properties page appears, displaying the properties associated with the selected form template. The Category property is the only property that you can edit on this page.

5. **In the Category name field, enter the category name for your template.**

6. **Click OK.**

   The Manage Form Templates page appears, which displays the category name in the Category column. To view your form templates grouped by their categories, click the By Category link in the List Views section of the Quick Launch.

Activating form templates

The upload process deploys your administrator-approved form template as a feature and pushes the associated feature files, including the form template, out to the Features directory of all the front-end Web servers in your farm. At this point in the deployment process, the form template isn't available for use because it hasn't yet been activated. During the activation process a number of things happen:

1. The feature associated with your form template is activated in the site collections that you specify.

2. The activated feature creates the form template in the Form Templates library of the site collection.

3. SharePoint creates a site content type in the site collection and maps it to the form template.

After you activate a form template to a site collection, the site collection members can begin to leverage the form template by using the site content type or by referencing the form template in the Form Templates library directly.

The feature definition file (Feature.xml) in the Feature folder shows that the feature is scoped to the site collection level and references an element manifest (Elements.xml) that, at the time of feature activation, creates the form template in the Form Templates library of the site collection.

Activating by using Central Administration

Follow these steps to activate an administrator-approved form template to a site collection by using Central Administration:

1. **Navigate to the Central Administration home page.**

2. **In the Quick Launch menu, select General Application Settings.**

The General Application Settings page appears.

3. **In the InfoPath Forms Services section, click Manage Form Templates.**

The Manage Form Templates page appears, listing all the uploaded form templates.

4. **Click the name of the form template that you want to activate, and then click Activate to a Site Collection.**

The Activate Form Template page appears, displaying the form template properties.

5. **In the Activation Location section, select the site collection to which you want to activate the form template.**

If the currently selected site collection is the site collection to which you want to activate the form template, skip to Step 6. Otherwise, follow these steps:

a. Click the current site collection to display a shortcut menu, and then click Change Site Collection.

The Select Site Collection page appears.

b. In the list of URLs, click the site collection to which you want to activate your form template.

If you don't see the site collection listed, click the current Web Application, then click Change Web Application, and select the Web Application that contains your site collection from the list.

c. Click OK.

The Activate Form Template page reappears.

6. **Click OK.**

SharePoint creates the form template in the Form Templates library of the site collection you selected in Step 5. You can verify that the activation was successful by checking the Form Templates library to see whether your newly activated form template is there.

SharePoint allows you to activate administrator-approved form templates from Central Administration to site collections that don't support InfoPath Forms Services, such as those created using the Basic Meeting Workspace template; however, even though it appears that the activation process is successful you won't be able to use the form templates in the site collection.

Activating by using PowerShell

Follow these steps to activate a form template by using PowerShell:

**Book III
Chapter 4**

Investigating
InfoPath Forms
Services

1. **From the Start menu, choose All Programs⇨Microsoft SharePoint 2010 Products⇨SharePoint 2010 Management Shell.**

2. **At the PowerShell command prompt that appears, type the following command, and then press Enter.**

   ```
   Enable-SPInfoPathFormTemplate -Identity "YourTemplateName.xsn" -Site
       http://urltoyoursitecollection
   ```

Activating from the Site Collection Features page

Follow these steps to activate an administrator-approved form template directly from a site collection:

1. **Navigate to the home page of the site collection.**

2. **In the Site Actions menu, select Site Settings.**

   The Site Settings page appears.

3. **In the Site Collection Administration section, click Site Collection Features.**

   The Site Collection Administration Features page appears, listing all the features activated or available for activation for the site collection.

4. **In the list of features, click the Activate button that appears next to the feature that represents your administrator-approved form template.**

   The feature has the same name as your form template (.xsn) file and has the description Microsoft InfoPath Form Template. When you click the Activate button, SharePoint creates the form template in the Form Templates library for the site collection. You can verify that the activation was successful by checking the Form Templates library to see whether your newly activated form template appears there.

   If you see a Deactivate button rather than an Activate button beside the form template feature, the form template is already activated for your site collection.

   If you don't see a feature that represents your form template, then the administrator-approved form template isn't deployed on the farm.

Deactivating form templates

You can deactivate an administrator-approved form template from a site collection. When you deactivate a form template, SharePoint performs a number of actions that may negatively impact your users. These actions include

✦ **The removal of the form template from all the libraries in the site collection, including the Form Templates library:** Users can't create new forms based on the form template, and they can't render forms that were created by using the form template.

✦ **The termination of any existing form-filling sessions:** All the data that a user has currently entered into an open form that's based on the form template is lost. You can allow existing sessions to finish before deactivation by using the Quiesce function in Central Administration. You can find out how to quiesce your form template in the "Quiescing form templates" section, later in this chapter.

Deactivating by using Central Administration

Follow these steps to deactivate an administrator-approved form template to a site collection by using Central Administration:

1. **Navigate to the Central Administration home page.**

2. **In the Quick Launch menu, select General Application Settings.**

The General Application Settings page appears.

3. **In the InfoPath Forms Services section, click Manage Form Templates.**

The Manage Form Templates page appears, listing all the uploaded form templates.

4. **Click the name of the form template that you want to deactivate, and then click Deactivate from a Site Collection.**

The Deactivate Form Template page appears, displaying the form template properties.

5. **In the Deactivation Location section, select the site collection from which you want to deactivate the form template.**

If the currently selected site collection is the site collection from which you want to deactivate the form template, then skip to Step 6. Otherwise, follow these steps:

a. *Click the current site collection to display a shortcut menu, and then select Change Site Collection.*

The Select Site Collection page appears.

b. *In the list of URLs, click the site collection from which you want to deactivate your form template.*

If you don't see the site collection listed, click the current Web Application, then click Change Web Application, and select the Web Application that contains your site collection from the list.

c. *Click OK.*

The Deactivate Form Template page reappears.

6. **Click OK.**

SharePoint removes the form template from the Form Templates library of the site collection you selected in Step 5. You can verify that the deactivation was successful by checking the Form Templates library to see whether your deactivated form template has been removed.

**Book III
Chapter 4**

**Investigating
InfoPath Forms
Services**

Deactivating by using PowerShell

Follow these steps to deactivate a form template by using PowerShell:

1. **From the Start menu, choose All Programs⇨Microsoft SharePoint 2010 Products⇨SharePoint 2010 Management Shell.**

2. **At the PowerShell command prompt that appears, type the following command, and then press Enter.**

   ```
   Disable-SPInfoPathFormTemplate -Identity "YourTemplateName.xsn" -Site
       http://urltoyoursitecollection
   ```

Deactivating from the Site Collection Features page

Follow these steps to deactivate an administrator-approved form template directly from a site collection:

1. **Navigate to the home page of the site collection.**

2. **In the Site Actions menu, select Site Settings.**

   The Site Settings page appears.

3. **In the Site Collection Administration section, click Site Collection Features.**

   The Site Collection Administration Features page appears and lists all the features activated or available for activation for the site collection.

4. **In the list of features, click the Deactivate button that appears next to the feature that represents your administrator-approved form template.**

   The feature has the same name as your form template (.xsn) file and has the description Microsoft InfoPath Form Template. When you click the Deactivate button, SharePoint removes the form template from the Form Templates library for the site collection. You can verify that the deactivation was successful by checking the Form Templates library to see whether your deactivated form template has been removed.

   If you see an Activate button rather than a Deactivate button beside the form template feature, then the form template is already deactivated for your site collection.

   If you don't see a feature that represents your form template, then the administrator-approved form template isn't deployed on the farm.

Removing form templates

When you remove an administrator-approved form template from the server farm, SharePoint removes the form template feature from each site collection, regardless of whether the form template feature is active. Removing the feature involves removing the associated feature files on the front-end Web servers, including the form template (.xsn) file.

Removing the form-template feature from the site collection doesn't remove the form template from the libraries in the site collection. The form template isn't accessible because the files are removed from the front-end Web servers; accessing the form template produces an error. In addition, the next time you upload the same form template, it's automatically activated in all the site collections where it was active when the form template was previously removed.

Follow these steps to remove an administrator-approved form template from the server farm by using Central Administration:

1. **Navigate to the Central Administration home page.**

2. **From the Quick Launch menu, click General Application Settings.**

The General Application Settings page appears.

3. **In the InfoPath Forms Services section, click Manage Form Templates.**

The Manage Form Templates page appears, listing all the uploaded form templates.

4. **On the Manage Form Templates page, click the name of the form template that you want to remove, and then click Remove.**

The Manage Form Templates page appears again, listing all the uploaded form templates. The status of the form template you chose to remove is changed to Deleting. The deletion process can take a while, depending on the size of your farm and the number of site collections SharePoint must traverse.

Follow these steps to remove a form template by using PowerShell:

1. **From the Start menu, choose All Programs⇨Microsoft SharePoint 2010 Products⇨SharePoint 2010 Management Shell.**

2. **At the PowerShell command prompt that appears, type the following command, and then press Enter.**

```
Uninstall-SPInfoPathFormTemplate -Identity "YourTemplateName.xsn"
```

Upgrading form templates

Upgrading an administrator-approved form template requires more thought and planning than simply uploading a form template. When you upgrade a form template that users are currently using, you have two options with respect to how to handle the existing sessions:

✦ Allow all existing browser-based form-filling sessions to complete by using the older version of the form template.

✦ Terminate all existing browser-based sessions, resulting in loss of data.

**Book III
Chapter 4**

**Investigating
InfoPath Forms
Services**

Although the second option may be a quicker route to getting your form template upgraded, it may not be very popular among the end-user community. Figure 4-6 shows the error message that a user receives when he or she tries to save the form data after the form template has been upgraded by using the option to terminate all existing browser-based sessions.

Even though you may have chosen to terminate the users' sessions, users can still fill in data on the form. If the form is considerably large, your users aren't notified that the session has been terminated until they contact the server, whether by clicking Save or initiating a postback within the form. Imagine the frustration if you went to the trouble of filling in a lot of data on a form, only to find that it had all been lost!

Figure 4-6:
Users
receive
an error
message
when trying
to save their
form.

To handle administrator-approved form template upgrades we recommend that you wait until the browser-based sessions are complete. You can achieve this by quiescing your form template; which we conveniently cover in the next section.

Quiescing a form template

Quiescing refers to the process of *temporarily* rendering a form template inactive. The quiescing capability in InfoPath Form Services allows you to disable a form template gradually, not abruptly. Disabling a form template gradually provides users with ample time to save their data and prepare for the template upgrade. Only administrator-approved and activated form templates have quiescing capabilities.

Follow these steps to quiesce an administrator-approved form template from the server farm by using Central Administration:

1. **Navigate to the Central Administration home page.**

2. **In the Quick Launch menu, select General Application Settings.**

   The General Application Settings page appears.

3. **In the InfoPath Forms Services section, click Manage Form Templates.**

   The Manage Form Templates page appears, listing all the uploaded form templates.

4. **On the Manage Form Templates page, click the name of the form template that you want to remove, and then click Quiesce Form Template.**

   The Quiesce Form Template page appears.

5. **In the Quiesce field, enter the time interval in minutes after which you want your form template to be quiesced.**

6. **Click Start Quiescing.**

   The form template's status changes to Quiescing. After the allotted time has passed, the form template is quiesced, which means

   - The form template status is updated to Quiesced.

   - New sessions are rejected.

   - Existing sessions are terminated.

   - Unsaved data is lost.

Follow these steps to quiesce a form template by using PowerShell:

1. **From the Start menu, choose All Programs⇨Microsoft SharePoint 2010 Products⇨SharePoint 2010 Management Shell.**

2. **At the PowerShell command prompt that appears, type the following command, and then press Enter.**

   ```
   Stop-SPInfoPathFormTemplate -Identity "YourTemplateName.xsn" --TimeLeft
       <yourtimeinminutes>
   ```

When a form template has the quiesced status, it means there are no open sessions using the template; therefore, you can successfully upgrade the form template without impacting users. Figure 4-7 shows the error that a user receives when he or she tries to save data on a form whose template is in the quiesced state.

After the new form has been successfully uploaded, you can release the form from its quiesced state by clicking the Reset Template button on the Quiesce Form Template page.

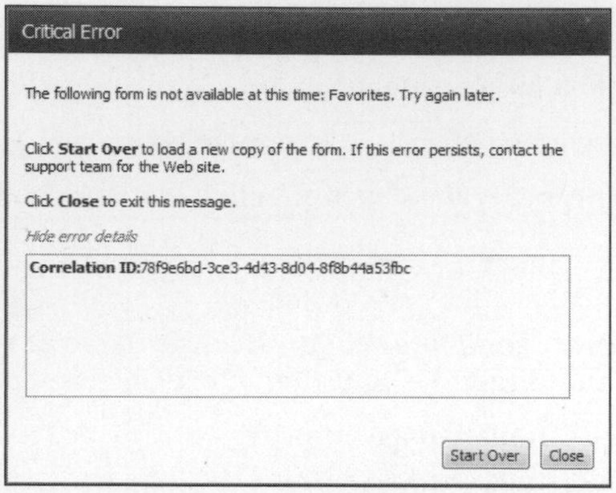

Figure 4-7:
You receive an error when you save a form that's in a quiesced state.

The Critical Error dialog box reads:

Critical Error

The following form is not available at this time: Favorites. Try again later.

Click **Start Over** to load a new copy of the form. If this error persists, contact the support team for the Web site.

Click **Close** to exit this message.

Hide error details

Correlation ID:78f9e6bd-3ce3-4d43-8d04-8f8b44a53fbc

Start Over   Close

Upgrading a form template

Follow these steps to upgrade a new form template by using Central Administration:

1. **Navigate to the Central Administration home page.**

2. **From the Quick Launch menu, click General Application Settings.**

   The General Application Settings page appears.

3. **In the InfoPath Forms Services section, click Upload Form Template.**

   The Upload Form Template page appears.

4. **Browse to and select the administrator-approved form template that you want to deploy.**

5. **Click Verify.**

   SharePoint verifies the form template and provides the status about whether the form template is ready to upload to the server.

6. **In the status-notification page, click OK.**

   If you received any errors or warnings during the verification process, correct them before going on to Step 7.

   After you click OK, the File Name field is blank again, so you have to browse to the file again.

7. **Browse to and select the administrator-approved form template that you want to deploy.**

8. **In the Upgrade section, select Upgrade the Form Template if it already exists.**

9. **Select how you want to handle existing browser-based form-filling sessions.**

You have two options:

- Allow existing browser-based form-filling sessions to complete by using the current version of the form template.

- Terminate existing browser-based form-filling sessions. Any data in those sessions is lost.

If you want to wait until all sessions of the form template are complete before you upgrade, you should first quiesce the form template (see the Quiescing a form template section of this chapter).

10. **Click Upload.**

InfoPath Forms Services provides status on the upload process. If the process went smoothly, you receive a status that notifies you when the form template has been successfully uploaded; otherwise you receive a status that notifies you of any errors that occurred during the upload process.

11. **In the status-notification page, click OK.**

SharePoint redirects you to the Manage Form Templates page, which lists all the uploaded form templates.

Chapter 5: Maneuvering the Managed Metadata Service

In This Chapter

- ✔ **Managing metadata — why and how it works**
- ✔ **Configuring the Managed Metadata Service**
- ✔ **Using Managed Metadata in SharePoint**

These days information is being captured at a remarkable rate, and in many different forms — we have blogs, we have vlogs, we have wikis, we have tweets, we have discussion forums, and we have good old e-mail. With this smorgasbord of content types, corporations can create, capture, store, and disseminate more data than ever before — making it easy to harness knowledge and retain intellectual property in-house.

The downside of all this data is that the more data you have, the more data you have to sift through to find the information you actually need. To truly benefit from all the information your organization takes in, you have to get at that juicy info — exactly when you need it, in a form you can use.

Microsoft SharePoint Server 2010 comes equipped with a variety of tools and services that help you manage and make use of the large corpus of data within your organization. One such offering — which lies at the heart of content management in SharePoint 2010 — is the Managed Metadata Service.

The Managed Metadata Service centralizes the management of how your organization describes its content. In essence, the service standardizes the terminology used in metadata files. The idea is for everyone in your organization to share a common language (at least where the content is concerned), which can help make the data more accurate and easier to find. If the standard terminology in your managed metadata changes, then those changes propagate automatically throughout your SharePoint farm.

Before your organization can start to reap the rewards of managed metadata, however, you have to configure the Managed Metadata Service. In the chapter you're now reading, we turn your focus to precisely that process — and show you how to get the service up and running in your organization.

Reviewing the Managed Metadata Lingo

Metadata refers to words or phrases that describe an item or an object in a database — information *about* your information resources.

For example, the metadata that describes an employee could consist of

✦ Employee ID

✦ First name

✦ Last name

✦ Job Title

✦ Office

Each item in a SharePoint list or library has accompanying metadata that describes the item. Each item of metadata also serves as a name for a column in SharePoint. For example, a document in a document library has several columns that describe it; these include columns for the document title, the creation date, and the author. However, these columns aren't considered managed metadata — not by themselves, anyway. SharePoint manages metadata by creating a hierarchical set of words or phrases (sort of like an automatic dictionary) that you can apply to all the items and content types in your SharePoint farm — and you control that set of words from a central location.

This may come as a shock, but not all metadata *needs* to be managed. For example, a project team may have a SharePoint list that keeps track of team members' hobbies and fun activities. The list may contain metadata that describes a list of pastimes, making it easy for the team members to contribute to the list and get a glimpse of what their colleagues get up to on weekends (the shareable stuff, anyway). This information helps team members build rapport with one another, which improves their working relationship and has a positive impact on their overall productivity. The pastimes data is useful in the context of the team, but is it crucial for the whole organization to sit down and determine a consistent vocabulary to use for each pastime? Probably not. (George Orwell can rest easy.)

Metadata that helps your users navigate the large corpus of data within your organization to find the information they need is deemed worthy of being managed. For example, if your organization is a record-label company that sells music by various artists, then having a consistent vocabulary to classify and describe music-business terms, such as genre, would be beneficial.

Before you start working with the Managed Metadata Service in SharePoint, it helps to pick up some of the metadata vernacular. Here's a quick overview (*not* alphabetical, mind you) of the words that the Managed Metadata Service uses to describe itself:

✦ **Term:** No, we're not kidding (about this, anyway). To SharePoint, a *term* is a word associated with an item. For example, if you have a list of Albums, the term Country can describe the type (or genre) of music that the album represents. A *managed term* is, in effect, a word with a standardized meaning that's accepted for use in metadata, so it's centrally managed and controlled by the Managed Metadata Service in SharePoint 2010. In general, the use of managed terms in metadata enables SharePoint to "know" exactly what you mean.

A term can contain multiple levels of detail, arranged in a hierarchy of related terms that help your users navigate through content. You can define a maximum of seven levels of detail for a term. For example, you could subdivide the term Country with other terms such as Bluegrass and Americana, each representing a different style of country music. Figure 5-1 shows an example of the term Country and its related terms, defined in the Managed Metadata Service.

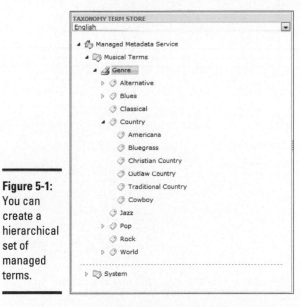

Figure 5-1: You can create a hierarchical set of managed terms.

Book III
Chapter 5

Maneuvering the
Managed Metadata
Service

When you create a term in SharePoint it is given a unique identifier, enabling you to associate multiple labels with a single term. You can use labels to represent synonyms for your terms; if you have a multilingual implementation of SharePoint, you can use labels to represent your term in each language.

✦ **Term set:** A hierarchical collection of related terms. For example, the term set Genre may contain a list of music genres such as Blues, Classical, Rock, Pop, and Country, with each individual genre representing a single term in the term set. Figure 5-1 shows an example of a Genre term set defined in the Managed Metadata Service.

You can define a maximum of 30, 000 terms per term set, with a combined total of one million per Term Store.

✦ **Group:** A collection of relatable term sets that share the same security requirements.

Figure 5-2 shows a group containing multiple term sets. In this example, the Locations group contains three term sets: Asia, Europe, and North America. Each term set represents a geographical region, and so contains terms for countries within the region — specifically those where our fictitious organization does business. Each individual country is further defined with more terms for its states or cities.

Figure 5-2: Groups provide a security boundary for your metadata.

When you create a group in your Term Store, you may specify the following security permissions:

- **Group Mangers:** The users you assign as Group Managers have Contributor rights; they can add, create, edit, and delete term sets and terms within the group. In addition, they can assign and revoke contributor permissions to the group.

- **Contributors:** The users you assign as Contributors may add, create, edit, and delete the term sets and terms within the group. They can't assign and revoke contributor permissions.

A group can contain a maximum of 1,000 term sets.

✦ **Taxonomy Term Store:** When you create your Managed Metadata Service application, a database is created to store all the managed metadata that you define — this database is the Taxonomy Term Store. (Hey, buddy, wanna buy a term? We've got 'em all here.)

There is only one Term Store per Managed Metadata Service application.

When you configure the Managed Metadata Service in your server farm, you define the following administrator roles:

- **Service Application Administrators:** The Managed Metadata Service administrator has full control over the Managed Metadata Service in Central Administration. Users granted this level of permission can manage all settings related to the service application.

- **Term Store Administrators:** The Term Store Administrators can create and manage the groups in the Term Store (as well as their associated contents), and can determine which users are assigned the Group Manager role.

A Term Store can contain a total of 1 million terms. Go ahead, include all the details that your business might find useful. Just keep 'em hierarchical, okay?

✦ **Enterprise Keywords:** When creating content in SharePoint, your users can associate *keywords* with their items — words or phrases that end users enter to describe their content so other users can find that content more easily. For example, if a SharePoint trainer in your organization uploads a How To guide that covers managing documents in SharePoint, associating keywords such as *SharePoint* and *training* can help other users find the document when they're browsing the SharePoint document repositories. Users can search and filter various document libraries and search results using the *enterprise keywords* (each of which has a standard meaning for the entire organization).

Enterprise keywords are enabled at two levels: the document library and the list. When they're enabled, an Enterprise Keywords column is added to the list or library — and the Enterprise Keywords control appears on the Create and Edit forms. You can use the control to add new keywords — or to select existing keywords and managed terms from the Managed Metadata Term Store. Figure 5-3 shows an example of the Enterprise Keyword control in action — keywords are separated with semicolons. As you start typing your keyword, SharePoint presents you with a list of suggestions from the Managed Metadata Services Term Store.

When you enter a new enterprise keyword, that keyword is stored as a term in the Managed Metadata Service Term Store — in the non-hierarchical Keywords term set. There it's accessible to other users and applications.

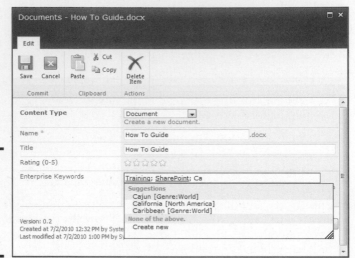

Figure 5-3:
You
separate
keywords
with
semicolons.

+ **Orphaned terms:** The Managed Metadata Service in SharePoint 2010 allows you to reuse terms in multiple term sets. The term set, or term in which a term is created is considered as the source term. If the source term is deleted, any reused terms linked to it are considered orphaned terms. The Managed Metadata Service displays a list of all orphaned terms in a single term set: the Orphaned Terms system generated term set. From the Orphaned Terms term set, you can assign new source terms to orphaned terms. Figure 5-4 shows an orphaned term's Member Of property, which lists the various term sets, and parent terms (a term that contains terms) in your Term Store that use the term. Here you can select the term set that you want to assign as the new source term for the orphaned term.

Figure 5-4:
You can
assign
orphaned
terms a new
source term.

When you're viewing the properties of an orphaned term, the Term Set Description informs you that the the source term was deleted, and allows you to assign a new owner simply by clicking the source term option for one of the shared terms in the list. In the example shown in Figure 5-4, clicking the source term option in the Genre parent term would make the Genre term the new term owner (source term), and the term would no longer be orphaned.

✦ **Tagging:** (No, this doesn't mean spraying graffiti on your information.) In the context of SharePoint, *tagging* refers to applying metadata to an item. The metadata can be in a variety of forms including a site column, a Managed Metadata column, or even a social tag. When you create a term set, a term, or a keyword, you can make it available for tagging by selecting (logically enough) the Available for Tagging setting.

Book I, Chapter 5 shows you the places where managed metadata surfaces (appears onscreen to meet the user's curious gaze) in SharePoint 2010.

Managing the Managed Metadata Service

Creating a service application for the Managed Metadata Service follows the standard rules and processes used for any service application. If those don't spring to mind just now, no problem: If you use the SharePoint Farm Configuration Wizard during your installation of SharePoint Server (whether the Standard or Enterprise Edition), you can choose to have the Managed Metadata Service service application and its associated proxies created automatically.

If you want to create the service application manually — or you want to associate the service application with another Web Application — jump to Book II, Chapter 8, which shows you how to work with service applications.

**Book III
Chapter 5**

When you have the service application up and running, you can control the Managed Metadata Service through Central Administration. Fortunately, the management interface of Managed Metadata Service is consistent with other SharePoint service applications — sharing a common look and feel with them — which makes administration of the service a lot more intuitive.

Maneuvering the
Managed Metadata
Service

Assigning Managed Metadata Administrators

When you configure the Managed Metadata Service, you must assign the Administrator role to one or more users. The Managed Metadata Service Administrator has full control over the Managed Metadata Service, exercised in Central Administration. Users granted this level of permission can manage all the settings related to the service application — including defining who gets to be a Term Store Administrator.

Follow these steps to assign a Managed Metadata administrator:

1. **Using your browser, navigate to the Central Administration home page.**

2. **In the Application Management section, click Manage service applications.**

3. **From the list of service applications, select the Managed Metadata Service.**

4. **On the Service Applications tab, in the Operations group, click Administrators.**

   The Administrators for Managed Metadata Service Web dialog box appears.

5. **In the People Picker, enter the name of the account you want to add as an Administrator, and then click Add.**

   The name you entered appears in the list of Administrators.

6. **In the Permissions box, select Full Control.**

7. **Click OK.**

   The user whose name you entered now has access to the Central Administration site, and can manage the settings related to the Managed Metadata Service.

Members of the Farm Administrators group always have the right to manage all service applications. The permission is assigned automatically to group members.

Accessing the Term Store Management Tool

When you create your Managed Metadata Service application, a Term Store is created that stores all the metadata associated with the service application. But back to basics: Your Managed Metadata Service can't provide business value until it actually contains metadata. To generate metadata, you need both Administrators and Contributors; more about those roles in a minute. For now, note that the Term Store Management Tool provides you with all the tools necessary to configure permissions and manage all the groups, term sets, and terms in the Term Store.

If you're a Term Store Administrator or a Term Store Contributor, you have a couple of ways to access the Term Store Management Tool.

Managing the service application in Central Administration

If you're a Term Store Administrator, you can access the Term Store Management Tool through the Managed Metadata Service application management pages. Follow these steps:

1. **Using your browser, navigate to the Central Administration home page.**

   The Service Applications management appears listing all the service applications available for managing.

2. **From the Application Management section, click Manage service applications.**

   The ribbon menu activates the commands that you can perform on the selected service. Instead of selecting the Managed Metadata service, you can simply click service which will open the Term Store Management Tool, effectively skipping Step 4.

3. **From the list of service applications, select the Managed Metadata Service.**

4. **On the Service Applications tab, in the Operations group, click Manage.**

   The Term Store Management Tool Web page appears.

Managing the service application at the SharePoint Site

If you're a Term Administrator, or have the Contributor role in a group and you have administrative rights to the site, you have a couple of ways to access the Term Store Management Tool:

✦ If you have access to the Site Settings page in your SharePoint site, you can use this process:

   1. *Using your browser, navigate to the home page of your site.*

   2. *From the Site Actions menu, click Site Settings.*

      The Site Settings page appears.

   3. *From the Site Administration section on the Site Settings page, click Term Store Management.*

      The Term Store Management Tool appears

✦ If you don't have access to the Site Settings page in your SharePoint site, you can access the Term Store Management Tool directly by navigating to the aspx page in the layouts directory of your site or site collection. The URL would look something like this:

   ```
   http://nut2craic.com/_layouts/termstoremanager.aspx
   ```

   Figure 5-5 shows an example of a user who has been assigned the Contributor role of the Musical Terms group in the Term Store. Here the user only has access to modify the Musical Terms group — and doesn't have access to modify any of the other groups (including the System group).

The Term Store Management Tool consists of a Taxonomy Term Store Navigation pane and a Details pane. The Taxonomy Term Store Navigation pane allows you to traverse the contents of your Term Store. When you move from one item to the next, the Details pane shows the currently selected item. For example, if you select the Managed Metadata Service item at the top of the Navigation pane, the Details pane displays the properties of the Managed Metadata Service (for example, Term Store Administrators).

If you click an item in the Navigation pane, a down arrow appears next to the item's name. If you click the down arrow, the menu commands associated with the item appear. For example, if you click the down arrow of a term in a term set, you're presented with options that include creating new terms and editing existing terms. Figure 5-6 shows the menu options that appear when you click the down arrow next to a term in the Term Store.

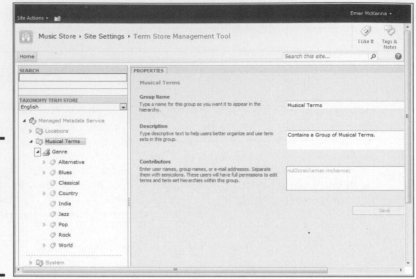

Figure 5-5:
You can access the Term Store Management Tool from your site.

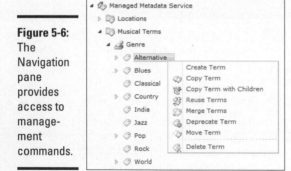

Figure 5-6:
The Navigation pane provides access to management commands.

Setting the Managed Metadata Service Properties

When you launch the Term Store Management Tool, you're presented with the properties associated with the Managed Metadata Service. Here's a quick list of the associated properties:

✦ **Available Service Applications:** A SharePoint site may use multiple metadata applications, each of which has a management page; you can use the Term Store Management Tool to navigate among those management pages. You use the Available Service Application property to select one of the metadata service applications to manage.

✦ **Term Store Administrators:** You use the Term Store Administrators setting to add users to (or remove them from) the list of Term Store Administrators. The users whose names you enter in this property become Administrators; not only can they create new term set groups, but they can also assign users to the Group Manager role for the currently selected metadata application.

✦ **Default Language:** You can use the Default Language property to select a default language for all metadata in the Term Store. You must define a label in the default language for all the terms in your Term Store.

✦ **Working Languages:** The Working Languages property section allows you to select translations to apply to terms in your Term Store — both language-specific labels and translations of your terms.

When you're satisfied with the settings of your Managed Metadata Service properties, you can click the Save button at the bottom of the Details pane to apply your changes.

Assigning Term Store Administrators

Controlling who has the access privileges necessary to add metadata is vital when you're trying to keep your taxonomy consistently effective in helping users find their information. That job falls to the Term Store Administrator, who can create and manage groups, term sets, and terms in the Term Store, as well as assign the Group Manager role to users.

Follow these steps to assign a Term Store Administrator:

1. **Using your browser, navigate to the Central Administration home page.**

2. **From the Application Management section, click Manage service applications.**

3. **From the list of service applications, select the Managed Metadata Service.**

4. **On the Service Applications tab, in the Operations group, click Manage.**

   The Term Store Management Tool appears.

5. **From the Taxonomy Term Store Navigation pane, select Managed Metadata Service.**

   The properties associated with the Managed Metadata Service appear.

6. **In the Term Store Administrators field, enter the user names, group names, or e-mail addresses of the users or groups you want to grant the Term Store Administrator role.**

Separate the entries with a semicolon at the end of each one.

7. **From the bottom of the Details pane, click Save.**

   The users or groups you entered can now manage groups and assign the Group Manager role to users.

Creating a group

If you're a Term Store Administrator, you can create groups in the Term Store. Follow these steps to create a new group:

1. **Using your browser, navigate to the Central Administration home page.**

2. **From the Application Management section, click Manage service applications.**

3. **From the list of service applications select the Managed Metadata Service.**

4. **On the Service Applications tab, in the Operations group, click Manage.**

   The Term Store Management Tool appears.

5. **From the Taxonomy Term Store Navigation pane, click Managed Metadata Service, and click the down arrow to display the menu.**

6. **From the menu, click New Group.**

7. **Enter the name of your group and press Enter.**

   The group properties appear in the Details pane.

8. **Enter a description for the group that will help users to organize their content and use the term sets in your group.**

9. **In the Group Managers field, enter the user names, group names, or e-mail addresses to be granted Group Manager permissions.**

   The users assigned Group Manager permissions have Contributor permissions; they can also add and remove users to and from the list of those who have the Contributor role.

10. **In the Contributors field, enter the user names, group names, or e-mail addresses to be granted Contributor permissions.**

    The users assigned Contributor permissions can now add, remove, and manage term sets and terms in the group.

11. **From the bottom of the Details pane, click Save.**

    Your group appears in the Taxonomy Term Store hierarchy.

Creating a term set

If you're a Term Store Administrator, a Group Manager, or a Contributor, you can create term sets in a group. Use the following steps to create a new term set:

1. **Using your browser, navigate to the Central Administration home page.**

2. **From the Application Management section, click Manage service applications.**

3. **From the list of service applications, select the Managed Metadata Service.**

4. **On the Service Applications tab, in the Operations group, click Manage.**

The Term Store Management Tool appears.

5. **From the Taxonomy Term Store Navigation pane, click the group in which you want to create the term set, and then click the down arrow to display the Group menu.**

6. **From the menu, click New Term Set.**

7. **Enter the name of your term set and press Enter.**

The term set's properties appear in the Details pane.

8. **Enter a description that will help users to understand your term set's intended use.**

9. **In the Owner field, enter the user name or group of your term set's primary owner.**

10. **In the Contact field, enter the e-mail address you want to use to receive term suggestions and feedback.**

If you leave this field blank, then the suggestion feature is disabled for this term set.

11. **In the Stakeholders field, enter the user names or groups to notify before anyone makes changes to the term set.**

Separate all the names you enter, both the user names and the group names, with semicolons.

12. **In the Submission Policy field, specify whether you want the term set to be Open or Closed.**

- A *closed term set* is structured metadata and falls into the taxonomy category (formal categorization). If the term set is closed, only metadata managers can add terms to the term set.

- An *open term set* is unstructured metadata and falls into the folksonomy category (informal, or user driven, categorization). If the term set is open, users can add terms to the term set.

13. **In the Available for Tagging field, select whether your term set is available for end users to use.**

    When this setting isn't selected, the term set isn't available to your users. If you unselect this setting after it has been in use for a while, you can still view any tags already applied to your items — but if you try to edit those items, the column associated with the term set is disabled.

14. **Click Save, to apply your changes and to save the term set.**

    You can now add terms to your term set. The following section shows you how.

Adding a term

If you're a Term Store Administrator, a Group Manager, or a Contributor, you can create new terms in a term set by following these steps:

1. **Using your browser, navigate to the Central Administration home page.**

2. **From the Application Management section, click Manage service applications.**

3. **From the list of service applications select the Managed Metadata Service.**

4. **On the Service Applications tab, in the Operations group, click Manage.**

    The Term Store Management Tool appears.

5. **From the Taxonomy Term Store Navigation pane, click the term set, or parent term in which you want to create the new term, and click the down arrow to display the term set menu.**

6. **From the menu, click Create Term.**

7. **Enter the name of your term, and press Enter.**

    After you press Enter the term is added to your term set and you can create another new term. You can repeat this process to create all your terms in your term set at once and then when you're finished you can go back over each term and update its properties.

    At this point in the process your term is available for use by your users — assuming the parent term set is available for tagging.

8. **Select the newly created term to display its properties.**

    The term set properties appear in the Details pane.

9. **In the Available for Tagging field, select whether your term is available to your users.**

   When this setting isn't selected, the term set is visible to your users, but cannot be used for tagging. If you unselect this setting after it has been in use for a while, you can still view any tags that have already been applied to your items. If you edit an item that uses a disabled tag, SharePoint highlights the field and informs you that the term isn't a valid term; if you want to save or update the item you must select a valid term.

   If you're creating a child term, selecting the Available for Tagging option will make the child term available for use by your users regardless of whether the parent term is available for tagging.

10. **In the Language field, select a language for your term.**

11. **Enter a description for your term that will help users to know when to use this term.**

    Providing your users with a good description of a term and its use will help them to differentiate between similar terms in your taxonomy.

12. **In the Default Label field, enter a label as the default for the selected language.**

13. **In the Other labels section, enter the synonyms or abbreviations for you term.**

    You can enter a word or phrase per line. Press Enter to move to a new line.

14. **Click Save, to apply your changes and to save the term.**

Sorting terms

By default, the terms you create in your term set are sorted alphabetically — in the default language (as you might expect). If you need to customize the sort order in which your terms appear, you can. Changing the sort order for the terms in your term set is easy: Just use the Custom Sort tab in the Details pane. The Custom Sort tab appears when you select a parent term — which only happens if the term or term set has child terms to sort. If those child terms exist, then the Custom Sort page allows you to sort them in a custom order. For example, Figure 5-7 shows Custom Sort details for the Genre term set.

Follow these steps to change the sort order of your child terms:

1. **Using your browser, navigate to the Central Administration home page.**

2. **From the Application Management section, click Manage service applications.**

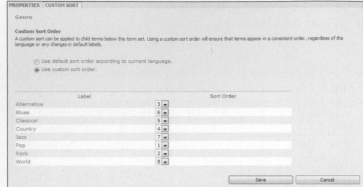

Figure 5-7:
You can
change the
sort order
of your child
terms.

3. **From the list of service applications select the Managed Metadata Service.**

4. **On the Service Applications tab, in the Operations group, click Manage.**

   The Term Store Management Tool appears.

5. **From the Taxonomy Term Store Navigation pane, click the term set or the parent term that you would like to sort.**

   The properties for the selected term or term set appear in the Details pane. If you've selected a parent term or term set, the Custom Sort tab appears next to the Properties tab.

   The custom sort order that you specify will apply to the child terms of the selected parent term or term set.

6. **Click the Custom Sort tab.**

7. **Click Use custom sort order.**

   The child terms appear in their current sort order. The sort-order number appears next to the label of each child term.

8. **Change the sort-order numbers to meet your needs.**

9. **Click Save to save the sort-order changes.**

   The sort order for the child terms is updated automatically in the taxonomy hierarchy to reflect your changes.

Moving terms

Sometimes you may want to move a term within a term set, or move it from one term set to another. For example, if you create a term and then realize that you created it at the wrong level in your hierarchy, you can use the Move Term command to move the term to its correct parent term. When you move a term, you also move all the child terms associated with that term.

Follow these steps to move a term:

1. **Using your browser, navigate to the Central Administration home page.**

2. **From the Application Management section, click Manage service applications.**

3. **From the list of service applications, select the Managed Metadata Service.**

4. **On the Service Applications tab, in the Operations group, click Manage.**

   The Term Store Management Tool appears.

5. **From the Taxonomy Term Store Navigation pane, click the term that you want to move, and then click the down arrow to display the Term menu.**

6. **From the Term menu, click Move Term.**

   The Term Move Web dialog box appears, displaying the Taxonomy Term Store's contents. The term you're moving doesn't appear in this display.

7. **Select the parent term or term set to which you want to move your term.**

   The OK button will be enabled when you select a valid destination for your term.

8. **Click OK.**

   The term moves to the new parent term and the taxonomy hierarchy reflects your changes.

Copying terms

You can copy a term within your term set, using either the Copy Term command or the Copy Term with Children command.

✦ The Copy Term command copies the selected term within the Term Store; the child terms aren't copied. SharePoint creates a copy of the term and prefaces the label with the words "Copy of". You can rename the term to suit your needs.

   The names of your terms must be unique at the same level in the hierarchy.

✦ The Copy Term with Children command behaves in the same way as the Copy Term command, except all the children of the term are also copied. The names of the child terms stay intact because they're still unique within their level of the taxonomy hierarchy.

Follow these steps to copy a term:

1. **Using your browser, navigate to the Central Administration home page.**

2. **From the Application Management section, click Manage service applications.**

3. **From the list of service applications, select the Managed Metadata Service.**

4. **On the Service Applications tab, in the Operations group, click Manage.**

   The Term Store Management Tool appears.

5. **From the Taxonomy Term Store Navigation pane, click the term you want to move, and then click the down arrow to display the Term menu.**

6. **From the Term menu, click either Copy Term or Copy Term with Children.**

   A copy of the term (and optionally its children) appears in the term set.

7. **Rename the copied term to suit your needs.**

   When you copy a term, its original name is prefaced with the words Copy of. Double-click the term to change its name.

Reusing terms

You can use the Reuse Term command to make use of a term from another term set. When you reuse a term, these conditions apply:

+ The original term becomes the owner (source term) term for the reused term.

+ If you disable (deprecate) the term you're reusing — whether the owner or the reused version — you disable it automatically in all the locations where it's reused.

+ If the reused term is deleted, the source term remains intact.

+ If the source term is deleted, the reused term becomes an orphaned term.

Follow these steps to reuse a term:

1. **Using your browser, navigate to the Central Administration home page.**

2. **From the Application Management section, click Manage service applications.**

3. **From the list of service applications select the Managed Metadata Service.**

4. **On the Service Applications tab, in the Operations group, click Manage.**

   The Term Store Management Tool appears.

5. **From the Taxonomy Term Store's Navigation pane, click the location in which you want to place the reused term, and then click the down arrow to display the Term menu.**

6. **From the Term menu, click Reuse Terms.**

   The Term Reuse Web dialog box appears, displaying the Taxonomy Term Store contents. The location in which you're reusing the term doesn't appear in the hierarchy.

7. **Select the term you want to reuse, and then click OK.**

   The term is reused in the chosen location; the term icon is updated in both term sets to indicate that the term is being used in multiple locations.

You can break the reuse link by deleting the term from the location(s) in which it is reused. Keep one more thing in mind, however . . .

Deleting the source term causes any reused terms to become orphaned terms.

Handing orphaned terms

If you delete the source term of a reused term, the reused terms are orphaned. They appear in the Orphaned Terms list in the System term set. To rectify this situation, you have to assign each orphaned term a new owner.

You can assign a new owner to an orphaned term by following these steps:

1. **Using your browser, navigate to the Central Administration home page.**

2. **From the Application Management section, click Manage service applications.**

3. **From the list of service applications select the Managed Metadata Service.**

4. **On the Service Applications tab, in the Operations group, click Manage.**

   The Term Store Management Tool appears.

5. **From the Taxonomy Term Store Navigation pane, expand the System group.**

6. **From the System group, expand the Orphaned Terms term set.**

   The terms that appear in this list are orphaned terms.

7. **Select the orphaned term that you want to correct.**

   The properties of the orphaned term appear in the Details pane.

8. **In the Member Of section of the properties page, select the term that you want to be the new source term for the orphaned item.**

9. **Click OK.**

   The term is no longer orphaned.

Surfacing Metadata in your Sites

When you have your Managed Metadata Service configured, the necessary permissions in place, and your taxonomy hierarchy created, you're ready to make use of your metadata in your SharePoint sites. That means *surfacing* the metadata — displaying it as needed, in a nice, neat, usable form.

Creating Managed Metadata Columns

You can create managed metadata columns in your SharePoint lists, libraries, and content types. When you create a column, you select Managed Metadata as the column type, and then select the term set or term hierarchy that you want the column to represent. When users enter data into the column, they are presented with a list of choices from the term hierarchy.

The following steps show you how to create a Managed Metadata site column:

1. **Using your browser, navigate to your SharePoint site.**

2. **From the Site Actions menu, click Site Settings.**

3. **From the Galleries section of the Site Settings page, click Site Columns.**

4. **From the Site Columns page, click Create.**

5. **Enter the name of your new column.**

6. **Select Managed Metadata as the data type for this column.**

7. **Select the site group in which you want to file the site column, or create a new site group.**

8. **From the Term Set Settings, select the term set or term hierarchy that you want the site column to represent.**

For example, an Instruments site column would represent the Instruments term set.

9. **Click OK.**

To start using the Managed Metadata column, you apply it to a content type, list, or library.

As soon as you add your Managed Metadata column to a list or library, your users can start putting the metadata in your Term Store to good use.

Keep in mind that the metadata won't show up in the Navigation pane until you've configured your site, along with its lists and libraries, for Metadata Navigation. The following section shows you how.

Configuring Metadata Navigation

When you add Managed Metadata to your list or library, you can navigate the content in the list or library by using Metadata Navigation — a feature enabled at the site level. This feature provides each list and library in your site with configuration pages where you choose settings for Metadata Navigation and Filtering. A metadata tree view of term hierarchies and filter controls helps you navigate and filter the content in your site so you can find your way to the content you want to see — fast. Figure 5-8 shows the Metadata Navigation control in action on a SharePoint list.

**Book III
Chapter 5**

Maneuvering the
Managed Metadata
Service

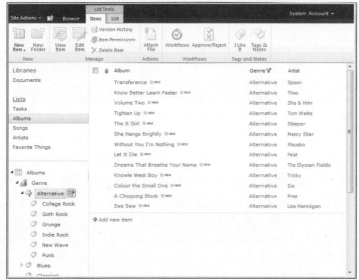

Figure 5-8:
Metadata Navigation helps you navigate and filter the content in your site.

The list in this example contains a Managed Metadata field that represents the Genre term set. The list has been configured to display the Genre column in the Metadata Navigation control, which appears directly under the Quick Launch bar (allowing easy and convenient interaction with your SharePoint lists and libraries). When you click a term in the Metadata Navigation control, the contents of your list or library are filtered accordingly.

Enabling Metadata Navigation for a site

Follow these steps to enable the Metadata Navigation feature on your SharePoint site:

1. **Using your browser, navigate to your SharePoint site.**

2. **From the Site Actions menu, click Site Settings.**

3. **From the Site Actions section of the Site Settings page, click Manage site features.**

    The Features page appears, listing all the available features of the site. If a feature is active in the site, you'll see a Deactivate button next to an Active status label. If the feature is inactive, you'll see an Activate button. (Always nice to have choices.)

4. **Locate the Metadata Navigation and Filtering feature, and then click Activate.**

    If the feature is already activated, the Deactivate Feature button is enabled (for later use), and your site now has Metadata Navigation and Filtering controls available for use.

To display these controls on your site, you must configure Metadata Navigation and Filtering on your lists and document libraries beforehand.

Configuring the Metadata Navigation settings

Follow these steps to configure the Metadata Navigation settings for a SharePoint list:

1. **Using your browser, navigate to your SharePoint list.**

2. **On the List tab, click Settings⇨List Settings.**

    The List Settings page appears.

    If you're configuring a SharePoint document library instead of a list, click Library Settings from the Library tab to display the Document Library Settings page.

3. **From the General Settings section, click Metadata navigation settings.**

    The Metadata Navigation Settings page appears.

TIP

If the settings option doesn't appear for Metadata Navigation, then the Metadata Navigation and Filtering feature isn't enabled on the site.

4. **In the Available Hierarchy Fields list, select the metadata that you want to appear in the Metadata Navigation control, and then click Add.**

5. **In the Available Key Filters list, select the fields that you want to appear in the Filtering control.**

    The fields you select in this setting appear underneath the Site hierarchy tree when a user views items in the list.

    Figure 5-9 shows an example of the Key Filter control configured for a SharePoint list. In this example, the control is configured to filter on the Created By and Created fields.

    If you don't have fields assigned to the Key Filter, the control doesn't appear.

Figure 5-9: Key filters appear underneath the site hierarchy in Metadata Navigation.

Enabling Enterprise Keywords

When you enable your list or document library to allow enterprise keywords, your users can add their own words or phrases (or select terms from the Term Store) to describe the content they add to your site. If some new words or phrases added by your users aren't in the Term Store, they're added automatically to the Keywords term set in the Term Store's System group.

Figure 5-10 shows an example of a picture library that has the Enterprise Keywords setting enabled. The user is tagging a picture uploaded with the keywords Easter and Children.

Figure 5-10:
Enterprise
Keywords
are
synchro-
nized with
the Term
Store.

Follow these steps to enable Enterprise Keywords in your SharePoint list or library:

1. **Using your browser, navigate to your SharePoint list.**

2. **On the List tab, click Settings ⇨ List Settings.**

   The List Settings page appears.

3. **From the Permissions and Management section, click Enterprise Metadata and Keywords settings.**

   The Enterprise Metadata and Keywords Settings page appears.

4. **Select the Enterprise Keywords setting to add an Enterprise Keywords column to your list and enable keyword synchronization.**

5. **Click OK.**

   Your users can now add keywords to items in the list, and those keywords will be synchronized with the Term Store.

Chapter 6: Submerging into Search

Searching online has become common enough that you'd have to call it, well, normal. Everyone frequently engages in it. But too much search activity inside a business is a sign that things aren't right — it may be an indication that the information you seek isn't easily findable. And that can mean you aren't exploiting your company's intellectual capital to its fullest. When that happens, the productivity of your information workers tends to dip — not only because of frustration but also because nobody is one-hundred-percent confident that the information they're working with is *really* the best and most relevant for the task at hand.

Successfully tackling such issues is vital to ensuring that your search capability aids information workers' productivity. Instead of a barrier, search becomes a valuable tool that you can rely on and use to achieve better business outcomes. In this chapter, we look at the search features in SharePoint — and explain how to build a search environment that helps users find the right information for whatever task they have in mind (sometimes literally!).

The Importance of Search

Of course you want to ensure that the information returned to a search query is the absolute best — but that's hard to do. Here's why:

✦ **Volume and scope of information sources:** Your organization's information assets tend to be massive and spread out through multiple repositories. Finding the best answer is usually akin to finding a needle in a haystack — with no metal detector.

✦ **Unevenly structured information sources:** Most businesses have a familiar dilemma: Some of their in-house information sources are highly structured — but others have no particular structure. This inconsistency affects how well information assets can be identified via *metadata* (data that describes the information — such as who its author is, what project it belongs to, and when was it created). Any given item can

- Strictly adhere to a known taxonomy (see Book III, Chapter 5)

- Have partial metadata that may not adhere to a taxonomy

- Have no metadata associated with it at all

✦ **Non-exhaustive listing of valuable content:** Your information assets aren't just documents. Search results should include the people who have the knowledge you seek. Also, information sources external to your organization may be able to assist users in achieving the goals that drive their queries.

✦ **Relevance requires a context:** If the person who executes a search query doesn't supply some *context* for the query — that is, the information sources that the query should execute against — then it's almost impossible to return the best information. Simply entering some keywords willy-nilly into a search box and expecting the best just won't do the job.

✦ **User context is generally unknown:** Users expect results relevant to their concerns, so different results must be returned for different people. For example if an engineer searches for `drawings`, then it's relevant to return engineering drawings; the same search by a painter should return works by artists.

✦ **Ambiguous and incomplete query terms:** Users expect the search engine to find the right thing as if by magic — so often they enter only minimal terms in the query request. They may also struggle to decide which terms are best to enter — and may not know how certain information assets are named in the system. For example users' first names and surnames can often be difficult to enter correctly if the spelling is uncommon or unfamiliar. All these factors make it even harder for the search engine to return the best information.

Given these difficulties, search shouldn't be viewed as something that always delivers the right results the first time. Instead, consider search as an interactive utility that guides the user through the information jungle to the appropriate destination in as few clicks as possible.

Search has been around in all the earlier versions of SharePoint — but the major focus of the 2010 release is on the issues just described. That's why the current version offers many improvements intended to bring better search results for the end user — especially in these areas:

✦ **Scale:** Support is provided for dramatically bigger scales of operation, which should handle the needs of most large enterprises.

✦ **User experience:** Many changes make it easier for the user to navigate search results and to be led to appropriate resources.

✦ **Social and People searches:** This feature taps into social networks and the expertise that exists inside your organization to take full advantage of the tacit knowledge and expertise your people possess.

✦ **Relevance:** Many improvements seek (a) to ensure that the returned items are relevant to the context of the query and (b) to promote what is considered the best information for particular queries.

✦ **Versatile and detailed content processing:** SharePoint 2010 can index many item types and apply some context to the contents found within those types.

Positioning search in SharePoint

Search is available in a range of Microsoft products — but they all have the same search architecture and the Service Application Framework in common. Although the search architecture is the same, the features available for building and managing the search environment differ among the offerings.

SharePoint Foundation 2010

Search in SharePoint Foundation is focused on the local content in a site collection. Although it does a good job of finding information within the current site collection, you don't have many ways to customize how it works. For example, you can't search external data sources, the search results page isn't customizable, and you can't control the frequency of the indexing process.

At least SharePoint Foundation lets you search on a grand scale: It adds multiple search-server roles, and each search server can index around 10 million items.

Search Server 2010 Express

Search Server 2010 Express is a free (and basic) product that's primarily focused on entry-level departmental needs. As such, it has only a limited scale of operation, mainly because it can't add multiple search servers. It can, however, index multiple data stores — including SharePoint sites, Web sites, file shares, Exchange Public Folders, and Lotus Notes databases.

You can not only customize the search results page, but also tweak the Federation feature (more about that later in the chapter) to return search results from other search engines that support the OpenSearch protocol. OpenSearch (also described later on) defines a way for Web sites and search engines to publish search results in a standard and accessible format, using aggregation and syndication.

Some organizations deploy Search Server 2010 Express in conjunction with SharePoint Foundation. They're looking to overcome the restriction in Foundation that limits search results to what's available in a site collection. By adding the SharePoint Foundation server farm as an external data source, to Express (neat trick, isn't it?), users can execute queries via Express against all content in the farm.

Book III Chapter 6

Submerging into Search

Express is designed to be easy to set up and manage — but it's limited in the number of items it can index. A version of SQL Server is required to configure Express; if you use the free SQL Server Express edition, you're limited to around 300,000 items. Using the industrial-strength version of SQL Server raises this limit to around 10 million items (but you have to pay a licensing fee).

Search Server 2010

Search Server 2010 provides much of the search functionality of SharePoint Server 2010 and is focused on the enterprise. You can scale it up to support as many as 100 million items — and provide redundancy of operations by deploying multiple index and query servers.

Consider using Search Server 2010 if you don't have much (or any) SharePoint content in your organization but want to provide a single, enterprise-wide search capability that can index multiple data stores.

You can customize and extend the search environment in Search Server 2010, and its administration and monitoring features are easy to use. (In fact, they're almost the same as those in SharePoint Server 2010.)

SharePoint Server 2010

Search in SharePoint Server 2010 is primarily focused on enterprise-wide hunts for content residing on your organization's intranet. The search capability is tightly integrated with other SharePoint Server 2010 features such as managed metadata and the use of social networking. SharePoint Server 2010 features are what set its search capability apart from that of Search Server 2010. For example, you can run People searches and guide your end users to results — just about painlessly — through what Microsoft calls a "conversational search experience". (Conversational, eh? What *do* you talk about with a corporation while you're ordering lunch?)

SharePoint Server 2010 has emerged as the product of choice for organizations that deploy SharePoint — for both its collaboration features and its enterprise-strength search capability. The search system is highly configurable and customizable; its scale can stretch to meet the needs of the largest of organizations. The product can handle up to around 100 million items and can support a multi-tenant deployment (where multiple companies can use the same SharePoint farm but have their searches restricted to returning results only from within their own internal sources).

FAST Search Server for SharePoint 2010

FAST offers, in effect, SharePoint Server 2010 search with superpowers (more about those later in this chapter). It's targeted at organizations that

✦ Demand a really grandiose scale

✦ Need specialized capabilities such as fine-tuning relevancy or sophisticated content processing (say, indexing Flash content).

FAST offers a highly flexible search platform; developers can use its features to build search-based applications for reputation analysis or full-featured research portals. It's also the vehicle that augments SharePoint Server 2010 with capabilities like these:

✦ **User context search:** Allows certain documents to be promoted/demoted to or from Best Bets for certain groups of employees.

✦ **Preview of returned content:** Allows users to look inside the search results to determine whether the returned content is what they seek.

✦ **Visual Best Bets:** Permits lighting up search results with visuals to call the user's attention to important content.

✦ **Deep refiners:** Allows precise counts of items to be displayed for each filter in a refinement panel.

Some basic FAST search technology is included in SharePoint Server 2010 to give you a taste of high-end features such as relevancy, refiners, and the use of filters to navigate through search results. But if you want to take full advantage of those higher-end search capabilities, then you essentially have to augment your SharePoint Server 2010 installation by installing FAST Search (and — yes — paying its license fee). Of course, that installation does provide a pretty luxurious search experience: FAST seamlessly takes over the processing of content and the serving of search queries after you've successfully configured your FAST server farm.

Oh, by the way: You can configure FAST to index more than 500 million items.

Major Search Concepts

The major job of the search engine is to create a full-text index of content and properties from a big tangle of structured and unstructured content — and to facilitate fast linguistic searches on that content. Many components are required to achieve this goal; they're shown in Figure 6-1.

The major concepts associated with search are as follows:

✦ **Content sources:** These host the actual content to which search results apply. You define the content sources you want indexed as part of your implementation.

✦ **Connectors:** These components know how to gather the content from content sources. They're used to present the content to the indexing engine for processing. You can extend the Connector framework by defining other content sources for indexing.

As a standard feature, SharePoint Server 2010 supports several connectors — such as file shares, Exchange Public Folders, and Business Connectivity Services — and FAST complements this with others such as Documentum and FileNet.

✦ **Crawling:** (Sounds like a "creature feature," doesn't it?) This is the process of traversing the URL namespace associated with content sources, looking for links to content that should be indexed.

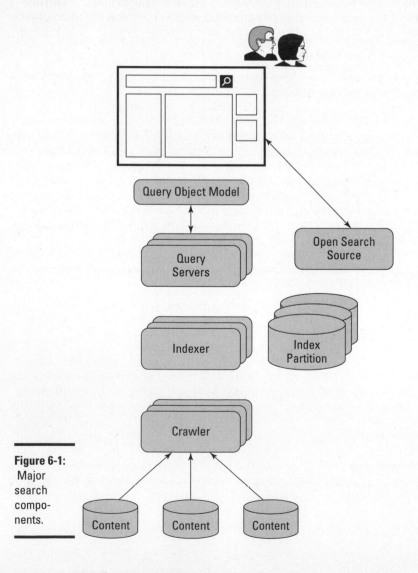

Figure 6-1:
Major search components.

✦ **Indexing:** This is what SharePoint does when it opens the items found by the crawler and stores the details in the index (also referred to as the *search catalog*). The index itself can also be partitioned if you want to scale it — or its partitions — up or down.

✦ **Querying:** Queries are handled by specialized servers (query servers) that process each query and return results to the requesting client.

✦ **Federation:** This feature supports the execution of the query on non-SharePoint search platforms.

Any search engine that supports the OpenSearch protocol can be configured to augment the results sent back to the requesting client application.

✦ **Search Center site:** Provides a user interface to allow users to formulate queries and to display the results. SharePoint also offers an object model (essentially an application programming interface) and Web services that can be used by developers for integrating search queries into applications.

Creating The End-User Experience

SharePoint brings a whole mob of features into play to create its characteristic end-user experience. This chapter highlights the major features available with a SharePoint Server 2010 installation.

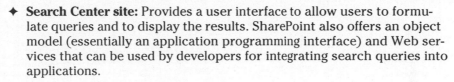

In Book IV, Chapter 8, we use an example to explore how you can configure most of these features to suit your own needs. We detail some of the additional features of FAST Search Server for SharePoint 2010 later in this chapter.

Building and executing queries

Figure 6-2 shows a typical search results page from SharePoint Server 2010. The following components control how the search is formed and executed.

Search Box

Users typically enter their search queries into a Search Box that's present on most SharePoint pages. The configuration of the Search Box ultimately controls the query that's executed — and the page on which the results are displayed. For example, the search box may offer the user custom capabilities such as

✦ Limiting the scope of a query to a subset of the overall index.

✦ Calling a custom search results page.

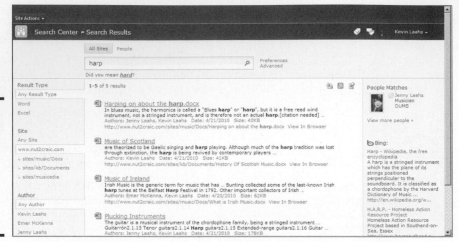

Figure 6-2:
SharePoint Server 2010 Enterprise Search Center results page.

Search scopes

Search scopes are filters on search results that you set by specifying extra criteria to use when SharePoint executes the search query. They are used to target the search query to specific content. Search scopes are applied either implicitly or explicitly, depending on (a) how the Search Box is configured and (b) the context in which the search is being performed.

Three types of search scopes might come into play:

✦ Standard scopes such as All Sites or People.

✦ Custom scopes that administrators can define.

✦ Contextual scopes derived from the situation at hand.

    For example, if you're searching from a view of a list or library, SharePoint knows it — and assumes a contextual scope limited to just that list or library.

Keyword query syntax

SharePoint supports a versatile query language that can use keyword-based queries to do various types of searches — full text, Boolean, and wildcard (which uses prefix matching), as well as operator- and property-based. Developers can tap into the full power of the language in their search applications; the search pages, both standard and advanced, give the user the advantage of the constructs most commonly required by search engines.

When SharePoint processes user input, it passes suitable query terms to the search results page. For example, Figure 6-3 shows the details entered by a user into an advanced search page — and Figure 6-4 shows the resulting query that was executed.

Figure 6-3:
Advanced
search
page.

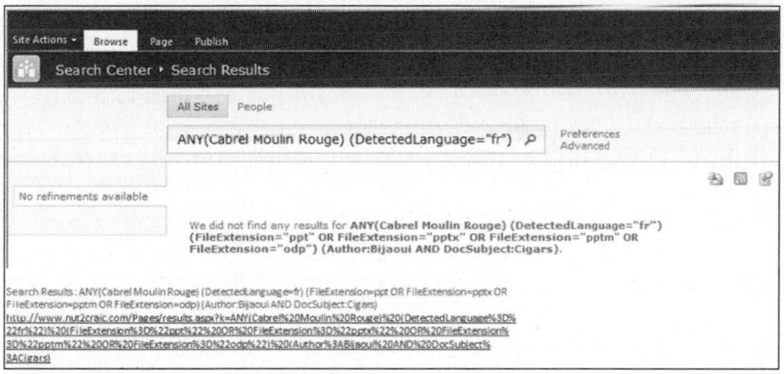

Figure 6-4:
Query from
advanced
search.

Typically, the default processing on the standard search page treats the entered keywords as a Boolean AND — meaning that all the entered search terms have to match before an item is considered a hit. As users become familiar with the search language, however, they can use the Search Box to specify different kinds of searches — property, Boolean, and wildcard. For example, entering Author:Laa* (using the asterisk wildcard) returns all items whose Author property begins with Laa.

Operator-based queries allow you to search for items using a property-based comparison. For example, if you have a Managed Property (see the next section) called Value, you could return all items whose Value property was greater than a certain value — say, 100 (Value>100).

**Book III
Chapter 6**

**Submerging
into Search**

Managed Properties

Here's a potentially intimidating thought: A typical SharePoint environment has literally millions of possible items that could be indexed — each containing structured *and* unstructured data, as well as its own properties (metadata). (Yikes.) Although the normal approach is to use keyword-based queries against the body of the indexed items, metadata is also a very important handle you can grab to find specific information. SharePoint uses crawled properties (discussed earlier in this chapter) to give you that grip.

With a large number of items comes many crawled properties — discovered in the course of indexing your content — and not all of these would be worth indexing. Two or more properties could be the same semantically but different in syntax — for example, Movies and Films.

As an administrator, you can control which crawled properties are stored in the index. These are known as *Managed Properties*, and they're the only properties that SharePoint lets you use (a) in search queries or (b) to define search scopes. When you define a Managed Property, you can map as many crawled properties to it as you like. For example, you could map a standard Managed Property called `Status` to two crawled properties: one from the Status column in an Issues list, and one from the Status column in a Task list.

Query Suggestions

The goal of Query Suggestions is to offer suggestions for query terms that have previously been known to return results.

Query Suggestions (as well as Did You Mean and Related Searches, which are covered later in the "Did You Mean & Related Searches" section) are available because SharePoint logs a couple of useful indicators:

✦ All user queries that generated results.

✦ All click-throughs done from the search results page.

Such indications that the search results did indeed return something are especially useful because they show that the users acted on the results. Two timer jobs — Query Logging and Prepare Query Suggestions — work together to give you this handy information.

Prepare Query Suggestions only runs once a day; you may have to run this job manually (through Central Administration) if you're testing this feature in a lab environment.

Query Suggestions comes into play before the query is executed — while the users are entering their search terms. It lists matching keywords from any previously entered queries that returned results — a nice feature when users want to see right away which query terms are likely to return the results they're looking for.

Phonetic and nickname matching

Microsoft Speech Server can augment your search results with phonetic matches to the entered query terms — or matches to a commonly used nickname. For example entering `Mike Smith` in the search box would return items related to `Michael Smith`. Similarly, entering `Kev Laz` would return items related to `Kevin Laahs`.

That kind of power can cut down your search hassles when you're trying to locate people. If (for example) you know how to pronounce someone's surname but not how to spell it, now you have discreet help from SharePoint. (Note, however, that you have to have installed Microsoft Speech Server Runtime — and the appropriate speech language packs — before you can use this feature.)

Understanding and Working with Search Results

After a query is entered, you have more options than a mosquito at the beach. SharePoint provides many features that can influence the display of the matching results — and options that give the end user just as many ways to interact with the result set.

Federating searches and using search locations

In SharePoint 2010, *federation* has nothing to do with government or *Star Trek*. It's a technique that saves you a lot of search time: You define locations, such as Internet search engines (or other repositories such as those defined via Business Connectivity Services — see Book II, Chapter 2), and then have SharePoint search them simultaneously for content. You can also apply federation when you search your local SharePoint content index — and use it to target your searches to specific scopes within the index.

SharePoint uses the concept of a *search location* to describe how to perform a search on a particular resource. Search locations have some really convenient attributes:

**Book III
Chapter 6**

✦ You can define locations as internal (the local SharePoint index) and external. External locations must conform to the OpenSearch protocol 1.0 or 1.1.

✦ What you get from using such federated locations is that you don't have to index the same content as all the other search engines. Those other search engines have already done that chore to a fare-thee-well.

✦ You can search the Internet for details of other search engines that support OpenSearch (such as YouTube) — and use those as federated search locations to direct searches against the desired content.

Submerging into Search

✦ Many Search Web Parts are configured to use particular search locations for a specific task — for example, the Core Results Web Part is configured to search against the Local Search Results location and you can set the Federated Web Part to search the Internet Search Results location.

A search location also defines what properties to return in the search results when different Web Parts use the location in various ways (say, as core search results, federated search results, or top federated results). The location also specifies how to use an XSL template to display the results. You can modify these definitions — and override configurations — on a per-Web-Part basis to suit your needs.

SharePoint gives you five standard defined search locations — but you can augment these with your own custom locations, or import definitions from other OpenSearch-compliant engines. Microsoft has an online gallery from which you can import sample location definitions such as YouTube. You can see the standard locations listed in Figure 6-5, alongside a custom search location called `Images`. Each location also displays data points (such as number of queries and click-through rates) that you can use to adjust your locations as needed.

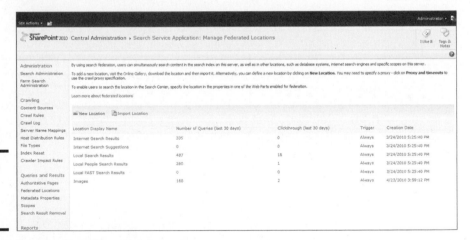

Figure 6-5:
Federated
search
locations.

The five standard locations are as follows:

✦ **Internet Search Results:** This OpenSearch location utilizes `search. live.com` to return search results. (This is the location used for the Federated Web Part shown at the right in Figure 6-2.)

✦ **Internet Search Suggestions:** This OpenSearch location utilizes `search.live.com` to offer related Internet-search suggestions.

✦ **Local Search Results:** This SharePoint location returns results from the entire index (that is, it's an *unscoped* search).

✦ **Local People Search Results:** This SharePoint location has a scope that's limited to show only People results.

✦ **Local FAST Search Results:** This location searches the local FAST index.

Before you can use this location, you have to have FAST Search Server for SharePoint 2010 installed, up, and running.)

You define search locations via the Search Service Application administrative options available in Central Administration. The following subsections describe the terms you use to define those locations.

Triggers

If you want to know when to execute a search against a location, first you have to define what will trigger the search. You can trigger a search for all search queries — or for only those queries that match a particular pattern, or only those that begin with a particular string. The Trigger option gives you the flexibility to target specific searches to equally specific locations.

If (for example) you wanted to call on a federated search engine to look up something to do with phone numbers, then you could define a pattern that matches only digits. Similarly, you may want to check for prefixes in searches related to a particular topic so you can target them to a federated location. For example, a user might enter `discography sinatra` — in which case, the word `sinatra` could be searched against a federated location that housed discography information.

Query templates

You use a *query template* to describe the actual search engine to which you want the entered search terms sent. What you enter is a URL that supports the entered search terms as query strings.

If you're using an external search engine, its federated location must support the OpenSearch protocol (1.0 or 1.1). That's because OpenSearch is designed to support syndication and aggregation — so generally you can use it to consume data from Web sites that support RSS or Atom. When defining your federated location, you indicate

✦ The URL you want used for executing the search.

✦ A More Actions link should the search return too many results.

Tokens within this URL are substituted before the search is executed. For example, here's the query template defined for the Internet Search Results:

```
http://search.live.com/results.aspx?q={searchTerms}&count={itemsPerPage}&first={s
    tartItem}&mkt={language}&format=rss&FORM=SHAREF
```

**Book III
Chapter 6**

**Submerging
into Search**

Display Information

For each search location, you define the properties that you want returned about the items that match the search query and some XSL to transform the returned XML into the HTML that will be displayed in the Web Parts that utilize search locations. Default XSL and property definitions (in XML) are provided for you but you can override these with your own definitions should you wish to. You can also specify different display information on a Web Part by Web Part basis.

Restrictions and Credentials

You can control whether a federated location is available to all sites in your farm or only to sites whose URL matches a particular namespace. If you're careful about how you name your sites, you can have particular types of federated searches target specific site types. For example, you may support sites that have something to do with medicine under a /medicine/ root. In this case you can allow all these sites to federate searches against an external medical search engine.

If the federated search engine requires authentication, then you have the option of using multiple authentication techniques and also using a single set of credentials (which you define) or to pass the current user's credentials.

Search Results Page

As previously mentioned, queries are formed via the Search Box — which subsequently passes the formed query to a search results page. The search results page is what executes the query and processes the results. Most search result pages are Web Part Pages that contain a subset of the available standard Search Web Parts.

SharePoint offers you the standard primary search pages shown in the following list — but you can also create your own and associate them via search scopes or by configuring a search box to use a named results page.

✦ SearchResults.aspx: This is the results page that you get in SharePoint Foundation. It's a non-customizable page that implicitly sets the search scope to be that of the site collection you are searching from or sets a contextual scope to the list/library you may be viewing. It's a non-customizable page so doesn't offer any of the advanced techniques for interacting with search results (such as Refiners).

✦ OSSSearchResults.aspx: This is the basic results page (the default, in fact) for a SharePoint Server 2010 team site. It's called when you execute a search across the site collection or search within a list or library. This Web Part page is locked down so you can't modify it by using traditional techniques such as the browser or SharePoint Designer. By default, its scope is the site collection; therefore its navigational aids (such as refiners) have the same scope.

You can configure a search within a site collection to use an alternate search results page under circumstances you specify. For example, you can choose to modify the search box so it displays a drop-down list of search scopes, and then expand the scope of your search beyond the local site collection.

✦ `Results.aspx`: This is the standard results page associated with a Search Center site. It's a customizable Web Part Page that provides the end user with the most functionality for dealing with search results and is typically associated with site collections to host the displaying of results sets that are scoped to wider than the site collection's content (see later for how to configure this).

   Three `results.aspx` pages are associated with Search Center sites, as follows:

   • Basic Search Center: A nontabbed page for a simple results display.

   • Enterprise Search Center: The most commonly used results page containing multiple tabs for targeting search results to more specific entities such as a People search and the capability to augment search results with Federated results. You can add extra tabs to this page to suit your needs.

   • FAST Search Center: This page contains FAST-specific features such as deep refiners and visual Best Bets.

✦ `Advanced.aspx`: This search results page is used for advanced searches.

✦ `PeopleResults.aspx`: Tailored to show details about people and to take advantage of social networking features.

   This page is covered in more detail in Book IV, Chapter 9.

The `results.aspx` page on an Enterprise Search Center site contains the following Web Parts, all of which you can customize to suit your needs:

✦ **Search Box:** This is where the user enters their basic search queries. By default, it's configured to not show any search scopes, to not augment the search with any pre-defined terms, and to show the Advanced search link. The search results page to use for the Advanced link is also set to advanced.aspx.

✦ **Search Summary:** This is where "Did You Mean" suggestions are displayed (see the "Did You Mean & Related Searches" section for more information).

✦ **Refinement Panel:** Positioned in the left navigation pane, this Web Part displays dynamic refiners for the search results (see the "Refiners" section of this chapter for details).

✦ **Search Statistics:** Displays the number of hits found and the range currently being displayed. You can also customize this Web Part to show search response times.

**Book III
Chapter 6**

**Submerging
into Search**

✦ **Search Action Links:** Displays actions that can be performed on the search results such as setting up an alert (see the "Search Actions" section for more details).

✦ **Search Best Bets:** Items marked as Best Bets for the keywords used in the search query are displayed here (see the "Keyword, Definitions, and Best Bets" section for more details on Best Bets). You can customize the display by modifying the XSL that is associated with this Web Part.

✦ **Top Federated Results:** Use this option to combine the top results from multiple federated searches in this Web Part. You can customize the display by modifying the XSL that is associated with this Web Part.

✦ **Search Core Results:** This option controls which search location is used to execute the search — and how the results are displayed. The default search location is the Local Search Results, which means all content in the index. You can customize the display by modifying (a) the properties that are returned and (b) the XSL associated with this Web Part.

✦ **Search Paging:** Use this option to page through the search results.

✦ **Related Queries:** This is where one click access is given to similar queries that have previously returned some results.

✦ **Federated Web Part:** Use this Web Part to show People Results — it uses search locations to execute a search whose scope is limited to People — and this is where the results of that search appear onscreen.

Did You Mean & Related Searches

Did You Mean suggestions are presented at the top of search results page after the query has been executed. These help the user re-execute with other query terms that are similar to the ones they entered — typically used to cover spelling mistakes or typographical errors. For example, executing a query for the word "Gitars" will result in a Did You Mean for the word "Guitars" if the word "Guitars" has previously been entered in a query that returned some results.

Related Searches are another post-query feature that lists other searches with similar query terms that at one time had returned results. These are listed on the search results page giving the user one click access to related searches.

Refiners

Refiners (also known in some circles as faceted search) are a key feature that allows users to further navigate the result set using what are essentially smart filters/groupings. Refiners are typically presented in the left navigation area of the search results page using the Refinements Web Part and facilitate the idea of a conversational user experience.

Refiners are dynamically determined according to the result set that the query returns, who the calling user is, and the search results page being used. In Figure 6-2 you can see three Refiners displayed — Result Type, Site, and Author — but there are more refiners presented such as Modified Date and Wiki Categories.

The dynamic nature of refiners can be understood best by looking at the By Result Type refiner in Figure 6-2. Here you see the capability to further filter the result set by either Word or Excel. This tells you that only Word and Excel items were returned in the search results but if, for example, a PowerPoint document was returned you would also see an option to filter by PowerPoint.

You can also navigate farther into some refiners — for example, the `Site` refiner (refer to Figure 6-2), where we've navigated into the `www.nut 2craic.com` namespace and found three site collections within. This discovery tells you a couple of handy things:

✦ The result set came from only these three site collections.

✦ You can therefore home in on the content you seek with a few clicks.

Tags that users have specified to mark content can also serve as refiners. (See Book I, Chapter 4 for details on tags.) In fact, you can navigate the result set to find pages that are being tagged by the whole community.

Pages that nearly everybody tags are usually very good candidates for relevant content; the community itself is highlighting their importance by looking for them in the search results.

Clicking a refiner value calls the search results page, using suitable query terms to ensure that only the refined content is returned. The `"r"` query string passes the desired refiner to the query. For example, the URL associated with the Excel refiner (as shown in Figure 6-2) is as follows:

```
http://www.nut2craic.com/Pages/results.aspx?k=harp&r=fileextension="o
    dc" fileextension="ods" fileextension="xls" fileextension="xlsb"
    fileextension="xlsm" fileextension="xlsx"
```

The Refinements Web Part displays the refiners; configuring this Web Part determines which refiners are listed for the current result set. XML associated with the Web Part is used to define *filter categories* — specific refiners mapped either to Managed Properties in the index or to managed metadata (defined in the Managed Metadata service application).

Book III
Chapter 6

Submerging into Search

Through this XML, you can control the functioning of the Web Part such as how to determine which refiners appear onscreen and how many refiners each category can contain. You can also define how to associate those items that match the search query with a particular filter category. For example the filter category for Result Type indicates that the `File Extension` Managed Property should be used and that extensions similar to `.xlsx` and `.xlsm` should be included in the `Excel` category.

The XML can also perform relative calculations on the value of a managed property to determine its filter category. For example, the `Modified Date` category compares the number of days that have passed since the value of the `Write` Managed Property to determine whether the item should be in the `Last Week`, `Last Month`, or `Last Year` category. Here's some sample XML for the `Modifed Date` category:

```
<Category Title="Modified Date" Description="When the item was
  last updated" Type="Microsoft.Office.Server.Search.WebControls.
  ManagedPropertyFilterGenerator"    MetadataThreshold="5"
  NumberOfFiltersToDisplay="6"    MaxNumberOfFilters="0"    SortBy="Custom"
  ShowMoreLink="True"    MappedProperty="Write"    MoreLinkText="show more"
  LessLinkText="show fewer" >
  <CustomFilters MappingType="RangeMapping" DataType="Date"
  ValueReference="Relative" ShowAllInMore="False">
    <CustomFilter CustomValue="Past 24 Hours">
        <OriginalValue>-1..</OriginalValue>
    </CustomFilter>
    <CustomFilter CustomValue="Past Week">
        <OriginalValue>-7..</OriginalValue>
    </CustomFilter>
    <CustomFilter CustomValue="Past Month">
        <OriginalValue>-30..</OriginalValue>
    </CustomFilter>
    <CustomFilter CustomValue="Past Six Months">
        <OriginalValue>-183..</OriginalValue>
    </CustomFilter>
    <CustomFilter CustomValue="Past Year">
        <OriginalValue>-365..</OriginalValue>
    </CustomFilter>
    <CustomFilter CustomValue="Earlier">
        <OriginalValue>..-365</OriginalValue>
    </CustomFilter>
  </CustomFilters>
</Category>
```

Keywords, Definitions, and Best Bets

Administrators can define keyword terms and synonyms to enhance search results by (a) associating a definition with the keyword and (b) assigning locations — such as links to Web sites and documents — that are deemed Best Bets (the best possible matches for that keyword). These definitions and Best Bets can be displayed prominently in the search results page if the query terms match any of the defined keywords.

Best Bets are typically used to promote a particular piece of content during the lifetime of a project such as a sales campaign. For example, if you a have a special offer on tickets for a show, you may want to promote the Web page that designates the show as a Best Bet if the search query contains any keywords that might relate to the show or its presenters.

Site administrators define not only the keywords for their site collections (Site Actions⇨Site Settings⇨Site Collection Administration⇨Search Keywords), but also the resources that are Best Bets for that keyword — and any definition for that keyword. Administrators also define a date range during which each Best Bet is active. (You can see a keyword definition in Figure 6-6.)

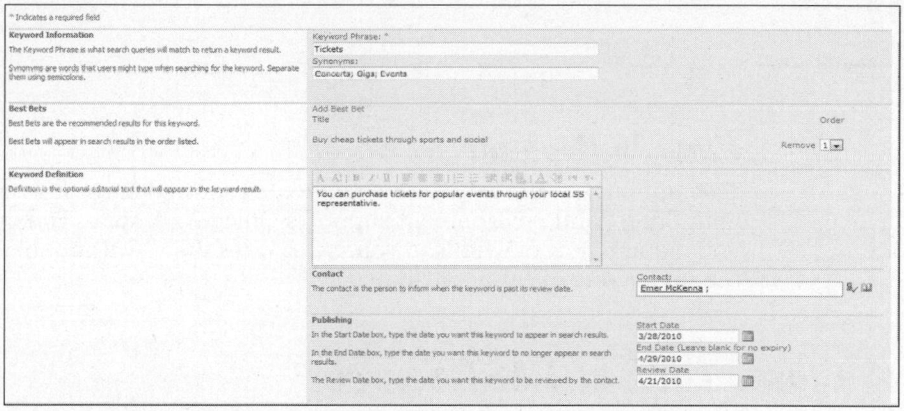

Figure 6-6:
Defining a
keyword
with its
definition
and
associated
Best Bets.

Search Actions

The Search Actions Web Part displays the icons you see in Figure 6-2 at the right side (in line with the search statistics). You can use these icons to perform the following actions related to the current search:

✦ **Alert:** This option notifies you when future content that matches the current search query is indexed. In effect, you can search the future!

✦ **RSS:** Use this option to set up an RSS feed to the search results so you can view future results in your favorite RSS reader.

✦ **Search via Windows Explorer:** Use this option to add the current search location to the Windows 7 Search Center so you can perform searches — and process their results — directly from Windows Explorer. Clicking this icon generates an OSDX file that's imported into the Windows 7 Search Center as a search connector. (You can see an example of the result in Figure 6-7.) The magic works because Windows 7 Search Center supports OpenSearch federation — and the OSDX file contains the federated definition for SharePoint.

Figure 6-7:
Searching
SharePoint
from
Windows
Explorer.

View In Browser

This option appears for Office documents returned in the search results if your SharePoint environment supports Office Web Apps. The option offers you a quick view of what's in your search results — without having to fire up the underlying client application.

A Closer Look at FAST Search Server for SharePoint 2010

FAST Search Server for SharePoint 2010 is an add-on product from Microsoft that brings with it a whole load of new search capabilities — and requires a separate server license and a separate installation. It also requires that users have an Enterprise Client Access License to access the FAST features.

Building on the overview of FAST offered earlier in this chapter, here's a quick look at its major new features that shape the end user's overall search experience. In a nutshell, FAST makes much greater use of concepts and contexts in its searches than does the search capability in SharePoint Server 2010.

✦ **Content Processing Pipeline:** This allows custom processing of content during the indexing process. You can use it to create a variety of search applications such as a reputation portal. As content is processed, you can analyze it to find patterns and references — and use these to create linkages between items of content.

This is the same functionality that was in the product called FAST Enterprise Search Platform (ESP).

✦ **Metadata Extraction:** You can use FAST to extract metadata from unstructured content and to use that metadata for features such as relevancy tuning, ranking, and refinements. If (for example) you have product names scattered through documents and presentations, you can use this feature to tag that content with a piece of metadata that defines the product it relates to.

✦ **Richer query language:** FAST provides more sophisticated searching on structured data (such as dates and numbers). One benefit is that developers can harness the full FAST Query Language (FQL) for their applications.

✦ **Deep refiners:** Run-of-the-mill refiners (as described in the "Refiners" section earlier in this chapter) are also known as *shallow refiners* because their scope is relatively limited. FAST adds the option of *deep refiners* that can work against search results of any size while retaining a precise count of the items associated with each refiner. Thus the user can see exactly how many items match a particular refiner — which can be an important decision-making criterion.

✦ **Document Thumbnails and Previews:** The idea of visual search is available by the capability to provide thumbnails for Word documents and graphical previewers for PowerPoint presentations directly from the search results. This significantly helps the end user judge what's relevant in the search results. You can also add Visual Best Bets to make the images most relevant to the content appear at the top of a search results page.

✦ **Custom search experiences (per user/profile):** This capability creates custom relevancy models tuned to differences in content sources, application needs, and user contexts. Different users can have different contexts — which you can use to optimize the search experience for their specific business needs. You can set the search sources, relevance rank profile, and other search features by user or by user group. That means a sales director (for example) can see different search results from those shown to a technical consultant — even when executing the same query that seeks information from the same content sources.

Chapter 7: User Profiles, Organization Profiles, and Audiences

In This Chapter

✔ Stocking up the User Profile Store

✔ Configuring User Profiles, organization profiles, and audiences

✔ Synchronizing profiles

There are many features in SharePoint that facilitate the ability for people to work together to create, and ultimately consume, information assets. A common challenge is in identifying the best people and the best information sources to use for a collaboration to produce a specific business outcome. This challenge arises due to multiple factors; and in large organizations a primary one isn't having knowledge of the skills that exist across the entire breadth of the company nor the linkages between people (that is the social networks) that might help you find the right skill.

SharePoint Server 2010 has a distinct focus on the social side of information sharing; it treats people as a major component of an organization's intellectual wealth — and provides many features to help you find the right people to do the right job. These features can help turn *tacit social networks* (those known only inside people's heads) into persistent information networks that the organization can use as a valuable business tool.

SharePoint social features rely on being able to find out information about the organization's people — and this is where the Profile Store comes into play. In this chapter, we look at how you can maintain a well-stocked Profile Store that can feed your organization's social networks.

In Book IV, Chapter 9, we take a closer look at the features of such a social network.

Understanding the User Profile Service Application

The User Profile Service Application is at the heart of SharePoint Server 2010's social networking features. It controls many people features and you manage these by choosing Central Administration⇨Manage service applications⇨User Profile Service Application. The page shown in Figure 7-1 appears, offering you some configuration options:

✦ **People:** Manage User Profiles and audiences.

✦ **Synchronization:** Control synchronization between your Profile Store and other directory services.

✦ **Organizations:** Manage organization profiles.

✦ **My Site Settings:** Control personal homepages and their contents.

✦ **Monitor status:** Keep track of the number of profiles, as well as audiences and synchronization status.

Provisioning a User Profile Service Application creates three databases in your SQL server to support its features:

✦ **ProfileDB:** Used to store user and organization profile information.

✦ **SocialDB:** Used to store social tags and notes that are created by users. Each social tag and note is associated with an entry in the User Profile.

✦ **SyncDB:** Used to store configuration and staging information for synchronizing profile data from external sources.

An often-used external source is the *Active Directory Directory Service* (AD DS). This redundant-sounding service typically holds information about people, which is vital to SharePoint social networking.

You can see these databases listed via SQL Server Management Studio in Figure 7-2 alongside the many other databases required to support all of the features of SharePoint Server 2010.

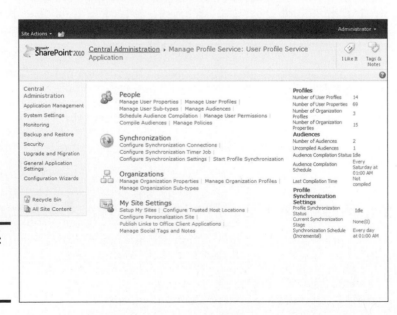

Figure 7-1:
The User
Profile
Service.

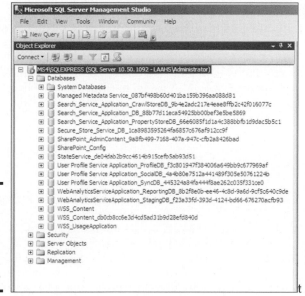

Figure 7-2:
SQL
databases
for
SharePoint
Server 2010.

Working with User Profiles

The User Profile is, in effect, the hub of all SharePoint social networking capabilities.

Think of the User Profile as a special-purpose SharePoint list that acts like a directory for people (this explains why the User Profile options in Figure 7-1 are grouped under People).

You can fuel this profile with content from multiple sources — for example, data can be imported from other directory sources that you might have in your organization, such as the Active Directory or other LDAP (Lightweight Directory Access Protocol — an industry standard protocol for accessing directory services) -compliant source. In addition, end users can update their own directory entries from their personal workspaces (each user has one, called a My Site).

Make sure that the data in each User Profile is as detailed, relevant, and up to date as needed. SharePoint provides plenty of tools and features to help you (and your organization) achieve this state of business bliss.

A common misconception is that User Profiles are required for authorizing access to a SharePoint site. Relax — it's not. The User Profile isn't even involved in authorization, and doesn't have to be implemented to authorize access to SharePoint content.

User Profile Properties and Profile Types

The User Profile is defined in terms of user properties. You can modify those properties to add or remove other pertinent properties.

Don't add properties to the User Profile unless you have a solid belief that they'll be usable, maintainable, and useful in a businesslike way. For example it is unlikely that someone's shoe size would add to the greater good of an organization. The idea is to add value. Typically, you'd add properties to hold data that can be

✦ Populated and maintained automatically

or

✦ Managed by the end users

Consider that end users must know the intended purpose of an added property or they can't provide pertinent data.

Previous versions of SharePoint had no way to offer different types of profiles for users — properties defined in the User Profile were applied to all users. In essence, you only had one type of user. In SharePoint Server 2010, you can assign properties to any number of User Sub-Types — so you can hold different data for different specified types of people.

All standard *and* custom properties are initially assigned to all User Sub-Types. SharePoint 2010 still defines just one standard User Sub-Type — called (logically enough) Default User Profile Subtype. When you create a new User Sub-Type, all existing properties are automatically assigned to that default subtype. Then you have to remove any existing properties that you don't want assigned.

Although the Default User Profile Subtype is selected automatically by default, you can choose which existing User Sub-Types to apply as you create new properties. For example, suppose you add a new sub-type for Contractors — and add a new property to hold the contract end date. Then you'd only apply the new property to the Contractors sub-type. (Logic can be beautiful.)

Technically, all User Profile properties are actually associated with every entry in the User Profile — and the User Sub-Type serves (in effect) as a filter to determine which properties to display. So if you change the User Sub-Type to which a User Profile entry is linked, and then change it back again, the properties retain their original values. This makes perfect sense (honest!) because user properties can be associated with more than one User Sub-Type.

A user property has many attributes that control where and how it's used. Here's a list of the most important attributes and considerations:

✦ **Type:** Defines the type of data that the property will hold. For example this can be set to Person to indicate that the property must contain a link to another User Profile.

✦ **Term Set:** String property types can be set to only allow values from a Term Set that has been defined for use in the Managed Metadata service.

This SharePoint feature helps ensure that the data in the property is used consistently which subsequently aids findability and usability.

✦ **Sub-type of Profile:** This is where you define the sub-types of User Profiles that the property is assigned to.

✦ **Policy Settings:** Defines whether the property requires a value, or whether the user can override the value and its privacy setting.

Privacy settings control who can see the property. You can specify one of the following values:

- Only Me
- My Manager
- My Team
- My Colleagues
- Everyone

For more about how SharePoint determines which of these groups a viewer belongs in, see Book IV, Chapter 9.

You can also set whether a property is replicable — whether its value shows up all over the place, replicated to user details held in site collections (such as team sites and blogs) that are defined in the SharePoint Farm. You can set a property to replicate only if

- The user isn't allowed to override its value (the idea here is to avoid inconsistencies).
- Its privacy policy is set to Everyone (necessary because there's no way to limit who can see user details in a site collection).

✦ **Display settings:** These control where the property is displayed.

One interesting setting here (refer to Book IV, Chapter 9) is whether to display updates to the property value in a user's *newsfeed* (which is like an RSS subscription to user activities so you can follow what other people are up to).

✦ **Search settings:** This where you can indicate if the property should be indexed for searching purposes. You can also set the property to be used as an alias which means it's treated as being equivalent to a user-name for operations that involve finding items by a particular user.

✦ **Synchronization settings:** These control whether the property is mapped to an external data source for import and/or export purposes.

✦ **Language considerations:** You can add native-language descriptions and display names for properties to support multilingual scenarios.

Creating a User Profile Sub-Type and User Properties

Here's an example of a practical business tweak to a user property: Suppose you have to identify a group of students in your User Profile Store and mandate that they indicate their primary preference from a predefined list of musical genres. The business objective is to be able to advertise each student's musical preference to any interested parties. The following steps show how to do that tweak. They assume that you've previously created a Term Set called Genre via the Managed Metadata Service. (Book III, Chapter 5 shows you how to create a Term Set.) Here's the drill:

1. **Create a User Sub-Type by choosing People⇨Manage User Sub-Types on the User Profile Service Application page.**

   The Manage User Sub-Type page appears.

2. **Enter** Student **for both the name and display name, and then click the Create button.**

3. **Navigate back to the User Profile Service Application page and create a user property by choosing People⇨Manage User Properties.**

   The Manage User Properties page appears, showing you all properties that have been defined.

4. **Click the *New Property* button at the top of the page.**

   The Add User Profile Property page appears.

5. **Set the following details in the text boxes on the page:**

   a. **Name:** MusicalGenre

   b. **Display Name:** Favorite Musical Genre

   c. **Type:** *string* (Single Value)

   d. Select the **Configure a Term Set check box:** This allows you to choose the terms to be used for this property.

   e. **Pick a Term Set for this property:** Genre

   f. **Sub-type of Profile:** For this example, choose only the Student check box.

   g. **Default privacy setting:** Everyone

   h. **Replicable**: Check this box.

   i. **Allow users to edit values for this property:** Choose this option.

   j. **Display Settings:** Choose all three check boxes in this section.

   k. **Indexed:** Check this box.

   l. **Click the OK button to create the property.**

Although your property is now created, it won't show up on the User Properties page until you choose a Student Sub-Type from the drop-down menu at the top of this page. When you've done that, the property appears in a list at the bottom of the page.

User Properties are grouped into sections that appear onscreen when the User Profile is displayed on a user's My Site. Feel free to use those laborious arrows to move the property up or down one line at a time to a section of your choosing (or create a new section if you like!).

Document the User Sub-Types that you've associated with new or changed user properties so you can find them easily from the User Properties page. That page doesn't show you all properties — it always filters by a specific User Sub-Type — you might as well be prepared!

Options for populating the User Profile

The method you use to initially populate User Profiles depends on the size of your organization — and on whether you have some other People directories deployed that might contain definitive information.

The following methods are the most common ways to fill up User Profiles:

✦ **Manually:** On the Manage User Profiles page, choose Use the New Profile.

✦ **Dynamically:** If a user has privileges that allow the Use Personal Features setting, then SharePoint creates a dynamic entry for that user in the User Profile the first time he or she accesses the My Site or My Profile option: Clicking the user's name in the top-right corner of a SharePoint page displays a drop-down list that offers both of those options.

See Book IV, Chapter 9 for more details on the Use Personal Features privilege.

✦ **Programmatically:** Your programming wizards can populate the User Profiles by using the object model and the User Profile Web Service.

✦ **Via Profile Synchronization:** This option uses LDAP to synchronize User Profiles with Active Directory and other LDAP-compliant repositories, and can use Business Connectivity Services to synchronize with other appropriate external sources.

Understanding Profile Synchronization

Large organizations usually have multiple repositories that contain information. These potential treasure troves include Human Resources databases, Enterprise Directory systems, and multipurpose stores such as the Active Directory (which has many roles, among them authentication store and directory store).

The User Profile Store is yet another place to store information about people — but it may not be the store you want to use as your definitive source of information. For example, many organizations use a centralized Enterprise Directory that feeds other stores as part of an established provisioning process. If that's your organization's approach, you may have to populate certain properties in your User Profile Store from one or more repositories scattered around the enterprise.

SharePoint Server 2010 provides a Profile Synchronization feature you can use to integrate user and group information, wherever it hangs out. Those places can include

✦ External LDAP directories services (such as the Active Directory).

✦ Business systems (such as SAP or Siebel) already defined via Business Connectivity Services

You define external information sources for synchronization with the User Profile Store by taking two general steps:

1. You map individual User Profile properties to appropriate properties in the external source.

2. You specify whether a user property is mapped for import or export — this essentially dictates who is the owner of the property (the external system or SharePoint).

• If the property is mapped for import then the external system feeds the SharePoint User Profile.

• If the property is mapped for export then the SharePoint User Profile feeds the external system

• Keep in mind that mapping a property for export to a Business Connectivity Service information source is not possible.

• Because you can map a property for export *and* allow users to edit specific User Profile properties, you can put the maintenance of those properties (in the external directory service, anyway) in the hands of your end users.

When you've configured the connections and mapped properties as necessary, the User Profile Synchronization Service detects changes in all the stores — and processes the changes accordingly.

Turn to Book III, Chapter 2 for further details of defining an external information source through Business Connectivity Services. For the time being, you can see a before-and-after Active Directory synchronization scenario in Figure 7-3 — for an imported (Email) and exported (Telephone) User Profile property.

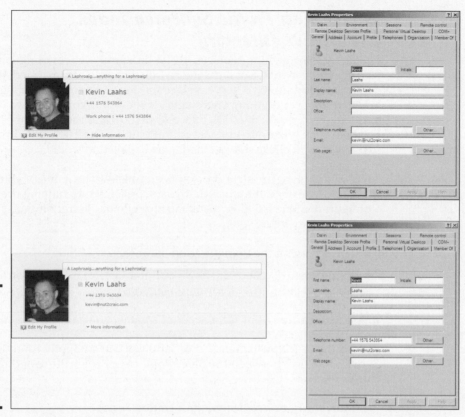

Figure 7-3:
Synchro-
nizing with
Active
Directory
(import and
export).

ForeFront Identity Manager (FIM) is the engine you use to execute and control the synchronization of the various directory sources. It acts as the central metadirectory for all directory services that are involved in synchronization. This feature isn't enabled by default — but it's installed as part of the overall configuration of the Profile Synchronization (as detailed in the next section of this chapter).

To further understand how synchronization works we will now walk through the necessary steps to configure Profile Synchronization with the Active Directory Directory Services (AD DS) for both user and group objects. Group objects are used to help people understand what they have in common with others (which sounds idealistic but is actually practical); we cover that in Book IV, Chapter 9.

Configuring Profile Synchronization with Active Directory

Profile synchronization requires that your SharePoint environment is installed as a farm rather than a standalone installation. Don't be alarmed; this does not mean you need multiple servers since for development and testing purposes, you can install everything on a single server — but you must install some version of SQL manually (SQL Express will do), and then run the SharePoint Configuration Wizard to connect SharePoint to SQL. The whole process takes just a few more clicks than a standalone installation would.

To configure synchronization, you need to know the name of your *farm account* — the account name that you supplied while running the SharePoint Configuration Wizard after installing SharePoint. SharePoint uses this account in two ways:

✦ For accessing the configuration database.

✦ As the identity used for the SharePoint Central Administration application pool in Internet Information Server.

If you've forgotten your farm account's name, you can retrieve it from IIS.

Executing the following tasks in order gives you a happily running Profile Synchronization between the SharePoint User Profile Store and the Active Directory:

1. Start the User Profile Synchronization Service.

2. Define your Active Directory connections.

3. Define the properties that will be mapped.

4. Invoke and monitor synchronization.

The following subsections look at these steps one at a time, in detail.

Starting the User Profile Synchronization Service

This service application does the heavy lifting of synchronization. As mentioned previously, it takes advantage of the Forefront Identity Manager Services (FIM) — which aren't enabled by default, so you'll have to get FIM up and running. Read on.

The first time you start the User Profile Synchronization Service, you are (in effect) completing the installation of the FIM services needed for synchronization. Don't be alarmed if this step takes some time. The FIM services run under the farm account; you have to provide some prerequisite permissions for this account so it can fully participate in synchronization.

Therefore — *before* you start the User Profile Synchronization Service — check to make sure that the following conditions are satisfied:

✦ **Your farm account must be a member of the local Administrators group on your SharePoint Server.** That's because the User Profile Synchronization Service will run there. Technically, this requirement is only needed for the initial provisioning of the FIM software. If absolutely necessary, you can remove the farm account from the local Administrators group after you get everything running smoothly — but here's something to keep in mind . . .

Removing the farm account from the local Administrators group after initial provisioning may disrupt later synchronizations. If that happens, try re-adding the farm account to the Admin group as a troubleshooting measure.

✦ **The farm account must be able to log on locally to the server upon which the User Profile Synchronization Service will run.**

✦ **If you're using a Windows Server 2003 AD DS forest, the farm account must be a member of the Pre-Windows 2000 Compatible Access group for the domain with which you're synchronizing.**

For more about resource forests, see "Defining Connections to the Active Directory" section, later in this chapter.

✦ **You have a User Profile Service application running in your farm.** Normally you'd set up that service application after installation, using the Farm Configuration Wizard. If you haven't yet configured your User Profile Service application, no problem — it's a quick process:

1. **Choose Central Administration➪Application Management➪Manage service applications.**

2. **On the page that appears, click the New button.**

Doing so creates an instance of the User Profile Service Application.

When you've confirmed the necessary pre-requisites you can now proceed to start the User Profile Synchronization Service.

1. **Choose Central Administration ➪System Settings➪Manage services on server.**

2. **Ensure that the chosen server at the top right of the page is the one on which your User Profile Service Application is running.**

3. **Scroll down the page, click the Start button for the User Profile Synchronization Service, and associate that service with the User Profile Service application.**

The status of the service changes to Starting. Now you have to sit back and be patient while the computer processes madly to configure the FIM services and the necessary connections to the relevant SQL databases. All this twiddling can take up to fifteen minutes (a minor Ice Age in computer time). You'll know it's successful when the status indicator of the service changes to Started.

4. **If Central Administration is running on the same server as the User Profile Synchronization Service and the User Profile Service, reset IIS on your server: Run the** `IISReset/noforce` **command in a command window.**

Here's where you can check to verify whether the configuration is complete:

✦ **Check the Forefront Identity Manager and Forefront Identity Manager Synchronization Windows services.** They should now be started, associated with your farm account, and have startup type set to Automatic. Forefront Identity Manager is the service that controls the configuration and administration of the Profile Synchronization, and Forefront Identity Manager Synchronization service performs the legwork of keeping the directories in sync.

Don't start these services manually — they must be started via the User Profile Synchronization Service.

✦ **Check the location that you reach via the following path:**

```
%Programfiles%\Microsoft Office Servers \14.0\Synchronization Service\
     MaData.
```
You should see empty folders created there.

✦ **Check the Windows application log and the SharePoint ULS (Unified Logging Service) for any error messages.** If you don't see any, you're good to go.

The SharePoint farm account must be added to the local Administrators group before starting the service for the first time. If you forget to add the farm account to the local Administrators group *before* you provision the synchronization service, then you have to bring the process to a screeching halt:

1. **Reboot your server.**

2. **Use PowerShell to stop the User Profile Synchronization Service:**

   a. *Use the* `Get-SPServiceInstance` *cmdlet to find out the service's GUID (Globally Unique Identifier).*

   b. *Pass this GUID into a* `Stop-SPServiceInstance` *cmdlet.*

   Shutting down the service this way ensures that everything is re-set correctly *before* you attempt to re-provision the service.

3. **Add the farm account to the local Administrators group.**

4. *Now* **Start the User Profile Synchronization Service as described above**

    Optional step: Breathe.

Defining Connections to the Active Directory

Synchronizing any two directory sources typically involves the following processes:

✦ **Identifying** the objects that you to keep in synch.

✦ **Linking** the objects together so you know which objects are related to which others.

✦ **Initially loading** the objects from one directory into the other.

- This step may be optional if your two directories are initially complete.

- The loading can be one-way or bidirectional — typically it's one-way, with the originating source designated as the Master.

✦ **Monitoring** for changes to the objects in either source.

✦ **Applying changes** to either source — in particular, additions, updates, and deletions.

The Profile Synchronization feature in SharePoint allows you to use the Active Directory Directory Services (AD DS) as a Master source for populating the SharePoint User Profile. This means that as user and group objects are created, updated, and deleted in the AD DS they are also created, updated, deleted in the SharePoint User Profile.

You identify the objects in the AD DS that you want to synchronize by defining a Synchronization Connection. Doing so also defines the type of directory service that's related to the connection. Table 7-1 lists the directory services supported by default, along with their names and synchronization capabilities (that is, whether they sync user objects and/or group objects, and whether they support incremental synchronizations).

**Book III
Chapter 7**

**User Profiles,
Organization Profiles,
and Audiences**

Table 7-1	Supported Directory Services		
Service	*Users*	*Groups*	*Incremental*
Active Directory Domain Services (AD DS) 2003 SP2, 2008	Yes	Yes	Yes
SunOne (LDAP) 5.2	Yes	No	Yes
Novell eDirectory (LDAP) 8.7.3	Yes	No	Yes
IBM Tivoli (LDAP) 6.2	Yes	No	Yes

A good working knowledge of the following information will help you prepare for creating an Active Directory connection:

✦ **Knowledge of your Active Directory:** You'd better know your stuff about your Active Directory — in particular, how it's structured in terms of resource forests (defined later in this list), domain controllers, and Organizational Units. You have to know which containers hold the user and group objects you want to synchronize with — mainly so you can point your connection at them. You also need to know whether any default port numbers for LDAP access have been changed — and whether you have to use an encrypted LDAP connection (if that's a yes, then you also have to implement the Secure Sockets Layer, as your nearest Active Directory guru can tell you).

✦ **Filtering of object may be required:** You can specify a filter to the connection that can be used to fine tune the objects and groups that you want to pull from the AD DS into the User Profile. If your organization includes an Active Directory property as part of a provisioning process that identifies which users to put in the SharePoint User Profile, then you need to know which AD property to use — and what its value should be.

✦ **Support for resource forests:** No, we're not talking trees or wildlife here. Many organizations use an AD *topology* that's called a *resource forest* because it contains details of resources that users access.

In this case, you actually have *two* Active Directory forests — one for authentication (this is the forest that users log on to, so it's known as the *account forest* or the *logon forest*) and one for resources (such as Microsoft Exchange or SharePoint). In this case, objects in the resource forest are suitably secured so users who log on to the account forest can access those objects.

Entries in the User Profile are linked to their counterparts in the Active Directory via the user's Security Identifier (SID), which is associated with his or her object in the account forest. If your system uses a resource forest, you'll want to link its objects together via the account forest — while taking most attributes that require synchronizing from the resource forest. That means setting up two connections — one for the account forest and one for the resource forest. The User Profile will then contain the SID for the object in the account forest and the SID from the associated object in the resource forest.

✦ **An account with suitable permissions:** You need an account to do the actual synchronization, which will be designated as the service account in the Metadirectory Services Active Directory Management agent — which goes by the name Forefront Identity Manager (FIM).

The account you use must fulfill these conditions:

- It must have Domain Administrative permissions.

- It must belong to the Domain Administrators group or be explicitly granted Replicating Directory Changes permissions for every domain of the forest that this management agent accesses.

- It must have an Access Control Entry to the domain object that grants your chosen account the Replicating Directory Changes permission.

  You can use an ACL editor or ADSIEDIT to add this Access Control Entry if necessary.

- If the NETBIOS name is different from the domain name, at least Replicate Directory Changes permission is also needed on the `cn=configuration` container.

  Refer to the PowerShell help files, specifically regarding the cmdlet `Get-SPServiceAppliction`, for more information about enabling NETBIOS names on a User Profile Service application.

- The account must be a member of the Farm Administrators group, or must be designated as a User Profile Service Administrator account.

- If you intend to export user properties from SharePoint into the AD DS, then the account also needs Replicating Directory Changes permission on each object (and all child objects) in the AD DS domains to which you want to export data.

- If you're exporting the `picture` property, then the container that stores the attribute you want to export also needs Read/Write permission. The `ThumbnailPhoto` attribute for profile pictures is an example of such a property.

When you have all the needed permissions in place, and have all the required information prepared and at your fingertips, you're ready for the next adventure: Take a deep breath and execute the following steps to create a Connection to the Active Directory:

1. **On the User Profile Service Application page of Central Administration, choose Synchronization⇨Configure Synchronization Connections.**

   The Synchronization Connections page appears.

2. **Click the Create New Connection button.**

3. **Give your connection a name and choose Active Directory as the type.**

   The Type drop-down list also allows you to choose other types, including those that support resource forests (in particular, Active Directory Logon Data and Active Directory Resource).

4. **Enter your Active Directory forest's name and then choose how you want to connect to the domain controller.**

Book III Chapter 7

User Profiles, Organization Profiles, and Audiences

You have two options:

- Enable automatic discovery of a suitable domain controller.
- Target the connection to a specific domain controller.

5. **Choose Windows Authentication as the Authentication Provider Type and then specify the name and password of the account you've chosen to act as the service account for the synchronization.**

6. **If your Active Directory has non-standard ports for LDAP access (and/ or requires an encrypted connection), enter the port number and select the SSL check box.**

   The Containers section is where you browse the containers that are within your Active Directory and choose those that contain the user and group objects that you want to synchronize. The next steps show this process.

7. **Click the Populate Containers button.**

   The Containers text box on the page is populated with details from your Active Directory.

8. **Navigate through the containers (using the + and – signs); click to put a check in the box next to the name of each container that holds an object you require.**

   Keep in mind that

   - You must choose at least one container.
   - Selecting a container automatically selects all the objects it contains (if you grab the box, you grab what's *in* the box).

   You can select individual objects at this stage, but a more common approach is to select the highest-level container(s) in which your desired objects reside — and *then* use a filter to extract only the relevant objects. If you get any error messages at this stage, then it's likely that

   - The details entered for your forest, domain controller, or service account are incorrect

     or

   - Your service account doesn't have the required permissions for viewing the Active Directory.

     Better check those two possibilities and troubleshoot before you go farther.

   You can see an example of a successful connection in Figure 7-4 — in this instance, we selected the Users container.

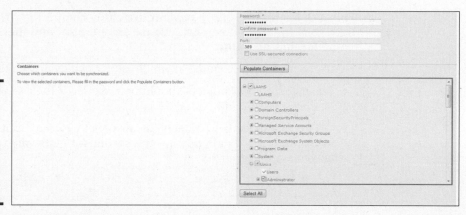

Figure 7-4:
Browsing
the Active
Directory
when
setting up a
connection.

As you browse the containers in your Active Directory from Central Administration, SharePoint is busy making LDAP calls to a domain controller. When you click the Populate button, the initial LDAP call has a starting node of the domain root — and a search scope of base, which returns a list of all the top-level containers. Clicking a container makes another LDAP call, with that container as the starting node and the search scope set to onelevel — which returns a list of all the objects in the container.

9. **Click the OK button.**

The definition of your Connection is complete. Now, that wasn't so painful, was it? (On second thought, don't answer that.)

With a successful connection up and running, the AD DS serves as a master directory for all objects that will be included in your User Profile. At this point, you've defined the containers in the AD DS that will be monitored for any additions, changes, and deletions. By default, if the AD DS finds any object in those containers that matches the LDAP search filter, it imports that object into your User Profile. The LDAP search filter looks like this:

```
(&(objectCategory=person)(objectClass=user)(objectClass=group))
```

To fine-tune the objects that end up imported to your User Profile — if, say, you want to import only enabled user objects, or import only those with a particular attribute set to a particular value (picky, aren't we?) — you have to create a filter to find only the objects you want. Here's how:

1. **On the Manage Connections page, hover your mouse pointer over your connection; when a drop-down list appears, click Edit Connection Filters.**

The Edit Connection Filters page appears. From there you can specify exclusion filters for both User and Group objects.

2. **For each exclusion filter you want to define, choose the AD DS attribute from the drop-down list, choose an operator, and then choose a value for that operator.**

   Figure 7-5 shows an example in which we set two exclusion filters:

   - We indicated that objects should be excluded if their `extensions Attribute1` wasn't equal to 1.

   - We excluded disabled objects because the AD DS attribute `user AccountControl` already has the second bit of its value set if an account is disabled.

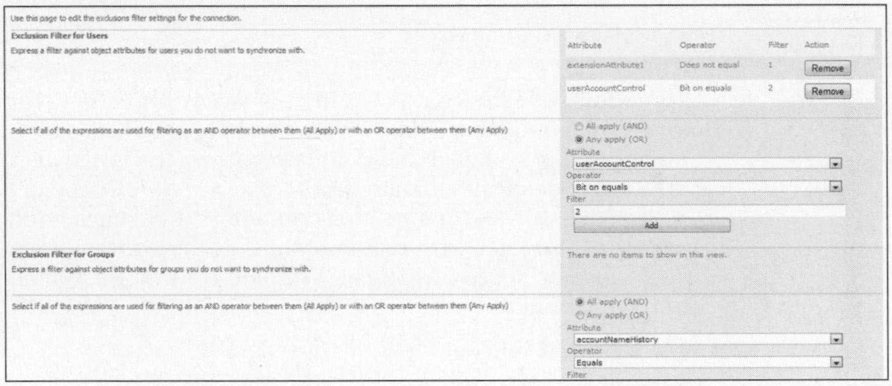

Figure 7-5:
Setting
exclusion
filters.

3. **After defining all your exclusion filters, choose how they handle the exclusion of objects from synchronization.**

   You have a choice between these options:

   - All filters' criteria must apply for an object to be excluded.

     or

   - One filter match suffices for an object to be excluded.

   Figure 7-5 shows a scenario that excludes an object from synchronization if any of the filters' criteria are `true`.

4. **Click OK to save your filter definitions.**

Defining properties to be mapped

The Connection settings define which objects participate in the synchronization — but the frenzy of configuring isn't done yet. (You probably expected as much.) The next level of fine detail to tweak is the User Profile Properties: You map them to AD DS attributes. You can do that mapping in one of two directions:

✦ **Import:** If you're importing properties, you write the AD DS attribute value into the mapped User Profile Property.

✦ **Export:** If you're exporting properties, you write the User Profile Property into the mapped AD DS attribute.

SharePoint provides a default set of mappings for an Active Directory Connection; user-specific mappings are listed in Table 7-2 (note that all default properties are marked as Import).

But defaults are no fun unless you can override them — and you *can* adjust most of these defaults to suit your needs. Here's an example: Suppose a user has edited her User Profile and then modified the value of the MusicalGenre property (discussed earlier in the "Creating a User Profile Sub-Type and User Properties" section). You find this change — and want to update an extension attribute in the user's Active Directory object. The idea is to make that property value available to other applications (such as Microsoft Exchange Server) that use the Active Directory as their directory. To do that job, you'd follow these steps:

1. **On the User Profile Service Application page, choose Manage User Properties.**

   The Manage User Properties page appears.

2. **Navigate to the property called Favorite Musical Genre.**

   This will work if you've followed this book's musical example with fierce tenacity (as, of course, you have).

3. **Hover your mouse pointer over the property; when a drop-down list appears, click Edit.**

   The Edit User Profile Property page appears.

4. **Scroll to the bottom of the page, choose the following options from the three drop-down lists, and then click the Add button:**

   a. **Source Data Connection:** *<name of your previously created AD Connection>*

   b. **Attribute:** extendionAttribute2

   c. Direction: Export

5. **Click OK to complete the editing of the property.**

Now the mapping is set. The next time a synchronization runs, the details from the Favorite Musical Genre user property are written into the extension Attribute2 of the user's Active Directory object.

Table 7-2	Default AD Attribute Mapping
AD DS attribute	*User Profile Property*
objectSID	SID
<logon id e.g. {domain}/{user}>	ADGuid
givenName	FirstName
msDS-PhoneticFirstName	PhoneticFirstName
Sn	LastName
msDS-PhoneticLastName	PhoneticLastName
displayName	Name
msDS-PhoneticDisplayName	PhoneticDisplayName
telephoneNumber	WorkPhone
Department	Department
Title	SPS-JobTitle
Manager	Manager
sAMAccountName	UserName
wWWHomePage	PublicSiteRedirect
proxyAddresses	SPS-SipAddress
Dn	SPS-DistinguishedName
msDS-SourceObjectDN	SPS-SourceObjectDN
Mail	WorkEmail
physicalDeliveryOfficeName	Office

Invoking and monitoring synchronization

Before we tell you how to execute a synchronization, we're going to invoke a little common wisdom: It's good practice to have thought through the whole process before you start synchronizing everything in sight. So . . .

✦ Think about the Active Directory containers that hold the desired objects.

✦ Think about how you will identify the objects you want to synchronize.

✦ Think about what exclusion filters you will utilize.

✦ Think about which custom properties you want to map before you dive in and do your first synchronization — especially if it's intended for a production system!

✦ Think about two weeks in the Bahamas when you're done. (Well, we can dream.)

The synchronization process has (as you've no doubt noticed) many stages — you'll have to look for changes in directory sources, and figure out what changes must be applied to which objects — in both directions! Don't be surprised if the synchronization process takes quite a while to run to completion. The metadirectory service has to chug through processing a boatload of changes — updates, additions, deletions — which is a lot of work, even for a computer system.

The Active Directory is essentially the master as far as replication goes. Therefore it determines which entries in the User Profile require updating, adding, or deleting.

SharePoint offers two modes in which you can execute synchronization:

+ **Full:** This is only required if you want to do a full reset of the User Profile. Barring disasters, it's pretty rare.

+ **Incremental:** This is the preferred method. It only processes objects that have changed in either directory source since the last synchronization.

During synchronization, any new Active Directory objects found in the mapped containers — if those objects aren't excluded by any filter rules — are added to the User Profile. Then the mapped attributes in Table 7-2 are set on the new (that is, updated) User Profile. Fortunately this happens automatically.

The metadirectory links the Active Directory user object and the User Profile by using the `objectSID` attribute to locate existing User Profiles for modified or deleted AD objects.

You can invoke synchronization manually and/or set up a schedule for an incremental synch to run routinely at a time of your choosing. Remember that synchronization uses a truckload of computer resources — so it's wisest and best to run this process during some time other than regular working hours. When the time is right and the moon is full (just kidding), you can execute a synchronization by choosing Start Profile Synchronization on the User Profile Service Application page.

When your synchronization is running, you can monitor its status from the right side of the User Profile Service Application page, under the Profile Synchronization Settings section. This section also allows you to stop the synchronization and to see how far along it is. The number of stages required to run the synch depends on the number and type of connections you've configured. The progress of each stage appears in the page that appears onscreen when you choose the Synchronization option (as shown in Figure 7-6).

**Book III
Chapter 7**

User Profiles,
Organization Profiles,
and Audiences

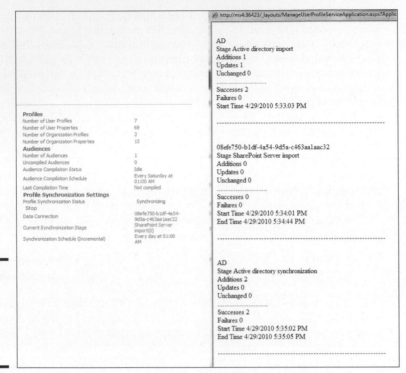

Figure 7-6:
The
Synchro-
nization
status bar
and log.

When synchronization is complete, you should find that the number of entries in your User Profile has increased — possibly dramatically, if your organization is big. You can view the User Profiles by choosing Manage User Profiles. Just don't get upset if nothing is displayed — that's the default. You can override it by typing in a filter string and then clicking the Filter button. A list of entries that match the string will humbly appear onscreen.

A good way to list all entries is to enter the domain name of your Active Directory objects as the filter string (sneaky but effective). This bit of magic works because all your User Profile entries have the domain name in the Account Name User Property.

Using Organization Profiles

Organization Profiles are new to SharePoint — but they are very similar in nature to User Profiles and use the same underlying architecture. They have the same concept of defining a set of properties and allocating those properties to Organization Sub-Types in order to support the needs of different types of organizations.

The idea behind Organization Profiles is to support information about ad-hoc teams and groups that transcend your organizational structure. Although SharePoint does show you strict reporting relationships (by maintaining details of who each user's manager is), the Organization Profile takes a wider view; it's more for describing business teams. After all, you may report to one manager but you may be involved in multiple projects, business units, or teams of people who wear many hats. Each Organization Profile can be maintained by a named individual who can identify members of that organization (either manually or through a reporting structure or group).

At the time of writing, the Organization Profiles feature is still incomplete — look for it to make a grander entry into SharePoint in the future. These profiles can only be maintained via Central Administration — and the only other place they show up is in the People Picker User Interface while somebody's modifying the membership of an Organization (as shown in Figure 7-7). At least the feature lets you see the organizations of which a user is a member. SharePoint provides a pre-defined organization called Root Organization — you can certainly add others if you like, but you may want to hold off on doing that for a while yet. As with many new things, let this functionality mature a little before you spend much time on it.

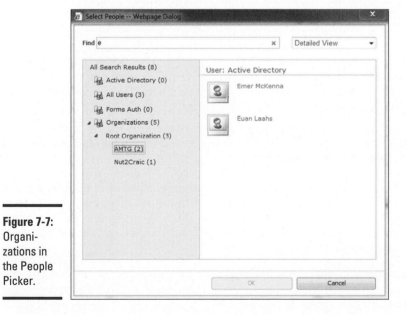

Figure 7-7: Organizations in the People Picker.

That said, developers can already access Organization Profiles via the object model and Web Services. In the longer term, expect to see them linked into People profiles as well — so you can browse *all* the Organizations that a user is a member of.

Audiences as targets for content

Audiences are a SharePoint feature that's been around for quite a while now. An *audience* is a rules-based mechanism for defining a target group of people so you can aim specific content at them. For example, you can insert a Web Part on a page and target it so it appears only to members of specific audiences.

Audiences are not a way to restrict access to content — they are more like an automatic filter used to display information selectively. If users have access to the underlying content, they can display it through other means, regardless of the audiences at which the content is targeted.

In SharePoint terms, audiences consist of one or more rules. You can configure whether one rule or all rules must be met before a person is considered part of the target audience. Each rule has an operand, an operator, and a value against which to check the result. The operand can either be a User or a Property from the User Profile; the operator depends upon which operand is used:

✦ **User:** The operator is one of Reports Under or Member Of. The Reports Under matches against the Manager property in the User Profile. The Member Of matches against any group that is defined — be it an Active Directory group that has been imported via the User Profile or the Members group of individual team sites.

✦ **Property:** The operator is determined by the type of the property chosen as the operator. All common operators are available — such as *contains*, *equals (=)*, not equal (<>), and is *present*.

Audiences must be compiled before they can be used. When you've successfully compiled an audience, you can view the names of its members to verify that it's picking up the people you expect it to. Figure 7-8 shows an example that defines an audience that includes all users whose Favorite Musical Genre is set to the value `Country` or `Rock`.

Audiences can be used to influence content as follows:

✦ **Fit the scope of the Web Part to the audience:** You can control the actual Web Parts that appear on a page by setting the Audiences in the Advanced Settings on the Web Part itself.

✦ **Filter the content that Web Parts display:** You can set the Web Part to show different items from a list or library to different audiences (the equivalent of, say, showing a catnip toy to a group of cats and a nice juicy bone to a group of dogs).

To achieve this versatility, you execute the following general steps:

1. **Enable audience targeting on the list itself.**

   From the Ribbon, you would choose the List Settings ⇨Audience Targeting Settings, and then check the box to enable audience targeting. Doing so creates a Target Audience column that you add to views of the list.

2. **Edit the properties of the items in the list that you want to target, and then set the appropriate audiences.**

3. **Configure a Web Part that is audience-aware and configure it to use the audience sctting(s) on individual items as a filter when it displays the items by user context.**

   The Content Query Web Part, for example, is audience-aware — and you can set it to receive input from any list or library in the site collection. For example, you may have items spread out in multiple lists in your site collection that are specific to particular musical genres. These could be displayed in a personalized fashion on a home page so the users see only the content that matches their own chosen genres.

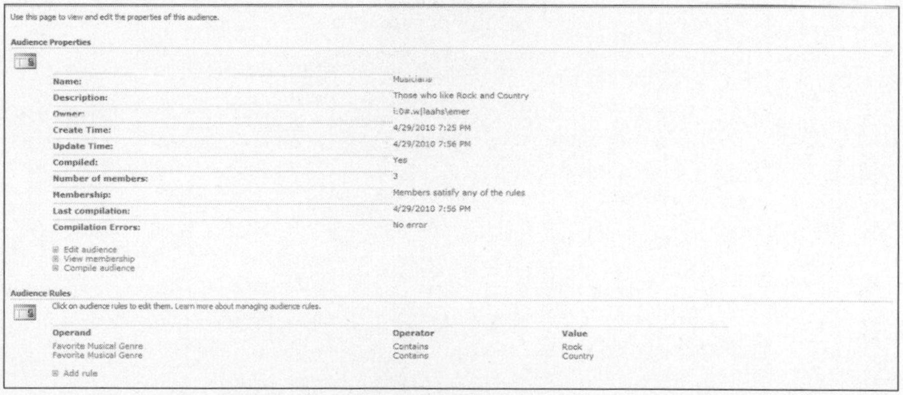

Figure 7-8:
Defining an audience.

Chapter 8: Considering PerformancePoint Services

In This Chapter

✔ Reviewing PerformancePoint Services

✔ Configuring PerformancePoint Services

✔ Understanding the role of the Secure Store Service

✔ Introducing the Dashboard Designer

SharePoint Server 2010 Enterprise Edition is a business-collaboration platform that offers your organization almost as many controls and gauges as you'd find on the dashboard of a starship (okay, when they're built, they'll probably *have* dashboards). You even get to choose which controls, gauges, and indicators to use — depending on what your business considers its most vital information assets. SharePoint Server also provides

✦ Integrated resources (including Communities, Composites, and Insights) you can draw upon to craft solutions to thorny business problems.

✦ Service applications such as PerformancePoint and Visio Services to help you develop insights into how your business is performing as a whole

✦ Tools that put up-to-date business information at your fingertips (or at least practically under your mouse button).

Using PerformancePoint Services, you can build SharePoint *dashboards* (arrays of indicators) that use various *metrics* (a fancy word for measurements) to show how specific areas of your business are performing. For example, metrics that show at a glance how well — or how not-so-well — your products are selling can help you make informed business decisions about whether to increase or decrease your inventory.

Tools that help you gain insight into your business through the monitoring, analysis, and reporting of data can be grouped under an umbrella term: *business intelligence (BI)*. With SharePoint 2010, Microsoft provides a slew of BI tools — including PerformancePoint Services, Visio Services, and Excel Services. In this chapter, we poke around in the PerformancePoint Services BI toolbox and show you how to get the service up and running in your SharePoint environment.

You can immerse yourself in the details of Visio Services in Book III, Chapter 9 — and those of Excel Services in Book III, Chapter 3, and Book IV, Chapter 4.

Reviewing PerformancePoint Services

Microsoft PerformancePoint Server 2007 was originally a standalone product that delivered business intelligence: It helped you analyze and monitor the performance of your organization with interactive software tools such as dashboards, scorecards, and reports. With the introduction of SharePoint Server 2010, PerformancePoint no longer stands alone; it's now fully integrated into SharePoint Server 2010 — and into the service–application architecture. Result: The tools you have available now are more like industrial-strength power tools.

PerformancePoint Services extends the capabilities of its predecessor — and takes full advantage of SharePoint by

✦ Storing all its content (such as data–source connections and dashboard templates) in SharePoint.

✦ Inheriting the SharePoint security model.

That's a great place to start. But how does SharePoint handle business intelligence? So glad you asked (well, okay, *we* did — but read on).

Peeking at the SharePoint Business Intelligence Center

Users get their hands on PerformancePoint Services in a special SharePoint site template: the Business Intelligence Center. This template is a new, improved, hot-rodded version of the Report Center site template offered in SharePoint Server 2007. Figure 8-1 shows the default home page of a site created using the Business Intelligence Center site template.

The Business Intelligence Center site template comprises the features, Web Parts, Web services, and Web pages that do the work of business intelligence in SharePoint. Here's a list of the big guns:

✦ **PerformancePoint Services:** The Business Intelligence Center site template includes the components that provide PerformancePoint functionality as a Web service (for example, Dashboard Designer). The template also includes sample Web pages that provide tutorials and instructions on how to use the PerformancePoint business intelligence tools.

✦ **Excel Services:** The Business Intelligence site template shows you how to publish your Excel workbooks to Excel Services. Excel Services, in turn, gives users access to SharePoint capabilities from within Excel 2010 workbooks — where they use a familiar interface to shape, manage, and share their information.

✦ **Reporting Services:** The Business Intelligence Center site template takes advantage of integrating Reporting Services with SharePoint: You can upload and publish Report Server content types to your SharePoint libraries, and then view and manage your reports directly from SharePoint.

✦ **Visio Services:** The Business Intelligence Center site template supports the integration of Visio Services so you can (for example) render your Visio diagrams through the browser and create strategy maps for business intelligence.

Understanding the PerformancePoint Lingo

Any hot new field generates buzzwords, and *business intelligence* (like military intelligence, a strategic use of information — only business-derived) is no exception. Often it goes by a nickname: BI. In SharePoint — especially in PerformancePoint Services — you're going to run into yet another barrage of vernacular. But relax: Under the buzzwords is the stuff you have to know to create *solutions* — the deployments of SharePoint capabilities and features needed to get business problems handled and specific jobs done.

The data used to produce this chapter's screenshots that illustrate PerformancePoint output come from a dynamic (and imaginary) corporation's BI setup: the Contoso BI Demo Dataset for Retail Industry. The dataset includes the Contoso Retail database and an Analysis Services database, which gives you a foundation on which you can test the BI capabilities of SharePoint and other Office products. You can download the dataset from the Microsoft Web site.

Book III
Chapter 8

Considering
PerformancePoint
Services

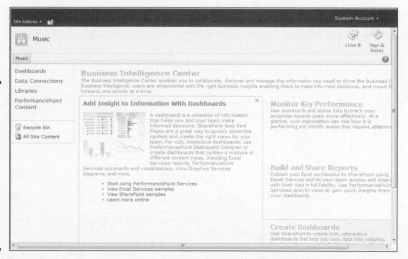

Figure 8-1: The Business Intelligence Center is where you tell PerformancePoint Services what to do.

Here's a quick overview of the PerformancePoint buzzwords you need to know:

✦ **Indicator:** A graphical representation that works like a gauge to show the status of one or more Key Performance Indicators (KPIs — more about those in a minute). For example, you could have color indicators of Red, Orange, and Green to give you a quick reading of whether a process is (respectively) off target, at risk, or on target.

Dashboard Designer provides a wide variety of Indicator Templates you can use to put such at-a-glance gauges on your business processes. Figure 8-2 shows you the Select an Indicator Template dialog box from Dashboard Designer.

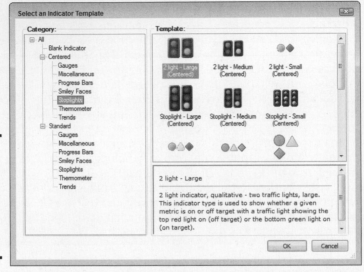

Figure 8-2:
Dashboard
Designer
provides
a large
selection of
indicators.

✦ **Data Source:** A *data source* is the connection to the underlying data that your dashboard and scorecards report on. You'll encounter these five *data–source types* in SharePoint Dashboard Designer:

- Analysis Services: These data sources pull data from an Analysis Services cube. A cube is a way of analyzing the data in a database from different points of view.

- Excel Services: These data sources pull data from data sources defined in Excel Services.

- Excel Workbook: These data sources pull data from an Excel Workbook.

- SharePoint List: These data sources pull data from a SharePoint list.

- SQL Server Table: These data sources pull data from a table in a SQL Server database.

With PerformancePoint Services, you can select different authentication options for each individual data source. An exception to this rule crops up if the data source is an Excel Workbook: The Excel Workbook data source type has no authentication model. (Ack.) Figure 8-3 shows an example of a data source connection being defined in Dashboard Designer. This particular data source connection uses the Unattended Service Account for its authentication method.

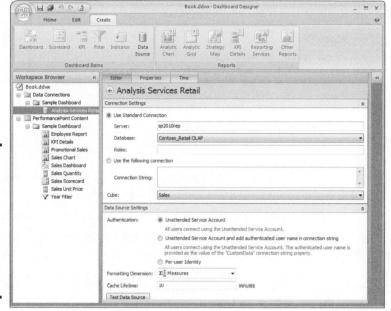

**Book III
Chapter 8**

Considering
PerformancePoint
Services

Figure 8-3:
Use the
Unattended
Service
Account
when
connecting
to data
sources.

✦ **KPI:** A KPI (Key Performance Indicator) is a measurement of a performance metric, displayed as a graphical image that shows you the status of that metric. For example, you could choose a Stop Light indicator to inform your users that a specific area of your business is off-target and needs urgent attention; you could choose a Green circle indicator to tell your users that everything's running as expected for that specific area of your business and it's on target. Whether the indicator is red or green depends on the number value of the particular KPI being measured (say, regional sales figures or stock values).

By default, a KPI is made up of two parts:

• The *Actual metric* measures what was actually achieved by the business.

• The *Target* is what the business wants to achieve, or the business goal, usually expressed as a number.

Figure 8-4 shows an example of a simple KPI (created in Dashboard Designer) that changes in response to a field named `Sales Quantity`.

A KPI also includes other PerformancePoint features that make it work, such as connections to data sources and indicators. You can map a KPI metric to a fixed value (such as a target sales figure) or connect it to a selected data source (such as a particular SQL database). If you have a KPI whose target doesn't change very often, you can use fixed values in your calculation. Figure 8-6 shows you how the same KPIs appear on a scorecard.

Figure 8-4:
KPIs provide
a graphical
repre-
sentation
of your
business
metrics.

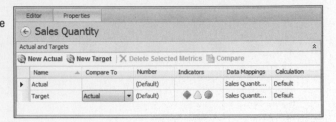

+ **Filters:** You use filters to control — or select for presentation — the data that appears on your dashboard. For example:

  • A date filter could show your users current data or historical data.

  • A region filter could display only data from a specific geographical region in your scorecard.

  When you create a filter, you can select a display method to specify how your filter appears in your dashboard. Most filters you create offer three display methods:

  • **List:** This option displays a drop-down list from which the user can select a single item.

  • **Tree:** This option displays a directory tree from which the user can select a single item.

  • **Multi-Select Tree:** This option displays a more sophisticated direc-tory tree from which the user can select multiple items.

  Figure 8-5 shows a dashboard page that filters the contents of the dash-board for a selected year. The filter display method in this case is set to List, displaying a drop-down list (the user selects a single item).

Figure 8-5:
Use filters
to create
dynamic,
interactive
dashboards.

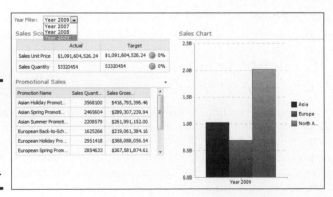

✦ **Scorecard:** A *scorecard* is one of the items that may appear on your dashboard; it measures the performance of your organization. A scorecard consists of PerformancePoint items such as connections to data sources and KPIs. PerformancePoint comes with a number of scorecard templates, including Balanced or Analytic (which gets the values it uses from Analysis Services).

If the standard SharePoint templates don't meet your needs, you can build a scorecard from scratch — and let your imagination run wild. For example, at the SharePoint Conference 2009, a Microsoft presenter demonstrated a scorecard that when zoomed out displayed a picture of the Mona Lisa by using custom indicators. (Most users, of course, have a more *businesslike* imagination, don't they?)

Typical scorecards present data in a table format containing rows and columns. Figure 8-6 shows an example of a very simple scorecard that measures the sales within an organization. The Actual and Target sales show how the company is performing against the expected metrics.

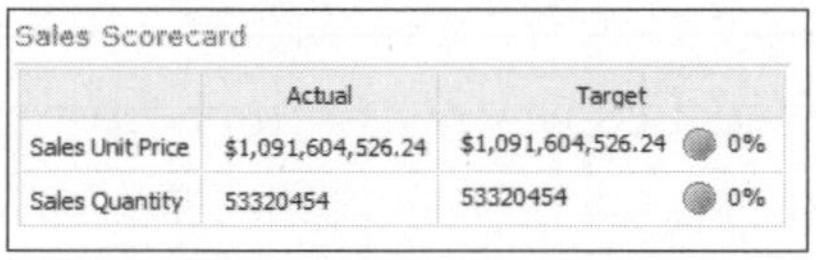

Figure 8-6:
Use
scorecards
to measure
performance
in your
organization.

Sales Scorecard				
	Actual	Target		
Sales Unit Price	$1,091,604,526.24	$1,091,604,526.24	⬤	0%
Sales Quantity	53320454	53320454	⬤	0%

✦ **Decomposition Tree:** No, it isn't a leftover prop from a horror movie. A Decomposition Tree is a data-visualization tool in PerformancePoint Services that helps users analyze complex data by showing them a view subdivided into hierarchical levels of detail — which makes relationships among items of data easier to see. For example, you could have a Decomposition Tree that shows the number of sales of a specific product, and then the tree hierarchy could break down the sales into region, office, and, ultimately, sales teams or individuals, giving you an accurate picture of what is actually driving the sales for that specific item.

You don't create or open a Decomposition Tree using Dashboard Designer. Instead, you open the Decomposition Tree from a view in a dashboard you've deployed to SharePoint. For example, right-clicking the middle bar (which represents Europe) on the sales chart shown in Figure 8-5 gets SharePoint to display a list of menu options — one of which is (well, hello, there!) Decomposition Tree. Clicking this option displays a Decomposition Tree of the chosen value on a separate Web page; Figure 8-7 shows an example of what appears. The tree subdivides the Europe value into more detailed levels, showing all countries in the database that are part of Europe.

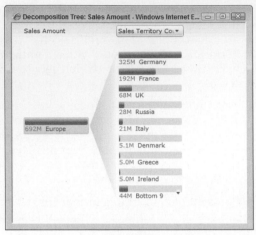

Figure 8-7:
The
Decomp-
osition Tree
can break
down a
value into a
hierarchical
view.

Decomposition Trees are offered for items or views that make use of SQL Server Analysis Services — for example, a scorecard based on Analysis Services, as well as analytic charts and grids. Whether the menu option appears depends on how you configure your scorecard (or for that matter, your analytic view). If your scorecard or view doesn't contain hierarchical data, (say, the list of product names in a Products table) the Decomposition Tree option isn't available.

You must have Microsoft Silverlight 3 installed on your computer in order to use the Decomposition Tree.

✦ **Reports:** Businesses need reports (lots of them) if the top brass expects to know what's going on (and they do). You can present various types of reports that provide information on specific areas of your business. For example, a KPI details report can provide more detailed information on a KPI — such as the thresholds for that KPI by defining what it means to be on target, off target, or at risk.

Dashboard Designer provides you with eight options for creating reports:

• **Analytic Chart:** Use the Analytic Chart report type to create an interactive bar, line, or pie chart of cube data.

• **Analytic Grid:** Use the Analytic Grid report type to create an interactive grid view of cube data.

• **Strategy Map:** Use Visio 2007 or later to create a Strategy Map report connected to a scorecard. A *strategy map* is a visual representation of an organization's goals and how it intends to achieve those goals. You can find out more information on how to create Strategy Maps in Book III, Chapter 9.

If your computer is a 64-bit model, be sure to install the 64-bit version of Visio.

- **KPI Details:** Use this report type to create a report that shows underlying information about a KPI. The KPI Details report works hand in hand with your scorecard. For example, if you have a scorecard that displays your company's Target sales for a given year, you can click the Target value on your scorecard to display details of the Actual sales in the KPI Details report.

- **Reporting Services:** Use the Reporting Services report type to create a reference to an existing SQL Server Reporting Services Report.

Alas, you may not avail yourself of this functionality unless you have SQL Reporting Services configured in your environment. Forsooth.

Figure 8-8 shows an example of a PerformancePoint report that corresponds to a Reporting Services (.rdl) report deployed to SharePoint. The report is presented on the page using the PerformancePoint Report Web Part.

Before you can create Reporting Services reports in Dashboard Designer you must have Microsoft Report Viewer 2008 installed on your computer. Microsoft Report Viewer enables .NET applications, such as Dashboard Designer, to display reports. The control is a free distributable available for download at the Microsoft Web site.

- **Other Reports: Excel Services:** Use the Excel Services report template from the Other Reports command to create a report view of an Excel Services workbook. In order to create an Excel Services report type, Excel Services must be up and running in your SharePoint environment.

- **Other Reports: ProClarity Analytics Server Page:** Use the ProClarity Analytics Server Page report template from the Other Reports command to create a report with a reference to an existing ProClarity Analytics Server Page.

Figure 8-8:
Use existing Reporting Services reports in your PPS reports and dashboards.

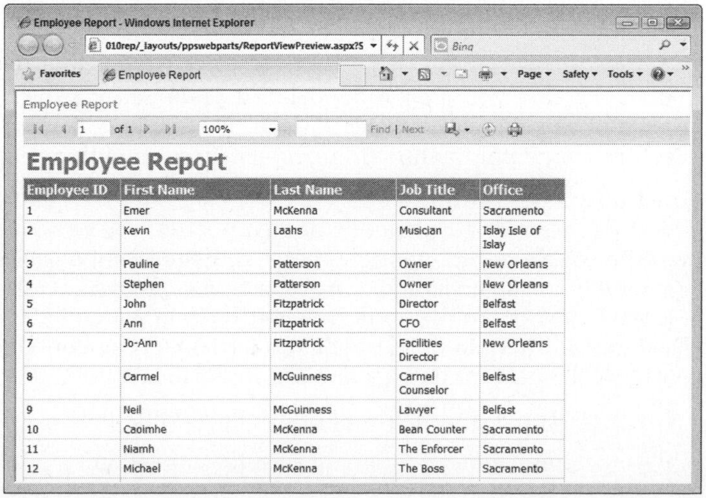

Employee ID	First Name	Last Name	Job Title	Office
1	Emer	McKenna	Consultant	Sacramento
2	Kevin	Laahs	Musician	Islay Isle of Islay
3	Pauline	Patterson	Owner	New Orleans
4	Stephen	Patterson	Owner	New Orleans
5	John	Fitzpatrick	Director	Belfast
6	Ann	Fitzpatrick	CFO	Belfast
7	Jo-Ann	Fitzpatrick	Facilities Director	New Orleans
8	Carmel	McGuinness	Carmel Counselor	Belfast
9	Neil	McGuinness	Lawyer	Belfast
10	Caoimhe	McKenna	Bean Counter	Sacramento
11	Niamh	McKenna	The Enforcer	Sacramento
12	Michael	McKenna	The Boss	Sacramento

- **Other Reports: Web Page:** Use the Web Page report template from the Other Reports command to create a report with a reference to an existing Web page.

✦ **Dashboard:** In PerformancePoint Services, a dashboard is simply a Web Part page (.aspx) that may contain scorecards, filters, and reports. It functions like the piece of fake wood that holds the gauges in a car, putting them where you can read them at a glance. As a BI tool, a dashboard gives you readings you can use to monitor and analyze performance in your organization; you even get to define specific criteria that trigger the gauges. A quick look at the dashboard tells you whether your organization or department is meeting its goals (provided, of course, you remembered to put your glasses on). Figure 8-9 shows an example of a PerformancePoint dashboard whipped up using the Dashboard Designer and deployed to SharePoint.

Figure 8-9: Dashboards are deployed to Web Part pages in SharePoint.

You can create your PerformancePoint dashboards using the Dashboard Designer. For more about the Dashboard Designer, see the "Introducing PerformancePoint Dashboard Designer" section of this chapter.

✦ **Dashboard Definition:** When you use Dashboard Designer to design and build your PerformancePoint dashboards, you're actually working with the dashboard definition item. Using the Dashboard Designer you can add PerformancePoint items to zones on your dashboard definition. Figure 8-10 shows a dashboard definition item edited in Dashboard Designer. In this example, the dashboard definition contains three zones with each zone containing a specific PerformancePoint item:

- Header zone: containing a PerformancePoint filter.

- Left column zone: containing a PerformancePoint scorecard.

- Right column zone: containing a PerformancePoint report.

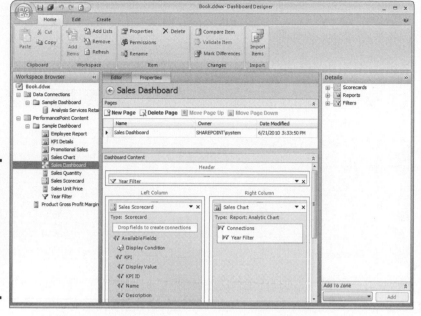

Figure 8-10: Use Dashboard Designer to create and edit your dashboard definition.

The items that appear in the dashboard definition aren't actually stored in the dashboard definition; instead, the dashboard definition stores a reference to the items. This enables the PerformancePoint items to be reused across multiple dashboards. When updates are made to any of the individual items, dashboard definitions that contain those items, and the dashboards deployed from the dashboard definition files, reflect the updated information.

The first time you save your dashboard to SharePoint, Dashboard Designer saves a dashboard definition as an item to your PerformancePoint Content List. Figure 8-11 shows the dashboard definition item as it appears in the PerformancePoint Content List.

You can edit your dashboard definition directly from the PerformancePoint Content List: Right-click the dashboard definition item in the list, and then click Edit in Dashboard Designer from the shortcut menu that appears.

The actual dashboard (*.aspx) *file* that produces the onscreen display your users see doesn't appear in SharePoint until you use the Deploy to SharePoint command from Dashboard Designer. When you deploy your dashboard to SharePoint, Dashboard Designer creates a Web Part page that represents your dashboard — and stores it in the SharePoint library you've defined as your Dashboards library.

When you edit your dashboard definition's SharePoint list item in Dashboard Designer and save your changes back to SharePoint, the changes apply *only* to the dashboard definition item in the PerformancePoint Content List. The changes aren't visible in the dashboard your users see until you deploy your changes (using the Deploy to SharePoint command). When you deploy the changes to your dashboard, SharePoint overwrites the old dashboard (`*.aspx`) file in the Dashboards library. If you've edited the dashboard's `*.aspx` file manually, those changes are overwritten.

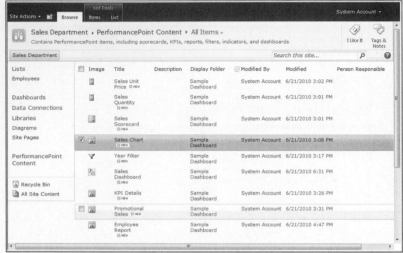

Figure 8-11:
Dashboard definitions are stored in the PerformancePoint Content List.

Storing PerformancePoint Content

PerformancePoint Services stores its contents in lists and document libraries within your SharePoint site. The great thing about this arrangement is that the PerformancePoint items you create are reusable: You can share them across multiple Web pages in a dashboard, and even across multiple dashboards. For example, you can define a connection to a data source and use this same data connection in multiple dashboards; if you have a set of custom indicators, you can use those in multiple dashboards as well.

PerformancePoint Services draws upon various libraries and lists in your SharePoint site, including these:

✦ **Dashboards library:** This library is where you store the Web Part pages, Status Lists, and PerformancePoint dashboards deployed from Dashboard Designer.

✦ **Data Connections For PerformancePoint library:** The Data Connections content library contains the data sources you can use when you're designing your dashboard. The data includes the connection and security information for each individual data source in the library. When you double-click a data source item in the Data Connection library, SharePoint launches the Dashboard Designer. From there you can edit the data source.

✦ **PerformancePoint Content List:** The PerformancePoint Content List contains the PerformancePoint items you create — such as KPIs, score-cards, reports, filters, and dashboards. When you create a new item, you can launch Dashboard Designer in two ways:

> Click the *Add new item* link in the Content List.
>
> or
>
> Open an existing item, and when a shortcut menu appears, clicking Edit.

> All items you create using the Dashboard Designer are stored in the PerformancePoint Content List.

SharePoint stores all items of content in lists and libraries. There the items automatically inherit the capabilities and advantages of the SharePoint lists and libraries that hold them. You can create views of entire lists or libraries to help you sort, filter, and better manage your PerformancePoint content. You can also apply permissions using the standard SharePoint security model.

The PerformancePoint Content List has several built-in views that help you organize your PerformancePoint content; for example, you can view items of a specific content type (such as KPIs). As with any SharePoint list, you can modify the existing views or create new views.

Reviewing the PerformancePoint content types

Activating PerformancePoint Services Site Collection Features in your SharePoint site deploys several content types to your site — categorized as follows in the PerformancePoint group (you'll notice a pattern here):

✦ **PerformancePoint Dashboard:** This content type represents a dash-board created using the Dashboard Designer.

✦ **PerformancePoint Scorecard:** This content type represents a scorecard created using the Dashboard Designer.

✦ **PerformancePoint KPI:** This content type represents a KPI created using the Dashboard Designer.

✦ **PerformancePoint Indicator:** This content type represents an indicator created using the Dashboard Designer.

✦ **PerformancePoint Report:** This content type represents a report cre-ated using the Dashboard Designer.

✦ **PerformancePoint Filter:** This content type represents a filter created using the Dashboard Designer.

So there you have it — the essential relationship between the Dashboard Designer and the PerformancePoint content types. (Hey, what it may lack in complexity it makes up for in consistency.)

If you create your SharePoint site using the Business Intelligence Center site template, you'll find the PerformancePoint lists, libraries, and content types all ready to use — neatly tucked into the PerformancePoint Content List.

Adding a new item is easy: On the Items tab of the Content List, click the New Item command. You're presented with a list of PerformancePoint content types (the very same ones just listed here, in fact); just choose the one you want your item to be. Figure 8-12 shows the content types as they appear on the New Item menu. (They may look hauntingly familiar.)

When you select a new item from the list of content types, SharePoint invokes the Dashboard Designer. When you save items in the Dashboard Designer, they appear as items in the PerformancePoint Content List. (Yep, there's definitely a pattern here.)

To find out more about the Dashboard Designer, jump to the "Introducing PerformancePoint Dashboard Designer" section of this chapter.

Figure 8-12:
You can launch the Dashboard Designer directly from the New Item menu.

Reviewing the PerformancePoint Web Parts

PerformancePoint Services provides several Web Parts that you can draw upon to enhance your reports and PerformancePoint Web pages, including these:

✦ **PerformancePoint Report Web Part:** Use this Web Part to display your PerformancePoint Reports on your Web page. The Dashboard Designer uses the Report Web Part when adding reports to your dashboard page.

✦ **PerformancePoint Filter Web Part:** This Web Part displays PerformancePoint filters. You can link the filters to other Web Parts on the Web page to filter their content — providing your users with a dynamic, interactive Web page. The Dashboard Designer uses the Filter Web Part to add filters to your dashboard page.

✦ **PerformancePoint Scorecard Web Part:** This Web Part displays a PerformancePoint scorecard. When configuring this Web Part, you simply associate it with a scorecard that exists in your PerformancePoint Content List (by setting the Location property of the Web Part to the URL of your published scorecard). The Dashboard Designer uses the Scorecard Web Part when adding scorecards to your dashboard page.

✦ **PerformancePoint Stack Selector:** You use this Web Part when you stack several graphs or charts on top of one another in a single Web Part page (or a single area of your Web page), and want to show only one chart at a time. Your users can select one of your graphs from a drop-down list, which brings the chosen graph to the front for viewing. The PerformancePoint Stack Selector Web Part helps you make the most efficient use of your Web-page real estate.

Using Web Parts to create dashboards manually

The Digital Designer isn't the only way to create dashboards. You can also do so manually — by creating a regular Web Part page in SharePoint and then adding your chosen PerformancePoint Web Parts to that page. (For more about Adding Web Parts to a Web Part page in SharePoint, see Book IV, Chapter 3.) If you venture into creating dashboards both in *and* out of Dashboard Designer, here's a list of things you should consider when deciding which method to use:

✦ If you've already created a dashboard manually, you can add non-PerformancePoint SharePoint Web Parts. For example, you can use the SharePoint Query String URL filter Web Part to add more filtering capabilities to your dashboard.

If you created a dashboard in Dashboard Designer and deployed it from there, *and* that dashboard is still connected to Dashboard Designer, *don't edit that dashboard manually.* Here's why:

• When you use Dashboard Designer to modify such a dashboard, and then deploy those changes to SharePoint, you overwrite the Web Part page (.aspx) that represents your dashboard with a new page that reflects your updates.

• If you use the SharePoint Edit Page command or use SharePoint Designer to edit your dashboard, then any changes you make are doomed if you then use Dashboard Designer to deploy the edited dashboard. That's because the deployment process overwrites the old dashboard — in this case, with a Dashboard Designer Web Part page you haven't edited.

✦ After you initially deploy a dashboard from Dashboard Designer, the dashboard has a corresponding Web Part page in your dashboards library. You can copy that Web Part page and store it in another library on your SharePoint site. You can then edit the dashboard copy manually, using either the SharePoint Edit Page in the browser, or using SharePoint Designer to add and remove Web Parts as needed.

✦ If you use Dashboard Designer to update items (such as a scorecard or report) on a stored dashboard copy, your changes apply to the dashboard copy automatically — the dashboard copy isn't overwritten. SharePoint retrieves any content needed for the dashboard copy's PerformancePoint Web Parts from the PerformancePoint Content List. That's because the Content List is updated whenever PerformancePoint items are saved or deployed from Dashboard Designer.

Bottom line: Exercise some caution when you create, deploy, and edit your dashboard. Make sure the methods you use for those tasks are consistent.

Examining the PerformancePoint Architecture

As with many of the service offerings in SharePoint Server 2010, PerformancePoint Services structures its architecture in three tiers that correspond to servers with different roles:

✦ **Front-end Web server:** Your front-end Web server hosts the PerformancePoint Services Web Parts, Web services, and the service-application proxy that communicates with the PerformancePoint Services service application (which sits on the next layer, the application server).

✦ **Application server:** This server hosts the PerformancePoint Services service application, and the Secure Store Service. The Secure Store Service stores the password for the PerformancePoint Services Unattended Service Account. (The what? You read right. See the sidebar, "Who's attending the account?")

✦ **Database server:** As the third tier of the PerformancePoint architecture, the database server hosts the SharePoint content database, the Secure Store database, and PerformancePoint Services database.

For more about three-tier architecture, see Book II, Chapter 1.

✦ **Dashboard Designer:** Although the Dashboard Designer isn't really a tier per se, it's the supreme tool in PerformancePoint Services; it's launched whenever you create a PerformancePoint item in SharePoint. Consider Dashboard Designer as your primary tool for creating and publishing dashboards (and their associated content) to SharePoint.

Figure 8-13 shows you a bird's-eye view of the PerformancePoint Services architecture.

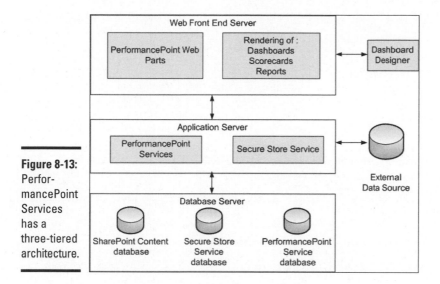

Figure 8-13:
Perfor-
mancePoint
Services
has a
three-tiered
architecture.

Managing PerformancePoint Services

Creating a PerformancePoint Services service application follows the standard service application rules and processes. You have two possible ways to get that job done:

Book III
Chapter 8

Considering
PerformancePoint
Services

+ **Create the service application manually:** For a refresher, with tips on associating a service application with another Web Application, flip to Book II, Chapter 8.

+ **Use the SharePoint Farm Configuration Wizard while installing SharePoint Server Enterprise Edition:** If you do so, you can select a handy option in the wizard that creates the PerformancePoint Services service application (and its associated proxies) automatically.

When you have the service application for PerformancePoint Services up and running, you can manage the service through Central Administration. Fortunately, the management interface of PerformancePoint Services is consistent with that of other SharePoint service applications. It shares a common look and feel with them, which makes administration intuitive.

Although you can start using PerformancePoint Services right away, you might as well set it up the way you like it before you take the plunge. Use numerous configuration settings to fine-tune your implementation. For example, you can specify the query time-out settings for the service. But first things first: The Manage PerformancePoint Services page in Central Administration is where you configure PerformancePoint Services. Here's how you get to it:

Who's attending the account?

Having an Unattended Service Account may seem crazy, but it enables PerformancePoint to use an account with the lowest privilege setting to connect seamlessly to data sources. PerformancePoint 2007 used the Application Pool Identity (see Book II, Chapter 1 for information on Application Pools) to connect to data sources — less than ideal because it can provide access to unauthorized data. The implementation of the Unattended Service Account is common across other business intelligence applications, such as Excel services and a welcome addition to the PerformancePoint architecture. (For more about the Unattended Service Account, see Book III, Chapter 3.)

1. **Navigate to the Central Administration home page.**

2. **From the Application Management section, click Manage service applications.**

The Service Applications page appears, listing all available service applications in alphabetical order.

3. **From the Ribbon menu, select PerformancePoint Services⇨Manage (or simply click PerformancePoint Services).**

The Manage PerformancePoint Services Web page appears.

Configuring the PerformancePoint Service Application Settings

The PerformancePoint Service Application Settings page is the place to configure PerformancePoint Services; your options include these:

✦ **Secure Store and Unattended Service Account:** The Secure Store and Unattended Service account section is where you select the service application that does the work of the Secure Store Service: storing data that the Unattended Service Account uses when authenticating itself with data sources. In addition, you specify the domain username and password of the Unattended Service Account.

Before you can take advantage of the Unattended Service Account, you must first configure the Secure Store Service. For details of that vital task, jump to the "Configuring the Secure Store" section of this chapter.

✦ **Comments:** In the Comments section, you specify settings for the comments that users (with appropriate permissions) can apply to annotations in the scorecard cells. Comments settings include

- **Enable comments:** This setting is enabled by default.

- **Maximum number of annotations:** The default value for this setting is 1000 cells.

- **Delete Comments by Date:** Here you set a date for the automatic deletion of comments.

✦ **Cache:** Here you enter the duration for items to remain in the cache. *Caching* refers to the process of temporarily storing items that are frequently accessed. Caching decreases the load times for future requests — but it also makes more demands on server resources. You can fine-tune the cache setting to suit your SharePoint implementation by entering the duration times (in seconds) for the KPI icon cache.

The default value for this setting is 10 seconds.

✦ **Data Sources:** Here you set the maximum duration for PerformancePoint to wait for a response before canceling a query. This interval is the *data source query timeout*.

The default value for this setting is 300 seconds.

✦ **Filters:** Here you specify values for the following settings:

- **Remember user filter selections for:** Use this setting to specify the number of days that PerformancePoint Services should retain user-selected filter values. When the number of days is reached, PerformancePoint clears the filters.

The default value for this setting is 90 days.

- **Maximum members to load in filter tree:** Use this setting to set the maximum number of members to retrieve into a filter of the Tree type. (For more about filter types, see the "Understanding the PerformancePoint Lingo" section at the start of this chapter.)

The default setting for this value is 5,000 members.

✦ **Select Measure Control:** Use the settings in the Select Measure Control section to define the maximum number of measures to retrieve into a dashboard's Select Measure control. A measure in PerformancePoint terminology represents the size, or scale of something that is of importance to an organization. For example, a Key Performance Indicator (KPI) is a predefined measure used to track the performance of a strategic goal or initiative.

The default setting for this value is 1,000 measures.

✦ **Show Details:** The Show Details section allows you to specify values for the following settings:

- **Initial retrieval limit:** Use the Initial retrieval limit setting to set a limit for the number of rows initially returned when a user clicks "Show Details".

The default value for this setting is 1,000 rows.

Book III Chapter 8

Considering PerformancePoint Services

- **Maximum retrieval limit: Fixed Limit:** Use the Maximum retrieval limit setting to set a fixed limit for the maximum number of rows that can be returned when a user clicks "Show Details".

  This setting is selected by default, with a default value of 10,000 rows.

- **Maximum retrieval limit: Limit controlled by Analysis Services:** Use the Limit controlled by Analysis Services setting to inform PerformancePoint Services that it should retrieve the maximum retrieval limit setting from SQL Analysis Services.

  This setting isn't selected by default.

✦ **Decomposition Tree:** Use the settings in the Decomposition Tree section to define the maximum number of individual items (per level) that PerformancePoint Services returns to the Decomposition Tree visualization. Values for this setting should be in the range of 0 to 1,000,000. A Decomposition Tree is a data visualization tool in PerformancePoint Services that helps users analyze complex data in a hierarchical view.

  The default value for this setting is 250 items.

Configuring PerformancePoint Security

The adoption of PerformancePoint Services into SharePoint Server 2010 means that PerformancePoint content and administration settings can be managed and monitored from a central point.

When you navigate to the PerformancePoint Services Management page you'll notice a number of settings that are specifically related to security. The following sections show you how to configure these settings according to your business needs.

Configuring the locations of trusted data sources

The PerformancePoint Services Site Features feature adds PerformancePoint lists and library templates to your SharePoint site. If you're using the Business Intelligence Center site, the lists and libraries are provisioned automatically; if not then you create each content location manually. One of the PerformancePoint libraries includes a Data Connections library, which is used to store the connection information to data sources that you want to use for your PerformancePoint dashboards.

Use the Trusted Data Source Locations page to specify the Data Connection libraries in your SharePoint environment from which PerformancePoint Services may retrieve its data-source information.

The default value for this setting is to trust all SharePoint locations, which means that PerformancePoint Services can retrieve data source information from any site in which the PerformancePoint Services features have been enabled. As an administrator you may want to change this setting so that you can control and limit the locations in which PerformancePoint Services retrieves its data source information. For example, for ease of administration you may want to dedicate one SharePoint site for the hosting of PerformancePoint data source information.

Follow these steps to configure the Trusted Data Source Locations setting to limit the location from which PerformancePoint Services may retrieve its data source information:

1. **Using your browser, navigate to the Central Administration home page.**

2. **From the Application Management section, click Manage service applications.**

   The Service Applications management page appears listing all the service applications in your SharePoint implementation.

3. **From the list of service applications, select PerformancePoint Service Application.**

4. **On the Service Application tab, in the Operations group, click Manage.**

   The Manage PerformancePoint Services: PerformancePoint Service Application page appears.

5. **Click Trusted Data Source Locations.**

   The Trusted Data Source Locations page appears, with the default setting set to All SharePoint locations.

6. **Click only specific locations, and click Apply.**

   The Trusted Data Source Locations page refreshes to display a new Add Trusted Data Source Location link.

7. **Click Add Trusted Data Source Location.**

   The Edit Trusted Data Source Location Web dialog box appears.

8. **In the Address field, enter the URL to the SharePoint site that hosts the trusted data source location.**

   The URL that you enter must be the URL to a valid SharePoint site collection, site, or document library. SharePoint will let you know if the URL is valid.

9. **In the Location Type section, select the type of location that matches the URL that you entered in step 8.**

   For example:

   • If you entered the URL to a site collection, then select Site Collection (and subtree) as your location type.

- If you entered the URL to a SharePoint site, then select Site (and sub-tree) as your location type.

- If you entered the URL to a data connection library in your SharePoint site, then select Document Library as your location type.

10. **Repeat Steps 7 through 9 for each trusted location that you want to add.**

If you try to add a data source in Dashboard Designer that isn't a PerformancePoint-trusted location, you get the curt little error message shown in Figure 8-14.

Figure 8-14:
Data Sources must be listed in the Trusted Data Source Locations.

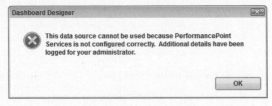

Configuring Trusted Content Locations

The PerformancePoint Services Site Features feature adds PerformancePoint lists and library templates to your SharePoint site. If you're using the Business Intelligence Center site, the lists and libraries are provisioned automatically; if not then you create each content location manually. One of the PerformancePoint lists includes a PerformancePoint Content List, which is used to store content such as dashboards and scorecards.

Use the Trusted Content Locations page to specify the lists in your SharePoint environment in which PerformancePoint Services may store its content.

The default value for this setting is to trust all SharePoint locations, which means that PerformancePoint Services can store its content in any site in which the PerformancePoint Services features have been enabled. As an administrator you may want to change this setting so that you can control and limit the locations in which PerformancePoint Services stores its content. For example, for ease of administration you may want to dedicate one SharePoint site for the hosting of PerformancePoint content.

Follow these steps to configure the Trusted Content Locations setting to limit the location in which PerformancePoint Services may store its content.

1. **Using your browser, navigate to the Central Administration home page.**

2. **From the Application Management section, click Manage service applications.**

   The Service Applications management page appears listing all the service applications in your SharePoint implementation.

3. **From the list of service applications, select PerformancePoint Service Application.**

4. **On the Service Application tab, in the Operations group, click Manage.**

   The Manage PerformancePoint Services: PerformancePoint Service Application page appears.

5. **Click Trusted Content Locations.**

   The Trusted Content Locations page appears, with the default setting set to All SharePoint locations.

6. **Clickly specific locations, and click Apply.**

   The Trusted Content Locations page refreshes to display a new Add Trusted Content Location link.

7. **Click Add Trusted Content Location.**

   The Edit Trusted Content Location Web dialog box appears.

8. **In the Address field, enter the URL to the SharePoint site that hosts the trusted content location.**

   The URL that you enter must be the URL to a valid SharePoint site collection, site, or list. SharePoint will let you know if the URL is valid.

9. **In the Location Type section, select the type of location that matches the URL that you entered in step 8.**

   For example:

   - If you entered the URL to a site collection, then select Site Collection (and subtree) as your location type.

   - If you entered the URL to a SharePoint site, then select Site (and subtree) as your location type.

   - If you entered the URL to a data connection library in your SharePoint site, then select List as your location type.

   Repeat Steps 7 through 9 for each trusted location that you want to add.

Configuring the Secure Store

Unless Kerberos is already defined in your environment, your PerformancePoint Services configuration will use a shared domain account, known as the Unattended Service Account, for authenticating to data sources.

PerformancePoint uses the Secure Store Service to store the password for the Unattended Service Account; the username information for the Unattended Service Account is stored in the PerformancePoint Services configuration database. You can think of the Secure Store Service as the SharePoint Server 2010 replacement for the Single Sign-On (SSO) feature that comes with SharePoint Server 2007. The SSO stored account names and passwords and associated them with their equivalents in SharePoint; the idea was, and is, to facilitate seamless connection to line-of-business applications.

Before you can take advantage of the Unattended Service Account in PerformancePoint, you have to configure the Secure Store Service so PerformancePoint Services can use it.

Follow these steps to configure the Secure Store Service for use with PerformancePoint Services:

1. **Using your browser, navigate to the Central Administration home page.**

2. **From the Application Management section, click Manage service applications.**

   The Service Applications management page appears listing all the service applications in your SharePoint implementation.

3. **From the list of service applications, select Secure Store Service Application.**

   The Secure Store Service management page appears. If this is the first time using the Secure Store Service, the page displays a message stating that before creating a new Secure Store Target Application, you must first generate a new key for the Secure Store Service. If you've already generated a key for your Secure Store Service, you can skip to step 5.

   If the Secure Store Service application doesn't appear in the list of service applications, you'll have to create the service application and its associated proxy. You can find instructions on how to create and configure service applications in Book II, Chapter 8.

4. **On the Edit tab, in the Key Management group, click Generate New Key.**

   The key is used to encrypt and decrypt the credentials that are stored in the Secure Store database. The Generate New Key Web dialog box appears, as shown in Figure 8-15, requesting a pass phrase from which a new key is generated.

5. **In the Pass Phrase field and the Confirm Pass Phrase field, enter your passphrase.**

The pass phrase is case-sensitive and must contain at least three of the following:

- Uppercase letters
- Lowercase letters
- Numerals
- At least one of the following special characters:

    "! " # $ % & ' ( ) * + , - . / : ; < = > ? @ [\ ] ^ _ ` { | } ~

The pass phrase that you enter isn't stored; you'll have to remember it the next time you have to refresh the key (for example, when you add a new application server to your server farm). Be sure you record the password securely so that you can enter the pass phrase successfully when needed.

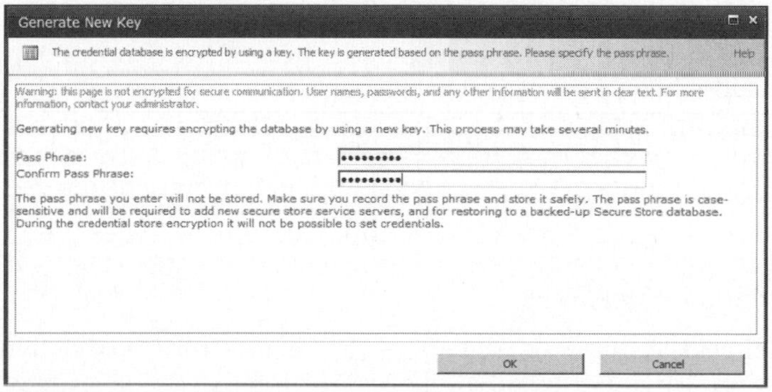

Figure 8-15:
Make sure you record the pass phrase that you use to generate your key.

When you've entered the pass phrase, the Secure Store Service generates a new key and can now accept requests from PerformancePoint Services. When you configure the Unattended Service Account from the PerformancePoint Services configuration page, PerformancePoint communicates with the Secure Store Service to create a target application in the Secure Store. The target application will be specific to PerformancePoint and is a container used to store the password securely so that you can ultimately access your data sources securely.

Configuring the Unattended Service Account

When you have your Secure Store Service configured correctly, you can configure the Unattended Service Account in PerformancePoint Services. The *Unattended Service Account* is what PerformancePoint uses — an account with the most restricted level of network privileges — to connect seamlessly to data sources. You can find the Unattended Service Account cropping up in other SharePoint service applications used for business intelligence (such as Excel Services).

Follow these steps to configure the Unattended Service Account for PerformancePoint Services:

1. **Using your browser, navigate to the Central Administration home page.**

2. **From the Application Management section, click Manage service applications.**

   The Service Applications management page appears, listing all the service applications in your SharePoint implementation.

3. **From the list of service applications, select PerformancePoint Service Application.**

   The ribbon menu activates the commands that you can perform on the selected service. Instead of selecting the PerformancePoint service, you can simply click the service which will open the PerformancePoint Service management page, effectively skipping Step 4.

4. **In the Operations group, on the Service Application tab, click Manage.**

   The Manage PerformancePoint Services: PerformancePoint Service Application page appears.

5. **Click PerformancePoint Service Application Settings.**

   The PerformancePoint Service Application Settings page appears.

6. **In the Secure Store Service Application field, enter the Secure Store Service application you want to use to store the Unattended Service Account Password.**

   SharePoint uses the default — the Secure Store Service in the current proxy group — automatically.

7. **In the User Name field, enter the domain account to use as the Unattended Service Account.**

8. **In the Password field, enter the password for the Unattended Service Account.**

   The password is stored in the Secure Store Service database, and the user name is stored in the PerformancePoint Service database.

9. **Click OK.**

   The Unattended Service Account is now configured and ready for use when connecting to data sources in Dashboard Designer.

Activating PerformancePoint Services

Before you can begin to take advantage of PerformancePoint Services, you must have its features — including the associated lists, libraries, content types, and Web Parts — up and running in your SharePoint site. As is often the case in SharePoint, you have two ways to get this job done:

✦ The quickest route is simply to create a PerformancePoint Services site using the Business Intelligence Center site template. (More about that approach in the next subsection of this chapter.)

✦ Alternatively, you can configure the required features manually. We get to that method a little later in this chapter.

With either approach, the goal is to get you up and running with PerformancePoint as quickly and painlessly as possible.

Creating a Business Intelligence Center Site

When you use the Farm Installation Wizards to install SharePoint 2010, the service applications for business intelligence — including PerformancePoint Services — are automatically configured and ready for use. When these services are up and running, you can take immediate advantage of the functionality they offer in your SharePoint sites.

Availing yourself of these service applications can be as easy as falling off the proverbial log: Create a SharePoint site based on the Business Intelligence Center site template. The Business Intelligence Center site provides a starting point: a PerformancePoint site template from which you can launch the Dashboard Designer and start building and managing your PerformancePoint data.

Here's how to create a Business Intelligence Center SharePoint site from Central Administration, step by step:

1. **Using your browser, navigate to the Central Administration home page.**

2. **From the Application Management section, click Create Site Collections.**

   The Create Site Collection Web page appears.

3. **Select the Web Application in which you want to create the new site.**

   If the Web Application that you want is not selected, click Change Web Application, and then click the Web Application in which you want to create your new site collection.

4. **Enter the Title and the Description for your new site.**

5. **In the Web Site Address section, enter the URL for your new site.**

6. **In the Template Selection section, click the Enterprise tab and then select the Business Intelligence Center site template.**

7. **In the Primary Site Collection Administrator section, enter the username for the person who will be the main Site Collection Administrator for your site.**

8. **In the Secondary Site Collection Administrator section, enter the username for the person who will be the Secondary Site Collection Administrator for your site.**

9. **Click OK.**

   SharePoint creates a SharePoint site based on the Business Intelligence Center site template. When the site has been successfully created, you'll receive a notification, along with a link to your new site. When you click the link, the Business Intelligence Center home page appears.

   Your new site automatically includes PerformancePoint capabilities.

Enabling PerformancePoint on an existing site

If you have a SharePoint site that was created using a site template *other* than that of the Business Intelligence Center, you can still enable PerformancePoint features by activating them manually on that site. The following subsections detail the procedure.

Activate the PerformancePoint Services Features

Follow these steps to enable PerformancePoint functionality in an existing SharePoint site:

1. **Using your browser, navigate to the home page of the root of your SharePoint site collection.**

2. **From the Site Actions menu, click Site Settings.**

3. **In the Site Collection Administration section, click Site collection features.**

   The Site Collection Administration Features page appears.

4. **Choose SharePoint Server Publishing Infrastructure, and click Activate.**

5. **Click the Activate button that appears next to the PerformancePoint Site Collection feature.**

   This site-collection feature installs the PerformancePoint site column, content types, and site definitions. (For more about the content types that are installed, flip to the "Reviewing the PerformancePoint Content Types" section of this chapter.)

   You can verify that the feature was activated successfully by examining the site's content types — if you find that the PerformancePoint group exists on the site, then the feature activation was a success.

6. **From the Site Actions menu, click Site Settings to navigate back to the Site Settings page.**

   Alternatively, you can click the Site Settings link on the breadcrumb trail to navigate back to the Site Settings page.

7. **From the Site Actions section, click Manage site features.**

   The site settings feature page appears.

8. **Click the Activate button that appears next to the PerformancePoint Services Site Features.**

   This site feature deploys the PerformancePoint lists and document library templates necessary for running PerformancePoint in your site.

   You can verify that the feature was activated successfully by examining the list and library templates available when you want to create a list or a library:

   a. *From the Site Actions menu, click More Options.*

   b. *In the Filter By section, click Library.*

   In the list of available libraries, if the Dashboards Library template appears then the feature activation was a success. The Dashboards library is where you store your dashboard definition files.

   c. *In the Filter By section, click List.*

   In the list of available lists, if the PerformancePoint Content List template appears, then the feature activation was a success. The PerformancePoint Content List triggers the Dashboard Designer.

Create the PerformancePoint List and Libraries

When you enable the PerformancePoint Services Site Features, several templates are added — representing each of the PerformancePoint stores. If your PerformancePoint site wasn't created using the Business Intelligence Center site template, then you'll have to set up those PerformancePoint stores manually. You'll have to create a list or library for each of the following:

✦ Data Connections or PerformancePoint library to store data source connections.

✦ Dashboards library to store the dashboards that you deploy from Dashboard Designer.

✦ PerformancePoint Content List to store the reusable PerformancePoint content that shows up in your dashboards, such as KPIs, scorecards, and reports.

Follow these steps to create the PerformancePoint Data Connections library:

1. **Using your browser, navigate to the SharePoint site in which you activated the PerformancePoint Services features.**

2. **From the Site Actions menu, click More Options.**

   The Create page appears listing all the available templates from which you can create your lists and libraries.

3. **From the Filter By section, click Library.**

   The list of available templates is filtered to show library templates.

4. **From the list of available templates, click Data Connections Library For.**

   Use the Data Connections Library For template to create a library that stores the connection information for the data sources PerformancePoint will use.

5. **In the Name field, enter the name of your Data Connections library, for example the Business Intelligence Center names its library Data Connections.**

6. **Click Create.**

   SharePoint creates your Data Connections library. When that's done, the Dashboard Designer recognizes the library as one of its data stores.

 Before PerformancePoint Services can use the data sources defined in your Data Connection library, the location must be trusted by PerformancePoint Services. You can find out how to set the trusted locations in the "Configuring locations for trusted data sources" section of this chapter.

Follow these steps to create the PerformancePoint Content List:

1. **Using your browser, navigate to the SharePoint site in which you activated the PerformancePoint Services features.**

2. **From the Site Actions menu, click More Options.**

   The Create page appears, listing all the available templates from which you can create your lists and libraries.

3. **From the Filter By section, click List.**

   The list of available templates is filtered to show list templates.

4. **From the list of available templates, click Performance Content List.**

   Use the PerformancePoint Content List template to create a SharePoint list that stores PerformancePoint data such as scorecards and reports.

5. **In the Name field, enter the name of your PerformancePoint Content List, for example the Business Intelligence Center names its list PerformancePoint Content.**

6. **Click Create.**

   SharePoint creates your PerformancePoint Content List, and then the Dashboard Designer recognizes the list as one of its data stores.

 Before PerformancePoint Services can use the content stored in your PerformancePoint Content List, the location must be trusted by PerformancePoint Services. You can find out how to set the trusted locations in the "Configuring Trusted Content Locations" section of this chapter.

Follow these steps to create the PerformancePoint Dashboards library:

1. **Using your browser, navigate to the SharePoint site in which you activated the PerformancePoint Services features.**

2. **From the Site Actions menu, click More Options.**

   The Create page appears, listing all the available templates from which you can create your lists and libraries.

3. **From the Filter By section, click Library.**

   The list of available templates is filtered to show library templates.

4. **From the list of available templates, click Dashboards Library.**

   Use the Dashboards Library template to create a library that stores the dashboards you deploy from the Dashboard Designer.

5. **In the Name field, enter the name of your Dashboards library.**

   For example, the Business Intelligence Center names its library Dashboards (hey, what do you want from a software feature — imagination?).

6. **Click Create.**

   SharePoint creates your Data Connections library, after which the Dashboard Designer recognizes the library as one of its data stores.

Introducing PerformancePoint Dashboard Designer

The Dashboard Designer is *the* PerformancePoint Services tool for creating your dashboard and the associated elements it contains (such as KPIs and scorecards).

Launching the Dashboard Designer

The first time you use the Dashboard Designer, SharePoint tends to basics: It downloads and installs the Dashboard Designer tool on your computer. The rest of this chapter shows how to get your Dashboard Designer up and running.

Dashboard Designer Prerequisites

Before you can install Dashboard Designer on your computer, you must have the following software installed:

✦ **.NET Framework 3.5 SP1:** Dashboard Designer is a .NET Framework ClickOnce application and as such requires the .NET Framework 3.5 SP1. The ClickOnce architecture means the application is hosted, and the client deployment doesn't require any installation or media files. If the .NET framework isn't installed, you'll see an error message indicating that the System.Data.Entity assembly doesn't exist (so you'd better not build anything on it). Figure 8-16 shows the error message that may appear.

✦ **Visio 2007 or 2010 Professional (optional):** Before you can create Strategy Maps using Dashboard Designer, you'll need to have Visio installed. Strategy maps are reports in PerformancePoint that you use to associate KPI data with shapes in Visio so your data is easier to visualize.

✦ **Report Viewer 2008 (optional):** Before you can create and edit SQL Server Reports, Report View 2008 has to be already installed.

Figure 8-16:
You receive an error if the .NET Framework 3.5 SP1 isn't installed.

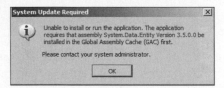

Installing Dashboard Designer

If you have a Business Intelligence Center site up and running, follow these steps to install Dashboard Designer on your computer:

1. **Navigate to the home page of your Business Intelligence Center site.**

2. **From the Web page content, click the Start using PerformancePoint Services link.**

   A link labeled *Start using PerformancePoint Services* appears in the center of the page as you hover your mouse pointer over each of the following instructional areas:

   • Monitor Key Performance

   • Build and Share Reports

   • Create Dashboards

   The PerformancePoint page appears, as shown in Figure 8-17, from which you can launch the Dashboard Designer, in addition to discovering more information on how to create PerformancePoint content.

3. **Click Run Dashboard Designer.**

   If this is your first time using the Dashboard Designer, the installation process will kick in — and an Application Run security warning will appear. Otherwise the Dashboard Designer application appears and you won't have to trudge through these installation steps.

4. **In the Application Run security dialog box, click Run to launch the** `DashboardDesigner.exe` **application.**

The `DashboardDesigner.exe` application runs — it installs the Designer on your computer, and then launches the Dashboard Designer application. Figure 8-18 shows the Dashboard Designer as it looks the first time it's launched — notice that it displays the Data Connections library and the PerformancePoint Content List in the Workspace browser that appears on the left. You can now begin creating your PerformancePoint dashboards.

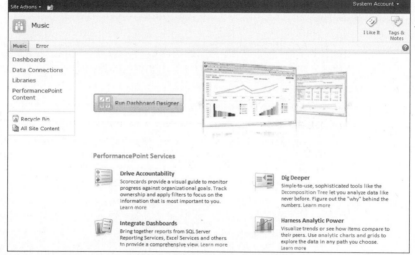

Figure 8-17: You can click Run Dashboard Designer directly from the Web page.

Book III Chapter 8

Considering PerformancePoint Services

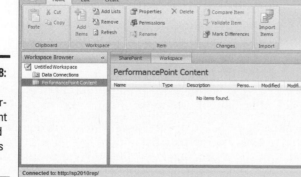

Figure 8-18: The first time PerformancePoint Dashboard Designer is launched.

If you don't have a Business Intelligence Center site up and running, but you do have PerformancePoint Services up and running in your SharePoint site, follow these steps to install Dashboard Designer on your computer:

1. **Using your browser, navigate to the PerformancePoint Content List.**

2. **Click Add new Item.**

   If this is your first time using the Dashboard Designer, the installation process will begin, and an Application Run security warning will appear. Otherwise the Dashboard Designer application appears and you won't have to slog on through these installation steps.

3. **In the Application Run security dialog box, click Run to allow the** `DashboardDesigner.exe` **application to execute.**

   The `DashboardDesigner.exe` application runs, installs the Designer on your computer, and then launches the Dashboard Designer application. You can now begin creating your PerformancePoint dashboards.

Opening Dashboard Designer from the Start menu

When you have the Dashboard Designer installed on your computer, you'll notice that a PerformancePoint Dashboard Designer shortcut appears in the SharePoint folder on the menu when you choose Start⇨All Programs.

To launch the Dashboard Designer, follow these steps:

1. **From your desktop, click the Start menu.**

2. **Click All Programs⇨SharePoint.**

3. **Click PerformancePoint Dashboard Designer.**

Opening from PerformancePoint Site Template

If you have a Business Intelligence Site Center up and running, follow these steps to launch the Dashboard Designer:

1. **Using your browser, navigate to the home page of your Business Intelligence Center site.**

2. **In the Create Scorecards with PerformancePoint Services section of the page, click Start using PerformancePoint Services.**

   The PerformancePoint page appears, as shown in Figure 8-17. From there you can not only launch the Dashboard Designer, but also find more information about creating PerformancePoint content.

3. **Click Run Dashboard Designer.**

   If this is your first time using the Dashboard Designer, the installation process blasts off and an Application Run security warning appears.

Otherwise the Dashboard Designer application appears, and you won't have to follow these installation steps to the bitter end.

Do you notice a certain family resemblance between these steps and the earlier ones in this chapter? Let's hear it for consistent look and feel!

Launching the Dashboard Designer this way loads *all* PerformancePoint content for the site into the Designer, rather than loading individual items.

Opening from PerformancePoint Content List

Follow these steps to launch the Dashboard Designer when you're creating a new item in the PerfomancePoint Content List:

1. **Using your browser, navigate to the PerformancePoint Content List in your SharePoint site.**

2. **From the Items Ribbon, click the arrow next to the New Item menu option, or click a link on the page labeled *Add new item.***

3. **Click the PerformancePoint content type that you want to create.**

   The Dashboard Designer loads and displays the wizard or pages associated with creating an item that fits the content type you chose to create. For example, if you chose to create a PerformancePoint Dashboard, then Dashboard Designer launches, presenting you with a dialog box from which you can select your dashboard layout.

Follow these steps to launch the Dashboard Designer to edit or view an existing item in the PerformancePoint Content List:

1. **Using your browser, navigate to the PerformancePoint Content List in your SharePoint site.**

2. **From the list of items, click the down arrow that appears next the item you want to open in the Dashboard Designer.**

   The item's shortcut menu appears.

3. **From the shortcut menu, click Edit in Dashboard Designer.**

   The Dashboard Designer loads the item for editing.

Introducing the Workspace Browser

When the Dashboard Designer opens, you're presented with the Workspace browser from which you can navigate the dashboard objects in your SharePoint site. In the center pane of the Designer, you can preview, edit, and configure your dashboard items. The Details pane appears on the right and presents you with a list of items that are relevant to the currently selected item.

The Workspace browser is context-sensitive, filtering the content that appears in the Designer according to the object you've selected. For example, if you navigate to the PerformancePoint Data Connections library in Dashboard Designer and click the Create tab, you'll notice that the Data Source command is the only command available on the Ribbon menu. Figure 8-19 shows the Dashboard Designer with the Data Source Connection item selected from the Data Connections library in the Workspace browser. The center pane is where you configure the data source settings; the Details pane displays the PerformancePoint items that make use of the current data source.

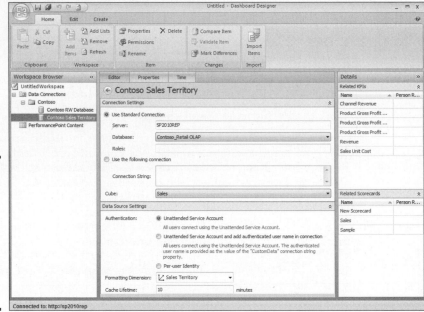

Figure 8-19: The menu options reflect the item selected in the Workspace Browser.

Reviewing the Ribbon Menu

PerformancePoint Dashboard Designer provides three tabs that contain the commands that you need to create your PerformancePoint items:

✦ **Home Tab:** The Home Tab offers commands that help you manage the PerformancePoint items in the Workspace and in your SharePoint PerformancePoint lists and libraries. For example, if you want to delete an item in your Workspace, you can do it in two steps:

    a. From the Workspace browser, click the item you want to delete.

    b. On the Home tab, in the Item group, click Delete.

✦ **Edit Tab:** The Edit tab is where you find commands that help you configure your PerformancePoint items. The commands that appear on the Edit tab vary, depending on the item you've selected. For example, if you're editing a PerformancePoint scorecard, the menu shows options that are specific to working with scorecards; for instance, Collapse All Rows collapses the scorecard view to display only the top level of rows in the scorecard.

✦ **Create Tab:** In the Create tab, you find commands that help you create your PerformancePoint items and reports. Figure 8-20 shows the Dashboard Designer Create tab in the Ribbon.

Figure 8-20:
You can create your PerformancePoint items from the Create tab.

Saving PerformancePoint Items

When you save your changes in PerformancePoint Dashboard Designer, your items are saved and updated in the SharePoint list or library associated with that item:

✦ **Data connections** are saved to the SharePoint Data Connections for PerformancePoint library.

✦ **Indicators** are saved to the SharePoint PerformancePoint Content List.

✦ **KPIs** are saved to the SharePoint PerformancePoint Content List.

✦ **Scorecards** are saved to the SharePoint PerformancePoint Content List.

✦ **Filters** are saved to the SharePoint PerformancePoint Content List.

✦ **Reports** are saved to the SharePoint PerformancePoint Content List.

✦ **Dashboard definition** items are saved to the SharePoint PerformancePoint Content List.

All logical enough. And here's yet more logic: Follow these steps to save your PerformancePoint items to SharePoint:

1. **From the Workspace browser, click the PerformancePoint item you want to save.**

2. **Right-click the item, and then click Save from the shortcut menu.**

Alternatively, you can click the Save icon from the Quick Launch bar that appears at the top of the Dashboard Designer.

If your PerformancePoint items have changes that haven't yet been saved to SharePoint, a pencil image appears on the icon as a quick reminder.

Deploying a dashboard to SharePoint

When you create and save your dashboard in Dashboard Designer, you're working with the dashboard definition. The dashboard (*.aspx) page that your users view is created when you deploy your dashboard to SharePoint.

Follow these steps to deploy your PerformancePoint dashboard to SharePoint:

1. **Launch PerformancePoint Dashboard Designer.**

2. **From the Workspace browser, right-click the dashboard item you want to deploy, and then click Deploy to SharePoint from the shortcut menu.**

Congratulations — now you have a snazzy new PerformancePoint dashboard right where you can see it.

Chapter 9: Considering Visio Services

In This Chapter

✓ **Reviewing Visio Services**

✓ **Configuring the Visio Graphics Service**

✓ **Understanding the role of the Secure Store Service**

✓ **Publishing Visio Diagrams to SharePoint**

✓ **Creating Workflow Blueprints**

✓ **Creating Strategy Maps with PerformancePoint Dashboard Designer**

Among the major tools for business intelligence (BI) in SharePoint Server 2010 Enterprise Edition are the service applications it includes. And being able to picture a business trend accurately can save words, time, and headaches — sometimes a little timely insight is better than aspirin.

Visio Services helps you translate business insights into a dynamic visual form by bringing interactive versions of your Visio diagrams into SharePoint. For example, you can Web enable a Visio diagram that contains an organization chart listing the employees in each department. The Visio diagram can be configured in such a way so that when you click a department — such as Sales — SharePoint presents a dashboard containing metrics to show how that department is performing as a whole.

Tools that help you gain insight into your business through the monitoring, analysis, and reporting of data make up a (presently hot) capability you'll encounter throughout this book: business intelligence (BI). SharePoint 2010 bristles with BI tools — PerformancePoint Services, Visio Services, and Excel Services prominent among them. (Business problems had just better look out.)

In this chapter, we turn your attention to Visio Services and show you how to get its service application up and running in your SharePoint environment. You can read information on PerformancePoint Services in Book III, Chapter 8 and on Excel Services in Book II, Chapter 3 and Book IV, Chapter 4.

If some of the procedures in this chapter seem a lot like those you may have followed in other chapters, that isn't deja vu — not exactly, anyway. It's just the miracle of consistent software design.

Reviewing Visio Services

Visio Services is a new service offering introduced with SharePoint Server 2010 Enterprise Edition, allowing you to render your Visio diagrams through the browser. The rendering capability is offered through the Visio Web Access Web Part, allowing you to view, zoom in and out of, and refresh your Visio Web drawing — directly from your browser.

Figure 9-1 shows an example of a Visio Web drawing that was published to SharePoint and rendered in the browser.

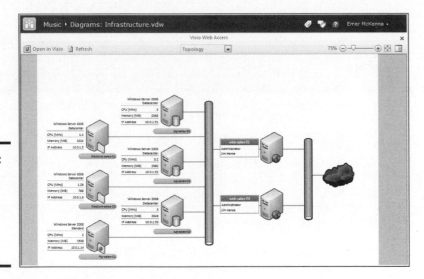

Figure 9-1: You can view your Visio Web drawings in your browser.

Installing Microsoft Silverlight gives you (and your users) the best interactive and visual experience with your Visio Web diagrams: Drawings load faster and appear clearer. If you don't have Silverlight installed, you'll see the Visio diagram in PNG format — adequate, but nothing to write home about.

One simple capability — publishing Visio diagrams for rendering in SharePoint — brings many immediate benefits to your organization:

✦ **Cost savings by removing dependency on the Visio client:** Only the authors of Visio diagrams actually need to have the Visio client application installed on their computers. No longer does your office receptionist need special software just to view your company's organization chart.

✦ **Diagrams are accessible and current:** When you can publish your Visio diagrams to SharePoint for rendering in the browser, one of the biggest advantages is that the version of the diagram your users are viewing through the browser is the most up-to-date version.

✦ **No need to convert your Visio diagrams:** Many organizations didn't deploy Visio on everyone's computers, but instead required Visio authors to convert, or publish their diagrams to a more accessible format, such as PDF. This meant that the Visio authors had to maintain multiple copies of their diagrams, and each time a change was made they had to go through the conversion and dissemination process. With Visio Services, your Visio authors can publish their Visio diagrams directly to SharePoint, removing the need for managing multiple files.

✦ **Manage Visio diagrams centrally:** When you deploy your Visio diagram to SharePoint, you have a centralized version of the diagram, allowing you to easily update, maintain, and back up your diagrams.

✦ **Make full use of SharePoint Foundation Platform:** With a Visio diagram deployed to SharePoint, you can take advantage of all the capabilities that come with the SharePoint platform. For example, you can control who has access to your Visio diagrams by applying permissions — just as you would for a document in a SharePoint document library — and you can use SharePoint document-management capabilities (such as version control and check-in/check-out) to prevent mutant versions of the diagrams from cropping up.

✦ **SharePoint Workflow Integration:** Visio Services provides integration with SharePoint Designer — so you can use your Visio diagrams as blueprints for SharePoint workflows. (Trust us, it's way better than drawing on a cocktail napkin.) In fact, Visio 2010 introduces a new Microsoft SharePoint Workflow Visio template. Here are some intriguing possibilities:

- You can drag and drop shapes onto your Visio diagram just as you would if you were creating a basic flowchart.

- When you've authored your workflow process, you can export the file in a format that SharePoint Designer understands, import this file into SharePoint Designer, and so attach your workflow process to SharePoint content.

- You can also export workflows designed in SharePoint Designer to a Visio diagram for visualization. You can then take this exported file and import it into Visio. There you can document your SharePoint workflows so your business stakeholders can verify and validate the workflow process before implementation.

✦ **Connect to data sources:** You can connect your Visio diagrams to data sources, enabling you to click elements in your diagram and retrieve more detail from the connected data source. By default, Visio Services refreshes the data from connected data sources — at an interval of once every minute — ensuring that the data presented to your users is accurate and up to date.

✦ **Interactive Web Pages:** You can create Web Part pages that connect data in your Visio diagrams to other data in your SharePoint site — bringing your diagrams to life by making them interactive. For example, clicking a shape in your Visio diagram and updating the value associated with the shape could update the content of another Web Part on the page — automatically.

✦ **Business Intelligence Integration:** Because Visio Services provides integration with PerformancePoint Services, you can publish strategy maps you created in Visio to PerformancePoint dashboards — or simply create your strategy maps in the PerformancePoint Dashboard Designer.

Keep a couple of points in mind when you use Visio with SharePoint:

✦ You don't need Visio installed on your computer if you want to simply view Visio diagrams published to Visio Services.

✦ If you want to author and publish your Visio diagrams to SharePoint Server 2010, you need either Visio Professional 2010 or Visio Premium 2010 installed on your computer. Other versions of Visio 2010 don't support publishing to SharePoint.

Managing the Visio Graphics Service

Creating a service application for the Visio Graphics Service follows the standard service application rules and processes. Here are your options:

✦ If you use the SharePoint Farm Configuration Wizard during your installation of SharePoint Server Enterprise Edition, you can choose an option that creates the service application for Visio Graphics Services — and the associated proxies — automatically.

✦ If you want to create the service application manually, or you want to associate the service application with another Web Application, jump to Book II, Chapter 7 for a refresher.

Whichever approach you use, when you have the Visio Graphics Service service application up and running, you can manage the service through Central Administration.

The management interface of the Visio Graphics Service shares a consistent look and feel with other SharePoint service applications, which helps keep administration of the service as intuitive as possible.

Configuring the Visio Graphics Service Settings

Although you can start using Visio Services right away, first things first: Have a look at the configuration settings and fine-tune your implementation before you charge ahead. (For example, you can specify the maximum size of a diagram that can be rendered by Visio Services.)

You can find the configuration settings for Visio Services on the Manage the Visio Graphics Service page in Central Administration. Here's how you get there:

1. **Navigate to the Central Administration home page.**

2. **From the Application Management section, click Manage service applications.**

    The Service Applications page appears, listing all available service applications in alphabetical order.

3. **Select Visio Graphics Services and, from the Ribbon menu, click Manage (or you can simply click Visio Graphics Services).**

    The Manage the Visio Graphics Services Web page appears.

4. **Click Global Settings.**

    The Visio Graphics Service Settings page appears, from which you can manage the performance, security, and data connection refresh settings.

On the Visio Graphics Services Application Settings page, you'll find these configuration settings for Visio Services:

✦ **Maximum Diagram Size:** You can use the Maximum Diagram Size setting to specify the maximum size (in MB) for a Web drawing that can be rendered in the browser. The larger the value used for this setting, the slower the performance you get on the server — especially if the server is under heavy load. Of course, if you set the limit too small, you may prevent more complex Web drawings from being rendered. Find the setting that best suits your organization and its IT infrastructure; that may take some trial and error.

    The default value for this setting is 5 MB; valid values for this setting range from 1 MB to 50 MB.

✦ **Minimum Cache Age:** You can use the Minimum Cache Age setting to specify the minimum number of minutes that a Web drawing is cached in memory. The smaller the value, the more frequent data refresh operations occur for your users; however, more refreshes increase CPU and memory usage on the server.

The default value for this setting is 5 minutes; valid values for this setting range from 0 to 34,560 minutes (24 days).

✦ **Maximum Cache Age:** You can use the Maximum Cache Age setting to specify the maximum number of minutes that a Web drawing is cached in memory. After the specified limit is reached, the Web drawings are purged from the cache. Larger values require fewer I/O operations and less CPU load on the server — but they do increase server memory usage.

The default value for this setting is 60 minutes; valid values for this setting range from 0 to 34,560 minutes (24 days).

✦ **Maximum Recalc Duration:** You can use the Maximum Recalc Duration setting to specify the number of seconds that elapse before a data-refresh operation times out.

The default value for this setting is 60 seconds; valid values for this setting range from 10 to 120 seconds.

✦ **External Data: Application ID:** You use the ApplicationID field in the External Data section to configure the Unattended Service Account that Visio Services uses to access the data sources connected to Visio diagrams.

To configure the Unattended Service Account for use with Visio Services, you must define a target application ID and associated account in the Secure Store Service. When you have the target application ID defined, you enter the ID in the Application ID field.

Configuring the Unattended Service Account

When a user accesses a Visio drawing that contains data connections to SharePoint lists or Excel Services, Visio Services uses the identity of the current user to access those resources.

When rendering drawings that contain data connections to data sources external to SharePoint, Visio Services can authenticate to the data source in a variety of ways:

✦ **Integrated Windows Authentication:** You can use this method of authentication if you have Kerberos up and running in your environment.

✦ **Secure Store Service:** You can use this method to map the current user's credentials to a different credential that provides access to the database. The Secure Store Service handles the mapping. This authentication method is only usable for drawings that define the connection data (including the target application used for credential mapping) in use in an ODC file.

✦ **Unattended Service Account:** Configuring Visio Services to use the Unattended Service Account is the easiest way to give your Visio drawings secure access to the data sources they use. (The humble-but-useful Unattended Service Account is a low-privilege account that has access to the data sources to which you want to connect.)

As an administrator, you can create a target application in the Secure Store that not only stores account details but also handles mapping all the approved users to the account. When connecting to an external data source from a Web drawing, Visio Services impersonates the Unattended Service Account to retrieve the data.

Create a Target Application ID in the Secure Store Service

In order to configure the Unattended Service Account for use with Visio Services, you first need to create a target application in the Secure Store Service.

Follow these steps to add a Target Application ID to the Secure Store:

1. **Using your browser, navigate to the Central Administration home page.**

2. **From the Application Management section, click Manage service applications.**

The Service Applications management page appears, listing all the service applications in your SharePoint implementation.

3. **From the list of service applications, select Secure Store Service Application**.

The Secure Store Service management page appears. If this is your first time using the Secure Store Service, the page displays a message stating that before creating a new Secure Store Target Application, you must first generate a new key for the Secure Store Service. (If you've already generated that key, proceed to the next step.)

4. **On the Edit tab, in the Manage Target Application group, click New.**

The Create New Secure Store Target Application page appears.

5. **In the Target Application ID field, enter a unique identifier for your application.**

   You use the Target Application ID field to map a service application (such as Visio Services or Excel Services) to the Unattended Service Account. The value you enter in this field is the same value that you enter in the Application ID setting on the Manage the Visio Graphics Service page.

6. **In the Display Name field, enter a descriptive name to use as the display name for the target application.**

7. **In the Contact e-mail field, enter a valid e-mail address for the person you want to be the contact for the target application.**

8. **In the Target Application Type field, select whether the application uses a group mapping or an individual mapping.**

9. **Select a value for the Target Application Page URL field.**

   You can use the Target Application Page URL field to set individual users' credential information for the target application.

10. **Click Next.**

    The Specify Credentials page appears, in which you can specify the fields to use when authenticating the Unattended Service Account.

11. **Add or remove the fields that you would like to use for authenticating the Unattended Service Account.**

    The default fields defined are

    - Windows User name
    - Windows Password fields

    You can remove a field by clicking the Delete icon next to the field.

    You can add more credential fields by clicking Add Field. When you do so, a new row appears on the page with two text boxes: one representing the Field Name and the other representing the Field Type.

12. **Click Next.**

    The Specify the Membership Settings page appears.

13. **In the Target Application Administrators field, enter the list of the users you want to have access privileges to manage the target application settings.**

14. **Click OK.**

    The Target Application is created, and you're returned to the Secure Store Service management page. You should see your newly created target application listed on the page.

The next step is to configure the credential mappings by using the Set Credentials option. For example, if your target application is configured with a Windows user name field and a Windows password field, you would use the Set Credential menu option to set the user name and password values. SharePoint uses credential information from the target application when it needs to access the Unattended Service Account for a service application mapped to the target application.

15. **Click the down arrow next to the name of your new target application.**

    A shortcut menu appears.

16. **From the shortcut menu, click Set Credentials.**

    The Set Credentials for Secure Store Target Application page appears.

17. **In the Credentials Owner field, enter the identity of the owner of the target application.**

18. **In the remaining fields, enter the valid credential settings for your Unattended Service Account.**

    If you used the default User Name and Password credential fields, then enter the user name and password of the account that you want to assume the role of the Unattended Service Account. The account that you specify must have access to the data sources to which you want Visio Services to connect.

19. **Click OK.**

    Your target application and the Unattended Service Account are now ready to be associated with the Visio Graphics Service. The next order of business is to add the Application ID to Visio Services. Stay tuned.

Add the Target Application ID to Visio Services

To use the Unattended Service Account when connecting to data sources in your Web drawings, you must configure the Visio Graphics Service with the application ID of the Secure Store Service target application that stores the Unattended Service Account credentials.

Follow these steps to map your Visio Graphics Service to a target application in your Secure Store:

1. **Navigate to the Central Administration home page.**

2. **From the Application Management section, click Manage service applications.**

    The Service Applications page appears, listing all of the available service applications in alphabetical order.

3. **Select Visio Graphics Services and, from the Ribbon menu, click Manage.**

   Alternatively, you can simply click the Visio Graphics Services link, which also brings you to the Manage Visio Graphics Services page.

   The Manage the Visio Graphics Services Web page appears.

4. **Click Global Settings.**

   The Visio Graphics Service Settings page appears, from which you can specify the application ID of the Secure Store Service target application.

5. **In the Application ID field, enter the application ID of the Target Application in the Secure Store that hosts the Unattended Service Account credentials.**

6. **Click OK.**

   The Unattended Service Account is now ready for use when connecting to data sources in your Web drawings.

Publishing Visio Diagrams to SharePoint

Visio Services enables you to publish, or save, your Visio diagrams to SharePoint in two formats:

✦ Drawing (*.vsd): This file type uses the Visio Drawing format.

✦ Web Drawing (*.vdw): Use this file type if you'll use your drawing with Visio Services; data you put in it is refreshable.

Saving your Visio Drawings to SharePoint

When you save your Visio diagram to SharePoint using the Visio drawing format, your Visio diagram is published to your chosen SharePoint library as a Visio file. When you click the file, it opens in the Microsoft Visio client application.

Follow these steps to publish your Visio diagram to SharePoint using the Visio drawing format:

1. **Open your Visio drawing, using the Microsoft Visio client application.**

2. **Click the File tab to present the Visio Backstage View.**

3. **From the Backstage View, click the Save & Send tab.**

4. **In the Save & Send section, click Save to SharePoint.**

5. **In the File Types section, click Drawing (*.vsd).**

6. **In the Locations section, double-click Browse for a location.**

7. **In the address bar of the Save As dialog box, enter the URL to the SharePoint document library to which you want to publish your Visio drawing.**

8. **Enter a file name for your file, and then click Save.**

   Visio contacts the SharePoint server and publishes the file in the document library specified in Step 7. You can navigate to the document library to verify that the file was published successfully.

Saving your Visio Web Drawings to SharePoint

When you save your Visio diagram to SharePoint using the Visio Web drawing format, your Visio diagram is published to your chosen SharePoint library as a Visio Web drawing file — and opens automatically in the browser for viewing. When you click the Web drawing file in the SharePoint library, the drawing opens in the browser.

Follow these steps to publish your Visio diagram to SharePoint using the Visio Web drawing format:

1. **Open your Visio drawing, using the Microsoft Visio client application.**

2. **Click the File tab to present the Visio Backstage View.**

3. **From the Backstage View, click the Save & Send tab.**

   Figure 9-2 shows the Visio Backstage View with the Save & Send tab active.

Figure 9-2:
Saving a
Visio Web
Drawing to
SharePoint.

4. In the Save & Send section, click Save to SharePoint.

5. In the File Types section, click Web Drawing (*.vdw).

6. In the Locations section, double-click Browse for a location.

7. In the address bar of the Save As dialog box, enter the URL to the SharePoint document library to which you want to publish your Visio drawing.

8. Enter a file name for your file, and then click Save.

   Visio contacts the SharePoint server and publishes the Web Drawing file to the document library specified in Step 7. SharePoint renders the Web drawing in the browser for you to review.

Integrating Visio with SharePoint Workflow

Microsoft Visio 2010 Premium comes with a Microsoft SharePoint Workflow template and a set of SharePoint Workflow shapes from which you can create workflow diagrams — or blueprints — for SharePoint Server 2010 and SharePoint Foundation 2010.

Figure 9-3 shows the Microsoft SharePoint Workflow template option that appears in the Visio Backstage View when you're creating a new Visio diagram.

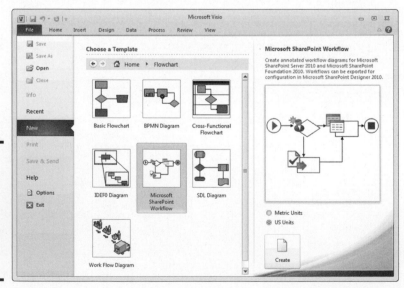

Figure 9-3:
You can use the SharePoint Workflow Template to create your blueprint.

When you generate workflow diagrams using the SharePoint shapes and template, you can export them from Visio — and then import them into SharePoint Designer for actual implementation and deployment.

You can find the digital stencils for the SharePoint Workflow shapes in the Flowchart category in Visio. They include these:

✦ **SharePoint Workflow Conditions:** This stencil includes shapes that represent various aspects of a SharePoint item or object that you may want to check — such as who created the item or the current user's permissions.

Figure 9-4 shows the SharePoint Workflow Conditions stencil that appears in Visio.

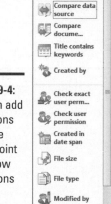

Figure 9-4:
You can add conditions from the SharePoint Workflow Conditions stencil.

✦ **SharePoint Workflow Actions:** This stencil includes shapes that represent various actions you may want to perform in your SharePoint Workflow, such as setting the value of a field or updating a list item.

Figure 9-5 shows the SharePoint Workflow Actions stencil that appears in Visio.

Creating a SharePoint workflow blueprint is as easy as creating a regular Visio diagram. Business users who are familiar with Visio — and accustomed to creating business process workflows and flowcharts in Visio — can now be an integral part of the development and implementation of workflows in SharePoint. Better yet, your business users don't have to know how workflows are implemented or developed in SharePoint; nor do they have to figure out how to use Microsoft SharePoint Designer. Instead, they can familiarize themselves with SharePoint workflow shapes in Visio — and use them to describe their business automation needs.

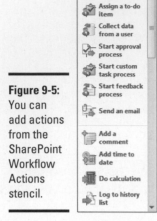

Figure 9-5:
You can
add actions
from the
SharePoint
Workflow
Actions
stencil.

Business stakeholders can review, modify, and approve the workflow blue-print before it even touches the SharePoint environment. This increases the likelihood that the actual implementation of the workflow process in SharePoint will meet the needs of the business unit and reduce overall development time and effort. (And that was the point, wasn't it?) Figure 9-6 shows a simple SharePoint workflow diagram that does four quick tasks:

✦ Checks to see whether the current item was created by a specific person.

✦ Checks the results of the condition.

✦ Sets the value of a specific field in the item.

✦ Commits the changes to the item in the SharePoint list.

Pretty smart, for a drawing.

When it comes time for deployment to SharePoint, the business users can export the diagram to the appropriate format and hand over the blueprint to the SharePoint development team for final implementation. (Of course, power users with the appropriate permissions can import the workflow diagram into SharePoint Designer *and* handle the implementation process. Do what works best for your organization.)

Visio 2010 provides commands on the Process tab of the Visio Ribbon that aid the export and import process:

✦ **Export:** This command appears in the SharePoint Workflow group on the Ribbon; use it to export your current Visio diagram to a Visio Workflow Interchange file (`*.vwi`), which is compatible with SharePoint Designer.

✦ **Import:** This command appears in the SharePoint Workflow group on the Ribbon; use it to import a Visio Workflow Interchange file (`*.vwi`) into Visio 2010 for further editing. You can export the Workflows you generate in SharePoint Designer and then import them into Visio, providing you with a quick and easy way to document your SharePoint workflows.

✦ **Check Diagram:** This command appears in the Diagram Validation group on the Ribbon; use it to check your Visio diagram for potential problems before exporting. Visio lists any issues it detects in an Issues dialog box that appears below the diagram by default. The description of the issues helps get you started correcting the problem.

You can't export ant item that contains errors (you know, "issues" — and we don't mean magazines). Trying to ignore issues produces the error message shown in Figure 9-7, which states flatly that the workflow diagram must be valid before you can export it.

Figure 9-8 shows an example of the potential issues you may run into as you create your workflow diagrams. In this example, we removed the connector lines from the condition that checks to see whether a particular user exists. (After all, you can't walk up to a user and ask, "Do you exist?" — unless you don't mind getting funny looks.)

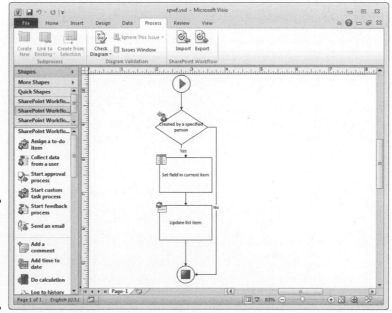

Figure 9-6:
You can design your SharePoint Workflow in Visio.

Figure 9-7:
You can't export your workflow diagram if it contains errors.

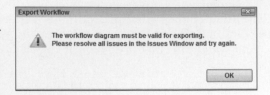

Figure 9-8:
Visio can detect any issues with your workflow and help you resolve them.

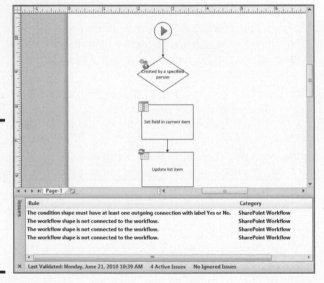

The SharePoint Workflow Template capability is offered with Visio 2010 Premium Edition only; Visio 2010 Professional doesn't provide the SharePoint Workflow template.

Creating a SharePoint workflow diagram

Follow these steps to create a SharePoint workflow diagram in Visio 2010:

1. **Launch Microsoft Visio 2010 Premium.**

You need Visio 2010 Premium edition in order to create SharePoint workflow diagrams; all other versions of Visio (including Visio 2010 Professional) don't support SharePoint workflow creation.

When you launch Visio, the client application opens to the File menu in Backstage View.

2. **From the Backstage View, click the New tab.**

   A list of available Visio templates appears.

3. **From the Template Categories section, click Flowchart to display the list of available flowchart templates.**

4. **From the list of available templates, click Microsoft SharePoint Workflow.**

   A description of the template appears to the right of the page, along with a Create button.

5. **Select whether you want to use Metric units or US units in your diagram.**

   This selection determines which stencils are added to Visio for you.

6. **Click Create.**

   Visio opens with the appropriate SharePoint workflow stencils loaded; you're now ready to create your workflow. Drag and drop the shapes you need onto your page, and then configure the connections between the shapes to define the process flow.

   When you've completed your design, you're ready for the export process.

Exporting your SharePoint workflow diagram

Follow these steps to export a SharePoint workflow diagram in Visio 2010:

1. **Open your Visio SharePoint Workflow Diagram in Visio.**

   Before you can export your workflow diagram, check to see whether it contains any errors that may prevent the export from working.

2. **On the Process tab, in the Diagram Validation group, click Check Diagram.**

   Visio checks your workflow diagram for potential issues; if it finds any, it lists them and offers guidance on how to resolve them.

   You must resolve any identified issues before you proceed to the next step, or you'll get that terse error message.

   If your diagram is valid, Visio informs you that the data validation is complete, and no issues were found in the current document.

3. **On the Process tab, in the SharePoint Workflow group, click Export.**

   The Export Workflow dialog box appears.

4. **Select the location in which you want to store your file.**

5. **In the file name field, enter a name for your Visio Workflow Interchange file.**

6. **Click Save.**

Your SharePoint Workflow diagram is saved as a Visio Workflow Interchange file (*.vwi), in the location you specified in Step 4. Your file is now ready to be imported into SharePoint Designer.

Importing Workflow into SharePoint Designer

Follow these steps to import a Visio SharePoint workflow diagram into SharePoint Designer:

1. **Using your browser, navigate to the home page of the SharePoint site in which you want to implement the workflow.**

2. **From the Site Actions menu, click Edit in SharePoint Designer.**

   Your SharePoint site opens in SharePoint Designer.

   Alternatively, you can launch SharePoint Designer from the Start menu, and open your SharePoint site directly from the Designer client application.

3. **From the Navigation bar, click Workflows.**

   The Ribbon menu changes to reflect the Workflow commands available in SharePoint Designer.

4. **On the Workflows tab, in the Manage group, click Import from Visio.**

   The Import Workflow from Visio Drawing Wizard appears.

5. **From the Import Workflow from Visio Drawing Wizard, browse to the SharePoint Workflow diagram that you exported from Visio.**

   The file should be a valid Visio Workflow Interchange (*.vwi) file.

6. **Click Next.**

   The wizard moves to the next stage of the import process, which involves specifying the workflow name and additional properties.

7. **In the Workflow Name field, enter a descriptive name for your workflow.**

8. **Select the workflow type.**

   If you want to attach your workflow to a specific SharePoint list or library, click List Workflow as the workflow type. Then select the list or library to which you want to attach the workflow.

   Alternatively, if you want to attach to a specific content type so you can reuse the workflow in multiple lists and libraries, click (you guessed it) Reusable Workflow — and then select the content type to which you want to attach the workflow.

9. **Click Finish.**

   The workflow opens in the SharePoint Designer Workflow Editor.

You are now free to complete the workflow implementation by setting your condition and action values. For example, if your workflow implements a condition that checks to see whether the current item was created by a specific person, then you set the Specific Person value; if your workflow contains an action to set the value of a field, you specify the field that's being updated and the value you want to assign to the field. Figure 9-9 shows the workflow generated in Figure 9-6, exported and imported into SharePoint Designer for completion.

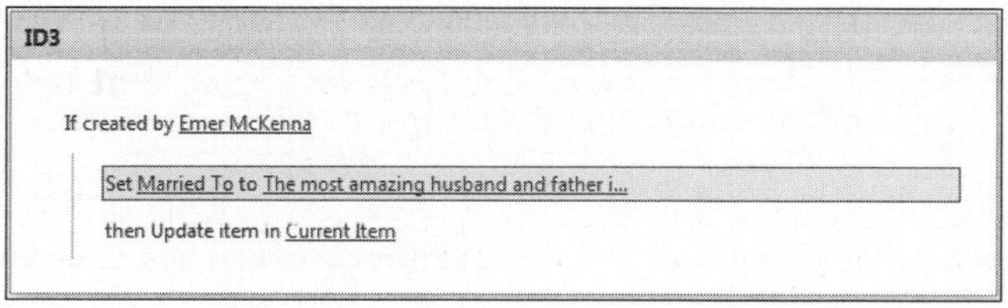

Figure 9-9:
You set the values for your conditions and actions in SharePoint Designer.

Publishing Visio Workflow to SharePoint

When you've defined all the conditions and actions in the workflow you've imported from Visio, you're ready to publish it to SharePoint — which attaches it to the list and makes it ready for use. When publishing your SharePoint workflow, make sure that you've configured its settings appropriately (for example, when the workflow should run).

Follow these steps to publish your Visio SharePoint workflow to SharePoint using SharePoint Designer:

1. **On the Workflow tab, in the Manage group, click Workflow Settings.**

The Workflow Settings page appears, from which you can view and manage the settings for your workflow.

2. **From the Workflow Information section, enter a description for your workflow.**

3. **From the Settings section, if you want to provide your users with a Visio visualization of the workflow in SharePoint, click Show workflow visualization on status page.**

If you enable this setting, SharePoint adds the Visio Web Access Web Part to the workflow status page — and displays a Web drawing of the workflow process. Now your users have a visual representation of what actually happened during the workflow process — which is great for troubleshooting purposes.

**Book III
Chapter 9**

Considering Visio Services

Figure 9-10 shows an example of the workflow visualization as it appears on the Workflow Status page in SharePoint.

4. From the Start Options section, select when you want your workflow to start.

These Start Options are available:

- *Allow this workflow to be manually started.*

  If you choose this option, users can run the workflow manually from the Start Workflow option in SharePoint. If you enable this option, you can limit this capability to only those users who have Manage List Permissions.

- *Start workflow automatically when an item is created.*

- *Start workflow automatically when an item is changed.*

5. On the Workflow Settings tab, in the Save group, click Save.

The changes you made to the workflow settings are saved.

6. On the Workflow Settings tab, in the Save group, click Publish.

SharePoint Designer runs through a series of steps that include

- Generating the workflow visualization.

- Generating and saving the workflow markup (.XOML) file.

- Associating the workflow.

Your workflow is now up and running in SharePoint, ready for use.

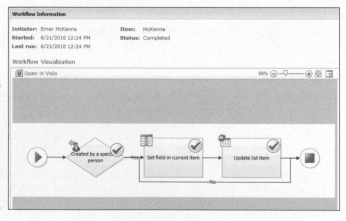

Figure 9-10:
The Visio workflow visualization tells you what happened.

Exporting your SharePoint Workflow to Visio

Integration between Visio and SharePoint Designer supports not only importing SharePoint workflow blueprints from Visio, but also exporting workflows created in SharePoint Designer — after such an export, you can then import them into Visio. This integration makes your SharePoint workflow processes surprisingly easy to document and explain in layman's terms. (After all, a happy layman is a productive layman.)

Follow these steps to export your SharePoint workflow to a Visio Workflow Interchange (*.vwi) file format:

1. **Open your SharePoint workflow in SharePoint Designer.**

2. **On the Workflow Settings tab, in the Manage group, click Export to Visio.**

The Export Workflow to Visio Drawing dialog box appears.

3. **Select the location in which you want to store your file.**

4. **In the File Name field, enter a name for your Visio Workflow Interchange file.**

5. **Click Save.**

Your SharePoint Workflow is saved as a Visio Workflow Interchange file (*.vwi) in the location you specified in Step 3. Your file is now ready to be imported into Visio 2010 Premium.

Importing your SharePoint Workflow into Visio

Follow these steps to import a SharePoint workflow diagram in Visio 2010:

1. **Launch Microsoft Visio 2010 Premium.**

You need Visio 2010 Premium edition in order to create SharePoint workflow diagrams; all other versions of Visio, including Visio 2010 Professional, don't support SharePoint workflow creation.

When you launch Visio, the client defaults to the File menu in Backstage View.

2. **From the Backstage View, click the New tab.**

A list of available Visio templates appears.

3. **From the Other Ways to Get Started section, click Blank Drawing to create a blank Visio diagram.**

A description of the template appears to the right of the page along with a Create button.

4. **Select whether you want to use Metric units or US units in your diagram.**

   This selection determines which stencils are added to Visio for you.

5. **Click Create.**

   Visio opens with a blank canvas. You are now ready to import your SharePoint workflow.

6. **On the Process tab, in the SharePoint Workflow group, click Import.**

   The Import Workflow dialog box appears.

7. **Select the file that you want to import, and click Open.**

   Visio imports the SharePoint workflow and converts it to a Visio drawing. If Visio has any problems during the import process, it gives you an error message.

Sometimes the error message is benign. For example, if an error message huffs that your workflow concepts couldn't be understood by Visio and the import failed — but the diagram appears correctly in Visio — well, that's just Visio's hard luck if couldn't understand great art. You can ignore that error message with impunity. You've already achieved the desired result — and you may continue editing and viewing the workflow in Visio.

Creating a Strategy Map

A strategy map is a visual representation of an organization's goals and how it intends to achieve those goals. A strategy map shows your organization's relationships and dependencies, and how they relate to the business metrics needed to measure and monitor your organization's performance.

The integration between PerformancePoint Services and Visio Services allows you to create a strategy map that you can publish to your business intelligence dashboard. You can map the shapes in your Visio diagrams to KPIs defined in PerformancePoint Services so that the color of your shapes change according to whether the associated value is on target with the defined KPIs. For example, if you have a strategy map that shows shapes mapped to branch offices on each continent, and the shapes are mapped to KPIs that measure whether each branch office is meeting its sales target, then the indicator is instant and simple in what it says: If (say) Europe's sales are on target, the shape that represents them is green.

If you're running the 64-bit version of Dashboard Designer, then you need the 64-bit version of Visio 2010 Premium installed before you use the Strategy Map feature. Likewise, the 32-bit version of Dashboard Designer needs the 32-bit version of Visio 2010 Premium. If you have a mismatched version of Visio installed, then any attempt to create a strategy map will make Dashboard Designer display an error message that complains about the incorrect version of Visio.

You can't install the 64-bit version of Visio on your computer if you have a 32-bit version of Microsoft Office installed. First you must remove the 32-bit version of Office. In addition, if you install the 64-bit version of Office, you can no longer use the Datasheet view when you're working with SharePoint lists. That's because the ActiveX control that provides the datasheet functionality isn't available in the 64-bit version of Office.

Follow these steps to create a strategy map and publish it to your PerformancePoint dashboard:

1. **Using Microsoft Visio 2010, create a Visio diagram that will be used for the visualization of your strategy map.**

You can create your strategy maps directly from the Dashboard Designer, using the Visio stencils — but it's much easier to create them in Visio first and *then* import them into the Dashboard Designer when you create your strategy map.

2. **From your Start Menu, click All Programs➪SharePoint➪Performance Point Dashboard Designer to launch the Dashboard Designer application.**

You can find alternative methods for launching the Dashboard Designer in the "Launching Dashboard Designer" section of this chapter.

3. **On the Create tab, in the Reports group, click Strategy Map.**

The Create a Strategy Map Report wizard launches.

4. **Select a scorecard to use for the strategy map, and then click Finish.**

5. **On the Edit tab, in the Report Editor group, click Edit Strategy Map.**

The Strategy Map Editor appears.

6. **From the Strategy Map Editor menu, click Import Visio File.**

The Open dialog box appears.

7. **From the Open dialog box, select the Visio drawing that you want to use for the strategy map, and then click Open.**

   The Visio diagram opens in the Dashboard Designer Strategy Map Editor. The next step is to connect the shapes in the Visio diagram to your PerformancePoint KPIs.

8. **For each shape in your Visio diagram, follow these steps:**

   a. *Select the shape you want to connect, and, from the menu, click Connect Shape.*

      The Connect Shape dialog box appears.

   b. *From the list of KPIs, select the KPI value to map to the shape, and click Connect.*

   c. *Click Close.*

9. **In the Strategy Map Editor, click Apply.**

   Your strategy map is created — and is now ready to insert into your PerformancePoint dashboard. Figure 9-11 shows a basic strategy map report, displayed in SharePoint via the browser. The color for each shape changes to reflect the color associated with the map's connected KPIs (for example, if the Sales Amount is off target, the shape is red).

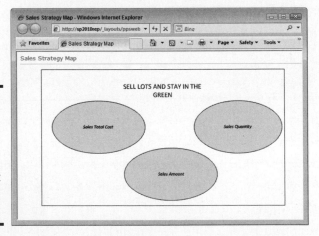

Figure 9-11:
Creating strategy maps with PerformancePoint Dashboard Designer.

Book IV

Using the SharePoint Services

The 5th Wave   By Rich Tennant

"Run Nigel! It's the mummy's cursor!"

Contents at a Glance

Chapter 1: Publishing Access Applications

In This Chapter

✔ Designing SharePoint-compatible Access Databases

✔ Understanding how your Access objects map to SharePoint

✔ Publishing your Access application to Access Services

✔ Creating your Access Web database site templates

Access Services is a new feature that comes with SharePoint Server 2010 Enterprise Edition, bringing the power and agility of Access applications into the flexible, scalable, and easily reachable SharePoint environment. When Access Services is up and running in your organization, here's what you get:

✦ You can extend the reach of your Access database applications to the Web by publishing them to SharePoint Server 2010.

✦ Integrating the Access client application with SharePoint's Access Services architecture means a single click gets Access up and running in SharePoint — providing all your users with a centrally managed, Web-accessible version of Access.

✦ Publishing your Access application to SharePoint means that you have only one instance of the application to manage — gone are the days of distributing multiple copies of your database software throughout your organization.

✦ When a user adds, removes, or modifies data, those changes are automatically accessible to all other users.

✦ You can easily control the roles and access permissions on your database application by using standard SharePoint permissions.

✦ Any functional or schematic updates you make to the database application can be seamlessly synchronized with SharePoint, ensuring that your users are always working with the most up-to-date version of your application.

In Book III, Chapter 1, we look at the architecture behind Access Services, and examine the settings that can help keep both your Access applications and your SharePoint environment running smoothly. In this chapter, we hop on board the Access Services train again to show you how easy it is to publish your Access applications to SharePoint Server 2010.

Designing SharePoint-Compatible Access Databases

Access 2007 provided the capability to publish an Access list into a SharePoint list — you could manage and control your data directly from SharePoint's browser interface. With the Access 2010 integration features, you can publish your entire database application into SharePoint — including all the forms, queries, and reports associated with your application.

Before you can publish your Access 2010 database application to SharePoint, it must be *compatible* (able to work seamlessly and play nice) with Access Services. Fortunately, Access 2010 provides a lineup of tools to help you ensure that compatibility:

✦ **Access 2010 Web Database client template:** When you create a new Access database, Access 2010 presents you with a list of templates you can use as the foundation of your database application. Selecting the Blank Web Database template creates an Access 2010 Web database application — which is compatible with Access Services by default (let's hear it for good software design!) and may be published to SharePoint.

All menu options in the Access client application are filtered automatically; the only options enabled are compatible with SharePoint — which helps keep your database application compatible. That way you're less likely to run into problems during the publishing process.

If you create your Access database application using another template (such as the Blank Database template), you can still convert that application to a Web database if it's compatible with Access Services: Simply publish it to SharePoint. If the database application publishes successfully, it becomes an Access Web database application automatically.

✦ **Web Compatibility Checker:** You can use this feature to check your database application before you publish it to SharePoint so you can make sure that all the objects, forms, reports, and code are compatible and translatable to Access Services. The Compatibility Checker identifies any issues that may prevent you from publishing your application successfully. Armed with this knowledge, you can troubleshoot the offending items before publishing to SharePoint. The idea is to keep that experience clean and simple.

Creating an Access Web database

Here's how to create an Access Web database from the Access 2010 client that can be published to Access Services:

1. **Launch the Access 2010 client.**

2. **From the File menu, click New.**

    A list of the available Access templates appears.

3. **From the list of available templates, select Blank Web Database and then click Create.**

    Figure 1-1 shows the list of available Access templates that appear in the Access 2010 client.

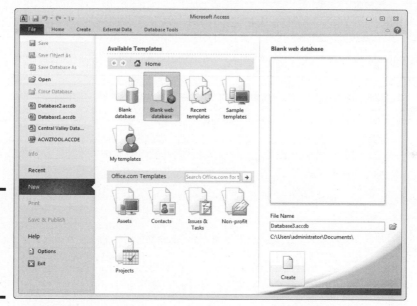

Figure 1-1:
Creating
an Access
Web
database
application.

When you click the Create button, the Access client opens and filters the menu options to present you with only Access Services-compatible commands. You're now ready to create your Access Web database application.

Creating an Access Web database from SharePoint

SharePoint 2010 provides a list of available Access Web database site templates from which you can create your SharePoint site. When you create a

SharePoint site based on one of these templates, you can publish, edit, customize, and synchronize your changes by using controls that appear in the Access 2010 client application.

Access Services is a new feature that comes with SharePoint Server 2010 Enterprise Edition. If you don't have an Enterprise license, the Access Web Database site templates won't appear in your SharePoint Gallery.

Figure 1-2 shows you a list of the templates available with SharePoint 2010.

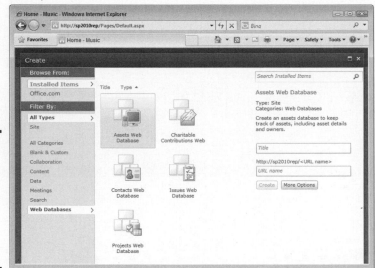

Figure 1-2:
You can create your Access Web database from SharePoint.

You have a range of Access Web database templates available:

✦ **Assets Web Database:** Use this database site template to create a database to keep track of assets. The information stored includes asset details and owners.

✦ **Charitable Contributions Web Database:** Use this site template to create a Web database to track information about fundraising campaigns — including donations made by contributors, campaign-related events, and pending tasks.

✦ **Contacts Web Database:** Use this site template to create a Web database for managing information about the people you and your team collaborate with, such as customers and business partners.

✦ **Issues Web Database:** Use this site template to create a Web database to help you manage a set of issues or problems, such as bug-tracking for an application under development. You can assign, prioritize, and follow the progress of issues from start to finish.

✦ **Projects Web Database:** Use this site template to create a project-tracking Web database that you can use to follow the progress of multiple projects stage by stage, and assign tasks to members of your team.

In addition to the standard templates that come with SharePoint, you can find a plethora of Access Web database templates on the Internet — not only from Microsoft, but also from third-party vendors. For example, the Microsoft Web site provides you with a sample Web database application (starring the intrepid imaginary company Northwind Traders) that's a virtually painless introduction to the process of publishing and synchronizing content from the Access client application to Access Services.

You can customize these templates to suit your business needs — and then upload them to your Site Template Gallery for use in your SharePoint environment. Alternatively, you can simply publish the Web database application to SharePoint creating a SharePoint Web application.

Using a template to create your Web database application means you don't have to create your application from scratch, which saves time; you can get your applications up and running as quickly as possible.

Follow these steps to create an Access Web database application directly from SharePoint:

1. **Using your browser, navigate to the home page of your SharePoint site.**

2. **From the Site Actions menu, click New Site.**

   The Create site page appears, displaying a list of the available SharePoint site templates sorted by category.

3. **From the list of categories, click Web databases.**

   The list of available Access Web database site templates appears.

4. **Select the Web database template that you want to use as the basis of your site.**

5. **In the Title field, enter the title for your site.**

6. **In the URL field, enter the URL to your site.**

7. **Click More Options.**

8. **In the description field, enter a description for your site.**

9. **Choose whether your new site will inherit permissions:**

   - *Use same permissions as parent site:* Choose this option if you want the new site to inherit the permission structure from its parent site.

   - *Use unique permissions:* Choose this option if you want to specify permissions for the new site.

   After the site is created, you can not only manage the site permissions through the browser interface, but also add and remove users and groups to suit your needs.

10. **From the Navigation Inheritance section, accept the default setting of No so the new site won't inherit the top link bar from the parent site.**

   Regardless of whether you select Yes or No for this setting, the top link bar from the parent site doesn't appear onscreen. Excluding the top link bar from the Web database application pages reduces possible user confusion because it helps give navigation a close resemblance to the familiar navigational structure of the client application. (We're convinced that this behavior must be "a feature, not a bug!" It's just too convenient.) You can still use the Options⇨Navigate Up command to get back to the parent site.

11. **Click Create.**

   Access Services creates the new Access Web database site ready for use.

After your Web database is created, you're free to start using the site as desired. If you want to customize the site or give it additional functionality, you can open it in the Access 2010 client locally. For example, you can add forms and reports, rename tables and fields, and change the navigational structure. When you've made your changes, simply save them and click the Synchronize button to apply them to your SharePoint site. (For more about the publishing and synchronization process, flip to the "Publishing to Access Services" section of this chapter.)

Access Web Database Objects

When you're creating a Web database application using the Access client, it helps to familiarize yourself with the various objects and tools at your disposal before you just start slinging electrons around. The creation of a typical Web database application includes one or more of the components we present in the following sections.

Tables and Fields

When you create your Access Web database, you're initially presented with the Table Designer from which you can design the first table in your Web database application.

Okay, we're not talking furniture here (but you knew that). In Access, a *table* is a database object that stores information about an entity. For example, an Employee table may store information relating to all the employees in your company. A table is a grid made up of *fields* — not grassy places for playing ball or growing corn, but smaller database objects that hold specific pieces of data — arranged in rows that represent the items that the fields describe. For example, an Employee table may contain multiple fields describing an employee — such as First Name, Last Name, Job Title, and Employee ID — and one row (containing all these fields) corresponds to one employee.

Fields are also commonly referred to as *attributes* or *columns* (because each one occurs at the same place in every row, and so stacks up as a column). Rows are also called *records* or (if you're being vague) *items*. At least one field in the table is used to uniquely identify an item or row. In our example, this unique field may be the Employee ID. For search purposes, this unique field is also known as the *primary key*.

Most database applications contain multiple tables, many of which have a relationship. For example, you may have a Jobs table that contains a list of all the jobs within your organization, including such information as the Job Title, Job Description, Job Classification, and Salary Range. The Employee table would contain a Job Title field that would retrieve the list of possible jobs from the Job table. In this case the Job Title field would be a lookup field with a relationship to the Jobs table.

Microsoft Access provides an intuitive designer to help you through the process of creating your database tables, and their associated fields and relationships.

Forms

When you create an application that requires users to enter data, you invariably need to create a form. The Forms Ribbon group, shown in Figure 1-3, provides a number of commands from which you can create your Web database forms.

Figure 1-3:
You can create many different form types in your Web database.

You can access the Forms Ribbon by clicking the Create tab in Access. The Form commands include these:

✦ **Form:** Creates a Web form that allows you to enter data one record at a time. Web forms can only be created for tables or Web queries.

✦ **Multiple Item:** Creates a Web form that shows multiple records at once. Continuous forms can only be created for table or Web queries.

✦ **Blank Form:** Creates a Web form that contains no controls or formatting. Blank forms can only be created for tables or Web queries.

✦ **Datasheet:** Creates a Web form that displays multiple records in a datasheet, with one record per row. Web datasheets can only be created for tables or Web queries.

✦ **Navigation:** Create a Web form that allows you to move between forms and reports in your database application.

Navigation

When you're creating a Web database application, you'll need to provide your users with a way to get around between the various forms and reports in your application. You can create your navigation system using Navigation Forms (as mentioned in the previous bullet list).

When you're creating a navigation form, Access provides you with a variety of navigation types, including these:

✦ **Horizontal Tabs:** Allows you to add a series of tabs horizontally across your Web page.

✦ **Vertical Tabs, Left:** Allows you to add a series of tabs vertically to the left of your Web page.

✦ **Vertical Tabs, Right:** Allows you to add a series of tabs vertically to the right of your Web page.

✦ **Horizontal Tabs, 2 Levels:** Allows you to add two levels of horizontal tabs across your Web page. Figure 1-4 shows an example of this type of navigation form.

✦ **Horizontal Tabs and Vertical Tabs, Left:** Allows you to add a series of tabs horizontally across your Web page, and a series of tabs vertically to the left of your Web page.

✦ **Horizontal Tabs and Vertical Tabs, Right:** Allows you to add a series of tabs horizontally across your Web page, and a series of tabs vertically to the right of your Web page.

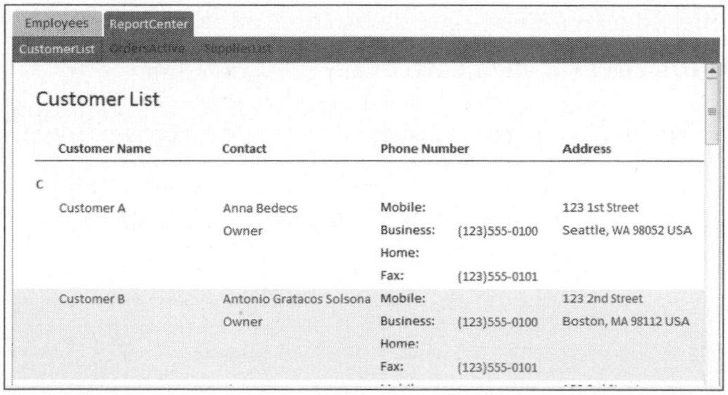

Figure 1-4:
You can
create a
two-level
navigation
bar.

Macros

Access 2010 provides a new and improved Macro Builder — also referred to
as the Macro Designer — to allow you to add logic to your database to automate repetitive tasks and create a more usable interface. Using the Macro
Builder you can quickly define conditions and actions for your macros.

When you're creating Web macros, the Macro designer filters out actions
and expressions that don't translate to Access Services, taking much of the
guess work out of creating macros and ensuring that the publishing process is as easy and efficient as possible. The designer allows you to expand
and collapse the macro data in much the same way you'd expand and collapse the elements of an XML file. When a macro appears in expanded view
it looks very similar to viewing code. Figure 1-5 shows an example of the
`zzzEraseOrders` macro from the Northwind Traders sample Access Web
database from Microsoft. The macro is being viewed in design view using the
Macro Builder. The Action Catalog appears on the right side from which you
can drag and drop the conditional statements and corresponding actions as
needed.

The In This Database node in the Action Catalog allows you to view all the
macros you've already created in the current database, in addition to other
objects in the database such as tables, forms, and reports. You can reuse the
logic created from other macros by simply dragging and dropping them from
this node onto your new macro.

Follow these steps to create a macro:

1. **Open your Web database application in Access 2010.**

2. **On the Create tab, in the Macros & Code group, click Macro.**

   Clicking the Macro command launches the Macro Builder, which you
   can use to build your business logic.

3. **Build your business logic using the Action Catalog.**

4. **On the File tab, click Save to save your macro.**

The macros that you create appear under the Macros in the navigation tree.

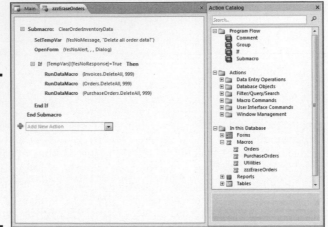

Figure 1-5:
You can drag and drop conditions and actions from the Action Catalog.

Data macros

Data macros are new with Access 2010 and allow you to add logic that is triggered when specific events occur on a table — such as adding, updating, or deleting data.

Data macros don't appear under the Macros command in the Access navigation pane. Instead you can find them by selecting a table in your database and then clicking the Table tab from the Ribbon menu. The Table tab gives you access to a number commands that allow you to create data macros:

✦ **Before Change:** Allows you to create logic that runs before a change is committed to the database. You can use this event to validate changes before saving them to the table.

✦ **Before Delete:** Allows you to create logic that runs before deleting a record. You can use this event to validate the delete function, or to cancel the deletion and raise an error.

✦ **After Insert:** Allows you to create logic that runs after a record has been added to the table.

✦ **After Update:** Allows you to create logic that runs after a record has been edited in the table.

✦ **After Delete:** Allows you to create logic that runs after a record has been deleted from the table.

✦ **Named Macro:** Allows you to create, edit, delete, or rename data macros that can be called from a macro or from event code.

Queries

Queries are the heart and soul of most database applications allowing you to extract and filter the information you need when you need it. You can use queries to extract data from a single table, or multiple tables, to perform calculations and to generate reports. Queries appear in the Access left navigation pane under the heading Queries. When you're working with Web database applications, the queries you create are called (with admirable clarity) *Web queries*.

Access provides a Query Designer that provides you with a visual representation of the tables in your query and their associated relationships. Using this feature, you can specify which fields will appear in your query results — as well as dictate the fields used to filter data and perform calculations on that data. Figure 1-6 shows the `SalesAnalysis` query from the Northwind Traders sample Web database application. The figure shows you all the relationships among the various tables that make up the query. When you add tables to a query, Access creates the relationship for you automatically in the Query Designer.

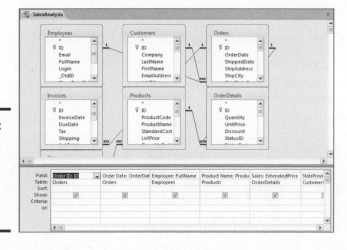

Figure 1-6: The Query Designer makes queries easy to create.

Reports

Reports help you present the data in your database visually — in the format your business users require. For example, you can create a report that makes use of charts and graphs if those get your point across best. Figure 1-7 shows an example of a Web report created for the Products table in the Northwind Traders sample Access Web database. (Impressive, isn't it?) Microsoft Access provides you with lots of tools to make sophisticated reports easy to create.

Figure 1-7: Access creates a sample layout when you create a report.

ID	Product Code	Product Name	Standard Cost	List Price	Quantity Per Unit
1	NWTDFN-7	Northwind Traders Dried Pears	$22.50	$30.00	12 - 1 lb pkgs.
2	NWTS-8	Northwind Traders Curry Sauce	$30.00	$40.00	12 - 12 oz jars
3	NWTDFN-14	Northwind Traders Walnuts	$17.44	$23.25	40 - 100 g pkgs.
4	NWTCFV-17	Northwind Traders Fruit Cocktail	$29.25	$39.00	15.25 OZ
5	NWTBGM-19	Northwind Traders Chocolate Biscuits Mix	$6.90	$9.20	10 boxes x 12 pieces
6	NWTB-1	Northwind Traders Chai	$13.50	$18.00	10 boxes x 20 bags
7	NWTCO-3	Northwind Traders Syrup	$7.50	$10.00	12 - 550 ml bottles
8	NWTCO-4	Northwind Traders Cajun Seasoning	$16.50	$22.00	48 - 6 oz jars
9	NWTO-5	Northwind Traders Olive Oil	$16.01	$21.35	36 boxes
10	NWTJP-6	Northwind Traders Boysenberry Spread	$18.75	$25.00	12 - 8 oz jars
11	NWTJP-7	Northwind Traders Marmalade	$60.75	$81.00	30 gift boxes
12	NWTBGM-21	Northwind Traders Scones	$7.50	$10.00	24 pkgs. x 4 pieces
13	NWTB-34	Northwind Traders Beer	$10.50	$14.00	24 - 12 oz bottles
14	NWTCM-40	Northwind Traders Crab Meat	$13.80	$18.40	24 - 4 oz tins
15	NWTSO-41	Northwind Traders Clam Chowder	$7.24	$9.65	12 - 12 oz cans
16	NWTB-43	Northwind Traders Coffee	$34.50	$46.00	16 - 500 g tins

You can create a report very quickly (if not quite "yesterday") by following these steps:

1. **Open your Web database application in Access 2010.**

2. **Click the Home tab to display the left navigation pane.**

3. **From the navigation pane, select the table or query you want to use to generate the report.**

4. **In the Reports group, on the Create tab, click Report to create a Web report.**

   Access creates a report automatically, and gives it a standard look and feel. You can customize the report as needed, changing the layout, color scheme, and adding or removing fields.

Setting the default form

When you publish your Web database application to Access Services, SharePoint accepts your application as a SharePoint site. When you navigate to that SharePoint site, you'll want to present your users with a form that acts as the launching pad for your application. The form should contain navigation components so your users can cruise easily from one form or report to another.

Here's how to set the default Web form that appears in your SharePoint site:

1. **Using your browser, navigate to the SharePoint site that hosts your Web database application.**

2. **From the title bar, click Options ⇨ Open in Access.**

   A local copy (which is a fancy way of saying on your computer) of your Web database application opens in Access 2010 ready for editing. Any changes that you make won't show up in SharePoint until you synchronize the local copy back to SharePoint.

3. **Click the File tab to present the Access Backstage View.**

4. **Click the Options command.**

   The Access Options dialog box appears.

5. **Click Current Database.**

   The options for the current database appear.

6. **In the Web Display Form drop-down list, select the form you want as the default form when users navigate to the SharePoint site.**

7. **Click OK.**

8. **Save your changes.**

   The changes are saved to the local copy of the Web database application, but won't show up in SharePoint until your synchronize them back to your SharePoint site.

9. **Click the Info tab, and then click Sync All.**

   Your changes are synchronized back to your SharePoint site. If you refresh the home page of the SharePoint site that hosts your Web database application, the new default Web form displays.

Publishing to Access Services

Access 2007 provided the capability to publish your Access list into a SharePoint list. Suddenly you could manage and control your data directly from SharePoint's browser interface. With Access 2010, you can use the integration features to publish your entire database application into SharePoint — along with its associated forms, queries, and reports — as a SharePoint site.

Microsoft Access 2010 provides enough tools and wizards that you can easily create sophisticated Web database applications without writing a single line of code. Publishing your database applications to Access Services extends their reach, which makes Microsoft Access a powerful development platform for SharePoint. Business units can maintain, customize, manage, and deploy their own databases — freeing up the IT staff to focus on running a stable, high-performance infrastructure. (That's the idea, anyway.)

Publishing Web applications to Access Services gives your users a common and familiar way to meet their business needs. For example, if your users are already taking advantage of SharePoint for collaboration and content management, you might as well give their productivity a boost by making their departmental Access database applications accessible in the same environment.

Mapping Access Objects to SharePoint Objects

When you publish your Access Web database application to SharePoint, Access Services kicks off a process that gives every Access object a corresponding object in SharePoint. Access Services enables your Access Web database applications to run the same way on both the server *and* the client machines. The conversion process also ensures that your users can get to and use your Access applications, regardless of which browsers they're running. That's because the conversion process steers clear of special ActiveX-type controls, using only standard Web HTML and JavaScript.

Here's a list of the Access client objects and how they're represented in SharePoint:

✦ **Access Web Database Application = SharePoint Site:** When you publish an Access Web database application to SharePoint, Access Services works behind the scenes to create a new SharePoint site for the Web database application.

✦ **Access Tables = SharePoint lists:** Tables in the Access Web database are implemented in SharePoint as SharePoint lists. The fields in an Access table are represented as columns in the SharePoint list, reflecting the appropriate data types. For example, if your Access Web database application contains an Employee table that has `First Name`, `Last Name` text fields and an `EmployeeID` integer field, each field becomes a column in the Employee list — with data types of Single Line of Text (for the text fields) and Integer (for the `EmployeeID` field).

✦ **Access Forms = ASPX pages:** Forms that you create in your Access Web database are implemented in SharePoint as standard `.ASPX` Web pages for rendering in the browser. If you need to modify any of your pages, you can implement the changes in the Access client application and synchronize 'em back to SharePoint as needed.

✦ **Access Reports = SQL Server Reporting Services Reports (`.rdl`):**
Reports that you create in your Access database application are converted to RDL files (Report Definition Language — you can find out more about that in Book III, Chapter 1). Then they're presented using SQL Server Reporting Services; the Report Viewer Web Part renders the reports in the browser.

✦ **Access User Interface Macros = JavaScript:** Macros attached to user interface objects (such as buttons, text boxes, forms, and reports) are known as *UI macros.* Data macros (see the next item in this list) are associated with tables. Use UI macros to automate a series of actions, such as opening a report when you click a navigation tab. UI macros in SharePoint use JavaScript that is attached to your Web pages.

✦ **Access Data Macros = SharePoint Workflows**: *Data macros* use and apply business-level Access macros at the level of individual tables. For example, if you want to update the content of a field in a table when the content of another field in another table changes, then you can easily achieve this using Data Macros. When you publish your application to SharePoint, the data macros you've defined in your application are converted to SharePoint workflows on the list.

Figure 1-8 shows you how SharePoint turns the data macros associated with the PurchaseOrders table in the Northwind Traders Web database application into workflows.

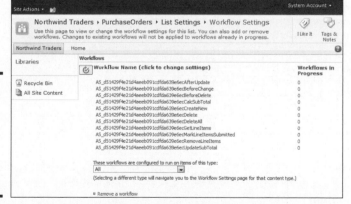

Figure 1-8:
Data macros are converted into SharePoint workflows.

✦ **Access Queries = System table:** If your Access database application contains queries, SharePoint puts them in the System table (that is, the `MSysASO` SharePoint list) in the SharePoint site, where the Access Services query processor renders the queries.

Checking Web compatibility

Your Access Web database applications can be shared across your organization by being published to Access Services. If your database contains items and settings that aren't compatible with Access Services, your application won't publish correctly.

Use the Compatibility Checker that Access provides to check your database before you publish it to SharePoint. If compatibility problems turn up, they land in a table called Web Compatibility Issues.

Most errors that the Checker identifies usually happen because some gremlin in the works tried to apply *client-only* features or settings (the ones that are supposed to be disabled when an Access database becomes a SharePoint site) to your database. You can avoid many of these errors entirely by selecting the Web database template when you initially create your database. Doing so filters out many of the client-only features preventing you from applying them to your database.

Follow these steps to check your Access database to see whether it's compatible with the Access Services:

1. **Open your Web database application in Access 2010.**

2. **Click the File tab to present the Access Backstage View.**

3. **Click the Save & Publish tab.**

   The save and publishing options appear.

4. **In the Publish section, click Publish to Access Services.**

   The Compatibility Checker option appears on the right.

5. **Click Run Compatibility Checker to check to see whether your Access Web database is Web-compatible.**

   If you have any objects open in your database, a dialog box appears and asks whether you want to close those objects. If you've saved all those objects, click Yes to have Access close them.

   The Compatibility Checker presents a dialog box that shows the progress as Access processes every object in the database to check for compatibility issues.

If your database is compatible with the Web, the Compatibility Checker displays a message to tell you so — and the Web Compatibility Issues button is disabled.

If your database is *in*compatible (oh, the shame!), the Compatibility Checker shows the following attributes:

✦ The Compatibility Checker is highlighted in red to indicate that errors turned up. (It's not embarrassed; it just looks that way.)

✦ This status message appears:

```
The database is incompatible with the Web. Press Web Compatibility Issues
     to see errors.
```

✦ The Web Compatibility Issues button is enabled.

Figure 1-9 shows the Compatibility Checker for a database that isn't Web-compatible.

Figure 1-9:
Access
lets you
know if your
application
isn't Web-
compatible.

When you click the Web Compatibility Issues button, Access displays a list of all Web-compatibility problems the Checker found, along with a description of each error (complete with Issue Type ID and a link to a Microsoft article that provides more information on the error and a possible resolution). Figure 1-10 shows an example of the compatibility error found in a database that uses on OLE data type for a field in one of its tables. Figure 1-11 shows details of the error as they appear on the Microsoft site.

Publishing your Access Web database

When you've made sure that your database application is Web-compatible, you're ready to publish the Web database application to Access Services (that is, SharePoint).

Figure 1-10:
Access
provides
a list of
compatibility
issues.

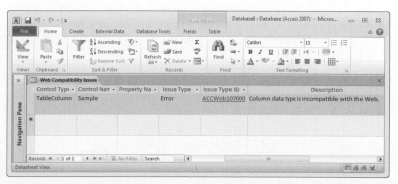

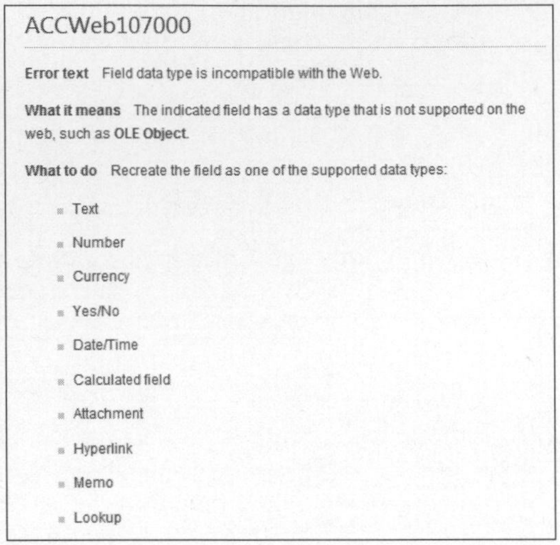

ACCWeb107000

Error text   Field data type is incompatible with the Web.

What it means   The indicated field has a data type that is not supported on the web, such as OLE Object.

What to do   Recreate the field as one of the supported data types:

- Text
- Number
- Currency
- Yes/No
- Date/Time
- Calculated field
- Attachment
- Hyperlink
- Memo
- Lookup

Figure 1-11: OLE Object data types aren't compatible with publishing to the Web. Oops.

The first time you publish your application to Access Services, you use the Publish to Access command to deploy your application. Follow these steps to publish your application:

1. **Open your Web database application in Access 2010.**

2. **Click the File tab to present the Access Backstage View.**

3. **Click the Save & Publish tab.**

The save and publishing options appear.

4. **In the Publish section, click Publish to Access Services.**

If this is your first time publishing the Web database application to Access Services, a Publish to Access Services section (complete with appropriate button) appears just below the Compatibility Checker option, as shown in Figure 1-12.

5. **In the Server URL field, enter the URL to the server running Access Services.**

6. **In the Site Name field, enter the name you want to give to the new SharePoint site that will represent your Access Web database application.**

7. **Click the Publish to Access Services button.**

The Synchronizing Web Application dialog box appears, showing you a status bar while the conversion process runs. If the publishing process is successful, you receive a success message, along with a link to the new SharePoint site. If the publishing process is unsuccessful, you'll see a message similar to the one in Figure 1-13. (Oh, well, the world hasn't ended yet. Try again.)

Figure 1-12:
The Publish
command
appears
under the
Compa-
tibility
Checker.

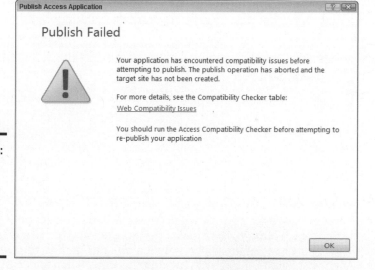

Figure 1-13:
Access
notifies
you if the
publishing
process
fails.

When your database application is published, the Publish to Access command is no longer available. The command that replaces it is the Sync All —
which synchronizes your changes with the SharePoint server. If you want to
tinker some more with your changes in Access and then synchronize those
changes back to SharePoint, we have just the place to look for instructions —
yes, the "Synchronizing your changes with SharePoint" section of this very
chapter.

Before you can publish your Access Web database application, you must have Designer permissions in the SharePoint site to which you want to publish.

Viewing the Application Log

In addition to the Compatibility Checker table, you can check for error notifications in the Application log (USysApplicationLog) for any server-side errors that may have occurred during the publishing process.

Follow these steps to view the Application log:

1. **Open your Web database application in Access 2010.**

2. **Click the File tab to present the Access Backstage View.**

3. **Click the Info tab.**

   General options relating to you application appear, including the application log options.

4. **In the Application log section, click View Application Log Table.**

   The application log table (UsysApplicationLog) appears. Figure 1-14 shows the View Application Log Table command as it appears in the Microsoft Access Backstage View.

Figure 1-14:
Server-side publishing errors show up in the Application Log Table.

Opening your Access Web database application

When you successfully publish your Access Web database application to Access Services, a SharePoint site is created, sporting the name you supplied during the publishing process. When you navigate to the site, the Web Access application appears, looking the way you specified as the site's default *Web display form*. If you haven't yet defined a default Web display form for the site, that's a minor gaffe, and see the Site Setting page below.

The publishing process stores the entire Access Web database application in SharePoint. Thus you can use SharePoint as your launching point for editing your application *in Access*. Even if you lose all the local copies of your database application, you can still open the application from SharePoint — which downloads a new copy of the application to you, linked to the server.

When you open your Access Web database application from SharePoint, you are (in effect) opening an offline copy of your database application. But not to worry: Any changes you make while offline can be synchronized back to the server.

Opening the database from the Site Settings page

Here's how to open your published Web database application in Access:

1. **Using your browser, navigate to your SharePoint Web database site.**

2. **From the Options menu, click Settings to display the site settings page.**

If you haven't defined a default Web display form for your site, you'll be staring at the Site Settings page (which will have appeared in Step 1) until you specify the pesky Web display form. Humor the machine and move on.

3. **Click the Modify this Web database, add new fields, customize forms and reports link.**

The File Download dialog box appears.

4. **Click Open.**

The Web database application opens in Access 2010. You can customize the database as needed. When you're ready to push your changes up to the server, flip ahead to the "Synchronizing your changes with SharePoint" section of this chapter and follow the instructions we left there.

Opening your database from the Options menu

You can use the following instructions to open your published Web database application in Access:

1. **Using your browser, navigate to your SharePoint Web database site.**

2. **From the Options menu, click Open in Access.**

The File Download dialog box appears.

3. **Click Open.**

The Web database application opens in Access 2010. You can customize the database as needed. When you're ready to synchronize your changes with the server, follow the steps in the "Synchronizing your changes with SharePoint" section of this chapter.

You can't use SharePoint Designer to open a Web-database SharePoint site. Instead, you have to use Access — just as you do if you're going to change or customize your database application.

Synchronizing your changes with SharePoint

After you've initially published your Access Web database to Access Services, the way you synchronize all subsequent database modifications and customizations with SharePoint is to use the Sync All command in the Access client application.

Here's how to synchronize your database application changes to SharePoint:

1. **Open your Web database application in Access 2010.**

2. **Click the File tab to present the Access Backstage View.**

3. **Click the Info tab.**

General options relating to your application appear, including the synchronize options.

4. **Click the Sync All command to synchronize all your changes with the server and reconnect all the tables.**

The Synchronizing Web Application dialog box appears, showing you a status bar so you can keep track of the conversion process.

Saving your Web Database as a Site Template

The integration between Microsoft Access 2010 and Access Services makes it easy to create an Access Web database template and implement it as a site template in SharePoint. SharePoint Server 2010 implements site templates as *solution files* (.wsp). If you haven't created a solution file yet, don't despair; there's an easy way . . .

With Access 2010 handy, you don't have to figure out how to package your database as a SharePoint solution file. Instead, you wave your magic wand (well, almost): You simply save your Web database as a regular Access template file (.accdt) and upload it to the SharePoint Solution Gallery. When you upload an Access database template to the SharePoint Solution Gallery, Access Services kicks into gear and wraps the template in a SharePoint solution file — automatically. (Gotta love it.)

Here's the process that deploys your Access Web database as a SharePoint site template:

1. **Open your Web database in Access 2010.**

2. **Click the File tab to present the Access Backstage View.**

3. **Click Save & Publish, and then click Save Database As.**

A list of database file types appears on the right, under the Save Database As section.

4. **From the list of file types, click Template (***.accdt**).**

   The Create New Template from This Database dialog box appears.

5. **Enter a Name and Description for your template.**

6. **Select an Icon that you'd like to use for your template.**

7. **In the Instantiation Form field, select the form you want to appear as the default display form.**

8. **If you want to include the data in the current database as part of the template, select Include Data in Template, otherwise leave the setting clear.**

9. **Click OK.**

   Note the location where your template is saved.

10. **Using your browser, navigate to the home page of the SharePoint site to which you want to deploy the template.**

11. **From the Site Actions menu, click Site Settings.**

12. **From the Galleries section, click Solutions.**

    The Solutions Gallery appears.

13. **Click the Solutions Gallery page to activate the Gallery Ribbon menu.**

14. **From the New Ribbon group, click Upload Solution.**

    The Solution Gallery Upload Solution dialog box appears.

15. **Browse to the Access Web database template file that you saved in Step 9.**

16. **Click OK to upload the file.**

    Access Services gets busy and wraps the template file in a SharePoint solution file (.wsp).

17. **Select the newly uploaded solution file and click the down arrow next to the file.**

    A shortcut menu appears.

18. **From the shortcut menu, click Activate.**

    The template now appears under the Web Databases category as a site template that you can select when you create a new site.

When you create a site based on your new Access site template, Access Services extracts the solution file and converts what's in it to a SharePoint site.

Chapter 2: Connecting to External Data

*B*usiness Connectivity Services (BCS) provides an easy, flexible, and extensible method of displaying content from external data sources (such as your custom line-of-business applications) SharePoint, allowing you to work with that content in much the same way you do native SharePoint content. At the center of all this magic lies the external content type. External content types provide configuration information that allows BCS to connect to a specific entity in an external system. For example, an employee external content type may represent an Employee table in a back-end database.

In this chapter, we explain the ins and outs of external content types and show you the steps involved in creating an external content type by using SharePoint Designer 2010.

Understanding External Content Types

Regardless of the type of SharePoint solution you're deploying, content is crucial to its success. Relevant, meaningful, current, and useful content is what makes users want to come back to your site. Content breathes life into your deployment and comes in all shapes and sizes, including

+ **A public-facing Internet site:** Informational Web pages and navigational components.

+ **A departmental collaboration portal:** Document libraries, calendars, and discussion boards

+ **A business intelligence dashboard:** Web pages that report and analyze data from external back-end systems.

You define content in SharePoint by using content types:

✦ **SharePoint content type:** A reusable package of information that describes a specific entity that resides in SharePoint, such as a document or a page layout. The package contains information such as the fields and behaviors associated with that specific type of content. For example, a document library dedicated to abstract submissions for an upcoming conference may have a content type named Abstract Submission that leverages a specific Word template. Fields such as Presenter Name, Presentation Title, and Abstract are associated with the content type, in addition to an approval workflow that triggers when an Abstract Submission is posted to the document library. The template, the fields, and the workflow are all components of the Abstract Submission content type.

✦ **External content type:** At the heart and soul of BCS, an external content type defines the fields and methods of the external data source to which you want to connect, in addition to how you want the external content type to behave in both SharePoint and Microsoft Office. External content types differ from SharePoint content types in that the entity they represent resides outside of SharePoint. For example, an external content type may represent an Employee table in an external SQL database.

External content type XML definition

When you create an external content type, you provide the Business Data Connectivity (BDC) service with an XML definition of the external content type which is stored in the BDC metadata store. The XML definition includes the following information:

✦ **Fields:** Identifies the fields of data that are associated with the object being defined. For example, an Employee external content type may contain fields such as Employee ID, First Name, Last Name, and Job Title.

Microsoft provides the following tools, which you can use to identify the fields for your external content type:

- *SharePoint Designer 2010:* Connect to the external data source and select the fields relevant to your external content type.

- *Microsoft Visual Studio 2010:* Contains a BDC project template that you can use to define your external content type fields.

✦ **Actions:** You can define the actions that a user can take on an object, which enables you to link your business data to external URLs. For example, if you have an external content type named Artists that's implemented in SharePoint as an external list, you can define an action that passes the name of the artist through to your favorite online search engine for more information about the artist.

Book 3, Chapter 2 shows you how to create an external content type action by using Central Administration.

✦ **Associations:** A relationship between two types of entities, such as a music artist and an album. Associations can be very complex. For example, an artist can belong to more than one genre, and a genre can represent multiple artists. Out of the box, BCS supports associations.

Microsoft provides the following tools with which you can create associations:

- *SharePoint Designer 2010:* Create simple associations, such as one-to-many associations and self-referential associations.

- *Microsoft Visual Studio:* Create simple and complex associations. Simple associations include one-to-many associations and self-referential associations, similar to those you can create with SharePoint Designer. Complex associations include many-to-many associations and multiple external-content-type associations.

✦ **Methods:** An operation that you perform on an object. You can define methods that can create, read, update, query, or delete the object.

Microsoft provides the following tools with which you can create methods:

- *SharePoint Designer 2010:* Define the appropriate Create, Read, Update, and Query operations for your external content type. When you define operations in SharePoint Designer, you create a method in the XML definition for the external content type.

  You can use the terms *method* and *operation* interchangeably. In this chapter, we use the term *operation* when we're using SharePoint Designer, and we use the term *method* when referencing the XML definition.

- *Microsoft Visual Studio:* Contains a BDC project template from which you can create your external content types, including any associated methods.

✦ **Parameters:** You can associate a set of parameters for the methods that you assign to an external content type. For example, the Read operation may take the unique identifier field for an item (such as ArtistId) as an input parameter and return additional fields (such as Artist Name and Genre) as return parameters.

Assigning parameters is part of the process when you create methods for an external content type, so you use the same tools.

✦ **Filter parameters:** In addition to being able to set the parameters associated with the methods of an external content type, you can also define filters for the methods. Filters are used to help you manage queries that have the potential to return a large number of items. For example, the Read List method returns a list of all the items from an external data source. You can reduce the number of items returned by allowing users to filter on the result set. This is like creating views in SharePoint — if you're using very large lists, you rarely need to return all the items in the list. Allowing users to filter the result set based on their needs creates a better user experience and much better performance.

You can create multiple filter parameters for a method. When you use large lists, apply a limit filter parameter on the method to ensure that not all items are returned with the result of the query. For example, if you're returning a list of Artists from a music database, you can limit the initial list to return the first 100 artists. A limit filter returns a subset of the items in your list; therefore, create additional filter types to allow your users to access the remaining items in your list. For example, you can create a filter on Genre that returns artists based on the genre in which they belong.

The filters that you define appear in the BDC Web Parts, such as the Business Data List Web Part. Figure 2-1 shows a simple Business Data List Web Part that allows users to filter the list of Irish artists by a specific genre; the genre in this particular example is set to filter on Folk.

Figure 2-1:
The
Business
Data List
Web Part
displays
filter
parameters.

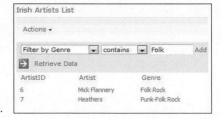

Add a limit filter to methods that return multiple items. If you don't apply a limit filter to the returned list, all the items for the list are returned — which may create a large result set, ultimately affecting performance.

Tooling for Business Connectivity Services

Microsoft provides a number of different tools that you can use to create external content types, including

✦ **Microsoft SharePoint Designer:** SharePoint Designer is the power tool when it comes to connecting to and using external data from SharePoint. It takes much of the legwork out of creating your external content types so that you can respond to requests from your business users much more expediently and efficiently. In fact, you can even pass this responsibility on to your users. Of course, where you place the responsibility depends on a number of factors, including how technically savvy your users are and whether they even want to crack open SharePoint Designer at all. For example, your users are probably busy enough doing their actual jobs and would much rather put in a request for what they want so that someone else makes it happen. Also, your IT department most likely has strict policies regarding what your SharePoint users can do; do you really want to allow all users to connect to external systems freely?

Regardless of whether you're an IT administrator, a SharePoint developer, or a business user, SharePoint Designer 2010 makes it incredibly easy to leverage Business Connectivity Services (BCS) in your SharePoint 2010 environment.

✦ **Microsoft Visual Studio:** Microsoft Visual Studio 2010 allows professional developers to create reusable components — such as external content types — and then package and deploy them to your Business Data Connectivity (BDC) service. Microsoft Visual Studio 2010 ships with many SharePoint project templates that can assist you in the creation of SharePoint entities.

You can use the BDC-model project template to kick-start the creation of your custom BDC models and external content types.

✦ **Import an application model into BCS.**

You probably develop and test your BDC models in separate development and test environments. After you're satisfied that your BDC model is ready for prime time, you need a method of deploying it to your production farm. Fortunately, Central Administration provides an easy mechanism for importing and exporting BDC models.

You can use Central Administration to import an application model for an external system into your BDC Services application. The application model that you import is an XML file known as the BDC model. The file

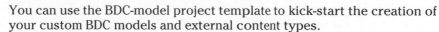

Book IV
Chapter 2

Connecting to
External Data

contains the definition of one or more external content types for a given external system. When you import a BDC model, all of its external content types are added to the BCS and are available for use.

Book 3, Chapter 2 shows you the steps involved in importing and exporting BDC models from Central Administration.

Creating External Content Types with SharePoint Designer

When it comes to creating external content types, SharePoint Designer provides an intuitive and flexible environment that allows you to get your connections up and running very quickly. The following sections walk you through the process of creating an external content type by using SharePoint Designer. This chapter assumes that you have all the necessary permissions in place to modify the Business Data Connectivity (BDC) model for the BDC Service application.

If you haven't set up your permissions or don't know what permissions you need, check out Book 3, Chapter 2.

Creating an external content type in SharePoint Designer involves the following high-level steps:

1. **Open your site in SharePoint Designer.**

   When you create an external content type by using SharePoint Designer 2010, you need to first open a site that has access to the BDC Service by using an account that has permissions to modify the BDC model to that specific BDC Service application.

2. **Launch the external content type designer.**

   When you create a new external content type or customize an existing external content type, the first page that appears displays summary information about your external content type:

   • General information, such as the display name and external connection

   • Operations defined for the external content type

   • Fields that were defined in the operations for the external content type

   • Permissions defined for the external content type

   • External lists bound to the external content type

If you're creating a new external content type, the information is unde-fined and awaiting your configuration settings. If you're modifying an existing external content type, you can use this page to view and manage the settings.

3. **Configure your new external content type general settings.**

   When you create a new external content type, you configure general set-tings, such as the display name and version number.

4. **Add a connection to the external system.**

   After you define the general settings, you add a connection to your external system. SharePoint Designer supports connections to the fol-lowing data source types:

   - *.NET Type:* Defines a connection to a .NET assembly.
   - *SQL Server:* Defines a connection to a SQL Server database.
   - *WCF Service:* Defines a connection to WCF/Web service.

   Figure 2-2 shows the Data Source Explorer window of the Operation Designer, which lists an example of a connection to each of the data-source types.

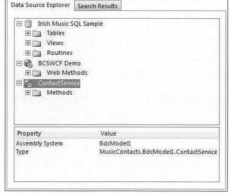

Figure 2-2: Connections appear in the Operation Designer Data Source Explorer window.

5. **Add operations or methods.**

   The data source type that you select when you configure your connec-tion determines the operations and methods that are available to create. For example, Figure 2-3 shows the operations available out of the box when you connect to an external SQL database.

The Create All Operations option allows you to create the Create, Read, Update, and Delete operations at the same time; however, it's available only when you're configuring operations against a SQL Server database connection. All remaining options, such as the New Read Item operation, are available to all three data source types.

Figure 2-3:
Creating operations when connecting to an external SQL database.

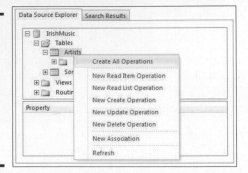

When creating the operations and method, you also create the parameters and filters associated with each operation. For example, the Read List operation typically has filter parameters and a return parameter defined.

6. **Save the external content type.**

When you create a new external content type or modify an existing external content type, your configuration settings aren't written to the BDC metadata store until you click Save.

7. **Assign permissions to your external content type by using Central Administration.**

After you have your external content type up and running, you can control who has the ability to manage and use the external content type. You manage permissions to an external content type by using Central Administration.

The preceding list of high-level steps outlines the tasks involved when you create an external content type. In the following sections, we expand on some of these tasks, providing step-by-step instructions.

Book 3, Chapter 2 shows you how to apply permission settings to an external content type by using Central Administration.

Opening your site in SharePoint Designer

Follow these steps to open a SharePoint site in SharePoint Designer:

1. **Launch Internet Explorer and navigate to your SharePoint site.**

2. **From the Site Actions menu, select Edit in SharePoint Designer.**

The Edit in SharePoint Designer option appears, regardless of whether you have SharePoint Designer installed. To open a SharePoint 2010 site in SharePoint Designer, you must first install SharePoint Designer 2010.

Alternatively, you can launch the SharePoint Designer 2010 application, and then select the Open Site option from the Sites menu.

Your site opens in SharePoint Designer. The left navigation pane displays a list of site objects that you can manage and customize for your site.

Launching the External Content Type Designer

Follow these steps to launch the External Content Type Designer, which you can use to create a new external content type or customize an existing external content type:

1. **From the SharePoint Designer left navigation bar, click External Content Types.**

A dialog box appears, notifying you that SharePoint Designer is retrieving information from the BDC Service application's BDC metadata store. This process may take some time.

SharePoint Designer presents a list of the external content types already defined in the BDC metadata store for the BDC Service to which you're connected. You see only the external content types that you have permission to see.

2. **If you're creating a new external content type, in the New group on the Ribbon menu, click External Content Type.**

This option presents you with the External Content Type Designer, which you can use to create your new external content type.

3. **If you're modifying an existing external content type, from the list of external content types that appears in the design window, click the external content type that you want to modify.**

External Content Type Designer appears, which you can use to customize your existing external content type.

Configuring your external content type general settings

When you create a new external content type, you provide information that describes both the fields and the behavior of the external content type.

Follow these steps to create and configure an external content type:

1. **Launch the External Content Type Designer.**

Follow the steps in the preceding section to create a new external content type and launch the designer.

2. **Enter the name of the new external content type in the Name text box.**

3. **Enter the display name of the external content type in the Display Name text box.**

4. **Enter the namespace for the new external content type in the Namespace text box.**

5. **Enter the version of the new external content type in the Version text box.**

6. **In the Office Item Type drop-down list, select the type that best represents your external content type.**

The item that you select from this list determines how your external content type behaves when you access it by using Microsoft Outlook. For example, if you select Contact as the Office Item Type, items in your external list appear in Outlook as Outlook contacts.

7. **In the Offline Sync for External List drop-down list, select Enabled or Disabled.**

If you select Enabled, your external list can be synchronized with Outlook and SharePoint Workspace; the options Connect to Outlook and Sync to SharePoint Workspace are enabled on the Ribbon menu.

If you select Disabled, your external list can't be synchronized, and those options are disabled on the Ribbon menu.

Connecting to an external SQL database

When you create a new external content type, you define the connection to your external system. SharePoint Designer supports connections to three types of data sources, including SQL databases. Figure 2-4 shows an example of the settings for connecting to an external SQL Server database.

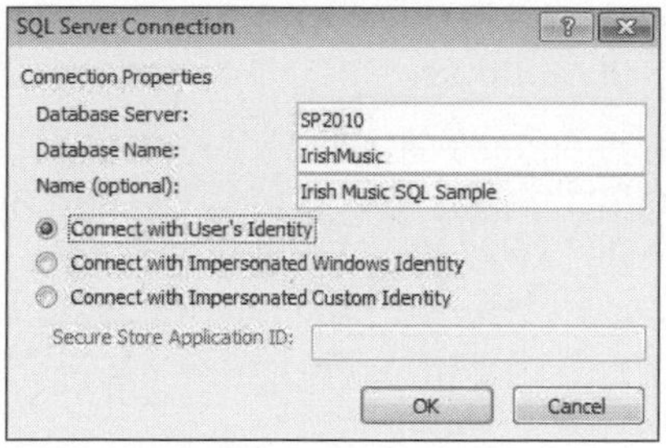

Figure 2-4:
Connecting
to an
external
SQL
database.

Follow these steps to add a connection to an external SQL database by using SharePoint Designer:

1. **Open your external content type in SharePoint Designer.**

   Follow the steps in the preceding sections to access an existing external content type or create a new external content type.

2. **In the Views group on the Ribbon menu, click Operations Design View.**

   The Operation Designer, which you can use to manage connections to external data sources and manage the operations for the external content type, opens.

3. **Click Add Connection.**

   The External Data Source Type Selection dialog box appears.

4. **From the Data Source Type drop-down list, select SQL Server.**

5. **Click OK.**

   The SQL Server Connection dialog box appears.

6. **Complete the connection fields that identify the SQL Server database.**

   The SQL Server Connection dialog box provides fields that define the connection properties to the SQL database. The fields that determine the database for your connection include

   - *Database Server:* Enter the name of the database server to which you're connecting.

   - *Database Name:* Enter the name of the database to which you're connecting.

   - *Name (Optional):* You can enter an optional name that allows you to easily identify your connection in the future.

7. **Select the authentication method that your users will use when they connect to the external SQL database.**

   The SQL Server Connection dialog box provides fields that determine the identity under which the connection occurs. You can select one of three authentication options to use for your connection:

   - *Connect with User's Identity.* Users interact with data in your external SQL Server database by using the identity with which they're currently logged on to SharePoint.

   - *Connect with Impersonated Windows Identity.* Users interact with data in your external SQL Server database by using a separate Windows identity whose credential information is stored in the secure store service.

   - *Connect with Impersonated Custom Identity.* Users interact with data in your external SQL Server database by using a separate custom identity, such as a claim, whose credential information is stored in the secure store service.

8. **Click OK.**

   The SQL Server Connection dialog box closes and you return to the Operations Designer. SharePoint Designer creates the new SQL database connection and displays it in the list of data sources in the External Content Type Data Source Explorer window of the Operations Designer.

Connecting to a Web service

When you create a new external content type, you define the connection to your external system. SharePoint Designer supports connections to three types of data sources, one of which is a Windows Communication Foundation (WCF) Service. WCF is a framework for building service-oriented applications; the WCF Service allows you to create a connection to a service that you have created that was built using the WCF framework . Figure 2-5 shows an example of the settings for connecting to an external WCF Service.

Follow these steps to add a connection to an external Web service by using SharePoint Designer:

1. **Open your external content type in SharePoint Designer.**

   Follow the steps in section "Creating External Content Types with SharePoint Designer," earlier in this chapter, to access an existing external content type or create a new external content type.

2. **In the Views group on the Ribbon menu, click Operations Design View.**

   The Operations Designer, which you can use to manage connections to external data sources and manage the operations for the external content type, opens.

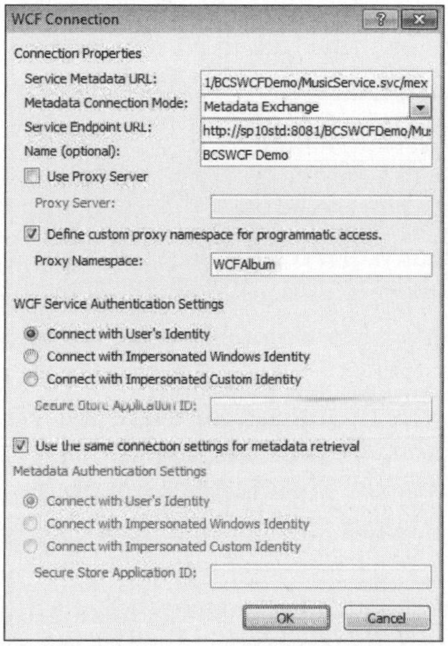

Figure 2-5:
Connecting
to an
external
WCF
Service.

3. **Click Add Connection.**

   The External Data Source Type Selection dialog box appears.

4. **From the Data Source Type drop-down list, select WCF Service.**

5. **Click OK.**

   The WCF Connection dialog box appears.

6. **Complete the connection fields that identify the WCF/Web Service connection.**

   The WCF Connection dialog box provides fields that define the connection properties to the WCF/Web Service. The fields that determine the WCF/Web Service for your connection include

**Book IV
Chapter 2**

Connecting to
External Data

- *Service Metadata URL.* If you're connecting to a WCF Service, enter the URL to the service endpoint that provides metadata (the endpoint exposed by using the Metadata Exchange contract).

  If you're connecting to a Web service, simply enter the URL to the Web Service Definition Language (WSDL).

- *Metadata Connection Mode.* Select WSDL to connect to a Web service. Select Metadata Exchange to connect to a WCF Service.

- *Service Endpoint URL.* Enter the URL to the service endpoint.

  If you're connecting to a Web service, simply enter the URL to the Web Service Definition Language (WSDL).

- *Name (Optional).* You can enter a name that allows you to easily identify your connection in the future.

- *Use Proxy Server.* If your WCF/Web Service uses a proxy server, then select Proxy Server and enter the proxy server name.

- *Define Custom Proxy Namespace for Programmatic Access.* Enter the proxy namespace for your project.

7. **Select the authentication method that your users will use when connecting to the WCF/Web Service.**

   The WCF Connection dialog box provides you with the option to select a different authentication method when a user requests or retrieves metadata from your WCF/Web Service.

   If you want to keep the authentication method the same for all interactions with the WCF/Web service, then select the Use the same connection settings for metadata retrieval check box. This setting is selected by default.

   To use a different authentication method for metadata retrieval, start by deselecting the Use the same connection settings for metadata retrieval check box. Next, select one of three authentication options to use for your connection:

   - *Connect with User's Identity.* Users interact with data in your WCF/Web Service by using the identity with which they're currently logged on to SharePoint.

   - *Connect with Impersonated Windows Identity.* Users interact with data in your WCF/Web Service by using a separate Windows identity whose credential information is stored in the secure store service.

- *Connect with Impersonated Custom Identity.* Users interact with data in your WCF/Web Service by using a separate custom identity, such as a claim, whose credential information is stored in the secure store service.

8. **Select the authentication method that your users will use when retrieving metadata from the WCF/Web Service.**

   The WCF Connection dialog box provides you with the option to select a different authentication method when a user requests or retrieves metadata from your WCF/Web Service.

   If you want to keep the authentication method the same for all interactions with the WCF/Web service, then select the Use the Same Connection Settings for Metadata Retrieval check box.

   To use a different authentication method for metadata retrieval, start by deselecting the Use the Same Connection Settings for Metadata Retrieval check box. Next, select one of three authentication options to use for your connection:

   - *Connect with User's Identity.* Users request or retrieve metadata from your WCF/Web Service by using the identity with which they're currently connected to SharePoint.

   - *Connect with Impersonated Windows Identity.* Users request or retrieve metadata from your WCF/Web Service by using a separate Windows identity whose credential information is stored in the secure store service.

   - *Connect with Impersonated Custom Identity.* Users request or retrieve metadata from your WCF/Web Service by using a separate custom identity, such as a claim, whose credential information is stored in the secure store service.

9. **Click OK.**

   The WCF Connection dialog box closes and you return to the Operations Designer. SharePoint Designer creates the new WCF/Web Service connection and displays it in the list of data sources in the External Content Type Data Source Explorer window of the Operations Designer.

Connecting to a .NET assembly

A .NET assembly is a file that contains your compiled code ready for deployment to the servers in your environment. Your .NET assembly is compiled as either a dynamic link library (.dll), or an executable (.exe). When you create a new external content type, you define the connection to your external system. SharePoint Designer supports connections to three types of data sources, one of which is a .NET type. The .NET Type option allows you to create an external content type that maps to an entity, or .NET class, defined in the .NET assembly. For example, if you had a .NET assembly that defines two classes — Artists and Songs — both classes appear in the Types drop-down list in the .NET Type Selection dialog box. From this drop-down list, you can select the class, or type, that you want to map to your external content type.

You can use .NET assemblies as a way to make your external systems accessible through your BDC Service application, which is particularly useful if you are connecting to a system that is not a SQL Server database, a WCF Service or a Web Service.

After you create your .NET assembly and publish it into the BDC metadata store, the assembly is available for use in applications such as SharePoint Designer. Figure 2-6 shows an example of the settings for connecting to a .NET assembly that's published to the BDC metadata store.

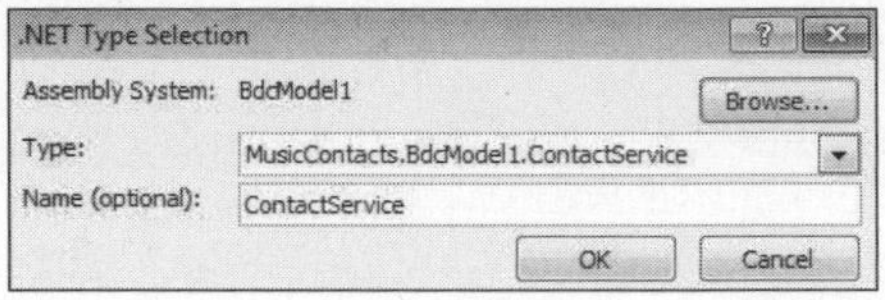

Figure 2-6: Connecting to a .NET assembly.

Follow these steps to add a connection to a .NET assembly by using SharePoint Designer:

1. **Open your external content type in SharePoint Designer.**

Follow the steps in section "Creating External Content Types with SharePoint Designer," earlier in this chapter, to access an existing external content type or create a new external content type.

2. **In the Views group on the Ribbon menu, click Operations Design View.**

The Operation Designer, which you can use to manage connections to external data sources and manage the operations for the external content type, opens.

3. **Click Add Connection.**

The External Data Source Type Selection dialog box appears.

4. **From the Data Source Type drop-down list, select .NET Type.**

5. **Click OK.**

    The .NET Type Selection dialog box appears.

6. **To populate the .NET Assembly System Selection drop-down list, click Browse.**

    SharePoint Designer connects to your BDC Service application and retrieves the list of .NET assemblies published to the BDC metadata store. If the Assembly System Selection drop-down list is blank, then your .NET assembly hasn't been published to the BDC metadata store. You need to publish your assembly before proceeding.

7. **From the Assembly System Selection drop-down list, select the system that contains the reference to your .NET assembly.**

8. **Click OK.**

    SharePoint Designer returns you to the .NET Type Selection dialog box and populates the Type drop-down list with the types available in the .NET assembly.

9. **From the Type drop-down list, select the .NET type that you want to use for your external content type.**

10. **(Optional) In the Name field, enter a name that allows you to easily identify your connection in the future.**

11. **Click OK.**

    The .NET Type Selection dialog box closes and you return to the Operations Designer. SharePoint Designer creates the new .NET assembly connection and displays it in the list of data sources in the External Content Type Data Source Explorer window of the Operations Designer.

Adding operations to an external content type

Before you can interact with your external content type, you must define the appropriate Create, Read, Update, and Delete (CRUD) operations. When you define an operation, you configure the appropriate input, return, and filter parameters specific to the operation. For example, when you define the Read List operation in SharePoint Designer, you can specify a limit filter parameter to ensure that all items aren't returned at the same time.

When you create an external content type by using SharePoint Designer, you must connect to an external system and define at least one operation before you can save the external content type.

Follow these steps to add an operation to an external content type by using SharePoint Designer:

1. **Open your external content type in SharePoint Designer.**

   Follow the steps in section "Creating External Content Types with SharePoint Designer," earlier in this chapter, to access an existing external content type or create a new external content type.

2. **In the Views group on the Ribbon menu, click Operations Design View.**

   The Operation Designer, which you can use to manage connections to external data sources and manage the operations for the external content type, opens.

3. **From the Data Source Explorer, right-click the entity for which you want to define an operation.**

   The entity you select depends on the type of connection with which you're working:

   - *External SQL Server database:* Expand the database tree and right-click the table that your external content type represents.

   - *WCF/Web Service:* Expand the WCF/Web Service tree and right-click the Web method for which you want to define an operation.

   - *.NET assembly:* Expand the .NET tree and right-click the Web method for which you want to define an operation.

   The Operations shortcut menu appears, listing the available operations. Figure 2-7 shows the operations shortcut menu for a WCF Service. (Figure 2-3 shows the Operations shortcut menu for a table in a SQL Server database.)

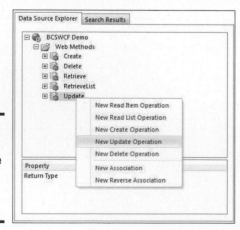

Figure 2-7: Creating a new Update operation for a WCF Service.

4. **In the Operations shortcut menu, click the operation that you want to define.**

   The operations that you define determine how your users can interact with your external data. For example, if you create an external list based on an external content type that has only the Read Item and Read List operations defined, users can read the content in the list, but they can't create, update, or delete items.

   The operations that you can define depend on the external system to which you're connecting. Here are some things to keep in mind:

   • When you define operations for SQL Server connections, SharePoint natively supports all CRUD operations. You don't need to define special stored procedures or code to handle the create, read, update, and delete tasks for your database.

   • When you define operations for WCF/Web Service connections, your WCF/Web Service must implement a Web method to support the operation you want to define. For example, if you want your users to be able to create new items by using your Web Service, then that Web Service must implement a Web method to provide Create functionality.

   • When you define operations for .NET assembly connections, your .NET assembly type must implement a method to support the operation that you want to define. For example, if you want your users to be able to delete new items by using your .NET assembly, then your assembly must implement a method to provide Delete functionality.

   The Create All Operations option is available only when you configure operations against a SQL Server database connection.

5. **Complete the fields in the Operation Configuration Wizard.**

   When you click the operation that you want to define from the Operations shortcut menu, the Operation Wizard for the type of operation you're defining appears. For example, if you're defining a Create operation, then the Create Operation Wizard appears. The operation properties that appear in the wizard reflect the operation type and the connection type. For example, if you're creating a Read operation on an external SQL data source, you can configure the input parameters and return parameters for the operation; if you're creating a Read List operation on an external SQL data source, you can configure filter parameters and their default values, along with return parameters.

   The Operation Configuration Wizard steps you through the process of defining the parameters for your operation. The following sections walk you through an example of how to define the CRUD operations for an external content type mapped to a particular SQL database. The actual parameters and filters that you apply to your external content types vary according to your needs and your external data source type, but the basic premise of how to define the operations remains the same.

Defining a Create operation

Follow these steps to define a Create operation for an external content type that's mapped to a specific SQL database:

1. **In the Create Wizard, enter the name and display name for the create operation, and then click Next.**

   If you want to accept the default name and display name, click Next without making changes.

   The Input Parameters Configuration page appears.

2. **In the Data Source Elements group, select the fields from the data source that you want to populate.**

   Ignore the warnings that indicate your identifier isn't mapped. You'll address that issue in Step 4.

3. **Click Next to display the Return Parameter Configuration page.**

4. **In the Data Source Elements group, select an identifier field.**

   Select the field that uniquely identifies an item in your external data source. For example, the EmployeeID field uniquely identifies an Employee entry in an Employee database.

5. **From the Properties group, select Map to Identifier.**

6. **Click Finish.**

   The Create Wizard closes and you return to the Operations Designer. SharePoint Designer creates the new Create operation and displays it in the list of operations in the External Content Type Operations window of the Operations Designer.

Defining a Read Item operation

Follow these steps to define a Read Item operation for an external content type that's mapped to a certain SQL database:

1. **In the Read Item Wizard, enter the name and display name for the read item operation, and then click Next.**

   If you want to accept the default name and display name, click Next without making changes.

   The Input Parameters configuration page appears.

2. **In the Data Source Elements group, select an identifier field.**

   Select the field that uniquely identifies an item in your external data source. For example, the EmployeeID field uniquely identifies an Employee entry in an Employee database.

3. **In the Properties group, select Map to Identifier.**

4. **Click Next to display the Return Parameter Configuration page.**

5. **In the Data Source Elements group, select all the fields from the data source that you want to return when an item is read.**

6. **In the Data Source Elements group, select an identifier field.**

   Select the field that uniquely identifies an item in your external data source. For example, the EmployeeID field uniquely identifies an Employee entry in an Employee database.

7. **In the Properties group, select Map to Identifier.**

8. **Click Finish.**

   The Read Item Wizard closes and you return to the Operations Designer. SharePoint Designer creates the new Read Item operation and displays it in the list of operations in the External Content Type Operations window of the Operations Designer.

Defining a Read List operation

Follow these steps to define a Read List operation for an external content type that's mapped to a particular SQL database:

1. **In the Read List Wizard, enter the name and display name for the Read List operation, and then click Next.**

   If you want to accept the default name and display name, click Next without making changes.

   The Filter Parameters Configuration page appears. We discuss filter parameters in the section "Defining filter parameters," later in this chapter.

   If you're using using a data type other than a SQL Server database, such as a WCF/Web Service, then the Input Parameters Configuration page may appear, rather than the Filter Parameters Configuration page.

2. **Click Next to display the Return Parameter Configuration page.**

3. **In the Data Source Elements group, select the fields from the data source that you want to display in your read list.**

   Ignore the warnings indicating that your identifier isn't mapped. You address that problem in Step 5.

4. **In the Data Source Elements group, select an identifier field.**

   Select the field that uniquely identifies an item in your external data source. For example, the EmployeeID field uniquely identifies an Employee entry in an Employee database.

5. **In the Properties group, select Map to Identifier.**

6. **Specify each field that you want to appear in the picker.**

   Follow these steps:

   a. *In the Data Source Elements group, select a field that you want to appear in the External Item Picker dialog box.*

      The External Item Picker provides an easy mechanism for resolving external items in SharePoint and in Office applications. You typically select fields that help the user differentiate between items. FirstName and LastName are examples of fields that would be useful in an External Item Picker.

   b. *In the Properties group, select Show in Picker.*

      If you don't select in the External Item Picker dialog box the fields that you want to appear, then by default, all fields appear.

7. **Click Finish.**

   The Read List Wizard closes and you return to the Operations Designer. SharePoint Designer creates the new Read List operation and displays it in the list of operations in the External Content Type Operations window of the Operations Designer.

Defining an Update operation

Follow these steps to define an Update operation for an external content type that's mapped to a certain SQL database:

1. **From the Update Wizard, enter the name and display name for the update operation, and then click Next.**

   If you want to accept the default name and display name, click Next without making changes.

   The Input Parameters configuration page appears.

2. **From the Data Source Elements group, select the fields from the data source that you want to populate.**

   Ignore the warnings that indicate your identifier isn't mapped. You address that issue in Step 4.

3. **From the Data Source Elements group, select an identifier field.**

   Select the field that uniquely identifies an item in your external data source. For example, the EmployeeID field uniquely identifies an Employee entry in an Employee database.

4. **From the Properties group, select Map to Identifier.**

5. **Click Finish.**

   The Update Wizard closes and you return to the Operations Designer. SharePoint Designer creates the new Update operation and displays it in the list of operations in the External Content Type Operations window of the Operations Designer.

Defining a Delete operation

Follow these steps to define a Delete operation for an external content type that's mapped to a specific SQL database:

1. **In the Delete Wizard, enter the name and display name for the delete operation, and then click Next .**

   The Input Parameters Configuration page appears.

2. **In the Data Source Elements group, select an identifier field.**

   Select the field that uniquely identifies an item in your external data source. For example, the EmployeeID field uniquely identifies an Employee entry in an Employee database.

3. **In the Properties group, select Map to Identifier.**

4. **Click Finish.**

   The Delete Wizard closes and you return to the Operations Designer. SharePoint Designer creates the new Delete operation and displays it in the list of operations in the External Content Type Operations window of the Operations Designer.

You can define only one Delete operation on an external content type.

Defining filter parameters

Some operations — such as the Read List operation for an external content type mapped to a specific SQL database — allow you to define filter parameters so that you can filter the content for that operation. For example, defining a limit filter on a Read List operation results in only a subset of the data being displayed to the user.

Filters allow you to define the default behavior of queries to your external content type and enable your users to customize how they navigate your data. You can combine multiple filters by using AND and OR operators when building your filters. If you combine two filters by using the AND operator and one filter is set to be the default filter, then both filters apply to the default view.

The power behind filters really lights up in the SharePoint BDC Web Parts. For example, the Business Data List Web Part provides a Filter drop-down list that displays the list of available filters and allows the users to build their filter dynamically. Figure 2-8 shows you an example of the BDC Business Data List Web Part that has multiple filters added by the user. The filters in the example are AND filters, which means that by adding the filters to the view, the user can narrow the results.

Figure 2-8:
Using multiple filters in the Business Data List Web Part.

You can find more information about how to use the BDC Web Parts in Book 4, Chapter 3.

Creating a limit filter

A limit filter allows you to specify the number of items, or rows, that an operation returns from your external data source. For example, if you're displaying a list of Artists from a music database, you can limit the initial list so that it returns only the first 100 artists.

Follow these steps to create a limit filter on a Read List operation for an external content type that's mapped to an external SQL database:

1. **Launch the Read List Wizard and click Next to display the Filter Parameters page.**

2. **Click Add Filter Parameter.**

   A new filter parameter is added to the list of filter parameters.

If this is the first time you're creating a filter parameter, then an empty filter parameter may already appear in the Filter Parameters dialog box. You can use that filter parameter, instead of adding an additional filter parameter.

3. **From the Data Source Element drop-down list in the Properties group, select a unique identifier field for your data source.**

   Select a field that uniquely identifies an item in your external data source. For example, the EmployeeID field uniquely identifies an Employee entry in an Employee database.

4. **From the Filter property, click Click to Add.**

   The Filter Configuration dialog box appears.

5. **In the New Filter text box, enter the name of your limit filter.**

6. **From the Filter Type drop-down list in the Properties section, select Limit.**

7. **Click OK.**

   The Filter Configuration dialog box closes and you return to the Filter Parameters page. Your new filter parameter appears in the Filter Parameters list box on the page, and in the Properties section, the Click to Add link next to the Filter property is replaced with the limit filter you specified in Step 5.

8. **In the Default Value property, enter the number of items that you want the Read List operation to return from the database.**

   The limit filter returns only a subset of the items in your list; consequently, you may want to create additional filter types to allow your users to access the remaining items in your list.

9. **Click Finish.**

   Clicking finish updates the operation only within the confines of SharePoint Designer. The filter isn't available for use until you save the changes back to the BDC metadata store.

10. **From the SharePoint Designer File menu, click Save to save your changes.**

    Your changes are saved to the BDC metadata store and your filter is available for use.

A limit filter returns a subset of the items in your list; consequently, you may want to create additional filter types to allow your users to access the remaining items in your list. For example, you can create a filter on Genre that returns artists based on the genre to which they belong.

When you use large lists, apply a limit filter parameter on the operation to limit the number of items your operations return.

When you define limit filters, ensure that the default value to which you set the limit filter is less than 5000. The BDC Service rejects the results of database connections that exceed 5000 rows, so it doesn't return any data from the external system. This process is known as throttling. If you need to return more than 5000 rows, then you need to increase the default resource throttling settings on the SharePoint server. Resource throttling settings are managed at the Web Application level, and you can change the default throttling settings by using Central Administration.

Creating a comparison filter

A comparison filter allows you to filter contents based on the exact value of a field. For example, if you define a comparison filter on the LastName field, your users can query for items in the external data source that have the LastName field equal to Smith.

Follow these steps to create a comparison filter on a Read List operation for an external content type that's mapped to an external SQL database:

1. **Launch the Read List Wizard and click Next to display the Filter Parameters page.**

2. **Click Add Filter Parameter.**

   A new filter parameter is added to the list of filter parameters.

   If this is the first time you're creating a filter parameter, then an empty filter parameter may already appear in the Filter Parameters dialog box. You can use that filter parameter, instead of adding an additional filter parameter.

3. **From the Data Source Element drop-down list in the Properties group, select the field to which you want to apply the filter.**

   Select a field that you want your users to use when filtering content from your external data source.

4. **From the Filter property, click Click to Add.**

   The Filter Configuration dialog box appears.

5. **In the New Filter text box, enter the name of your comparison filter.**

6. **From the Filter Type drop-down list in the Properties section, select Comparison.**

7. **Ensure the Filter Field setting maps to the field on which you want to filter.**

   The Filter Field setting maps to the field you selected in Step 3. If you didn't select a field in Step 3, then this setting automatically defaults to the first field in the list. Change the filter field to map to the correct field by selecting the field you want in the Filter drop-down list.

8. **Specify whether you want SharePoint to ignore the filter if the filter matches a specific value.**

   Select the Ignore Filter if Value Is check box if you want SharePoint to ignore the filter when the field is set to a specific value. If you select this check box, you have two options from which to choose:

   - *Null:* Your external content type bypasses the filter if the value on which to filter is set to Null.

   - *Custom Value:* Your external content type bypasses the filter if the value on which to filter is set to the value that you enter in the Custom Value text box.

   If you're using large lists, use the Ignore Filter setting with a limit filter to prevent an operation from returning too many items at the same time.

9. **Select the Is Default check box if you want the filter to be the default filter.**

   The *default filter* is the filter applied to the default view when you create an external list for the external content type. If you combine two filters by using the AND operator and one filter is set to be the default filter, then both filters apply to the default view.

10. **Select the Case Sensitive check box if you want the filter query to be case sensitive.**

11. **Select the User to Create Match List in External Item Picker check box if you want the filter to be available from the External Item Picker.**

    Figure 2-9 shows the External Item Picker behavior after setting this option on the Filter by Artist and Filter by Genre filter parameters.

12. **Click OK.**

    The Filter Configuration dialog box closes and you return to the Filter Parameters page. Your new filter parameter appears in the Filter Parameters list box on the page, and in the Properties section, the Click to Add link next to the Filter property is replaced with the comparison filter you specified in Step 5.

13. **In the Default Value drop-down list box, enter a default value.**

    If you want your list to begin unfiltered, then set the default value to the setting you specified in the Ignore Filter if Value Is field in Step 8.

14. **Click Finish.**

    If you need to add additional filters, you don't need to click Finish: You can continue adding and removing filters from the Filter Parameters page.

    Clicking finish updates the operation only within the confines of SharePoint Designer. The filter isn't available for use until you save the changes back to the BDC metadata store.

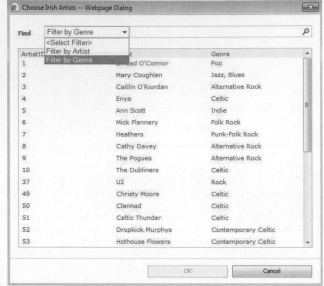

Figure 2-9:
You can
display
the filter
parameters
in the
External
Item Picker
dialog box.

15. **From the SharePoint Designer File menu, choose Save to save your changes back to the BDC metadata store.**

    Your changes are saved to the BDC metadata store and your filter is available for use.

Creating a wildcard filter

A *wildcard filter* is a comparison filter that has a much broader usage scope. When you define a wildcard filter, your users can narrow or broaden their filtering by using the following search criteria:

✦ Starts With

✦ Ends With

✦ Contains

✦ Equals

When you create your wildcard filters, choose fields that work well with the filter criteria. For example, a Name field is a good candidate for a wildcard field because users often want to search for names by using a Starts With and Contains query.

Follow these steps to create a wildcard filter on a Read List operation for an external content type that's mapped to an external SQL database:

1. **Launch the Read List wizard and click Next to display the Filter Parameters page.**

2. **Click Add Filter Parameter.**

   A new filter parameter is added to the list of filter parameters.

   If this is the first time you're creating a filter parameter, then an empty filter parameter may already appear in the Filter Parameters dialog box. You can use that filter parameter, instead of adding an additional filter parameter.

3. **From the Data Source Element drop-down list in the Properties group, select the field to which you want to apply the filter.**

   Select a field on which you'd like your users to perform wildcard searches.

4. **From the Filter property, click Click to Add.**

   The Filter Configuration dialog box appears.

5. **In the New Filter text box, enter the name of your wildcard filter.**

6. **From the Filter Type drop-down list in the Properties section, select Wildcard.**

7. **Ensure the Filter Field setting maps to the field on which you want to filter.**

   The Filter Field setting maps to the field you selected in Step 3. If you didn't select a field in Step 3, then this setting automatically defaults to the first field in the list. Change the filter field to map to the correct field.

8. **Specify whether you want SharePoint to ignore the filter.**

   Select the Ignore Filter if Value Is check box if you want SharePoint to bypass the filter when the field is set to a specific value. If you select this field, you have two options from which to choose:

   - *Null:* Your external content type bypasses the filter if the value on which to filter is set to Null.

   - *Custom Value:* Your external content type bypasses the filter if the value on which to filter is set to the value that you enter as the Custom Value.

   If you're using large lists, use the Ignore Filter setting with a limit filter to prevent an operation from returning too many items at the same time.

9. **Select the Is Default check box if you want the filter to be the default filter.**

   The *default filter* is the filter applied to the default view when you create an external list for the external content type. If you combine two filters by using the AND operator and one filter is set to be the default filter, then both filters apply to the default view.

10. **Select the Case Sensitive check box if you want the filter query to be case sensitive.**

11. **Select the Use to Create Match List in External Item Picker check box if you want the filter to be available from the External Item Picker.**

    Figure 2-9 shows the External Item Picker behavior after setting this option on the Filter by Artist and Filter by Genre filter parameters.

12. **Click OK.**

    The Filter Configuration dialog box closes and you return to the Filter Parameters page. Your new filter parameter appears in the Filter Parameters list box on the page, and in the Properties section, the Click to Add link next to the Filter property is replaced with the wildcard filter you specified in Step 5.

13. **In the Default Value property, enter a default value.**

    If you want your list to begin unfiltered, then set the default value to the setting you specified in the Ignore Filter if Value Is field in Step 8.

14. **Click Finish.**

    If you need to add additional filters, you don't need to click finish: You can continue adding and removing filters from the Filter Parameter filter page.

    Clicking finish updates the operation only within the confines of SharePoint Designer. The filter isn't available for use until you save the changes back to the BDC metadata store.

15. **From the SharePoint Designer File menu, choose Save to save your changes.**

    Your changes are saved to the BDC metadata store and your filter is available for use.

Editing operations for an external content type

After you create an operation on an external content type, you can easily go back and change the configurations settings or add additional settings, such as adding a filter.

Follow these steps to edit an existing operation by using SharePoint Designer.

1. **Open your external content type in SharePoint Designer.**

   Follow the steps in the preceding sections to access an existing external content type.

2. **In the External Content Type Operations section of the page, click the operation you want to modify.**

   The External Content Type section appears near the bottom of the External Content Type Details page.

3. **In the Operation group on the Ribbon menu, click Edit Operation.**

   You can also simply double-click the selected operation to gain edit access.

   The Operations dialog box specific to the operation you chose to modify in Step 2 appears.

4. **Modify the operation, as desired, and click Finish when you're done.**

5. **From the SharePoint Designer File menu, choose Save to save your changes back to the BDC metadata store.**

Removing operations for an external content type

After you create an operation on an external content type, you can easily delete the entire operation.

Follow these steps to delete an existing operation by using SharePoint Designer:

1. **Open your external content type in SharePoint Designer.**

   Follow the steps in the preceding sections to access an existing external content type.

2. **In the External Content Type Operations section of the page, click the operation you want to modify.**

   The External Content Type section appears near the bottom of the External Content Type Details page.

3. **In the Operation group on the Ribbon menu, click Remove Operation.**

   The Operational Removal Confirmation prompt appears.

4. **To continue the delete process, click Yes; otherwise, click No.**

   If you choose to proceed with the removal of the operation, the operation no longer appears in the External Content Type Operations section. However, the operation hasn't yet been removed from the BDC metadata store.

5. **From the SharePoint Designer File menu, choose Save to save your changes back to the BDC metadata store.**

Saving an external content type

When you create a new external content type by using SharePoint Designer, the external content type isn't accessible until you save it to the BDC metadata store. Similarly, when you modify an existing external content type, the changes aren't applied until you save the external content type back to the BDC metadata store. Fortunately, saving your external content type to the BDC metadata store is as easy as clicking the Save button.

Follow these steps to save your external content type and its changes back to the BDC metadata store by using SharePoint Designer:

1. **Open your external content type in SharePoint Designer.**

Follow the steps in section "Creating External Content Types with SharePoint Designer," earlier in this chapter, to open an existing external content type in SharePoint Designer.

2. **From the SharePoint Designer File menu, choose Save to save your changes back to the BDC metadata store.**

Before you can save an external content type to the BDC metadata store by using SharePoint Designer, your external content type must be connected to an external system, and it must have at least one operation defined.

Chapter 3: Using External Content

*I*n this chapter, we show you how to work with your external data directly from SharePoint by leveraging external lists, external data columns, and the Business Data Web Parts. We also show you how you can extend the reach of your external data to your mobile workforce by taking your external lists offline.

Creating an External List

Creating an external content type enables you to interact with your external data just like you do a regular SharePoint list. To use this functionality, you must first create an external list based on your external content type.

SharePoint provides you with two interfaces for creating external lists:

✦ SharePoint browser user interface

✦ SharePoint Designer

When you create an external list, it appears in your site content, along with native SharePoint lists, such as the tasks list and calendaring. Figure 3-1 shows a SharePoint team site that contains two external lists: Irish Artists and Songs. The word External in the Item count column helps you easily distinguish an external list from a native SharePoint list.

When accessing an external list through the SharePoint browser user interface, the external list looks and feels like a native SharePoint list — it shares the same Ribbon menu and many of the capabilities. Users work with external list items in the same way they do native SharePoint list items. For example, if you want to edit an external item, you can right-click the item and select Edit Item from the shortcut menu that appears. Figure 3-2 shows an external list that has a list item's shortcut menu displayed in the SharePoint browser user interface. You can create views and manage list settings like you do for a native SharePoint list.

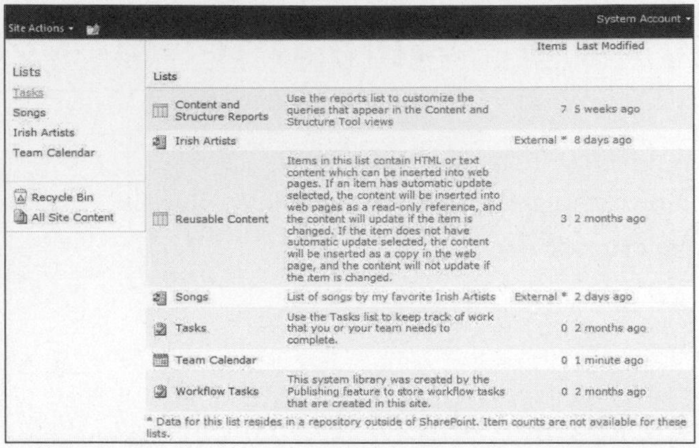

Figure 3-1:
External lists appear alongside the native SharePoint lists.

Figure 3-2:
You can work with external items like you do native SharePoint items.

The menu options that are enabled on the Ribbon menu reflect the external content type configuration. For example, if the external content type supports offline synchronization of the external data, then the Sync to SharePoint Workspace option is enabled on the Connect & Export menu.

Creating an external list with the browser interface

Follow these steps to create an external list by using the SharePoint browser user interface:

1. **Browse to the home page of the SharePoint site where you want to create the external list.**

2. **From the Site Actions menu, choose More Options.**

   The Create page appears, listing the types of content you can create within your SharePoint site. If you have Silverlight installed, a screen similar to that shown in Figure 3-3 appears.

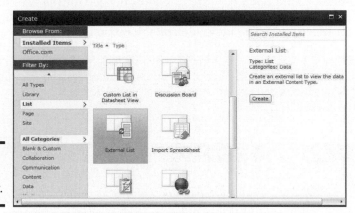

3. **In the List types section, click External List.**

   The right column provides information about the type of content that you're creating, such as the category it maps to and a description. An external list maps to the Data category and allows you to view and interact with data in an external content type.

4. **Click Create.**

   The New page appears, requesting the information necessary to create your external list.

5. **In the Name and Description section of the New page, enter the name and description of your new external list.**

6. **In the Navigation section, click Yes or No to specify whether you want to display the external list on the Quick Launch.**

   If you click Yes, a link to your external list appears on the Quick Launch navigation panel.

7. **In the Data Source Configuration section, select the external content type that you want to use as the data source for your external list.**

   Click the Database icon next to the External Content Type Picker field to browse the list of available external content types.

8. **Click Create.**

SharePoint creates the external list and displays content from the external data source that the external list represents.

The menu options available when you interact with items in your external list depend on the operations, or methods, defined for the external content type. For example, if only Read and Read List operations are defined, then the Edit Item and New Item options on the Ribbon menu are disabled.

Figure 3-4 shows the content for an external list that connects to a back-end SQL database. The external content type has all operations defined, which means that users can create, read, update, and delete items directly from the external list.

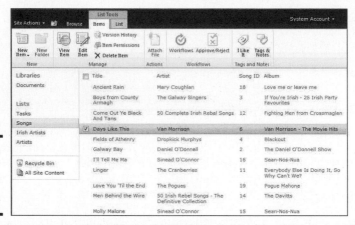

Figure 3-4:
Interacting
with an
external list.

Creating an external list with SharePoint Designer

Follow these steps to create an external list by using SharePoint Designer:

1. **Open your site in SharePoint Designer.**

2. **In the left navigation bar, click External Content Types.**

3. **From the list of External Content Types that appears, select the external content type from which you want to create your external list.**

4. **From the Ribbon menu, select External List.**

The Create External List dialog box appears.

If you don't see an External List option on the menu, you may be in the External Content Type Designer. If that's the case, then follow these steps:

a. *In the Lists & Forms group on the Ribbon menu, click Create Lists & Forms.*

The Create List and Form dialog box for the external content type appears.

b. *Select the Create New External List option.*

5. **Enter the name and description for your new external list in the List Name and List Description text boxes.**

6. **Click OK.**

SharePoint Designer creates your new external list and displays the List Settings page in SharePoint Designer, where you can view and manage the settings for the list. If you're presented with the External Content Type Designer page, then your new external list will appear in the External Lists section of the External Content Type Designer page.

Figure 3-5 shows the External Content Type Designer displaying an external list titled Songs for the Irish Music – Songs external content type.

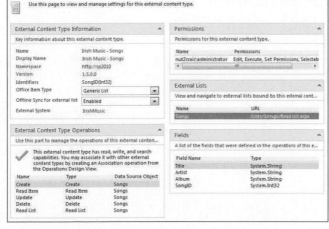

Figure 3-5: You can view all the external lists for a given external content type.

Creating External Data Columns

External data columns allow you to include fields from your external data source into native SharePoint lists. For example, if you have a document library that contains Word documents that include biographical information of musical artists, you can reuse the fields from an external Artists database table and display them as content in the document library, as well as inside the actual biography Word documents.

Follow these steps to create an external data column by using the SharePoint browser user interface:

1. **Browse to the SharePoint document library or list to which you want to add the external data column.**

2. **Click the Library tab or the List tab.**

3. **From the Settings group on the Ribbon menu, click Library Settings or List Settings.**

4. **From the Columns section, click Create column.**

5. **In the Column Name field, enter the name.**

6. **From the list of available types, click External Data.**

7. **In the External Content Type field, browse to and select the external content type that contains the field to which you want to map the external data column.**

8. **Select Display the Actions Menu check box to display the actions associated with the external content type.**

9. **Select the Link This Column to the Default Action of the External Content Type check box, if desired.**

10. **From the Additional Column Settings section, select the check box next to each additional field from the external content type for which you want to add an external data column.**

11. **Select Add to Default View check box if you want to display the external data column(s) in the default view for the library or list.**

12. **Click OK.**

    The external data column is added to the native SharePoint library or list.

Figure 3-6 shows you an example of a native SharePoint list — named Favorites — that contains two external data columns: Song and Music Artist. An icon at the top of each column indicates that it's an external data column. When you edit or create a new item in the list, each of the external data column fields has an icon beside it that gives you access to the External Item Picker.

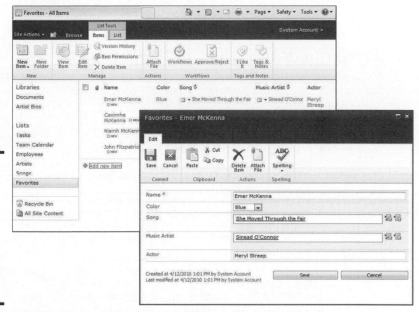

Figure 3-6:
You can display external data columns in your native SharePoint lists.

Taking External Content Offline

Business Connectivity Services (BCS) extends the accessibility of your external data by allowing you to take your external lists offline. Microsoft provides a number of tools that support offline access to SharePoint lists (including external lists), such as:

✦ **Microsoft SharePoint Workspace 2010:** Provides a rich SharePoint client, similar to the experience that Outlook provides to its server counterpart, Microsoft Exchange Server.

✦ **Microsoft Outlook 2010:** SharePoint Workspace 2010 is the powerhouse when it comes to working offline with SharePoint content; however, Microsoft Outlook is a better fit for specific types of content, such as calendaring items and contacts.

In Book I, Chapter 6, we discuss the synchronization process for both Microsoft Outlook and SharePoint Workspace. In the following sections, we show you how this synchronization capability applies to your external content.

Enabling offline sync for your external lists

Regardless of which method you use to access your external data offline, you must first ensure that your external content type supports offline synchronization.

Follow these steps to configure your external content type to support offline synchronization by using SharePoint Designer:

1. **Open your site in SharePoint Designer.**

2. **In the left navigation bar, click External Content Types.**

3. **From the list of external content types that appears, select the external content type from which you want to enable offline synchronization.**

   The External Content Type Details page appears.

4. **If you plan to synchronize your external list with Microsoft Outlook, from the Office Item Type drop-down list, select the item type, and then map your fields to the appropriate Office property field.**

   The Office Item Type selection appears in the External Content Type Information section of the External Content Type designer. Select the Office field that best represents your external content type. For example, if your external content type stores contact-type information (such as first name, last name, and address), then select Contact as the appropriate item type for your list.

5. **From the Offline Sync for External List drop-down list, select Enabled.**

   The Offline Sync for External List selection appears in the External Content Type Information section of the External Content Type Designer page. Figure 3-7 shows the Offline Sync for External List setting for the Employees external content type.

6. **From the SharePoint Designer File menu, choose Save to save your changes back to the BDC metadata store.**

   You can now take your list offline by using Microsoft Outlook or Microsoft SharePoint Workspace.

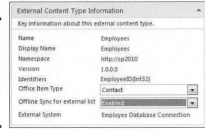

Figure 3-7:
Set the
Offline Sync
for External
List setting
to Enabled.

If you encounter errors when you try to connect or synchronize your data offline, check your external content type to ensure its configuration supports offline synchronization. Setting the Offline Sync for External List option to Enabled doesn't necessarily mean that your external content type supports this behavior. Other settings — such as the operations, associations, and filters that you define — affect offline support.

Connecting your external list to Microsoft Outlook

Follow these steps to connect your external list to Outlook by using the SharePoint browser user interface:

1. **Using your SharePoint browser, navigate to your external list in your SharePoint site.**

2. **Click the List tab.**

3. **In the Connect & Export group in the Ribbon, click Connect to Outlook.**

   If your external list supports offline synchronization, SharePoint works with the Office client to set up the connection between your external list and Outlook. SharePoint installs the Office customization necessary to create the connection.

   If this is the first time you're connecting your external list to Outlook, a prompt appears, asking whether you're sure you want to install this customization:

   a. *Click Install to continue installing the customization.*

   b. *When you receive the notification that the customization was successfully installed, click Close to return to the page displaying your SharePoint list.*

   If your external list doesn't support offline synchronization with Outlook, you receive an error message, rather than a prompt.

4. **Open Microsoft Outlook and set the view to Folder List.**

   The connection to your external list appears below SharePoint External Lists. Figure 3-8 shows you an example of a connected external list in Microsoft Outlook 2010. The item in our example appears as a contact item because we set the Office Item Type for the external content type to Contact.

After your external list is connected to Outlook, you can work with your items in Outlook like you do regular Outlook items. Any updates or deletions that you make within Outlook are committed to the external data source. If you're offline at the time you make changes, then those changes are cached and committed to the external data source the next time you're online.

Synchronizing to SharePoint Workspace

Follow these steps to synchronize your external list to a SharePoint Workspace by using the SharePoint browser user interface:

1. **Using your SharePoint browser, navigate to your external list in your SharePoint site.**

2. **Click the List tab.**

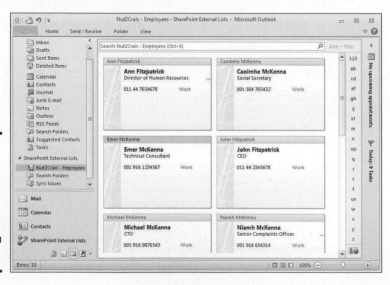

Figure 3-8:
You can update the items in an external data source directly from Outlook.

3. **From the Connect & Export group in the Ribbon, click Sync to SharePoint Workspace.**

   The Sync to SharePoint Workspace dialog box appears.

4. **Verify that you're synchronizing the correct list, and then click OK.**

   SharePoint Workspace creates a local cached copy of the external list.

   If this is the first time you're synchronizing your external list to SharePoint Workspace, you receive a prompt from the Microsoft Office Customization Installer, asking whether you're sure you want to install this customization. Follow these steps:

   a. *Click Install to continue installing the customization.*

      The installation may take several minutes.

   b. *When you receive the notification that the customization was success-fully installed, click Close to continue the synchronization process.*

5. **From the Sync to SharePoint Workspace dialog box, click Open Workspace.**

   The SharePoint Workspace client opens, and SharePoint Workspace displays your synchronized external list. Figure 3-9 shows an example of a synchronized external list as it appears in SharePoint Workspace. The external list appears below the External Lists heading in the Content column.

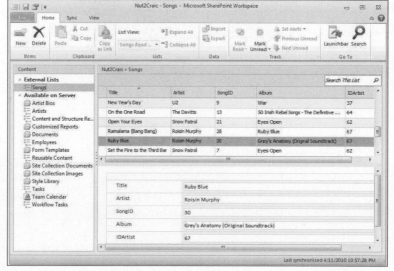

Figure 3-9:
Open the
Workspace
to display
the
synchronized
external list.

Any updates or deletions that you make within SharePoint Workspace are committed to the external data source. If you're offline when you make changes, then those changes are cached and committed to the external data source the next time you're online.

After you create a connection between SharePoint Workspace and your SharePoint site you can initiate synchronization with your external lists directly from the SharePoint Workspace client.

Synchronizing from SharePoint Workspace

Follow these steps to connect to an external list from SharePoint Workspace:

1. **Launch SharePoint Workspace.**

2. **From the SharePoint Workspace Launch bar, right-click your SharePoint Workspace, and then select Open from the pop-up menu that appears.**

   The SharePoint Workspace opens, displaying the list with which you were last working. The external lists to which SharePoint Workspace is currently connected appear below the External Lists heading.

   If you haven't yet established a SharePoint workspace for your SharePoint site, you can do so by following these steps:

   a. *From the Launch bar menu, choose New⇨SharePoint Workspace.*

      The New SharePoint Workspace dialog box appears.

   b. *In the location field, enter the URL to your external list and click OK.*

3. **From the Available on Server section, click the external list that you want to connect.**

   The Details pane notifies you that the list isn't currently on this computer. Figure 3-10 shows an example of the message in SharePoint Workspace.

4. **From the Details pane, click Connect *"Your External List Name"* to Server.**

   The Details pane displays a message that indicates SharePoint Workspace is initializing the SharePoint synchronization and that the process may take a few minutes.

   SharePoint Workspace creates a local cached copy of the external list.

If this is the first time you're connecting to your external list, you receive a prompt from the Microsoft Office Customization Installer, asking whether you're sure you want to install this customization:

a. *Click Install to continue installing the customization.*

   The installation may take several minutes.

b. *When you receive the notification that the customization was success-fully installed, click Close.*

The external list appears below the External Lists heading in the Content column.

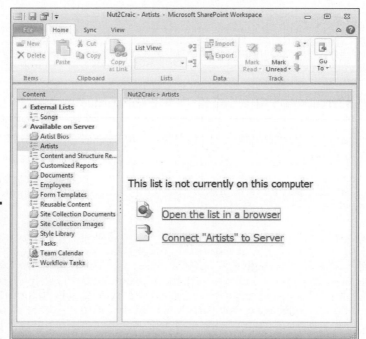

Figure 3-10:
You can connect to an external list directly from SharePoint Workspace.

Using the Business Connectivity Services Web Parts

You don't need to create an external list in order to interact and work with your data — instead, you can create Web pages and add Business Connectivity Services (BCS)–specific Web Parts to display your external data. SharePoint ships with six Business Data Web Parts that you can use to add external data to your SharePoint Web pages:

✦ **Business Data Actions Web Part:** Displays a list of actions associated with an external content type. The Web Part retrieves the list of actions from the Business Data Connectivity (BDC) metadata store.

When you connect the Business Data Actions Web Part to the Business Data Item Web Part, you create a URL-based external content type action. When you click an action that's connected to an item, it's like you right-clicked the item in an external list and clicked the action.

✦ **Business Data List Web Part:** Displays a list of items from the external data source to which an external content type is connected.

✦ **Business Data Related List Web Part:** Displays a list of items related to one or more parent items from an external data source.

✦ **Business Data Connectivity Filter Web Part:** Filters the contents of Web Parts by using a list of values defined in the BDC metadata store.

✦ **Business Data Item Web Part:** Displays one item from an external data source. The Data Item Web Part sends the URL of the identifier to other Business Data Web Parts.

✦ **Business Data Item Builder Web Part:** Creates a Business Data Item from parameters in the query string and provides the item to other Web Parts. The Web Part extracts the identifier for the item from the current URL and passes it to the Web Parts to which it's connected, allowing those Web Parts to filter their contents accordingly.

The Business Data Web Parts are available in SharePoint Foundation Server, as well as SharePoint Server 2010.

You can see some of the Business Data Web Parts in action by editing the profile page for your external content type. A profile page provides a BDC-specific Web page that appears when you view an external item in SharePoint. Figure 3-11 shows a default profile page in Design mode. The default profile page uses the Business Data Item Web Part and the Business Data Item Builder Web Part, which is a hidden Web Part that's connected to the Business Data Item Web Part. The Business Data Item Builder Web Part's job is to figure out the specific data item from the identifier information in the URL, and then send the data item to the Business Data Item Web Part for display. You can add additional Business Data Web Parts to your profile pages, or create your own custom Web pages and add the Business Data Web Parts necessary to display your external data.

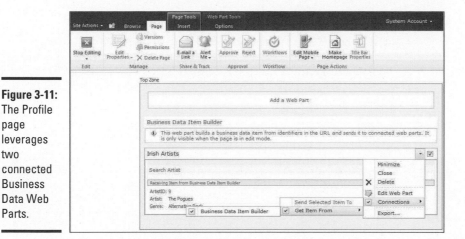

In the following sections, you can display your external data by using the Business Data Web Parts.

Creating a blank Web Part page

To make the steps easier to follow in the following sections, we start by walking you through the process of creating a blank Web page; however, you can add Business Data Web Parts where you see fit, including any existing pages in your SharePoint deployment.

Follow these steps to create a blank Web Part page by using the SharePoint browser user interface:

1. **Using your SharePoint browser, navigate to your SharePoint site.**

2. **From the Site Actions menu, choose More Options.**

3. **From the Filter By section, click Page.**

4. **Click the Web Part Page type.**

5. **Click Create.**

   The New Web Part Page page appears.

6. **In the Name field, enter the Name of your Web Part page.**

7. **From the list of available layout tempaltes, select a layout template for your Web Part page.**

8. **In the drop down that appears in the Save Location section, select the location to which you want to save your Web Part page.**

9. **Click Create.**

   Your Web Part Page appears in Edit mode. You can begin adding your Web Parts. Figure 3-12 shows a Web Part page in Edit mode. To add a Web Part, you simply click the Add a Web Part link in the zone to which you want to add your Web Part.

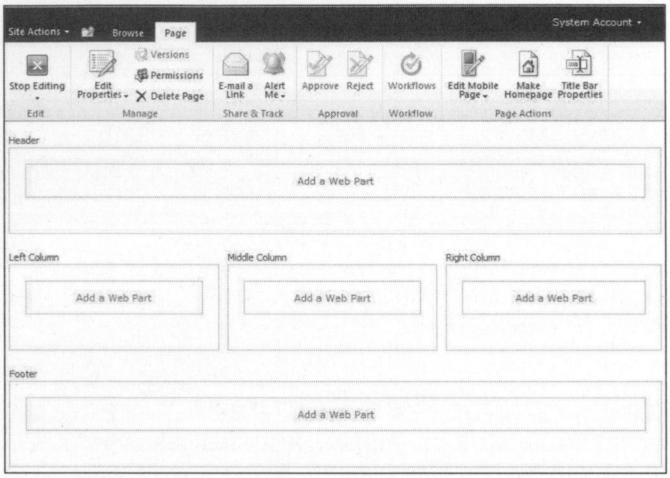

Figure 3-12: Click the Add a Web Part links to add Web Parts to zones on your page.

Adding the Business Data List Web Part

The Business Data List Web Part displays a list of data from an external data source and allows you to configure the view that appears, including which columns to display and in what order.

Follow these steps to add a Business Data List Web Part to a Web Part page by using the SharePoint browser user interface:

1. **Using your SharePoint browser, navigate to the Web Part page in your SharePoint site to which you want to add the Web Part.**

2. **Click the Page tab.**

3. **From the Edit group in the Ribbon menu, click Edit Page.**

4. **The Web Part zone that you want to place your Web Part, click Add a Web Part.**

   A list of Web Parts appears below the Ribbon menu.

5. **In the Categories column, click Business Data.**

The Web Parts related to the Business Data category appear, including the six BCS Web Parts.

6. **In the Web Parts column, click Business Data List.**

The About the Web Part column provides you with information about the selected Web Part and shows you the zone where it will be added.

7. **Click Add.**

The Business Data List Web Part is added to the Web Part page. At this stage, it hasn't been configured.

8. **In the contents of the Business Data List Web Part, click Open the Tool Pane.**

The Web Part Tool pane appears, where you can define the Web Part settings.

Alternatively, you can edit a Web Part by following these steps:

a. *On the right side of the Web Part title, click the down arrow to display the Web Part pop-up menu.*

b. *From the Web Part menu, select Edit Web Part.*

9. **In the Type property, click the External Content Type icon.**

The External Content Type Picker dialog box appears.

10. **Select the external content type that you want to display in the Business Data List Web Part.**

11. **Click OK.**

12. **In the View property, select the view that you want to display in the Web Part.**

13. **In the Display Toolbar property, specify whether to display the toolbar.**

If you select the Display Toolbar setting the following links appear:

- *Actions link:* Lists the actions associated with the external content type.

- *Page Navigation links:* Allow you to traverse through the list, displaying a batch of items on each page. If you disable the toolbar for the Web Part, you need to provide a way for all your data to be accessible.

- *Edit View link:* Allows you to determine which fields to display and in what order. This link is available only in Edit mode.

14. **In the Display Animation While Loading property, specify whether to inform users when the page is loading the data.**

If you select this property, a moving line appears that lets your users know that something is happening on the page, which can be reassuring if building the list takes a long time.

15. **Click OK.**

The Business Data List Web Part appears on your Web Part page.

The data that appears in the Business Data List Web Part is static — you can't select an item to display more detail about the item. To make the list come alive, you can connect it to other Business Data Web Parts, such as the Business Data Item Web Part (discussed in the following section).

Adding the Business Data Item Web Part

The Business Data Item Web Part displays information related to a specific item in an external data source. The Web Part can be *static*, displaying information for only a specific instance of data in the external data source, or it can be *dynamic*, presenting information relative to the currently selected item in a Business Data List Web Part.

Configuring a Business Data Item Web Part

Follow these steps to add a Business Data Item Web Part to a Web Part page by using the SharePoint browser user interface:

1. **Using your SharePoint browser, navigate to the Web Part page in the SharePoint site to which you want to add the Web Part.**

2. **Click the Page tab.**

3. **From the Edit group in the Ribbon menu, click Edit Page.**

4. **In your chosen Web Part zone, click Add a Web Part.**

   A list of Web Parts appears below the Ribbon menu.

5. **In the Categories column, click Business Data.**

   The Web Parts related to the Business Data category appear, including the six BCS Web Parts.

6. **From the Web Parts column, click Business Data Item.**

   When you select a Web Part the About the Web Part column provides you with information about the Web Part and shows you the zone where it will be added. In this particular instance, the About the Web Part column provides information about the Business Data List Web Part.

7. **Click Add.**

   The Business Data Item Web Part is added to the Web Part page. At this stage, it hasn't been configured. The next steps configure it.

8. **In the contents of the Business Data Item Web Part, click Open the Tool Pane.**

    The Web Part Tool pane opens, from which you can define the Web Part settings. Alternatively, you can display the Web Part Tool pane by following these steps:

    a. *On the right side of the Web Part title, click the down arrow to display the Web Part pop-up menu.*

    b. *From the Web Part pop-up menu, click Edit Web Part.*

9. **In the Type field, click the External Content Type icon.**

    The External Content Type Picker dialog box appears.

10. **From the External Content Type Picker dialog box, select the external content type that you want to display in the Business Data Item Web Part.**

11. **Click OK.**

12. **In the Item property, if you want to select a specific instance of an item in the external data source, then browse and select the instance; otherwise, ignore this setting.**

13. **In the Display Animation While Loading property, specify whether to inform users when the page is loading the data.**

    If you select this property, a moving line appears that lets your users know that something is happening on the page.

14. **In the Fields section, click Choose.**

15. **Select the fields that you want to appear in the Business Data Item Web Part.**

16. **Click OK.**

17. **In the Actions section, click Choose.**

18. **Select the actions that you want to appear in the Business Data Item Web Part.**

19. **Click OK.**

20. **Click OK to apply the changes.**

    The settings for your Web Part are saved. If you left the Item property blank, you need to connect your Business Data Item Web Part to another Web Part in order to display the contents.

**Book IV
Chapter 3**

**Using External
Content**

Connecting a Business Data Item Web Part

Follow these steps to connect a Business Data Item Web Part to a Business Data List Web Part on the same page by using the SharePoint browser user interface:

1. **On the right side of the Business Data Item Web Part title, click the down arrow to display the Web Part pop-up menu.**

2. **From the Web Part pop-up menu, select Edit Web Part.**

   If you're already in Edit mode, you can skip to Step 3.

3. **From the Web Part menu, choose Connections⇨Get Item From⇨<Your Business Data List Web Part>.**

   The Business Data List Web Part now displays an icon to the left of each item in the list, indicating that the Web Part is connected and you can interact with the items in the list. You must select an item in the Business Data List Item Web Part to display content in the Business Data Item Web Part.

   You may also connect the Business Data Item Web Part to a Business Data Related List Web Part, if necessary.

4. **Select an item in the Business Data List Web Part to display that item in the Business Data Item Web Part.**

   The Business Data Item Web Part dynamically reflects the selection by displaying the relevant data.

Creating associations by using SharePoint Designer

Before you can take advantage of the Business Data Related List Web Part, you must define associations between the related external content types. An *association* is a relationship between two entities, such as a musical artist and songs. Using tools such as SharePoint Designer and Microsoft Visual Studio, you can define associations between your external content types, and then view the associated data with the Business Data Web Parts.

Follow these steps to create an association between two external content types by using SharePoint Designer:

1. **Open your SharePoint site in SharePoint Designer.**

2. **Open the external content type from which you want to create the association.**

   When creating a one-to-many association, create the association from the external content type that represents the many side of the equation. For example, if you have an Artists external content type and a Songs external content type where an artist is associated with multiple songs, then you create the association from the Songs external content type. In this example, the Songs external content type contains a foreign key that maps it to a specific artist in the Artists external content type.

In other words, create the association from the external content type that contains the foreign keys.

3. **In the Views group on the Ribbon menu, click Operations Design View.**

4. **From the Data Source Explorer, right-click the data source or Web method on which you want to create the association.**

   What you do depends on what you're creating an association for:

   - *SQL database connection:* Right-click the table that represents your external content type.

   - *WCF Service connection:* Right-click the appropriate Web method.

   The Operations shortcut menu appears, listing the available operations, one of which is the New Association operation.

5. **In the Operations shortcut menu, select New Association.**

   The Association Wizard appears and walks you through the process of defining the association properties, input parameters, filter parameters, and return parameters.

6. **Enter names in the Association Name and Display Name text boxes.**

   The association name appears in the list of operations in SharePoint Designer. The display name appears when you view an external content type in Central Administration and when you reference the association in the Business Data Web Parts.

7. **Click Browse and select the related external content type to which you're connecting.**

   In the example of the Artists and Songs external content types, you create the association from the Songs external content type and browse to the Artists content type.

8. **In the Related Identifier column, select the primary key of the related content type.**

9. **In the Field column, select the foreign key of the current external content type that maps to the primary key of the related external content type.**

   If the name of your foreign key is the same as the related identifier field, that field is preselected.

10. **Click Next.**

The Input Parameters page appears.

11. **In the Data Source Elements group, select the foreign key's field.**

12. **In the Properties group, select Map to Identifier and set the Identifier field to be the primary key (or *identifier*) of the related external content type.**

13. **Click Next.**

If you're creating an association for an existing SQL database connection, the Filter Parameters page appears. You can't create filter parameters for WCF Service associations.

14. **Add filters, as desired, and click Next.**

Most associations don't require filters. But you may find filters beneficial in certain situations — for example, if you want to filter the Songs-to-Artists association to a specific genre of music.

After you click Next, the Return Parameter page appears.

15. **In the Data Source Elements group, select the identifier (or *primary key*) of the current external content type.**

16. **In the Properties group, select Map to Identifier and set the Identifier field to be the primary key of the related external content type.**

To configure what's returned from the association, you need to map the field of the external content type to the identifier of the current external content type. The wizard typically handles this mapping automatically.

17. **In the Data Source Elements group, select the foreign key's field.**

18. **In the Foreign Identifier property of the Properties group, click Click to Add.**

If you don't see the Click to Add link next to the Foreign Identifier property, and instead see a URL to the identifier of the related external content type (such as `http://sp2010.Artists.ArtistId`), then the wizard has preconfigured this setting for you. The wizard typically configures the foreign-key relationship if the foreign key and the related external-content-type identifier use the same name; otherwise, you need to configure the relationship manually.

Follow these steps to add the foreign identifier:

a. *In the Foreign Identifier dialog box, select the Select a Foreign Identifier option.*

    b. In the Referenced External Content Type property, click Click to Add.

    The External Content Type Selection dialog box appears.

    c. Select the external content type to which you're connecting.

    The current content type has Current next to its name. Select any external content type except for that one.

    d. Click OK.

    e. From the Association External Content Type property, click Click to Add.

    The External Content Type Selection dialog box appears.

    f. Select the current external content type.

    Again, the current content type has Current next to its name.

    g. Click OK.

    The Association property is automatically populated.

    h. Click OK.

    The foreign key identifier is mapped to the identifier of the related external content type.

19. **Click Finish.**

Your new association appears in the list of operations for your external content type.

20. **From the SharePoint Designer File menu, choose Save to save your external content type changes to the BDC metadata store.**

You can now take advantage of your associations by using the Business Data Related List Web Part (as described in the following section).

Adding the Business Data Related List Web Part

The Business Data Related List Web Part brings your external content type associations to life. For example, if you have a Business Data List Web Part on your page that displays a list of Artists, you can add to the page a Related List Web Part that's been mapped to the Songs external content type and connect it to the Artists Business Data List Web Part. When a user clicks an artist in the Artists Business Data List Web Part, the list of songs associated with that artist automatically appears in the Songs Business Data Related List Web Part.

**Book IV
Chapter 3**

**Using External
Content**

To enable this type of interaction between two external content types, you must first create an association between the external content types. After you have the association up and running, you can add your Business Data Related List Web Part.

Configuring a Business Data Related List Web Part

Follow these steps to add a Business Data Related List Web Part to a Web Part page by using the SharePoint browser user interface:

1. **Using your SharePoint browser, navigate to the Web Part page in your SharePoint site to which you want to add the Web Part.**

2. **Click the Page tab.**

3. **In the Edit group in the Ribbon menu, click Edit Page.**

4. **In your chosen Web Part zone, click Add a Web Part.**

A list of Web Parts appears below the Ribbon menu.

5. **In the Categories column, click Business Data.**

The Web Parts related to the Business Data category appear, including the six BCS Web Parts.

6. **In the Web Parts column, click Business Data Related List.**

The About the Web Part column provides you with information about the selected Web Part and shows you the zone where it will be added.

7. **Click Add.**

The Business Data List Web Part is added to the Web Part page. At this stage, it hasn't been configured.

8. **In the contents of the Business Data Related List Web Part, click Open the Tool Pane.**

The Web Part Tool pane, where you can define the Web Part settings, opens.

Alternatively, you can edit a Web Part by using the following method:

a. *On the right side of the Web Part title, click the down arrow to display the Web Part pop-up menu.*

b. *From the Web Part pop-up menu, select Edit Web Part.*

9. **In the Type property, click the External Content Type icon.**

The External Content Type Picker dialog box appears.

10. **Select the external content type that you want to display in the Business Data Related List Web Part.**

    SharePoint contacts the BDC metadata store and filters the list of available external content types to display only those that have an association defined.

11. **Click OK.**

12. **In the Relationship property, select the association that represents the relationship for this Web Part.**

13. **In the Display Toolbar property, specify whether to display the toolbar.**

    If you select the Display Toolbar setting, the following links appear:

    - *Actions link:* Lists the actions associated with the external content type.

    - *Page Navigation links:* Allow you to traverse through the list, displaying a batch of items on each page. If you choose to disable the toolbar for the Web Part, you need to provide a way to make all your data accessible.

    - *Edit View link:* Allows you to determine which fields to display and in what order. This link is available only in Edit mode.

14. **In the Display Animation While Loading property, specify whether to inform users when the page is loading the data.**

    If you select this property, a moving line appears that lets your users know that something is happening on the page.

15. **Click OK.**

    The settings for your Web Part are saved. You need to connect your Business Data Related List Web Part to a Web Part that displays content from the associated external content type, such as a Business Data Item List Web Part or a Business Data Item Web Part.

Connecting a Business Data Related List Web Part

Follow these steps to connect a Business Data Related List Web Part to another Web Part on the same page by using the SharePoint browser user interface:

1. **On the right side of the Business Data Related List Item Web Part title, click the down arrow to display the Web Part pop-up menu.**

2. **From the Web Part pop-up menu, select Edit Web Part.**

   If you're already in Edit mode, you can skip to Step 3.

3. **In the Web Part menu, choose Connections⇨Get Item From⇨<*Your Associated External Content Type Business Data List or Item Web Part*>.**

4. **Select or display an item in the connected Web Part to display the associated data in the Business Data Related List Web Part.**

   The Business Data Related List Web Part dynamically reflects the selection by displaying the relevant data. Figure 3-13 shows an example of a Business Data List Web Part (Irish Artists List) connected to a Business Data Related List Web Part (Irish Music – Songs List).

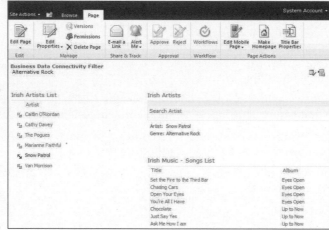

Figure 3-13: You can connect multiple Business Data Web Parts on the same page.

Adding the Business Data Actions Web Part

The Business Data Actions Web Part displays the list of actions defined for a specific external content type.

To use the Business Data Actions Web Part, you must connect it to another Web Part that provides it with an external data instance. Web Part candidates include the Business Data Item Web Part, the Business Data List Web Part, and the Business Data Related List Web Part.

If you add the Business Data Actions Web Part to a Web Part that already lists the actions in its toolbar, you may want to consider disabling the toolbar on the other Web Parts or reconsider the need to add the Business Data Actions Web Part.

Configuring a Business Data Actions Web Part

Follow these steps to add a Business Data Actions Web Part to a Web Part page by using the SharePoint browser user interface:

1. **Using your SharePoint browser, navigate to the Web Part page in your SharePoint site to which you want to add the Web Part.**

2. **Click the Page tab.**

3. **In the Edit group in the Ribbon menu, click Edit Page.**

4. **In your chosen Web Part zone, click Add a Web Part.**

   A list of Web Parts appears below the Ribbon menu.

5. **In the Categories column, click Business Data.**

   The Web Parts related to the Business Data category appear, including the six BCS Web Parts.

6. **In the Web Parts column, click Business Data Actions.**

   The About the Web Part column provides you with information about the selected Web Part and shows you the zone where it will be added.

7. **Click Add.**

   The Business Data Actions Web Part is added to the Web Part page. At this stage, it hasn't been configured.

8. **In the contents of the Business Data Actions Web Part, click Open the Tool Pane.**

   The Web Part Tool pane, from which you can define the Web Part settings, opens.

   Alternatively, you can edit a Web Part by following these steps:

   a. *In the right side of the Web Part title, click the down arrow to display the Web Part pop-up menu.*

   b. *In the Web Part pop-up menu, select Edit Web Part.*

9. **In the Type property, click the External Content Type icon.**

   The External Content Type Picker dialog box appears.

10. **Select the external content type for which you want to display the Actions.**

11. **Click OK.**

12. **If you want to select a specific instance of an item in the external data source, in the Item property, browse and select the instance; otherwise, ignore this setting.**

13. **In the Actions section, click Choose.**

14. **Select the actions that you want to appear in the Business Data Actions Web Part.**

15. **Click OK.**

16. **In the Style property, select how you want your Actions to appear in the Web Part.**

    You have three styles to choose from out of the box:

    - *Bulleted list:* Displays the actions in a list with a bullet to the left of the action name

    - *List:* Displays the actions in a simple list without bullets

    - *Tool Bar:* Displays the actions as a toolbar, with an action appearing horizontally across the Web Part, along with any associated icons for the action

17. **Click OK to apply the changes.**

    The settings for your Web Part are saved. If you left the Item property blank, you need to connect your Business Data Actions Web Part to another Web Part (which we talk about in the following section) in order to display the contents.

Connecting a Business Data Actions Web Part

Follow these steps to connect a Business Data Actions Web Part to a Business Data List Web Part on the same page by using the SharePoint browser user interface:

1. **On the right side of the Business Data Actions Web Part title, click the down arrow to display the Web Part pop-up menu.**

2. **From the Web Part pop-up menu, select Edit Web Part.**

    If you're already in Edit mode, you can skip to Step 3.

3. **From the Web Part menu, choose Connections⇨Get Item From⇨*<Your Business Data List/Item Web Part>*.**

    You must select an item in the Business Data List Item Web Part to display content in the Business Data Actions Web Part.

    You can also connect the Business Data Actions Web Part to a Business Data Related List Web Part.

4. **Select an item in the Business Data List Web Part to display an item in the Business Data Actions Web Part.**

    The Business Data Actions Web Part dynamically reflects the selection by displaying the relevant data.

Adding the Business Data Connectivity Filter Web Part

The Business Data Connectivity Filter Web Part allows you to filter the contents of the list-type Web Parts on the same page. You don't need to have filters defined on your operations in order to use this Web Part.

To be use the Business Data Connectivity Filter Web Part, you need to connect it to another Web Part on the same page, such as the Business Data List Web Part.

Configuring a Business Data Connectivity Filter Web Part

Follow these steps to add a Business Data Connectivity Filter Web Part to a Web Part page by using the SharePoint browser user interface:

1. **Using your SharePoint browser, navigate to the Web Part page in your SharePoint site to which you want to add the Web Part.**

2. **Click the Page tab.**

3. **In the Edit group in the Ribbon menu, click Edit Page.**

4. **In your chosen Web Part zone, click Add a Web Part.**

   A list of Web Parts appears below the Ribbon menu.

5. **In the Categories column, click Business Data.**

   The Web Parts related to the Business Data category appear, including the six BCS Web Parts.

6. **In the Web Parts column, click Business Data Connectivity Filter.**

   When you select a Web Part, the About the Web Part column provides you with information about the selected Web Part and shows you the zone where it will be added. In this instance, the column provides information about the Business Data Connectivity Filter Web Part.

7. **Click Add.**

   The Business Data Connectivity Filter Web Part is added to the Web Part page. At this stage, it hasn't been configured. The following steps configure the Business Data Connectivity Filter Web Part.

8. **From the contents of the Business Data Connectivity Web Part, click Open the Tool Pane.**

   The Web Part Tool pane, from which you can define the Web Part settings, opens.

   Alternatively, you can display the Web Part Tool Pane by following these steps:

a. On the right side of the Web Part title, click the down arrow to display the Web Part pop-up menu.

b. From the Web Part pop-up menu, select Edit Web Part.

9. **In the Filter Name text box, enter the name of your filter.**

The Filter Name appears on the Web Part page, so make the name descriptive, such as Filter by Genre.

10. **In the Type field, click the External Content Type icon.**

The External Content Type Picker dialog box appears.

11. **Select the external content type for which you want to display the Actions.**

12. **Click OK.**

The External Content Type Picker dialog box closes and you are returned to the Web Part Tool Pane. The Type text box is populated with the external content type that you selected in the previous step.

13. **In the View property, select the view that you want to display in the Web Part.**

14. **In the Value Column drop-down, select the field value that you want to use for the filter.**

The Value Column drop-down list displays the external content type's fields.

15. **In the Description Column drop-down, select the field description value that you want to use for the filter.**

The Description Column drop-down list displays the external content type's fields.

16. **In the Advanced Filter options, set the width of the Web Part.**

Leaving the value for this setting at 0 (zero) tells SharePoint to auto-size the field. You can experiment with this value to get the exact look you want.

17. **In the Advanced Filter options, select the Require User to Choose a Value check box if you want to make the filter mandatory; otherwise, deselect this setting.**

18. **In the Advanced Filter options, set the default value for the filter, if needed.**

If you want to automatically filter on a specific value, then you can set the Default Value setting to that value. Set this value if you require your users to choose a filter value; otherwise, use as desired.

19. **Click OK to save your settings.**

The settings for your Web Part are saved, but the filter remains inactive until you connect it to another Web Part (which we explain in the following section).

Connecting a Business Data Connectivity Filter Web Part

Follow these steps to connect a Business Data Connectivity Filter Web Part to another Web Part on the same page by using the SharePoint browser user interface:

1. **On the right side of the Business Data Connectivity Filter Web Part title, click the down arrow to display the Web Part pop-up menu.**

2. **From the Web Part pop-up menu, click Edit Web Part.**

   If you're already in Edit mode, you can skip to Step 3.

3. **From the Web Part menu, choose Connections⇨Send Filter Values To⇨<Your Associated External Content Type Business Data List or Item Web Part>.**

   The Choose Connection dialog box appears. When you send filter values from a Business Data Connectivity Filter Web Part to another Web Part, you have two connection types from which to choose:

   - *Get Filter Values From:* Map your filter to a specific field in the connected Web Part.

   - *Get Query Values From:* Map your filter to a specific filter parameter in the connected Web Part. You can use this type of connection only if your external content type has filter parameters defined.

   Book IV, Chapter 2 shows how to define filter parameters by using SharePoint Designer.

4. **Select the connection type in the Choose Connection dialog box, then click Configure.**

   The Connection dialog walks you through a series of steps to set up your connection. The steps will vary depending on the type of connection you select.

   If you select the Get Filter Values From connection type, follow these steps:

   a. *From the Consumer Field Name drop-down list, select the field on which you want to filter.*

   b. *Click Finish.*

   If you select the Get Query Values From connection type, follow these steps:

   a. *From the Consumer Field Name drop-down list, select the filter parameter on which you want to filter.*

   b. *Click Finish.*

   Your filter is ready to use. To test your filter connection, click the Filter icon from the Web Part and select the filter value that you want to apply to your connected Web Parts.

Chapter 4: Working with Excel Services

In This Chapter

✔ **Creating your Excel Workbooks**

✔ **Publishing your Excel Workbooks to Excel Services**

✔ **Modifying with workbooks in Edit mode**

✔ **Getting handy with the Excel Web Access Web Part**

✔ **Working with Excel Web App**

*E*ven the standard capabilities of Microsoft Excel 2010 can make your data come to life. For example, you can create PivotTables and PivotCharts to provide a graphical summary of your business data that you can filter according to your needs. Features such as Visual Slicers (new with Excel 2010) offer easy ways to filter the data in your PivotTables and PivotCharts. Excel Services understands these new Excel 2010 capabilities, and takes them into account when you publish a workbook to SharePoint: What you see through the browser looks and feels just like the Excel client application. If you want to have that same high-fidelity viewing experience when you're editing Excel workbooks through the browser, you can install Office Web Apps in your server farm — and edit your workbooks to your heart's content, using the Excel Web App functionality.

Workbooks that you publish to Excel Services immediately inherit all the capabilities of the SharePoint environment. For example, if you've enabled versioning in the document library to which you publish your workbook, then SharePoint keeps track of the versions of your workbook. You can roll back to a previous version if necessary, and workbooks published to Excel Services are available for use by other services — in particular, PerformancePoint Services. This integration of PerformancePoint Services and Excel Services allows you to create PerformancePoint dashboards and reports that display data and charts from your Excel workbooks. (You can find more about PerformancePoint Services in Book III, Chapter 8.)

In Book III, Chapter 3, we discuss the Excel Services architecture and take you through a tour of the associated configuration settings. In this chapter, we get you started using Excel Services and managing your published workbooks.

Reviewing a Snapshot of Excel 2010 New Features

Before you can leverage Excel Services, you must first create an Excel workbook. The Excel workbook is the driving force of the Excel Services architecture. Without it, Excel Services is meaningless.

Creating a workbook is a simple matter of firing up the Excel client. The ins and outs of using Excel 2010 are beyond the purview of this book; however, there are a few new features that ship with Excel 2010 that are supported in Excel Services that deserve a quick mention. These features include:

✦ **Slicers**

Slicers in Excel 2010 are visual controls that allow you to quickly filter the data in your PivotTable. When working with PivotTables, you can select the PivotTable, then click the Insert Slicer command to insert a slicer directly into your workbook. You can determine which items from the PivotTable that you want your slicer to filter. For example, if you have a PivotTable that displays information on the product sales for each quarter, you can insert a slicer that allows you to filter your data by on the products. From a functional perspective, slicers behave similarly to search refiners and metadata navigation in SharePoint, because they allow you to narrow your dataset to show only the data that interests you.

Figure 4-1 shows an example of an Excel workbook that has been published to SharePoint and is being viewed in the browser. The workbook contains a slicer, which appears to the right of the PivotTable. We have selected three product items in the slicer (Ravioli Angelo, Sir Rodney's Marmalade and Teatime Chocolate Biscuits), which filters the contents of the PivotTable to display data related to the selected product items. When you are viewing your workbooks using the browser, the slicer functionality provides a visually pleasing and usable experience when it comes to filtering data in your workbooks.

✦ **Sparklines**

Sparklines in Excel 2010 allow you to visually represent trends in your data through the use of small charts that fit in cells alongside the data that they are describing. When you create your Sparklines in Excel 2010 and then publish your workbook to Excel Services, SharePoint knows how to display the Sparklines in the browser, again offering a visually pleasing and effective way of surfacing your data through SharePoint. At a glance, business executives can quickly spot trends in company data, such as product sales, which can help when forecasting results.

Figure 4-2 shows an example of an Excel workbook that has been published to SharePoint and is being viewed in the browser. The workbook contains a Sparkline, which appears to the right of the PivotTable. At a quick glance, you can see that the sales of Alice Mutton and Jack's New England Clam Chowder have been on a steady rise throughout the whole year; the sales of other products, such as Gorgonzola Telino, weren't as predictable.

The Sparkline measures the trend of the product sales for each quarter to produce a visual representation of the sales trend for the year.

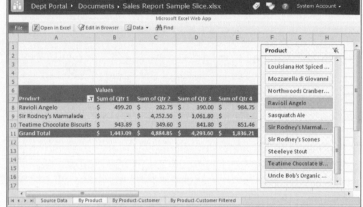

Figure 4-1:
You can filter your PivotTables quickly using the Slicer functionality.

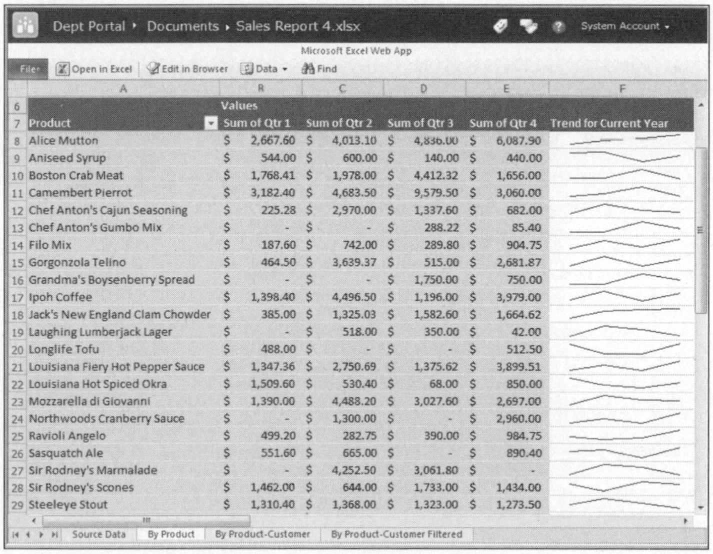

Figure 4-2:
You can represent trends in your data visually using Sparklines.

✦ **Show Value As**

Excel 2010 provides a quick and easy way for you to perform calculations on data in your PiviotTable through the introduction of the Show Value As functionality. With Show Value As, you can click on an entry in your PivotTable and apply a ready-made formula to the data. For example, if you have a PivotTable that displays product sales broken down by customer, you can use the Show Value As % of Parent Total to display the product sales for each customer as a percentage of the overall sales for that specific product. Figure 4-3 illustrates the Show Value As % of Parent formula in action. The four columns containing the percentages represent each four quarters in the year, and the product column is grouped by customer sales. At a quick glance, we can see that the customer WARTH was responsible for approximately 63 percent of the sales of Ravioli Angelo in Q1, and the customer AROUT was responsible for almost 80 percent of the sales of the same product in Q4.

✦ **Named Sets**

When you're working with data from an Analysis Services cube (a data structure that allows data to be analyzed quickly) you may find yourself using the same sets of fields over and over again to produce your PivotTables. Excel 2010 provides a way to capture those fields as a single item: a *named set*. When you've created your named set of fields, those fields still appear in the PivotTable Field List task pane along with all the other fields for the data source. But when you select the set, the fields' named set is applied to your PivotTable automatically — and the data is filtered accordingly.

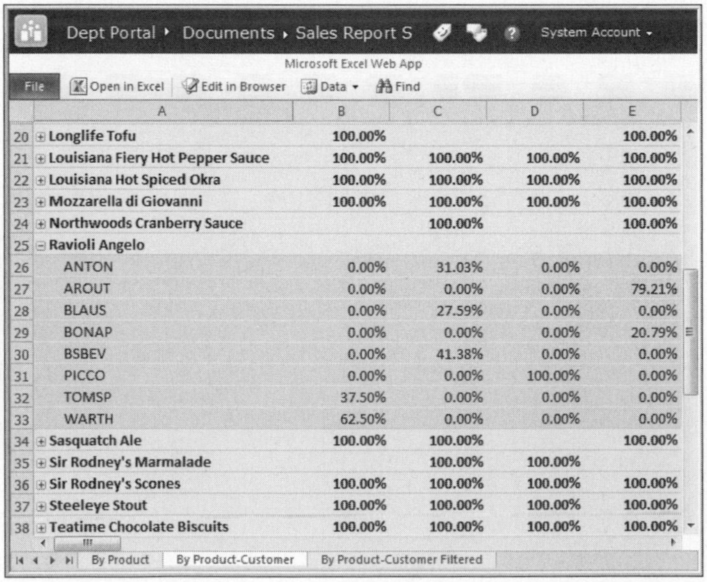

Figure 4-3:
You can display values based on percentages.

	A	B	C	D	E
20	⊞ Longlife Tofu	100.00%			100.00%
21	⊞ Louisiana Fiery Hot Pepper Sauce	100.00%	100.00%	100.00%	100.00%
22	⊞ Louisiana Hot Spiced Okra	100.00%	100.00%	100.00%	100.00%
23	⊞ Mozzarella di Giovanni	100.00%	100.00%	100.00%	100.00%
24	⊞ Northwoods Cranberry Sauce		100.00%		100.00%
25	⊟ Ravioli Angelo				
26	ANTON	0.00%	31.03%	0.00%	0.00%
27	AROUT	0.00%	0.00%	0.00%	79.21%
28	BLAUS	0.00%	27.59%	0.00%	0.00%
29	BONAP	0.00%	0.00%	0.00%	20.79%
30	BSBEV	0.00%	41.38%	0.00%	0.00%
31	PICCO	0.00%	0.00%	100.00%	0.00%
32	TOMSP	37.50%	0.00%	0.00%	0.00%
33	WARTH	62.50%	0.00%	0.00%	0.00%
34	⊞ Sasquatch Ale	100.00%	100.00%		100.00%
35	⊞ Sir Rodney's Marmalade		100.00%	100.00%	
36	⊞ Sir Rodney's Scones	100.00%	100.00%	100.00%	100.00%
37	⊞ Steeleye Stout	100.00%	100.00%	100.00%	100.00%
38	⊞ Teatime Chocolate Biscuits	100.00%	100.00%	100.00%	100.00%

Figure 4-4 shows a sample PivotTable generated from an Analysis Services cube in Microsoft's Contoso BI Demo Dataset, as viewed in the browser. We generated a named set for the PivotTable that filters the data to display product sales from North America only.

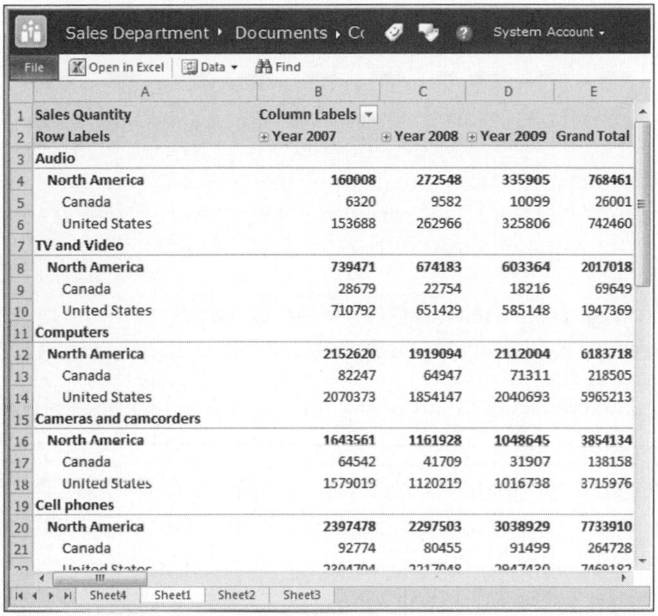

Figure 4-4:
You can use named sets to filter data in an OLAP Pivot Table

	A	B	C	D	E
1	Sales Quantity	Column Labels			
2	Row Labels	Year 2007	Year 2008	Year 2009	Grand Total
3	**Audio**				
4	North America	160008	272548	335905	768461
5	Canada	6320	9582	10099	26001
6	United States	153688	262966	325806	742460
7	**TV and Video**				
8	North America	739471	674183	603364	2017018
9	Canada	28679	22754	18216	69649
10	United States	710792	651429	585148	1947369
11	**Computers**				
12	North America	2152620	1919094	2112004	6183718
13	Canada	82247	64947	71311	218505
14	United States	2070373	1854147	2040693	5965213
15	**Cameras and camcorders**				
16	North America	1643561	1161928	1048645	3854134
17	Canada	64542	41709	31907	138158
18	United States	1579019	1120219	1016738	3715976
19	**Cell phones**				
20	North America	2397478	2297503	3038929	7733910
21	Canada	92774	80455	91499	264728
22	United States	2304704	2217048	2947430	7469182

Sheet4 Sheet1 Sheet2 Sheet3

You can use the Sales Report sample template that ships out-of-the-box with Excel 2010, and the Contoso BI Demo Dataset Analysis Services cube to quickly test drive the new Excel 2010 functionality.

Publishing Your Excel Workbooks

Publishing your workbook to Excel Services is as simple as clicking the Save button in Excel; however, before you publish your spreadsheet there are a number of checks that you need to take to ensure the publishing process goes smoothly. You can group the preparation into two main categories:

✦ **Preparation on the client**

Preparation on the client involves making sure your workbooks publish and run successfully in the browser. This includes

- Checking to make sure the features you implement in your workbook are supported in Excel Services

- Ensuring that the connections to your external data sources are configured to support Excel Services

✦ **Preparation on the server**

Preparation on the server involves making sure that SharePoint can successfully display your workbook in the browser and handle all the user interactions. This includes

- Ensuring that you have the appropriate permissions to publish to the document library in SharePoint

- Ensuring that Excel Services has the document library listed as trusted location

- Ensuring that Excel Services knows how to connect to, and trusts your external data sources

Checking for compatibility issues

Excel Services provides you with a great experience when interacting with your workbooks through the browser; however, there are some features that work in the Excel client that won't necessarily work in the browser. For example, Excel Services doesn't support the direct interaction with PivotChart reports, because the PivotChart is represented as a static image in Excel Services. However, if you have a PivotChart on the same worksheet as your PivotTable, your interaction with the PivotTable will drive the image that appears in the PivotChart.

A word to the wise: When you're creating your workbooks and preparing to publish them to SharePoint, check to see whether Excel Services actually supports the features you've set up your workbooks to use

In deference to its ancestors, Microsoft Excel 2010 comes equipped with a compatibility checker to determine whether your current workbook is (well, yes) compatible with previous Excel versions. Unfortunately, unlike other Office client applications (such as Microsoft Access and Microsoft InfoPath), Excel can't check to see whether your spreadsheet is compatible with Excel Services — which it has to be if it's going to work the way you want it to in SharePoint. In order to check for compatibility with Excel Services you'll have to do the work manually, or invest in an Add-In to do the job for you

It would be nice to be able to automatically detect compatibility issues prior to publication, but don't worry, all is not lost. If your workbook contains features that are unsupported by Excel Services, you are still able to publish your workbook, and you are still able to view the workbook using the browser. This is a big improvement over Excel Services 2007; if your workbook contained unsupported functionality then Excel Services wouldn't even open the workbook. Better yet, when you view the workbook in the browser, Excel Services displays a status bar across the top of the page notifying you if your workbook contains unsupported features. The status bar contains a

Details button that, when clicked, lets you know what unsupported features your workbook contains and provides a link to a Microsoft online article with information regarding the issue. Figure 4-5 shows a workbook in the browser that contains external query table functionality that isn't supported by Excel Services; the details button on the status bar that appears across the top of the workbook page has been clicked to display information on the issue.

The Microsoft Office Web site has an article that provides information on what is supported in Excel Services and what isn't supported. You can access the article using the Help functionality in Excel 2010, or by simply entering the article title: "Differences between using a workbook in Excel and Excel Services", in your favorite online search engine. Note that there are two versions of this article online, one specific to Excel Services 2007 and one specific to Excel Services 2010, so ensure that the article that you are reading is for 2010.

Of course, if you're in a hurry, you can go ahead and publish your workbooks to SharePoint, unsupported features and all — and alert your users to ignore the features that Excel Services doesn't support. If your users click an icon to expand a query and get an error message that says a feature is unsupported, they can ignore the error, dismiss the message, and "just don't do that again"; they can still view and interact with the data. Of course, if your users really want to get their hands on that particular piece of forbidden functionality, they can download the workbook to their computers — assuming they have the appropriate permissions — and open it up in its full glory in the Excel client application.

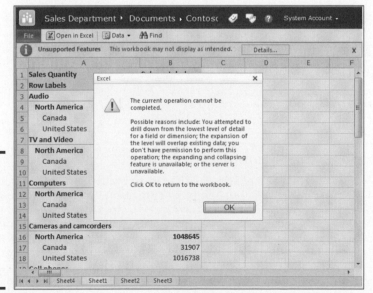

Figure 4-5: Excel Services informs you if any incompatibilities exist.

Configuring your external connections

If your workbook contains connections to external data sources then you need to ensure that Excel Services can work with and trust those connections. By default Excel Services is configured to allow embedded connections and connections stored in data connection libraries for workbooks uploaded to SharePoint. If your Excel Services implementation is configured in this way, then when Excel Services opens a workbook that contains connections, it will first check to see if there are connections embedded into the workbook, and then check for data connection library connections.

When configuring your data connections, regardless of whether they are embedded or stored in a data connection file, you can select one of three authentication options:

✦ **Integrated Windows Authentication**

> You may use Windows Authentication if you've configured Kerberos in your environment (for more about Kerberos, see Book II, Chapter 2). If Kerberos is absent when you try to use this option for your data connections, Excel Services runs into delegation problems when it tries to authenticate with the data source. Figure 4-6 shows an example of the error message you receive when you configure your data connection to use Windows Authentication in an environment that isn't configured to use Kerberos.

Figure 4-6: Use Windows Authentication only if you have Kerberos configured.

✦ **Secure Store Service (SSS)**

> If your environment isn't configured to use Kerberos then you can use the Secure Store Service to handle the authentication to your external data sources. The Secure Store Service stores the credential information that Excel Services can use to connect to your external data sources. You must have a target application configured in the Secure Store Service and Excel Services, and know the application ID in order to leverage this option in your data connections; you use the application ID that is mapped to Excel Services in your data connection.

✦ **None**

If you configure your data connection to use None for its authentication, this informs Excel to get its connection data from the connection string data that is defined as a property of the data connection in Excel. In order to protect the server environment from malicious attacks, Excel Services impersonates the unattended service account to connect to the data source. In order for this method to successfully connect to your data source, the unattended service account would need to have access to the data source.

Granting the unattended service account access to sensitive data sources isn't recommended. Doing so enables the Excel users within your organization to access data from the data sources when selecting None as the authentication method in their workbook. Instead, it is recommended that you use the Secure Store Service and configure specific target applications for per user or per group access to your data sources.

Finding the Secure Store Service Application ID

When you are configuring your workbook data connection to use the Secure Store Service, you need to know the application ID that is listed in the Secure Store Service for accessing your application. You can discover this information by contacting your SharePoint administrator, or the person that is responsible for maintaining the Secure Store Service target application.

If you are the administrator, or the person responsible for managing the target application in the Secure Store, then you can use the following steps to discover the application ID needed for the data connection:

1. **Using your browser, navigate to Central Administration.**

2. **From the Application Management section, click Manage service applications.**

The Service Application management page appears, listing the service applications to which you have access.

3. **From the list of service applications, select Secure Store Service.**

4. **On the Service Application tab, in the operations group, click Manage.**

Alternatively, you can simply click the service application name to display the management page for that service.

A list of target applications appears, showing the target application ID, the type and the target application name.

5. **Find the target application that you need for your data connection, and take note of the Target Application ID.**

The Target Application ID is the field that you enter into the Secure Store setting in your Excel workbook. If you don't see a target application that represents your data connection, you will need to create one before you can use the Secure Store Service to connect to the data source. The Configuring the Secure Store section of Book III, Chapter 3 shows you how to create a target application in the secure store.

Configuring the authentication options

You can use the following instructions to access and configure the authentication settings for existing data connections in your workbook:

1. **Using Excel 2010, open the workbook or Office Data Connection file that contains your data connection.**

You can open ODC files directly in Excel and update the connection settings as you would a regular workbook.

2. **On the Data tab, in the Connections group, click Connections.**

The Workbook Connections dialog appears from which you can manage your existing connections and add new connections.

3. **Select the data connection for which you would like to configure the authentication settings, and click Properties.**

The Connection Properties dialog appears.

4. **From the Connection Properties dialog, click the Definition tab.**

The definition tab displays the properties that make up the Office Data Connection (ODC) file. The Authentication Settings button appears at the end next to the Excel Services label.

5. **Click Authentication Settings.**

The Excel Services Authentication Settings dialog appears.

6. **Select the authentication option that you want Excel Services to use when connecting to your data sources.**

If you don't have Kerberos configured in your environment, then it is recommended that you use the Secure Store Service (SSS) setting. You will need to know the target application ID created in the Secure Store Service in order to use this option.

For more about Kerberos, see Book II, Chapter 2.

7. **Click OK.**

8. **Click OK to save your changes to the data connection**

9. **From the Quick Launch bar at the top of the Excel application, click the Save icon.**

   Your changes are saved to your ODC file or your Excel worbook.

Verifying the Unattended Service Account

If you don't want to use the Secure Store Service option, and instead just want Excel Services to figure out how to handle the authentication, then you will need to make sure that the unattended service account is configured for Excel Services.

If you are the administrator of the Excel Services service application, you can use the following steps to verify that the unattended service account is configured correctly:

1. **Using your browser, navigate to Central Administration.**

2. **From the Application Management section, click Manage service applications.**

   The Service Application management page appears, listing the service applications to which you have access.

3. **From the list of service applications, select Excel Services.**

   The Manage Excel Services Application page appears with a list of links to the various Excel Services management pages.

4. **From the Manage Excel Services Application page, click Global Settings.**

   The Excel Services Application Settings page appears.

5. **From the External Data section, make a note of the value in the Application ID field.**

   The value set in the Application ID field maps to a target application in the Secure Store. The target application holds the credential information for the unattended service account. You need to make sure that the corresponding target application exists in the Secure Store Service.

   If the Application ID field is blank, then the unattended service account hasn't been configured properly for Excel Services. If that is the case, then the Configuring the Unattended Service Account section in Book III, Chapter 3 shows you how to configure the unattended service account for Excel Services.

6. **Click Cancel to exit out of the Excel Services Application Settings page.**

7. **From the Quick Launch, click Application Management.**

   The Application Management page appears.

8. **From the Service Applications section, click Manage service applications.**

   The Service Application management page appears listing all the service applications to which you have access.

9. **From the list of service applications, select Secure Store Service.**

10. **On the Service Applications tab, in the Operations group, click Manage.**

    Alternatively, you could simply click on the Secure Store Service application in the list.

    The Secure Store Service management page appears listing the target applications defined for SharePoint.

11. **Verify that the application ID that you took note of in Step 5 appears in the list of target applications.**

    If the matching target application isn't listed, then the unattended service account hasn't been configured properly for Excel Services. If that is the case, then the Configuring the Unattended Service Account section in Book III, Chapter 3 shows you how to configure the unattended service account for Excel Services.

Exporting data connection files to SharePoint

When accessing external data in your workbooks Excel Services supports the use of embedded connections and connections from data connection files stored in a trusted location. Using data connection files in your workbooks has its advantages including:

✦ **Reusable**

   When you define data connections in an Office Data Connection (ODC) file, you can reuse the same connection information in multiple workbooks; you don't need to redefine the same connection steps over and over again.

✦ **Centrally managed**

If you use a data connection file in multiple workbooks and need to change your data connection information, you simply update the file and all workbooks linked to that file will automatically receive the new connection information.

✦ **More secure**

You can store your data connection files used by Excel Services in a trusted SharePoint library. By doing so your data connection files automatically inherit the security and functionality of SharePoint. You can apply permissions on each data connection file, ensuring that only the right users have access to the right data connection information.

The easiest way to create your data connection files for uploading to SharePoint is to first create them in Excel using the Data Connection Wizard. When creating your data connection in this way, you should ensure that the authentication settings are configured correctly and that the Always attempt to use this file to refresh data setting is selected. Selecting this setting will ensure that Excel Services doesn't use the embedded data connection stored in the workbook when connecting to the external data source, which means that if the connection information changes, then Excel Services will automatically use the correct information when opening and refreshing your workbook. Figure 4-7 shows the Data Connection Wizard with the Always attempt to use this file to refresh data setting selected. Once you have your data connection created, you can export it directly to your SharePoint library for use by Excel Services.

Figure 4-7:
Create
your data
connection
using
the Data
Connection
Wizard.

The following steps show you how to export a data connection file and save it directly to your SharePoint library:

1. **Using Excel 2010, open the workbook or Office Data Connection file that contains your data connection.**

   You can open ODC files directly in Excel and update the connection settings as you would a regular workbook.

2. **On the Data tab, in the Connections group, click Connections.**

   The Workbook Connections dialog appears from which you can manage your existing connections and add new connections.

3. **Select the data connection for which you would like to configure the authentication settings, and click Properties.**

   The Connection Properties dialog appears.

4. **From the Connection Properties dialog, click the Definition tab.**

   The definition tab displays the properties that make up the Office Data Connection (ODC) file.

5. **From the Connection file settings, ensure that the Always use connection file setting is selected.**

6. **From the bottom of the Connection Properties dialog, click Export Connection File.**

   The File Save dialog appears which you can use to save your data connection file directly into your SharePoint library.

7. **In the address bar, enter the URL to the SharePoint library to which you want to save your data connection file and click the right-arrow next to the address to navigate to the SharePoint library.**

   You must have write permissions to the SharePoint library that you are saving to in order to store your data connection library in that file.

8. **In the File Name, enter the name that you would like to give your data connection file.**

9. **Click Save.**

   Your data connection file is saved in Microsoft Office Data Connection (ODC) format. Figure 4-8 shows an example of a data connection file being saved to a SharePoint library.

 After your data connection file is saved to the SharePoint library, you can use SharePoint's permission management functionality to control which users can use your data connection in their workbooks. If you give your users Read access to the file, they will be able to use your data connection in their workbooks.

Figure 4-8:
You can export your data connection file directly to SharePoint.

Checking Trusted Resources

Part of the publishing process entails checking to make sure that Excel Services knows that your workbooks and data connection files are safe to use. Excel Services keeps a list of the trusted resources, defined by the service administrator, that it considers safe. If you want Excel Services to be able to load your workbook and refresh its external data, you will need to verify that the libraries that contain your workbook and associated data connection files are listed as trusted resources.

Verifying your SharePoint library is trusted

When you publish your workbook to a SharePoint library you can edit and view your workbook in the Excel client without any additional steps. If you want to view and interact with your workbook using the browser, Excel Services must trust the library in which you store your workbook. If you use the Farm Configuration wizard to create and configure the services within your farm, then Excel Services will automatically trust all SharePoint library locations within the farm by default. If you have modified the default configuration or manually configured your services, then you should verify that Excel Services trusts the SharePoint library to which you are uploading your workbooks.

If you are the administrator of the Excel Services service application, you can use the following steps to verify that the library containing your data connection files is trusted:

1. **Using your browser, navigate to Central Administration.**

2. **From the Application Management section, click Manage service applications.**

   The Service Application management page appears, listing the service applications to which you have access.

3. **From the list of service applications, select Excel Services.**

   The Manage Excel Services Application page appears with a list of links to the various Excel Services management pages.

4. **From the Manage Excel Services Application page, click Trusted File Locations.**

   The Trusted File Locations page appears, listing the file locations that Excel Services trusts.

5. **Verify that your SharePoint library appears in the list of trusted file locations.**

   If your SharePoint library appears in the list, it is already trusted and Excel Services will open and refresh workbooks stored in the library. If your SharePoint library doesn't appear in the list then you need to add it to the list of trusted connections. The Defining your Trusted File Locations section of Book III, Chapter 3.

Verifying your data connection library is trusted

If you want Excel Services to leverage data connection files stored in a SharePoint library, then the library must be listed as a trusted data connection library in Excel Services. If your workbook uses a data connection file from a library that isn't trusted by Excel Services, you will receive an error message similar to the error shown in Figure 4-9.

Figure 4-9:
Data
connection
files must
be stored
in a library
trusted
by Excel
Services.

If you are the administrator of the Excel Services service application, you can use the following steps to verify that the library containing your data connection files is trusted:

1. **Using your browser, navigate to Central Administration.**

2. **From the Application Management section, click Manage service applications.**

   The Service Application management page appears, listing the service applications to which you have access.

3. **From the list of service applications, select Excel Services.**

   The Manage Excel Services Application page appears with a list of links to the various Excel Services management pages.

4. **From the Manage Excel Services Application page, click Trusted Data Connection Libraries.**

   The Trusted Data Connection Libraries page appears, listing the SharePoint document libraries that host data connections that you can use in your workbooks.

5. **Verify that your data connection library appears in the list of trusted data connection libraries.**

   If your data connection library doesn't appear in the list, proceed to the next step. If your data connection library appears in the list, it is already trusted and you can use the connection files in your workbooks.

6. **Click Add Trusted Data Connection Library.**

   The Add Trusted Data Connection Library page appears.

7. **In the Address field, enter the URL to the SharePoint library that hosts the data connection files.**

8. **In the Description field, enter the description of the purpose of the data connection library.**

9. **Click OK.**

   Excel Services will now open data connections from your SharePoint library.

Configuring your Publishing Options

When publishing your workbooks to SharePoint you don't have to publish the entire workbook; instead, you can use the Publish Options dialog to tell Excel only to publish a worksheet, or even a single PivotTable from your workbook.

The Publish Options dialog provides a very simple interface that has two tabs:

✦ **Show**

The Show tab, as its name suggests, allows you to configure what items in your workbook you would like Excel Services to show when viewing through the browser. You can choose to show any of the following:

• **Entire Workbook**

This option publishes the entire workbook, in all its glory, to SharePoint. You can use the browser interface to navigate between worksheets and scroll through the data.

• **Sheets**

This option allows you to select one or more worksheets in your workbook that you would like to publish. For example, if your workbook only contains one worksheet, there's no point in rendering the entire workbook in the browser; instead, you can select the Sheets option and select the worksheet from the list of worksheets to display.

• **Items in the Workbook**

This option allows you to select one or more items in your workbook that you would like to publish. For example, if your workbook contained two PivotTables, three Named Ranges and two PivotCharts, you could decide to only publish one PivotTable and two Named Ranges. The items that you select from the Items in the Workbook list appear in the View drop-down navigation menu at the top right of the Excel Web Access Web Part. You can navigate between items using this drop-down.

✦ **Parameters**

Use this tab to set individual cells in your workbook as parameters. Cells that have been identified as parameters during the publishing process (the buzzword is "parameterized") are editable when viewed through the browser. You can use the Parameters pane in the browser to edit those parameterized cells. Parameters are useful if you want to give your users the option of doing what-if analyses changing the actual data or workbook file.

Before you can select a cell as a parameter, you must first define a named range for the cell in Excel.

When you publish your workbook to Excel Services, you can specify specific cells as editable when viewing through the browser. To do this you must perform the following steps:

1. **Define a name for your cell in Excel**

2. **Add the named range as a parameter in the Publish Options, when publishing your workbook.**

Naming Cells for Editing

You can use the following steps to name the cells you want to mark as editable in Excel:

1. **Using Excel 2010, open the workbook you want to publish to SharePoint.**

2. **Select the cell that you wish to mark as editable when viewing in the browser.**

3. **On the Formulas tab, in the Define Names group, click Define Name.**

   The New Name dialog appears from which you can specify the name for your cell.

4. **Enter the Name that you want to give the parameter and display in the browser.**

   The name that you enter is what your users see in parameters pane when they view your workbook in the browser. With that in mind, ensure that you use meaningful names.

5. **Select the scope from which you would like the parameter to be available.**

6. **Enter a description of the parameter in the Comment field.**

   The description field appears in the Publish Options dialog and provides a good reminder as to the purpose and function of the named cell.

7. **Click OK.**

   Your named cell is ready to add as a parameter when publishing to SharePoint.

Using the Publish Options Dialog

You can use the following steps to determine what parts of your workbook to show in SharePoint, and to add your named cells as parameters in Excel Services:

1. **Using Excel 2010, open the workbook you want to publish to SharePoint.**

2. **Click the File tab to present the Backstage View.**

   The Backstage view holds the commands that help you manage your Excel workbooks and view any properties, metadata, and options associated with your workbook.

3. **Click the Save & Send tab to display the Excel Save options.**

   The Save & Send page displays showing you the different locations to which you can save and send your Excel files.

4. **From the Save & Send section on the page, click Save to SharePoint.**

   The Save to SharePoint details pane appears to the right.

5. **Click Publish Options to select which items to publish.**

   The Publish Options dialog appears, from which you can select to publish the entire workbook or only sections of your workbook. In addition, you can add parameters based on Named cells defined in your workbook.

6. **On the Show tab, in the drop-down list, select the items that you want to publish to Excel Services.**

7. **On the Parameters tab, click Add to add parameters to represent editable cells in your workbook.**

   The Add Parameters dialog appears, listing the available named cells in your workbook that you can add as parameters in Excel Services. Parameters allow you to designate cells in your workbook that you can edit when viewing through the browser with Excel Services.

8. **Select the parameters you want to make available in Excel Services, and click OK.**

   You return to the Publish Options dialog, and any parameters you selected appear in the list of parameters.

9. **Click OK to save your Publish Options for this workbook, and return to the Save & Send page in Excel.**

   Now that your publishing options are all set, you are ready to publish your workbook to SharePoint.

Publishing your workbook

After you have completed all the publishing prep work, the actual publishing process is very simple. You can use the following steps to publish your Excel workbook to your SharePoint library:

1. **Using Excel 2010, open the workbook you want to publish to SharePoint.**

2. **Click the File tab to present the Backstage View.**

   The Backstage view holds the commands that help you manage your Excel workbooks and view any properties, metadata, and options associated with your workbook.

3. **Click the Save & Send tab to display the Excel Save options.**

   The Save & Send page displays showing you the different locations to which you can save and send your Excel files.

4. **From the Save & Send section on the page, click Save to SharePoint.**

   The Save to SharePoint details pane appears to the right. Figure 4-10 shows an example of the Save & Send page with the Save to SharePoint option selected.

Figure 4-10:
You can
use the
Backstage
view to
publish your
workbook to
SharePoint

5. **If you need to configure your publishing options using the Publish Options button, jump to the Configuring your Publishing Options section of this chapter before proceeding to Step 6.**

6. **From the Save to SharePoint details pane, double-click Browse for a location.**

   Alternatively, if your SharePoint location appears in the Recent Locations list, simply double-click it to open the SharePoint library and skip to Step 8.

7. **In the address bar, enter the URL to the SharePoint library to which you want to save your data connection file and click the right-arrow next to the address to navigate to the SharePoint library.**

   You must have write permissions to the SharePoint library to which you are saving your workbook, in order to store your data connection library in that file.

8. **In the File Name, enter the name that you would like to give your data connection file.**

9. **Click Open with Excel in the browser, if you want Excel Services to open your workbook in the browser once you publish it to SharePoint; otherwise skip to Step 10.**

10. **Click Save.**

    Your SharePoint workbook is saved to your SharePoint library ready to be accessed by the users with the appropriate permissions. If you selected the Open with Excel in the browser option, Excel Services opens your browser and displays your workbook.

After your workbook is saved to the SharePoint library, you can use SharePoint's permission management functionality to control which users can access your workbook. You can set permissions at the library, folder, and file level to make sure that the right people see the right information at all times.

You can use the SharePoint View Only permissions to confine the use of your workbook to Excel Services. View only permissions allows users that have been assigned that permission, to open and interact with your workbook in Excel Services, but prevents them from opening the workbook in the Excel client. Data connections defined in the Excel workbook are accessible to Excel Services, allowing users to view and interact with the external data in the workbook using the browser only.

Viewing Your Workbooks in the Browser

After you have published your workbooks successfully to SharePoint, you can open and interact with your workbook in the browser.

The browser interface is made up of a SharePoint Web Part page with the Excel Access Web Part added. The Excel Access Web Part loads your workbook for rendering in the browser.

The Web Part page is a special page that is used to load each workbook that you view in the browser; SharePoint doesn't create a separate Web Part page for each workbook. If you want to create a separate page to display the contents of your workbook, you would create a Web Part page and manually add and configure the Excel Web Access Web Part to display your workbook. The Working with the Excel Web Access Web Part section of this chapter shows you how to configure the Excel Web Access Web Part

You can use the following steps to open your workbook in the browser:

1. **Using your browser, navigate to the SharePoint library that stores your workbook.**

2. **Click on the workbook to open it in your browser.**

   Alternatively, hover over the file name, click the down@arrow to display the shortcut menu, and then click View in Browser.

   Your Excel workbook appears in the browser, and you are now able to interact with it filtering and sorting data as needed.

Figure 4-11 shows an example of a published workbook viewed in the browser.

Figure 4-11: Excel Services provides a high-fidelity viewing experience.

Reviewing the Excel Web Access Menu Options

Excel Services provides a set of menu options across the top of the page that you can use when working with your workbook through the browser.

Excel Web Access and Excel Web App are two different offerings that are driven by Excel Services. Excel Web Access represents the Excel Web Access Web Part and refers to the browser viewing experience that comes out of the box with Excel Services. Excel Web App ships as part of Office Web Apps, and provides you with the ability to edit your workbooks in the browser in the same way you would on the client. An additional Edit in Browser menu option appears in the Excel Web Access menu bar if Excel Web App is up and running in your SharePoint environment. If you don't see the Edit in Browser menu option, then Excel Web App isn't available.

At a glance, the Excel Web Access menu options include:

✦ **File⇨Open in Excel.**

You can use this menu option to open the workbook that you are currently viewing in the Excel client. This option is the same as clicking the Open in Excel menu option that appears directly on the menu bar. The Open in Excel menu option doesn't appear if you have View Only, or Read only permissions on the workbook.

✦ **File⇨Download a Snapshot**

You can use this menu option to download a simple copy of the current workbook that contains only the values and formatting.

✦ **File⇨Download a Copy**

You can use this menu option to download a copy of the workbook to your computer. This option doesn't appear if you have View Only or Read only permissions to the workbook.

✦ **File⇨Reload Workbook**

You can use this menu option to reload the workbook from its file location. This option is just like clicking View in browser again.

✦ **Data⇨Refresh Selected Connection**

You can use this option to refresh the data connection for the currently selected PivotTable. If the data in your external data source has changed, your PivotTable will update accordingly.

✦ **Data⇨Refresh All Connections**

You can use this option to refresh all the data connections in your workbook. If the data in your external data sources has changed your workbook data will update accordingly.

In addition to refreshing your data, this option is a great way to verify if your data connections are actually working in Excel Services.

✦ **Data⇨Calculate Workbook**

You can use this menu option to reload the workbook from its file location. This option is just like clicking View in browser again.

✦ **Find**

You can use this option to search for data in the cells of your workbook.

Using the Parameter Pane

If your workbook contains editable cells defined as parameters, (as with the example shown in Figure 4-12), the Parameters pane appears; it's to the right of the workbook. You can toggle between hiding and displaying the Parameters pane by clicking the right arrow and left arrow respectively, they also appear to the right of the workbook.

Figure 4-12: You can use parameters to test what-if scenarios in your workbook.

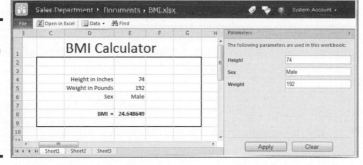

You can update the cells associated with your parameters by simply entering the data in the parameter fields and clicking Apply.

When you use parameters to edit cells in a workbook through the browser, the changes are only seen by you. You aren't actually changing the core workbook stored in the SharePoint library; instead, you are viewing the copy of the workbook that Excel Services generated especially for you when viewing the workbook in the browser. This is great because it allows you to perform "What If" type scenarios with your data without disrupting other users and, more importantly, annoying the workbook author.

**Book IV
Chapter 4**

**Working with Excel
Services**

Configuring the Excel Web Access Web Part

When you view a workbook in the browser from a SharePoint library, you are presented with a SharePoint page that renders your workbook. The component on the page that handles the rendering is the Excel Web Access Web Part. The Excel Web Access Web Part ships with Excel Services and allows you to render Excel workbooks in your SharePoint Web pages. You can create a Web Part page in SharePoint and add the Excel Web Access Web Part to the page. You can configure the Web Part to display your workbook, and to turn on and off menu items and other options, such as interactivity. You can connect the Web Part to other Web Parts on the page to provide your users with a dynamic, interactive, dashboard type of experience.

Excel Web Access Web Part Settings

The Excel Web Access Web Part has a number of settings that you can configure that control its behavior and appearance in the browser. The settings include:

✦ **Workbook**

Use the Workbook setting to define the workbook that you want to appear in the Excel Web Access Web Part. The Workbook field stores the URL to the workbook that you want to display.

You can connect your Excel Web Access Web Part to another Web Part that feeds the workbook URL to the Excel Web Access Web Part, allowing you to dynamically update the workbook that appears in the Web Part as the user changes the selection in the connected Web Part.

✦ **Named Item**

Use the Named Item setting to specify a named item in your workbook that you want to display in the Web Part. For example, if your workbook contained multiple PivotTables and PivotCharts, and you only wanted to display one of the PivotTables, you would enter the name of that PivotTable in the Named Item setting.

✦ **Autogenerate Web Part Title**

Select this Autogenerate Web Part Title to let Excel Services automatically create the title of the Web Part. If this setting is selected, Excel Services appends the name of your workbook to the Web Part title bar. If you clear this setting, then Excel Services displays the contents of Title field in the Appearance section.

The Microsoft documentation states that Excel Services builds the Web Part title by appending the workbook name to the value assigned to the Title field in the Appearance section of the Web Part. In the actual version of SharePoint that Microsoft released, however, the Web Part simply appends the workbook name to the "Excel Web Access" text. It's a small, nitpicky issue — but it has the potential to cause frustration. If you don't want your Web Part to display the "Excel Web Access" phrase in its title, then clear the Autogenerate Web Part Title setting.

✦ **Autogenerate Web Part Title URL**

Select this option to tell Excel Services to create the URL associated with the Web Part Title. Excel Services replaces the value in the Title URL field that's in the Advanced section of the Web Part. Then, when you click the title of the Web Part, you navigate to the URL as defined by Excel Services.

If you don't want Excel Services to automatically generate the URL, clear the Autogenerate Web Part Title URL setting. If you want to specify your own custom URL, enter it into the Title URL field in the Advanced section of the Web Part.

✦ **Type of Toolbar**

Use the Type of Toolbar to select the menu options, and view options that you want to appear in the Web Part.

- **Full** displays the full Excel Web Access menu in your Web Part. The menu options that appear are controlled by the settings that you enable and disable in the Toolbar Menu Commands section of the Web Part. For example, if you clear the Open in Excel, Download a Copy, Download a Snapshot setting, each of those menu commands will be hidden from the File menu in the Excel Web Access Web Part, with only the Reload Workbook command remaining.

- **Summary** displays a subset of the menu options and includes the View drop-down list displaying named items in the workbook.

- **Navigation Only** removes the menu options and only displays the View related information to navigate between named items in your workbook.

- **None** hides all menu and worksheet navigation options from the menu. This is a good option to choose if you want to control how your users interact with your workbook.

✦ **Open in Excel, Download a Copy, Download a Snapshot**

Select this setting to enable the associated commands on the File menu in the toolbar. This setting works in conjunction with the Type of

Toolbar setting. For example, if you have this setting enabled but have the Type of Toolbar set to None, you will not see the Open in Excel, Download a Copy and Download a Snapshot commands on the Excel Web Access menu because the menu will be hidden.

Clear this setting to hide these commands from the Excel Web Access toolbar in your Web Part.

✦ **Refresh Selected Connection, Refresh All Connections**

Select this setting to enable the associated commands on the Data menu in the toolbar. This setting works in conjunction with the Type of Toolbar setting. For example, if you have this setting enabled but have the Type of Toolbar set to None, you will not see the Refresh Selected Connection and the Refresh All Connections commands on the Excel Web Access menu because the menu will be hidden.

Clear this setting to hide these commands from the Excel Web Access toolbar in your Web Part.

✦ **Calculate Workbook**

Select this setting to enable the Calculate Workbook command on the Data menu in the toolbar. This setting works in conjunction with the Type of Toolbar setting. For example, if you have this setting enabled but have the Type of Toolbar set to None, you will not see the Calculate Workbook command on the Excel Web Access menu because the menu will be hidden.

Clear this setting to hide the Calculate Workbook command from the Excel Web Access toolbar in your Web Part.

✦ **Named Item Drop-Down List**

Select this setting to display the View drop-down menu listing the named items selected when publishing the workbook. The View drop-down menu appears on the right side of the toolbar menu, and will only be shown if your workbook contains named items and those items have been published using the Items in the Workbook option on the Show tab in the Publish Options dialog.

This setting works in conjunction with the Type of Toolbar setting. For example, if you have this setting enabled but have the Type of Toolbar set to None, you will not see the View drop-down on the Excel Web Access menu because the menu will be hidden.

Clear this setting to hide the View drop-down from the Excel Web Access toolbar in your Web Part.

✦ **Hyperlinks**

Select this setting to enable hyperlinks to link to locations within the workbook or to files and documents outside the workbook.

Clear this setting to disable all hyperlinks in the workbook, regardless of their target location.

✦ **All Workbook Interactivity**

Select this setting to enable interactivity for your workbook. You can further customize the interactivity settings be enabling and disabling the following settings:

• **Parameter Modification**

Select this setting to allow user to edit parameters using the Parameter task pane.

• **Display Parameters Task Pane**

If the Parameter Modification setting is selected, select this setting to show the Parameters Task Pane, allowing users to edit values.

Clear this setting to hide the Parameters Task Pane to prevent users from editing parameters directly. You can use this option if you wanted to feed the parameter values to the Web Part from another connected Web Part instead of allowing users to input values.

• **Sorting**

Select this setting to enable sorting of cells, tables, and PivotTables in your workbook.

Clear this setting to prevent users from sorting of cells, tables, and PivotTables in your workbook.

• **Filtering**

Select this setting to enable filtering of cells, tables, and PivotTables in your workbook.

Clear this setting to prevent users from filtering of cells, tables, and PivotTables in your workbook.

• **All PivotTable Interactivity**

Select this setting to enable the expanding and collapsing of levels, sorting and filtering in PivotTables. In order for sorting and filtering to work, you need to have the previous sorting and filtering settings enabled.

- **Periodically Refresh if Enabled in Workbook**

  Select this setting to enable periodic refreshes of the external data in your workbook.

  Clear this setting to disable periodic refreshes of the external data in your workbook.

  If you clear the Workbook Interactivity setting all of the interactivity settings are automatically disabled, and no interactivity is permitted in the workbook.

✦ **Close Session Before Opening a New One**

  Select this setting to close the current workbook session before opening a new session. Enabling this setting may improve performance if you have a lot of users view the workbook. However, users will lose their state information when they open a new workbook; this means that any cached settings, such as filters or parameter values, are discarded.

Adding the Excel Web Access Web Part

You can use the following steps to add an Excel Web Access Web Part to your Web Part page:

1. **Using your browser, navigate to the Web Part page in your SharePoint site to which you want to add the Web Part.**

2. **Click the Page tab.**

3. **From the Edit group in the ribbon menu, click Edit Page.**

4. **From your chosen Web Part zone, click Add a Web Part.**

   A list of Web Parts appears below the ribbon menu.

5. **From the Categories column, click Business Data.**

   The Web Parts related to the Business Data category appear, including the Excel Web Access Web Part.

   If the Excel Web Access Web Part doesn't appear in the listing, then you may not have Excel Services configured in your organization or for your site collection. You can read more information on how to configure Excel Services for your environment in Book III, Chapter 3.

6. **From the Web Parts column, click Excel Access Web Part.**

   The About the Web Part column provides you with information about the selected Web Part, and shows you the area on the Web Part Page, more commonly referred to as the Zone, in which it will be added.

7. **Select the zone you want, and then click Add.**

   The Excel Access Web Part is added to your Web Part page. At this stage, it hasn't been configured.

8. **From the contents of the Excel Access Web Part, click the link to open the tool pane.**

   This will open the Web Part tool pane from which you can define the Web Part settings. Alternatively, you can edit a Web Part using the following method:

   a. From the right hand side of the Web Part title, click the down arrow to display the Web Part menu.

   b. From the Web Part menu, click Edit Web Part.

9. **In the Workbook field, browse to the workbook that you want to appear in the Web Part.**

10. **Complete the remaining fields as needed.**

    You can find out information what each field means in the Excel Web Access Web Part Settings section of this chapter.

11. **Click OK.**

    The Excel Web Access Web Part appears on your Web Part page, and displays your workbook.

Understanding Excel Web App

Excel Services includes the Excel Web Access Web Part out of the box which allows you to view and interact with your Excel workbooks using the browser. The Excel Web Access Web Part provides limited edit capabilities through the use of parameters. When users apply edits using parameters, they aren't really editing the Excel workbook; instead, they are working with their own cached version of the workbook. The underlying workbook remains untouched. This is very nice; however, at the end of the day it is safe to say that the Excel Web Access Web Part is for viewing purposes, and out of the box, Excel Services doesn't provide interactive, high-fidelity editing in the browser. And that is exactly where Excel Web App comes into the picture.

Excel Web App ships with Office Web Apps and builds on top of the Excel Services architecture to enable the editing of Excel workbooks directly from your browser. Book I, Chapter 6 takes you on a tour of the Office Web Apps suite and explains the architectural components involved. When you have Office Web Apps installed and configured in your SharePoint farm, a new menu option (Edit in Browser) appears in the Microsoft Excel Web App toolbar. When you edit a workbook using the Edit in Browser menu option, the changes you make are automatically applied to the actual workbook. Figure 4-13 shows the Edit in Browser menu option that appears when viewing a workbook in the browser. Clicking the Edit in Browser menu opens the workbook in edit mode

Figure 4-13:
Excel Web
App adds
the Edit in
Browser
option to the
menu.

If you click the Edit in Browser menu option, Excel Services opens your workbook in the browser and presents you with an array of editing and formatting tools that can help you with the changes that you need to make. The changes that you make are immediately applied to the original file — there is no Save button when editing your workbooks through the browser. Figure 4-14 shows the workbook from in Figure 4-13 now being edited in the browser.

If you have been viewing your workbook in the browser and have been interacting with the workbook by filtering, sorting, and applying parameter values, and then you click the Edit in Browser menu option, all the changes such as sorting and filtering, are immediately applied to the physical workbook file.

Because your edits are applied immediately, there is no Save button when editing in the browser.

To prevent you from inadvertently overwriting your original workbook, you should get into the habit of selecting the File⇨Reload Workbook menu option. You should also consider enabling version control on the library that contains your workbooks, so that you can roll back to the previous version if you accidentally overwrite your workbook file.

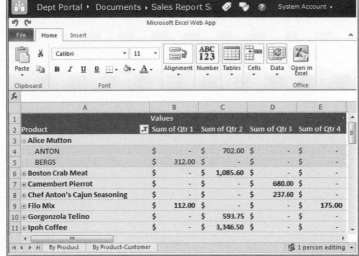

Figure 4-14: With Excel Web App you can edit your workbooks directly in the browser.

Chapter 5: Investigating InfoPath Designer 2010

In This Chapter

☞ **Understanding InfoPath roles**

☞ **Touring the InfoPath client**

☞ **Understanding form templates**

Microsoft Office InfoPath 2010 (InfoPath 2010) is a client application that allows you to develop sophisticated XML-based forms that can be optionally Web browser–enabled so that it can render them in SharePoint Server 2010. The integration between InfoPath and SharePoint has evolved considerably over the years, and with SharePoint Server 2010, using InfoPath Designer 2010 has become the default method for customizing the native SharePoint list forms.

In this chapter, we take you on a tour of InfoPath Designer 2010 (Microsoft's form designer tool that comes with the Office suite), and then explain the designer template offerings that are available in SharePoint out of the box and can help you get your forms up and running as quickly as possible.

Understanding InfoPath Roles

When you use forms, whether paper or electronic, you typically fall into one of two roles:

✦ **Filler:** You fill out a form.

✦ **Designer:** You author the form.

These roles aren't mutually exclusive — a person who designs forms may also need to fill out forms; however, when you're filling out a form, your environment doesn't need to be cluttered with the tools required to design a form. Microsoft addresses this need for de-cluttering with the installation of InfoPath 2010. Microsoft Office InfoPath 2010 ships as a single application, with a single executable (`InfoPath.exe`); however, when you install the application, the InfoPath 2010 installation adds two program options to your Program menu, representing your two possible roles:

✦ **Microsoft InfoPath Filler 2010:** When you're filling out a form. The Microsoft InfoPath Filler program option is a shortcut link to the `InfoPath.exe` application file.

✦ **Microsoft InfoPath Designer 2010:** When you're authoring, or designing, a form.

Accessing InfoPath Filler 2010

If you browse to the Office directory and double-click the InfoPath executable, the application opens in InfoPath Filler mode.

Figure 5-1 shows the InfoPath Filler Backstage view — this view is common across all Office 2010 client applications and is the place where you manage the files associated with the application you're running. From an InfoPath Filler perspective, the Backstage view provides instant access to the forms that are available for you to fill out.

Figure 5-1: You can use InfoPath Filler 2010 to fill out InfoPath Forms.

You can launch InfoPath Filler in a number of ways:

✦ **Launch directly from the Program menu.** Choose Start➪All Programs➪Microsoft Office➪Microsoft InfoPath Filler 2010.

✦ **Double-click a form template (.xsn) file.** If you have access to the form template that you need to fill out, then a simple double-click does the trick. Double-clicking a template file opens a new version of the form in InfoPath Filler.

✦ **Double-click a form (.xml) file.** If you've already saved a form, and want to reopen it to make changes or simply view the content, double-clicking the form file opens the form in InfoPath Filler.

Accessing InfoPath Designer 2010

The Microsoft InfoPath Designer 2010 program option is a shortcut link to the `InfoPath.exe` application file with a design command line switch. For example, running the following command launches InfoPath Designer and presents you with the Backstage view (replace `C` with the appropriate drive letter for your Office installation):

```
"c:\Program Files\Microsoft Office\Office14\InfoPath.exe" /design
```

When you're using InfoPath Designer, the Backstage view provides instant access to the design template options that are available to you, which you can use as a foundation for your InfoPath forms — consider this view the launch pad for building your form templates. Figure 5-2 shows the InfoPath Designer Backstage view, listing the available templates that you can use when designing your forms. If you find a template that matches your needs, simply select the template, click the Design Form button, and start designing your form in the window that appears. We explain each of the template options in the following section.

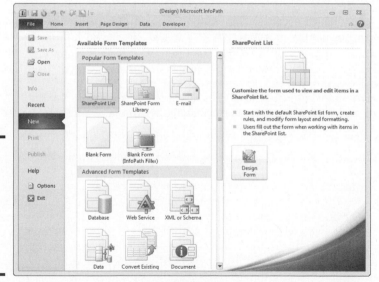

Figure 5-2:
The
Backstage
view
displays
the design
template
options.

You can launch InfoPath Designer 2010 in a number of ways:

✦ **Launch directly from the Program menu.** Choose Start➪All Programs➪ Microsoft Office➪Microsoft InfoPath Designer 2010.

✦ **Select the Design option from the shortcut menu on a form template (.xsn) file.** If you have access to an existing form template that you want to further customize, you can right-click the `.xsn` file and select Design from the shortcut menu that appears.

✦ **Click the Customize List menu option from SharePoint.** SharePoint Server 2010 provides increased integration capabilities with InfoPath, including allowing you to customize native SharePoint list forms and leverage one-click publishing within InfoPath to make your customizations live.

You can find how to use the Customize List option in Book III, Chapter 8.

Touring InfoPath Designer 2010

Microsoft Office InfoPath Designer 2010 is the application to use when you design form templates that can be deployed to SharePoint. InfoPath 2010 provides a rich user interface that's intuitive to most people already familiar with Microsoft Office applications, such as Word and Excel, and Microsoft development tools, such as Microsoft Visual Studio.

InfoPath Designer Backstage view

Like with most Office 2010 client applications, the Backstage view in InfoPath Designer is the place where you manage your form templates. The navigation component of the Backstage view has quick commands and ribbon tabs. The quick commands include those commands that you use frequently, such as Save and Close. The ribbon tabs group together tasks that you can perform on your form template as a whole. For example, the Publish tab reveals the publishing options that are available to you when you're ready to publish your form template.

At a quick glance, the Backstage view ribbon tabs include

✦ **Info:** Find information about your form at a glance, as well as quick links to the more commonly used commands, such as Publish. A very useful option on the information page is the Form Options command that provides you with quick access to the advanced properties of your form template. From the Form Options dialog box, you can check to make sure that your form template is browser-compatible and manage your property mappings with SharePoint columns.

✦ **Recent:** Get quick access to recently used form templates.

✦ **New:** Create a new form template. The New page that appears presents you with a variety of form template designs on which you can base your new template form. Figure 5-2 shows the Backstage view with the New tab selected. The section "Considering the Designer templates," later in this chapter, explains what each template represents.

✦ **Print:** Access the print activities associated with your form template, including previewing how your form will print.

✦ **Publish:** Manage all the publishing activities associated with your form template. After you initially publish your form template, the Quick Publish option becomes active, which means that you don't have to go through the entire Publishing Wizard again if your publishing needs remain the same.

✦ **Help:** Get access to Help resources, discover version information about InfoPath, and check Microsoft Office for available updates.

At the bottom of the navigation pane are two additional commands:

• *Options:* Also accessible from the Help page. This command gives you access to the general options associated with the form template, such as whether you want background colors and pictures to appear when printing your form.

When you create browser-compatible forms, you may need to override the user's Internet options to ensure your form works as expected. For example, if your form accesses data from a Web site that's outside its own domain, then you can set the Internet security options and add the site to your Trusted Sites zone. So, when a user accesses your form, the form temporarily overrides the Internet security settings, and the user doesn't receive a security message. Or if you want to make sure that Auto Complete is turned off for your form template, regardless of the setting the user has in his or her browser, you can use the Options button to override the Auto Complete setting.

• *Exit:* Close the InfoPath application. If you're in the middle of designing your form template, InfoPath prompts you to save your changes.

When you create or open a form template in the Backstage view, you're brought *into* the designer application. Figure 5-3 shows you a sample form template opened in InfoPath Designer. The designer has a set of menu options, task panes, and a Design page. You can create your form layout by using tables and formatting tools, and you drag and drop controls and fields directly onto your Design page. The following sections take you on a tour of the design tools and task panes that make designing form templates in InfoPath Designer very easy.

**Book IV
Chapter 5**

Investigating
InfoPath Designer
2010

Figure 5-3:
Easily
accessible
tools help
you design
your form
templates.

InfoPath ribbon tabs

InfoPath 2010 has been revamped to take full advantage of the ribbon functionality and navigational components of the Microsoft Office 2010 product suite. The InfoPath Designer ribbon includes several tabs that contain specific task groupings that provide you with the tools you need to design your form templates.

The Quick Access Toolbar, which appears at the very top of the InfoPath Designer window, is a customizable toolbar that contains frequently used commands. By default, the Quick Access Toolbar displays the following commands:

✦ **Save (Ctrl+S):** Save the changes you make to the form template that you're currently designing.

✦ **Quick Publish:** If you've published your form template at least once, you can use this command to quickly publish by using the same publishing settings. This command is enabled after you publish the form template once.

✦ **Undo (Ctrl+Z):** Undo the changes you made in your form template, the same way you undo your changes in other Office applications, such as Microsoft Word.

✦ **Redo (Ctrl+Y):** Redo the changes you made in your form template, the same way you redo your changes in other Office applications.

✦ **Preview (F5):** See how your form looks and behaves before you deploy it.

✦ **Design a Form Template:** Takes you to the New tab on the Backstage view, where you can select a template design on which you want to base your form template.

Navigating the Home tab

The Home tab provides access to tools that can help you perform tasks such as formatting the text that appears on your form and adding controls to your form template. The menu options on the Home tab are arranged into the following groupings:

+ **Clipboard:** Clipboard commands, such as Copy and Paste.

+ **Format Text:** Text formatting commands, such as alignment, bolding, and font-size commands.

+ **Font Styles:** Font-style selection commands.

+ **Controls:** Controls that you can add to your form template. The controls available depend on the type of form template you're designing. For example, browser-compatible form templates contain a subset of the controls available for InfoPath Filler form templates.

+ **Rules:** The Rules task pane, which you can use to add and manage rules (including business rules and logic) associated with the controls or fields on your form. For example, you can set up rules to perform field validation or calculations when the value of another field changes.

+ **Editing:** Editing commands, such as spell check and Find functions.

+ **Form:** An alternative way to access the Preview command, which allows you to see how your form looks and behaves before you actually deploy it.

Navigating the Insert tab

The Insert tab provides access to tools that can help you perform common insertion tasks, such as inserting tables and pictures.

The menu options on the Insert tab are arranged into the following groupings:

+ **Tables:** Quickly add a wide range of table formats to your page. If you don't find a table that matches the format you need, then you can create a custom table and specify the columns, rows, and layouts, as desired.

+ **Illustrations:** Insert pictures and clip art onto your page.

+ **Links:** Insert hyperlinks onto your page.

+ **Page Format:** Insert a page break or a horizontal line onto your page.

+ **Symbols:** Insert characters that aren't supported on your keyboard, such as copyright and trademark symbols.

Navigating the Page Design tab

The Page Design tab provides access to tools that help you perform page design tasks, such as applying themes and adding headers and footers to a page. The menu options on the Page Design tab are arranged into the following groupings:

✦ **Views:** Create and manage views for your form template. A form template has one or more views. You use views to arrange the contents of your form so that different views are presented at different times during the form-filling process, or to different users. You can also use the view commands to configure the print view of your form if you want it to have a different layout than the form-filling view.

✦ **Page Layouts:** Insert table templates or custom templates into the current view of the form template. Table templates help you organize the content of your form and enable form-template theming.

✦ **Themes:** A large selection of themes that you can apply to the tables in your form template.

✦ **Headers:** Edit the header or footer of your form template. The information in the header or footer appears at the top or bottom, respectively, of each printed page of your form.

Navigating the Data tab

The Data tab provides access to tools that can help you perform tasks related to the data sources associated with your form template. The menu options on the Data tab are arranged into the following groupings:

✦ **Form Data:** Manage the form data associated with your form template, including fields, resource files, and default field values. The Show Fields command allows you to display the Fields task pane, which you can use to view and manage the data fields for your entire form template.

✦ **Get External Data:** Create and manage the data connections associated with your form. For example, the From SharePoint Server command launches the Data Connection Wizard, which steps you through the process of creating a connection with your SharePoint Server. The Data Connections command launches the Data Connections dialog box, which you can use to view and manage all the data connection for your form template.

✦ **Submit Form:** Submit data from your form to an external data source, such as a SharePoint list. The Submit Options command allows you to manage the submit sessions for the form or configure advanced submit capabilities, such as what to do after you submit the form.

✦ **Rules:** Configure and manage the business rules associated with your form template. The Rule Inspector allows you to view the details of all rules in your form template.

✦ **Roles:** If you're designing InfoPath Filler form templates, you can define unique form behavior for different users or groups. This command isn't accessible for browser-compatible form templates.

Navigating the Developer tab

The Developer tab provides access to tools to help you perform development tasks, such as writing code that runs when your form is loaded or when you switch to a different view. The menu options on the Developer tab are arranged into the following groupings:

✦ **Code:** Language Settings and Code Editor commands. The Language Setting command launches the Form Options dialog box, with the Programming category selected. In this dialog box, set the preferred programming language that you want to use for your form template, such as C# or Visual Basic. The Code Editor command launches Visual Studio Tools for Applications, which you can use to write or edit code for your form template.

The first time you launch InfoPath Visual Studio Tools for Applications, it creates a project folder to store your code.

✦ **Events:** Write code for specific events, such as when your form loads or when a user switches to another form view. Sign events and context-changed events aren't supported with browser-compatible form template.

✦ **Control Events:** Write code for events specific to the controls on your form template. You can write code for three types of control events:

- *Changing Event:* Code that runs when the contents of the selected field are edited by a user and before the changes are committed to the connected data source.

  Changing Events aren't supported for browser-compatible form templates.

- *Validating Event:* Code that runs when the data in the selected field is validated and before the changes are committed to the connected data source.

- *Changed Events:* Code that runs after the contents of the selected field are edited by a user and after the changes are committed to the connected data source.

✦ **Add-Ins:** Manage the available COM Add-Ins for your form template. The COM Add-Ins dialog box allows you to view, add, and remove COM Add-Ins.

**Book IV
Chapter 5**

Investigating
InfoPath Designer
2010

Navigating the Layout tab

The Layout tab provides access to table tools that help you manage the layout and appearance of the tables on your form template. The menu options on the Layout tab are arranged into the following groupings:

+ **Table:** Access table commands, such as Select and Table Properties. The Change To command allows you to change a table to a repeating table. The Repeating Table option appears when you select a table.

+ **Rows & Columns:** Manipulate the rows and columns in the tables on your form template by using table commands such as Insert and Delete.

+ **Merge:** Merge and split your table cells.

+ **Cell:** Change the height and width of your table cells.

+ **Alignment:** Align and pad the contents of your table cells.

+ **Color:** Format the borders and shading of your selected text, objects, or layout elements.

+ **Draw:** Draw and erase borders on your tables.

Accessing the Designer task panes

InfoPath Designer provides several task panes that can help improve your productivity when you design form templates. The task panes give you quick and easy access to commands usually associated with repetitive tasks, such as adding controls to your form. For example, if you have a form that requires numerous controls of several types, then having the Controls task pane open reduces the number of mouse clicks you need to make to design your form (and positively contributes to your productivity and patience).

Task panes typically appear to the right of your form template page; however, you can drag and drop them in another location in your designer window, if you prefer.

Fields task pane

Form templates contain one or more connections to data sources. The default data source is the main data source, which stores the data entered onto the form by your users. The main data source is made up of fields and groups. Groups contain fields — you can think of them as folders for your fields — and help you organize related fields for easier manageability. For example, if you have a set of fields at the top of your form that store contact information — such as name, address, and telephone number — you can place those fields into a group named ContactInfo.

The Fields task pane appears by default when you open your form template in InfoPath Designer. This task pane displays the list of groups and fields associated with your form, including any fields from secondary data sources.

If you don't see the Fields task pane, click Show Fields in the Data tab.

You can use the Fields task pane to perform the following tasks:

✦ **Add fields and groups to your form template's main data source.** You can't add fields or groups to a secondary data source. Figure 5-4 shows the Fields task pane displaying the fields and groups for the form template's main data source. You can tell that the fields that appear are associated with the main data source because Main is the current selection in the Data Source drop-down list on the Fields task pane.

The Data Source drop-down list appears only if your form template has a secondary data source defined; otherwise, the main data source's content is automatically displayed in the Fields task pane.

You can find out how to add fields and groups to your form template in Book III, Chapter 8.

Figure 5-4:
Use the Fields task pane to drag and drop fields onto your form template.

✦ **View and modify field and group properties.** After you create a field or group, you can use the Fields task pane to view or modify the associated properties at any time during the design process.

To view and modify the properties of a field or group, simply right-click the field or group, and select Properties from the pop-up menu that appears.

✦ **Drag and drop fields onto your form template.** You can drag and drop fields — including those from your secondary data sources — from your Fields task pane directly onto your form template. InfoPath selects the appropriate control based on the field's data type. For example, if you add a Birthday field that uses the Date data type, and then drag and drop the field from the Fields task pane onto your form template, InfoPath binds the field to a Date Picker control.

✦ **Manage data connections and secondary data sources.** In the Fields task pane, you can click Manage Data Connections to access the Data Connections dialog box. After you define a connection to a secondary data source, you can view the associated fields directly from the Fields task pane. To view the fields of a secondary data source, simply select your secondary data source from the Data Source drop-down list.

Figure 5-5 shows the Data Source drop-down list for a form template that has three secondary data sources defined: Colors, Drink, and Food.

You can't add fields or groups to a secondary data source.

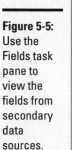

If you see a padlock on the icon of a field or a group in the task pane, it means that you can't modify the field or group.

Figure 5-5: Use the Fields task pane to view the fields from secondary data sources.

Rules task pane

Rules allow you to apply business logic and validation to your form templates. For example, you can use rules to automatically populate fields on your form. Selecting the Manage Rules ribbon command in the Rules section on the Home tab launches the Rules task pane.

The Rules task pane provides you with an easy way to add, remove, and keep track of the rules for your form template. The Copy and Paste commands allow you to copy your rules from one field and paste them to another — which is very helpful when you need to apply the same rules to multiple fields on your form template.

You can create three types of rules by using the Rules Wizard:

✦ **Validation:** Check that the data entered meets specific criteria. For example, you can check to make sure a date field is within a specific range. When a user enters data incorrectly, you can display a message about the error that provides guidance about how to enter a correct value. Data validation rules are executed when the user enters data — the user doesn't have to wait until he or she submits the form to find out whether the data was entered correctly.

✦ **Formatting:** Apply specific formatting when a certain condition is met. For example, you may have a hidden field or section of your form that becomes visible when another field contains a specific value.

✦ **Action:** Perform a specific action when your field meets specific criteria. For example, you can add a rule that specifies when a user enters data into a field, that action triggers a calculation in another field.

Figure 5-6 shows an example of the Rules task pane with two rules defined:

✦ **Action rule:** Calculates age based on the data that the user enters in the birthday field, and then performs an action to update the age field with the calculated value. You can see the details of the action rule in Figure 5-6.

✦ **Form validation rule:** Checks the Age field to see whether the person entering the form is over 18.

TIP

You can find out how to add rules to the fields in your form template in Book III, Chapter 8.

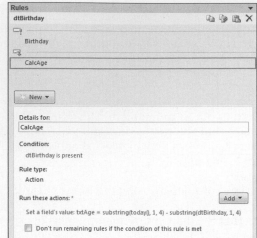

Figure 5-6:
You can use action rules to set values in another field.

Paragraph task pane

The Paragraph task pane provides you with quick and easy access to tools that help you format the text on your form.

The formatting options on the task pane include these settings:

✦ Alignment

✦ Background color

✦ Left- and right-indentation

✦ Before, after, and line spacing

You can launch the Paragraph task pane by clicking the small arrow to the right of the Format Text grouping label.

Controls task pane

When you first create your form template, a list appears of available form template designs that you can use as the basis for your form template. The design template that you select determines the type of form template you're creating. For example, the SharePoint Form Library Designer template is a browser-compatible form template.

The type of form template determines what controls are available for your form template. For example, if you select the SharePoint Form

Library Designer template, the form template that you create is automatically browser-enabled and supports only those controls that SharePoint Server 2010 InfoPath Forms Services supports. The controls that appear for browser-compatible form templates are a subset of those available for InfoPath Filler form templates.

When you click the Controls ribbon command (in the Controls section of the Home tab), a list of available controls that are compatible with your form template type appear.

The following input controls are available out of the box for browser-compatible form templates:

+ **Text Box:** Enter plain text.

+ **Rich Text Box:** Enter formatted text, hyperlinks, tables, and pictures.

+ **Drop-Down List:** Select from a list of choices in a drop-down list. The drop-down list control isn't editable.

+ **Combo Box:** Similar in function to the Drop-Down List control, except that users can either type a value directly into the control or select a value from the list of choices.

+ **Check Box:** Select or deselect a check box to show whether you (the user) select an item.

+ **Option Button:** Select from a set of mutually exclusive choices.

+ **Date Picker:** Type or select a date from a calendar display.

+ **Date and Time Picker:** Type a date and time, or select a date from a calendar display.

+ **Multiple-Selection:** Select multiple options from a scrollable list.

+ **List Box:** Make a selection from a scrollable list of options.

+ **Bulleted List:** Enter text in a bulleted list.

+ **Numbered List:** Enter text in a numbered list.

+ **Plain List:** Enter text in a plain list.

+ **Person/Group Picker**: Type or select a person from a SharePoint User list.

+ **External Item Picker**: Type or select items from external systems by using Business Connectivity Services (BCS).

**Book IV
Chapter 5**

Investigating
InfoPath Designer
2010

The following object controls are available out of the box for browser-compatible form templates:

✦ **Button:** Trigger an action, such as submitting a form or querying a database, or trigger rules and custom code in your form template.

✦ **Picture Button:** Similar in function to the Button control, except the Picture Button control allows you to use a picture, rather than the usual button icon.

✦ **Calculated Value:** Insert a control that displays read-only data, such as text, the value of a field, or a calculation that you define.

✦ **File Attachment:** Attach a file to the form.

✦ **Picture:** Insert a picture in the form.

✦ **Hyperlink:** Insert a hyperlink in a form by entering a URL and display text.

The following container controls are available out of the box for browser-compatible form templates:

✦ **Section:** A control that contains other controls and is bound to a group.

✦ **Optional Section:** A control that contains other controls but doesn't usually appear by default. Users can insert and remove optional sections when filling out the form.

✦ **Repeating Section:** A control that contains other controls and repeats, as needed. Users can insert additional sections when filling out the form.

✦ **Repeating Table:** Display repeating information in a table. When filling out a form, users can add or delete rows in the repeating table. For example, a form that asks you to list your previous employer information may include a repeatable form because the number of previous employers varies from person to person.

✦ **Choice Group:** Works hand in hand with the Choice Section control. When you add a Choice Group control to your form template, InfoPath automatically adds two Choice Section controls inside the Choice Group. The Choice Section control allows the user to choose a section to include in the form. Each section can contain one or more controls. When filling out the form, users can replace the default section with a different section.

✦ **Choice Section:** A section in a Choice group that can contain one or more controls. When filling out the form, users can replace the default section with a different section.

Design Checker task pane

When you design browser-compatible form templates, you may run into compatibility issues from time to time. For example, some controls aren't supported in the browser — such as the Ink Picture control — so they can lead to problems or unexpected behavior during the publishing process.

InfoPath tries its best to help you avoid compatibility issues by filtering the available controls and commands based on the form type you select. However, you can change your form type at any point during the design process, so there's nothing to stop you from having your form type set to an InfoPath Filler Form initially, which allows you to add controls such as the Ink Picture control to your form, and then switching the form type to a Web Browser Form with the Ink Picture control still present on your form, even though it's not supported. If you forgot that the controls you added to your form weren't browser-compatible, you probably expect your form to still work in the browser.

To help you figure out potential problems and compatibility issues with your form *before* you publish it, InfoPath provides a Design Checker. The Design Checker highlights any areas of concern and provides guidance about how to resolve the problems. For example, Figure 5-7 shows the Design Checker command on the InfoPath Backstage view. In this example, the Design Checker notifies the form author that errors have been found for this form type.

Figure 5-7: InfoPath highlights the Design Checker if it detects potential problems.

Book IV Chapter 5

Investigating InfoPath Designer 2010

Clicking the Design Checker command opens the Design Checker task pane. Figure 5-8 shows this task pane, which lists one error and one warning.

Figure 5-8: The Design Checker lists errors and warnings about potential issues.

At the top of the task pane, InfoPath displays the current form type for the form template — which, in Figure 5-8, is set to Web Browser Form; the error message indicates that the Ink Picture control isn't supported with the current form type. If you select the Verify on Server check box, you can check your form template against a server that's running InfoPath Forms Services so that you can see whether your form has any additional problems. If you select this setting, provide InfoPath with the URL to the server that's running InfoPath Forms Services by entering the URL in the Compatibility settings for the form template. (Clicking the Change Settings link at the bottom of the Design Checker opens the Compatibility category in the Form Options dialog box.) You can find out how to set the compatibility settings for your form in the "Browser-compatible form templates" section, later in this chapter.

If you're designing browser-compatible forms, select the Verify on Server check box on the Design Checker task pane so that you can see errors and warnings generated by InfoPath Forms Services, in addition to the errors and warnings generated by the InfoPath client.

If you click an item in the Design Checker list, InfoPath displays a dialog box that contains more information about the specific error or warning, along with information or guidance about how to resolve the issue. For example, Figure 5-9 shows the additional information that InfoPath provides for the warning that appeared in Figure 5-8. In this particular example, the form template has three drop-down list boxes that pull their selection choices from secondary data sources. The warning informs the form author that to provide users with a good offline experience, the data associated with the drop-down list boxes should be stored with the form template; otherwise, Offline mode should be disabled. Based on the information provided by InfoPath, the form author can now update the settings in his or her form template to address these potential problems before a user has even interacted with the form.

Figure 5-9:
InfoPath describes the issue and offers guidance about potential resolutions.

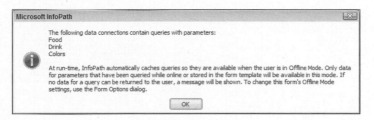

Follow these steps to access the Design Checker:

1. **Open your form template in InfoPath Designer.**

2. **Click the File tab to display the Backstage view.**

3. **In the Info tab, click Design Checker.**

The Design Checker task pane appears.

Exploring Form Templates

InfoPath includes numerous form templates that you can use to create forms. The rest of this chapter shows you what's inside a form template when you crack it open.

Understanding what makes up a form template can help you troubleshoot problems when forms don't behave the way you expect them to.

Understanding form templates

An InfoPath form template is a single file that contains several supporting files that define the presentation and behavior of the form template. The file is basically a cabinet (CAB) file with an .xsn file extension; in fact, if you rename an `InfoPath.xsn` file with a `.cab` extension, you can examine the files and components that comprise the template. Figure 5-10 shows you the contents of a form template (`Favorites.xsn`) that has been renamed to a CAB file (`Favorites.cab`).

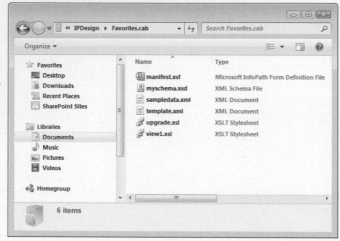

Figure 5-10: You can open your form template as a `.cab` file to see what's inside.

In this particular example, the form template includes the following files:

✦ **Manifest.xsf:** The InfoPath form definition file, which is automatically created by InfoPath and contains all the information about the form template, such as the location of all the files and resources associated with the template.

✦ **Myschema.xsd:** The form schema file, which contains schema-related information, such as the form field elements and their associated data types.

✦ **Sampledata.xml:** Defines the default values that you want the controls on your form to display when a user first loads your form.

✦ **Template.xml:** A blank form that InfoPath uses when creating an instance of your form template.

✦ **Upgrade.xsl:** An XSL Transformation (XSLT) file that handles the presentation between old and new versions of your form template. For example, if you create a form template and your users are happily creating forms (`.xml` files) based on that template, but you then add some additional controls to your form template and republish, InfoPath needs to be able to transform the older forms into the new template.

The first time you save your form template, the template doesn't contain, or need, an `upgrade.xsl` file.

✦ **View1.xsl:** A form template contains at least one visual representation of the form data, known as a *view*. When you design your forms, you may need to provide different views of your form to different users. For example, you may have views that represent different languages or that provide some users with a subset of data and others with a more elaborate view of the data. Views are basically XSL files that transform the form and its associated data into an HTML representation so that your users can fill it out.

A form template is associated with a main data source, such as a SharePoint list, that stores the data entered onto the form by the user. Additional data sources can be associated with the form to help populate different components, such as a drop-down list box. You configure these secondary data sources in the Data Connections dialog box. Each data source that you connect to your form has an associated set of XML schema (.xsd) files that define the elements and attributes of the data connection.

You can find out how to create data connections in Book III, Chapter 8. Form template files may contain additional resource files, such as images and picture files, that you can associate with your form template.

Cracking open the form template

When you develop InfoPath form templates, you'll likely introduce an error at some point that prevents you from even opening your form template in the InfoPath Designer, let alone using it. If this happens to you, don't despair because, in most cases, you can resolve the problem by cracking open the form template and removing the offender from one of the template files we discuss in the preceding section. The error messages that InfoPath and InfoPath Forms Services display are, in general, very helpful and provide a lot of information that takes you about half way to your resolution. For example, if you have fields, such as signature fields, that you want to remove from your form template but the interface shows that the fields are locked, you can remove the fields by editing the form schema file (myschema.xsd) directly.

Extracting the CAB files

Follow these steps to extract the files from a form template, make modifications, and save the modifications back to the form template:

1. **Using Windows Explorer, navigate to the form template that you want to edit.**

2. **Make a copy of your current form template for backup purposes.**

Before modifying form template files, always have a copy of the file *before* you make any changes.

**Book IV
Chapter 5**

Investigating
InfoPath Designer
2010

3. **Rename your form template file so that it has a `.cab` extension, rather than an `.xsn` extension.**

   For example, `Favorites.xsn` becomes `Favorites.cab`.

4. **Double-click the `.cab` file to open it and expose its contents.**

   A list of files, similar to the list shown in Figure 5-10, appears.

5. **Select all the files, right-click, and then select Extract from the pop-up menu that appears.**

6. **Select a folder or create a new folder to which you want to extract the form template files.**

7. **Click Extract.**

   The files are extracted to the folder you chose in Step 6. After the files are extracted, you can view and customize them by using your favorite editor, such as `Notepad.exe`.

Saving changes to the CAB files

Follow these steps to save the modifications you made to an extracted CAB files back to the form template:

1. **Using Windows Explorer navigate to the folder that contains your form template's CAB files.**

2. **Right-click the form definition file (`manifest.xsf`) and select Design from the pop-up menu that appears.**

   The form template appears with your new modifications applied. Save the form template like you normally do. Your form template has now been updated successfully — you no longer need the CAB files.

3. **Delete the CAB files.**

   To clean up your customizations, you can now delete the CAB files that you had previously extracted.

Considering the Designer templates

When you launch InfoPath Form Designer to create a new form template, Designer opens in the Backstage view. The out-of-the-box Designer templates are a great starting point because they provide you with a basic form layout and wizards that guide you through the design steps, such as connecting your form to a specific Web service.

The Designer templates available out of the box include

✦ **SharePoint List:** A new form template option, introduced with InfoPath 2010 and SharePoint Server 2010, that allows you to customize the form in which a user views and edits items in a SharePoint list. The template steps you through a Data Connection Wizard that helps you build an InfoPath form from a SharePoint list.

You can't use this template to connect to an external list; in order to connect to an external list, you must create your InfoPath form by using SharePoint Designer 2010.

✦ **SharePoint Form Library:** Design a form that collects data and saves it to a SharePoint form library. This template is browser-compatible by default, which allows the users of your form to fill it out by using either the browser or InfoPath Filler. The template provides a built-in layout to which you can add controls, assign rules, and apply formatting.

✦ **E-Mail:** Design a form that can be distributed and submitted through e-mail.

✦ **Blank Form:** Design a form template from scratch. You can choose your own layout, add controls, create rules, and apply formatting.

This template is browser-compatible by default, which allows the users of your form to fill it out by using either the browser or InfoPath Filler.

✦ **Blank Form (InfoPath Filler):** Design a form template from scratch. You can choose your own layout, add controls, create rules, and apply formatting. This template isn't browser compatible, which means that users must use InfoPath Filler to fill out your form; they can't fill the form out by using the browser.

✦ **Database:** Design a form to collect data that's stored in an Access or Microsoft SQL Server database. InfoPath automatically creates a form based on a database table and provides a built-in layout to which you can add controls, assign rules, and apply formatting. The Data Connection Wizard helps you set up the connection and map to the data source of your choice. This template isn't browser compatible, which means that users must use InfoPath Filler to fill out your form; they can't fill the form out by using the browser.

✦ **Web Service:** Design a form to query from and submit to a Web service. InfoPath automatically creates a form based on a Web service and provides a built-in layout to which you can add controls, assign rules, and apply formatting. The Data Connection Wizard helps you define how the Web service works and whether its primary action is to submit or receive data. This template isn't browser compatible, which means that users must use InfoPath Filler to fill out your form; they can't fill the form out by using the browser.

✦ **XML or Schema:** Design a form based on an XML or schema file. InfoPath automatically creates a form that contains the fields from the XML or schema file. You can then modify the layout of the form, add controls, create rules, and apply formatting. The Data Connection Wizard helps you build the form template. This template isn't browser compatible,

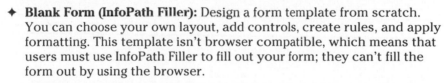

Book IV
Chapter 5

Investigating
InfoPath Designer
2010

which means that users must use InfoPath Filler to fill out your form; they can't fill the form out by using the browser.

✦ **Data Connection File:** Design a form that queries a SharePoint data source defined in a data connection file. InfoPath automatically creates a form based on a SharePoint data source. You can then modify the layout of the form, add controls, create rules, and apply formatting. The Data Connection Wizard helps you map to the data connection stored in your SharePoint data connection library. You can find out more about data connections in Book III, Chapter 6 and how to use the Data Connection Wizard to create a connection to your data sources in Book III, Chapter 8.

✦ **Convert Existing Form:** Automatically convert an existing form that was created in another application, such as Microsoft Word or Microsoft Excel, into an InfoPath form template. The InfoPath Import Wizard steps you through the conversions process. In addition to importing Word and Excel forms, you can also search for third-party form-template import converters on Office Marketplace.

After you import the converted form into InfoPath, you can modify the layout of the form, add controls, create rules, and apply formatting.

✦ **Document Information Panel:** Microsoft provides a panel across the top of Office applications, such as Word, that you can use to edit the properties of documents stored in a SharePoint library. You can create a custom document information panel to replace the default document control panel in your documents.

✦ **Blank 2007 Form:** Design an InfoPath 2007–compatible form template from scratch. You can choose your own layout, add controls, create rules, and apply formatting. This template is browser compatible by default, which allows the users of your form to fill it out by using either the browser or InfoPath Filler.

✦ **Blank 2007 Form (InfoPath Filler):** Design an InfoPath 2007–compatible form template from scratch. You can choose your own layout, add controls, create rules, and apply formatting. This template isn't browser compatible, which means that users must use InfoPath Filler to fill out your form; they can't fill the form out by using the browser.

Understanding template parts

When you want to create a new form template, the Designer templates provide the option to create a template part. A *template part* is a part of a template that you can reuse from one form template to another.

For example, if you're developing an account registration application that consists of several forms, several of the forms probably contain an address section with identical fields in each form. In this situation, it makes sense to create a template part that contains all the appropriate address fields, and then insert that part into each form template that needs the address information.

Browser-compatible form templates

To create a form template, you first select a Designer template that you want to use as the starting point for your form template design. The Designer template provides you with the layout and structure of your form template and presets form options, including the browser-compatibility settings.

For example, if you select the Blank Form Designer template, the form type is set to Web Browser Form, whereas if you select the Blank Form (InfoPath Filler) Designer template, the form type is set to InfoPath Filler Form. You can view or change the compatibility settings for your form at any time during the form creation process.

The compatibility settings provide five form types that you can use for your form template:

✦ **Web Browser Form:** Browser compatible. Users can fill out forms based on your template by using InfoPath Filler or InfoPath Forms Services 2010. Your form template isn't compatible with the InfoPath 2003 or InfoPath 2007 clients, or InfoPath Forms Services 2007.

✦ **InfoPath Filler Form**: Not browser compatible. Users can fill out forms based on your template only by using InfoPath Filler. Your form template isn't compatible with the InfoPath 2003 or InfoPath 2007 clients, InfoPath Forms Services 2007, or InfoPath Forms Services 2010.

✦ **Web Browser Form (InfoPath 2007):** Browser compatible. Users can fill out forms based on your template by using InfoPath Filler, InfoPath 2007, or InfoPath Forms Services (both 2007 and 2010 versions). Your form template isn't compatible with the InfoPath 2003 client.

✦ **InfoPath 2007 Filler Form:** Not browser compatible. Users can fill out forms based on your template by using InfoPath Filler and InfoPath 2007. Your form template isn't compatible with the InfoPath 2003 client, InfoPath Forms Services 2007, or InfoPath Forms Services 2010.

✦ **InfoPath 2003 Filler Form:** Not browser compatible. Users can fill out forms based on your template by using InfoPath Filler, InfoPath 2007, or InfoPath 2003.Your form template isn't compatible with InfoPath Forms Services 2007 or InfoPath Forms Services 2010.

Although users can view or edit form templates that aren't browser compatible by using the browser, you can still publish them to SharePoint and access them in a SharePoint form library by using the InfoPath client.

Follow these steps to view or change the browser-compatibility settings at any time during the form creation process:

1. **Open your form template in InfoPath Designer.**

2. **Click the File tab to open the Backstage view.**

3. **In the Info tab, click Form Options.**

   The Form Options dialog box appears.

4. **Click the Compatibility category.**

5. **In the Form Type, select the form type for your form template.**

   For example, Web Browser Form means that users can view and edit your form by using the browser.

6. **In the Server Validation field, enter the URL of the server that's running InfoPath Forms Services.**

   • If you select either of the Web Browser Form options as your form type, the Server Validation section is enabled; otherwise, it's disabled.

   • If you select Web Browser Form as your form type, enter the URL of a server that's running InfoPath Forms Services 2010.

   • If you select Web Browser Form (InfoPath 2007) as your form type, you can enter the URL of a server that's running InfoPath Forms Services 2010 or InfoPath Forms Services 2007.

7. **If necessary, select the Allow Code to Use Features That Work Only When Filling Forms with InfoPath Filler setting.**

   Enable this setting if you need to run code when your users have your form open in InfoPath Filler, but not in a Web browser.

8. **Click OK.**

InfoPath embraces a design-once philosophy when it comes to designing browser-compatible form templates, meaning that you can use your browser-compatible form template in both InfoPath Filler and the browser, with no need to design a separate form to cater for each scenario. If you decide that users need to fill out your form by using only InfoPath Filler (meaning it's not browser compatible), then InfoPath Designer provides access to an extended set of features and tools that can be used on your form. For example, signature lines and vertical labels aren't supported when you design browser-compatible form templates that will run in InfoPath Forms Services; however, those are available when you design InfoPath Filler form templates.

If you're designing a form template and aren't sure why a command is disabled, or why a control is missing from the selection of available controls, check your compatibility settings — the form type you selected may not support those commands.

If you publish a form template to a SharePoint form library and your form template isn't browser compatible, SharePoint automatically opens forms based on that form template by using the InfoPath client.

Chapter 6: Designing Browser Compatible Forms

In This Chapter

✔ Customizing SharePoint List Forms

✔ Creating and deploying InfoPath Forms

✔ Getting the hang of with the InfoPath Form Web Part

*W*herever you may roam in this book, you'll see that we consider SharePoint 2010 an impressive application with a ton of standard functionality — including integration with such Microsoft Office applications as Word, Excel, PowerPoint, Outlook, and — relevant to this chapter — InfoPath. This capacity for integration is what makes SharePoint a natural choice for many organizations — especially Microsoft shops — on a quest to boost their employees' productivity and streamline their business processes.

Book IV, Chapter 5 provides an introduction to InfoPath Designer 2010 and its capabilities. In this chapter, we turn the focus to designing form templates for InfoPath Forms Services, showing you how to get your own browser-compatible form templates up and running in your SharePoint farm. When designing form templates, there are practices that you can adopt to reduce the overall design effort and to aid in the design of efficient and, more importantly, usable forms. For example, putting multi-column tables in your forms can help you keep scrolling to a minimum. Simple design practices such as these help keep your users happy, increasing the likelihood that (a) they'll fill out the form and (b) you'll get the data you need. Throughout this chapter we offer you tips and guidance on how best to design your forms, and then show you how to publish them to SharePoint.

Designing Web Browser InfoPath Forms

If you're designing browser-compatible form templates with InfoPath Designer 2010, here's a bird's-eye view of the the basic tasks in this process:

1. Add fields and groups

The first step to designing your form template is to figure out what data fields you will need and to group those fields that share a common function. For example, if you want to capture address information from the user you can group all the address fields together. Once you have defined your fields and grouped them accordingly you can move on to designing the layout and structure of your form template. You will find that the fields and groups that you have defined will drive the layout of your form. The Adding fields and groups section of this chapter shows you how to create your data fields and organize them into groups.

2. Design the layout and structure

Once the fields and groups are defined, you can begin designing the layout and the basic structure that your form template will adopt. This stage of the design process involves tasks such as adding tables, columns, and rows to your form. Depending on which design template you chose from the Backstage view, some layouts and tables may have already been added to your form; however, you will more than likely need to customize this further to suit your needs. The "Designing your form layout" section of this chapter describes the various tools that are available to you when designing your forms.

3. Add controls

When you have all the data fields for your form template defined, you can add controls to your form and then bind them to their matching fields. As you choose controls to map to your fields, look for the controls that best represent what you want the user of your form to do. For example, if you want the user to pick a person's name from a list, use the People Picker control; if you want the user to choose one option from a finite set of options, use an Option control. (If you want the user to go get you a sandwich, sorry — there's no control for that.) The "Adding controls to your form" section of this chapter shows you how to put a control into your form template — and then bind the control to the appropriate data field.

4. Create additional form views

You can use views to present a different view of your form to different users, or to split up a large form into a more usable format. You can also create a special type of view for printing purposes — referred to as a print view. For each additional form view that you create, repeat steps 2 and 3. The "Creating form views" section of this chapter shows you how to add a form view and a print view to your form template.

5. Add secondary data sources

If you want to populate some of the controls on your form with data from an external data source, such as a SharePoint list, you will need to configure the appropriate data connections. For example, if you have a drop-down list that contains a set of choices, you can pull those choices from a SharePoint list. The "Adding secondary data sources" section of this chapter shows you how to create data connections to secondary data sources and how to leverage those data sources in your form.

6. **Add business logic**

   The next step in the design process is to create the business logic associated with the form (the processes that keep your organization running) including rules and any required code. For example, you can validate the data entered by your users by applying validation rules to the data fields on the form. The "Adding business rules and logic" section of this chapter shows you how to add logic to your forms.

7. **Configure security and trust settings**

   When deploying your forms it is important to make sure that you define the appropriate security and trust settings. For example, your form template may contain code requiring Full Trust and a code-signing certificate. The "Configuring Security and Trust" section of this chapter shows you how to define the security and trust settings for your form.

8. **Verify your form template**

   You can check for potential problems *prior* to deployment of your form by verifying your form template with the Design Checker. For example, if you're creating a browser-compatible form template, the Design Checker can check your form against InfoPath Form Services and highlight any inconsistencies that it finds. The "Verifying your form template" section shows you how to use the Design Checker to check your form for errors or compatibility issues.

Once the verification process is complete, and you're happy with the content, layout, and behavior of your form, you're ready to move from the design phase to the publishing and deployment phase. The "Deploying Form Templates" section of this chapter walks you through the process of publishing your form templates to InfoPath Forms Services 2010.

Creating a browser compatible form

Before you begin designing your browser-compatible form template with InfoPath Designer, you need to first select a designer template on which you want to base your form template. The out-of-the-box designer templates that ship with InfoPath Designer 2010 are a great starting point providing you with the basic form layout and preconfigured settings for your form template. The "Considering the designer templates" section of Book IV, Chapter 5 describes each of the available designer templates.

All browser-compatible form templates are rendered in the browser by InfoPath Forms Services. You can configure your form template to be browser compatible by setting the compatibility options in InfoPath Designer 2010 or InfoPath 2007. InfoPath Designer 2010 provides several designer templates that are preconfigured to be browser compatible. These designer templates include:

✦ **SharePoint Form Library**

The SharePoint Form Library designer template is browser compatible by default and provides a built-in layout to which you can add controls, create rules, and apply formatting. This option reveals all the controls that are supported by InfoPath Forms Services 2010, including the Combo Box — the Combo Box control isn't supported with InfoPath Forms Services 2007.

✦ **Blank Form**

The Blank Form designer template is similar to the SharePoint Form Library template in that it is browser compatible by default and supports publishing to InfoPath Forms Services 2010. The difference between this template and the SharePoint Form Library template is Blank Form template doesn't provide any layout or formatting — you start with a blank canvas.

✦ **Blank 2007 Form**

The Blank 2007 Form designer template also provides a blank canvas and is browser compatible by default; however, this designer template only supports publishing to InfoPath Forms Services 2007. Using the Blank 2007 Form designer, InfoPath Designer only reveals those controls that are supported by InfoPath Forms Services 2007. For example, the Combo Box control doesn't appear in the list of available controls.

The following steps show you how to create a new browser-compatible form template using InfoPath Designer 2010.

1. **Launch InfoPath Designer 2010 directly from the Program Menu**

Click the Start menu ➪ All Programs ➪ Microsoft ➪ Microsoft InfoPath Designer 2010.

InfoPath Designer 2010 opens in Backstage view.

2. **From the list of available form templates, select a browser-compatible designer template.**

The browser compatible form templates include:

- SharePoint Form Library

- Blank Form

- Blank 2007 Form

A description of the designer template that you select appears in the right pane.

3. **Click Design Form.**

Your new form template opens in InfoPath Designer, ready for you to add your data fields.

Adding fields and groups

The default data source in your form template is referred to as the main data source. The main data source is made up of fields and groups. Groups contain fields allowing you to organize related fields for ease of use and manageability. This is similar to the file and folder paradigm — files reside in folders, and fields reside in groups. When you create a field, you determine the group in which it will reside. If you change your mind later, you can easily move a field from one group to another.

The following steps add a group to your main data source:

1. **From the Fields task pane, select the Main data source from the drop-down list.**

2. **Select the top-level group (for example, myFields), and then click the down arrow to display the shortcut menu.**

3. **From the shortcut menu, click Add...**

   The Add Field or Group dialog box appears.

4. **In the Name field, enter the Name of your group.**

5. **Change the Type field to Group.**

6. **Click OK.**

You can use the following steps to add a field to your main data source:

1. **From the Fields task pane, select the Main data source from the drop-down list.**

2. **Select the group to which you want to add your field and then click the down arrow to display the shortcut menu.**

3. **From the shortcut menu, click Add...**

   The Add Field or Group dialog box appears.

4. **In the Name field, enter the Name of your field.**

5. **In the Data type field, select the data type for your field.**

   For example, a Birthday field may have the Date data type.

6. **(Optional) In the Default value field, enter the value that you want to appear in this field when a user loads your form for the first time.**

7. **Specify if you want the field to be a repeating field.**

   For example, if you want to collect the user's top five favorite songs, you could define a repeating field named FavoriteSong.

Book IV
Chapter 6

**Designing Browser
Compatible Forms**

TIP

Field and group names can't contain spaces or other special characters. They must begin with an alphabetic character, or underscore, and can only contain alphanumeric characters, underscores, hyphens, and periods.

Designing your form layout

Once you have your data fields and their associated groups defined, you're ready to create the basic layout and structure of your form. InfoPath provides formatting and layout tools out of the box that help you to create the layout of your form. Creating your form layout typically involves the following tasks, with each task represented by a tool in the InfoPath client:

✦ **Adding tables**

You can add and remove tables from your form template in the same way you would add and remove tables from other Microsoft Office applications, such as Microsoft Word.

Use the Insert tab on the Ribbon menu to access the table options, including a slew of preformatted tables and a command for inserting your custom tables. The great thing about using the preformatted tables is that they automatically reflect your theme color scheme.

Limiting the use of nested tables on your form will improve the performance of your forms — nested tables increase the complexity of the HTML that has to be rendered in the browser, and the more complex the form, the longer it takes to load.

✦ **Adding page layouts**

InfoPath Designer 2010 provides a set of form templates that combine preformatted table layouts with headers and columns. The page layouts allow you to quickly design the layout of your form template and its associated views. Page layouts support template theming, automatically updating the tables and headings it contains to reflect the current theme. Page layouts are particularly useful when you're working with a blank canvas, as is the case if you're creating either of the following:

• A new form template based on the Blank Form designer template.

• A new view within your form template.

Use the Page Design tab on the Ribbon menu to access the Page Layouts Templates command.

✦ **Adding themes**

InfoPath Designer provides a large selection of themes that you can apply to your form templates. Themes provide a consistent look and feel across tables and layouts in a form template view, including coordinating colors with matching backgrounds, fonts, and effects. When you apply a theme within InfoPath Designer, the theme is applied to the current form template view, allowing different views of your form template to have different color schemes.

InfoPath provides five out-of-the-box theme categories:

- **SharePoint:** Theming your forms with one of the SharePoint themes ensures that your InfoPath form template shares a consistent look and feel with the rest of the SharePoint browser interface.

- **Professional:** The themes in the Professional category are designed for business use and typically fit with the culture of a professional organization. They provide a classic, traditional corporate look and feel to your forms.

- **Industrial:** The themes in the Industrial category are also designed for business use, providing a very clean-cut look and feel with limited use of colors.

- **Playground:** The themes in the Playground category, as their name suggests, are designed to be playful in nature, providing brighter color schemes and breaking away from the more structured corporate style designs.

- **Modern:** The themes in the Modern category also break away from the confines of the traditional corporate style, adding more excitement to your overall form look and feel.

Theming in InfoPath relies on your use of tables, page layouts, and font styles in your form. For example, if you add one of the out-of-the-box multi-column tables to your form template, the tables will automatically reflect the theme that you select. If you format your text without using a font style, then your text will not reflect your theme selection.

✦ **Formatting text**

You can format the text in your tables and controls in your form template in much the same way you would format content in other Microsoft Office applications, such as Microsoft Word.

Use the Home tab on the Ribbon menu to access the Format Text options, including alignment and indentation settings.

Where possible use the existing font styles, tables, and page layouts so that your form will pick up the current theme selection.

When designing your form layout, keep your design as efficient as possible by grouping related fields together, leveraging multi-column tables and page layouts. Most users are turned off by large scrolling forms, so keep your design compact and look for opportunities to take advantage of form views to break the monotony of large forms. You can find more information on form views in the "Creating Form Views" section of this chapter.

Adding controls to the page

No, you won't be adding steering wheels or joysticks to your forms. Controls are visual representations of your data fields; they respond to user input in a way that captures information from your users. When you place a control on your form, you map it to a specific data field — a process known as data binding. When users enter data into a control, they populate the field to which the control is mapped.

When selecting the controls you want to use on your form, choose the control most specific to the data you're trying to capture from the user. For example, if you want the user to select a date, use the Date Picker control; if you want the user to select from a list of available choices, then use a drop-down list box that shows the available items from which the user can select.

When placing controls on your form, it's helpful to group your related fields together and display them in the same section of your form; that way your users can jump immediately to whatever section interests them. If you want your users to skip certain sections if they provide certain specified data, then you can design your form so your users see only what they need to see while they're filling out the form. For example, if your form asks for a shipping address and a billing address, you can group the billing address information in one section and provide the user with a check-box field that asks whether the billing address is the same as the shipping address. If the user checks that box, then your preparation pays off: Because you've grouped your billing fields in a single section, you can simply hide or disable the billing-address fields after the user checks the box (because the user doesn't need to fill out this data). Result: The form is easier to fill out.

InfoPath Designer doesn't limit the amount of data that a user can place in the Rich Text Box control; consequently, the Rich Text Box control has the potential to generate a large number of HTML elements in your form behind the scenes, which may negatively affect the performance of your browser.

Consider using the Multi-line Text Box control instead of the Rich Text control where possible. If you need to use multiple Rich Text controls on your form, then try to use multiple views instead of placing all the Rich Text controls in a single view. Separating the controls spreads the load across multiple pages, which reduces the amount of HTML render with each view.

Using the Fields task pane

If you're working with the Fields task pane, you have two methods for adding controls to your form:

✦ **Drag and drop data fields from the Fields task pane.**

With the drag and drop technique, InfoPath attempts to figure out the control that best represents the data field, places the control on your form, and binds it to your data field. This is very handy for simple text data fields, such as First Name, because InfoPath will map your data field to a Text Box control. However, there will be times when InfoPath's selection doesn't meet your needs. For example, if you have a Gender data field with a Text data type and you want to represent the Male/Female choices with two option buttons, then dragging and dropping the data field onto the form will not meet your needs.

✦ **Right-click the data field and select the control to insert.**

Right-clicking the data field in the Fields task pane and selecting the correct control to insert directly onto the page is a very efficient technique for adding controls to your form.

This method has a number of advantages:

- InfoPath presents you with a list of available controls that support the selected data field type. For example, if your data field has a Text (string) data type, then you can't map it to a Date and Time Picker control — the Date and Time Picker control requires a Date and Time (dateTime) data type; consequently, the Date and Time Picker control doesn't appear in the list of available controls. This removes a lot of the guess work from you as the designer — you won't run into the issue where you select a control only to get an error message stating that it isn't supported. Removing the guesswork equates to reduced effort from an overall design perspective.

- You get to choose the exact control that you best represents your data field. For example, if you have a Gender data field with a Text data type, you can choose to insert an Option Button control. InfoPath will prompt you for configuration details of the control, and will then bind the control to the Gender data field and place it into the currently selected area of your form.

- InfoPath is able to handle the binding as part of the add process, because it has all the information it needs to perform the binding — it knows the specific data field and the specific control.

The following add a control to your form using the Fields task pane and bind it to a data field. These steps assume that the data binding process is set to happen manually.

1. **Click the location on your form in which you want to place your control.**

2. **From the Fields task pane, right-click the field that you want the control to represent.**

A shortcut menu appears listing the controls that suit the data type of the selected data field. If the Fields task pane isn't visible, you can display it by clicking the Show Fields command from the Form Data group on the Data tab.

3. **Click the control that you want to add to your form.**

The control is added to your form. To further configure the control properties, right-click the control and click <control> properties, where <control> represents the type of control you're configuring.

Using the shortcut menu on the Fields task pane is a convenient and efficient way to add controls to your forms. It fully leverages the effort that you put into configuring your fields and groups.

Using the Controls task pane

When it comes to adding controls on your form using the Controls command on the Ribbon menu or the Controls task pane, you have two options for how you want the data binding to occur:

✦ **Automatically**: When you add a control to your form, InfoPath automatically creates a new data field for you and binds it to the control. The data field has the name: field<n> where n is a unique number for the control — which you will most likely want to rename. Fields created using this method are created under the default top level group for your Main data source — which means that you must move it to the appropriate group within your data source.

Fields created using this method pop into existence under the default top-level group for your Main data source — where they probably won't do you much good, so you'll have to move those fields to the appropriate group(s) in your data source.

✦ **Manually:** When you add a control to your form, InfoPath prompts you for the data field to which you want to bind the control. This allows you to configure and organize all your data fields upfront, preventing you from having to rename and move data fields and groups respectively.

The Automatically create data source setting on the Controls task pane determines whether binding will be automatic (checked) or manual (unchecked). This setting is checked by default. Figure 6-1 shows the Controls task pane with Automatically create data source setting, at the bottom of the task pane, unchecked.

If you're using the Controls command on the Ribbon menu or the Controls task pane to add controls to your form, create your data fields first and then manually bind them to your controls when you place them on your form. To use this method, clear that pesky check box that says *Automatically create data source*.

Follow these steps to use the Controls task pane add a control to your form and bind the control to a data field. These steps assume that you want the data-binding process to happen manually (not automatically). Here goes:

1. **On the Home tab, click the arrow to the right of the Controls group to launch the Controls task pane.**

2. **Uncheck the Automatically create data source setting.**

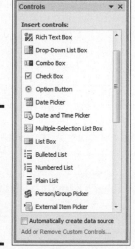

Figure 6-1:
Use the
check box
to turn
off the
automatic
creation of
data fields.

3. **Click the control that best represents the data field to which you want to map.**

   The Binding dialog box for the control appears as shown in Figure 6-2.

4. **From the Data source drop-down list, select Main.**

5. **From the list of fields and groups, select the field to which you want to map the control.**

6. **Click OK.**

   The control is added to your form and is bound to the chosen data field.

If you need to change the data binding for you control, you can do so easily by simply right-clicking the control and selecting the Change Binding command. The Binding dialog box appears as before.

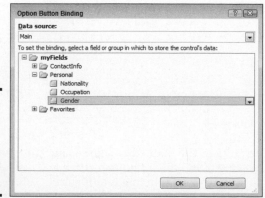

Figure 6-2:
InfoPath
prompts
you for the
data binding
information.

**Book IV
Chapter 6**

**Designing Browser
Compatible Forms**

The controls that appear in the Controls task pane may not support the data field's data type. When you try to bind a control to an incompatible data field, InfoPath will display an error message.

Adding secondary data sources

InfoPath form templates may contain one or more connections to data sources. If you use more than one data source, keep these points in mind:

+ **The main data source is the default data source; it stores the data that the user enters into the form.**

+ **You can connect additional — that is, secondary — data sources — to your form template; these add to your form's function and its business logic.**

For example, you may have a list box on your form that retrieves its contents from a SharePoint list when the form is opened. InfoPath Designer provides a connection wizard that enables you to configure your secondary data sources very quickly. In addition to retrieving data, you can configure your secondary data sources to submit data to a destination data source, such as a SharePoint document library.

You can receive (query) data from and submit data to the following external data sources:

+ Any Microsoft Office Access database

+ Any Microsoft SQL Server database

+ Any Web service

+ Any SharePoint list or library

+ Any XML file

    Although you can query and submit data to a SharePoint library, you can't submit data to a SharePoint list (you can only query the list). The Data Connection Wizard doesn't support submissions to the list, but if you really want to submit data anyway, you could (a) write custom code to do the job or (b) connect to a Web Service and have it submit data to the SharePoint list for you (sneaky but effective).

When you add secondary data sources to your form template, the Fields task pane displays a drop-down list box showing all the configured data sources you can use on your form template. (Data sources to which you can submit data don't appear in this list.)

The drop-down list defaults to the main data source, and the remaining data sources get a (Secondary) suffix, which trumpets their role as secondary data sources (without embarrassing them a bit). Figure 6-3 shows you the

Fields task pane with a secondary data source selected: an external list in SharePoint. This external list uses Business Connectivity Services to pull data from an external SQL database into SharePoint. In effect, these data connections are transparent; you can retrieve data from an external list just as you would from a native SharePoint list.

Figure 6-3:
External lists are treated just like regular SharePoint lists.

Adding a data connection to retrieve data from SharePoint

The following steps show you how to add a secondary data source to receive data from a SharePoint list:

1. **Open your form template in InfoPath Designer.**

2. **On the Data tab, in the External Data group, click From SharePoint List.**

   The Data Connections Wizard appears, prompting for the URL of your SharePoint site.

3. **Enter the URL to the SharePoint site that contains the library or list, and click Next.**

   A list of the available libraries and lists in the specified SharePoint site appears.

4. **Select the list or library from which you wish to retrieve data, and click Next.**

5. **From the list of SharePoint fields, select the fields that you want to access in your SharePoint form template.**

6. **In the Sort by and Sort order fields, select the field that you wish to sort by and the order you want the data sorted, and click Next.**

7. **Determine whether you want to store a copy of the data from the secondary data source in your form template.**

If your form will only be filled out in the browser, then you may leave this option unchecked. Offline query support doesn't apply to forms running in the browser. But if you want to configure the InfoPath Filler client application so its users can fill in the form while offline, select this setting.

8. **Click Next.**

9. **Enter the name of your data connection.**

10. **Determine whether to Automatically retrieve data when the form is opened.**

    Leave this setting checked only if you want to have access to the data in the secondary data source the moment your form opens.

    Your form will open more quickly if you delay data queries until the data is actually needed. You can leverage rules, buttons, or code to retrieve data when a specific action occurs.

11. **Click Finish.**

    The Data Connection Wizard closes and the Data Connections dialog box reappears displaying your new data connection in the list of data connections for the current form template. When you've seen what you need to see to check your results, you can click OK to close the Data Connection dialog box.

Adding a data connection to submit data to SharePoint

The following steps add a secondary data source to submit data to a SharePoint document or form library:

1. **Open your form template in InfoPath Designer.**

2. **On the Data tab, in the Submit Form group, click To SharePoint Library.**

    The Data Connections Wizard appears.

3. **Enter the URL to the document library to which you will submit the form.**

4. **Enter the filename that you wish to give the newly submitted form.**

5. **Determine whether to overwrite the file should it already exist, and click Next.**

6. **Enter the name of your data connection, and determine whether you want it to be the default submit connection.**

7. **Click Finish.**

    The Data Connection Wizard closes, and the Data Connections dialog box reappears displaying your new data connection in the list of data connections for the current form template. You can click OK to close the Data Connection dialog box.

If you select a secondary data source from the drop-down list, the query and data fields associated with the data source appear in the Fields task pane. You can now leverage your secondary data sources in your form controls and logic. For example, you can use the content from a specific field in your secondary data source to populate a drop-down list control on your form.

Mapping a secondary data source to a control

The following steps populate the choices for a drop-down list using a secondary data source:

1. **From the form template right-click the control that you wish to populate, and then click Drop-down List Box properties.**

   The Drop-down List Box Properties dialog appears. Figure 6-4 shows a drop-down list that retrieves its list contents from a SharePoint list data connection.

2. **In the List box choices, select Get choices from an external data source.**

   The Data Source drop-down list box appears.

3. **In the Data Source drop-down list, select the secondary data source that you want to use to populate the list choices.**

4. **Click the button to the right of the Entries field.**

   The Select a Field or Group dialog box appears.

5. **Expand the tree and select the repeating group for your data source.**

6. **Click OK.**

   InfoPath returns you to Drop-down List Box Properties dialog box.

7. **In the Display Name field, select the field from the external data source that you want to present in the list of choices.**

8. **In the Value field, select the field from the external data source that you want to use to populate the main data source field that is bound to the control.**

   In most cases, the Value field and the Display Name field will be the same.

9. **If you only want to display unique names, select the Show only with unique display names check box.**

10. **Click OK to save your changes.**

If you're connecting to a SharePoint list from which you only want to retrieve a subset of the data, consider leveraging SharePoint list views to filter the data for your connection. This will ensure that you only retrieve the data you need from the SharePoint list further optimizing your form.

Creating form views

You can use form views to present different pages in your form to different users, or to split up a large form into a more usable format. You can also create a special type of view for printing purposes — a print view.

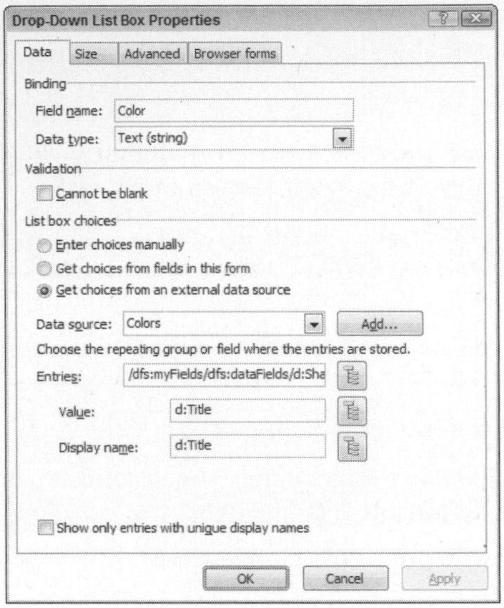

Figure 6-4:
You can use secondary data sources to populate controls on your form.

Creating a new form view

When you create a new form view, you can add fields, controls, and logic to it in the same way you would with the default form view. You will need to provide additional rules and controls to help your users navigate between your views.

You can use the following steps to create a new form view in your form template:

1. **On the Page Design tab, in the Views group, click New View.**

The Add View dialog box appears.

2. **Enter the name of the new form view.**

A blank form view page appears ready for you to design.

Creating a print view

If you want your users to be able to print out paper copies of their online forms, make sure that your form template fits your available paper stock acceptably when it's printed. For example, you have to make sure that the form fits within the page margins. Print view allows you to set up a separate print version of your form without altering the way your form template appears in the browser. (A very cool trick, that one.)

You can use the following steps to create a new Form view in your form template:

1. **Create a new view that you want to be the printed version of your form.**

   This is the view that you will set as the Print View for your other form views. You can use the view properties dialog box to specify the margins, header, and footer settings for the print view.

2. **On the Page Design tab, in the Views group, select the view to which you wish to apply the Print View that you created in step 1.**

3. **On the Page Design tab, in the Views group, click Properties.**

   The View Properties dialog box appears.

4. **From the View Properties dialog box, click the Print Settings tab.**

5. **In the Designate Print View section, select the Print View that you created in step 1 as the view to use when printing the current view.**

6. **Specify the other print settings such as whether to print Portrait or Landscape.**

7. **Click OK.**

The addition of views to your form increases the number of postbacks to the server — each time a user switches to a different view, the form posts data back to the server. However, your users may have a better experience, especially if your form is large and complex. When adding additional views you should weigh the cost associated with the additional load on the server against the improved browser performance for the end user.

Storing connections in a Data Connection Library

Of course, after you've established data connections, you have to put them somewhere — and still be able to get at them. Secondary data sources are configured through the use of data connections. When you first create your connections to your secondary data sources, each connection is stored with your form template. But what if you want to check multiple data connections? Well, you'll have a lot of files to open.

If you'd rather have all your data connections available in one place, you can convert your data connections to files and store them in a Data Connection Library — a special type of SharePoint library reserved for this purpose. InfoPath provides a Data Connection Wizard that helps you convert your secondary data-source connections to data-connection files — known as UDC files — that have the .udcx file extension.

Storing your data connection information in a data connection library has its advantages, including:

✦ **Share connection information**: Storing your connection information in a data connection file allows you to share the same data connection information among many form templates, without requiring each template to store its own copy of the connection information.

✦ **Easier to maintain and update**: Storing your connection information in a data connection file within your data connection library improves the maintenance and upkeep of connection information. Should the data source move, you simply update the data connection file; all form templates that leverage that data connection are automatically updated.

Creating a data connection library

Before you can store your form's data connection information in SharePoint, you must first create a data connection library. The following steps show you how to create a data connection library in your SharePoint site:

1. **Using your browser, navigate to the SharePoint site in which you want to create the data connection library to host you connection files.**

2. **From the Site Actions menu, click More Options.**

3. **From the list of available libraries, click Data Connection Library.**

4. **Enter the name of your Data Connection Library, and click Create.**

    Your data connection library is ready for use.

Converting your Data Connection

Once your data connection library is up and running, you can convert your form's data connections to a connection file and store it in the library. The Data Connection Wizard creates the connection file and stores it for you in the data connection library that you specify.

The following steps convert your data connection to a connection file stored in your data connection library:

1. **Open your form template in InfoPath Designer.**

2. **On the Data tab, in the External Data group, click Data Connections.**

    The Data Connections dialog box appears. You can also display the Data Connections dialog box by clicking the Manage Data Connections link at the bottom of the Fields task pane.

3. **Select the connection that you wish to convert and click Convert to Connection File.**

    The Convert Data Connection dialog box appears.

4. **In the URL field, enter the URL to the data connection library in which you want to create your data connection file.**

If you enter the start of the URL to the SharePoint site and click Browse, InfoPath presents you with a list of the available libraries in the site from which you can select your Data Connection Library.

5. **In the Connection link type, click Relative to site collection.**

   Clicking this option tells InfoPath and InfoPath Forms Services that the connection information for the specific data connection is in a data connection library relative to the site collection in which the form resides.

6. **Click OK.**

Adding business rules and logic

The power of electronic forms becomes immediately apparent when you apply rules and logic to your forms, helping you to capture accurate information. For example, on a paper form, there's nothing to prevent a person from entering their name in a field that requests today's date; with an electronic form, you can apply validation rules that automatically populate fields — such as today's date — and perform field validation that prevents your users from submitting invalid data.

There are three types of rules that you can apply to the fields on your form:

✦ **Validation**: Allow you to validate the data entered in a field to ensure it meets a specific format.

✦ **Formatting**: Allows you to apply specific formatting when a certain condition is met.

✦ **Action**: Allows you to perform a specific action when your form meets a specific condition.

When you create and configure your fields, you can assign them a default value so the field is populated with a value when a user loads your form. Default values may be considered as form logic that you apply to your form; however, they aren't defined using the Rules task pane, so we have left them off the list for now.

There are four user-initiated events in your forms to which rules apply:

✦ **When users change the value on a field on your form.**

   You can apply rules to the controls and fields on your form so that, as users populate the form, they are notified instantly of any corrections they need to make, and allows you to automatically set the values in other fields based on the data the users just entered — which is handy when building cascading drop-down lists.

✦ **When users click a button on your form.**

If you add buttons to your forms, you can configure a rule to handle the actions that occur when users click the button. The Button and Rule combination has many advantages, including:

- Instead of retrieving all the data from your secondary data sources when the form loads, you can use buttons to let your users decide when to retrieve the data. This can boost your form's performance, especially while it's loading (less stuff to put up onscreen) — which in turn can improve the amount of data you get back: If your form takes too long to open, there's an increased risk that your users will abandon it altogether.

- You can use buttons to switch between your form views. Views also aid the performance of your form, allowing you to spread your controls across multiple pages, ultimately reducing the amount of HTML that the browser has to work with at one time. Buttons help your users to easily navigate between your views.

- You can use buttons to calculate and update the values of other fields automatically.

✦ **When users submit your form.**

You can create rules that will run when users submit your form. The Form Submit command, in the Rules group, on the Data tab allows you to define the actions that you want to occur upon form submission. For example, if you wanted to submit a form to a Web service or a SharePoint library, you can create a Submit Data action in the Form Submit rule, which would submit the form to the specified location.

The Form Submit option is enabled if your form has been configured to perform a custom action using rules. You can find out how to create a Form Submit rule in the "Creating Form Submit Rules" section.

✦ **When users load your form.**

You can create rules that trigger when your users open your form. For example, when users open your form you can check to see who they are and filter the presentation of the form accordingly — rules allow you to do all this without code!

You can find out how to create a Form Load rule in the "Creating Form Load Rules" section.

InfoPath provides a couple of techniques for you to create your rules:

✦ **Quick Rules**

InfoPath Designer provides you with out-of-the-box rules, known as Quick Rules, to allow you to set your rules.

You can access Quick Rules by clicking the Add Rules command from the Rules group on the Home tab.

✦ **Rules Task Pane**

The Rules task pane is your go-to place for managing and configuring rules in your form template. If the rule you want to create doesn't match any of the InfoPath Quick Rules, then the Rules task pane is the place you want to be, allowing you to be as creative as you need to be with your rules.

You can access the Rules task pane by clicking the Manage Rules command from the Rules group in the Home tab.

Creating a Validation Rule

Although you can't know for sure whether the data that a user enters on your forms is correct, validation rules can get you as close as possible to that goal. For example, if you need to capture the user's business telephone number you can't guarantee that the phone number actually belongs to the user entering the data. However, you can apply validation rules so that users enter their phone number in an accepted format — such as 999-999-9999 — thus eliminating common typos and formatting errors often experienced when filling out forms.

When adding data validation rules to your form, ensure that you add a screen tip to provide the user with guidance on the value and format that you're expecting them to enter. This prevents the user from getting frustrated, throwing their hands up, and abandoning your form altogether.

The following steps show you how to apply a validation rule to a field on your form using Quick Rules:

1. **Open your form template in InfoPath Designer.**

2. **Click the control on your form to which you want to apply the validation rule.**

3. **On the Home tab, in the Rules group, click Add Rule.**

   A series of conditions appear in a shortcut menu. If you don't see a condition that meets your needs, use the Rules task pane instead (details coming up soon) to create your rule.

4. **Select the condition that you want to use.**

   For example, "Is equal To".

5. **From the list of Actions, click Show Validation Error.**

   The Rule Details dialog box appears if your validation rule requires more information. If it doesn't appear, then your validation rule is complete and appears in the Rules task pane.

6. **Fill in the information to complete your rule.**

   You can use the Insert Formula dialog box to build the condition that you want to be met.

7. **Click OK.**

Okay, here's the manual method. It's a bit more of a pane (the Rules task pane, in fact), but it works well. Follow these steps to use the Rules task pane to apply a validation rule to a field on your form:

1. **Open your form in InfoPath Designer.**
2. **In the form view, click the control to which you want to apply the validation rule.**
3. **On the Home tab, in the Rules group, click Manage Rules.**

   The Rules task pane appears.
4. **From the task pane, click New.**
5. **From the shortcut menu, click Validation.**
6. **Enter a descriptive name for your Rule.**
7. **To apply a condition to the rule, click the None link.**

   If you see a link other than None in the Condition section, then you already have a condition defined. You can click the link to add to, remove, or modify the current condition.
8. **From the Condition dialog box, use the And/Or operators to build your condition, and then click OK.**
9. **Enter a screen tip to provide your users with some guidance on the data you want them to enter.**

   If you click the Show options button, you see that you can enter a dialog-box message in addition to a ScreenTip. (At least the Rules task pane says you can — but it's fibbing. Dialog-box messages aren't supported for browser based forms.)

Creating a formatting rule

Conditional formatting rules are very useful for controlling the information that a user sees on the form, and providing them with a personalized experience when filling out your forms. For example, when a user selects a certain value, you can use conditional formatting to trigger the form to display additional fields that were previously hidden.

The following steps show you how to apply a formatting rule to a field on your form using Quick Rules:

1. **Open your form in InfoPath Designer.**
2. **In the form view, click the control to which you want to apply the formatting rule.**
3. **On the Home tab, in the Rules group, click Add Rule.**

A series of condition options appear in a shortcut menu. If you don't see a condition that meets your needs then use the Rules task pane instead to create your rule.

4. **Select the condition that you want to use.**

   For example, "Is equal To".

5. **From the list of Formatting options, click the format that comes closest to the form you want.**

   If you don't see a format that meets your needs, you can either select the closest and customize it further using the Rules task pane, or create your rule from scratch using the Rules task pane.

6. **Fill in the information to complete your rule.**

   You can use the Insert Formula dialog box to build the condition that you want to be met.

7. **Click OK.**

The following steps show you how to apply a formatting rule to a field on your form using the Rules task pane:

1. **Open your form in InfoPath Designer.**

2. **In the form view, click the control to which you want to apply the formatting rule.**

3. **On the Home tab, in the Rules group, click Manage Rules.**

   The Rules task pane appears.

4. **From the task pane, click New.**

5. **From the shortcut menu, click Formatting.**

6. **Enter a descriptive name for your Rule.**

7. **To apply a condition to the rule, click the None link.**

   If you see a link other than None in the Condition section, then you already have a condition defined. You can click the link to add to, remove, or modify the current condition.

8. **From the Condition dialog box, use the And/Or operators to build your condition, and then click OK.**

9. **In the formatting section, choose the format that you want your rule to apply.**

   The formatting options are similar to those you would find in other Office applications, such as Microsoft Word. In addition to the typical Office formatting commands, you have the ability to hide or disable the control.

   Once you apply the formatting that you want, your rule is ready.

Creating an Action Rule

Action rules allow you to perform a specific action when your user changes the value of your field. For example, if you have a series of drop-down lists, you can create a cascading effect by using action rules to filter the selection choices of other drop-down list boxes when a user selects a value.

The Show Validation Error appears under the list of actions from the Quick Rule menu, and we showed how to use the Show Validation Error option in the "Creating a Validation Rule" section earlier in this chapter. In addition to the Show Validation Error, the Quick Rules menu provides three actions from which you can base your rule:

✦ **Set a Field's Value:** Allows you to populate the value in the current field, or another field in the form.

✦ **Submit Data:** Allows you to submit the form to a data source of your choice.

✦ **Query for Data:** Allows you to retrieve data from a data source of your choice, and populate the controls that are bound to the data connection that you specify in your query.

The following steps apply an action rule to a field on your form using Quick Rules:

1. **Open your form in InfoPath Designer.**

2. **In the form view, click the control to which you want to apply the action rule.**

3. **On the Home tab, in the Rules group, click Add Rule.**

   A series of condition options appear in a shortcut menu. If you don't see a condition that meets your needs, then use the Rules task pane instead to create your rule.

4. **Select the condition that you want to use.**

   For example, "Is equal To".

5. **From the list of Actions, click the action that you want your rule to perform.**

   If you want to send data to a Web Part, you can create your action rule using the Rules task pane.

   The Rule Details dialog box appears.

6. **In the Rule Details dialog box, fill in the information to complete your rule.**

   You can use the Insert Formula dialog box to build the condition that you want to be met.

   If you're defining a Set a Field's Value action, enter the Field that you want to populate and the value that you want to set.

If you're defining a Submit Data action, select the data connection to which you want to submit data.

If you're defining a Query Data action, select the data connection from which you want to receive data.

7. Click OK.

Follow these steps to use the Rules task pane to apply an action rule to a field on your form:

1. Open your Form in InfoPath Designer.

2. In the Form view, click the control to which you want to apply the action rule.

3. On the Home tab, in the Rules group, click Manage Rules.

The Rules task pane appears.

4. From the task pane, click New.

5. From the shortcut menu, click Action.

6. Enter a descriptive name for your Rule.

7. To apply a condition to the rule, click the None link.

If you see a link other than None in the Condition section, then you already have a condition defined. You can click the link to add to, remove, or modify the current condition.

8. From the Condition dialog box, use the And/Or operators to build your condition, and then click OK.

9. Click the Add button and from the menu, click the action that you want your rule to perform.

The Rule Details dialog box appears.

10. In the Rule Details dialog box, fill in the information to complete your rule.

You can use the Insert Formula dialog box to build the condition that you want to be met.

If you're defining a Set a Field's Value action, enter the Field that you want to populate and the value that you want to set.

If you're defining a Submit Data action, select the data connection to which you want to submit data.

If you're defining a Query Data action, select the data connection from which you want to receive data.

If you're defining a Send data to Web Part action, select the fields that you want to make available as Web Part connection parameters.

11. Click OK.

If you have several actions that share the same condition, consider grouping them together in a single rule. Actions that have unique conditions, or don't have conditions at all, should be kept separate in their own rule

You can build forms that have tabs using Rules and Views. You can create a button that has a rule applied that says, when the user clicks this button then switch the view.

Creating Form Submit Rules

If you want to leverage the form submission functionality of InfoPath to invoke specific actions, you can use the Form Submit command. For example, if you want to submit your form to more than one location you can achieve this through the Form Submit command.

The Form Submit command is located in the Rule group on the Data tab. If the command is disabled, you can enable if from the Submit Options dialog box.

You can use the following steps to enable the Form Submit rules command:

1. **On the Data tab, in the Submit Form group, click Submit Options.**

   The Submit Options dialog box appears.

2. **Select the Allow users to submit this Form check box.**

3. **Set the submit option to Perform custom action using Rules.**

4. **If you want the Submit button to appear in both the Ribbon and the Info tab in the InfoPath Filler, select the check box and enter the label that you would like to represent the Submit function.**

   If your users will only be filling out your form using the browser, then this setting doesn't apply.

5. **Click the Advanced button and optionally enter the message that you would like users to receive when the form submission is successful, or if it fails.**

6. **In the After submit field, select whether the form should close, open a new form, or stay open.**

7. **Click OK.**

   The Form Submit button is enabled and the Rules task pane appears to the right of your form, ready for you to create your Form Submit rule.

You can use the following steps to create a Form Submit rule to submit your form to a SharePoint list:

1. **On the Data tab, in the Rules group, click Form Submit.**

2. **Click New ⇨ Action.**

   You can create multiple actions for the Form Submit rule.

3. **Enter a name for your rule.**

4. **If you want to apply a condition to your submission, click Condition and configure the details of the condition; otherwise, skip to step 5.**

   For example, if you want to allow your users to optionally submit a copy of their form to an archive area, you could set a condition on the action that submits data to the archive location; the condition would check to see if the archive check box was selected.

5. **Click the Add button and from the menu, click Submit data.**

   The Rule Details dialog box appears.

6. **If you haven't yet defined your Submit to SharePoint Library data connection, click Add and step through the Data Connection Wizard; otherwise, select the data connection you want to use and click OK.**

   Use the following steps to configure your data connection:

   a. *Select the Create a new connection to Submit data option, and click Next.*

   b. *For the destination to which you want to submit your data, select To a document library on a SharePoint site, and click Next.*

   c. *Enter the URL to your destination document library.*

   d. *Enter the Filename formula that you want to use for your files.*

      Ensure that the formula you use provides a unique filename for each user submitting the form. For example, when a user submits a timesheet form, you can get the file name to include the user name of the person filling out the form by using the following command:

      ```
      concat("Timesheet for - ", username())
      ```

   e. *Click Next.*

   f. *Enter the name for you new data connection.*

   g. *Click Finish.*

7. **Click OK.**

Creating Form Load Rules

You can use Form Load rules to trigger a specific action immediately when your form opens. For example, if you're using multiple views for your form you can set a Form Load rule to display a specific view depending on the user that opened the form.

The Form Load command is located in the Rules group on the Data tab. You can use the following steps to create a Form Load rule that switches the form view:

1. **On the Data tab, in the Rules group, click Form Load.**

   The Rules task pane appears.

2. Enter a name for your rule.

3. If you want to apply a condition to your submission, click Condition and configure the details of the condition; otherwise, skip to Step 4.

   For example, if you want to switch to a different view depending on the user you can set a condition to check the username.

4. Click the Add button and from the menu, click Switch views.

   The Rule Details dialog box appears.

5. Select the view that you wish to display when the form loads and meets the specified condition.

6. Click OK.

Configuring Security and Trust

When you design your form template, InfoPath automatically sets the security and trust settings for you with the minimal level of trust. You can override the default setting and choose a different level of security.

InfoPath provides three trust levels from which you can choose:

+ **Restricted**: The form can't access content outside the form.

  This is the level of minimal trust. (You probably suspected that.)

+ **Domain**: The form can access content from the domain in which it is located.

+ **Full Trust**: The form has access to files and settings on the computer.

You can use the following steps to set the security level for your form template:

1. Click the File tab to present the Backstage view.

2. From the Info tab, click Form Options.

3. From the Category list, click Security and Trust.

4. Clear the Automatically determine security level setting, and select the trust level for your form template.

5. If you have selected Full Trust, select the Sign this form template and specify a code-signing certificate to digitally sign your form template.

   You will need an authenticated code signing certificate from a certification authority, such as VeriSign or DigiCert.

6. Click OK.

If your form template requires Full Trust security — which is the case if your form runs code — you will need to digitally sign your template with a trusted root certificate before users can use it in the browser. A trusted root certificate is a certificate that is trusted by your browser. Certificates that are trusted by most browsers are typically issued by well known companies such as Verisign, Thawte, or Digicert.

Web browser forms that are configured with Full Trust security must be deployed to InfoPath Forms Services by an administrator.

Verifying your form template

When you think that you're ready to deploy your form template you can use the Design Checker to verify that your form doesn't contain errors and is compatible with InfoPath Forms Services.

If you're creating a browser-compatible form template, you can configure the Design Checker to verify your form against a server running InfoPath Forms Services to make sure that you form works correctly in the browser. In order to do this, you must first specify the URL of a server running InfoPath — you enter this URL in the compatibility settings for your form template.

You can use the following steps to configure the Web browser settings for your form template:

1. **Click the File tab to present the Backstage view.**

2. **From the Info tab, click Form Options.**

3. **From the Category list, click Compatibility.**

4. **Ensure that your Form type is set to either Web Browser Form, or Web Browser Form (InfoPath 2007).**

5. **Enter the URL to the SharePoint server running InfoPath Forms Services.**

If you enter the URL to the server running InfoPath Forms Services, InfoPath will figure out the complete URL for you. For example, if you enter `http://nut2craic.com` as the URL, when you click OK InfoPath will append the location of the FormsServices Web service to the URL:

```
http://nut2craic.com/_vti_bin/FormsServices.asmx
```

6. **Click OK.**

The Design Checker task pane appears, presenting any compatibility issues, errors, or warnings that your form may have.

You can use the following steps to verify your design:

1. **Click the File tab to present the Backstage view.**

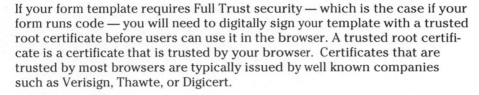

Book IV
Chapter 6

Designing Browser
Compatible Forms

2. **From the Info tab, click Design Checker.**

The Design Checker task pane appears, presenting any compatibility issues, errors, or warnings that your form may have. Figure 6-5 shows an example of the messages that the Design Checker displays.

Figure 6-5:
The Design Checker checks for compatibility issues.

3. **Select the Verify on server setting, and click Refresh.**

InfoPath contacts InfoPath Forms Services to check for inconsistencies.

Deploying Form Templates

When it comes to deploying form templates to InfoPath Forms Services, there are two paths you can follow:

✦ User-deployed forms

✦ Administrator-approved forms

Developers and form authors fall into the "user" category. As long as the Allow users to browser-enable form templates setting is enabled in the InfoPath Forms Services configuration settings, users can deploy form templates to InfoPath Forms Services. You can find out more information on this setting in Book III, Chapter 4. Form templates that have one of the following characteristics qualify for deployment by an administrator:

✦ The security level of the form template is set to full trust.

✦ The form template contains managed code. This goes hand-in-hand with the previous setting; browser-compatible form templates require full trust security if they contain managed code.

✦ Cross-domain data connections are defined directly in the form template; the form template doesn't leverage UDC files.

✦ The data connections used by the form template are located in the centrally managed connection library.

User-deployed form templates are stored in the SharePoint content database, whereas administrator-approved form templates are stored on the local disk of each front-end Web servers. Consequently, administrator-approved form templates provide better performance than user-deployed form templates, as they don't have to be retrieved from the SQL database.

You must have the Enterprise edition of SharePoint Server 2010 to deploy your InfoPath browser-compatible forms to your SharePoint farm.

Publishing User Form Templates

Assuming that your form template doesn't require administrator approval, you can publish your template to a variety of locations, one of which is InfoPath Forms Services. The form template deployment to InfoPath Forms Services is initiated by selecting the SharePoint Server command from the Publish tab in the Backstage view, followed by entering the URL to the location of the site in which you want to deploy the form template.

Once you enter the URL, InfoPath contacts the SharePoint server and then presents you with a number of publishing options:

✦ **Form Library:** Allows you to publish your form template as a template in a form library that will store forms based on your form template. Users can open and fill out forms in your form library. When publishing to a form library you can specify which fields in the template will appear as columns in the library.

✦ **Site Content Type (advanced):** Allows you to publish your template to a site content type, which means that your template can be used in multiple libraries and sites. When publishing to a site content you can specify which fields in the template will appear as site columns. InfoPath places the site columns in the Microsoft InfoPath group.

✦ **Administrator-approved form template (advanced):** Allows you to prepare your form template so that it can be subsequently deployed by an administrator.

Publishing to a form library

If you're publishing your form template to a form library, you can create your form library up front and map the form template to it during the publishing process, or let InfoPath create the form library for you from scratch.

The following steps publish a form template to a form library:

1. Click the File tab to present the Backstage view.

2. From the Publish tab, click SharePoint Server.

3. Enter the URL of the SharePoint site to which you want to publish your form template, and click Next.

4. Select the Enable this form to be filled out by using a browser check box.

5. Select Form Library, and then click Next.

6. Select whether to create a new form library or use an existing form library, and click Next.

   If you want to use an existing form library, InfoPath provides you with a list of all the available libraries in your site from which you can select.

7. If you're creating a new form library, enter the name and description for the form library and click Next; otherwise, skip to step 8.

8. In the first list box on the page, for each field that you want to add as a column in your form library, click Add.

   In the Field to display as column, select the field from your form template. You can then map your field to the column in SharePoint. When mapping your fields you have the following choices:

   - Let InfoPath create a new column in your form library.

   - Map your field to an existing column in your form library.

   - Map your field to an existing site column in SharePoint.

   Determine whether you want to allow users to edit the data in this field by using the datasheet or properties page in SharePoint. If you set this option, rules and code that you have mapped to the field will not run.

   Once you have selected your mapping choices click OK, and then repeat this step for each field you want to represent as a column in SharePoint.

   Figure 6-6 shows you an example of the property promotion page of the Publishing Wizard, listing fields that will be promoted to SharePoint columns.

9. In the second list box on the page, for each field that you want to make available as a connection parameter in the InfoPath Form Web Part, click Add.

   In the Field to use as Web Part Connection Parameter, select the field that you want to promote, and then choose the Parameter type. You have three options for the Parameter Type:

   - Input: the parameter can retrieve data from other Web Parts.

   - Output: data from this parameter can be sent to other Web Parts.

   - Input and Output: the parameter can be used to both send and receive data to and from other Web Parts.

Once you have selected your parameter type, click OK, and then repeat this step for each field you want to make available as a Web Part connection parameter.

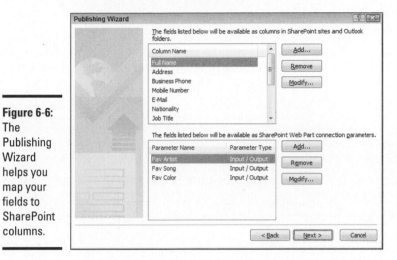

Figure 6-6:
The Publishing Wizard helps you map your fields to SharePoint columns.

Figure 6-6 shows you an example of the property promotion page of the Publishing Wizard, listing the fields that will be promoted as Web Part connection parameters.

10. **Click Next.**

11. **Verify the form information. If everything is the way you want it, click Publish; otherwise, use the Back button to make your changes.**

The publishing process may take a while. Once complete, you will receive a notification that your form was completed successfully. You can click the Open this form in the browser to see your form working in SharePoint.

12. **Close.**

Publishing to a site content type

When publishing your form template to a site content type, you can create your site content type upfront and map the form template to it during the publishing process, or let InfoPath create the site content type for you from scratch.

The following steps publish a form template to a site content type:

1. **Click the File tab to present the Backstage view.**

2. **From the Publish tab, click SharePoint Server.**

3. **Enter the URL of the SharePoint site to which you want to publish your form template, and click Next.**

4. **Select the Enable this form to be filled out by using a browser check box.**

5. **Select Site Content Type (advanced), and then click Next.**

6. **Select whether to create a new site content type or use an existing site content type, select the content type from the list and then click Next.**

   If you want to use an existing site content type, InfoPath provides you with a list of all the available content types from which you can select.

   If you want to create a new site content type, InfoPath provides you with a list of available content types on which you can base your new site content type.

   In each case, select a content type from the list of available content types.

7. **If you're creating a new site content type, enter the name and description of the site content type, and click Next; otherwise, skip to step 8.**

8. **Enter the URL for the location and filename for the form template that will be associated with the content type, and click Next.**

   You can use the browse button to select the form library that you wish to store your form template for the content type. When entering a name for the form template file, use a descriptive name that accurately represents the function of the form.

   The form template must be published to a location on the same site as the content type. Publish your form template to a library that you use to manage the user deployed form templates for your site.

   After you click Next, the property promotion page of the Publishing Wizard appears.

9. **In the first list box on the page, for each field that you want to add as a site column in your content type, click Add.**

   In the Field to display as column, select the field from your form template. You can then map your field to the column in SharePoint. When mapping your fields you have the following choices:

   • Let InfoPath create a new site column in your site.

   • Map your field to an existing site column.

   Determine whether you want to allow users to edit the data in this field by using the datasheet or properties page in SharePoint. If you set this option, rules and code that you have mapped to the field will not run.

   Once you have selected your mapping choices click OK, and then repeat this step for each field you want to represent as a site column in SharePoint.

Figure 6-6 shows you an example of the property promotion page of the Publishing Wizard, listing fields that will be promoted to SharePoint columns.

10. In the second list box on the page, for each field that you want to make available as a connection parameter in the InfoPath Form Web Part, click Add.

In the Field to use as Web Part Connection Parameter, select the field that you want to promote, and then choose the Parameter type. You have three options for the Parameter Type:

- Input: the parameter can retrieve data from other Web Parts.
- Output: data from this parameter can be sent to other Web Parts.
- Input and Output: the parameter can be used to both send and receive data to and from other Web Parts.

Once you have selected your parameter type, click OK, and then repeat this step for each field you want to make available as a Web Part connection parameter.

Figure 6-6 shows you an example of the property promotion page of the Publishing Wizard, listing the fields that will be promoted as Web Part connection parameters.

11. Click Next.

12. Verify the form information and if you're content that everything is the way you want it, click Publish; otherwise, use the Back button to make your changes.

The publishing process may take a while. Once complete, you will receive a notification that your form template was published successfully.

Click the Manage this Content Type link to view the site content type in SharePoint.

Click the Open this form in the browser to see your form working in SharePoint.

13. Close.

Adding your site content type to a form library

When your form template is published as a site content type, you can use it in any of the form libraries of your SharePoint site.

You can use the following steps to add a form template that was published as a site content type to your form library.

1. Using your browser, navigate to the SharePoint form library in your SharePoint site.

2. On the Library tab, click Settings ⇨ Library Settings.

The Form Library Settings page appears.

3. Click the Advanced Settings link to display the Advanced Settings page.

4. In the Content Types section, select Yes to allow the management of content types.

5. Leave all other settings with their default values, unless you have a specific need to change them.

6. Click OK, to return to the Form Library Settings page.

7. In the Content Types section, click Add from existing site content types.

   The Add Content Types page appears.

8. Set the Select site content types from drop-down list to Microsoft InfoPath.

9. In the list of available site content types, select the site content type to which you published your form template, and click Add.

10. Click OK, to return to the Form Library Settings page.

   Your form template is available for use in your form library.

Preparing a form template for administrator approval

A form template that requires full trust to the domain must be approved and deployed by an administrator. The approval and deployment process requires that the administrator verifies, uploads, and activates the form template. Once the form template is activated it is available for activation by the site collection administrator.

Although the administrator is actually the person to deploy your form template in this scenario, you must take certain deployment steps to prepare your form template for administrator approval and ultimate deployment; the Publishing Wizard steps you through the required tasks.

You need to prepare your form template for administrator approval if the following are true:

✦ **The farm has been set so that users can't publish their form templates to InfoPath Forms Service.**

   If the Allow users to browser-enable form templates InfoPath Forms Services setting is unchecked in Central Administration, users can't deploy their own form templates into SharePoint, regardless of the form templates trust setting.

✦ **Your form template requires full trust to the domain.**

The following instructions prepare your form for administrator approval and deployment:

1. Click the File tab to present the Backstage view.

2. **From the Publish tab, click SharePoint Server.**

3. **Enter the URL of the SharePoint site to which you want to publish your form template, and click Next.**

4. **Select the Enable this form to be filled out by using a browser check box.**

5. **Select Administrator-approved form template (advanced), and then click Next.**

   If the trust level of your form template is set to Full Trust, this will be the only publishing option available to you.

6. **Specify a location and file name for your form template, and click Next.**

   Place the form template in a location on your computer or network share that your administrator has access to for approval and deployment, and then let your administrator know that your form template is ready for deployment.

7. **In the first list box on the page, for each field that you want to add as a site column in your content type, click Add.**

   When the administrator deploys your form template, it is deployed as a new site content type under the Microsoft InfoPath group, and promoted fields are represented by site columns.

   In the Field to display as column, select the field from your form template. You can then map your field to the column in SharePoint. When mapping your fields you have the following choices:

   • Let InfoPath create a new site column in your site.

   • Map your field to an existing site column.

   Determine whether you want to allow users to edit the data in this field by using the datasheet or properties page in SharePoint. If you set this option, rules and code that you have mapped to the field will not run.

   Once you have selected your mapping choices, click OK, and then repeat this step for each field you want to represent as a site column in SharePoint.

   Figure 6-6 shows you an example of the property promotion page of the Publishing Wizard, listing fields that will be promoted to SharePoint columns.

8. **In the second list box on the page, for each field that you want to make available as a connection parameter in the InfoPath Form Web Part, click Add.**

   In the Field to use as Web Part Connection Parameter, select the field that you want to promote, and then choose the Parameter type. You have three options for the Parameter Type:

   • Input: The parameter can retrieve data from other Web Parts.

   • Output: Data from this parameter can be sent to other Web Parts.

- Input and Output: The parameter can be used to both send and receive data to and from other Web Parts.

Once you have selected your parameter type, click OK, and then repeat this step for each field you want to make available as a Web Part connection parameter.

Figure 6-6 shows you an example of the property promotion page of the Publishing Wizard, listing the fields that will be promoted as Web Part connection parameters.

9. Click Next.

10. Verify the form information and if you're content that everything is the way you want it, click Publish; otherwise, use the Back button to make your changes.

The publishing process may take a while, and once complete you will receive a notification that your form template was published successfully to the file location your specified in step 6.

In order to make your form template available for use in SharePoint, the form administrator must approve and deploy the form template. The Managing Administrator-approved Form Templates section of Book III, Chapter 4 shows the steps involved for an administrator to deploy administrator-approved form templates.

11. Close.

Property Promotion

During the publishing process, the Publishing Wizard presents you with a property promotion page in which you select the fields that you want to promote as columns in SharePoint, and as Web Part Connection parameters for use with the InfoPath Form Web Part. You can use the Form Options dialog box to access your property promotion mappings at any time during the form template design process.

The following steps access the property promotion settings when designing your form:

1. Click the File tab to present the Backstage view.

2. From the Publish tab, click Form Options.

3. From the list of categories, click Property Promotion.

You can add, modify, and remove your property mappings as desired.

Quick Publishing

Once you have successfully published your form template, the Quick Publish command becomes available to you for future publishing. Quick Publish saves you from having to go through all the configuration steps that you went through when you initially published your form template.

You can access the Quick Publish command from several locations within InfoPath:

✦ From the Info tab in the InfoPath Backstage View.

✦ From the Publish tab in the InfoPath Backstage View.

✦ From the Publish icon on the title bar of the InfoPath Designer client.

Chapter 7: Examining the InfoPath Forms Services Tools

In This Chapter

✔ **Customizing SharePoint List Forms**

✔ **Creating InfoPath Forms for External Lists**

✔ **Making effective use of with the InfoPath Form Web Part**

✔ **Taking your forms offline**

InfoPath Services 2010 brings to the table many exciting new features that bring your forms to life in your SharePoint sites. For example, the InfoPath Web Part provides an easy way to let your users interact with your forms in the context of other Web Parts on the page — data can be passed to and from your form to other Web Parts on the page as sources or destinations, dynamically updating what the user sees.

Book IV, Chapter 5 provides an introduction to InfoPath Designer 2010 and its capabilities, and Book IV, Chapter 6 shows you how to design browser-compatible forms. In this chapter, focus on the cool features that extend beyond the InfoPath Designer Shell and bring your applications to life.

Customizing SharePoint List Forms

SharePoint Server 2010 and its InfoPath integration capabilities make it easy to customize the way users interact with data in SharePoint lists. In SharePoint lists, several forms are involved when you're viewing, editing, and updating your list items. They're .aspx pages that work like dialog boxes:

✦ **DispForm.aspx**: This page appears when viewing an item in a SharePoint list.

   This page corresponds to the View Item command on the Items menu.

✦ **EditForm.aspx**: This page appears when editing an item in a SharePoint list.

   This page corresponds to the Edit Item command on the Items menu.

✦ **NewForm.aspx**: This page appears when creating a new item in a SharePoint list.

   This page corresponds to the New Item command on the Items menu.

The out-of-the-box forms list fields in a single column scrolling view. Figure 7-1 shows the default View Item form in a simple Contacts list. The default form is clean and simple, and may meet the needs of your organization, but if your list has many fields, a single column scrolling view may prove to be too cumbersome for your users. You can change the order of the fields on the page, using the List Settings page; however, if your customization needs go beyond field ordering, that's where InfoPath comes into play.

Figure 7-1: The default View Item form displays a single column scrolling view.

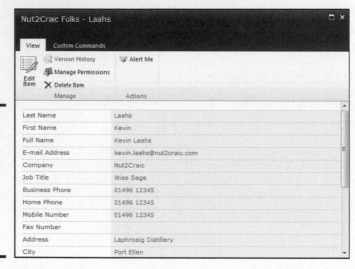

SharePoint Server 2010 provides a customization menu with a set of tools to help you customize your SharePoint lists. You can access the set of tools by clicking the Customize List command on the List tab. Figure 7-2 shows the customization options that are available from the menu.

Figure 7-2: You have many customization tools at your disposal.

The tools include:

✦ **Customize Form:** Allows you to use InfoPath 2010 to create custom forms for adding, editing, and viewing list items.

You must have InfoPath 2010 installed in order to use this tool.

✦ **Form Web Parts:** Allows you to modify the Web Parts in the forms associated with the list, including both the default SharePoint list forms and any custom InfoPath forms. The dialog box that displays your form is a Web Part page that includes a Web Part that presents the list form or InfoPath form. You can change the Web Part settings as you would with other Web Parts, and you can add additional Web Parts to the page and connect it with the form Web Part. The Web Part that displays the InfoPath form is known as the InfoPath Form Web Part.

✦ **Edit List:** Allows you to use SharePoint Designer to edit the list, including editing the list settings, adding or removing columns, and creating new views, forms, workflows, and custom actions.

✦ **New Quick Step:** Uses SharePoint Designer to help you create your own workflow-powered Ribbon button to perform a custom action on items in your list. This tool will add a button to the Quick Steps group on the Items tab.

The Customize Form command opens your list form in InfoPath Designer, providing you with a very quick and versatile way to customize your SharePoint list form to suit your needs. Using InfoPath Designer, you can customize a SharePoint list form as you would a regular InfoPath form. For example, you can change the page layout, add and remove fields, add rules to your fields, and create additional form views to give your users a tabbed form experience.

Book IV, Chapter 5 provides you with a tour of InfoPath Designer and Book IV, Chapter 6 shows you how to use the InfoPath Designer tools to design browser-compatible forms. The same design capabilities are available when customizing your SharePoint list forms. Figure 7-3 shows the Contacts form opened in InfoPath Designer. The Fields task pane appears to the right of the form and displays all the columns for your list, including any custom columns that you may have added. If you examine the data connections for the list you will see that the main data source is the SharePoint list that you're editing, and that the connection is configured to retrieve and submit data to and from the list.

**Book IV
Chapter 7**

Examining the
InfoPath Forms
Services Tools

Figure 7-3:
Customize
Form
opens the
SharePoint
list form in
InfoPath
Designer.

The InfoPath Fields task pane provides two views for looking at your
SharePoint list columns:

✦ **Basic view:** shows you the fields with descriptive icons representing the
type of field. For example, the Web Page fields display a HyperLink icon.
When viewing your fields with Basic view, you can add additional columns
to your SharePoint list.

✦ **Advanced view:** shows you the node tree display of the data source
fields. You can't add additional fields to your list using this view.

InfoPath tailors the menu commands and form options specifically for
working with SharePoint list forms. For example, if you launch the Form
Options dialog box you will see that the following categories *aren't* available:

✦ Property Promotion

✦ E-mail attachments

✦ Digital Signatures

✦ Security and Trust

✦ Preview

✦ Programming

By disabling these options. Microsoft provides a clean, uncluttered SharePoint specific view of your list forms in InfoPath Designer.

Customizing your SharePoint list form has never been easier:

+ **Adding new fields:** You can add fields to your form view by simply dragging them from the task pane and dropping them onto your form.

+ **Removing fields:** You can remove fields from your form view by selecting the control and hitting the delete key.

+ **Reordering fields:** You can reorder your fields by dragging and dropping them around your form view.

+ **Changing color scheme:** You can change the color scheme by selecting a new theme, and by using the formatting commands.

+ **Customize table layout:** You can add more columns and rows to the existing tables in your form view, insert new tables using either the preformatted tables or your own custom tables, and remove tables from your form view all in the matter of a few clicks.

+ **Change your page layout:** You can delete the entire content of the default SharePoint list form — be brave, just hit Ctrl-A to select all the content and then hit the delete key — and insert a new page layout, and add the tables, theme, and fields you want.

+ **Rules rule:** You can add your own rules to your fields, as you would with a regular InfoPath form. Now you can get your SharePoint lists to behave exactly the way you want without having to resort to writing code!

+ **Add additional views:** You can add multiple views to your form separating your fields across views, or even providing different users a different view of your SharePoint list form.

+ **Change the display view:** The Display view is what a user sees while staring at an existing list item — which is to say (by default) the Edit Item view. If you want to change what the user sees to another view you've created, you can. If you like, your users can see one version of your form when they're viewing an item, and another version when they're editing an item.

+ **Preview:** You can check out your new design — prior to publishing it to SharePoint — by clicking the preview button.

+ **Quick Publish:** When publishing your form, the publishing connection is already there for you; you simply click the Quick Publish button on the menu and your changes are instantly published to your SharePoint list.

You can find details on designing your forms with InfoPath Designer in Book IV, Chapter 6.

**Book IV
Chapter 7**

Examining the
InfoPath Forms
Services Tools

Apprehensive about customizations? You really can't go wrong when customizing your SharePoint list forms with InfoPath Designer; InfoPath disables those commands and features that aren't supported with your list form and SharePoint provides an option for you to revert the form back to the default SharePoint form.

The following instructions show you how to open your SharePoint list form in InfoPath Designer:

1. **Using your browser, navigate to your SharePoint list.**

2. **From the Ribbon menu, click the List tab.**

3. **From the Ribbon menu, click Customize List⇨Customize Form.**

The following steps revert a customized list form back to the default SharePoint list form:

1. **Using your browser, navigate to your SharePoint list.**

2. **From the Ribbon menu, click the List tab.**

3. **From the Ribbon menu, click Settings⇨List Settings.**

   The List Settings page appears.

4. **From the General Setting column, click Form Settings.**

   The Form Setting Page appears. If you haven't yet customized your SharePoint list form with InfoPath, you get only one option — Customize the current form using Microsoft InfoPath. When selected, this option launches the default SharePoint list form in InfoPath for you to customize — and because you don't want to customize your SharePoint list form with InfoPath, you can simply click Cancel.

   If you have customized your SharePoint list form with InfoPath, two options will be available:

   • Modify the existing InfoPath Form (enabled by default)

   • Use the default SharePoint form

5. **Select Use the default SharePoint form.**

   If you want to keep a copy of the customized template on the server in case you may want to revisit your customization attempt, then leave the Delete the InfoPath Form from the server setting unchecked. The next time you click the Customize Form button, the customized file you were working on will appear in InfoPath ready for you to continue your customizations.

   Alternatively, if you want to delete your customized form from SharePoint, select the Delete the InfoPath form from the server setting.

The next time you click the Customize Form button, the default SharePoint list form will appear in InfoPath ready for you to customize.

6. **Click OK.**

The form reverts back to its default existence SharePoint list form.

Save a copy of the form template file to your computer or network location for safe keeping. You can do this by clicking the Save button in the InfoPath client and saving the Template.xsn file. If you have a copy saved and someone with the appropriate privileges inadvertently deletes the copy on the server, you can simply open your Template.xsn file with InfoPath Designer and Quick Publish back to your SharePoint list.

Once you have your SharePoint list form open in InfoPath Designer, you can begin designing your list form to get the appearance and behavior you want. When you're ready to publish your changes back to the list, simply click the Quick Publish command on the title bar — you can also find the command on the InfoPath Designer Backstage view. Figure 7-4 shows you a customized view of the default SharePoint contacts form shown in Figure 7-1 — the design looks considerably different, and only took a few minutes to produce.

Figure 7-4: It only takes a few minutes to make changes to your form.

Before you can use the Customize Form command to modify SharePoint list forms, you must have Microsoft Office InfoPath 2010 installed on your computer. (You might be surprised at how many people forget they have to install the software before they try to use its tools.)

Embedding InfoPath Forms in Web Pages

SharePoint Server 2010 is the first SharePoint version with the InfoPath Form Web Part: Now you can present your browser-compatible InfoPath form in a Web Part on your SharePoint page and connect it to other Web Parts on your page. If you're creating your forms with InfoPath Designer — and this includes SharePoint list forms — you can promote your fields, which makes them available as parameters to other connecting Web Parts.

This is particularly useful when you have multiple lists of data with relatable fields. For example, you may have a SharePoint list that contains a list of albums and their associated information — such as the production date and recording artist — and another SharePoint list that contains a list of songs and the albumId of the album on which the song appears. Both lists are connected with the albumId field, so you can navigate to the songs list, find a song you like, take note of the albumId, and then view the second list, find the albumId and see who the artist is that sings the song. You would most likely agree that, while you eventually get the information you want, it is quite a cumbersome process. SharePoint Server 2010 offers lots of possibilities for presenting this data in a more efficient form, including:

✦ **Connecting SharePoint List View Web Parts:** You can add the List View Web Parts for your lists to your page, and then connect them to enable filtering of data between lists. Although this option is very easy to configure, it may not present the information to your users in the way you would like.

✦ **Connecting DataView Web Part:** You can convert the default List View Web Parts to DataView Web Parts; that way you can use SharePoint Designer to manipulate the layout to get the look and feel you want. The DataView Web Part gives you lots of flexibility in the ways you present data to your users; you can, for example, create views and sub-views of relatable data.

✦ **InfoPath Form Web Part:** The InfoPath forms you create can filter information as needed before presenting it to your users in the browser. This capability gives you more ways to display the form libraries and lists that use your InfoPath forms, and offers users more browsing features they can apply.

The following sections show you how to leverage the InfoPath Form Web Part to display information from a SharePoint list or library.

Creating a blank Web Part page

To make the steps easier to follow, we start by walking you through the process of creating a blank Web page; however, you can add the InfoPath Form Web Part where you see fit and that includes any existing pages in your SharePoint deployment.

The following steps create a blank Web Part page using the SharePoint browser user interface:

1. **Using your browser, navigate to your SharePoint site.**

2. **From the Site Actions menu, click More Options.**

3. **Filter by Page.**

4. **Click Web Part Page⇨Create**

   The New Web Part Page page appears.

5. **Enter the Name of your Web Part page.**

6. **Select a layout template for your Web Part page.**

7. **Select the location to which you want to save your Web Part page, and click Create.**

   Your Web Part Page appears in edit mode. You can now begin adding your Web Parts. Figure 7-5 shows a Web Part Page in edit mode. To add a Web Part you simply click on the Add a Web Part link from the zone to which you want to add your Web Part.

Figure 7-5: Click the Add a Web Part link to add a Web Part to zones on your page.

Adding the InfoPath Form Web Part

If you customize your SharePoint list form with InfoPath Designer, the page that appears when you click on an item is actually a Web Part page that uses the InfoPath Form Web Part to display your form. You can insert the InfoPath Web Part page onto your own custom Web Part pages as well.

The following steps show you how to add the InfoPath Web Part to a Web Part page using the SharePoint browser user interface:

1. **Using your browser, navigate to the Web Part page in your SharePoint site to which you want to add the Web Part.**

2. **Click the Page tab.**

3. **From the Edit group in the Ribbon menu, click Edit Page.**

4. **From your chosen Web Part zone, click Add a Web Part.**

   A list of Web Parts appears below the Ribbon menu.

5. **From the Categories column, click Forms.**

   The Web Parts related to the Forms category appears, including the InfoPath Form Web Part.

   A Web Part Zone is an area of the Web page in which you can insert Web Parts.

6. **From the Web Parts column, click InfoPath Form Web Part.**

   The About the Web Part column provides you with information about the selected Web Part, and shows you the zone in which it will be added.

7. **Click Add.**

   The InfoPath Form Web Part is added to your Web Part page. At this stage it hasn't been configured.

8. **From the contents of the InfoPath Form Web Part, click the link to open the tool pane.**

   This will open the Web Part tool pane from which you can define the Web Part settings. Alternatively, you can edit a Web Part using the following method:

   a. *From the right hand side of the Web Part title, click the down arrow to display the Web Part menu.*

   b. *From the Web Part menu, click Edit Web Part.*

9. **From the List or Library drop-down list, select the list or library that contains the InfoPath form.**

10. **Select the content type that you wish to display in the InfoPath Form Web Part.**

11. **Determine whether to display a read-only form.**

    This option is only valid for InfoPath forms associated with a SharePoint list. Selecting this property means that users will not be able to edit data in the Web Part.

12. **Determine whether to display the InfoPath Ribbon or toolbar.**

    If you select this setting, a Form tab appears on the toolbar providing access to the InfoPath Ribbon menu.

13. **Determine whether to send data to connected Web Parts when the page loads.**

14. **Select the form view that you want to display in the Web Part.**

    The default setting is the Edit Item view.

15. **Determine what you want to happen when a user submits the form**

    You can choose one of three options:

    • Leave the form open: This is the default setting and saves your changes back to the list or library, and leaves the item open in the form for additional changes or viewing.

    • Open a new form: Saves your changes back to the list or library, and opens a new blank form.

    • Close the form: Saves your changes back to the list or library, and closes the form.

16. **Click OK.**

    The InfoPath Form Web Part appears on your Web Part page, and a new Form tab appears on the toolbar.

At this stage, you can fill out the form in your InfoPath Form Web Part — assuming your InfoPath Form Web Part hasn't been set to read-only — and submit the data to your SharePoint list or library. Note, however, that you can't display the information from forms that have already been filled out. In order to wake up the InfoPath Form Web Part so it makes your form more dynamic, you can connect it to other Web Parts, such as the List View Web Part. More about that coming right up.

Connecting the InfoPath Form Web Part

To bring your InfoPath form alive, you don't need a castle laboratory filled with mad-scientist devices; all you have to do is connect it to other Web Parts. For example, if you've customized the SharePoint list form for the Contacts list, and you want to create a Web page that you can easily browse through the contacts and view their contact information, using the InfoPath Form Web Part can help you achieve this blissful state. Here's an overview of all you need to do:

1. Create a view in your Contacts list that displays only the names of your contacts.

2. Create a Web Part Page.

3. Set the view to display only the names of your contacts.

4. Add the Contacts List View Web Part to the page.

5. Add the InfoPath Form Web Part and configure it to map to the Contacts list.

6. Connect the Contacts List View Web Part to the InfoPath Form Web Part so the Contacts List View is sending data to the InfoPath Form Web Part.

The following steps connect a List View Web Part to your InfoPath Form Web Part:

1. **From the right hand side of the InfoPath Form Web Part title, click the down arrow to display the Web Part menu.**

2. **From the Web Part menu, click Edit Web Part.**

   If you're already in Edit mode, you can skip to the next step.

3. **From the Web Part menu, click Connections⇨Get Form From⇨<*your List View Web Part*>.**

4. **Select an item in the List View Web Part to display an item in the InfoPath Form Web Part.**

   The InfoPath Form Web Part dynamically reflects the selection by displaying the relevant data.

Before you can use InfoPath Forms Services and all the tools it has to offer — including the InfoPath Form Web Part — you must have the Enterprise Edition of SharePoint Server 2010 — and not just sitting around in its box or its download file. It has to be installed and running in your environment. (Okay, you knew that. Just saying.)

Using InfoPath Forms with External Lists

You can use Business Data Connectivity Services to surface external data in a special SharePoint list referred to as an external list. If you want to customize the default SharePoint form for a SharePoint list, you can't use the Customize Form option from the Customize List menu in SharePoint. Instead, you must perform the following high-level steps:

1. Open the external list in SharePoint Designer.

2. Launch InfoPath Designer from within SharePoint Designer.

3. Publish your changes to the list.

It seems like a convoluted way to go about publishing your form, doesn't it? But it works well for external lists. That's because SharePoint Designer is the tool you're most likely to use when you create your external content types and external lists in the first place.

Here are the the up-close-and-personal steps you take to design InfoPath forms for your external lists:

1. **Using your browser, navigate to your SharePoint list.**

2. **From the Ribbon menu, click the List tab.**

3. **From the Ribbon menu, click Customize List⇨Edit List.**

The Edit List command allows you to edit your list, including external list, in SharePoint Designer. SharePoint Designer opens your external list to a page from which you can view and manage the settings for the list.

4. **On the List Settings tab, in the Actions group, click Design Forms in InfoPath⇨Item.**

    The Design Forms in InfoPath command launches InfoPath Designer allowing you to replace the existing browser forms with InfoPath forms.

5. **Customize your form as needed.**

6. **On the title bar, click the Save icon.**

    You must first save your form template before you can publish it to the external list. You can save the template to your local computer because the publishing process saves it to your external list.

7. **On the title bar, click the Quick Publish icon.**

    SharePoint Designer saves the form template to the external list and the Publish dialog box appears notifying you that your template was published successfully.

8. **To view your form in action click the Open this form in the browser link; otherwise, skip to step 9.**

9. **Click OK.**

10. **Close InfoPath Designer.**

Working Offline with InfoPath Forms

SharePoint Workspace 2010 provides offline access to your SharePoint content and native support for InfoPath. When you take a SharePoint list offline, SharePoint Workspace creates a synchronized copy of your list on your computer. The synchronized copy includes any custom InfoPath forms that your list uses. When you interact with your list offline, SharePoint Workspace presents your data in the same InfoPath form, providing you with a consistent experience while online and offline.

The following steps show you how to synchronize a SharePoint list to your SharePoint Workspace using the SharePoint browser user interface.

1. **Using your browser, navigate to your external list in your SharePoint site.**

2. **Click the List tab.**

3. **From the Connect & Export group in the Ribbon, click Sync to SharePoint Workspace.**

    The Sync to SharePoint Workspace dialog box appears.

4. Verify that you're synchronizing the correct list, and click OK.

SharePoint Workspace creates a local cached copy of the external list.

a. *If this is the first time you're synchronizing your external list to SharePoint Workspace you will receive a prompt from the Microsoft Office Customization Installer asking if you're sure you want to install this customization.*

b. *Click Install to continue installing the customization.*

The installation may take several minutes.

c. *When you receive the notification that the customization was successfully installed, click Close.*

5. From the Sync to SharePoint Workspace dialog box, click Open Workspace.

Clicking Open Workspace opens the SharePoint Workspace client and displays your synchronized external list. Figure 7-6 shows an example of a synchronized contacts list as it appears in SharePoint Workspace. The contacts list has a custom InfoPath form, which is used to view and edit data in the list while offline.

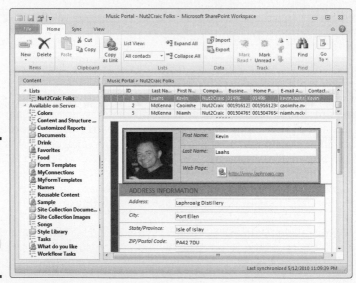

Figure 7-6:
The InfoPath form appears in the synchronized list.

SharePoint Workspace displays the custom InfoPath form when you browse, view, edit, or create an item in your synchronized list.

Once you have a connection with your SharePoint site, you can initiate synchronization with your SharePoint lists — both internal and external — directly from the SharePoint Workspace client.

Chapter 8: Designing and Administering Search

In This Chapter

✓ **Building a search results page**

✓ **Administering search**

In Book III, Chapter 6, we describe the main components of the SharePoint search architecture and the core end-user features that are available out of the box. In this chapter we show you how to implement many of the search features.

Designing the Search Experience

To show you how to leverage various search features we walk through the configuration steps to produce the search results shown in Figure 8-1. The top part of this figure shows the search query that was executed from within a team site (`http://www.nut2craic.com/sites/music`), and the bottom half shows the results page (`http://www.nut2craic.com/pages/instruments.aspx`).

The main features used to create the page in Figure 8-1 are

✦ **Search scopes:** Defined for use within the team site.

✦ **Search results landing page:** Page for a specific search scope.

✦ **Top federated search:** Result from the Internet.

✦ **Federated search location:** Retrieve and display images.

✦ **Refiner:** Based on a custom property.

We describe the configuration of these main components in the following sections.

Figure 8-1:
A custom
search
page.

Creating an Enterprise Search Center site

An Enterprise Search Center site hosts the search results page queries that users execute. This site can be either in its own site collection or a subsite, and it can reside on any SharePoint farm to which your users have read access. For the example shown in Figure 8-1, we created the Enterprise Search Center site at the root of the www.nut2craic.com Web Application. Create your Enterprise Search site (from Central Administration or from within an existing site collection) by using the Enterprise Search Center template.

After you create your site, you need to give all users read access. Follow these steps to grant users read access:

1. **From your site, choose Site Actions⇨Site Permissions and click the Grant Permissions task in the Ribbon.**

2. **In the dialog box that appears, type in "Authenticated Users" in the Users/Groups text box.**

3. Select the *<Site Name>* Visitors group from the "Grant Permissions" drop-down menu to grant permissions.

4. Deselect the "Send welcome e-mail to the new users" check box and click OK. You are now returned to the Site Permissions page.

Defining a search scope

You need to define a search scope that can be used by the Search Box drop-down list so that you can target the query at a particular subset of the overall index and display the search results on a specific results page.

Search scopes can be local or shared:

✦ **Local:** Defined at the site-collection level. These search scopes can be used only within that site collection.

To create a local search scope choose Site Actions⇨Site Settings⇨Site Collection Administration.

✦ **Shared:** Defined at the Search Service Application level and useable within any site collection that uses the Search Service

You create shared search scopes using Central Administration. From Central Administration Choose Manage Service Applications⇨Search Service Application, then select the Scopes option in the Queries and Results section.

Whether a scope is local or shared, you follow the same process to define it, and both the preceding options take you to a View Scopes page. In the shared View Scopes page, any local scopes that have been defined elsewhere are listed. To create a shared scope called Instruments that can target search results to a specific search results page (`Instruments.aspx`), follow these steps:

1. Click the New Scope button.

   The dialog box appears.

2. Enter the name Instruments, **and enter a description of your choosing.**

3. In the Target Results page, select Specify a Different Page for Searching This Scope and enter Instruments.aspx **in the accompanying text box.**

After you define a shared scope, you need to add rules to it. These rules determine what items from the index any search query that uses the scope should query against. You can apply different types of rules, and you can control which rules must match for an item in the index to be considered part of the scope.

Figure 8-2 shows the dialog box that you use to add a rule.

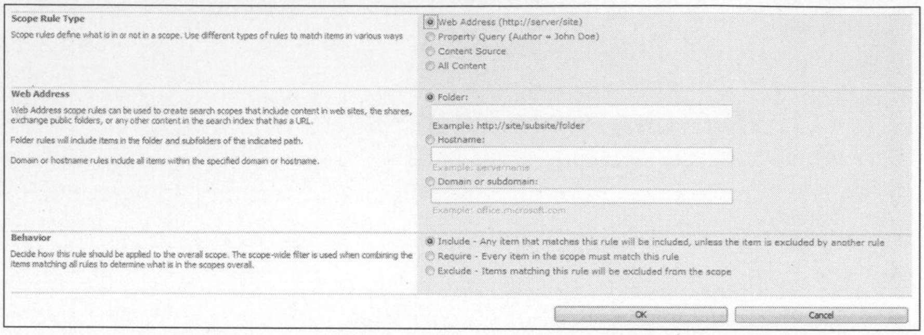

Figure 8-2: The search-scope rule options.

As you can see, you can choose from the following rule types:

✦ **Web Address:** Uses the URL of an item as the criteria that enables you to target any folder, hostname, or fully qualified domain name. For example, you can add a rule that targets a specific document library in a specific team site.

✦ **Property Query:** Can use any managed property that has been defined as useable in a search query as the criteria. By using this rule type, you have the flexibility to target only content that has a particular value for a particular property. For example, you can add a rule that targets only content that a named person has authored.

✦ **Content Source:** Can use any content source that your SharePoint administrator has defined within the Search Service application. You can use this rule type to target specific repositories that you're indexing, such as a Lotus Notes database, a file share, or an external Web site.

✦ **All Content:** Specifies all content. You typically use this rule type with another rule that excludes specific content. For example, the All Site content source includes two rules — one that includes All Content and one that uses a property query to exclude people item types.

The Instrument content source that we used in our example is shown in Figure 8-3 — it includes All Content, except People item types and any content from the site collection `http://www.nut2craic.com/sites/music`. You can create similar rules by using the New Rule option at the bottom of the Scope properties and rules page (`viewscopesettings.aspx`), which appears after you click your search scope in the View Scopes page.

The system compiles rules as a background task that runs every 15 minutes. You can't use your search scope until this task has been completed.

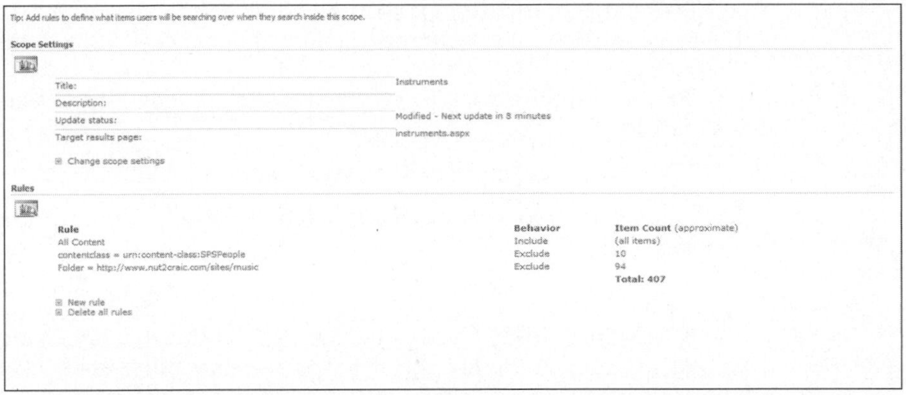

Figure 8-3:
View the
Scope
Settings and
Rules for the
Instruments
Search
Scope.

Associating the search scope with a team site

After you define a shared search scope and the Scopes Update job compiles it, you can then use it within a site collection. Search groups gather together scopes that should be used for particular circumstances. Out of the box, SharePoint comes with two search groups defined for each site collection:

+ **Search Dropdown:** Scopes in this group appear in the Search drop-down list control which is part of the Search Box Web Part.

+ **Advanced Search:** Scopes in this group are shown in the Advanced Search page, which is a component of the Search Box Web Part.

The View Scopes page shows you which scopes are in each group, which scopes are shared, and which shared scopes aren't being used within the site collection. It also shows you an estimate of the number of items associated with each scope and the update status of the scope, as shown in Figure 8-4.

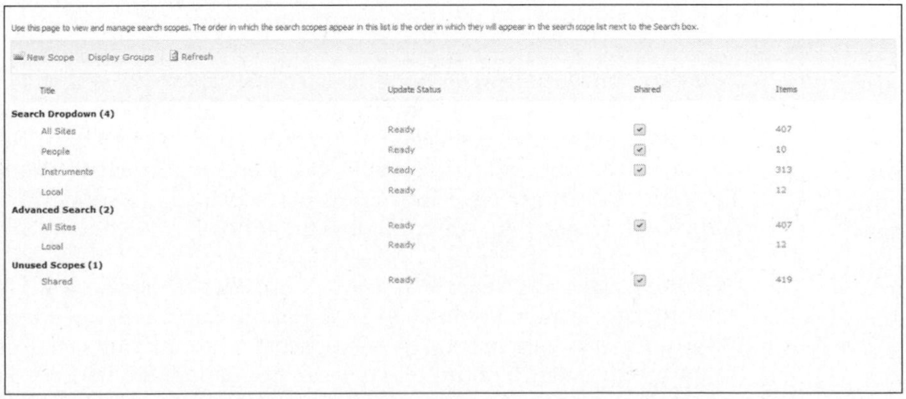

Figure 8-4:
Search-
groups
and search
scopes in
the View
Scopes
page.

To associate the Instrument search scope with the team site so that the Search drop-down list contains the Instrument scope, follow these steps:

1. **From the home page of your team site, choose Site Actions⇨Site Settings.**

    The Site Settings page (`settings.aspx`) appears.

2. **Select the Search Scopes option in the Site Collection Administration section.**

    The View Scopes page (`viewscopes.aspx`) appears.

3. **Click the Display Groups button and, in the Display Groups page (`listdisplaygroup.aspx`) that appears, click the Search Dropdown link.**

    The Edit Scope Display Group web page (`scopedisplaygroup.aspx`) appears.

4. **Select the Instrument scope, which you want to include in the Search Dropdown group.**

    You can also configure the order of scopes and which scope should be the default one by using the Position from Top and Default scope controls.

5. **Click OK and you are returned to the Display Groups page.**

Configuring the search dialog box on team site pages

By default, a team site limits its searches to items in the site collection and uses the out-of-the-box `OSSSearchResults.aspx` page to display the results. The Search Box Web Part actually controls which page is used to display search results, so you have to configure the search settings for the site collection to indicate that you want particular searches to be executed by using a different search results page — thus allowing you to execute wider searches than just the current site collection.

You can configure how to handle searches that are based on contextual scopes (meaning searches in This List, This Site, and so on) and Custom Scopes (such as the example Instrument scope) by using the Search Settings option in the Site Collection Administration section of the Site Settings page. The Search Settings page (`enhancedSearch.aspx`) appears, as shown in Figure 8-5, where you can configure the following:

✦ **Site Collection Search Center:** Control whether you want to support custom scopes. If you select the Enable Custom Scopes radio button, then your custom scopes can present search results that point to content outside of the current site collection. So, you need to direct the search results for such scopes to a search results page that's tailored for such a result set. Enter the page's address in the Center text box.

Typically, you use an Enterprise Search Center site for this purpose, as Figure 8-5 shows (set to `http://www.nut2craic.com/pages`).

✦ **Site Collection Search Dropdown Mode:** Control the contents of the drop-down list that appears in the Search Box Web Part. In the Specify the Dropdown Mode for Search Boxes drop-down list, you can choose to show all the scopes that are in the Search Dropdown group, include or exclude contextual scopes, and control the default scope. You may want to include contextual scopes, as well as custom scopes, in the drop-down list to allow users to first search the local content (for example, using the This List option in the Search Dropdown control) and to promote their search to a wider scope (for example, using the All Sites option in the Search Dropdown control) if the initial results don't include what they're looking for. For the example in Figure 8-1, we chose to show all search scopes.

✦ **Site Collection Search Results Page:** Control how SharePoint displays searches against contextual scopes. By default, this option is set to the `OSSSearchResults.aspx` page because contextual searches usually show only items from the current site. If you want to show the same search result, regardless of whether the search is contextual, then set this page to be the same as the one that you use in the Site Collection Search Center section.

By default, the Search Box Web Part takes its settings from the Site Collections settings, but you can configure the Web Part itself to override these settings. You may want to configure the Web Part if you build custom search pages.

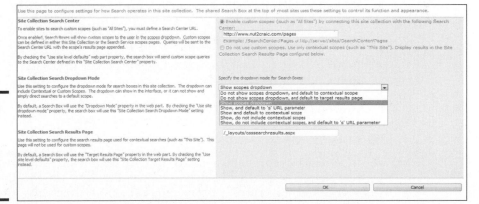

Figure 8-5: Specify your site-collection search settings.

Book IV
Chapter 8

Designing and Administering Search

Creating a custom search landing page

The search landing page controls how the search query is executed and how the results are displayed. You can use any page as a search landing page, but be sure to use a page that contains the Search Web Parts that meet your needs.

You can most simply create a landing page that already has many commonly used Search Web Parts in it by selecting the Site Actions/New Page option from an Enterprise Search Center site, which makes the New Page dialog appear, where you can create a multi-tabbed search results page. After you create your new page, you can customize the individual Web Parts that it contains, and add or remove any content that you want to.

To create the instrument landing page shown in Figure 8-1, follow these steps:

1. **From the home page of your Enterprise Search Center site, choose New Page from the Site Actions menu.**

2. **In the dialog that appears, enter the name** Instrument **in the New page name text box and click Create.**

    The resulting page opens in Edit mode.

3. **Click the arrow next to a Web Part and select Edit Web Part from the pop-up menu that appears.**

    The Web Part Editor dialog box appears at the right side of the page, as shown in Figure 8-6.

    Alternatively, you can select the check box next to the Web Part and use the Web Part Tools options in the Ribbon to access the Web Part Editor dialog.

4. **Configure the Web Part, as desired.**

    Each Web Part has different configuration options.

5. **Click OK.**

6. **Repeat Steps 3 through 5 for each Web Part that you want to edit.**

7. **You will still be in Edit mode on your new search page where you click the Add New Tab link at the top of the page.**

8. **In the** Newform.aspx **page that appears, enter the name** Instrument **in the Tab name text box and enter** Instrument.aspx **in the Page text box.**

    This step adds a new tab onto your new search page.

9. **Click Save.**

10. **In your new search page edit the Search Box Web Part at the top of the page as described in steps 3 to 5 and remove the Display advanced search link and Display user preferences link check boxes in the Miscellaneous section of the Web Part Editor dialog. Click OK to save these changes to the Web Part.**

    You can also choose to show the Scopes drop-down list in the Search Box Web Part via the Scopes dropdown section of the Web Part Editor dialog.

11. Remove the People Matches Web Part from the right zone by clicking the arrow next to it and selecting the Delete option from the drop-down menu that appears.

12. Move the Top Federated Results Web Part above the Search Core Results Web Part. You do this by dragging and dropping the Web Part. Click and hold your left mouse button on the title of the Web Part until a line appears above it. At this point you have grabbed the Web Part and can now move it to the desired location and then release the mouse button.

13. Access the Web Part Editor dialog as before to configure the Top Federated Results Web Part to show results from an Internet search. In the Location properties section select Internet Search Results from the Location drop-down list. Click OK to save your changes to the Web Part.

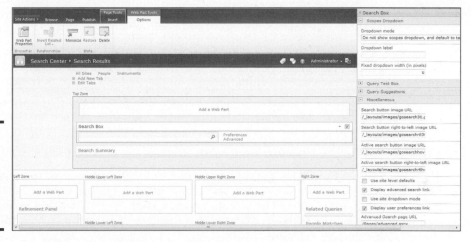

Figure 8-6: Editing a Web Part on a search results page.

Creating a federated search location for images

The images that appear on the right side of Figure 8-1 actually come from a Yahoo! search. Yahoo! (www.yahoo.com) supports the OpenSearch protocol, as do many other search providers, such as YouTube (www.youtube.com), Bing (www.bing.com), Google (www.google.com), and so on. To display search results from such providers, you have to first create a federated search location that defines how to execute the query and how to display the results.

To create a federated search location that can be used to retrieve images that match the entered search terms, follow these steps:

1. **From Central Administration, click the Manage service applications link from the Application Management section and click the Search Service Application from the resulting list of service applications that are displayed to access the Search Service Application Settings page. Click the Federated Locations link that appears in the Queries and Results section.**

   The Manage Federated Locations page (`managedfederatedlocations.aspx`) appears.

2. **Click the New Location button.**

   You can also import a location if you've downloaded an FDL (Federated Definition Location) file from a provider that supports OpenSearch. The FDL file contains all the necessary information to configure a new search location.

3. **In the Add Federated Location page (`addfederatedlocation.aspx`) that opens, enter** Images **in both the Location Name text box and the Display Name text box, and enter a description for the location in the Description text box.**

4. **In the Triggers section (which you have to scroll down the page to find), specify when the search location should be triggered by selecting one of the Always, Prefix or Pattern check boxes.**

   For this example, you can just use the default (which is Always), but you can further control when the search location is used by selecting one of the other two options.

5. **In the Location Type section, select the OpenSearch 1.0/1.1 check box.**

6. **In the Query Template section, enter the address of the template that will execute the search for images against Yahoo! in the Query Template text box. Note you can click the "..." button next to the text box to bring up a text editor for ease of entering and modifying the query template address..**

   This is the template address:

   ```
   http://api.search.yahoo.com/ImageSearchService/rss/imageSearch.xml?appid=
       yahoosearchimagerss&query={searchTerms}
   ```

   Note the text in the Query Template section that states "The URL specified should return structured XML (typically RSS or Atom results). It should not consist of a URL that shows an HTML-based search results page." Structured XML is required because the search results are passed through an XSL template for display processing. You should check that the query templates for any provider of a federated search does indeed produce RSS or Atom; otherwise, the Federated Web Part won't show any results.

7. **The Display Information section is where you select the properties that you want returned from the search and the XSL that will translate the returned XML into displayable HTML. The properties and XSL are specified by entering correctly formatted XML into the XSL and Properties text boxes.**

   Search results can be displayed in three Search Web Parts:

   - Federated Search Results Web Part
   - Core Search Results Web Part
   - Top Federated Search Results Web Part

   As the Use default formatting check box in the Display Information section indicates, the default properties and XSL that are provided are suitable for most scenarios.

8. **Uncheck the Use default formatting check box and then Click the "..." button next to the XSL text box. In the resulting text editor dialog that appears replace the single `<xsl:for-each>` loop in the default XSL that processes each property returned for an item with the following code.**

   ```
   <xsl:for-each select="$Rows">
     <xsl:variable name="CurPosition" select="position()" />
   <xsl:variable name="CurrentId" select="concat($IdPrefix,$CurPosition)" />
   <xsl:variable name="link">
     <xsl:call-template name="GetLink">
        <xsl:with-param name="Type" select="$Type"/>
     </xsl:call-template>
   </xsl:variable>
   <img src="{$link}" width="75" height="75"/>
   </xsl:for-each>
   ```

   In our example, the default XSL is insufficient because it shows the link, title, and description of the images, but you want to show the actual image to which the link points. You therefore need to customize the XSL for the Federated Search Results Web Part so that it doesn't show the title and description, and uses different XSL for the link property.

9. **In the Restrictions and Credentials section, use the radio buttons to control which sites can use the search location and which authentication method to use when executing the search.**

   The default settings work for our example.

After you define your search location, it appears (along with the others) in the Federated Locations page, as shown in Figure 8-7.

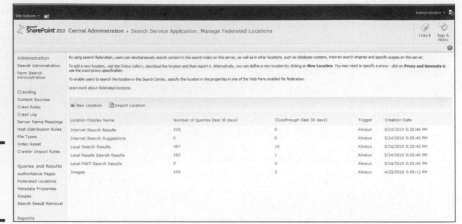

Figure 8-7:
Federated
search
locations.

This page also shows you details such as the number of queries that have been executed against the location and the number of click-throughs that have occurred.

Configure a Federation Web Part to display the images

After you define a search location, you can use it in a Federated Web Part in your search results page. Open your `Instruments.aspx` page in Edit mode and click the Add a Web Part link to add a Federated Web Part to the right zone, as shown in Figure 8-8. You can now edit the Web Part and set its Location property to Images, which will appear in the drop-down list of available search locations in the Location properties section of the Web Part Editor dialog.

You can override the display settings that are associated with the search location for each Web Part if you need to. In our example, you already set the search location itself to display the images correctly, so you don't need to override the settings.

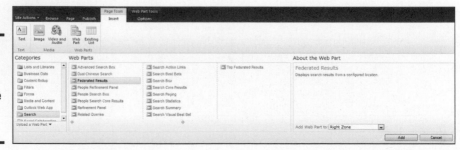

Figure 8-8:
Adding a
Web Part
by using the
Web Part
Gallery.

Creating a managed property for a custom site column

The refiner shown on the left in Figure 8-1 is based on a custom site column called Instrument that we created to use across our site collections. It's a simple text column that allows the user to type in any text, and we applied it to many of the content types that we use in our site collections. By editing items that were based on these content types, we typed in some values for the custom site column for items that were located across our site collections. If you've followed our example in the preceding sections of this chapter, then you can now create your own site column and apply it to content somewhere in your site collections.

Many features need columns to be indexed before those features can use the columns — the Refinement Web Part is a good example of such a feature because it only ever deals with information from the index. However, although the index engine crawls site columns, the index stores those columns only if they've been marked as managed properties. Only storing managed properties means that SharePoint does not have to unnecessarily store all properties in the index, regardless of whether they're subsequently used anywhere. Therefore, as an administrator, you need to promote properties to managed properties by following these steps:

1. **The search engine has to have crawled your site collections at least once after you create and apply your custom site column before you can promote it to a managed property.**

The search engine has to first discover your site column before you can mark that column as a managed property. By default, your local SharePoint content is crawled once every 20 minutes, but you can enforce an update immediately by following these steps:

a. In Central Administration, click Manage Service Applications.

The list of service applications appears on the Manage Service Applications page (`serviceapplications.aspx`)

b. Click the Search Service Application link and from the resulting page click the Content Sources link in the Crawling section. The Manage Content Sources page appears.

The Crawling section appears in the left navigation pane.

c. Hover your mouse over Local SharePoint Sites and, click the arrow that appears. From the resulting menu that appears, select Start Incremental Crawl.

You can monitor the status of your crawl from the Manage Content Sources page that you are on by clicking the Refresh button

2. **After your crawl finishes, click the Metadata Properties link below the Queries and Results section of the Search Service Application page that you accessed in step 1b above**

   The Metadata Property Mappings page (`listmanagedproperties.aspx`) appears. The Metadata Property Mappings page allows you to toggle between viewing crawled properties and managed properties. You can actually map crawled properties to a managed property from either page, but first you need to create a new Managed Property.

3. **Click the New Managed Property button.**

   The New Managed Property (`managedproperty.aspx`) page appears.

4. **Enter the name for your managed property in the Property name text box and indicate its type by selecting an appropriate radio box. Identify those crawled properties that should be mapped to it by using the Add Mapping button.**

   You can map any number of crawled properties to a managed property, which you may want to do if different properties describe the same data — for example, if two site collection administrators create a site column for the same purpose but with different names. Figure 8-9 shows our mapped property, which has two crawled properties mapped to it.

   If you've mapped multiple crawled properties, then you can assign the values from all of them for an item to the mapped property or only map a single value based on a preference order. On the New Managed Property page, you define whether a mapped property can be used in a property query-based search-scope rule by selecting the 'Allow this property to be used in scopes' check box (which we discuss in the section "Defining a search scope" earlier in this chapter).

All properties belong to a namespace (called Categories in the SharePoint user interface), and the namespace for SharePoint site columns is `ows_`. Therefore, when you map your crawled property, look for a property that has the name `ows_<Site Column Name>`.

Configuring a Refinement Web Part to use a managed property

After you define your managed property, you can use it in the Refinement Web Part. The details that are displayed by this Web Part when it is placed on a Web Part Page are primarily controlled via an XML configuration that's stored as a property of the Web Part itself (as discussed in Book III, Chapter

6). You can view the default XML by editing the Web Part (as discussed previously in this chapter) and viewing the Filter Category Definition in the Refinement section of the Web Part Editor dialog, as shown in Figure 8-10.

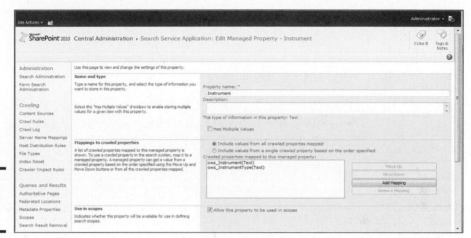

Figure 8-9:
A managed property.

Our example search page limits the Web Part to show a single filter category for the managed property called Instrument, and the Refinement Web Part displays the filter categories in alphabetical order. You can enter the following XML in the Filter Category Definition of the Web Part Editor for the Refinement Web Part to achieve this result:

```
<?xml version="1.0" encoding="utf-8"?>
<FilterCategories>
  <Category Title="Instrument"
Description="Type of instrument" Type="Microsoft.Office.Server.Search.
    WebControls.ManagedPropertyFilterGenerator"
MetadataThreshold="5"
NumberOfFiltersToDisplay="10"
MaxNumberOfFilters="0"
SortBy="Name"
SortDirection="Ascending"
SortByForMoreFilters="Name"
SortDirectionForMoreFilters="Ascending"
ShowMoreLink="True"
MappedProperty="Instrument"
MoreLinkText="show more"
LessLinkText="show fewer"/>
</FilterCategories>
```

**Book IV
Chapter 8**

Designing and
Administering
Search

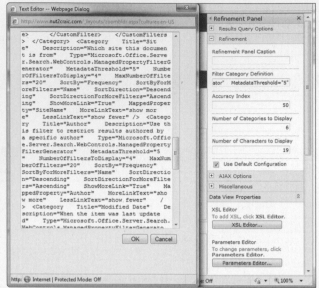

Figure 8-10:
The XML
configuration
for a
Refinement
Web Part.

You can apply many attributes to the Category node of the XML to control the refiners that appear in the Refinement Web Part. These attributes refer to properties that you can set on a FilterCategory WebControl. Check the Microsoft Developer Network website for more details. In the preceding example code, the most important attributes are

✦ **Type:** Controls what's used to determine the contents of the filters. In our example, the Type is ManagedPropertyFilterGenerator. Some filter types, such as TaxonomyFilterGenerator for Managed Metadata, are available out of the box, and developers can add other filter types.

✦ **MetadataThreshold:** Controls the minimum number of items that must be returned in the search results before the refiner will activate.

✦ **NumberOfFiltersToDisplay:** Controls the number of filters that appear in this filter category. If the search results have more filters available than this number, then a More link appears (if you set the ShowMoreLink attribute in to True in XML node for the filter category).

✦ **SortBy and SortDirection:** Controls the sort order of the displayed filters. You can set SortBy to Frequency, NumericValue, Name, or Custom. SortDirection can be Ascending or Descending.

✦ **MappedProperty:** Controls the managed property that the Refinement Web Part uses to build the list of filters for this filter category.

After we apply this XML to configure the Refinement Web Part in our example search page (shown in Figure 8-1), the search results contain items that have either the Instrument or InstrumentType site column set to Bagpipes, Cittern, Guitar, or Piano.

The Refinement Web Part also supports XSL to transform the display, so you can modify the default display to suit your needs. For example, in Figure 8-11, we replace the text of the filters with images.

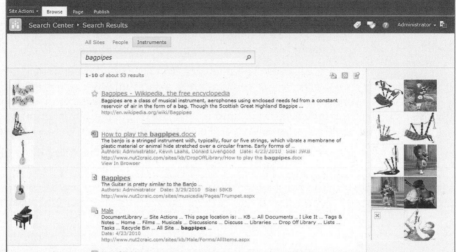

Figure 8-11: This modified XSL displays visual refiners.

Administrating and Monitoring Search

In previous versions of SharePoint, the administration experience was rather unwieldy, and you had to navigate through numerous pages to perform search-related administration tasks. SharePoint Server 2010 introduces the Search Management Dashboard, which delivers a more streamlined user interface for the SharePoint administrator. In the following sections, we take a look at the Dashboard and some of the main features it offers.

The Search Management Dashboard

If you've worked through any of the examples in this chapter, you've already visited the Dashboard, which you access by clicking the Search Service Application link from the Manage service applications page in Central Administration. Figure 8-12 shows the home page of the Dashboard, which is actually a Web Part page. You can modify this page and add other Web Parts to it to suit your needs.

The Dashboard gives you a one-page view of the state of the Search Service and links to the most common operations that you need when you administer search. The three main Web Parts on the Dashboard are

✦ **System Status:** The overall status of the search system. In this section, you can see details such as

   • The speed of the crawling process

   • How many items are in the index

   • The current response time for queries

   You can also control whether query logging is enabled. You need query logging enabled if you want to offer search features such as related searches (discussed in Chapter III, Book 6) to your end users.

✦ **Crawl History:** The most recent crawls that have been executed across all your content sources. In this section, you can get a good feel for how healthy each crawl is (in terms of how many errors were experienced during each crawl) and easily link to the individual content sources for further processing such as invoking a crawl or viewing crawl logs.

✦ **Search Application Topology:** The current topology of your Search Service, in terms of what servers and databases are required. This section shows you where certain components of your Search Service are running and which SQL Servers hold the necessary databases. You need to scroll to the bottom of the dashboard to see the topology.

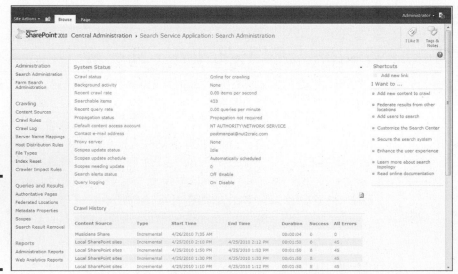

Figure 8-12:
The Search
Admini-
stration
Dashboard.

The links in the left navigation of the Dashboard are grouped according to function:

+ Administration

+ Crawling

+ Queries and Results

+ Reports

We cover some of these links, such as Scopes (in the "Defining a search scope" section) and Federated locations (in the "Creating a federated search location for images" section), earlier in this chapter. In the following sections, we take a look at some of the other major options that you can use to administer your overall Search Service.

Content sources

Content sources define the location of content that the indexing engine ultimately crawls. Defining a content source effectively builds the list of URLs that the crawler should start to process. From these URLs, the crawler can link to other URLs that it finds and, as an administrator, you can configure the content source from the Search Administration Dashboard to indicate how many links deep it should go and whether to follow links to other URL namespaces.

Out of the box, SharePoint has one content source defined, called Local SharePoint Sites. You can see its definition in Figure 8-13. This content source has three URLs associated with it. The first two are for the two Web Applications defined in the SharePoint farm, and the third one (sps3://ms5) crawls People-specific items in the farm. the first part of the URL defines the type of connector that crawls the content, and sps3 refers to a legacy-style protocol handler.

You can create as many content sources as you want to meet your needs, and you can build custom connectors to crawl any content sources that aren't covered by the out-of-the-box connectors.

 As well as being stored in the Search Administration database (the name of which you can see in the Topology section of the Dashboard), your index servers also store many of the configuration details of the search components in the Windows registry (on each Index server). For example, content sources are stored at HKEY_LOCAL_MACHINE\SOFTWARE\Microsoft\Office Server\14.0\Search\Applications\<appid>\Gather\Portal_Content\ContentSources, and crawl rules are stored at HKEY_LOCAL_MACHINE\SOFTWARE\Microsoft\Office Server\14.0\Search\Applications\<appid>\Gather\Portal_Content\Sites*\Paths.

Crawl rules

Crawl rules allow you to specifically include or exclude content based on a URL, so you can omit a particular subsection of a content source. For example, you may want to index your corporate portal but omit the financial section of that portal.

You can also use crawl rules to specify that different credentials be used for different URLs being crawled, as well as whether complex URLs (those with query parameters) are crawled. You can also use regular expressions to fine-tune the included or excluded URLs and choose whether the index engine should perform alphabetical case matching (useful if you crawl content, such as a Unix system, that supports case sensitivity in file names).

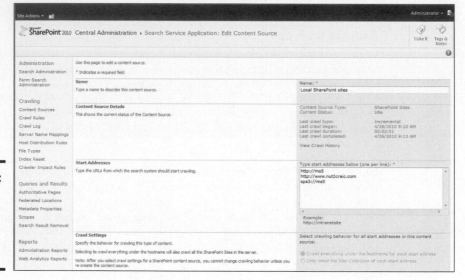

Figure 8-13:
The local SharePoint Sites content source.

Regular-expression support allows you to exclude content, regardless of where it's stored in your content sources, and to omit content that might be sensitive. For example, you may have filenames that contain information someone can use to identify people (such as employee badge numbers or Social Security numbers). Similarly, you may have links in Web pages that use specific query strings for sensitive purposes, so you want to omit those links.

Table 8-1 lists the regular-expression operators that you can use in your crawl rules.

You can't use regular expressions as the protocol part of a URL (so, for example, you can't enter `*//www.nut2craic.com/*` in the text box on the Manage Crawl Rules page). Click the Test button on the Crawl Rules page to ensure that your regular expressions match the target addresses you require. Here's an example of a crawl rule that uses a regular expression:

```
http://server/(9){3,}-(1){2}.asp(x)? will match http://server/99999-11.aspx but
    will not match http://server/99-11.asp
```

Table 8-1 Regular Expression Operators for Crawl Rules

Operator	Symbol	Description
Group	()	Group characters in round brackets; any operator applies to all the characters in the group.
Match Any Character	.	Matches any character except NULL.
Match Zero or One	?	The target either has the expression or doesn't.
Match Zero or More	*	The target can have no repetitions, or one or more repetitions, of the expression.
Match at Least One	+	The target must have the expression.
Exact Count	{num}	A number inside curly brackets; for example, {3}. The target must have this exact number of repetitions of the expression.
Minimum Count	{num,}	A number inside curly brackets, followed by a comma; for example, {4,}. The target must have at least this number of repetitions of the expression.

(continued)

Table 8-1 *(continued)*

Operator	Symbol	Description
Range Count	{*num1,num2*}	Two numbers inside curly brackets, separated by a comma; for example, {2,4}. The number of repetitions of the expression in the target must be within the range specified by the two numbers.
Alternation	|	The target must match one, and only one, of two expressions.
List	[*<list of chars>*]	The target can match any of the characters contained in the list. The list can be specified as an explicit list of characters; for example [1,2,3,4], and also as as a range; for example, [1-9].

Crawl log

The crawl log allows you to see what's been indexed and identify any errors that have occurred. Various options allow you to view the log in an appropriate way — such as by content source, URL, or hostname — so that you can easily navigate to the part of the log that you're interested in.

The ability to filter the log by error message allows you to quickly find content that has the same type of errors and then take appropriate action. In Figure 8-14, we select Remove the Item from the Index to omit the problematic item. Behind the scenes, the index engine removes the existing item from the index and creates a crawl rule that explicitly excludes the item in question from future crawls.

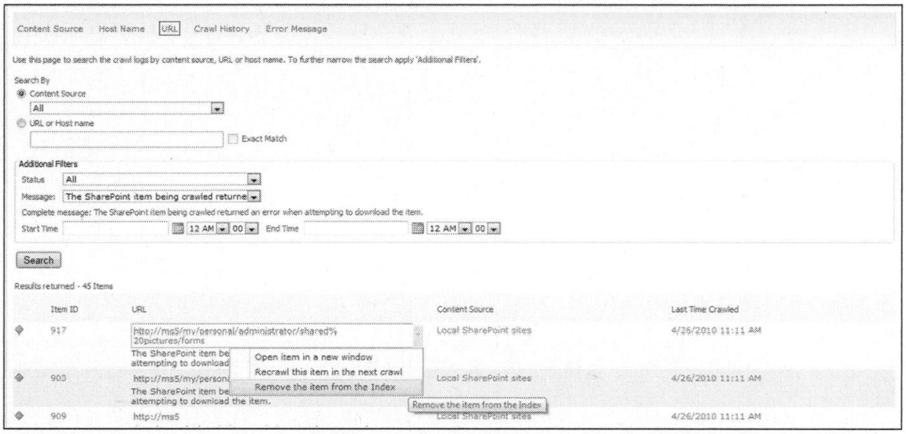

Figure 8-14:
In the crawl log, you can remove an item from the index.

Chapter 9: SharePoint Gets Social

In This Chapter

✔ Leveraging SharePoint's social features

✔ Making the most of My Sites

You can't build a social network that ultimately delivers value just by installing SharePoint. Everyone needs to buy into the plan so everyone can leverage the full wealth of the organization. So, everyone needs to be willing to enter details about themselves and the projects they're working on, which allows other people to discover this information and build linkages out of it.

The designers of SharePoint know that most human beings won't generally go out of their way to keep personal and project information up to date. So, SharePoint provides tools that are geared towards automatically keeping certain information up to date and presenting the user with opportunities to update other pertinent information in a seamless and simple fashion. In this chapter, we look at the tools that can help you and your users easily discover who knows who, who knows what, and who's doing what in your organization, creating a vibrant (and therefore worthwhile) social network.

Understanding People-centricity in SharePoint

People are a first-class object in SharePoint: They're just as important as the documents and other collateral that might be living inside your SharePoint farms. And SharePoint takes a people-centric view when it interacts with your collateral and resources by always looking for linkages between the current situation and other people and resources.

So, when you search for collateral, SharePoint presents any people that may be relevant to your quest so that they're just one click away. Furthermore, the relationships between other people and yourself appear on the search results page so that you can understand the social context inside — or outside — your organization. Understanding these social contexts can help you foster stronger relationships with others — others whom you may not have known anything about before you searching for collateral relevant to the task you have in mind.

Every end user needs to be able to maintain and display relevant information about him- or herself so that others can discover that user's expertise and interests. SharePoint supports a personal home page for each and every user, in which users can view and maintain their own information, as well as find out about what other people are up to. This home page is generally known as a My Site.

My Site at the Center

A user can potentially access three feature areas in his or her My Site, and permissions control the availability of these features. By default, all the areas are enabled for all authenticated users, but if you don't want all users to have unlimited access, highlight All Authenticated Users in the User Profile Service application (shown in Figure 9-1) and click Remove. You can then add your own users and/or groups, specifying the necessary permissions for your purpose.

To access the User Profile Service application, in Central Administration, select the Manage User Permissions option on the User Profile Service Application Settings page. You can adjust the following permissions:

✦ **Use Personal Features:** Advertise details about yourself to others via a public profile page. You can maintain some of the details that appear (such as your About Me information) and control certain aspects of the details (such as who's allowed to view them).

You can access this feature set by clicking in the My Profile tab of your personal home page.

✦ **Create Personal Site:** A standard team site that's created for your own personal use. You can store personal documents and documents that you want to share with others.

Access this feature set by clicking in the My Content tab of your personal home page.

✦ **Use Social Features:** Social features include social tagging and colleagues. You can also have an activity feed that shows the activities your colleagues have recently been doing.

You can access these features in many places, such as the My Newsfeed tab of your personal home page.

Quickly access your personal home page by clicking your name in the top-right corner of most SharePoint pages. A drop-down list appears, which includes options to visit your personal site or your public profile. Figure 9-2 shows a user's public profile page. While you navigate particular areas of SharePoint, clicking many of the links that you encounter takes you to the public profile of other users. For example, if a search result relates to a person, then clicking the search results link takes you to his or her profile page.

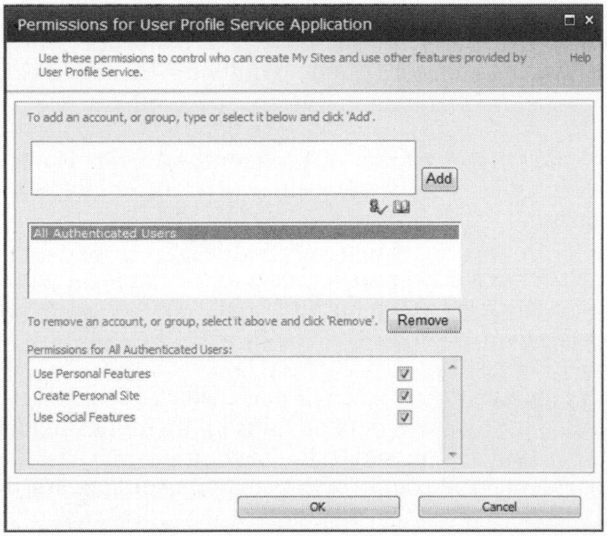

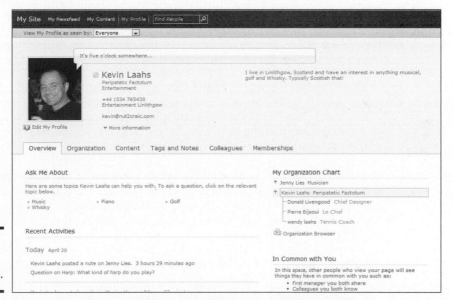

Figure 9-1:
Setting permissions for My Site usage.

Figure 9-2:
A user's profile page.

Understanding the My Profile page

The page that renders the profile page (`person.aspx`) resides in a site collection known as the My Site Host. Each User Profile Service application is associated with one My Site Host. You can control the My Site Host

Location by selecting the Setup My Sites option on the User Profile Service Application Settings page, and typing the desired location into the My Site Location text box that appears on the resulting Web page as shown in Figure 9-10.

If you want to change the default location for the My Site Host, you need to create the site collection by using either a blank template or the My Site Host site template.

You must ensure that a site actually exists at the top level of the Web Application that you use for the My Site Host; otherwise, the search engine doesn't index the People profiles.

Each user has only one `person.aspx` page, which has multiple tabs. The details that this page displays depend on who the requesting user is and the query strings that are passed to the page. If `person.aspx` is called with no query strings, then the profile of the current user appears, as shown in Figure 9-2.

The `person.aspx` page also shows a user's public profile to other users. In this case, the details that appear depend on the relationship that exists between the two users. For example, Figure 9-3 shows the result of the user Kevin Laahs viewing the profile of the user Jenny Lies. SharePoint called the person.aspx page by using this hyperlink:

```
http://<My Site Host>/person.aspx?AccountName=laahs\jenny
```

The Overview tab of the profile now displays things that the two users have in common, such as the colleagues they both know, interests they both enjoy, and the memberships they share.

But there's more to the displayed details than meets the eye because each user can control what information other people can see. To determine what information a user is allowed to see, SharePoint identifies the relationship between the calling user and the target user, placing the calling user into one of the following groups:

✦ **My Manager:** The calling user is listed as the manager in the target user's profile.

✦ **My Team:** The calling user is listed in the target user's Colleague list with the My Team column set to Yes.

✦ **My Colleague:** The calling user is listed in the target user's Colleague list, and the My Team column is set to No.

✦ **Everyone:** None of the preceding is true.

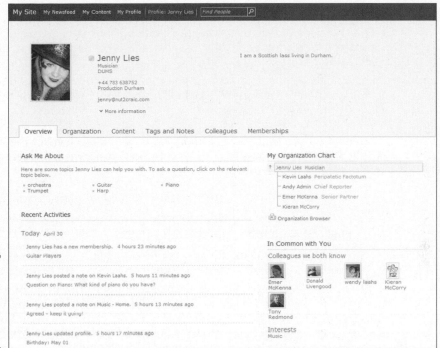

Figure 9-3:
Viewing
another
person's
profile page.

Each property in the user profile has a privacy setting that defines what group is allowed to see that property, and each property has a default value of Everyone set. If the end user has permission to change the property's privacy setting, then that user can edit his or her profile and change the group allowed to view the property. Additionally, each user can toggle the view of his or her own profile to see what it'll look like from the perspective of someone else by clicking the View My Profile as Seen By link at the top of the profile page.

This privacy feature extends to more than just user profile properties because, in your profile, you can also control who can see each of your colleagues, the site itself, and group memberships that you have. You can control which objects are subject to privacy settings and whether users can override the default setting by using policies. Administrators can manage these policies by using the Manage Policies option of the User Profile Service Application Settings page in Central Administration.

By maintaining his or her profile and keeping properties such as Interests and Skills up to date, each user makes a crucial contribution to the overall intellectual wealth of the organization because Sharepoint uses these properties when seeking expertise and building the links that make up the social networks within your organization.

Understanding the Overview tab of a profile page

The Overview tab displays the information about what a user has in common with another (as discussed in the preceding section), plus the following features:

✦ **My Organization Chart:** The user's position in the organizational hierarchy.

The user's peers and immediate manager are shown in the Organization Chart section on the Overview page and a link to the Organization browser is displayed underneath the Organization Chart (discussed in the following section).

✦ **Recent Activities:** The user's most recent activities.

Activities are covered in the section "Understanding the My Newsfeed page," later in this chapter.

✦ **Ask Me About:** Lists the user's interests that appear in his or her user profile and includes a link that you can click to ask the user a question about a particular topic. Each user has a noteboard associated with his or her profile, and any entries that are posted to this noteboard appear in that user's newsfeed. Users can also scroll to the bottom of the Overview tab and use the Previous and Next buttons to step through each note that's been placed on the board.

Writing on a SharePoint user's noteboard is very similar to writing on someone's wall in Facebook.

Understanding the Organization tab of a profile page

In the Organization tab, you can explore in more detail the user's position in the organizational hierarchy. If your Web browser has Silverlight support enabled, then you can use a very nice visual interface, as shown in Figure 9-4. This interface allows you to home in on individuals so that you can see the hierarchy from their perspectives. If your Web browser does not have Silverlight installed an informational message is displayed in the web page along with a link to allow you to perform an installation.

SharePoint determines the hierarchy itself by using the Manager property in the user's profile — users who have the same manager are classed as Peers in the organizational display.

Understanding the Content tab of a profile page

The Content tab shows recent content that the user has authored, such as blog entries, as well as a comprehensive list of documents that he or she has authored across the SharePoint farm.

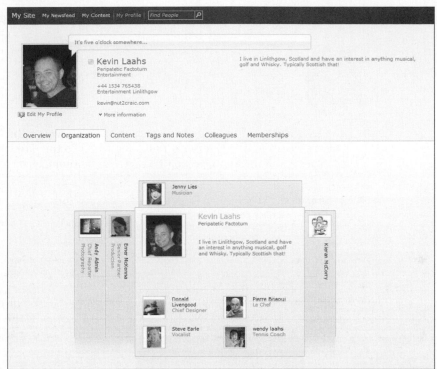

Figure 9-4:
The
Organization
browser.

The Content tab allows a visiting user to quickly home in on collateral from a specific SharePoint site because each site that contains content authored by the user appears in the SharePoint Content list.

Understanding the Tags and Notes tab of a profile page

Tags and Notes are described in Book I, Chapter 4. This tab allows users to quickly navigate their tag clouds and view recent notes and activities. If you click a tag term, the note and activities associated with that tag appear under the Activities section of the page.

In the Tags and Notes tab, the user can implement a tool that allows the user to tag external Web sites and add notes. You place the tool itself as a link in your Web browser Favorites or Bookmarks (just as you would any other link into your Web browser's favorites list). The link calls some JavaScript that brings up a dialog box, which you can use to enter Tags and Notes against the page that's currently displayed in your browser. You can see the net result of clicking a tag term in Figure 9-5. The first item displayed below Activities refers to an external Web site that the user browsed and decided to tag with the word Heaven.

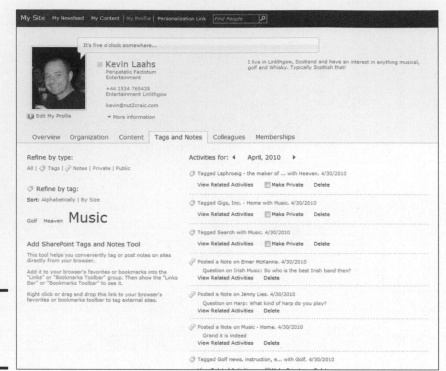

Figure 9-5:
The Tags
and Notes
tab.

Understanding the Colleagues tab of a profile page

Many of the SharePoint social features rely on knowing whom a user considers to be his or her colleagues. Armed with this knowledge, SharePoint can establish relationships between two people, such as the social distance between them — that is how many intermediaries would be required to establish a connection between the two people. This information can help build stronger social networks — for example, you may not know a particular person, but SharePoint can tell you if one of your colleagues (or one of your colleagues' colleagues) knows that person, which tells you whom you should ask for an introduction to that person.

Each user has a list of colleagues that's maintained both manually and automatically. SharePoint makes it easy for end users to add colleagues to their list by providing links in appropriate places — for example, from a search result that contains people.

By default, any user who has the same Manager in his or her user profile or who reports to you is automatically added as a Colleague and marked as being a member of your profile's My Team. In this way, SharePoint automatically maintains your Colleague list. SharePoint also provides the end user with suggested colleagues, and the user can then decide whether to include any of the suggested colleagues in his or her Colleagues list.

Suggested colleagues are derived from the user's messaging habits — whom the user sends e-mail to and receives e-mail from. The Microsoft SharePoint Server Colleague Import Add-In is available in Outlook 2010 (see Figure 9-6). It scans the user's Sent Items folder for names and keywords, along with the frequency of those names (colleagues) and keywords (colleague's area of expertise). These suggestions are then imported to SharePoint when the user visits their own personal home page.

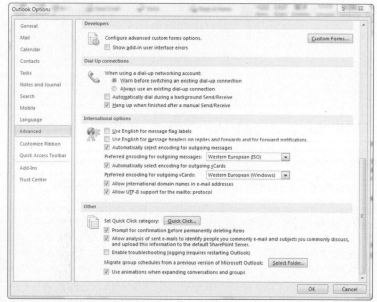

Figure 9-6:
Set the
Outlook 2010
option for
SharePoint
suggested
colleagues.

Colleague suggestions are stored in a file called `spscoll.dat` in the users' Windows profile. This file contains a list of e-mail addresses and a ranking for each address to determine how much the user has been communicating with these people. This list is imported to SharePoint so that it can offer suggested colleagues to the user when that user next visits the Colleagues tab on his or her personal home page.

Although SharePoint imports the suggestions, adding the suggestions to your colleague list is an opt-in feature: The user has to decide which people to add to their list of colleagues and which keywords to add to their list of expertise areas. Also, the Suggested Colleagues section, shown in Figure 9-7, is visible only if SharePoint has actually imported any new suggestions. And the e-mail addresses contained in the suggestions list must also already exist in the user's SharePoint user profile if that user wants to add them as colleagues.

**Book IV
Chapter 9**

**SharePoint
Gets Social**

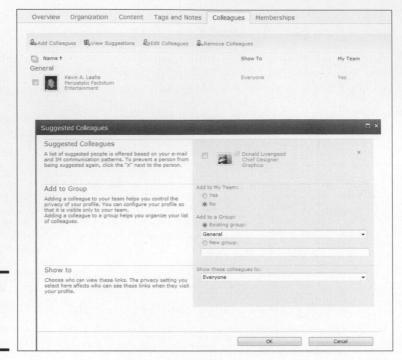

Figure 9-7:
Adding a
suggested
colleague.

Microsoft Office Communicator also contributes to your suggested colleagues list by analyzing your instant messaging practices.

Another place in the Office ecosystem allows you to easily add colleagues — the Outlook Social Connector. This Outlook 2010 feature allows you to hook up to social network services (such as Facebook, LinkedIn, and so on) and display information from those social networks directly in Outlook. The My Site connector is the only connector that comes with it. After you configure it to point to your My Site, you can simply add colleagues from the Social Connector pane that appears at the bottom of each Outlook message window. This pane also shows you information from the social network, as shown in Figure 9-8, which displays the sender's activity.

All colleagues (no matter how you attempt to add them) must exist in the SharePoint User Profile (see Book III, Chapter 7) ; otherwise, you will receive an error message indicating that you cannot add them to your list of colleagues.

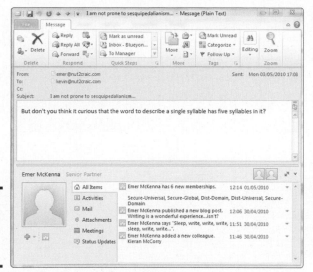

Figure 9-8:
The Outlook
Social
Connector.

Understanding the Memberships tab of a profile page

The Membership tab displays details of the groups to which the user is a member (shown in Figure 9-9). The following group details are displayed:

✦ **SharePoint Sites:** Only those SharePoint sites to which the user is explicitly granted access via the SharePoint Members group. A user can granted access to a SharePoint site via many other routes, such as being an Owner or a member of an Active Directory Security Group that's been added to the Members group of a site but, in these cases, the SharePoint site will not be listed here.

The tab also shows the number of members in each site, but this number reflects only the users who have been explicitly added to the Members group of the site. So, you can't trust this number to reflect the actual number of users who have some sort of access to the SharePoint site.

A background job that, by default, runs hourly updates the sites of which a user is a member. The job is called User Profile Service Application – User Profile to SharePoint Full Synchronization.

✦ **Distribution Lists:** The Active Directory Distribution Groups of which the user is a member.

TECHNICAL STUFF

The Distribution List section doesn't show Security Groups (even though SharePoint recognizes Security Group membership because such membership appears in a user's activity feed!).

The User Profile Synchronization job initially determines Active Directory Group membership, so ensure that it's running in your SharePoint Farm by monitoring the farm's service applications if you want to keep the details displayed in this section up to date.

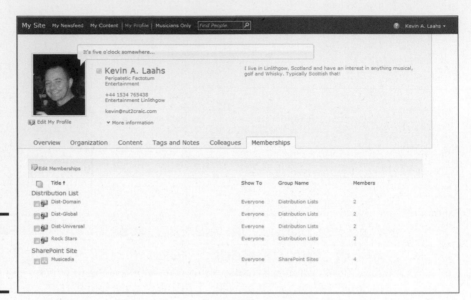

Figure 9-9:
The Member-ships tab.

Understanding the My Content page

Users who have the permission to create a personal site can access the My Content page. You grant this permission so that users can establish a team site that's linked to their profiles. This team site is designed as a place where users can store personal documents or documents that they want to share with others. SharePoint treats the My Content page as just a standard team site to which the user is granted owner permissions. SharePoint uses standard permissions on the libraries within the team site so that other users can access the content.SharePoint dynamically provisions a personal site the first time a user clicks the My Content link. An administrator configures the root location of the personal site by using the Personal Site Location text box in the User Profile Service Application Settings page, as shown in Figure 9-10. By default, the Personal Site Location is a managed path called Personal on the same Web Application that hosts the My Site Host site collection. The personal site is provisioned as a site collection from this path.

You can modify your personal site to suit your needs by leveraging all SharePoint's customization capabilities. For example, you can add Web Parts, such as the My Links Web Part. This Web Part lists those links to SharePoint sites and libraries that you created by using the Connect to Office option on the Ribbon, as discussed in Book I, Chapter 6.

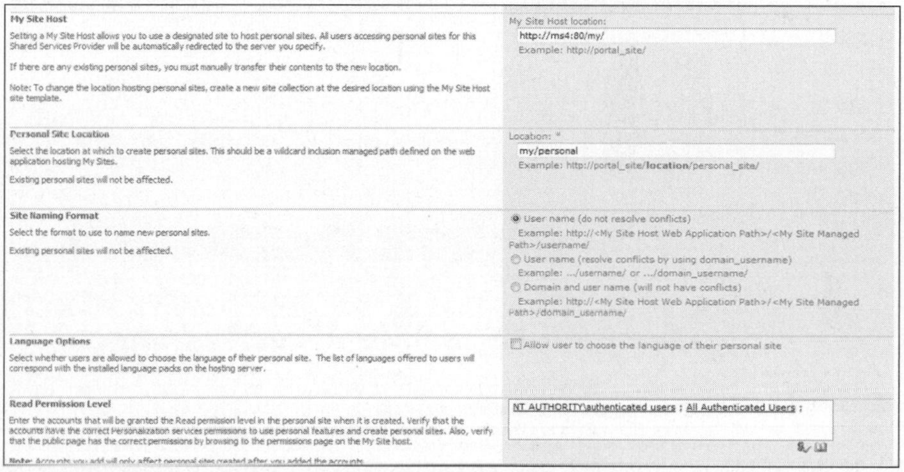

Figure 9-10: Setting up My Sites.

Understanding personalization links

Personalization links allow administrators to target navigation links to all users or to a specific set of users by using Audiences. These navigation links appear at the top of a user's personal home page.

To create personalization links, select Configure Personalization Site in the My Site Settings section of the User Profile Service Application Settings page. The dialog box that appears allows you to specify the following:

✦ URL of the link

✦ Display name

✦ Owner of the link

✦ Audience to which the link should be targeted (optional)

Figure 9-11 shows the Configure Personalization Site dialog box and a target user's top navigation bar within his or her personal home page.

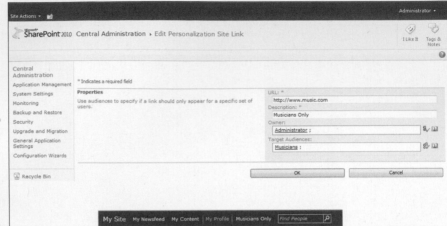

Figure 9-11: Configure personalization links for users' home pages.

Understanding the My Newsfeed page

In the My Newsfeed page (see Figure 9-12), you can keep up with what others are doing. If your colleagues show interest in something, then SharePoint thinks that you can benefit from knowing about it. For example, if a colleague tags some content that relates to your interests, then you may want to go and investigate that content. By keeping up with the activities of your colleagues, you can stay on top of information important to you.The My Newsfeed page lists both implicit and explicit activities relating to your colleagues:

✦ **Implicit:** Something the user hasn't actually done him- or herself, but something that has affected him or her. So, for example, a SharePoint site owner may have added the user as a member of a new SharePoint site or the user's reporting relationship may have changed, which means new peers are established for that user.

✦ **Explicit:** Actions the user has taken directly, such as commenting on someone's note board or updating the Interests and Expertise properties that appear in their My Profile page.

End users control what activities they want to appear in their My Newsfeed pages by editing their own profiles and selecting those activities that can be monitored. Here are the activities that you can receive notifications about:

✦ **Tagging by My Colleague:** When one of your colleagues adds a tag to some content. Tags surface the most popular content because individuals surface that content via tagging. Following your colleagues' tags usually takes you to the most useful content, so you don't have to search for it.

✦ **Note Board Post:** A note added to an internal page, an external page, or another user's note board by one of your colleagues.

Figure 9-12:
My
Newsfeed.

+ **Tagging with My Interests:** Tagging content that includes a keyword you have listed as one of your interests.

+ **Rating:** One of your colleagues rates some content.

+ **Status Message:** A colleague changes his or her status message.

+ **Upcoming Workplace Anniversary:** Lets you know when a colleague has almost completed another year in the organization. By letting you know in advance, SharePoint reminds you to prepare a celebration, if you want.

+ **Workplace Anniversary:** Lets you know that you forgot to prepare a celebration. (Oops!)

+ **New Colleague:** A new colleague has been automatically added to your list of colleagues. Most typically, you get a new colleague this way when the user's manager is changed in the system so that you now have the same manager.

+ **Job Title Change:** A colleague changes his or her job title.

+ **Manager Change:** A colleague's manager details are changed in the system.

✦ **New Blog Post:** A colleague has authored a new blog post.

✦ **New Membership:** A colleague has been added as a member to either an Active Directory Group (either a Distribution or Security group) or a SharePoint site.

✦ **Sharing Interests:** A colleague has updated his or her profile's list of Interests.

✦ **Profile Update:** A colleague has updated his or her profile.

✦ **Upcoming birthday:** Buy a present for the colleague who's turning a year older!

✦ **Birthday:** Hand over the present to the lucky colleague.

Updates to each user's newsfeed is processed by a background job called User Profile Service Application – Activity Feed Job, which runs daily by default. You may want to increase the frequency of this job if you want to capture activities in a timelier fashion. Make this change via the Recurring Schedule section of the Check Job Status option in Central Administration.

Activities also appear in the Outlook Social Connector, as shown in Figure 9-8.

 The preceding discussion on the social aspects of SharePoint adds value only if everyone participates in keeping their profile information up to date. Without regular updates, newsfeeds become stale and add no value to the overall intellectual wealth of the organization. By default, SharePoint sends out e-mail to users on a monthly basis to remind them to keep their profiles up to date. (Because sending these e-mails is a scheduled job, you can disable it by using the Disable button for the User Profile Service Application – My Site Suggestions Email Job via the Check Job Status option in Central Administration.) But, sadly, because technical solutions rarely seem to correct behavioral problems, you need to both lead by example and constantly encourage people to keep their profiles active.

Searching for People

SharePoint Server 2010 automatically provides a landing page that's tailored to show pertinent information about people — for example, the most-common interests among the people displayed in search results. This page (`people results.aspx`) is the landing page associated with the People tab on the default search results page. An example of a People search is shown in Figure 9-13.

The `peopleresults.aspx` page features two interesting Web Parts:

Figure 9-13:
A People
search
results
page.

✦ **People Search Core Results:** Uses the Local People Search Results search location. You can modify this Web Part to override the default properties returned for this location and/or tweak the XSL so that the results appear in a different way.

This Web Part also supports the following features:

• *Social Distance:* The results show you how far, in the SharePoint social hierarchy, you are from the users who appear in the result set by displaying their relationships to you below their pictures. For example, SharePoint may tell you that a particular user is a Colleague or a Colleague's Colleague.

• *Vanity Search:* When the user who's doing the search shows up in the search results (usually because that user deliberately searches for him- or herself!). To encourage users to keep their profiles up to date, the vanity result shows the users how many times other people have clicked their names and what keywords people use to find them. You can see this in the Help People Find Me section at the bottom of Figure 9-13. And, because SharePoint wants to make it easy for users to keep their information up to date, a user can click the Update My Profile link to go directly to his or her profile.

• *Add to Colleagues:* A single click allows you to add a person you've found through search to your list of colleagues.

- *View in Organization Browser:* Click the Browse in organizational chart link to see where the user exists in the organizational hierarchy.

- *More About the User:* If you hover over the By <User> link, a pop-up window appears that tells you more about the user, as well as displaying other information that the user has published.

✦ **People Refinement Panel:** Displays suitable refiners based on the search results. Unlike the refinement Web Part on the normal search results page, you can't modify the refiners that ultimately appear in the navigation bar. But SharePoint does a pretty good job of showing you the most relevant refiners based on the result set.

Figure 9-13 and Figure 9-14 show two examples of people search results. Figure 9-13 returned more users that had less in common with each other than Figure 9-14, and so the refiners were based on Job Title and Schools. For the search results in Figure 9-14, the two users that the search returned had some mutual interests, so the search results page displayed Interests as a refiner. Clicking one of the interests SharePoint then searches for all people in the organization who share that interest. This SharePoint Server 2010 feature lets you find the expertise you need quickly.

Figure 9-14:
A People search that has fewer results and different refiners.

If you want to get the most out of the social-networking features of SharePoint Server 2010, then you must encourage a culture in which people willingly update their user profiles on a regular basis with rich and relevant information.

Index

Numbers & Symbols

- (hyphen), 306
$ (dollar sign), 308
() (round brackets), 829
* (asterisk), 306
. (period), 829
? (question mark), 829
_ (underscore), 308
{} (curly brackets), 829–830
+ (plus sign), 829

A

AAM (Alternate Access Mappings), 31, 134, 200
Access 2010
  Web compatibility checker, 608
  Web database client template, 608
  working with lists, 129
Access Control Entry, 531
access control list (ACL), 215
Access forms, 620
Access reports, 620
Access Services. *See also* Access Web database
  Application log, 622–626
  architecture, 366–368
  creating Access Web database, 609–612
  data access layer, 367
  default form, 618–619
  description, 173
  even handlers, 367
  forms and reports, 367
  in-memory cache, 367
  Lists and Queries settings, 369–370
  managing, 368–369
  mapping Access objects to SharePoint objects, 620–621
  Memory Utilization settings, 371–372
  opening Access Web database application, 626–628
  overview, 365–366, 607
  project datasheet, 367

publishing Access Web database to, 623–625
  publishing to, 619–629
  query processor, 367
  running Reporting Services, 372–381
  session, 367
  Session Management settings, 371
  in SharePoint, 269
  SharePoint-compatible Access databases, 608
  Template settings, 372
  Web compatibility checker, 621–623
  Web database objects, 612–618
  Web service, 367
Access tables, 620
Access Web database. *See also* Access Services
  creating, 609
  creating from SharePoint, 609–612
  data macros, 616–617
  default form, 618–619
  fields, 612–613
  forms-based authentication, 613–614
  macros, 615–616
  navigation, 614–615
  objects, 612–618
  opening, 626–627
  publishing, 623–625
  queries, 617
  reports, 618
  saving as site template, 628–629
  in SharePoint, 620
  synchronizing changes with SharePoint, 628
  tables, 612–613
account forest, 530
ACL (access control list), 215
action rules, 773, 777–780
actions, 388, 632–633
Active Directory
  connections, 529–541
  importing user profile content from, 519
  user and group limits, 216
Active Directory Directory Services. *See* AD DS

C

M

Q

Notes

Notes

Notes

Notes

Apple & Macs

iPad For Dummies
978-0-470-58027-1

iPhone For Dummies,
4th Edition
978-0-470-87870-5

MacBook For Dummies, 3rd
Edition
978-0-470-76918-8

Mac OS X Snow Leopard For
Dummies
978-0-470-43543-4

Business

Bookkeeping For Dummies
978-0-7645-9848-7

Job Interviews
For Dummies,
3rd Edition
978-0-470-17748-8

Resumes For Dummies,
5th Edition
978-0-470-08037-5

Starting an
Online Business
For Dummies,
6th Edition
978-0-470-60210-2

Stock Investing
For Dummies,
3rd Edition
978-0-470-40114-9

Successful
Time Management
For Dummies
978-0-470-29034-7

Computer Hardware

BlackBerry
For Dummies,
4th Edition
978-0-470-60700-8

Computers For Seniors
For Dummies,
2nd Edition
978-0-470-53483-0

PCs For Dummies,
Windows
7 Edition
978-0-470-46542-4

Laptops For Dummies,
4th Edition
978-0-470-57829-2

Cooking & Entertaining

Cooking Basics
For Dummies,
3rd Edition
978-0-7645-7206-7

Wine For Dummies,
4th Edition
978-0-470-04579-4

Diet & Nutrition

Dieting For Dummies,
2nd Edition
978-0-7645-4149-0

Nutrition For Dummies,
4th Edition
978-0-471-79868-2

Weight Training
For Dummies,
3rd Edition
978-0-471-76845-6

Digital Photography

Digital SLR Cameras &
Photography For Dummies,
3rd Edition
978-0-470-46606-3

Photoshop Elements 8
For Dummies
978-0-470-52967-6

Gardening

Gardening Basics
For Dummies
978-0-470-03749-2

Organic Gardening
For Dummies,
2nd Edition
978-0-470-43067-5

Green/Sustainable

Raising Chickens
For Dummies
978-0-470-46544-8

Green Cleaning
For Dummies
978-0-470-39106-8

Health

Diabetes For Dummies,
3rd Edition
978-0-470-27086-8

Food Allergies
For Dummies
978-0-470-09584-3

Living Gluten-Free
For Dummies,
2nd Edition
978-0-470-58589-4

Hobbies/General

Chess For Dummies,
2nd Edition
978-0-7645-8404-6

Drawing
Cartoons & Comics
For Dummies
978-0-470-42683-8

Knitting For Dummies,
2nd Edition
978-0-470-28747-7

Organizing
For Dummies
978-0-7645-5300-4

Su Doku For Dummies
978-0-470-01892-7

Home Improvement

Home Maintenance
For Dummies,
2nd Edition
978-0-470-43063-7

Home Theater
For Dummies,
3rd Edition
978-0-470-41189-6

Living the
Country Lifestyle
All-in-One
For Dummies
978-0-470-43061-3

Solar Power Your Home
For Dummies,
2nd Edition
978-0-470-59678-4

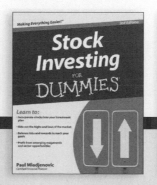

Available wherever books are sold. For more information or to order direct: U.S. customers visit www.dummies.com or call 1-877-762-2974.
U.K. customers visit www.wileyeurope.com or call (0) 1243 843291. Canadian customers visit www.wiley.ca or call 1-800-567-4797.

Internet

Blogging For Dummies,
3rd Edition
978-0-470-61996-4

eBay For Dummies,
6th Edition
978-0-470-49741-8

Facebook For Dummies,
3rd Edition
978-0-470-87804-0

Web Marketing
For Dummies,
2nd Edition
978-0-470-37181-7

WordPress
For Dummies,
3rd Edition
978-0-470-59274-8

Language & Foreign Language

French For Dummies
978-0-7645-5193-2

Italian Phrases
For Dummies
978-0-7645-7203-6

Spanish For Dummies,
2nd Edition
978-0-470-87855-2

Spanish
For Dummies,
Audio Set
978-0-470-09585-0

Math & Science

Algebra I
For Dummies,
2nd Edition
978-0-470-55964-2

Biology For Dummies,
2nd Edition
978-0-470-59875-7

Calculus For Dummies
978-0-7645-2498-1

Chemistry For Dummies
978-0-7645-5430-8

Microsoft Office

Excel 2010 For Dummies
978-0-470-48953-6

Office 2010 All-in-One
For Dummies
978-0-470-49748-7

Office 2010 For Dummies,
Book + DVD Bundle
978-0-470-62698-6

Word 2010 For Dummies
978-0-470-48772-3

Music

Guitar For Dummies,
2nd Edition
978-0-7645-9904-0

iPod & iTunes For
Dummies, 8th Edition
978-0-470-87871-2

Piano Exercises
For Dummies
978-0-470-38765-8

Parenting & Education

Parenting For Dummies,
2nd Edition
978-0-7645-5418-6

Type 1 Diabetes
For Dummies
978-0-470-17811-9

Pets

Cats For Dummies,
2nd Edition
978-0-7645-5275-5

Dog Training For Dummies,
3rd Edition
978-0-470-60029-0

Puppies For Dummies,
2nd Edition
978-0-470-03717-1

Religion & Inspiration

The Bible For Dummies
978-0-7645-5296-0

Catholicism For Dummies
978-0-7645-5391-2

Women in the Bible
For Dummies
978-0-7645-8475-6

Self-Help & Relationship

Anger Management
For Dummies
978-0-470-03715-7

Overcoming Anxiety
For Dummies,
2nd Edition
978-0-470-57441-6

Sports

Baseball
For Dummies,
3rd Edition
978-0-7645-7537-2

Basketball
For Dummies,
2nd Edition
978-0-7645-5248-9

Golf For Dummies,
3rd Edition
978-0-471-76871-5

Web Development

Web Design
All-in-One
For Dummies
978-0-470-41796-6

Web Sites
Do-It-Yourself
For Dummies,
2nd Edition
978-0-470-56520-9

Windows 7

Windows 7
For Dummies
978-0-470-49743-2

Windows 7
For Dummies,
Book + DVD Bundle
978-0-470-52398-8

Windows 7 All-in-One
For Dummies
978-0-470-48763-1

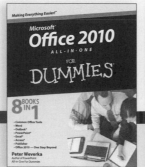

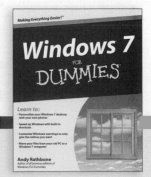

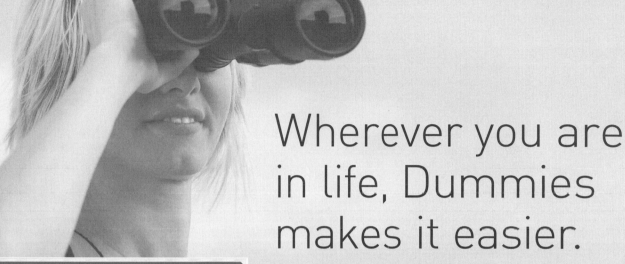

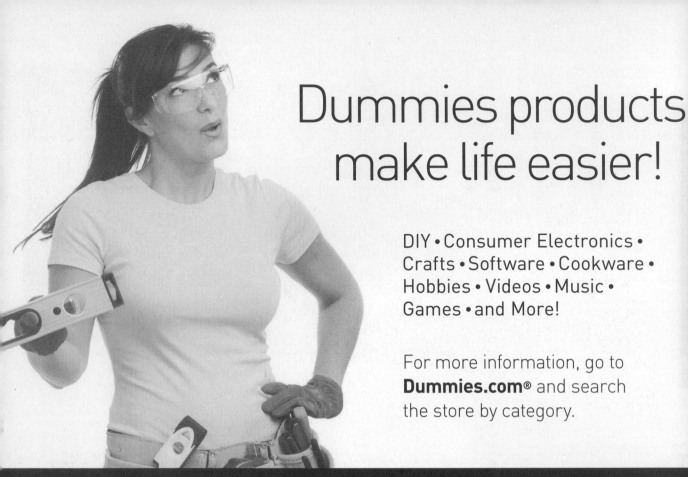

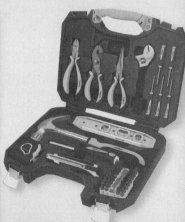